# South Asian Perspectives in Mental Health and Psychology

**Series Editors**

S. M. Yasir Arafat, Bangladesh Specialized Hospital Limited, Dhaka, Bangladesh

Sujita Kumar Kar, Department of Psychiatry, King George's Medical University, Lucknow, Uttar Pradesh, India

This series of books is an endeavor to gather and present a comprehensive understanding of the various aspects of mental health that are relevant to people living in South Asia. The books aim to provide in-depth guidance and practical solutions to the mental health challenges that are unique to these areas. The content covers a wide range of topics, including but not limited to, climate change and its impact, prison mental health, perinatal mental health, social psychiatry, mental health and disorder among the elderly population, psychiatry education and training, suicide, SDGs and mental health, trauma, addiction, and social isolation. The books also emphasize the importance of early intervention and provide resources for seeking help. The ultimate goal of this series is to empower individuals and communities to take proactive steps toward enhancing their mental wellbeing. The proposed books will fill the existing unmet need in the region with huge populations in low and middle-income country (LMIC) settings.

South Asia, home to about 2 billion people, is a region of diverse cultures, languages, and religions. It caters to about 25% of the global population. This densely populated region faces a myriad of challenges, both natural and man-made. The frequent occurrence of natural disasters, such as earthquakes, floods, and landslides, threaten the lives and livelihoods of millions of people. War, terrorism, and political instability have caused significant disruptions to the region's socio-political fabric. Poverty, migration, and tropical infectious diseases remain major challenges that hinder progress towards sustainable development. Climate change exacerbates these challenges, causing widespread environmental degradation, food insecurity, and water scarcity. Despite these obstacles, South Asian people have shown remarkable resilience and strength in the face of adversity.

Mental health issues in the South Asian region significantly contribute to the global burden of mental illnesses. However, the region faces plenty of challenges such as high stigma, low mental health literacy, poor budgetary allocation, high out-of-pocket expense for mental health services, lack of adequate infrastructure, and limited human resources are significant barriers in mental healthcare. The majority of research on mental health issues is produced by the western countries which may not fit all in the South Asian culture, albeit evidence is needed to test. There is a paucity of research and evidence-based strategies that are region-specific. This series of books is an attempt to compile the important dimensions of mental health that will benefit the regional people.

S. M. Yasir Arafat · Sujita Kumar Kar
Editors

# Ecological and Social Determinants of Suicidal Behavior

Springer

*Editors*
S. M. Yasir Arafat
Department of Psychiatry
Bangladesh Specialized Hospital
Dhaka, Bangladesh

Sujita Kumar Kar
Department of Psychiatry
King George's Medical University
Lucknow, Uttar Pradesh, India

ISSN 3059-3646 ISSN 3059-3522 (electronic)
South Asian Perspectives in Mental Health and Psychology
ISBN 978-981-96-4027-0 ISBN 978-981-96-4028-7 (eBook)
https://doi.org/10.1007/978-981-96-4028-7



This Springer imprint is published by the registered company Springer Nature Singapore Pte Ltd.
The registered company address is: 152 Beach Road, #21-01/04 Gateway East, Singapore 189721, Singapore

*To our beloved family members*
*SMYA—Asma Khatun, Yashfi Islam, and Orhan Adri*
*SKK—Sarvodaya Tripathy, Advik Kar, and Aritrika Kar*

# Preface

Suicide is a global public health problem. According to the World Health Organization (2024), more than 726,000 people die by suicide every year in the world. The number of suicide attempts is more than 20 times higher than suicides. Suicidal behavior is an extremely complex human behavior. It is an outcome of complex interaction among multiple factors like gene and environment, biopsychosocial, proximal, and distal factors. Several risk factors such as psychiatric disorders, life events, social deprivation, personality disorders, and substance abuse have been identified even though those vary based on culture, time, country, and methods of assessment.

So far, no single risk factor has been identified that directly correlates with suicidal behavior. However, various socio-ecological factors, such as the Human Development Index, a country's income category, the GINI Index, religion, climate change, environmental quality, and legal status regarding suicide attempts, have shown associations with this behavior. Determining these associations accurately is difficult due to the presence of numerous confounding variables and mediators. Against this backdrop, we aimed to review the current evidence and expertise regarding the impact of social and ecological determinants on suicidal behavior. This book is the first of its kind to explore the relationship between ecological and social variables and suicidal behavior. It examines the complexities and directions of these associations and discusses preventive measures for suicide, focusing on ecological and social perspectives.

We began the book with an introductory chapter explaining the different models and theories of suicide focusing on the links and how socio-ecology has been linked to suicide. Then, the social structure and suicide chapter discusses the association of suicidal behavior with multiple social variables. Then we included chapters on climate change and its impact on suicidal behavior in the community, how urbanization and environmental pollution influence suicide, associations of suicidal behavior and economic recession, war and suicide, religion and suicidal behavior, pandemics, and suicidal behavior, political milieu and suicide, protest suicide in response to environmental stimuli, impact of media on suicidal behavior, nutrition, mental health and suicidal behavior, sports and suicide, marginal life state and suicide, suicidal behavior among prisoners, social views on assisted suicide, suicide promoting groups, legal status and suicidal behavior, and suicide prevention focusing the social and ecological factors.

This book is an initial attempt to explore the role of social and ecological variables in suicidal behavior and its prevention. It will be useful for researchers, academics, policymakers, and professionals in the field of suicidology, environmental science, mental health, public health, economics, non-governmental organizations, epidemiology, social work, ecologists, and social science.

Dhaka, Bangladesh S. M. Yasir Arafat
Lucknow, Uttar Pradesh, India Sujita Kumar Kar

# Contents

# About the Editors

**Dr. S. M. Yasir Arafat** is currently working as an associate consultant of Psychiatry at Bangladesh Specialized Hospital, Dhaka, Bangladesh. He is affiliated with Dnet as an honorary research fellow and Biomedical Research Foundation, Bangladesh as a senior research fellow. He was affiliated with the University of Bristol, UK as a visiting senior research associate, (August 2021–2023). He completed MD in Psychiatry, MPH in Health Economics, MBA in Marketing and MBBS. Dr. Arafat has (co)authored more than 350 peer-reviewed articles and book chapters, and (co)edited more than ten books with Springer. He has been included in the global 2% researcher list in 2021, 2022, and 2023. He is acting as an editorial member in more than 10 leading journals in mental health published by Elsevier, Wiley, Springer, and Taylor and Francis. His research focused on mental health, suicidal behavior, psychometrics, panic buying, and psycho-sexual disorders.

**Dr. Sujita Kumar Kar** is currently working as an additional professor of Psychiatry at King George's Medical University, Lucknow, Uttar Pradesh, India. He is the editor-in-chief of *Indian Journal of Health, Sexuality, and Culture*. He is also the editorial board member and reviewer of various national and international journals. He had written 74 book chapters and more than 500 articles in various national & international journals and made 70 presentations at various national and international conferences. He has been included in the global 2% researcher list released by Stanford University in 2021, 2022, 2023, and 2024. His research interests include brain stimulation, neuropsychiatry, and suicide prevention.

# List of Figures

**Chapter 20**

# List of Tables

# Chapter 1
# Theoretical Models of Suicide

**Ravi Philip Rajkumar**

**Abstract** Suicidal behaviour is a complex phenomenon that has biological, psychological, social and even environmental roots. Theories of suicide are constructs that attempt to understand an individual's transition from a "non-suicidal" state to suicidal ideation and attempts. Biological theories focus either on the dysregulation of biological pathways or on the evolutionary roots of suicidal behaviour. Psychological-interpersonal theories attempt to understand suicide in terms of concepts such as psychological pain, hopelessness and cognitive constriction in response to the frustration of normal psychological needs. Sociological theories emphasize the role of culture and social integration on suicidal behaviour, while anthropological perspectives emphasize the uniqueness of a given cultural context and the meaning of suicidal behaviour embedded in that context. Various attempts have been made to reduce these models to certain common factors or dimensions or to integrate them into a higher-order model that provides a bio-psycho-social understanding of suicide. Ecological systems theory offers a promising framework for such an integration, improving cultural and ecological validity and conceptual clarity while fostering inter-disciplinary research into suicide. This chapter highlights the theoretical models that explain suicidal behaviour.

**Keywords** Suicide · Theoretical model · Ecology · Biopsychosocial model · Psychache · Interpersonal-psychological theory · Sociology · Evolutionary psychology

## 1 Introduction

*There is only one really serious philosophical problem, and that is suicide.*
*- Albert Camus, "The Myth of Sisyphus"*

R. P. Rajkumar (✉)
Department of Psychiatry, Jawaharlal Institute of Postgraduate Medical Education and Research (JIPMER), Puducherry, India
e-mail: ravi.psych@gmail.com

 
S. M. Y. Arafat and S. K. Kar (eds.), *Ecological and Social Determinants of Suicidal Behavior*, South Asian Perspectives in Mental Health and Psychology,
https://doi.org/10.1007/978-981-96-4028-7_1

*Self-existence, or the suicide that terminates it, is not the central question of philosophy. The hypothalamic-limbic complex automatically denies such logical reduction by countering it with feelings of guilt and altruism.*

*- E. O. Wilson, "Sociobiology: The New Synthesis"*

The contrast between the two quotations presented above illustrates the complexities involved in formulating theoretical models of suicide. From a philosopher's perspective, it is possible to debate whether suicide is ethically permissible, or even a rational response to a hostile or meaningless world. However, from the biologist's perspective, suicide is a puzzle and a paradox. If there is an evolutionarily driven imperative towards survival, how can this be reconciled with the phenomenon of human suicidal behaviour? Why is this behaviour seen across countries and cultures, even in those with a high material standard of living? If there are innate "defences" against suicide embedded in neural circuits, how are they overcome? Researchers and theorists from different fields have tried to answer this question from diverse perspectives—biological, psychological, social-cultural, or some combination thereof. This has resulted in the formulation of a wide range of models of suicidal behaviour.

In science, the term "model" refers to an attempt to represent a part of the existing world, and to understand or explain it, based on available observations (Frigg & Hartman, 2024). In the more restricted sense used in suicide research, a model is "an attempt to fit the established data into an overarching theory." Ideally, such a model should fulfil three criteria. First, it should be consistent with the available data. Second, it should address the relationship between internal (psychological) and external (interpersonal, social-cultural, environmental) factors. Third, it should provide insights into how "background" factors interact with immediate "triggers" leading to suicidal ideation and behaviour; if possible, it should have some predictive value (Barzilay & Apter, 2014).

Such models have a significance that transcends the purely theoretical. According to the latest data from the Global Burden of Disease studies, over 750,000 people die by suicide per year, yielding a global annual suicide rate of 9–10 per 100,000 population. In other words, suicide accounts for around 1.3% of global deaths. Gender differences in completed suicide are a striking and consistent finding across cultures and time periods, with a male-to-female ratio of approximately 2.2:1. In the period 2000–2019, there has been a modest decrease in the global suicide rate (around 2.4%), but suicide rates remain high in several regions, including Africa, Europe and South-East Asia. Over three-fourths of deaths due to suicide occur in low- and middle-income countries, and it is the fourth leading global cause of death in the age group of 15–29 years (Ilic & Ilic, 2022; Yip et al., 2022). Against this background, there is clearly a need for models of suicide that can inform efforts at prevention in clinical and community settings. At the individual level, such a model should inform our understanding of the dynamic interplay between risk and protective factors, and how these can be used to prevent initial or subsequent suicide attempts (Mitchell et al., 2017). At the community level, such a model should be able to identify groups or populations at a high risk of suicide due to social, cultural or economic vulnerabilities and provide leads towards effective prevention programmes (Oast & Zitrin, 1975;

Pirkis et al., 2024). The question that then arises is whether a single model will suffice, or whether we need separate models to address individuals and communities. Because most suicide research has been based on data from individual subjects, many models have focused on variables that influence suicide risk at the individual level (Rodríguez-Otero et al., 2022). However, some experts have attempted to model the relationship between "macro"-level demographic or economic variables and regional or national suicide rates (Lester, 1988).

The purpose of this chapter is to provide an overview of existing models of suicide, the evidence supporting them and their applications. Points of agreement and divergence between these models will be outlined, and the strengths and limitations of each model will be outlined. Following this, an attempt will be made to bridge the "micro" (individual) and "macro" (population) levels of suicide models using an ecological systems perspective.

## 2 Levels of Analysis in Models of Suicide

Before describing and evaluating models of suicide, a brief overview of the levels of analysis involved in these models is in order. In simple terms, suicide can be understood as arising from the interaction between an individual's vulnerability—which can be either innate or acquired—and factors in the external environment, particularly those of a stressful or traumatic nature. Models that make use of this perspective are known as *stress-diathesis models* and are widely used in the field of mental health (Booij et al., 2013). Initially, the stress-diathesis model of suicide was envisaged as a single entity, in which biological vulnerability, conceptualized in terms of genetic or biochemical factors, interacted with stressful events and the individual's appraisals of them to determine suicide risk (Rubinstein, 1986). With the passage of time and the accumulation of data, it is now clear that "stress-diathesis" is best used not to refer to a single model, but to a broad category of models that include these two elements. For example, a model that examines the interaction between multiple genetic loci and stress is a "stress-diathesis" model—but so is a model that examines the interaction between cognitive errors or deficits and specific life events (van Heeringen, 2012). As will be seen in the next section, most of the existing models of suicide are stress-diathesis models, differing mainly in terms of the way in which "diathesis" is construed.

The last statement brings us to a consideration of the biopsychosocial model and its relevance to suicide models. The biopsychosocial model was originally formulated by George Engel as a general framework for medical practice (Engel, 1977). This model was intended to be holistic rather than reductionistic and has been applied to a wide range of health conditions. Though there is no single "biopsychosocial model" of suicide, Engel's concept is useful in identifying the different *levels* at which risk or protective factors for suicide can be studied, namely the biological, psychological and the social. The study and modelling of these factors and levels generally occur when studying the individual's *diathesis* (Tio et al., 2024). Examples of factors at the *biological level* include genetic, epigenetic, neuroendocrine, immune-inflammatory, gut-brain axis or sleep-related biomarkers (Abou Chahla et al., 2023). Examples of factors at the *psychological level* include cognitive appraisals or variations in capabilities such as emotion regulation and theory of mind. Psychological variables often reflect a particular orientation—for example, a model based on cognitive theory would emphasize cognitive errors and distortions, while one based on psychodynamic theories would emphasize unconscious conflicts (Draper & Margolis, 1976; Prezant & Neimeyer, 1988). Examples of *social-level* factors include cultural values, religious beliefs and practices and economic circumstances (Mueller et al., 2021). These three levels do not exhaust the potential factors that can be considered in a model of suicide. For example, there is recent evidence linking environmental factors, such as climate change, with suicide (Cuijpers et al., 2023). There is also evidence linking particularly dietary patterns or constituents with suicide risk (Hibbeln & Gow, 2014). These findings highlight the need for considering an *environmental level* that is not encompassed by the other three levels. In a similar way, the status of *life events* in this scheme is ambiguous. Life events that are temporally correlated with suicidal ideation or behaviour can be considered "stressors" or "triggers," but the situation is not so simple regarding remote stressful or traumatic events (such as childhood abuse) or an ongoing chronic stressor (such as marital disharmony or workplace stress). Should these be placed on the "diathesis" or "stress" side of the equation? In the case of childhood adversity, it is customary to consider them as part of the diathesis, by invoking intermediate biological or psychological variables. For example, childhood adversity (exposure) leads to increased intolerance of uncertainty (intermediate variable) which increases the risk of suicide (outcome) (Jones et al., 2024). The exact placement of chronic stress in this schema remains unresolved.

It should also be noted that at each level—biological, psychological, social or environmental—both risk and protective factors exist. Sometimes, these are simple inverses of each other—for instance, social support reduces suicide risk whereas social isolation or loneliness increase it (Darvishi et al., 2024). In other cases, such as with genetic variants, dietary or environmental exposures and childhood events, these factors may be distinct or interrelated in complex ways. As an example, childhood sexual abuse is a risk factor for subsequent suicidality, whereas positive parenting is a protective factor—but positive parenting can also reduce the risk of experiencing abuse (Angelakis et al., 2020; Yilmaz & Bohara, 2021).

From the above discussion, it is evident that the theorist or researcher trying to construct a theory of suicide is faced with a rapidly increasing and interrelated list of variables that are difficult to model. For this reason, most models do not try to encompass every level of analysis: rather, they attempt a sort of "first-order approximation" by considering only certain salient variables, or by collapsing several variables into a single factor or dimension. For example, social factors such as support, number of household members, affiliation with a specific religious or cultural group, and participation in community activities can be "reduced" to a single dimension of *positive social connectedness* (Fässberg et al., 2012). Though there is some loss of precision in doing this, it is compensated for by greater simplicity and tractability of the model in real-world settings. This limitation must be kept in mind when describing, comparing and evaluating models of suicide. Another important fact to be kept in mind is that, because suicide models largely draw on the same "pool" of empirical data, there is a significant overlap between them. It may therefore be possible to "integrate" components of different models to obtain a single model that has greater explanatory power (Kleiman et al., 2014). One way of achieving this goal will be discussed at the end of this chapter.

## 3 Biological Models of Suicide

There is no single, integrated biological model that attempts to explain or predict suicidal behaviour. Different researchers have focused on the links between specific biomarkers or biological systems and suicidality and have formulated models to account for specific clinical or epidemiological observations. For example, it is well-known that completed suicide is more frequent in men than in women. Two biological hypotheses have been advanced to account for this. Lester (1987), based on earlier work by Skutsch (1981), hypothesized that this was due to the antagonism between oestrogen and dopamine. According to this hypothesis, high central levels of dopamine are associated with suicidal behaviour in patients with depression, and this effect is more marked in men because oestrogen inhibits dopamine release in women. More recently, Lenz et al. (2019) have proposed an "androgen model of suicide completion" based on clinical and research data. In this theory, both prenatal exposure to androgens and higher androgen levels during adult life are predictive of suicide. These researchers suggest that the association with androgen levels is specific to completed suicide, and not to instances of suicidal ideation or behaviour in general. Along similar lines, it has been found that men who make suicide attempts have higher cerebrospinal fluid (CSF) and plasma levels of testosterone, and that the CSF ratio of testosterone to the "stress hormone" cortisol was associated with impulsive and aggressive behaviour (Stefansson et al., 2016).

Among neurotransmitters, attention has been focused on serotonin, a monoamine transmitter implicated both in depression and in impulsive-aggressive behaviour (Jauhar et al., 2023; Moffitt et al., 1998). Broadly speaking, it is hypothesized that altered serotonergic transmission leads to depressed mood—which can trigger suicidal ideation—and lowers the threshold for impulsive or violent acts, facilitating the progression from ideas to suicide attempts (Picouto et al., 2015). There is some evidence to support this hypothesis. First, cerebrospinal fluid levels of both serotonin and its metabolite 5-hydroxyindoleacetic acid (5-HIAA) are lower in both suicide attempters and in post-mortem studies of persons who have died by suicide (Asberg, 1997; Musshoff et al., 2004). Second, functional variations in genes related to serotonergic transmission, such as the serotonin transporter *SLC6A4* and the tryptophan hydroxylase enzyme *TPH2*, have been associated both with suicidal behaviour and with intermediate phenotypes such as hopelessness (Du et al., 2001; Lazary et al., 2012; Ottenhof et al., 2018). However, other attempts to assess central serotonergic function have yielded mixed or negative results in patients exhibiting suicidal behaviour (Correa et al., 2002; Picouto et al., 2015). Moreover, in some cases, the use of antidepressants in an attempt to normalize serotonergic transmission has itself resulted in paradoxical suicidal acts (Healy & Whitaker, 2003). Overall, it appears that the link between serotonin and suicide is non-linear, and that a simplistic "serotonin model" of suicide is not tenable (de Leon et al., 2015).

Several other candidate biomarkers for suicide have been proposed. For example, some studies have found evidence of dexamethasone non-suppression in patients with suicidal ideation or behaviour, suggesting dysregulation of the hypothalamic–pituitary–adrenal (HPA) axis involved in stress sensitivity. However, results pertaining to this neuroendocrine axis, or to others such as the hypothalamic-pituitary-thyroid (HPT) axis, have been inconsistent and lack discriminant or predictive power (Weiss & Coccaro, 1997). Likewise, some researchers have found evidence of a link between patterns of circadian functioning (chronotype) and suicide. Their results suggest that an "eveningness" chronotype is associated with suicidal ideation or behaviour. However, this effect is influenced by other factors, such as depressed mood, and needs to be replicated in larger samples (Mokros et al., 2021; Park et al., 2018). More recently, elevations in pro-inflammatory cytokines, and elevated markers of oxidative stress, have also been demonstrated in persons who have made suicide attempts, suggesting a link between increased peripheral and central inflammation and suicidality. Though the strength of this evidence is much greater than that for serotonin, endocrine or chronobiological markers, much of it is derived from patients with an underlying psychiatric diagnosis (Vasupanrajit et al., 2021). It is unclear to what extent inflammation is linked to suicide in those without clear evidence of a mental disorder.

Novel molecular and statistical methods have also been used to identify biological vulnerability factors for suicide. For example, genome-wide association studies (GWAS) have been used to search for "suicide risk" genes without any theoretical presuppositions. Such research has identified genetic variants linked to neurotransmitters (dopamine and glycine) as well as novel loci related to synaptic function, protein transcription and cleavage, and a voltage-dependent calcium channel (Docherty et al., 2023). Developments in neuroimaging techniques have allowed a better characterization of functional brain networks—the connectome—in persons with a suicide attempt and their relatives. There is preliminary evidence of global deficits in brain connectivity and functioning, implicating the prefrontal and anterior cingulate cortices as well as the thalamus, striatum, in these individuals. Such deficits may be partially genetically determined (Wagner et al., 2019). Imaging techniques have also been used to infer increased microglial activation and inflammation in persons with suicidal ideation. These results have been used to construct a tentative hypothesis linking stress to increased conversion of tryptophan to quinolinic acid in lieu of serotonin, oxidative stress, neuroinflammation and disruption of the blood–brain barrier in individuals with suicidality (Baharikhoob & Kolla, 2020). However, a common limitation of these results and speculations is that they are not specific to suicide: similar genetic, connectomic and inflammatory results have been observed in individuals with other mental disorders, such as depression and nicotine dependence, and are not necessarily associated with suicidality in these disorders (Docherty et al., 2023; Wagner et al., 2019).

## 3.1 Evolutionary Models of Suicide

At a higher level of biological explanation, some theorists have attempted to understand suicidal behaviour from the perspective of evolutionary theory. At first glance, suicide is a "puzzle" from an evolutionary point of view, as it goes against the requirement for survival and reproduction (Aubin et al., 2013). However, there are certain circumstances in which suicidal behaviour could be construed as evolutionarily adaptive (Chatterjee & Rai, 2021).

Denys de Catanzaro was the first to propose a rigorous, mathematically modelled, evolutionary theory of suicide. He suggested that suicidal ideation and behaviour could be related to inclusive fitness. If individuals perceive themselves as being a burden to their relatives, and to have low reproductive potential, suicide is comprehensible as a means of increasing the availability of resources to these relatives, reducing the demand on their resources, and promoting their survival. In this model, suicide represents an example, albeit a dramatic one, of kin selection. This model has some support from empirical research and can explain suicide in circumstances such as chronic illness, old age, resource scarcity or the breakup of a marital relationship (de Catanzaro, 1984, 1986).

A similar but more restrictive hypothesis, proposed by Tanaka and Kinney (2011), suggests that evolutionary pressures favour suicidal behaviour in individuals with an infectious disease, as a means of preventing transmission to kin and thereby enhancing their survival. There is some ecological evidence supporting this model—for example, suicide rates are higher in regions with a higher infectious disease burden, or in those whose work exposes them to a risk of infection. Moreover, the immune-inflammatory changes triggered by infection can induce depressive-like symptoms and suicidal ideation. A major limitation of this hypothesis is that most suicides do not occur in individuals with infections. This model may be of use in explaining suicidality in very specific circumstances, such as the recent COVID-19 pandemic (Yan et al., 2023), but it cannot serve as a general evolutionary explanation for suicide.

A third hypothesis operating at the level of kin invokes the concept of aposematism, in which specific characteristics of an organism are both highly noticeable and act as a deterrent. In this model, proposed by Wiley (2020), it is suggested that suicidal behaviour, and particularly suicide, sensitizes members of a community towards the seriousness of suicidal threats or gestures. This would lead them to take such statements or acts more "seriously," and even to institute protective measures against suicide. In earlier times, such communities would have been composed of closely genetically related individuals. Thus, the death of an individual through suicide would promote kin survival indirectly, through a reduction in future suicide attempts among kin. There is some ecological support for this hypothesis, and it explains the persistence of suicidality as a trait across time. It does not account for phenomena such as suicide clusters (Haw et al., 2013). Besides, the notion of psychological aposematism—as opposed to the physical aposematism demonstrable and testable in insects—remains speculative, and it is unclear if the proposed benefits outweigh the losses incurred through the death of the individual.

At the individual level, evolutionary models of suicide focus on the interaction between inescapable pain and human cognitive capacities. The two major models based on this consideration are the "pain-brain model" and the "bargaining model" (also referred to as the "suffering ape hypothesis"). In both models, suicidal ideation and behaviour are triggered by chronic or severe pain from which the individual sees no chance of escape. Such pain may be physical, psychological or social in origin. According to the pain-brain theory, humans—unlike other animals—have a brain complex enough both to understand the permanence of death, and to devise methods of "self-killing." When these two factors are strong enough to overcome evolved tendencies towards self-preservation (known as "fenders" and "keepers"), the result is suicidal behaviour motivated by a desire to escape (Humphrey, 2018; Soper, 2023). In contrast, according to the bargaining model, suicide—or non-suicidal self-injury—is used to signal the distress caused by this pain to kin and to the wider community. This evokes responses that provide physical, emotional, or social support, and thereby correct the underlying trigger or situation (Syme et al., 2016; Steinkopf, 2023). A variant of the bargaining model sees suicide as a "costly form of apology" used to indicate one's remorse and desire to make reparations after a serious violation of social norms or laws (Syme & Hagen, 2019). The concept of seemingly maladaptive behaviours serving the purpose of communicating a need is not unique to suicide and was originally designed by Hagen (1999) to explain post-partum depression. Therefore, there is a certain lack of specificity in this model, though it does possess explanatory power across a wide range of cultures.

The final evolutionary hypothesis to be considered, which involves neither individual not kin selection, is the "parasite manipulation" hypothesis. Some parasites induce self-harming behaviour in their hosts in order to complete their life cycle. In this scenario, suicidal behaviour is deleterious to the host, but beneficial to the parasite. The most frequently cited example of such an interaction involves the protozoan *Toxoplasma gondii*. When *T. gondii* infects rats, it reduces their aversion to the odour of cats and their avoidance of or vigilance towards them. This leads to infected rats being killed by cats, which are the definitive host of *T. gondii*. The mechanism through which this occurs is thought to involve parasitic infection of rodent brain areas, such as the amygdala, involved in fear and threat perception (Postolache et al., 2021). This parasite can be transmitted to humans, particularly those who keep cats as pets. Existing human research suggests that there is a correlation between human *T. gondii* infection, as indicated by seropositivity for specific antibodies, and suicidal ideation or attempts (Zerekidze et al., 2024). However, there are some inconsistencies in this data, and it is not clear to what extent seropositivity correlates with brain infection or behavioural changes (Amouei et al., 2020; Wu & Chen, 2021). The seroprevalence of *T. gondii* infection in humans is high, ranging from 30 to 60%, and is often asymptomatic (Rahmanian et al., 2020); seropositivity has been non-specifically associated with several other mental disorders and not only with suicide (Hurley & Taber, 2012). Therefore, the "parasite manipulation" hypothesis is unlikely to have explanatory power as a general model of suicidality in humans. It may be applicable to individual cases where there is contact with cats, or with other routes of exposure to *T. gondii*.

## 4 Summary of Biological Models of Suicide

From this brief overview, it is evident that the neurobiology of suicide is complex, involving the interaction of multiple vulnerability genes with environmental stressors, and mediated through several biological pathways involving specific neurotransmitters, neurohormones, immune-inflammatory mediators, and alterations in biological rhythms. These may be best understood as "mechanisms" than as final "causes." Biological factors may explain certain group-level variations in suicide, such as gender differences, but they lack predictive or explanatory power at the individual level. As Mishara and Weisstub (2021) state, "it is impossible to predict the (suicidal) behaviors of individuals" even with the best available genetic or neurobiological methods. Even if such methods can be refined to yield more accurate probabilities, there are ethical challenges surrounding their use.

Evolutionary models of suicide are of interest in explaining how suicidal behaviour has persisted over "evolutionary time," but they must be subjected to rigorous testing in real-world settings. The best-supported models—the "inclusive fitness," "pain-brain" and "bargaining" models—overlap significantly with empirically validated psychological models of suicide and can be fruitfully integrated with them. For example, the "pain-brain" model overlaps with the "psychache," "social pain" and "predicament" models of suicide, while elements of the "inclusive fitness" and "bargaining" models dovetail with the interpersonal-psychological model. The integration of biological, evolutionary and psychosocial perspectives will be discussed more fully at the end of this chapter.

## 5 Psychological Models of Suicide

There are several models of suicide that are based primarily on intrapsychic factors, either alone or in combination with social or interpersonal factors. Lester (1994, 1998) enumerated 15 different theories or models of suicide that could be described as psychological. He also attempted to compare them by applying them to the suicides of well-known public figures, such as writers, actors or scientists, by extracting information from published biographies of these figures and "fitting" them to the elements of each model. The results of this study will be summarized later in this chapter (Sect. 6). For now, it is crucial to that these models vary not only based on included variables or factors but also on the theoretical orientation of their originators. Subsequent to Lester's work, several prominent models of suicide have been developed

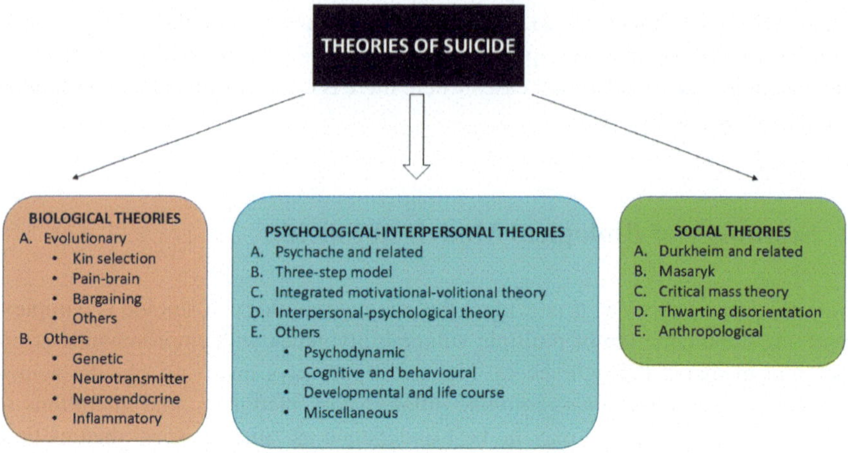


**Fig. 1** An overview of theoretical models of suicide

that fit into this category, such as the Interpersonal-Psychological Theory of Suicide (IPTS). These have sometimes been classified into "first" and "second" generation psychological theories on chronological grounds, but there is conceptual continuity between them (Yöyen & Keleş, 2024).

A brief summary of the various models of suicide is provided in Fig. 1. In the overview that follows, certain models will be covered in more detail due to their influence or historical importance. This should not be taken to imply that other models are less significant or valid: it is often the case that a model attains prominence because of temporal priority, novelty or a larger body of associated empirical research.

## *5.1 Shneidman: Psychache and Suicide*

One of the earliest and most influential psychological models of suicide was proposed by Edwin Shneidman. In his words, "suicide is caused by psychache." *Psychache* is defined as "psychological pain or anguish" and occurs in relation to emotions such as shame, guilt, anxiety or social situations such as humiliation or isolation. Though such emotions and experiences are part of the human condition, they can lead to suicide if the individual considers them "unbearable." Central to this model is the notion that there is marked inter-individual variation in the threshold for tolerating psychache, and this accounts for inter-individual variations in suicide risk. Elaborating further on this model, Shneidman describes it as predominantly psychological in focus, and traces several steps in the progression to suicide. First, there is the experience of stressful or adverse life events. Second, there is the appraisal of these events as psychologically painful. Third, there is a perception of this psychological pain, or psychache, as intolerable. Fourth, there is the thought that death is the only solution or "escape" from intolerable psychache. Fifth, there is a lowered threshold for enduring psychache, which may be innate, acquired, or both. Finally, there is the suicidal outcome, namely a completed suicide, resulting from the thought that the individual cannot live with the current level of pain (Shneidman, 1993). Elaborating on the concept of psychache, Shneidman specifies that it arises from "frustrated psychological needs" for privacy, identity, love, belonging, mastery, meaning or protection from humiliation (Shneidman, 1998). Though this model's primary focus is on intrapsychic phenomena, it is not reductionist: it can be extended to incorporate biological and social factors. Biological variables may influence an individual's threshold to tolerate psychache (i.e., the diathesis), while social factors may both sensitize an individual to psychache and serve as its source (i.e., they figure on both the stress and diathesis sides of the equation) (Shneidman, 2011). From the perspective of suicide prevention at the individual level, the psychache model emphasises the need for therapists to address psychological pain by identifying the specific need that is thwarted and tailoring psychotherapeutic techniques to it. From a public health perspective, Shneidman observes that "the explanation of suicide in humankind is the same as the explanation of the suicide of any particular human" (Shneidman, 1993). This implies that attempts to reduce suicide at a population level should focus on reducing the social roots of psychache, and improving the "psychological pain threshold" of vulnerable or at-risk groups.

Two key merits of this model are its simplicity and its support from empirical research in clinical and community settings. By introducing the concept of psychache as a conceptual bridge between stress and diathesis, Shneidman's model permits the consideration of multiple risk factors while focusing attention on the immediate circumstances surrounding a suicide attempt. His description of the transition from acute psychological pain to suicidal behaviour is very similar to contemporary descriptions of the "suicide crisis syndrome" characterized by feelings of entrapment, mood changes, increased arousal, social withdrawal and a loss of higher-level control over suicidal ideas or impulses (Melzer et al., 2024). Empirical research from both "Western" and "Eastern" cultures has confirmed the hypothesis that mental or psychological pain is both a precursor and a predictor of suicidal ideation and behaviour (Demirkol et al., 2024; El Keshky, 2024; Ielmini et al., 2022; Marcinkevičiūtė et al., 2024; Siau et al., 2024). More recently, researchers have attempted to integrate the concept of psychache into the IPTS, showing that these two theories are isomorphic to a certain extent: constructs such as "thwarted belongingness" and "perceived burdensomeness" in the IPTS correspond to Shneidman's "frustrated psychological needs." Both these constructs appear to predict levels of psychache (Brooks et al., 2024).

### 5.1.1 Variants and Elaborations of the Psychache Model

Some more recent models of suicide, though starting from different perspectives, are very similar to the psychache model and can be considered variants of it. The *predicament model* of suicide, developed by Pridmore and colleagues, suggests that suicidal behaviour originates from an uncomfortable and intolerable situation (the predicament) from which the individual sees little or no chance of escape. In this model, the predicament can be either internal (a mental or physical illness), external (circumstances such as financial loss or maltreatment) or both. Though the concept of psychache is not explicit in this model, the predicament model does emphasize the relationship between painful and unescapable conditions and suicide—in other words, the "final common pathway" to suicide is unbearable mental pain (Pridmore & Jamil, 2009; Pridmore & McArthur, 2010; Pridmore et al., 2015). The *strain model* postulates that suicidal ideas and behaviour arise not from a single stressor or predicament, but from the *strain* that an individual caught between two "competing stresses" experiences. Such strain can be related to values, aspirations, deprivation, or inability to cope with a critical life situation. Being under such a strain induces negative emotions, ideas of hopelessness, and ultimately mental pain (in other words, psychache). Such pain, in conjunction with other psychological or social factors, leads to suicidality (Zhang, 2016; Zhang et al., 2017).

At this juncture, it is also worth examining two models that are, in a sense, more sophisticated versions of the psychache model. The *social pain model* combines perspectives from psychology, neurobiology and evolutionary theory. This model postulates that experiences of social exclusion or rejection can lead to negative social cognitions and the experience of social pain, which triggers suicide-related cognitions. Social pain also reduces the threshold for acting on such cognitions, leading to suicidal behaviour (Gunn, 2017). The social pain model can be seen as a neurobiological update to the psychache model, based on recent research showing an overlap between the neural circuits for physical pain and pain caused by adverse social experiences (Courtet & Olie, 2017; Eisenberger, 2012). The *cry of pain model* sees suicide as the outcome of perceived "entrapment" in stressful circumstances from which there is no foreseen escape or help from others (Williams, 2014). A central construct in this model is the notion of "arrested flight," in which an animal encounters defeat but is unable to escape from it. When humans find themselves in similar situations, the result is unbearable mental anguish (in other words, psychache) resulting in suicide as an expression of this pain (Rasmussen et al., 2010). Like the social pain model, the cry of pain model represents a synthesis of ethological, evolutionary and psychological theories. Both these models illustrate how the seemingly simple psychache model can be elaborated and grounded more firmly both in theory and in empirical evidence. They are also fully consistent with the "pain-brain" evolutionary model of suicide.

## 5.2 *Klonsky and May: The Three-Step Model of Suicide*

It is well-known that many individuals experience suicidal ideation without acting on it: a recent meta-analysis found that only 3%–37% of ideators in the general population "transition" to a suicide attempt (Haregu et al., 2023). Research has also shown that the risk factors for suicidal ideation and attempts are not necessarily the same

(Li et al., 2022). What causes suicidal ideas to arise and persist over time? Are they caused by rising levels of mental pain, or does ideation precede mental pain? Is there a certain "threshold" at which mental pain causes the individual to move from suicidal ideas to acts? One of the drawbacks of the psychache model and its variants is that they do not fully succeed at answering such questions. For this reason, Klonsky and May suggested that a complete theory of suicide should use an "ideation-to-action" framework, with equal attention paid to two processes: (i) the origin and development of suicidal ideas and (ii) the transition from ideas to attempts. Building on this guiding principle, these researchers developed the *three-step theory of suicide*, sometimes abbreviated 3ST (Klonsky & May, 2014, 2015). As its name suggests, this theory is based on three sequential steps. First, suicidal ideation arises due to pain (mental, physical, or social) and ideas of hopelessness. Second, suicidal ideas intensify in individuals with low connectedness. Here, *connectedness* is understood broadly as including both connections with other people and attachments to a task, an institution, or even an idea or belief that confers a sense of purpose. Third, in the presence of strong suicidal ideation, additional factors influence the *capability* for suicide. These may be innate (for example, traits such as impulsivity, pain sensitivity, or the cognitive ability to plan an attempt), acquired (exposure to situations involving pain, trauma, or death), or practical (knowledge of, and access to, means such as firearms or pesticides). As capability increases, the likelihood of an attempt increases (Klonsky et al., 2021). An obvious advantage of this model is that it encompasses psychache-related models: it assigns a key role to psychological pain in the genesis of suicidal ideas, as well as in the acquired capacity for suicide attempts, but acknowledges the importance of other factors such as hopelessness, social support, a sense or meaning or purpose and the role of genetic and situational factors. Empirical research has provided support for various facets of the 3ST and provides support for its validity, it's utility as a conceptual framework and its predictive value, with certain caveats (Brown et al., 2021; Guo et al., 2024; Kelly et al., 2023; Tsai et al., 2021). There is also preliminary evidence that it is applicable across cultures (Ahmadboukani et al., 2023; Siau et al., 2024; Yang et al., 2019). From a practical standpoint, a virtue of this model is that it supports and informs multifaceted suicide prevention strategies that can target each step of the suicidal process. These include cognitive techniques to address ideas of hopelessness (Brown et al., 2005), existential or salutogenic interventions to develop a sense of purpose (Wilchek-Aviad & Cohen-Louck, 2022), enhancing social support to improve interpersonal connectedness (Hou et al., 2022) and reducing access to specific means of suicide (Noghrehchi et al., 2024). Another possible advantage of this model is that though its basic framework is simple, it can be used to organize a wide range of biological, psychological, social and environmental risk factors for suicide, and to explain at which step they act. Thus, for example, genetic factors may affect the innate capacity for suicide through their influence on temperamental factors, while social rejection can trigger suicidal ideation through its effects on mental pain (Klonsky, 2018).

### 5.3 O'Connor: The Integrated Motivational-Volitional Model of Suicide

Another "three-stage" model of broad scope is the Integrated Motivational-Volitional (IMV) model of suicide, developed by O'Connor and colleagues (O'Connor, 2011; O'Connor & Kirtley, 2018). As its name suggests, this model attempts to integrate a wide range of risk factors at different levels and to understand the transition from motivation (i.e., suicidal ideas or intentions) to volition (i.e., suicide attempts). The latter objective is similar to that of the 3ST, but a crucial difference between the IMV and the 3ST is the way in which the suicidal process is conceptualized. The first "step" in IMV is the *pre-motivational phase*. This involves "background events and triggering factors" that precede the formation of suicidal ideas or plans and involves interactions between individual diathesis (e.g., genetic or developmental factors), environmental variables, and current life events. At this stage, genetic, developmental, and environmental variables act as temporally remote "predisposing factors," while current life events act as "triggering factors" (O'Connor, 2011). The second stage, known as the *motivational phase*, is triggered by experiences of defeat or humiliation. This leads to perceived entrapment, as in Williams' cry of pain model. Perceived entrapment leads to the formation of suicidal ideas and the intent (motivation) to end one's life. The transition from defeat/humiliation to entrapment is moderated by *"threat to self" moderators*, which determine whether a given negative life event is perceived as leading to entrapment. These moderators are largely intrapsychic in origin and include capacities for problem-solving and coping, negative ruminations, and biases in recall of past life events. The transition from entrapment to suicidal ideation and motivation is moderated by *"motivational" moderators* which can be either internal (e.g., life goals, resilience) or external (e.g., social support, cultural norms and values). In this model, motivational moderators also include the constructs of *thwarted belongingness* and *burdensomeness*, derived from the IPTS. These concepts will be explained in the description of the IPTS. The final *volitional phase* involves the movement from suicidal ideation and intent to suicidal acts. Factors that influence this transition are known as *volitional moderators*. Like motivational moderators, these can be either internal (e.g., pain sensitivity, fear of death, past suicide attempts) or external (access to specific means, exposure to the suicide of others).

This model is slightly more complex than the 3ST and is eclectic in that it incorporates elements of several other psychological models, both within and outside the field of suicidology. These include the theory of planned behaviour (Ajzen, 1991), the stress-diathesis models (Rubinstein, 1986), the arrested flight model (Gilbert & Allan, 1998), the cry of pain model (Williams, 2014) and the IPTS (Ribeiro & Joiner, 2009; Van Orden et al., 2010). An advantage of this approach is that it considers evidence from a wide range of fields, including clinical practice, cognitive psychology, behavioural psychology and evolutionary psychology. The IMV attempts to delineate the specific moderators that influence transitions from one phase of the suicidal process to another, and it does so in a more "fine-grained" manner than the 3ST. Because of this, it has practical implications in terms of interventions that could address each set of moderator variables. Motivational moderators could be modified either through individual therapies, focused on developing resilience and identifying life goals as "reasons for living," or by providing social support at crucial moments. Volitional moderators, particularly those external to the patient—such as access to means of suicide or exposure to suicidal deaths in the media—can be addressed through public health or legislative measures designed to curtail them.

Empirical research has found that the IMV is valuable in understanding several aspects of the suicidal process in clinical and community settings. It has been used to identify those variables, such as social defeat, perceived entrapment and perceived burdensomeness, that differentiate between suicidal and non-suicidal self-harm in a hospital setting (Cleare et al., 2021). The volitional moderators outlined by the IMV, such as exposure to others' suicide and impulsivity, reliably distinguished persons with suicidal ideation from those who had made a suicide attempt (Branley-Bell et al., 2019). Likewise, the motivational moderators of the IMV were found to predict the emergence of suicidal ideation in young adults followed up for a year (Wetherall et al., 2021), and a latent class analysis based on the IMV model was used to identify suicide risk in this population over 3 years (van Eijk et al., 2023).

## 5.4 Joiner: The Interpersonal-Psychological Theory of Suicide

Perhaps the most "popular" theory or model of suicide, as measured by the quantity of research related to it, is the interpersonal-psychological theory of suicide (IPTS) (Hjelmeland & Knizek, 2019). The initial version of this model, known as the interpersonal theory of suicide, was elaborated by Joiner (2005). Subsequently, this model was extended and refined into the current form of the IPTS (Joiner et al., 2021; Van Orden et al., 2010). In its most basic form, the IPTS states that suicidal behaviour occurs if two conditions are fulfilled: "the desire to die and the capability to act on this desire" (Ribeiro & Joiner, 2009). These two conditions are separate from each other. The *desire to die* in the IPTS is understood to arise from two constructs of an interpersonal nature. The first of these, *thwarted belongingness*, corresponds to the individual's perception that they are alone, isolated or abandoned. It arises from a "sense of disconnection from others," loneliness and a lack of supportive or caring relationships. The second, *perceived burdensomeness*, refers to the individual's view of themselves as a burden to others. Such a perception is often out of proportion to a person's actual circumstances. Both these can lead to "passive" suicidal ideation. In addition, both of these, if severe enough, lead to ideas of *hopelessness*, the sense that current circumstances will "never change." This leads to the desire to die. The capability for suicide, or more specifically the *acquired capability*, is also viewed in terms of two internal constructs. The first, *lowered fear of death*, influences the transition from the desire to die to actual suicidal intent. The second, *increased pain tolerance*, influences the transition from suicidal intent to suicide attempts. Apart from these two constructs, capability for suicide is also influenced by genetic vulnerability and the availability of specific means of suicide (Joiner et al., 2021; Van Orden et al., 2010).

This theory has certain similarities to the IMV, particularly in the concept of specific moderators that influence transitions from one stage of the suicidal process to another: in fact, the developers of the IMV have acknowledged their debt to the IPTS (O'Connor and Kirtley, 2018). In terms of implications for suicide prevention, Joiner et al. (2021) have emphasized the importance of "caring follow-up contact" during a suicide crisis or following a suicide attempt, which should include both caring communication and the provision of points of contact, such as a telephone helpline, for further care and support. They also discuss the utility and acceptability of "means safety" (as opposed to "means restriction") as a method of reducing suicide risk. Thus, if the use of firearms or pesticides is part of a region's culture, strict regulation measures may meet with resistance from the local population. Instead, individuals, families and communities can be taught methods of handling these "means of suicide" safely.

There is a large body of research examining the validity, predictive properties and real-world utility of the IPTS in diverse populations. Two meta-analyses have synthesized this evidence and reviewed it critically. The first (Ma et al., 2016) examined data from 66 studies. It found significant evidence to support a link between perceived burdensomeness and suicidal ideation, and some evidence that hopelessness mediated the link between thwarted belongingness and suicidal ideation. Associations between acquired capacity and suicide attempts were mixed, and studies that tested the entire model, looking for interactions between all four factors, yielded inconsistent results. The second (Chu et al., 2017) examined data from 122 independent samples. It found that the interaction between both interpersonal constructs was associated with suicidal ideation, and that the interaction between these constructs and capability for suicide was linked to the number of suicide attempts. However, the magnitude of each of these effects was small, and there was evidence of bias in the reporting of certain results. Overall, there is some empirical evidence to support the individual "nodes" of the IPTS, but relatively less for the model in its entirety.

As might be expected for a popular and influential model, the IPTS has been subjected to significant criticism. Perceived limitations of the model include exaggerated claims of its accuracy, selective presentations of empirical evidence, an undue emphasis on individual perceptions as opposed to external realities, a neglect of social and cultural factors, inconsistencies regarding the role of pain tolerance, possible concerns regarding conflicts of interest and publication bias and the observation that suicides can and do occur even if none of the components of the IPTS are substantially present (Hjelmeland & Knizek, 2019). In addition, it has been noted that there is a discordance between the IPTS and evolutionary models of suicide (Soper, 2024). Prescinding from these specific criticisms, a general critique of the IPTS is that it is overly reductionist and does not capture the heterogeneity and complexity of suicidal behaviour (Paniagua et al., 2010). The developers of the IPTS have responded to these criticisms at some length, pointing to the evidence base in support of it while acknowledging that there is substantial "room for improvement" (Joiner et al., 2021; Robison et al., 2024). After carefully reviewing the arguments for or against, the following tentative conclusions can be reached. First, the IPTS cannot explain or predict every case of suicide, this is inherent in the very concept of a model, which is a simplified representation of reality that is meant to be useful as a heuristic and not as the "final truth" regarding the phenomenon under consideration. Second, there is a need to compare the usefulness of the IPTS with other models in diverse settings, and to attempt to integrate its best-verified components with those of others (Robison et al., 2024). Third, while certain criticisms of the IPTS are grounded in evidence, it remains a useful model for research and a guide to clinicians and public health experts, provided that its accuracy and predictive power are not overstated (Stanley et al., 2016).

## 5.5 *Other Psychological Models of Suicide*

The four models described above are probably the ones most frequently invoked and cited in the literature on suicide. Though it is not feasible to describe every other psychological model at length, a brief overview of these, organized roughly according to theoretical orientation, is presented below.

### 5.5.1 Psychodynamic Models of Suicide

Psychodynamic models of suicide are those that assign a central role to unconscious psychological conflicts, repression and defence mechanisms. These are based on concepts originally developed by Sigmund Freud and his collaborators but have evolved significantly over the past century (Meissner, 1977; Rangell, 1988). Though Freud did not directly attempt to model suicide, he linked suicidal behaviour to his theory of melancholia. According to this model, a state of pathological mourning arises from anger or aggression towards a lost loved object, such as a parental figure, that is ambivalently viewed and internalized or "introjected." As a result of this, anger is directed towards the self, resulting in depression, morbid guilt and suicidal ideation and behaviour (Freud, 2005).

Karl Menninger elaborated on this by postulating that suicide results from both an aggressive element, as in Freud's theory, and the "submissive" element of a "wish to die." He identified three components of the suicidal act: "killing, dying and being killed." In a subsequent monograph, "Man Against Himself," he extended this theory to explain not only suicidal behaviour but also non-suicidal self-injury or self-mutilation, accidents, mental disorders such as depression, and even certain physical illnesses that have a putative psychological component (Menninger, 1933, 1938).

Alfred Adler, a prominent dissenter from Freud's views, also emphasized the link between anger or aggression and suicide. However, he situated this anger in a social rather than an intrapsychic context, considering that suicide had a "social intention," namely, "to cause sorrow" to others or to "force them to appreciate what they have lost." This anger is directed towards a person or persons whom the individual believes has "slighted" or undervalued them. Thus, Adler viewed suicide as a form of maladaptive or paradoxical communication with an aggressive intent. This view is, in some ways, reminiscent of evolutionary theories of suicide as a form of social signalling (Adler, 1927; Ansbacher, 1969). Adler also linked suicide to a "neurotic form of thinking" characterized by cognitive errors (Neuringer, 1974). In a sense, his work can be seen as bridging the gap between earlier psychodynamic theories of suicide and later cognitive and interpersonal models.

Other psychodynamic explanations for suicidal behaviour have been advanced in the literature, including a "plea for love" in the face of social or sexual failure or rejection, a "path to glory" (as seen, for example, in kamikaze pilots or suicide bombers), or as a defence against an unconscious fear of castration, or more generally, as a defence against a "fate worse than death" (Rangell, 1988). Psychodynamic theories have fallen out of fashion, both because of their eclipse by biological, cognitive and interpersonal models, and due to the difficulty in empirically measuring unconscious psychological processes. Nevertheless, many aspects of these models—for example, the links between childhood adversity and suicide, the understanding of suicide as an "escape" from an intolerably painful or insoluble situation and the relationships between suicide, non-suicidal self-injury and depression are still relevant to contemporary suicidology. Contemporary models linking suicide to psychological pain, or to thwarted psychological needs, still contain echoes of psychodynamic concepts.

### 5.5.2 Cognitive and Cognitive-Behavioural Models of Suicide

In contrast to psychodynamic theories, cognitive and cognitive-behavioural models of suicide focus on thoughts and behaviours that are observable and accessible to scientific investigation. Aaron Beck, the founding father of cognitive-behavioural therapy, highlighted the link between hopelessness and suicide. Through empirical research in persons who had made a suicide attempt, he and his collaborators found that hopelessness was a better predictor of suicide risk than depressive symptoms (Kovacs et al., 1975) and that hopelessness mediated the relationship between depression and suicide (Beck et al., 1975). Though he did not formulate a single model of suicide, his work can be seen as anticipating several components of later models, such as the importance of suicidal intent in the transition from suicidal ideas to attempts (Bedrosian & Beck, 1979; Kovacs & Beck, 1977), the role of losses in early life as a risk factor for suicide in the face of later losses (Lester & Beck, 1976), the importance of social factors such as unemployment (Brown et al., 2000), and the utility of cognitive therapy in reducing the risk of suicide by correcting erroneous ideas about oneself, the external world, and the future (Brown et al., 2005; Rush & Beck, 1978). He also highlighted the complex and heterogeneous nature of suicidal phenomena (Beck et al., 1976) and the possible role of some suicide attempts as a form of communication (Beck & Lester, 1976).

These insights have been incorporated into more systematic models of suicide by later workers with a cognitive-behavioural orientation. One of these, which combines insights from cognitive theory with elements of the psychache and psychodynamic models, was proposed by Antoon Leenaars. In his model, suicide arises from a conjunction of intrapsychic and interpersonal processes: it is "an intrapsychic drama on an interpersonal stage." The *intrapsychic processes* include intolerable psychological pain, cognitive constriction (characterized by logical errors and rigidity in thinking), indirect expressions of unconscious processes or drives (such as ambivalence, aggression, or a desire for punishment), a low capacity to adjust to challenging situations, and low ego strength. The *interpersonal processes* include current interpersonal problems, acute experiences of loss or rejection, an identification with the lost or rejecting person, and a desire to "escape" from the pain caused by the interpersonal trauma. This model is in some ways similar to the IPTS, but places a much greater emphasis on psychodynamic constructs such as low ego strength, a harsh superego, and Freud's notion of aggression directed towards an internalized and ambivalently viewed "love object" (Leenaars, 1996).

A different cognitive model of suicide was proposed by Rudd (2000). This model draws on the fundamental concepts defined by Beck to propose a construct known as the *suicidal mode*. This mode includes components from four systems—cognitive, affective, behavioural and physiological. The cognitive component, which is the most central in this model, is a *suicidal belief system* based on Beck's cognitive triad—negative views of the self ("I am useless," "I am a burden to others"), others ("no one cares about me") and the future ("my situation cannot improve," "I cannot bear this anymore"), along with specific assumptions and compensatory strategies, leading to specific suicidal thoughts. The affective component involves mixed negative effects of sadness, anger, anxiety, shame and the like, collectively referred to as "dysphoria." The behavioural component includes suicidal planning and preparatory behaviours, while the physiological component involves autonomic and sensorimotor activation. The suicidal belief system is triggered by specific stressful circumstances, as well as the individual's appraisal of these circumstances. This model also gives importance to predisposing factors such as mental illness, past suicidal behaviour, early life adversity, and observation of suicidal behaviour in one's parents. A very similar model was developed by Rickelman and Houfek (1995). This model does not provide a detailed characterization of a suicidal mode or belief system but emphasizes interactions between Beck's cognitive concepts (cognitive errors, negative automatic thoughts, maladaptive schemata), biological factors, ongoing life stress or adversity, the presence of mental illness or substance abuse, past suicide attempts and demographic factors such as age, gender and ethnicity. Depending on the nature of these interactions and the severity of external circumstances, cognitive errors lead to negative affective states, suicidal ideation and suicide attempts.

A cognitive model that is not explicitly based on Beck's ideas is the *active inference* model proposed by Krupnik and Danilova (2024). This theory is based on the principle that biological systems must minimize their *variational free energy*, which is a measure of the "surprise" or "uncertainty" of sensory states. The brain is considered to be a "generative model" of the environment that receives both internal and external sensory inputs and makes predictions based on them. Under exposure to stress, interoceptive signals of stress, such as changes in cardiovascular, respiratory or endocrine parameters, signal a "prediction error" to the brain. When combined with sensory signals related to external stressors, this results in a "stream of prediction errors" that must be resolved. Individual self-efficacy then generates behaviours that are meant to address the stressor and return to a homoeostatic, low-error state. However, if prediction errors markedly exceed or overwhelm the capacity for precise predictions, self-efficacy may bias an individual towards self-destructive (suicidal) behaviour to minimize free energy. There is some indirect support for this model in the psychological literature, in which higher levels of "grit," a measure of self-efficacy and perseverance, have been associated with a greater transition from non-suicidal self-injury to suicide attempts (Anestis & Selby, 2015). An important prediction of this model is that therapies aimed at enhancing self-efficacy may sometimes have a paradoxical effect on suicidal behaviour. The developers of this model suggest that therapies for suicide prevention, based on cognitive-behavioural techniques, should be "skilfully" tailored to individual characteristics such as impulsivity and the current level of suicidal ideation.

Most of the foregoing discussion has focused on cognitive variables. Bostock and Williams (1975) used behavioural principles, based on operant conditioning, to model suicide attempts. Their theory is not meant to account for suicidal ideation or initial attempts, but for the well-known observation that past suicidal behaviour is a robust predictor of future suicidal behaviour. In this model, a suicide attempt is an operant (an individual's attempt to manipulate the environment). Subsequent responses from the social environment—either from significant others and caregivers, or from the healthcare system—may reinforce this behaviour, thereby increasing its likelihood in the future. Based on these principles, they recommend that hospital staff should avoid inadvertent reinforcement of suicidal threats or behaviour, while providing positive reinforcement for "alternative" (non-suicidal) behaviour. These principles should also be communicated to caregivers to ensure generalization to real-world settings, and patients should be encouraged to use cognitive methods of "self-reinforcement." Though this model is theoretically plausible, it has not been systematically evaluated and is somewhat reductionistic in its view of the triggers for repeated suicide attempts. Moreover, it is difficult to rigorously practice the sort of differential reinforcement that this model calls for in real-world hospital or clinic settings.

### 5.5.3 Developmental and Life Course Theories of Suicide

It is well documented that rates of suicidal behaviour vary across the life span: they are low in childhood, increase during adolescence and are markedly increased in late life (Ryan & Oquendo, 2020). Certain models based on developmental and life cycle considerations have been developed to account for this variation. Erik Erikson, one of the pioneers of a life course approach to psychology, emphasized the link between identity formation and suicide in adolescents. According to his model, adolescence is a stage characterized by the psychosocial crisis of *identity versus role diffusion*. Failure to successfully navigate this stage leads to a state of *identity diffusion*, which can predispose to suicidal behaviour (Erikson, 1950; Leenaars et al., 2001; Zimmerman, 1992). In more general terms, each of Erikson's developmental stages has its own associated crisis, and failure to navigate it may increase the risk of suicide (Maris, 1995).

Draper (1976) proposed a developmental model of suicide based on psychodynamic concepts. According to this model, the roots of suicidal behaviour later in life lie in experiences of one's mother being physically or emotionally unavailable, which can be due to death, separation or physical or mental illness. If such experiences occur between the ages of 4 and 12 months, they constitute a "suicidogenic trauma." If such a person is exposed to experiences of loss or separation from a "loved object" at later stages in their life (e.g., the breakup of a romantic relationship in adolescence or divorce or widowhood in adult life), this can precipitate a suicide attempt. This model also postulates that suicides due to physical illness are related to this phenomenon, as they are perceived as threatening the individual with separation from a loved object through their own death. This model is "developmental" in that it connects early developmental experiences with later suicidal behaviour, but it does not specifically explain the increased risk of suicide at certain stages of the life cycle.

Chew and McCleary (1994) suggested that variations in suicide across the lifespan were related to changes in motivation and opportunity at each stage of life. In this model, an individual's suicide risk at a given time of life is a product of three factors: motivation, surveillance, and access to means of suicide. In childhood, suicidal behaviour is low due to relatively few motives and low opportunity (increased surveillance by parents and other adults, low access to means). Suicide risk rises in adolescence and young adulthood due to an increase in the number of motives (academic, occupational, interpersonal), increased access to means and increased privacy (which implies lower surveillance). The nature of the motive changes in middle and late life, but access to means remains high. This model has been used to explain variability in suicide both across age groups and across time.

Ludwig et al. (2017) have proposed a "life span model" of suicide that integrates genetic and epigenetic research with the IPTS. In this model, the "diathesis" component is the individual's genome, with several genetic variants, each of small effect, influencing the risk of suicide (Docherty et al., 2023). The "stress" component refers to epigenetic changes—changes in gene expression brought about by painful, stressful or traumatic situations that the individual experiences throughout their lifespan. These neurobiological processes are reflected in higher-order cognitive and affective changes, such as the "thwarted belongingness" and "perceived burdensomeness" of the IPTS or the "psychological pain" of the psychache-based models. In this model, emphasis is laid on the cumulative effect of exposure to environmental adversity—in other words, the risk of suicide evolves across the life cycle. Though this model does not directly explain variations in suicide across developmental stages, it emphasizes the need to consider the totality of an individual's life experiences and their effects on biological and psychological processes.

### 5.5.4 Other Models of Suicide

Certain models of suicide cannot easily be classified into the above categories but are of theoretical or historical significance nonetheless. The first of these to be considered, advanced by Henry and Short (1954), combines psychodynamic, behavioural and sociological principles. According to this model, suicidal behaviour occurs in individuals who fulfil the following criteria: they are not significantly subjected to external restraints, have weak interpersonal relationships, and have had a complex relationship with their parents characterized by high expectations, a predominance of psychological over physical punishment, harsh punishment of any expression of anger, and experiencing punishment from the parent who was their primary attachment figure. They further hypothesized that such a parent–child relationship would be more common in single-parent families. According to this model, such circumstances would lead to the formation of a harsh, punitive superego and the learning of maladaptive behaviours. In their final analysis, suicide is seen as an act of aggression that becomes self-directed (as in Freud's model) because the child's primary tendency to express aggression outwards has been inhibited by their childhood experiences. This model is no longer an active focus of interest in suicidology, mainly because it is not supported by empirical evidence. It remains a thought-provoking early attempt to integrate psychological and sociological theories of suicide (Lester, 1968).

Ronald Maris' model of suicide (Maris, 1982, 1983, 1986) is important because of its depth and its overlap with the psychache, IPTS and existential models. According to Maris, "suicide is a solution to the problem of life itself"; in other words, human existence itself, or "the human condition," forms the basis for suicide. This view is in line with existentialist and absurdist philosophical views, in which suicide is seen as a "rational" response to a life that is meaningless or absurd (Roberts & Lamont, 2014). Like Menninger, Maris envisaged a "panorama of self-destructive behaviours" that included risk-taking or other forms of "indirect suicide." At a fundamental level, he considered that suicide was due to either an inability or a refusal to accept the "terms of the human condition." From the point of view of the attempter, suicide is "rational." In this model, the likelihood of suicide is increased in a cumulative manner by factors that interfere with "adaptation to the human condition." Such factors include biological vulnerability, early life adversity, physical illness, depression and life stressors associated with failure or social rejection. Suicide risk is also increased by "non-suicidal" self-destructive behaviours, such as substance use. Though this model does not explicitly examine the transitions from suicidal ideation to attempts, it is an integrative model much like the 3ST, IMV and IPTS.

In a more general sense, existential theories of suicide view suicidal behaviour as a "confession" on the part of the attempter that "life possesses no worth or value" in the face of struggles and contradictions. Moreover, the attempt to artificially impose meaning or worth on an "absurd" human condition, when there is no such actual meaning, may itself lead to frustration and a sense of nihilism (Roberts & Lamont, 2014). This view is somewhat at odds with the finding that a sense of meaning, purpose, or connection reduces the risk of suicidal ideation or repeated suicide attempts (Drum et al., 2017; Sjöström et al., 2012). Nevertheless, there is merit in existential theories' emphasis on the need to address the individual's sense of meaninglessness and to find a way to move beyond it in the context of their specific life situation. This may be feasible within a cognitive-behavioural or dialectical behavioural therapy framework (Heidenreich et al., 2021).

Orbach (1994) hypothesized that suicide was linked to the process of dissociation. In this model, "dissociation" is defined as a break in conscious experience characterized by two components: a sense of "splitting or detachment," and a loss of control over the ability to monitor one's behaviour. He highlighted the similarities between this state and the "cognitive constriction" or "tunnel vision" that precedes suicide in Shneidman's and Leenaars' models. In this model, early life adversity increases both sensitivity to stress and the likelihood to experience dissociation as a form of self-defence. Continued stress leads to a dissociative state aimed at reducing psychological pain, which also reduces sensitivity to physical pain. In conjunction with ideas of hopelessness and helplessness, this leads to self-injurious or suicidal behaviour. There is some support in the literature for a link between childhood abuse, dissociation, and suicidality, but this appears to be significant only in a subset of those attempting suicide (Calati et al., 2017).

Finally, the *fluid vulnerability theory* is a novel model that emphasizes the "non-linear" and "dynamic" nature of suicidality (Bryan et al., 2020). In this model, suicide is seen as an emergent process, arising from the interaction of multiple factors in a non-linear manner. Suicide risk is characterized in terms of two dimensions: *baseline* (stable risk factors that persist over time) and *acute* (factors that change in response to external circumstances). The first of these dimensions sets the individual's "base" risk of suicide: for example, an individual may have a genetic predisposition that increases their risk over that of the general population. The second is highly contingent on environmental factors and internal states and varies significantly over time. Complex interactions between these two dimensions can lead to the emergence of the *suicidal mode*, as described by Rudd (2000). This model attempts to account for the complex observed relationships between external events and suicide, and to emphasize the many pathways that can lead to a suicidal outcome. For example, a relatively "mild" stressor may trigger an attempt in one individual, while a more "severe" stressor may not have that effect in another. One implication of this model is that some individuals may move directly to a suicide attempt without a prior period of suicidal ideation, making prediction difficult; another is that suicide prevention strategies should be broad-based and multifaceted. This model also accounts for the fact that most suicide prediction tools and models have only modest accuracy, as it postulates the existence of multiple suicide-related processes that cannot be captured by a single model.

## 6 Sociological Models of Suicide

The division between "psychosocial" and "sociological" models of suicide is somewhat artificial. It is not possible, strictly speaking, to separate these two elements in a given individual experiencing a suicidal crisis (Melzer et al., 2024). Nevertheless, because of the influence of Emile Durkheim's theories, there is some conceptual justification for separating purely social theories of suicide from those which integrate intrapsychic and interpersonal processes (Selkin, 1983). A key aspect of sociological models is that they often incorporate population- or "macro"-level factors such as population density, unemployment, cultural values, and religious affiliation. Because of this, these models are often invoked to explain variations in suicidal behaviour across countries or regions or to examine trends in suicide in a population based on variations in these factors over a specified period (Bastiampillai et al., 2020; Yeom, 2021). However, sociological models have also been used to study suicidal behaviour in individuals, either alone or in conjunction with psychological theories (Na et al., 2022; Ozbilgin et al., 2024).

In his pioneering work, *Le Suicide: Etude de Sociologie*, published in 1897, Emile Durkheim outlined his views on the social roots of suicide. According to him, biological, intrapsychic and environmental factors play a very limited role in most cases of suicide, and cannot be used to explain population-level variations and trends in completed suicide. Though he concedes that suicide can sometimes be the result of a severe mental illness, he considers such cases rare in comparison to the total number of suicides in a country or region. Instead, most suicides are caused by an imbalance between two sets of social "forces": social *integration* and social *control*. Social integration refers to the strength of social ties between members of a community. Such ties provide members of the community with a sense of belonging and meaning. Social control, or social regulation, refers to the strength, clarity, and consistency of social norms in a community.

Based on these two sets of forces, Durkheim suggested that there were four types of suicide. A low level of integration, resulting in isolation, leads to *egoistic suicide*. An excessively high level of integration may lead to individual suicide for the "good" of the collective, known as *altruistic suicide*. A low level of regulation, caused by a societal collapse, crisis, or rapidly changing norms and values, leads to *anomic suicide*. Excessive regulation, when it amounts to coercion of individuals to conform with social norms, can lead to *fatalistic suicide* (Durkheim, 2006).

In Durkheim's original schema, egoistic and anomic suicides were thought to be the predominant types of suicide, while egoistic and fatalistic suicides were considered rare, and were considered to occur in more "primitive" societies. It was later shown that this view was only partially correct, as Durkheim's observations were largely derived from European countries during the nineteenth century, a period of rapid social change and increasing urbanization and industrialization. Fatalistic suicides were found to be more common than Durkheim envisaged, particularly in collectivistic cultures, under totalitarian regimes, in women who feel "trapped" by restrictive social norms, and in some migrant populations (Aliverdinia & Pridemore, 2009; Iga, 1981; Johnson, 1979; Lester, 1991; Stack, 1979). Likewise, altruistic suicide, though relatively rare—as Durkheim correctly hypothesized—may still occur at a substantial rate in specific closed communities or sub-cultures, though the study of such cases is difficult in practice (Leenaars, 2006).

Specific elements of Durkheim's work have been criticized on methodological grounds. Foremost among them is the difficulty in generalizing from population data to individuals, known as the ecological fallacy. Other concerns include the neglect of psychological factors and of the possible negative role of social norms and regulations for those in marginalized communities. Because both sociology and psychology were in their infancy at the time Durkheim wrote, he was not able to provide a conceptual or mechanistic "bridge" between broader social forces and an individual's suicidal behaviour. Nevertheless, Durkheim's insights remain invaluable, and his fundamental concepts are still used in suicide research to date (Mueller et al., 2021).

One apparent prediction of Durkheim's model is that suicide rates would increase over time due to modernization and social fragmentation, which would lead to anomie and reduced social integration. Evidence for this prediction has been inconsistent: cross-national research suggesting that specific variables, such as population growth, may be stronger predictors of suicide than "modernization" in general (Zhang, 1998). This has led some experts to suggest that Durkheim's theory should be integrated with more recent sociological insights into modernity (Cumming & Lazer, 1981). One explanation for this finding, advanced by Condorelli (2016), is that human social systems may be more robust than was apparent when Durkheim formulated his views. Instead of moving into a state of disorder when confronted with a crisis, they may be able to "adapt" to changes and even to evolve new, unexpected, "emergent" properties that affect suicide rates in a non-linear manner. In some cases, major social changes may be buffered by such "emergences"; in others, even a relatively minor perturbation may have a marked effect on suicide rates. This view has some similarities to the "fluid vulnerability" theory of individual suicides and implies that the relationships between social integration, social regulation and suicide may not be as direct as Durkheim considered them to be.

There have been other attempts to model suicidal behaviour in relation to social factors without reference to Durkheim's theories. In 1881, the Czech philosopher and stateman Tomas Masaryk attempted to explain rising suicide rates in Europe based on contemporary educational practices and the declining influence of religion. According to him, suicide resulted from a "moral defect" caused by a lack of religious and spiritual beliefs and practices. Such a defect, according to him, makes individuals more likely to experience hopelessness in the face of adverse life events. Generalizing from the individual to the collective case, he considered that modern educational systems placed undue emphasis on academics and not enough on spirituality: this led to a state of collective "irreligiosity" which correlated with the group suicide rate. Like Durkheim, Masaryk discounted the role of biological, social and environmental factors, though he did provide a psychological bridge—hopelessness or "despair"—between his hypothesized causal social factor and suicidal behaviour (Lester, 1997). Though Masaryk's theory has not been fully supported by subsequent evidence, and its specifics are open to criticism, it deserves credit for drawing attention to the links between religion (and spirituality) and suicide. Subsequent research has shown that variations in religiosity do correlate negatively with suicide rates in relation to age and gender, but not to location. In addition, specific religious traditions may protect against suicide in a manner that varies with a community's level of social disadvantage (Clarke et al., 2003; Seto, 2022).

From Durkheim's perspective, imitation or social learning played a relatively unimportant role in influencing suicide rates. However, subsequent research has shown that suicide contagion is a real phenomenon, occurring in relation to either (a) the suicide of a known person, (b) the suicide of a celebrity or public figure, or (c) reporting of suicides through conventional or social media (Calvo et al., 2024; Domaradzki, 2021; Walling, 2021). Generalizing from this phenomenon, Lester proposed a *critical mass theory* of suicide at the national level, in which countries with a higher suicide rate would also show a greater increase in their suicide rate over time. He hypothesized that above a certain suicide rate, the likelihood of suicide contagion would increase to such an extent that suicidal behaviour would become "self-sustaining" and even accelerate. A cross-national analysis of data from 28 countries found some support for a "critical mass" effect, though this needs to be replicated in larger samples over different time periods (Lester, 1988). An important implication of this hypothesis, if true, is that reducing the national suicide rate beyond the "critical" level would have the opposite effect, leading to a "deceleration" of the suicide rate over time.

From an anthropological perspective, suicide should be understood through an ethnographic approach, understanding local norms, beliefs, values, social relationships and even language in specific communities. Such an approach would deepen our understanding of those factors that are common to suicide across populations and cultures, and those that are unique to a given population. In this view, there is no place for a single "model of suicide" or a "theory of everything": rather, suicide should be understood and addressed in its social and cultural context. For example, the concepts of Durkheim's theory, such as anomie and egoism, may not have relevance, or even linguistic equivalents, in some non-European cultures. This implies that suicide prevention should be adapted to local ground realities, and that what works in one population or country will not necessary be effective in another (Staples & Widger, 2012).

More recently, there have been attempts to integrate sociological theories with biological or psychological models of suicide. An early attempt in this regard is the *thwarting-disorientation theory* of suicide, developed by Naroll and empirically verified by Krauss and Krauss. According to this model, certain specific cultural traits, known as *thwarting-disorientation situations* (TDS), increased the weakening or rupture of social ties in such a way that the disruption could be blamed on a particular individual. This would lead to both frustration and aggression towards that individual, leading to a suicide attempt. For example, in a society where men are free to divorce women without providing them with support (the TDS), an abandoned wife would experience both a rupture of social ties (personal frustration) and aggression directed towards the person responsible (the husband). This could lead to suicidal behaviour (Krauss & Krauss, 1968; Krauss & Tesser, 1971). Though not without its limitations, this theory is a sound attempt to link cultural situations to individual psychological distress and thence to suicide.

Jollant and Macdonald (2015) examined high suicide rates among strongly endogamous and isolated sub-groups. While this could be explained in terms of a lack of social integration or excessive regulation, these authors suggested that endogamy could act as an "amplifier" both in genetic terms, favouring the retention of suicide risk alleles, and in terms of perpetuating cultural values that favour suicide. Mobley and Taasoobshirazi (2022) examined variations in suicide rates across counties of the United States and found that these were best predicted by measures of financial stability, economic opportunity, and mental health. They explained these findings by combining Durkheim's concept of anomie with the IPTS. Along similar lines, a recent systematic review of the link between social isolation and suicide suggested that the evidence was best explained by a combination of Durkheim's (reduced social integration) and Joiner's (thwarted belongingness and perceived burdensomeness) concepts (Motillon-Toudic et al., 2022). These findings, and other like them, suggest that it is both possible and valuable to integrate psychological and sociological models of suicide.

## *6.1 Environmental Models of Suicide: A Missing Link Between Modernization and Suicide?*

Sociological theories often examine the relationship between modernization and suicide in terms of effects on social norms and cohesion. Though these factors are undoubtedly important, there is emerging evidence that the environmental changes caused by urbanization and modernization can also influence the risk of suicide. For example, access to "green spaces," such as forests and parks, has been associated with a reduced risk of suicide in some high-income countries (Helbich et al., 2018; Mendoza et al., 2023). This apparent protective effect has not been observed for proximity to "blue spaces" such as seas and lakes (Helbich et al., 2022). On the other hand, environmental changes of anthropogenic origin, such as air pollution and rising temperatures, have been associated with increases in suicidal behaviour (Radua et al., 2024). Likewise, certain aspects of the "built environment" (i.e., housing) have been significantly associated with suicidal behaviour (Jiang et al., 2021). The exact mechanisms through which these factors exert their beneficial or harmful effects is unknown, though air pollution has been found to trigger neuroinflammation and neuronal loss in animal models. These findings suggest that there may be a role for "environmental models of suicide," in which demographic, psychological and social risk factors interact with certain components of an individual's local environment to influence suicidal outcomes (Jiang et al., 2021). Even if a separate "environmental model" of suicide cannot be developed, these results underline the need to incorporate urban ecology-based factors into future theories and models of the suicidal process.

They also have public health implications, as they suggest that measures to mitigate climate change, reduce air pollution and improve urban planning may have a modest but significant effect on suicide prevention.

## 7 Integrating the Various Theoretical Models of Suicide

With so many theoretical models of suicide available to the clinician and the researcher, it is natural to ask which, if any, are of practical use. There is ample empirical evidence to support both the IPTS and models based on psychache/psychological pain, but this does not mean that other models are of less value: it simply indicates that they have been subjected to less formal testing and evaluation. Certain limitations of these models must be acknowledged. Even the models or theories with the largest evidence base have only a modest accuracy in terms of predicting suicidal outcomes in real-world settings, or in corresponding to the antecedents of an actual suicide attempt or suicide; in other words, they have limited *ecological validity*. Many patients do not proceed through well-defined stages of a theorized suicide process (Bryan et al., 2020; Penney & Simpson, 2022). There are many "roads" to suicide, and "suicide" itself is not a unitary construct but a dynamic process. A single framework, whether it is the IPTS or another model, may not be able to capture the many "pathways" through suicidal ideation and behaviour in real life (Bryan et al., 2020; Coppersmith et al., 2024; Martin et al., 2020). An additional problem in constructing viable models of suicide is the role of unknown variables or confounding factors, even if appropriate statistical methods are used to deal with these (Cero et al., 2021). The *cross-cultural validity* of suicide models has also not been conclusively established. Most models of suicide are derived from psychological concepts or data that have their origins in high-income European or North American (so-called "Western" or "WEIRD") countries. Some of these, such as the IPTS, 3ST and strain models, have been tested in Asian countries, but only to a limited extent. From an anthropological perspective, it is unlikely that a model of suicide constructed in a given culture can be "ported" to another without substantial adjustments (Staples & Widger, 2012).

Though these limitations seem daunting, they are common to most models in the behavioural and social sciences and should not be seen as unique to the field of suicidology (Glass & McAtee, 2006). Even if theoretical models of suicide do not perform well from a predictive viewpoint, they do have substantial explanatory power, and provide valuable leads to suicide prevention strategies at the individual and community levels. It may be possible to improve the accuracy and applicability of these models by identifying commonalities between them and integrating them into a broader model or "meta-model" (Kleiman et al., 2014). Such a model might be better able to embrace the wider range of factors that influence suicidal ideation and behaviour, leading to a closer approximation to real-world data.

An early attempt to identify common themes across diverse models of suicide was carried out by Lester (1994). In his study, 15 existing models of suicide were summarized using 10 statements each, and these statements were coded "present" or "absent" using the biographies of 30 notable individuals who committed suicide. Factor analysis of this data yielded a five-factor solution:

- The first factor corresponded to the *psychoanalytic theories* of Freud and Menninger.
- The second had strong loadings from *cognitive theories* such as Beck and Leenars' models.
- The third was related to items addressing *childhood learning* in relation to suicidal behaviour and was based on Adams and Short's model.
- The fourth, which encompassed Maris' theory, was related to failures in *coping*.
- The fifth was related to Adler's theory of suicide as related to self-centeredness and a need to overcome perceived inferiority, and was labelled *narcissistic*.

When specific theories were matched with biographies, the three models with the best descriptive accuracy were the cognitive (Beck), psychache (Shneidman) and failed coping (Maris) theories of suicide. A subsequent paper by the same author, using the death of the poet Sylvia Plath as a case study, found that her suicide was best understood using the models of Shneidman, Beck and Leenars (Lester, 1998).

This work has obvious limitations from today's vantage point: it is based on second-hand biographical reports of public figures, which are subject to bias and missing data, and it does not account for more recent or "second-generation" models of suicide such as the IPTS, 3ST, IMV or for evolutionary perspectives on suicide. However, as an initial step towards a higher-order model of suicide, it is invaluable, as it suggests that a combination of psychache-related, cognitive and coping models would best be able to explain a significant number of suicides from a retrospective point of view.

Subsequent to this work, several of the newer theories or models of suicide have taken an integrative perspective. For example, the IMV integrates elements of the IPTS and psychache models, while lifespan theory integrates biological models of suicide, based on genetics and epigenetics, with the IPTS. A promising line of research would be to examine whether such models have better explanatory or predictive power than the psychache-related or IPTS models, making use of first-hand information from individuals who are experiencing suicidal ideation or have made a suicide attempt.

Another approach towards constructing a "meta-model" of suicide is based on the general framework proposed by Finkel and Hall (2018) for the analysis of any given behaviour. This meta-model postulates that a given behaviour is influenced by three processes, which can be viewed as roughly orthogonal dimensions. These are *instigation*, *impellance* and *inhibition*. Instigation refers to immediate environmental stimuli that trigger a given behaviour (such as a stressful event triggering a suicide attempt). Impellance refers to "situational or dispositional factors" that increase the probability of engaging in the behaviour (for example, a genetic vulnerability towards suicide, or access to means). Inhibition is the opposite of impellance, consisting of those factors that reduce the likelihood of the behaviour (such as coping skills or social support). When instigation and impellance are strong and inhibition is weak, the result is a "perfect storm" that markedly increases the risk or probability of the given behaviour. This framework has been used to understand suicidal behaviour in vulnerable communities during the COVID-19 pandemic (Brown & Schuman, 2021). It is broadly similar to the traditional description of "predisposing," "protective" and "precipitating" factors that forms part of routine psychiatric training, practice and research on suicide (Favril et al., 2022), though it lends itself to more rigorous statistical modelling.

It has also been suggested that the precision of suicide models can be improved through technological advances, such as real-time monitoring of biobehavioural parameters, natural language processing, and machine learning. Real-time data on patients' subjective mood states and thoughts could be obtained through "ecological momentary assessments," which record periodically using a mobile application, while physiological parameters such as activity level, sleep–wake patterns, heart rate variability and skin conductance could be measured using real-time sensors. Such data could be correlated to identify dynamic changes in suicidal ideation and their psychophysiological correlates more precisely than through a routine clinical or research interview (Sedano-Capdevila et al., 2021). Individuals' text messages or social media posts could also be analysed to look for themes suggestive of hopelessness, psychological pain, or suicidality (Arowosegbe & Oleyade, 2023). These data, taken together, could be used to test various models of suicide and compare their performance. Alternatively, such data could be subjected to machine learning methods to derive a suicide model that is free from theoretical preconceptions. While there are significant methodological and ethical challenges involved in such research, they hold the promise of being able to confirm or refute existing models, or even to construct innovative models of suicide from the bottom-up (Bernert et al., 2020; Nordin et al., 2022).

## 8 Ecological Systems Theory as a Candidate for a Higher-Order Model of Suicide

As discussed in the previous section, there are various ways in which the multiple models of suicide can be analysed and incorporated into higher-order models. Ideally, such a higher-order model should have the following properties:

- it should incorporate biological, psychological, social and environmental levels of explanation,
- it should attempt to explain how these levels interact with and influence each other,
- it should improve our understanding of way in which remote and recent factors influence suicidal ideation and behaviour,
- it should account for the different "roads" or trajectories that lead to the final outcome of a suicide attempt or completed suicide,
- it should have cross-cultural and ecological validity.

One way of accomplishing this, which has attracted the attention of suicide researchers over the past two decades, is through *ecological systems theory* (EST). EST, originally developed to study "the ecology of human development" across an individual's lifespan, is an explanatory framework that consists of two components. The first is a description of the processes through which a given genotype is "transformed" into a phenotype throughout the course of development (Bronfenbrenner & Ceci, 1994). The second is a description of the various nested levels of the ecological environment in which developing humans find themselves (Bronfenbrenner, 1977). Both these components are of equal significance: without them, EST can be misunderstood as a simple description of these levels and their interactions, omitting the crucial role of the individual at the centre of these nested levels (Darling, 2007). The first component, also referred to by Bronfenbrenner as the *bioecological model*, examines the "biopsychological" interactions between an individual's inherent potentialities, defined in terms of genetics, and the "persons, objects, and symbols in its immediate environment" (Bronfenbrenner & Ceci, 1994). These interactions are referred to as *proximal processes* and vary in relation to the individual, the environment and the specific "developmental outcome" being studied. The second, which is sometimes referred to as EST by itself, describes the ecological environment in terms of four levels:

- The *microsystem* refers to the relations between the developing individual and their environment in a particular "setting," such as home or school.
- The *mesosystem* refers to the relations between the major "settings" encountered by the individual at that stage in their development—for example, interactions between family and school. In other words, it is composed of microsystems.
- The *exosystem* is an extension of the mesosystem that includes "formal and informal social structures" that influence the "settings" directly or indirectly—for example, government agencies or the media can influence the school "setting."
- Finally, the *macrosystem* encompasses the "institutional patterns" of the culture or subculture that the individual lives in, and that the micro-, meso- and exosystems subsist in. It carries values and beliefs that provide "meaning and motivation" to the other three levels of the ecological environment.

Though these models were originally devised to study development in general, they can be applied—with suitable modifications—to the study of the suicidal process. Suicidal behaviour has its antecedents in interactions between the genotype and the external environment, both in childhood and across the life cycle. Moreover, it can be influenced by various levels of the individual's environment, ranging from the microsystem (e.g., the family or workplace) to the macrosystem (e.g., the influence of cultural attitudes and values on the risk of suicide). The *proximal processes* could be understood in terms of the psychological processes outlined in various theories—psychological pain, cognitive errors, failures in coping and the consequent emergence of suicidal ideation. *Thus, from an EST perspective on suicide, psychological models can be seen as the "bioecological" component that determines the outcome of gene-environment interactions at specific stages of the life cycle, while sociological models*

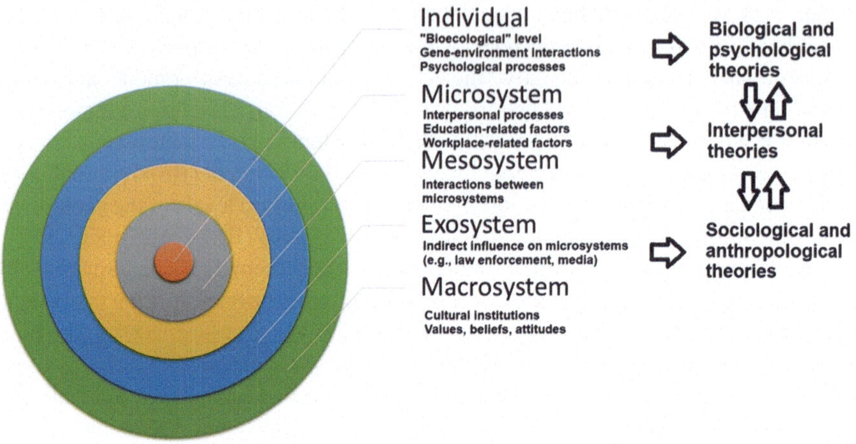


**Fig. 2** An outline of an ecological systems model of suicide, illustrating the different system levels and the theories related to them

*could elucidate the influences in the micro-, meso-, exo- and macrosystems.* This is depicted graphically (Fig. 2).

Though this outline is tentative in nature, it illustrates how the two components of EST can be used to construct a higher-order model of suicide with wide applicability. At the centre of this schema is the individual experiencing suicidal ideas or making a suicide attempt. These phenomena are the result of interactions between the genotype and events at various points in the life cycle, mediated through both biological processes (Sect. 3) and psychological processes (Sect. 4). Surrounding the individual are the various levels of the social ecosystem, beginning with the settings of immediate or close relationships (microsystems) and ending with the culture or subculture in which the individual lives (the macrosystem). As one moves outwards from the centre of Fig. 2, it becomes evident that different theories or models are best suited to account for specific levels. Biological, evolutionary and psychological theories perform best at describing individual "proximal processes," such as neurotransmitter changes or psychological pain. Psychological-interpersonal theories are appropriate for describing the relationships between the individual, microsystems and mesosystems, and how strains in these relationships can trigger suicidal ideation or behaviour. Finally, broader sociological theories are best suited to understand exo- and macrosystems and how they impinge on the "inner" circles of the individual's life. The ESM also allows for an understanding of suicide as a process, beginning with predisposing factors (genetics and early life experiences) and ending with precipitating factors arising from microsystems. Each level of the ESM also contains protective factors, whose strength relative to predisposing factors and stressors influences the likelihood of a suicidal outcome.

Though such a model is understandably more complex than any individual theory of suicide, it has several advantages both practically and from a research perspective.

First, it offers a logical framework for integrating biological, psychological, interpersonal and sociological theories of suicide. Second, it highlights the need to identify those mechanisms that bridge each level of the suicidal individual's ecosystem, allowing for fruitful collaboration between researchers from diverse fields (Calabrese et al., 2024). Third, it recognizes the unique nature of the micro-, meso-, exo- and macrosystems that constitute an individual's social environment. At the "inner" levels of the model, this allows for a personalized approach to suicide prevention; at the "outer" levels, it improves cross-cultural validity by making room for the wide range of values, beliefs, customs and institutions that can influence suicide across countries and regions. Fourth, it avoids unduly reductionistic views of suicide, such as those seen in the serotonin, predicament and psychodynamic models. Fifth, such a model lends itself to analysis through advanced statistical techniques, such as network analysis (de Beurs et al., 2021; Karnick et al., 2022). Finally, it provides a rationale for the development and evaluation of suicide prevention strategies at each ecological system level; such strategies may act synergistically to reduce the risk of suicide in individuals and communities.

Despite these many advantages, it must be acknowledged that research on suicide from an EST perspective is still in its early stages. EST-based models have been used to analyse risk and protective factors for suicidal behaviour in diverse settings, including in the general population in Asian countries (Jha et al., 2023; Rahman Khan & Shimul, 2024), in military personnel (Langhinrichsen-Rohling et al., 2019) and in vulnerable populations such as immigrants, the homeless and sexual minorities (Boyas et al., 2019; Garcia and Saewyc, 2007; Gattis, 2013). Though valuable as a starting point for further enquiry, this body of research is limited in scope because it focuses only on the second, four-level component of Bronfenbrenner's model. Constructing and testing a complete ESM for suicide, incorporating both the bioecological and ecological systems components would be quite a complex task. This difficulty notwithstanding, there is sufficient reason to believe that it would yield substantial advantages over existing models of suicide.

## 9 Conclusion

Suicide is a complex and heterogeneous phenomenon, and it is unlikely that a single theory or model would be able to capture it in all its diversity and depth. Nevertheless, theoretical models of suicide have been helpful in incrementally advancing our understanding of the biological changes, psychological processes, and wider social factors that contribute to suicidal ideation and behaviour. While certain "first generation" models have fallen out of favour due to changes in theoretical orientation, or a lack of support from research, they have served as stepping-stones to better and more empirically valid "second generation" models. Models of suicide have also served as a useful basis for suicide prevention strategies. All existing models have their inherent limitations, which underline the need for a higher-order model that incorporates the "best" of each model. Advances in technology and data analysis may help in this process but are unlikely to achieve this aim on their own. The ecological systems model is a promising framework that could potentially integrate the various levels of factors involved in suicide while improving cross-cultural and ecological validity and fostering better collaboration among biologically and psychosocially oriented researchers. Ultimately, the development of a better theoretical model of suicide can lead to better suicide prevention and treatment strategies, which would be of immense benefit to individuals, families and communities.

## References


Abou Chahla, M. N., Khalil, M. I., Comai, S., Brundin, L., Erhardt, S., & Guillemin, G. J. (2023). Biological factors underpinning suicidal behaviour: An update. *Brain Sciences, 13*(3), 505. https://doi.org/10.3390/brainsci13030505

Adler, A. (1927). *Understanding human nature*. Routledge.

Ahmadboukani, S., Kivi, H. G., Kiani, A., & Rezaeisharif, A. (2023). A structural test of the three-step theory (3ST) of suicide in the Iranian population: From ideation to action. *Health Science Reports, 6*(11), e1697. https://doi.org/10.1002/hsr2.1697

Ajzen, I. (1991). The theory of planned behavior. *Organizational Behavior and Human Decision Processes, 50*(2), 179–211.

Aliverdinia, A., & Pridemore, W. A. (2009). Women's fatalistic suicide in Iran: A partial test of Durkheim in an Islamic Republic. *Violence against Women, 15*(3), 307–320. https://doi.org/10.1177/1077801208330434

Amouei, A., Moosazadeh, M., Chegeni, T. N., Sarvi, S., Mizani, A., Pourasghar, M., Teshnizi, S. H., Hosseininejad, Z., Dodangeh, S., Pagheh, A., Pourmand, A. H., & Daryani, A. (2020). Evolutionary puzzle of Toxoplasma gondii with suicidal ideation and suicide attempts: An updated systematic review and meta-analysis. *Transboundary and Emerging Diseases, 67*(5), 1847–1860. https://doi.org/10.1111/tbed.13550

Anestis, D., & Selby, E. A. (2015). Grit and perseverance in suicidal behavior and non-suicidal self-injury. *Death Studies, 39*(1–5), 211–218. https://doi.org/10.1080/07481187.2014.946629

Angelakis, I., Austin, J. L., & Gooding, P. (2020). Association of childhood maltreatment with suicide behaviors among young people: a systematic review and meta-analysis. *JAMA Network Open, 3*(8), e2012563. https://doi.org/10.1001/jamanetworkopen.2020.12563

Ansbacher, H. L. (1969). Suicide as communication: Adler's concept and current applications. *Journal of Individual Psychology, 25*(2), 174–180.

Arowosegbe, A., & Oyelade, T. (2023). Application of natural language processing (NLP) in detecting and preventing suicide ideation: A systematic review. *International Journal of Environmental Research and Public Health, 20*(2), 1514. https://doi.org/10.3390/ijerph20021514

Asberg, M. (1997). Neurotransmitters and suicidal behavior. The evidence from cerebrospinal fluid studies. *Annals of the New York Academy of Sciences, 836*, 158–181. https://doi.org/10.1111/j.1749-6632.1997.tb52359.x

Aubin, H.-J., Berlin, I., & Kornreich, C. (2013). The evolutionary puzzle of suicide. *International Journal of Environmental Research and Public Health, 10*, 6873–6886. https://doi.org/10.3390/ijerph10126873

Baharikhoob, P., & Kolla, N. J. (2020). Microglial dysregulation and suicidality: A stress-diathesis perspective. *Frontiers in Psychiatry, 11*, 781. https://doi.org/10.3389/fpsyt.2020.00781

Barzilay, S., & Apter, A. (2014). Psychological models of suicide. *Archives of Suicide Research, 18*, 295–314. https://doi.org/10.1080/13811118.2013.824825

Bastiampillai, T., Allison, S., Looi, J. C., Tavella, A., & Agis, U. (2020). Why are Australia's suicide rates returning to the hundred-year average, despite suicide prevention initiatives? Reframing the problem from the perspective of Durkheim. *The Australian and New Zealand Journal of Psychiatry, 54*(1), 12–14. https://doi.org/10.1177/0004867419872815

Beck, A. T., Kovacs, M., & Weissman, A. (1975). Hopelessness and suicidal behaviour. An overview. *JAMA, 234*(11), 1146–1149.

Beck, A. T., & Lester, D. (1976). Components of suicidal intent in completed and attempted suicides. *The Journal of psychology, 92*(1), 35–38. https://doi.org/10.1080/00223980.1976.9921330

Beck, A. T., Weissman, A., Lester, D., & Trexler, L. (1976). Classification of suicidal behaviors. II. Dimensions of suicidal intent. *Archives of General Psychiatry, 33*(7), 835–837. https://doi.org/10.1001/archpsyc.1976.01770070065006

Bedrosian, R. C., & Beck, A. T. (1979). Cognitive aspects of suicidal behavior. *Suicide & Life-Threatening Behavior, 9*(2), 87–96.

Bernert, R. A., Hilberg, A. M., Melia, R., Kim, J. P., Shah, N. H., & Abnousi, F. (2020). Artificial intelligence and suicide prevention: A systematic review of machine learning investigations. *International Journal of Environmental Research and Public Health, 17*(16), 5929. https://doi.org/10.3390/ijerph17165929

Booij, L., Wang, D., Lévesque, M. L., Tremblay, R. E., & Szyf, M. (2013). Looking beyond the DNA sequence: The relevance of DNA methylation processes for the stress-diathesis model of depression. *Philosophical Transactions of the Royal Society of London. Series B, Biological Sciences, 368*(1615), 20120251. https://doi.org/10.1098/rstb.2012.0251

Bostock, T., & Williams, C. L. (1975). Attempted suicide: An operant formulation. *Australia and New Zealand Journal of Psychiatry, 9*(2), 107–110. https://doi.org/10.3109/00048677509159832

Boyas, J. F., Villarreal-Otálora, T., Alvarez-Hernandez, L. R., & Fatehi, M. (2019). Suicide ideation, planning, and attempts: The case of the Latinx LGB youth. *Health Promotion Perspectives, 9*(3), 198–206. https://doi.org/10.15171/hpp.2019.28

Branley-Bell, D., O'Connor, D. B., Green, J. A., Ferguson, E., O'Carroll, R. E., & O'Connor, R. C. (2019). Distinguishing suicide ideation from suicide attempts: Further test of the Integrated Motivational-Volitional Model of Suicidal Behaviour. *Journal of Psychiatric Research, 117*, 100–107. https://doi.org/10.1016/j.jpsychires.2019.07.007

Bronfenbrenner, U. (1977). Towards an experimental ecology of human development. *American Psychologist, 32*(7), 513–531. https://psycnet.apa.org/doi/https://doi.org/10.1037/0003-066X.32.7.513

Bronfenbrenner, U., & Ceci, S. J. (1994). Nature-nurture reconceptualized in developmental perspective: A bioecological model. *Psychological Review, 101*(4), 568–586.

Brooks, B. D., Dangel, T. J., Kaniuka, A. R., Jaszczak, E., Limdi, A., Webb, J. R., & Hirsch, J. K. (2024). Thwarted belongingness and suicide risk in primary care: Perceived burdensomeness and psychache as mediators. *Journal of Clinical Psychology in Medical Settings, 31*(1), 122–129. https://doi.org/10.1007/s10880-023-09960-6

Brown, G. K., Beck, A. T., Steer, R. A., & Grisham, J. R. (2000). Risk factors for suicide in psychiatric outpatients: A 20-year prospective study. *Journal of Consulting and Clinical Psychology, 68*(3), 371–377.

Brown, G. K., Ten Have, T., Henriques, G. R., Xie, S. X., Hollander, J. E., & Beck, A. T. (2005). Cognitive therapy for the prevention of suicide attempts: A randomized controlled trial. *JAMA, 294*(5), 563–570. https://doi.org/10.1001/jama.294.5.563

Brown, L. A., Denis, C. M., Leon, A., Blank, M. B., Douglas, S. D., Morales, K. H., Crits-Christoph, P. F., Metzger, D. S., & Evans, D. L. (2021). Number of opioid overdoses and depression as a predictor of suicidal thoughts. *Drug and Alcohol Dependence, 224*, 108728. https://doi.org/10.1016/j.drugalcdep.2021.108728

Brown, S., & Schuman, D. L. (2021). Suicide in the time of COVID-19: A perfect storm. *The Journal of Rural Health, 37*(1), 211–214. https://doi.org/10.1111/jrh.12458

Bryan, C. J., Butner, J. E., May, A. M., Rugo, K. F., Harris, J., Oakey, D. N., Rozek, D. C., & Bryan, A. O. (2020). Nonlinear change processes and the emergence of suicidal behavior: A conceptual model based on the fluid vulnerability theory of suicide. *New Ideas in Psychology, 57*. https://doi.org/10.1016/j.newideapsych.2019.100758. https://doi.org/10.1016/j.newideapsych.2019.100758

Calabrese, T. M., Hamilton, J. G., Benton, T. D., & Standley, C. J. (2024). Suicide prevention takes a nation: Collaborative approaches to universalize suicide prevention. *Child and Adolescent Psychiatric Clinics of North America, 33*(3), 423–435. https://doi.org/10.1016/j.chc.2024.02.003

Calati, R., Bensassi, I., & Courtet, P. (2017). The link between dissociation and both suicide attempts and non-suicidal self-injury: Meta-analyses. *Psychiatry Research, 251*, 103–114. https://doi.org/10.1016/j.psychres.2017.01.035

Calvo, S., Carrasco, J. P., Conde-Pumpido, C., Esteve, J., & Aguilar, E. J. (2024). Does suicide contagion (Werther effect) take place in response to social media? A systematic review. *Spanish Journal of Psychiatry and Mental Health*, S2950–2853(24)00032–2. Advance online publication. https://doi.org/10.1016/j.sjpmh.2024.05.003

Cero, I., Mitchell, S. M., & Morris, N. M. (2021). Causal inference in suicide research: When you should (and should not!) control for extraneous variables. *Suicide & Life-Threatening Behavior, 51*(1), 148–161. https://doi.org/10.1111/sltb.12681

Chatterjee, D., & Rai, R. (2021). Choosing death over survival: A need to identify evolutionary mechanisms underlying human suicide. *Frontiers in Psychology, 12*, 689022. https://doi.org/10.3389/fpsyg.2021.689022

Chew, K. S., & McCleary, R. (1994). A life course theory of suicide risk. *Suicide & Life-Threatening Behavior, 24*(3), 234–244. https://doi.org/10.1111/j.1943-278X.1994.tb00748.x

Chu, C., Buchman-Schmitt, J. M., Stanley, I. H., Hom, M. A., Tucker, R. P., Hagan, C. R., Rogers, M. L., Podlogar, M. C., Chiurliza, B., Ringer, F. B., Michaels, M. S., Patros, C. H. G., & Joiner, T. E. (2017). The interpersonal theory of suicide: A systematic review and meta-analysis of a decade of cross-national research. *Psychological Bulletin, 143*(12), 1313–1345. https://doi.org/10.1037/bul0000123

Clarke, C. S., Bannon, F. J., & Denihan, A. (2003). Suicide and religiosity–Masaryk's theory revisited. *Social Psychiatry and Psychiatric Epidemiology, 38*(9), 502–506. https://doi.org/10.1007/s00127-003-0668-6

Cleare, S., Wetherall, K., Eschle, S., Forrester, R., Drummond, J., & O'Connor, R. C. (2021). Using the integrated motivational-volitional (IMV) model of suicidal behaviour to differentiate those with and without suicidal intent in hospital treated self-harm. *Preventive Medicine, 152*, 106592. https://doi.org/10.1016/j.ypmed.2021.106592

Condorelli, R. (2016). Social complexity, modernity and suicide: An assessment of Durkheim's suicide from the perspective of a non-linear analysis of complex social systems. *Springerplus, 5*, 374. https://doi.org/10.1186/s40064-016-1799-z

Coppersmith, D. D. L., Kleiman, E. M., Millner, A. J., Wang, S. B., Arizmendi, C., Bentley, K. H., DeMarco, D., Fortgang, R. G., Zuromski, K. L., Maimone, J. S., Haim, A., Onnela, J. P., Bird, S. A., Smoller, J. W., Mair, P., & Nock, M. K. (2024). Heterogeneity in suicide risk: Evidence from personalized dynamic models. *Behaviour Research and Therapy, 180*, 104574. https://doi.org/10.1016/j.brat.2024.104574

Correa, H., Romano-Silva, M. A., Duval, F., Campi-Azevedo, A. C., Lima, V., & Macher, J.-P. (2002). Research on serotonin and suicidal behavior: Neuroendocrine and molecular approaches. *Dialogues in Clinical Neuroscience, 4*(4), 408–416. https://doi.org/10.31887/dcns.2002.4.4/hcorrea

Courtet, P., & Olie, E. (2017). Social pain at the core of suicidal behavior. *L'encephale, 45*, S7–S12. https://doi.org/10.1016/j.encep.2018.09.005

Cuijpers, P., Miguel, C., Ciharova, M., Kumar, M., Brander, L., Kumar, P., & Karyotaki, E. (2023). Impact of climate events, pollution, and green spaces on mental health: An umbrella review of meta-analyses. *Psychological Medicine, 53*(3), 638–653. https://doi.org/10.1017/S0033291722003890

Cumming, E., & Lazer, C. (1981). Kinship structure and suicide: A theoretical link. *The Canadian Review of Sociology and Anthropology, 18*(3), 271–282. https://doi.org/10.1111/j.1755-618x.1981.tb00055.x

Darling, N. (2007). Ecological systems theory: The person in the center of the circles. *Research in Human Development, 4*(3–4), 203–217. https://doi.org/10.1080/15427600701663023

Darvishi, N., Farhadi, M., & Poorolajal, J. (2024). The role of social support in preventing suicidal ideations and behaviors: A systematic review and meta-analysis. *Journal of Research in Health Sciences, 24*(2), e00609. https://doi.org/10.34172/jrhs.2024.144

de Beurs, D., Bockting, C., Kerkhof, A., Scheepers, F., O'Connor, R., Penninx, B., & van de Leemput, I. (2021). A network perspective on suicidal behavior: Understanding suicidality as a complex system. *Suicide & Life-Threatening Behavior, 51*(1), 115–126. https://doi.org/10.1111/sltb.12676

de Catanzaro, D. (1984). Suicidal ideation and the residual capacity to promote inclusive fitness: A survey. *Suicide & Life-Threatening Behavior, 14*(2), 75–87. https://doi.org/10.1111/j.1943-278x.1984.tb00339.x

de Catanzaro, D. (1986). A mathematical model of evolutionary pressures regulating self-preservation and self-destruction. *Suicide & Life-Threatening Behavior, 16*(2), 166–181. https://doi.org/10.1111/j.1943-278x.1986.tb00350.x

de Leon, J., Baca-Garcia, E., & Blasco-Fontecilla, H. (2015). From the serotonin model of suicide to a mental pain model of suicide. *Psychotherapy and Psychosomatics, 84*, 323–329. https://doi.org/10.1159/000438510

Demirkol, M. E., Tamam, L., Namlı, Z., Yeşiloğlu, C., & Yılmaz, H. (2024). Validity and reliability study of the Turkish version of the Orbach Mikulincer mental pain scale-8 in a clinical population. *Neuropsychiatric Disease and Treatment, 20*, 429–438. https://doi.org/10.2147/NDT.S449012

Docherty, A. R., Mullins, N., Ashley-Koch, A. E., Qin, X., Coleman, J. R. I., Shabalin, A., Kang, J., Murnyak, B., Wendt, F., Adams, M., Campos, A. I., DiBlasi, E., Fullerton, J. M., & Ruderfer, D. M. (2023). GWAS meta-analysis of suicide attempt: identification of 12 genome-wide significant loci and implication of genetic risks for specific health factors. *The American Journal of Psychiatry, 180*(10), 723–738. https://doi.org/10.1176/appi.ajp.21121266

Domaradzki, J. (2021). The Werther effect, the Papageno effect or no effect? A literature review. *International Journal of Environmental Research and Public Health, 18*(5), 2396. https://doi.org/10.3390/ijerph18052396

Draper, E. (1976). A developmental theory of suicide. *Comprehensive Psychiatry, 17*(1), 63–80. https://doi.org/10.1016/0010-440x(76)90058-4

Draper, D., & Margolis, P. (1976). A psychodynamic approach to suicide prevention. *Community Mental Health Journal, 12*(4), 376–382. https://doi.org/10.1007/BF01411076

Drum, D. J., Brownson, C., Hess, E. A., Burton Denmark, A., & Talley, A. E. (2017). College students' sense of coherence and connectedness as predictors of suicidal thoughts and behaviors. *Archives of Suicide Research, 21*(1), 169–184. https://doi.org/10.1080/13811118.2016.1166088

Du et al., 2001 Du, L., Faludi, G., Palkovits, M., Bakish, D., & Hrdina, P. D. (2001). Serotonergic genes and suicidality. *Crisis, 22*(2), 54–60. https://doi.org/10.1027//0227-5910.22.2.54

Durkheim, E. (2006). *On suicide.* Transl. Buss, R. Penguin Books.

Eisenberger, N. I. (2012). The neural bases of social pain: Evidence for shared representations with physical pain. *Psychosomatic Medicine, 74*(2), 126–135. https://doi.org/10.1097/PSY.0b013e3182464dd1

El Keshky M. E. S. (2024). Risk and protective factors for suicidal ideation among Saudi adolescents: A network analysis. *The International Journal of Social Psychiatry*, 207640241277164. Advance online publication. https://doi.org/10.1177/00207640241277164

Engel, G. L. (1977). The need for a new medical model: A challenge for biomedicine. *Science, 196*(4286), 129–136. https://doi.org/10.1126/science.847460

Erikson, E. (1950). *Childhood and society.* W. W. Norton and Co.

Fässberg, M. M., van Orden, K. A., Duberstein, P., Erlangsen, A., Lapierre, S., Bodner, E., Canetto, S. S., De Leo, D., Szanto, K., & Waern, M. (2012). A systematic review of social factors and suicidal behavior in older adulthood. *International Journal of Environmental Research and Public Health, 9*(3), 722–745. https://doi.org/10.3390/ijerph9030722

Favril, L., Yu, R., Uyar, A., Sharpe, M., & Fazel, S. (2022). Risk factors for suicide in adults: Systematic review and meta-analysis of psychological autopsy studies. *Evidence-Based Mental Health, 25*, 148–155. https://doi.org/10.1136/ebmental-2022-300549

Finkel, E. J., & Hall, A. N. (2018). The I3 Model: A metatheoretical framework for understanding aggression. *Current Opinion in Psychology, 19*, 125–130. https://doi.org/10.1016/j.copsyc.2017.03.013

Freud, S. (2005). *On murder, mourning and melancholia.* Penguin Books.

Frigg, R., & Hartman, S. (2024). Models in science. In E. N. Zalta & U. Nodelman (Eds.), *The Stanford encyclopedia of philosophy.* https://plato.stanford.edu/archives/fall2024/entries/models-science/

Garcia, C. M., & Saewyc, E. M. (2007). Perceptions of mental health among recently immigrated Mexican adolescents. *Issues in Mental Health Nursing, 28*(1), 37–54. https://doi.org/10.1080/01612840600996257

Gattis, M. N. (2013). An ecological systems comparison between homeless sexual minority youths and homeless heterosexual youths. *Journal of Social Service Research, 39*(1), 38–49. https://doi.org/10.1080/01488376.2011.633814

Gilbert, P., & Allan, S. (1998). The role of defeat and entrapment (arrested flight) in depression: An exploration of an evolutionary view. *Psychological Medicine, 28*(3), 585–598. https://doi.org/10.1017/s0033291798006710

Glass, T. A., & McAtee, M. J. (2006). Behavioral science at the crossroads in public health: Extending horizons, envisioning the future. *Social Science & Medicine, 62*, 1650–1671. https://doi.org/10.1016/j.socscimed.2005.08.044

Gunn III, J. F. (2017). The social pain model. *Crisis, 38*(5), 281–286. https://doi.org/10.1027/0227-5910/a000510

Guo, J. W., Kimmel, J., & Linder, L. A. (2024). Text analysis of suicide risk in adolescents and young adults. *Journal of the American Psychiatric Nurses Association, 30*(1), 169–173. https://doi.org/10.1177/10783903221077292

Hagen, E. H. (1999). The functions of postpartum depression. *Evolution and Human Behavior, 20*, 325–359. https://doi.org/10.1016/S1090-5138(99)00016-1

Haregu, T., Cho, E., Spittal, M., & Armstrong, G. (2023). The rate of transition to a suicide attempt among people with suicidal thoughts in the general population: A systematic review. *Journal of Affective Disorders, 331*, 57–63. https://doi.org/10.1016/j.jad.2023.03.063

Haw, C., Hawton, K., Niedzwiedz, C., & Platt, S. (2013). Suicide clusters: A review of risk factors and mechanisms. *Suicide & Life-Threatening Behavior, 43*(1), 97–108. https://doi.org/10.1111/j.1943-278x.2012.00130.x

Healy, D., & Whitaker, C. (2003). Antidepressants and suicide: Risk-benefit conundrums. *Journal of Psychiatry & Neuroscience: JPN, 28*(5), 331–337.

Heidenreich, T., Noyon, A., Worrell, M., & Menzies, R. (2021). Existential approaches and cognitive behavior therapy: Challenges and potential. *International Journal of Cognitive Therapy, 14*(1), 209–234. https://doi.org/10.1007/s41811-020-00096-1

Helbich, M., de Beurs, D., Kwan, M. P., O'Connor, R. C., & Groenewegen, P. P. (2018). Natural environments and suicide mortality in the Netherlands: A cross-sectional, ecological study. *The Lancet. Planetary Health, 2*(3), e134–e139. https://doi.org/10.1016/S2542-5196(18)30033-0

Helbich, M., Browning, M. H. E. M., White, M., & Hagedoorn, P. (2022). Living near coasts is associated with higher suicide rates among females but not males: A register-based linkage study in the Netherlands. *The Science of the Total Environment, 845*, 157329. https://doi.org/10.1016/j.scitotenv.2022.157329

Henry, A. F., & Short, J. F. (1954). *Suicide and homicide.* Free Press.

Hibbeln, J. R., & Gow, R. V. (2014). The potential for military diets to reduce depression, suicide, and impulsive aggression: A review of current evidence for omega-3 and omega-6 fatty acids. *Military Medicine, 179*(11 Suppl), 117–128. https://doi.org/10.7205/MILMED-D-14-00153

Hjelmeland, H., & Knizek, B. L. (2019). The emperor's new clothes? A critical look at the interpersonal theory of suicide. *Death Studies, 44*(3), 168–178. https://doi.org/10.1080/07481187.2018.1527796

Hou, X., Wang, J., Guo, J., Zhang, X., Liu, J., Qi, L., & Zhou, L. (2022). Methods and efficacy of social support interventions in preventing suicide: A systematic review and meta-analysis. *Evidence-Based Mental Health, 25*(1), 29–35. https://doi.org/10.1136/ebmental-2021-300318

Humphrey, N. (2018). The lure of death: Suicide and human evolution. *Philosophical Transactions of the Royal Society B, 373*, 20170269. https://doi.org/10.1098/rstb.2017.0269

Hurley, R. A., & Taber, K. H. (2012). Latent Toxoplasmosis gondii: Emerging evidence for influences on neuropsychiatric disorders. *The Journal of Neuropsychiatry and Clinical Neurosciences, 24*(4), 376–383. https://doi.org/10.1176/appi.neuropsych.12100234

Ielmini, M., Lucca, G., Trabucchi, E., Aspesi, G. L., Bellini, A., Caselli, I., & Callegari, C. (2022). Assessing mental pain as a predictive factor of suicide risk in a clinical sample of patients with psychiatric disorders. *Behavioral Sciences, 12*(4), 111. https://doi.org/10.3390/bs12040111

Iga, M. (1981). Suicide of Japanese youth. *Suicide & Life-Threatening Behavior, 11*(1), 17–30. https://doi.org/10.1111/j.1943-278x.1981.tb00996.x

Ilic, M., & Ilic, I. (2022). Worldwide suicide mortality trends (2000–2019): A joinpoint regression analysis. *World Journal of Psychiatry, 12*(8), 1044–1060. https://doi.org/10.5498/wjp.v12.i8.1044

Jauhar, S., Cowen, P. J., & Browning, M. (2023). Fifty years on: Serotonin and depression. *Journal of Psychopharmacology, 37*(3), 237–241. https://doi.org/10.1177/02698811231161813

Jha, P., Subedi, S., Paudyal, S., & Panta, P. P. (2023). Suicidal attempt among psychiatry patients presented to the department of emergency of a tertiary care centre: a descriptive cross-sectional study. *JNMA; Journal of the Nepal Medical Association, 61*(261), 442–445. https://doi.org/10.31729/jnma.8156

Jiang, B., Shen, K., Sullivan, W. C., Yang, Y., Liu, X., & Lu, Y. (2021). A natural experiment reveals impacts of built environment on suicide rate: Developing an environmental theory of suicide. *The Science of the Total Environment, 776*, 145750. https://doi.org/10.1016/j.scitotenv.2021.145750

Johnson, K. K. (1979). Durkheim revisited: "Why do women kill themselves?" *Suicide & Life-Threatening Behavior, 9*(3), 145–153. https://doi.org/10.1111/j.1943-278X.1979.tb00559.x

Joiner, T. (2005). *Why people die by suicide*. Harvard University Press.

Joiner, T. E., Jeon, M. E., Lieberman, A., Janakiraman, R., Duffy, M. E., Gai, A. R., & Dougherty, S. P. (2021). On prediction, refutation, and explanatory reach: A consideration of the Interpersonal Theory of Suicidal Behavior. *Preventive Medicine, 152*, 106453. https://doi.org/10.1016/j.ypmed.2021.106453

Jollant, F., & Macdonald, C. (2015). Endogamy and suicide: An observation-based hypothesis. *Medical Hypotheses, 85*(5), 542–547. https://doi.org/10.1016/j.mehy.2015.07.010

Jones, E. E., Blandl, F., Kreutzer, K. A., Bryan, C. J., Allan, N. P., & Gorka, S. M. (2024). Childhood adversity and youth suicide risk: The mediating role of intolerance of uncertainty. *Personality and Individual Differences, 216*, 112405. https://doi.org/10.1016/j.paid.2023.112405

Karnick, A. T., Fergerson, A. K., Caulfield, N. M., Buerke, M., Albanese, B. J., Schmidt, N. B., & Capron, D. W. (2022). Toward an integrative model of transdiagnostic risk factors and suicide: A network comparison of psychiatric outpatients. *Journal of Psychiatric Research, 154*, 252–260. https://doi.org/10.1016/j.jpsychires.2022.07.050

Kelly, L. M., Swenson, L. P., & Wolff, J. C. (2023). Application of the three-step ideation-to-action theory to passive and active suicidal ideation in college students. *Minerva Psychiatry, 64*(1), 1–12. https://doi.org/10.23736/s2724-6612.21.02263-6

Kleiman, E. M., Law, K. C., & Anestis, M. D. (2014). Do theories of suicide play well together? Integrating components of the hopelessness and interpersonal psychological theories of suicide. *Comprehensive Psychiatry, 55*, 431–438. https://doi.org/10.1016/j.comppsych.2013.10.015

Klonsky, E. D., & May, A. M. (2014). Differentiating suicide attempters from suicide ideators: A critical frontier for suicidology research. *Suicide & Life-Threatening Behavior, 44*(1), 1–5. https://doi.org/10.1111/sltb.12068

Klonsky, E. D., & May, A. M. (2015). The Three-Step Theory (3ST): A new theory of suicide rooted in the "ideation-to-action" framework. *International Journal of Cognitive Therapy, 8*(2), 114–129. https://doi.org/10.1521/ijct.2015.8.2.114

Klonsky, E. D. (2018). Toward a parsimonious understanding of suicide: Comparing the Three Step Theory to Malhi and colleagues' Integrated Model. *Bipolar Disorders, 20*(6), 568–569. https://doi.org/10.1111/bdi.12672

Klonsky, E. D., Pachkowski, M. C., Shahnaz, A., & May, A. M. (2021). The three-step theory of suicide: Description, evidence, and some useful points of clarification. *Preventive Medicine, 152*(Pt 1), 106549. https://doi.org/10.1016/j.ypmed.2021.106549

Kovacs, M., Beck, A. T., & Weissman, A. (1975). Hopelessness: An indicator of suicidal risk. *Suicide, 5*(2), 98–103.

Kovacs, M., & Beck, A. T. (1977). The wish to die and the wish to live in attempted suicides. *Journal of Clinical Psychology, 33*(2), 361–365. https://doi.org/10.1002/1097-4679(197704)33:2%3c361::aid-jclp2270330207%3e3.0.co;2-h

Krauss, H. H., & Krauss, B. J. (1968). Cross-cultural study of the thwarting-disorientation theory of suicide. *Journal of Abnormal Psychology, 73*(4), 353–357. https://doi.org/10.1037/h0026084

Krauss, H. H., & Tesser, A. (1971). Social contexts of suicide. *Journal of Abnormal Psychology, 78*(2), 222–228. https://doi.org/10.1037/h0031984

Krupnik, V., & Danilova, N. (2024). To be or not to be: The active inference of suicide. *Neuroscience and Biobehavioral Reviews, 157*, 105531. https://doi.org/10.1016/j.neubiorev.2023.105531

Langhinrichsen-Rohling, J., Snarr, J. D., Slep, A. M. S., & Heyman, R. E. (2019). Risk for suicide attempts among United States Air Force active duty members with suicide ideation: An ecological perspective. *Journal of Consulting and Clinical Psychology, 87*(12), 1124–1136. https://doi.org/10.1037/ccp0000435

Lazary, J., Viczena, V., Dome, P., Chase, D., Juhasz, G., & Bagdy, G. (2012). Hopelessness, a potential endophenotype for suicidal behavior, is influenced by *TPH2* gene variants. *Progress in Neuro-Psychopharmacology and Biological Psychiatry, 36*, 155–160. https://doi.org/10.1016/j.pnpbp.2011.09.001

Leenaars, A. A. (1996). Suicide: A multidimensional malaise. *Suicide & Life-Threatening Behavior, 26*(3), 221–236. https://doi.org/10.1111/j.1943-278X.1996.tb00608.x

Leenaars, A. A., De Wilde, E. J., Wenckstern, S., & Kral, M. (2001). Suicide notes of adolescents: A life-span comparison. *Canadian Journal of Behavioural Science, 33*(1), 47.

Leenaars, A. A. (2006). Altruistic suicide: Update. *Archives of Suicide, 10*(1), 99. https://doi.org/10.1080/13811110500406235

Lenz, B., Rother, M., Bouna-Pyrrou, P., Muhle, C., Tektas, O. Y., & Kornhuber, J. (2019). The androgen model of suicide completion. *Progress in Neurobiology, 172*, 84–103. https://doi.org/10.1016/j.pneurobio.2018.06.003

Lester, D., & Beck, A. T. (1976). Early loss as a possible "sensitizer" to later loss in attempted suicides. *Psychological Reports, 39*(1), 121–122. https://doi.org/10.2466/pr0.1976.39.1.121

Lester, D. (1968). Henry and short on suicide: A critique. *The Journal of Psychology, 70*, 179–186.

Lester, D. (1987). A physiological theory of sex differences in suicide. *Medical Hypotheses, 25*(2), 115–117. https://doi.org/10.1016/0306-9877(88)90028-x

Lester, D. (1988). A critical-mass theory of national suicide rates. *Suicide & Life-Threatening Behavior, 18*(3), 279–284. https://doi.org/10.1111/j.1943-278x.1988.tb00164.x

Lester, D. (1991). Totalitarianism and fatalistic suicide. *The Journal of Social Psychology, 131*(1), 129–130. https://doi.org/10.1080/00224545.1991.9713831

Lester, D. (1994). A comparison of 15 theories of suicide. *Suicide & Life-Threatening Behavior, 24*(1), 80–88.
Lester, D. (1997). An empirical examination of Thomas Masaryk's theory of suicide. *Archives of Suicide Research, 3*(2), 125–131. https://doi.org/10.1023/A:1009638904342
Lester, D. (1998). Theories of suicidal behavior applied to Sylvia Plath. *Death Studies, 22*(7), 655–666. https://doi.org/10.1080/074811898201344
Li, X., Mu, F., Liu, D., Zhu, J., Yue, S., Liu, M., Liu, Y., & Wang, J. (2022). Predictors of suicidal ideation, suicide attempt and suicide death among people with major depressive disorder: A systematic review and meta-analysis of cohort studies. *Journal of Affective Disorders, 302*, 332–351. https://doi.org/10.1016/j.jad.2022.01.103
Ludwig, B., Roy, B., Wang, Q., Birur, B., & Dwivedi, Y. (2017). The life span model of suicide and its neurobiological foundation. *Frontiers in Neuroscience, 11*, 74. https://doi.org/10.3389/fnins.2017.00074
Ma, J., Batterham, P. J., Calear, A. L., & Han, J. (2016). A systematic review of the predictions of the Interpersonal-Psychological Theory of Suicidal Behavior. *Clinical Psychology Review, 46*, 34–45. https://doi.org/10.1016/j.cpr.2016.04.008
Marcinkevičiūtė, M., Vilutytė, L., & Gailienė, D. (2024). Experience of pre-suicidal suffering: Insights from suicide attempt survivors. *International Journal of Qualitative Studies on Health and Well-Being, 19*(1), 2370894. https://doi.org/10.1080/17482631.2024.2370894
Maris, R. (1982). Rational suicide: An impoverished self-transformation. *Suicide & Life-Threatening Behavior, 12*(1), 4–16.
Maris, R. W. (1983). Suicide: Rights and rationality. *Suicide & Life-Threatening Behavior, 13*(4), 223–230.
Maris, R. W. (1986). Basic issues in suicide prevention: Resolutions of liberty and love (The Dublin Lecture). *Suicide & Life-Threatening Behavior, 16*(3), 326–334.
Maris, R. W. (1995). Suicide prevention in adults (age 30–65). *Suicide & Life-Threatening Behavior, 25*(1), 171–179.
Martin, J., LaCroix, J. M., Novak, L. A., & Ghahramanlou-Holloway, M. (2020). Typologies of suicide: A critical literature review. *Archives of Suicide Research, 24*(sup1), 25–40. https://doi.org/10.1080/13811118.2018.1564100
Meissner, W. W. (1977). Psychoanalytic notes on suicide. *International Journal of Psychoanalytic Psychotherapy, 6*, 415–447.
Melzer, L., Forkmann, T., & Teismann, T. (2024). Suicide crisis syndrome: A systematic review. *Suicide & Life-Threatening Behavior, 54*(3), 556–574. https://doi.org/10.1111/sltb.13065
Mendoza, H., Rodriguez-Loureiro, L., Gadeyne, S., Lefebvre, W., Vanpoucke, C., & Casas, L. (2023). Urban green spaces and suicide mortality in Belgium (2001–2011): A census-based longitudinal study. *Environmental Research, 216*(Pt 1), 114517. https://doi.org/10.1016/j.envres.2022.114517
Menninger, K. A. (1933). Psychoanalytic aspects of suicide. *The International Journal of Psychoanalysis, 14*, 376–390.
Menninger, K. (1938). *Man against himself*. Harcourt Brace Jovanovich.
Mishara, B. L., & Weisstub, D. N. (2021). Genetic testing for suicide risk assessment: Theoretical premises, research challenges and ethical concerns. *Preventive Medicine, 152*, 106685. https://doi.org/10.1016/j.ypmed.2021.106685
Mitchell, S. M., Brown, S. L., Roush, J. F., Bolaños, A. D., Littlefield, A. K., Marshall, A. J., Jahn, D. R., Morgan, R. D., & Cukrowicz, K. C. (2017). The clinical application of suicide risk assessment: A theory-driven approach. *Clinical Psychology & Psychotherapy, 24*(6), 1406–1420. https://doi.org/10.1002/cpp.2086
Mobley, K., & Taasoobshirazi, G. (2022). Predicting suicide in counties: Creating a quantitative measure of suicide risk. *International Journal of Environmental Research and Public Health, 19*(13), 8173. https://doi.org/10.3390/ijerph19138173
Mokros, L., Nowakowska-Domagala, K., Koprowicz, J., Witusik, A., & Pietras, T. (2021). The association between chronotype and suicidality among students of the medicine and psychology

faculties – the mediating role of general mental health indices. *Chronobiology International, 38*(4), 509–517. https://doi.org/10.1080/07420528.2020.1865393

Moffitt, T. E., Brammer, G. L., Caspi, A., Fawcett, J. P., Yuwiler, A., & Silva, P. (1998). Whole blood serotonin relates to violence in an epidemiological study. *Biological Psychiatry, 43*(6), 446–457. https://doi.org/10.1016/s0006-3223(97)00340-5

Motillon-Toudic, C., Walter, M., Séguin, M., Carrier, J. D., Berrouiguet, S., & Lemey, C. (2022). Social isolation and suicide risk: Literature review and perspectives. *European Psychiatry: The Journal of the Association of European Psychiatrists, 65*(1), e65. https://doi.org/10.1192/j.eurpsy.2022.2320

Mueller, A. S., Abrutyn, S., Pescosolido, B., & Diefendorf, S. (2021). The social roots of suicide: Theorizing how the external social world matters to suicide and suicide prevention. *Frontiers in Psychology, 12*, 621569. https://doi.org/10.3389/fpsyg.2021.621569

Musshoff, F., Menting, T., & Madea, B. (2004). Postmortem serotonin (5-HT) concentrations in the cerebrospinal fluid of medicolegal cases. *Forensic Science International, 142*(2–3), 211–219. https://doi.org/10.1016/j.forsciint.2004.02.023

Na, P. J., Bommersbach, T., Pietrzak, R. H., & Rhee, T. G. (2022). Durkheim's theory of social integration and suicide revisited: Is it diversity of social networks or perceived strength of social support that matters? *The Journal of Clinical Psychiatry, 84*(1), 22m14477. https://doi.org/10.4088/JCP.22m14477

Neuringer, C. (1974). Validation of the cognitive aspect of Adler's theory of suicide. *Journal of Individual Psychology, 30*(1), 59–64.

Noghrehchi, F., Dawson, A. H., Raubenheimer, J., Mohamed, F., Gawarammana, I. B., Eddleston, M., & Buckley, N. A. (2024). Restrictions on pesticides and deliberate self-poisoning in Sri Lanka. *JAMA Network Open, 7*(8), e2426209. https://doi.org/10.1001/jamanetworkopen.2024.26209

Nordin, N., Zainol, Z., Mohd Noor, M. H., & Chan, L. F. (2022). Suicidal behaviour prediction models using machine learning techniques: A systematic review. *Artificial Intelligence in Medicine, 132*, 102395. https://doi.org/10.1016/j.artmed.2022.102395

O'Connor, R. C. (2011). The integrated motivational-volitional model of suicidal behavior. *Crisis, 32*(6), 295–298. https://doi.org/10.1027/0227-5910/a000120

O'Connor, R. C., & Kirtley, O. J. (2018). The integrated motivational-volitional model of suicidal behaviour. *Philosophical Transactions of the Royal Society of London. Series B, Biological Sciences, 373*(1754), 20170268. https://doi.org/10.1098/rstb.2017.0268

Oast, S. P., & Zitrin, A. (1975). A public health approach to suicide prevention. *American Journal of Public Health, 65*(2), 144–147. https://doi.org/10.2105/ajph.65.2.144

Orbach, I. (1994). Dissociation, physical pain, and suicide: A hypothesis. *Suicide & Life-Threatening Behavior, 24*(1), 68–79. https://doi.org/10.1111/j.1943-278X.1994.tb00664.x

Ottenhof, K. W., Sild, M., Levesque, M. L., Ruhe, H. G., & Booij, L. (2018). *TPH2* polymorphisms across the spectrum of psychiatric morbidity: A systematic review and meta-analysis. *Neuroscience and Biobehavioral Reviews, 92*, 29–42. https://doi.org/10.1016/j.neubiorev.2018.05.018

Ozbilgin, M. F., Erbil, C., Demirbağ, O., Gündoğdu, N., & Şimşek Demirbağ, K. (2024). Institutional suicide as anomie: Decedents speak out for work-related suicides through a Durkheimian exploration of suicide notes in a context without institutional responsibilization for suicide prevention. *Frontiers in Sociology, 9*, 1309119. https://doi.org/10.3389/fsoc.2024.1309119

Paniagua, F. A., Black, S. A., Gallaway, M. S., & Coombs, M. A. (2010). *The interpersonal-psychological theory of attempted and completed suicide: conceptual and empirical issues.* AuthorHouse.

Park, H., Lee, H.-K., & Lee, K. (2018). Chronotype and suicide: The mediating effect of depressive symptoms. *Psychiatry Research, 269*, 316–320. https://doi.org/10.1016/j.psychres.2018.08.046

Penney, S. R., & Simpson, A. I. F. (2022). Suicide risk assessment. *The Lancet Psychiatry, 9*(12), 938. https://doi.org/10.1016/S2215-0366(22)00313-3

Picouto, M. D., Villar, F., & Braquehais, M. D. (2015). The role of serotonin in adolescent suicide: Theoretical, methodological, and clinical concerns. *International Journal of Adolescent Mental Health, 27*(2), 129–133. https://doi.org/10.1515/ijamh-2015-5003

Pirkis, J., Dandona, R., Silverman, M., Khan, M., & Hawton, K. (2024). Preventing suicide: a public health approach to a global problem. *The Lancet. Public Health, 9*(10), S2468–2667(24)00149-X. https://doi.org/10.1016/s2468-2667(24)00149-x

Postolache, T. T., Wadhawan, A., Rujescu, D., Hoisington, A. J., Dagdag, A., Baca-Garcia, E., Lowry, C. A., Okusaga, O. O., & Brenner, L. A. (2021). Toxoplasma gondii, suicidal behavior, and intermediate phenotypes for suicidal behavior. *Frontiers in Psychiatry, 12*, 665682. https://doi.org/10.3389/fpsyt.2021.665682

Prezant, D. W., & Neimeyer, R. A. (1988). Cognitive predictors of depression and suicide ideation. *Suicide & Life-Threatening Behavior, 18*(3), 259–264. https://doi.org/10.1111/j.1943-278x.1988.tb00161.x

Pridmore, S., & Jamil, M. Y. (2009). Two models of suicide. *Australasian Psychiatry: Bulletin of Royal Australian and New Zealand College of Psychiatrists, 17*(6), 466–471. https://doi.org/10.1080/10398560903281824

Pridmore, S., & McArthur, M. (2010). An observer's typology of suicide. *Australasian Psychiatry: Bulletin of Royal Australian and New Zealand College of Psychiatrists, 18*(1), 46–48. https://doi.org/10.3109/10398560903314591

Pridmore, S., Auchincloss, S., & Walter, G. (2015). Predicament suicide: An update. *Australasian Psychiatry: Bulletin of Royal Australian and New Zealand College of Psychiatrists, 23*(4), 411–414. https://doi.org/10.1177/1039856215588227

Radua, J., De Prisco, M., Oliva, V., Fico, G., Vieta, E., & Fusar-Poli, P. (2024). Impact of air pollution and climate change on mental health outcomes: An umbrella review of global evidence. *World Psychiatry, 23*(2), 244–256. https://doi.org/10.1002/wps.21219

Rahman Khan, A., & Shimul, S. M. A. K. (2024). Men's suicide in Bangladesh: Impressions from the socio-ecological system theory. *Omega*, 302228241257135. Advance online publication. https://doi.org/10.1177/00302228241257135

Rahmanian, V., Rahmanian, K., Jahromi, A. S., & Bokaie, S. (2020). Seroprevalence of Toxoplasma gondii infection: An umbrella review of updated systematic reviews and meta-analyses. *Journal of Family Medicine and Primary Care, 9*(8), 3848–3855. https://doi.org/10.4103/jfmpc.jfmpc_753_20

Rangell, L. (1988). The decision to terminate one's life: Psychoanalytic thoughts on suicide. *Suicide & Life-Threatening Behavior, 18*(1), 28–46. https://doi.org/10.1111/j.1943-278x.1988.tb00139.x

Rasmussen, S. A., Fraser, L., Gotz, M., MacHale, S., Mackie, R., Masterton, G., McConachie, S., & O'Connor, R. C. (2010). Elaborating the cry of pain model of suicidality: Testing a psychological model in a sample of first-time and repeat self-harm patients. *The British Journal of Clinical Psychology, 49*(Pt 1), 15–30. https://doi.org/10.1348/014466509X415735

Ribeiro, J. D., & Joiner, T. E. (2009). The interpersonal-psychological theory of suicidal behavior: Current status and future directions. *Journal of Clinical Psychology, 65*, 1291–1299. https://doi.org/10.1002/jclp.20621

Rickelman, B. L., & Houfek, J. F. (1995). Toward an interactional model of suicidal behaviors: Cognitive rigidity, attributional style, stress, hopelessness, and depression. *Archives of Psychiatric Nursing, 9*(3), 158–168. https://doi.org/10.1016/s0883-9417(95)80039-5

Roberts, M., & Lamont, E. (2014). Suicide: An existentialist reconceptualization. *Journal of Psychiatric and Mental Health Nursing, 21*, 873–878. https://doi.org/10.1111/jpm.12155

Robison, M., Udupa, N. S., Rice, T. B., Wilson-Lemoine, E., Joiner, T. E., & Rogers, M. L. (2024). The interpersonal theory of suicide: State of the science. *Behavior Therapy*. https://doi.org/10.1016/j.beth.2024.04.008

Rodríguez-Otero, J. E., Campos-Mouriño, X., Meilán-Fernández, D., Pintos-Bailón, S., & Cabo-Escribano, G. (2022). Where is the social in the biopsychosocial model of suicide prevention?

*The International Journal of Social Psychiatry, 68*(7), 1403–1410. https://doi.org/10.1177/00207640211027210
Rubinstein, D. H. (1986). A stress-diathesis theory of suicide. *Suicide & Life-Threatening Behavior, 16*(2), 182–197. https://doi.org/10.1111/j.1943-278x.1986.tb00351.x
Rudd, M. D. (2000). The suicidal mode: A cognitive-behavioral model of suicidality. *Suicide & Life-Threatening Behavior, 30*(1), 18–33. https://doi.org/10.1111/j.1943-278X.2000.tb01062.x
Rush, A. J., & Beck, A. T. (1978). Cognitive therapy of depression and suicide. *American Journal of Psychotherapy, 32*(2), 201–219. https://doi.org/10.1176/appi.psychotherapy.1978.32.2.201
Ryan, E. P., & Oquendo, M. A. (2020). Suicide risk assessment and prevention: Challenges and opportunities. *Focus, 18*(2), 88–99. https://doi.org/10.1176/appi.focus.20200011
Sedano-Capdevila, A., Porras-Segovia, A., Bello, H. J., Baca-García, E., & Barrigon, M. L. (2021). Use of ecological momentary assessment to study suicidal thoughts and behavior: A systematic review. *Current Psychiatry Reports, 23*(7), 41. https://doi.org/10.1007/s11920-021-01255-7
Selkin, J. (1983). The legacy of Emile Durkheim. *Suicide & Life-Threatening Behavior, 13*(1), 3–14. https://doi.org/10.1111/j.1943-278x.1983.tb00001.x
Seto, C. (2022). Saving grace? Religious ecology and deaths of despair. *Social Science & Medicine, 293*, 114642. https://doi.org/10.1016/j.socscimed.2021.114642
Shneidman, E. S. (1993). Suicide as psychache. *The Journal of Nervous and Mental Disease, 181*(3), 145–147. https://doi.org/10.1097/00005053-199303000-00001
Shneidman, E. S. (1998). Perspectives on suicidology. Further reflections on suicide and psychache. *Suicide & Life-Threatening Behavior, 28*(3), 245–250. https://doi.org/10.1111/j.1943-278X.1998.tb00854.x
Shneidman, E. S. (2011). Suicidology and the university: A founder's reflections at 80. *Suicide & Life-Threatening Behavior, 31*(1), 1–8. https://doi.org/10.1521/suli.31.1.1.21314
Siau, C. S., Klonsky, E. D., Kõlves, K., Huen, J. M. Y., Chan, C. M. H., Fariduddin, M. N., Ibrahim, N., Tan, Y. K., Jia, C., Zhang, J., & Lew, B. (2024). Psychache, hopelessness, and suicidal ideation and behaviors: A cross-sectional study from China. *International Journal of Environmental Research and Public Health, 21*(7), 885. https://doi.org/10.3390/ijerph21070885
Sjöström, N., Hetta, J., & Waern, M. (2012). Sense of coherence and suicidality in suicide attempters: A prospective study. *Journal of Psychiatric and Mental Health Nursing, 19*(1), 62–69. https://doi.org/10.1111/j.1365-2850.2011.01755.x
Skutsch, G. M. (1981). Manic depression – a disorder of central dopaminergic rhythm. *Medical Hypotheses, 7*(6), 737–746. https://doi.org/10.1016/0306-9877(81)90085-2
Soper, C. A. (2023). An integrated general theory of psychopathology and suicide. *Evolutionary Psychological Science, 9*, 491–511. https://doi.org/10.1007/s40806-023-00373-0
Soper, C. A. (2024). Ethological problems with the interpersonal theory of suicide. *Omega, 89*(1), 292–314. https://doi.org/10.1177/00302228211073010
Stack, S. (1979). Durkheim's theory of fatalistic suicide: A cross-national approach. *The Journal of Social Psychology, 107*(2), 161–168. https://doi.org/10.1080/00224545.1979.9922694
Stanley, I. H., Hom, M. A., Rogers, M. L., Hagan, C. R., & Joiner, T. E. (2016). Understanding suicide among older adults: A review of psychological and sociological theories of suicide. *Aging & Mental Health, 20*(2), 113–122. https://doi.org/10.1080/13607863.2015.1012045
Staples, J., & Widger, T. (2012). Situating suicide as an anthropological problem: Ethnographic approaches to understanding self-harm and self-inflicted death. *Culture, Medicine and Psychiatry, 36*(2), 183–203. https://doi.org/10.1007/s11013-012-9255-1
Steinkopf, L. (2023). The suffering ape hypothesis. *The Behavioral and brain sciences, 46*, e78. https://doi.org/10.1017/S0140525X2200190X
Syme, K. L., Garfield, Z. H., & Hagen, E. H. (2016). Testing the bargaining vs. inclusive fitness models of suicidal behavior against the ethnographic record. *Evolution and Human Behavior, 37*(3), 179–192. https://doi.org/10.1016/j.evolhumbehav.2015.10.005
Syme, K. L., & Hagen, E. H. (2019). When saying "sorry" isn't enough: Is some suicidal behavior a costly signal of apology? *Human Nature, 30*, 117–141. https://doi.org/10.1007/s12110-018-9333-3

Stefansson, J., Chatzittofis, A., Nordstrom, P., Arver, S., Asberg, M., & Jokinen, J. (2016). CSF and plasma testosterone in attempted suicide. *Psychoneuroendocrinology, 74*, 1–6. https://doi.org/10.1016/j.psyneuen.2016.08.009

Tanaka, M., & Kinney, D. K. (2011). An evolutionary hypothesis of suicide: Why it could be biologically adaptive and is so prevalent in certain occupations. *Psychological Reports, 108*(3), 977–992. https://doi.org/10.2466/02.12.17.pr0.108.3.977-992

Tio, E. S., Misztal, M. C., & Felsky, D. (2024). Evidence for the biopsychosocial model of suicide: A review of whole person modelling studies using machine learning. *Frontiers in Psychiatry, 14*, 1294666. https://doi.org/10.3389/fpsyt.2023.1294666

Tsai, M., Lari, H., Saffy, S., & Klonsky, E. D. (2021). Examining the three-step theory (3ST) of suicide in a prospective study of adult psychiatric inpatients. *Behavior therapy, 52*(3), 673–685. https://doi.org/10.1016/j.beth.2020.08.007

van Eijk, N. L., Wetherall, K., Ferguson, E., O'Connor, D. B., & O'Connor, R. C. (2023). A latent class analysis using the integrated motivational-volitional model of suicidal behaviour: Understanding suicide risk over 36 months. *Journal of Affective Disorders, 336*, 9–14. https://doi.org/10.1016/j.jad.2023.05.028

van Heeringen, K. (2012). Stress-diathesis model of suicidal behavior. In Y. Dwivedi (Ed.), The neurobiological basis of suicide. CRC Press/Taylor & Francis. Available online at: https://www.ncbi.nlm.nih.gov/books/NBK107203/

Van Orden, K. A., Witte, T. K., Cukrowicz, K. C., Braithwaite, S., Selby, E. A., & Joiner, T. E. (2010). The interpersonal theory of suicide. *Psychological Review, 117*(2), 575–600. https://doi.org/10.1037/a0018697

Vasupanrajit, A., Jirakran, K., Tunvirachaisakul, C., & Maes, M. (2021). Suicide attempts are associated with activated immune-inflammatory, nitro-oxidative, and neurotoxic pathways: A systematic review and meta-analysis. *Journal of Affective Disorders, 295*, 80–92. https://doi.org/10.1016/j.jad.2021.08.015

Wagner, G., de la Cruz, F., Kohler, S., Pereira, F., Richard-Devantoy, S., Turecki, G., Bar, K.-J., & Jollant, F. (2019). Connectomics-based functional network alterations in both depressed patients with suicidal behavior and healthy relatives of suicide victims. *Scientific Reports, 9*, 14330. https://doi.org/10.1038/s41598-019-50881-y

Walling, M. A. (2021). Suicide contagion. *Current Trauma Reports, 7*(4), 103–114. https://doi.org/10.1007/s40719-021-00219-9

Weiss, D., & Coccaro, E. F. (1997). Neuroendocrine challenge studies of suicidal behavior. *The Psychiatric Clinics of North America, 20*(3), 563–579. https://doi.org/10.1016/s0193-953x(05)70330-0

Wetherall, K., Cleare, S., Eschle, S., Ferguson, E., O'Connor, D. B., O'Carroll, R. E., & O'Connor, R. C. (2021). Predicting suicidal ideation in a nationally representative sample of young adults: A 12-month prospective study. *Psychological Medicine, 52*(14), 3168–3175. https://doi.org/10.1017/S0033291720005255

Wilchek-Aviad, Y., & Cohen-Louck, K. (2022). Testing the effectiveness of a salutogenic model for reducing suicidal tendencies in a population of elderly and young adults. *Omega, 84*(4), 1081–1099. https://doi.org/10.1177/0030222820919186

Wiley, J. C. (2020). Psychological aposematism: An evolutionary analysis of suicide. *Biological Theory, 15*, 226–238. https://doi.org/10.1007/s13752-020-00353-8

Williams, M. (2014). *Cry of pain: Understanding suicide and the suicidal mind*. Little, Brown.

Wu, H., & Chen, H.-L. (2021). Insufficient evidential basis for the association between Toxoplasma gondii and suicide attempts. *Transboundary and Emerging Diseases, 68*(6), 2993–2994. https://doi.org/10.1111/tbed.13995

Yan, Y., Hou, J., Li, Q., & Yu, N. X. (2023). Suicide before and during the COVID-19 pandemic: A systematic review with meta-analysis. *International Journal of Environmental Research and Public Health, 20*(4), 3346. https://doi.org/10.3390/ijerph20043346

Yang, L., Liu, X., Chen, W., & Li, L. (2019). A test of the three-step theory of suicide among Chinese people: A study based on the ideation-to-action framework. *Archives of Suicide Research: Official Journal of the International Academy for Suicide Research, 23*(4), 648–661. https://doi.org/10.1080/13811118.2018.1497563

Yeom, Y. (2021). Analysing spatial and temporal dynamics of suicide in South Korea: An application of the dynamic spatial panel data model. *Geospatial Health, 16*(1). https://doi.org/10.4081/gh.2021.964. https://doi.org/10.4081/gh.2021.964

Yilmaz, S. K., & Bohara, A. K. (2021). A step back from the edge: Empirical modeling of the role of social integration on suicide and associated deleterious health outcomes across adolescents from six middle-income countries. *Social Psychiatry and Psychiatric Epidemiology, 56*(5), 793–805. https://doi.org/10.1007/s00127-020-01987-6

Yip, P. S. F., Zheng, Y., & Wong, C. (2022). Demographic and epidemiological decomposition analysis of global changes in suicide rates and numbers over the period 1990–2019. *Injury Prevention: Journal of the International Society for Child and Adolescent Injury Prevention, 28*(2), 117–124. https://doi.org/10.1136/injuryprev-2021-044263

Yöyen, E., & Keleş, M. (2024). First- and second-generation psychological theories of suicidal behaviour. *Behavioral Sciences, 14*(8), 710. https://doi.org/10.3390/bs14080710

Zerekidze, A., Li, M., Refisch, A., Shameya, J., Sobanski, T., Walter, M., & Wagner, G. (2024). Impact of Toxoplasma gondii and human microbiome on suicidal behavior: A systematic review. *Journal of Clinical Medicine, 13*(2), 593. https://doi.org/10.3390/jcm13020593

Zhang, J. (1998). Suicide in the world: Toward a population increase theory of suicide. *Death Studies, 22*(6), 525–539. https://doi.org/10.1080/074811898201380

Zhang, J. (2016). From psychological strain to disconnectedness: A two-factor model theory of suicide. *Crisis, 37*(3), 169–75.

Zhang, J., Liu, Y., & Sun, L. (2017). Life satisfaction and degree of suicide intent: A test of the strain theory of suicide. *Comprehensive Psychiatry, 74*, 1–8. https://doi.org/10.1016/j.comppsych.2016.12.002

Zimmerman, J. M. (1992). Adolescent suicide: An analysis using Erikson's developmental framework. *Wisconsin Medical Journal, 91*(7), 351–357.

# Chapter 2
# Social Structure and Suicidal Behavior

**S. M. Yasir Arafat and Sujita Kumar Kar**

**Abstract** Suicide is an outcome of the complex interplay between multiple risk factors. Factors from personal areas like genetic loading and mental illness to wide socioeconomic domains like poverty, development indices, war, and pandemics affect suicidal behavior in the community. The risk factors vary based on the geographical location and socio-cultural structure. Available evidence revealed that wide ecological variables affect suicidality even though the association differs in strength and variations in directions. In this chapter, we highlight the role of different enduring structural factors of the society in suicide focusing on multiple components like HDI, income category of the country, and educational attainment.

**Keywords** Suicide · Suicidal behavior · Income · Poverty · Education and suicide · Suicide prevention

## 1 Introduction

Suicide, a global public health challenge, is an outcome of complicated interactions of multiple factors (World Health Organization, 2021, 2014). Among the 703,000 global suicides in 2019, 77% happened in low and middle-income countries (LMICs) in 2019 (World Health Organization, 2021).

Along with the clinical risk factors like psychiatric disorder and past self-harm attempts sociodemographic variables, family history, and adverse life events also play significant roles (Favril et al., 2022). A systematic review identified that the prevalence of psychiatric disorders in suicidal behavior is lower among LMICs than in high-income countries (Knipe et al., 2019). Despite the variations, personal factors have a significant role in suicidal behavior.

S. M. Y. Arafat (✉)
Department of Psychiatry, Bangladesh Specialized Hospital, Dhaka, Bangladesh
e-mail: arafatdmc62@gmail.com

S. K. Kar
Department of Psychiatry, King George's Medical University, Lucknow, India



S. M. Y. Arafat and S. K. Kar (eds.), *Ecological and Social Determinants of Suicidal Behavior*, South Asian Perspectives in Mental Health and Psychology,
https://doi.org/10.1007/978-981-96-4028-7_2

On the other hand, wider social variables also affect suicidality. One recent study with data from 183 countries identified that the national suicide rate is negatively associated with the Happy Planet Index ($|r| = 0.26–0.30$) and positively associated with Democracy Index ($r = 0.18$, $p = 0.028$) (Rajkumar, 2023). Another study with data from 46 Islamic countries identified that the suicide rate was significantly higher in democratic Islamic countries than in other political system [monarchy, military, and Sharia-based] countries (Arafat et al., 2022a, 2022b). A study from Brazil found that suicide was associated with the Gini Index, unemployment rate among persons above 18 years old, local HDI, illiteracy rate among persons above 18 years old, per capita income, proportion of individuals in homes with inadequate walls, inadequate water supply, and vulnerable to poverty who travel for more than 1 h for job (Silva et al., 2022). A study utilizing the German Microcensus with 149,033 German suicides from 1997 to 2010 assessed the association of suicide with sociodemographic variables (Näher et al., 2020). It found a positive association of suicide rate with regional unemployment and one-person one-person-households and a negative association with income (Näher et al., 2020). Low income, unemployment, and financial problems are revealed as risk factors for suicidality in South Korea (Raschke et al., 2022).

Based on this background, in this chapter, we highlight the role of social structure on suicide focusing on the multiple components like HDI, income category of the country, and educational attainment of individuals.

## 2 Human Development Index (HDI) and Suicidal Behavior

It is a composite indicator considering life expectancy, educational attainment, and per capita income. Associations between HDI and suicidality can be potential indicators of the influence of wider social variables on suicidality. One study with data from 46 Muslim-majority countries revealed that suicide (total, male, female) rate was significantly higher among countries with low income, and low Human Development Index (HDI) than high income and high HDI (Arafat et al., 2022a, 2022b). It found an inverse association between income category and HDI of the country with a steeper graph for female suicide rate indicating that females are more affected in poor Islamic countries (Arafat et al., 2022a, 2022b). Similar findings were noted in studies conducted in Brazil and Iran. Suicide was negatively associated with the local HDI in Brazil. The study found a 4% reduction in risk for each 0.01 increase in local HDI levels [$OR = 0.02$] (Ruiz et al., 2023). One study assessed suicide mortality and ecological factors in different provinces of Iran between 2006 and 2010 (Kiadaliri et al., 2014). It found that higher HDI was associated with a lower suicide rate. Another study from Iran found that the HDI rate was negatively related to the rate of suicide by self-burning (Veisani & Khazaei, 2018).

Other studies revealed different findings. One study with data from 91 countries irrespective of religious majority assessed the relationship between suicide and HDI (Khazaei et al., 2017). It found that suicide was significantly higher in countries with high development (13.94/100,000 people, $p = 0.004$) followed by countries with very high development (11.64/100,000 people and lower in countries with medium development (7.93/100,000 people) (Khazaei et al., 2017). The association doesn't follow a linear pattern. It also found that HDI affects suicide among males significantly. The assessment of the association in older populations revealed a different picture. One study assessed the relationship between the elderly suicide rate and HDI in 86 countries (Shah, 2009). The study found a curvilinear (inverted U-shaped curve) association between suicide rates in elderly males and the HDI.

## 3 Socio-Economic Status and Suicidal Behavior

Socioeconomic status and living conditions affect suicidality among community people (Ju et al., 2016; Kang et al., 2022; Madigan & Daly, 2023; Stack, 2021). One systematic review of 31 studies from nine LMICs in South and Southeast Asia suggested that low socioeconomic conditions are likely to raise the risk of suicidal behavior (Knipe et al., 2015). A systematic review of 221 data sets from 86 articles published between 1897 and 2004 assessed the suicide rate and socioeconomic status of the area (Rehkopf & Buka, 2006). It revealed that suicide was higher in the areas with low socioeconomic status (55% of studies yielded a non-significant association, 32% a significant and inverse association, and 14% a significant and direct association). Another study from Brazil found that the suicide rate was positively associated with the Gini Index indicating that the higher the inequality the higher the suicide (Silva et al., 2022). One study from Iran noted that income inequality and economic instability were positive and employment was negatively associated with suicide (Sezavar et al., 2023). The lower socioeconomic condition was associated with an increased risk of non-fatal (suicide) attempts in rural Sri Lanka (Knipe et al., 2017) and suicidal thoughts among males in Australia (Pirkis et al., 2017).

Sometimes the interactions are complex and difficult to explain. For example, one study in Brazil found that the suicide rate (total, male, female) was higher in the wealthiest and mid-income groups than the poorest in Brazil and the city of São Paulo (Bando et al., 2012). However, the association was reversed when the area was restricted to the state of São Paulo. One study in the US found that suicide was positively associated with the income of the population (Liang & Su, 2022).

One systematic review assessed the role of poverty on suicidal behavior in LMICs. It found that lower socioeconomic status and unemployment increase the risk of suicidal behavior at the individual level (Iemmi et al., 2016). On the other hand, no association was noted between poverty and suicidal behavior at the country level. The suicide rate is lower in Islamic countries than the global rate (World Health Health Organization, 2021; Arafat et al., 2024). However, among the 49 Muslim-majority territories, the rate of suicide is higher in African Muslim Countries than the global average (Arafat et al., 2024). All the 12 sub-Saharan countries have LMIC backgrounds.

## 4 Educational Attainment and Suicidal Behavior

Educational attainment and cognitive status of an individual affect suicidality (Rosoff et al., 2020). A study of the Norwegian Population Register between 1975 and 2014 with 2871 male and 1202 female suicides identified that low academic attainment increases the risk for suicides in both sexes whilst higher academic attainment decreases the risk for suicide in males (Øien-Ødegaard et al., 2021). Lower educational attainment was associated with an increased risk of suicide attempts in the European population (Zhu et al., 2024). The suicide rate was higher among low educational attainment in Taiwan (Li, 1972), in the US (Abel & Kruger, 2005), Koria (Kim et al., 2016), and in Europe (Katrňák & Hubatková, 2022). Suicide rate was negatively associated with educational attainment in Rio Grande do Sul State of Brazil indicating the protective role of education of suicide (Faria et al., 2006).

One study compared the educational attainment between suicide and natural deaths from 2006 to 2008 extracting data from the Italian Mortality Database (Pompili et al., 2013). It revealed that educational attainment was significantly higher among suicide deaths in both sexes between 15 and 64 years compared to natural deaths. A positive correlation between educational attainment and suicide was found in India also (Kar et al., 2024; Sharma, 2022). Other studies also revealed complicated pictures indicating interactions among multiple social variables (Assari et al., 2019; Lorant et al., 2021; Shah & Bhandarkar, 2009; Shah & Chatterjee, 2008).

## 5 Family Dynamics and Suicidal Behavior

Family is an integral part of life. There is a change in family structure globally. The number of joint families is declining drastically. A shift in family structure also alters the family support system. It may have a bearing on mental well-being and suicidal behavior. Family milieu and interactions among family members can affect suicidal behavior. It can trigger or prevent a suicide attempt (Arafat et al., 2022a, 2022b). A study reported that among the suicide attempters, the majority were the only child (Cornutiu, 2014). It indicates that not having a sibling can be a risk factor for suicide. Similarly, it has been found that living in families that have strong cohesion and support systems reduces the risk of suicide (Denney & Teachman, 2010). The risk of suicide is also found to be higher among persons who stay with persons who are unrelated to them, than those who stay with their family (Denney & Teachman, 2010). Family plays as a role model for an individual within the family. Suicide in the family increases the risk of suicidal behavior in the family members which is possibly imitative (Joe et al., 2007). This can also have biological reflection and genetic leading. Parents having any psychiatric illness may increase the risk of suicide in a family (Garber et al., 1998; Joe et al., 2007). It has also been seen that when an adolescent is living away from both parents, it increases the risk of suicide in the adolescent (Ang & Ooi, 2004; Joe et al., 2007). The quality of communication within the family also plays a significant role in the development of suicidality. It has been found that children and adolescents, who have low-quality (less satisfying) communication with their parents, have a higher risk of suicide (Evans et al., 2004; Joe et al., 2007). The closeness between family members is a protective factor for suicide (Joe et al., 2007; O'Donnell et al., 2003). Racial and geographic differences do exist in the association of family dynamics with suicidal behavior (Joe et al., 2007). In a study involving the Chinese population with suicidal ideation, it was found that poor family structure, harsh parenting styles, unstable employment of the parents, maladaptive family dynamics, and negative family environment are associated with suicidal behavior (Zhai et al., 2015). Family functioning needs to be optimal for mental well-being. Family functioning includes family rules, quality of communication between family members, quality of family bonding, coping and adaptation of the family to challenges, and family support system (Yang et al., 2022). Impairment of family functioning increases the risk of suicide (Yang et al., 2022). Any dysfunctional relationship between the adolescent and any of the parents is a risk factor for suicide among youths (Hunt et al., 2022).

## 6 Marriage and Suicidal Behavior

Several marital factors are found to be associated with suicidal behavior. Generally, marriage is considered to be a protective factor against suicide (Corcoran & Nagar, 2010; Mallory, 2022; Øien-Ødegaard et al., 2021), and this pattern is evident across the age and between the genders. Marriage is considered a social tie that protects against suicide (Øien-Ødegaard et al., 2021). An Irish study reports that widowhood after the age of 55 years significantly increases the risk of suicide among males (Corcoran & Nagar, 2010). Suicide was directly associated with marital separation and divorce in Rio Grande do Sul State of Brazil (Faria et al., 2006). However, this association may vary. One systematic review and meta-analysis found that married persons died more than others while single individuals had more attempts than married persons in South Asian countries (Arafat et al., 2023). Early marriage was found to be a cause of significant stress. Early marriage and stressful life events play a complex role in the development of suicidality (Fakhari et al., 2022). Same-sex marriage is not acceptable in many societies and countries, which produces significant distress among same-sex couples (Erlangsen et al., 2020; Kennedy et al., 2021). People with same-sex marriage were found to have a higher suicide rate in comparison to those with opposite-sex marriage (Erlangsen et al., 2020). This trend is also reported in countries that accept same-sex marriage and are tolerant to it (Björkenstam et al., 2016). It has been seen that the legalization of same-sex marriage reduces the risk of suicide (Kennedy et al., 2021).

Studies explored domestic violence in a marital relationship as a risk factor for suicide (Devries et al., 2011; Kavak et al., 2018; Rahmani et al., 2019). Women who experience peace in life or living with their mother or father-in-law are found to have lower suicidal risk (Rahmani et al., 2019). Several predictors of suicide attempts have been identified among women, which are (Devries et al., 2011; Rahmani et al., 2019):

- Infidelity
- Threat by husband for physical assault
- Jealousy of husband
- Past attempts to divorce
- Ever being divorced
- Intimate partner violence

## 7 Population Density and Suicidal Behavior

Population density is an important influencer of suicidal behavior (Stark et al., 2007). However, different studies identified different associations indicating even opposite directions (Lester, 1995). Additionally, the strength of the association also varies. A study conducted in the US found that a higher population density was negatively associated with both male and female suicide (Lester, 1995). A study on the Italian population reported that there is an inverse correlation between population density and suicide rates among males (Vichi et al., 2020), but the association among females is not found to be significant. However, contradicting evidence is also present, which reveals a positive association of population density with suicide rate, indicating the negative impact of urbanization on mental health (Werneck & Silva, 2020; Yamasaki et al., 2008). An Irish study found a weak positive relationship between population density and suicide among females in the 15 to 39-year-old age group (O'Farrell et al., 2016). An Iranian study also found a positive relationship between population density and suicide risk among women (Rostami et al., 2021).

## 8 Religious Beliefs and Suicidal Behavior

Religion is an integral part of society, which significantly influences human behavior. Different religions have different views on suicide (Gearing & Alonzo, 2018; Lizardi & Gearing, 2010). A large-scale multinational survey involving 82,898 participants following Buddhism, Christianity, Hinduism, Islam, and other non-specific religions reports gross variations in the views towards suicide (Saiz et al., 2021). A study among participants from 11 Muslim countries revealed that there is a negative association between religiosity and acceptability of suicide (Eskin et al., 2020). It was also found that negative religious coping is significantly associated with suicide attempts as it unwinds the protective effect of religion (Eskin et al., 2020). Religious affiliation is found to have a protective role against suicidal ideation, but it does not protect against suicidal attempts (Lawrence et al., 2016). Religions serve as a social way of preventing suicide as they facilitate social networking, social integration, following the religious recommendations of not killing oneself, and religious commitment (Norko et al., 2017). A recent meta-analysis that included 63 articles involving 8,053,697 participants found an inverse relation between religiosity and suicidal ideation, suicide plan, suicide attempt, and completed suicide (Poorolajal et al., 2022). A similar, protective effect of religion against suicide, was found in a previous meta-analysis (Wu et al., 2015). It indicates that religion has a protective effect against suicidal behavior. Though sexual minority communities like gays, bisexuals, and lesbians face an identity crisis and increased tendency to experience homophobia, but suicide attempts are less (Kralovec et al., 2014). However, religion may play the role of a risk factor as well as a protective factor among the sexual minority community strictly following a religion (Kralovec et al., 2014).

## 9 Unemployment and Suicidal Behavior

Unemployment is associated with suicidal behavior (Platt, 1984; Nordt et al., 2015; DeFina & Hannon, 2014; Breuer, 2014; Qin et al., 2003; Milner et al., 2013a, 2013b). It is positively associated with suicidality among both males and females (Amiri, 2022; Björkman, 2022; Gunnell et al., 1999; Huikari & Korhonen, 2021; Iglesias-García et al., 2017; Kposowa, 2001; Kposowa et al., 2019). Unemployment is associated with the financial crisis. Financial crisis may lead to suicidal behavior, which has been reported in Europe during the economic crisis in the last decade (Fountoulakis, 2017; Kamekis et al., 2021; Roelfs & Shor, 2023; Stuckler et al., 2009). Unemployment was positively associated with suicide with a rate of 1% increase of unemployment will increase 0.8% suicides below 65 years of age (Stuckler et al., 2009). The impact was more marked in Greece (Madianos et al., 2014). Similar incidences of suicidal behavior associated with job loss and unemployment were reported globally during the time of the COVID-19 pandemic (Ando & Furuichi, 2022; Mathieu et al., 2022). Low paid employments are also important contributing factors to financial hardship and are associated with suicidal behavior (Min et al., 2015). One study assessed data from the population census of New Zealand in 1991 and found that unemployment increased the risk of suicide 2–threefold compared to employed persons (Blakely et al., 2003). Considering the duration of unemployment, one meta-analysis revealed that the risk of suicidal death is greater in the initial 5 years which reduces later risk levels compared to employed persons (Milner et al., 2013a, 2013b). A similar positive association between suicide and unemployment has been noted in Japan (Chen et al., 2012) and South Korea (Kim & Yoon, 2018; Raschke et al., 2022). Like unemployment, underemployment is also found to be an important risk factor for suicide (Skinner et al., 2023). Another study in New Zealand found that exclusion from employment increased the risk of suicide and self-harm in both males and females (Cunningham et al., 2022).

Similarly, highly stressful professions may cause burnout and increase the risk of suicidal behavior (Dyrbye & Shanafelt, 2016; Milner et al., 2018). Workplace stress may result in mental illness and increase the risk of suicide (Milner et al., 2018).

Prevention strategies targeting unemployment have shown promising results in a reduction of suicide among males indicating the mitigating role of unemployment strategies for the association between unemployment and suicide (Shand et al., 2022).

## 10 Conclusion

Suicide is mysterious. There is a complex interaction among the risk factors of suicide. In this chapter, we discussed the relationship between suicide and wider social variables. We examined the association between suicidal behavior and HDI, socio-economic status, educational attainment, family dynamics, marriage, population density, religious beliefs, and employment. The detailed discussion revealed that there are some associations between suicide and wider social structural variables. However, the associations are inconclusive and inconsistent (except for unemployment and low socioeconomic status) based on study place, time, and methods. It is also challenging to determine the associations between wider ecological variables and suicidal behavior due to the complex interaction between man and the environment. This pattern of association puts further challenges for suicide prevention in the community. Additional studies are warranted with replications to consider the associations in prevention strategies.

## References


Abel, E. L., & Kruger, M. L. (2005). Educational attainment and suicide rates in the United States. *Psychological Reports, 97*(1), 25–28. https://doi.org/10.2466/pr0.97.1.25-28

Amiri, S. (2022). Unemployment and suicide mortality, suicide attempts, and suicide ideation: A meta-analysis. *International Journal of Mental Health, 51*(4), 294–318. https://doi.org/10.1080/00207411.2020.1859

Ando, M., & Furuichi, M. (2022). The association of COVID-19 employment shocks with suicide and safety net use: An early-stage investigation. *PLoS One, 17*(3), e0264829. https://doi.org/10.1371/journal.pone.0264829

Ang, R. P., & Ooi, Y. P. (2004). Impact of gender and parents' marital status on adolescents' suicidal ideation. *The International Journal of Social Psychiatry, 50*(4), 351–360. https://doi.org/10.1177/0020764004050335

Arafat, S. M. Y., Marthoenis, M., Khan, M. M., & Rezaeian, M. (2022). Association between suicide rate and human development index, income, and the political system in 46 Muslim-majority countries: An ecological study. *European Journal of Investigation in Health, Psychology and Education, 12*(7), 754–764. https://doi.org/10.3390/ejihpe12070055

Arafat, S. M. Y., Saleem, T., Edwards, T. M., Ali, S. A., & Khan, M. M. (2022). Suicide prevention in Bangladesh: The role of family. *Brain and Behavior, 12*(5), e2562. https://doi.org/10.1002/brb3.2562

Arafat, S. M. Y., Menon, V., Khan, M. A. S., Htay, M. N. N., Singh, R., Biyyala, D., Krishnamoorthy, Y., & Mynampally, K. (2023). Marital status and suicidal behavior in South Asia: A systematic review and meta-analysis. *Health Science Reports, 6*(12), e1781. https://doi.org/10.1002/hsr2.1781

Arafat, S. M. Y., Rezaeian, M., & Khan, M. M. (2024). Suicidal behavior in Islamic countries: An overview. In: S. M. Y. Arafat, M. Rezaeian, M. M. Khan (Eds.), *Suicidal behavior in Muslim majority countries*. Springer. https://doi.org/10.1007/978-981-97-2519-9_1

Assari, S., Schatten, H. T., Arias, S. A., Miller, I. W., Camargo, C. A., & Boudreaux, E. D. (2019). Higher educational attainment is associated with lower risk of a future suicide attempt among non-hispanic whites but not non-hispanic blacks. *Journal of Racial and Ethnic Health Disparities, 6*(5), 1001–1010. https://doi.org/10.1007/s40615-019-00601-z

Bando, D. H., Brunoni, A. R., Benseñor, I. M., et al. (2012). Suicide rates and income in São Paulo and Brazil: A temporal and spatial epidemiologic analysis from 1996 to 2008. *BMC Psychiatry, 12*, 127. https://doi.org/10.1186/1471-244X-12-127

Björkenstam, C., Andersson, G., Dalman, C., Cochran, S., & Kosidou, K. (2016). Suicide in married couples in Sweden: Is the risk greater in same-sex couples? *European Journal of Epidemiology, 31*(7), 685–690. https://doi.org/10.1007/s10654-016-0154-6

Björkman, E. (2022). *Does unemployment increase the risk of suicide?: Empirical evidence from the OECD countries*. Masters thesis, Umea University. Retrieved July 13, 2024, from https://www.diva-portal.org/smash/get/diva2:1673467/FULLTEXT01.pdf

Blakely, T. A., Collings, S. C., & Atkinson, J. (2003). Unemployment and suicide. Evidence for a causal association? *Journal of epidemiology and community health, 57*(8), 594–600. https://doi.org/10.1136/jech.57.8.594

Breuer, C. (2014). Unemployment and suicide mortality: Evidence from regional panel data in Europe. *Health Economics, 24*(8), 936–950. https://doi.org/10.1002/hec.3073

Chen, J., Choi, Y. C., Mori, K., Sawada, Y., & Sugano, S. (2012). Recession, unemployment, and suicide in Japan. *Japan Labor Review, 9*(2), 75–92.

Corcoran, P., & Nagar, A. (2010). Suicide and marital status in Northern Ireland. *Social Psychiatry and Psychiatric Epidemiology, 45*(8), 795–800. https://doi.org/10.1007/s00127-009-0120-7

Cornutiu, O. (2014). EPA-1105—The relationship between family structure and suicide attempts. *European Psychiatry, 29*, 1. https://doi.org/10.1016/S0924-9338(14)78377-4

Cunningham, R., Milner, A., Gibb, S., Rijnberg, V., Disney, G., & Kavanagh, A. M. (2022). Gendered experiences of unemployment, suicide and self-harm: A population-level record linkage study. *Psychological Medicine, 52*(16), 4067–4075. https://doi.org/10.1017/S0033291721000994

DeFina, R., & Hannon, L. (2014). The changing relationship between unemployment and suicide. *Suicide and Life-Threatening Behavior, 45*(2), 217–229. https://doi.org/10.1111/sltb.12116

Denney, J. T., & Teachman, J. (2010). Family and household formations and suicide in the United States. *Journal of Marriage and Family, 72*(1), 202–213.

Devries, K., Watts, C., Yoshihama, M., Kiss, L., Schraiber, L. B., Deyessa, N., Heise, L., Durand, J., Mbwambo, J., Jansen, H., Berhane, Y., Ellsberg, M., Garcia-Moreno, C., & WHO Multi-Country Study Team. (2011). Violence against women is strongly associated with suicide attempts: Evidence from the WHO multi-country study on women's health and domestic violence against women. *Social Science & Medicine (1982), 73*(1), 79–86. https://doi.org/10.1016/j.socscimed.2011.05.006

Dyrbye, L., & Shanafelt, T. (2016). A narrative review on burnout experienced by medical students and residents. *Medical Education, 50*(1), 132–149. https://doi.org/10.1111/medu.12927

Erlangsen, A., Drefahl, S., Haas, A., Bjorkenstam, C., Nordentoft, M., & Andersson, G. (2020). Suicide among persons who entered same-sex and opposite-sex marriage in Denmark and Sweden, 1989–2016: A binational, register-based cohort study. *Journal of Epidemiology and Community Health, 74*(1), 78–83. https://doi.org/10.1136/jech-2019-213009

Eskin, M., Baydar, N., El-Nayal, M., Asad, N., Noor, I. M., Rezaeian, M., Abdel-Khalek, A. M., Al Buhairan, F., Harlak, H., Hamdan, M., Mechri, A., Isayeva, U., Khader, Y., Khan, A., Al Sayyari, A., Khader, A., Behzadi, B., Öztürk, C. Ş., Agha, H., … Khan, M. M. (2020). Associations of religiosity, attitudes towards suicide and religious coping with suicidal ideation and suicide attempts in 11 muslim countries. *Social Science & Medicine (1982), 265*, 113390. https://doi.org/10.1016/j.socscimed.2020.113390

Evans, E., Hawton, K., & Rodham, K. (2004). Factors associated with suicidal phenomena in adolescents: A systematic review of population-based studies. *Clinical Psychology Review, 24*(8), 957–979. https://doi.org/10.1016/j.cpr.2004.04.005

Fakhari, A., Allahverdipour, H., Esmaeili, E. D., Chattu, V. K., Salehiniya, H., & Azizi, H. (2022). Early marriage, stressful life events and risk of suicide and suicide attempt: A case-control study in Iran. *BMC Psychiatry, 22*(1), 71. https://doi.org/10.1186/s12888-022-03700-0

Faria, N. M., Victora, C. G., Meneghel, S. N., de Carvalho, L. A., & Falk, J. W. (2006). Suicide rates in the State of Rio Grande do Sul, Brazil: Association with socioeconomic, cultural, and agricultural factors. *Cadernos De Saude Publica, 22*(12), 2611–2621. https://doi.org/10.1590/s0102-311x2006001200011

Favril, L., Yu, R., Uyar, A., Sharpe, M., & Fazel, S. (2022). Risk factors for suicide in adults: Systematic review and meta-analysis of psychological autopsy studies. *Evidence-Based Mental Health, 25*(4), 148–155. https://doi.org/10.1136/ebmental-2022-300549

Fountoulakis, K. N. (2017). Employment insecurity, mental health and suicide. *Psychiatrike = Psychiatriki, 28*(3), 259–264. https://doi.org/10.22365/jpsych.2017.283.259

Garber, J., Little, S., Hilsman, R., & Weaver, K. R. (1998). Family predictors of suicidal symptoms in young adolescents. *Journal of Adolescence, 21*(4), 445–457. https://doi.org/10.1006/jado.1998.0161

Gearing, R. E., & Alonzo, D. (2018). Religion and suicide: New findings. *Journal of Religion and Health, 57*(6), 2478–2499. https://doi.org/10.1007/s10943-018-0629-8

Gunnell, D., Lopatatzidis, A., Dorling, D., Wehner, H., Southall, H., & Frankel, S. (1999). Suicide and unemployment in young people. Analysis of trends in England and Wales, 1921–1995. *The British Journal of Psychiatry : The Journal of Mental Science, 175*, 263–270. https://doi.org/10.1192/bjp.175.3.263

Huikari, S., & Korhonen, M. (2021). Unemployment, global economic crises and suicides: Evidence from 21 OECD countries. *Applied Economics, 53*(13), 1540–1550. https://doi.org/10.1080/00036846.2020.1838430

Hunt, Q. A., Krauthamer Ewing, E. S., Weiler, L. M., Ogbaselase, F. A., Mendenhall, T., McGuire, J. K., Monet, M., Kobak, R., & Diamond, G. S. (2022). Family relationships and the interpersonal theory of suicide in a clinically suicidal sample of adolescents. *Journal of Marital and Family Therapy, 48*(3), 798–811. https://doi.org/10.1111/jmft.12549

Iemmi, V., Bantjes, J., Coast, E., Channer, K., Leone, T., McDaid, D., Palfreyman, A., Stephens, B., & Lund, C. (2016). Suicide and poverty in low-income and middle-income countries: A systematic review. *The Lancet. Psychiatry, 3*(8), 774–783. https://doi.org/10.1016/S2215-0366(16)30066-9

Iglesias-García, C., Sáiz, P. A., Burón, P., Sánchez-Lasheras, F., Jiménez-Treviño, L., Fernández-Artamendi, S., Al-Halabí, S., Corcoran, P., García-Portilla, M. P., & Bobes, J. (2017). Suicide, unemployment, and economic recession in Spain. *Revista De Psiquiatria y Salud Mental, 10*(2), 70–77. https://doi.org/10.1016/j.rpsm.2016.04.005

Joe, S., Clarke, J., Ivey, A. Z., Kerr, D., & King, C. A. (2007). Impact of familial factors and psychopathology on suicidality among African American adolescents. *Journal of Human Behavior in the Social Environment, 15*(2–3), 199. https://doi.org/10.1300/J137v15n02_12

Ju, Y. J., Park, E. C., Han, K. T., Choi, J. W., Kim, J. L., Cho, K. H., & Park, S. (2016). Low socioeconomic status and suicidal ideation among elderly individuals. *International Psychogeriatrics, 28*(12), 2055–2066. https://doi.org/10.1017/S1041610216001149

Kamekis, A., Rachiotis, G., Markaki, A., Samara, V., & Symvoulakis, E. K. (2021). Employment and suicidal rates during economic recession: A country-targeted integrative review. *The International Journal of Social Psychiatry, 67*(6), 801–815. https://doi.org/10.1177/0020764020969740

Kang, S., Jeong, Y., Park, E. H., & Hwang, S. S. (2022). The impact of household economic deterioration caused by the COVID-19 pandemic and socioeconomic status on suicidal behaviors in adolescents: A Cross-sectional Study using 2020 Korea youth risk web-based survey data.

*Journal of Preventive Medicine and Public Health, 55*(5), 455–463. https://doi.org/10.3961/jpmph.22.241

Kar, S. K., Naskar, C., Marthoenis, M., Tomer, S., Menon, V., & Arafat, S. M. Y. (2024). Suicide and socio-demography: An ecological study from India. *Indian Journal of Psychological Medicine*. https://doi.org/10.1177/02537176241262696

Katrňák, T., & Hubatková, B. (2022). Does educational expansion decrease suicide rates in European countries? The compositional effect in educational stratification of suicides. *Quality and Quantity, 56*, 923–947. https://doi.org/10.1007/s11135-021-01160-4

Kavak, F., Aktürk, Ü., Özdemir, A., & Gültekin, A. (2018). The relationship between domestic violence against women and suicide risk. *Archives of Psychiatric Nursing, 32*(4), 574–579. https://doi.org/10.1016/j.apnu.2018.03.016

Kennedy, A., Genç, M., & Owen, P. D. (2021). The association between same-sex marriage legalization and youth deaths by suicide: A multimethod counterfactual analysis. *The Journal of Adolescent Health: Official Publication of the Society for Adolescent Medicine, 68*(6), 1176–1182. https://doi.org/10.1016/j.jadohealth.2021.01.033

Khazaei, S., Armanmehr, V., Nematollahi, S., Rezaeian, S., & Khazaei, S. (2017). Suicide rate in relation to the human development index and other health related factors: A global ecological study from 91 countries. *Journal of Epidemiology and Global Health, 7*(2), 131–134. https://doi.org/10.1016/j.jegh.2016.12.002

Kiadaliri, A. A., Saadat, S., Shahnavazi, H., & Haghparast-Bidgoli, H. (2014). Overall, gender and social inequalities in suicide mortality in Iran, 2006–2010: A time trend province-level study. *British Medical Journal Open, 4*(8), e005227. https://doi.org/10.1136/bmjopen-2014-005227

Kim, J., & Yoon, S. Y. (2018). Association between socioeconomic attainments and suicidal ideation by age groups in Korea. *The International Journal of Social Psychiatry, 64*(7), 628–636. https://doi.org/10.1177/0020764018792592

Kim, J. L., Kim, J. M., Choi, Y., Lee, T. H., & Park, E. C. (2016). Effect of socioeconomic status on the linkage between suicidal ideation and suicide attempts. *Suicide & Life-Threatening Behavior, 46*(5), 588–597. https://doi.org/10.1111/sltb.12242

Knipe, D. W., Carroll, R., Thomas, K. H., Pease, A., Gunnell, D., & Metcalfe, C. (2015). Association of socio-economic position and suicide/attempted suicide in low and middle income countries in South and South-East Asia—A systematic review. *BMC Public Health, 15*, 1055.

Knipe, D. W., Gunnell, D., Pieris, R., Priyadarshana, C., Weerasinghe, M., Pearson, M., Jayamanne, S., Dawson, A. H., Mohamed, F., Gawarammana, I., Hawton, K., Konradsen, F., Eddleston, M., & Metcalfe, C. (2017). Is socioeconomic position associated with risk of attempted suicide in rural Sri Lanka? A cross-sectional study of 165 000 individuals. *British Medical Journal Open, 7*(3), e014006. https://doi.org/10.1136/bmjopen-2016-014006

Knipe, D., Williams, A. J., Hannam-Swain, S., Upton, S., Brown, K., Bandara, P., Chang, S. S., & Kapur, N. (2019). Psychiatric morbidity and suicidal behaviour in low- and middle-income countries: A systematic review and meta-analysis. *PLoS Medicine, 16*(10), e1002905. https://doi.org/10.1371/journal.pmed.1002905

Kposowa, A. J. (2001). Unemployment and suicide: A cohort analysis of social factors predicting suicide in the US National Longitudinal Mortality Study. *Psychological Medicine, 31*(1), 127–138. https://doi.org/10.1017/s0033291799002925

Kposowa, A. J., Aly Ezzat, D., & Breault, K. (2019). New findings on gender: The effects of employment status on suicide. *International Journal of Women's Health, 11*, 569–575. https://doi.org/10.2147/IJWH.S216504

Kralovec, K., Fartacek, C., Fartacek, R., & Plöderl, M. (2014). Religion and suicide risk in lesbian, gay and bisexual Austrians. *Journal of Religion and Health, 53*(2), 413–423. https://doi.org/10.1007/s10943-012-9645-2

Lawrence, R. E., Oquendo, M. A., & Stanley, B. (2016). Religion and suicide risk: A systematic review. *Archives of Suicide Research: Official Journal of the International Academy for Suicide Research, 20*(1), 1–21. https://doi.org/10.1080/13811118.2015.1004494

Lester, D. (1995). An extension of the association between population density and mental illness to suicidal behavior. *The Journal of Social Psychology, 135*(5), 657–658. https://doi.org/10.1080/00224545.1995.9712

Li, W. L. (1972). Suicide and educational attainment in a transitional society. *Sociological Quarterly, 13*(2), 253–258.

Liang, A., Su, E., (2022). Does money buy enough happiness: Investigating the relationship between income and suicide rates. *Honors in Management, 8*. https://openscholarship.wustl.edu/bsba/8

Lizardi, D., & Gearing, R. E. (2010). Religion and suicide: Buddhism, Native American and African religions, Atheism, and Agnosticism. *Journal of Religion and Health, 49*(3), 377–384. https://doi.org/10.1007/s10943-009-9248-8

Lorant, V., Kapadia, D., Perelman, J., & DEMETRIQ study group (2021). Socioeconomic disparities in suicide: Causation or confounding?. *PLoS One, 16*(1), e0243895. https://doi.org/10.1371/journal.pone.0243895

Madianos, M. G., Alexiou, T., Patelakis, A., & Economou, M. (2014). Suicide, unemployment and other socioeconomic factors: Evidence from the economic crisis in Greece. *The European Journal of Psychiatry, 28*(1), 39–49. https://doi.org/10.4321/S0213-61632014000100004

Madigan, A., & Daly, M. (2023). Socioeconomic status and depressive symptoms and suicidality: The role of subjective social status. *Journal of Affective Disorders, 326*, 36–43. https://doi.org/10.1016/j.jad.2023.01.078

Mallory, A. B. (2022). Dimensions of couples' sexual communication, relationship satisfaction, and sexual satisfaction: A meta-analysis. *Journal of Family Psychology : JFP : Journal of the Division of Family Psychology of the American Psychological Association (Division 43), 36*(3), 358–371. https://doi.org/10.1037/fam0000946

Mathieu, S., Treloar, A., Hawgood, J., Ross, V., & Kõlves, K. (2022). The role of unemployment, financial hardship, and economic recession on suicidal behaviors and interventions to mitigate their impact: A review. *Frontiers in Public Health, 10*, 907052. https://doi.org/10.3389/fpubh.2022.907052

Milner, A., Page, A., & LaMontagne, A. D. (2013). Long-term unemployment and suicide: A systematic review and meta-analysis. *PLoS One, 8*(1), e51333. https://doi.org/10.1371/journal.pone.0051333

Milner, A., Hjelmeland, H. M., Arensman, E., & De Leo, D. (2013). Social-environmental factors and suicide mortality: A narrative review of over 200 articles. *Sociology Mind, 3*, 137–148. https://doi.org/10.4236/sm.2013.32021

Milner, A., LaMontagne, A. D., Spittal, M. J., Pirkis, J., & Currier, D. (2018). Job stressors and employment precarity as risks for thoughts about suicide: An Australian study using the ten to men cohort. *Annals of Work Exposures and Health, 62*(5), 583–590. https://doi.org/10.1093/annweh/wxy024

Min, K.-B., Park, S.-G., Hwang, S. H., & Min, J.-Y. (2015). Precarious employment and the risk of suicidal ideation and suicide attempts. *Preventive Medicine, 71*, 72–76. https://doi.org/10.1016/j.ypmed.2014.12.017

Näher, A. F., Rummel-Kluge, C., & Hegerl, U. (2020). Associations of suicide rates with socioeconomic status and social isolation: Findings from longitudinal register and census data. *Frontiers in Psychiatry, 10*, 898. https://doi.org/10.3389/fpsyt.2019.00898

Nordt, C., Warnke, I., Seifritz, E., & Kawohl, W. (2015). Modelling suicide and unemployment: A longitudinal analysis covering 63 countries, 2000–11. *The Lancet. Psychiatry, 2*(3), 239–245. https://doi.org/10.1016/S2215-0366(14)00118-7

Norko, M. A., Freeman, D., Phillips, J., Hunter, W., Lewis, R., & Viswanathan, R. (2017). Can religion protect against suicide? *The Journal of Nervous and Mental Disease, 205*(1), 9–14. https://doi.org/10.1097/NMD.0000000000000615

O'Donnell, L., Stueve, A., Wardlaw, D., & O'Donnell, C. (2003). Adolescent suicidality and adult support: The reach for health study of urban youth. *American Journal of Health Behavior, 27*(6), 633–644. https://doi.org/10.5993/ajhb.27.6.6

O'Farrell, I. B., Corcoran, P., & Perry, I. J. (2016). The area level association between suicide, deprivation, social fragmentation and population density in the Republic of Ireland: A national study. *Social Psychiatry and Psychiatric Epidemiology, 51*(6), 839–847. https://doi.org/10.1007/s00127-016-1205-8

Øien-Ødegaard, C., Hauge, L. J., & Reneflot, A. (2021). Marital status, educational attainment, and suicide risk: A Norwegian register-based population study. *Population Health Metrics, 19*(1), 33. https://doi.org/10.1186/s12963-021-00263-2

Pirkis, J., Currier, D., Butterworth, P., Milner, A., Kavanagh, A., Tibble, H., Robinson, J., & Spittal, M. J. (2017). Socio-economic position and suicidal ideation in men. *International Journal of Environmental Research and Public Health, 14*(4), 365. https://doi.org/10.3390/ijerph14040365

Platt, S. (1984). Unemployment and suicidal behaviour: A review of the literature. *Social science & medicine (1982), 19*(2), 93–115. https://doi.org/10.1016/0277-9536(84)90276-4

Pompili, M., Vichi, M., Qin, P., Innamorati, M., De Leo, D., & Girardi, P. (2013). Does the level of education influence completed suicide? A nationwide register study. *Journal of Affective Disorders, 147*(1–3), 437–440. https://doi.org/10.1016/j.jad.2012.08.046

Poorolajal, J., Goudarzi, M., Gohari-Ensaf, F., & Darvishi, N. (2022). Relationship of religion with suicidal ideation, suicide plan, suicide attempt, and suicide death: A meta-analysis. *Journal of Research in Health Sciences, 22*(1), e00537. https://doi.org/10.34172/jrhs.2022.72

Qin, P., Agerbo, E., & Mortensen, P. B. (2003). Suicide risk in relation to socioeconomic, demographic, psychiatric, and familial factors: A national register-based study of all suicides in Denmark, 1981–1997. *The American Journal of Psychiatry, 160*(4), 765–772. https://doi.org/10.1176/appi.ajp.160.4.765

Rahmani, F., Salmasi, S., Rahmani, F., Bird, J., Asghari, E., Robai, N., Asghari, M., & Gholizadeh, L. (2019). Domestic violence and suicide attempts among married women: A case-control study. *Journal of Clinical Nursing, 28*(17–18), 3252–3261. https://doi.org/10.1111/jocn.14901

Rajkumar, R. P. (2023). The association between nation-level social and economic indices and suicide rates: A pilot study. *Frontiers in Sociology, 8*, 1123284. https://doi.org/10.3389/fsoc.2023.1123284

Raschke, N., Mohsenpour, A., Aschentrup, L., et al. (2022). Socioeconomic factors associated with suicidal behaviors in South Korea: Systematic review on the current state of evidence. *BMC Public Health, 22*, 129. https://doi.org/10.1186/s12889-022-12498-1

Rehkopf, D. H., & Buka, S. L. (2006). The association between suicide and the socio-economic characteristics of geographical areas: A systematic review. *Psychological Medicine, 36*(2), 145–157. https://doi.org/10.1017/S003329170500588X

Roelfs, D. J., & Shor, E. (2023). Financial stress, unemployment, and suicide—a meta-analysis. *Crisis, 44*(6), 506–517. https://doi.org/10.1027/0227-5910/a000908

Rosoff, D. B., Kaminsky, Z. A., McIntosh, A. M., Davey Smith, G., & Lohoff, F. W. (2020). Educational attainment reduces the risk of suicide attempt among individuals with and without psychiatric disorders independent of cognition: A bidirectional and multivariable Mendelian randomization study with more than 815,000 participants. *Translational Psychiatry, 10*(1), 388. https://doi.org/10.1038/s41398-020-01047-2

Rostami, M., Jalilian, A., Mahdavi, S. A., & Bagheri, N. (2021). Spatial heterogeneity in gender and age of fatal suicide in Iran. *Journal of Research in Health Sciences, 22*(1), e00541. https://doi.org/10.34172/jrhs.2022.76

Ruiz, A. M. P., Fernandez, M. R. B., Komoda, D. S., Treichel, C. A. D. S., & Cordeiro, R. C. (2023). Risk and protective factors for suicide: A populational case-control study, Brazil, 2019. *Revista de saude publica, 57*, 16. https://doi.org/10.11606/s1518-8787.2023057004606

Saiz, J., Ayllón-Alonso, E., Sánchez-Iglesias, I., Chopra, D., & Mills, P. J. (2021). Religiosity and suicide: A large-scale international and individual analysis considering the effects of different religious beliefs. *Journal of Religion and Health, 60*(4), 2503–2526. https://doi.org/10.1007/s10943-020-01137-x

Sezavar, F., Firoozy, M., & Sezavar, M. (2023). The effect of economic and social factors on the suicidal behavior of society in Iran (with emphasis on risk and economic instability). *Social Welfare Quarterly, 23*(90), 53–88. https://doi.org/10.32598/refahj.22.86.622.2

Shah, A. (2009). The relationship between elderly suicide rates and the human development index: A cross-national study of secondary data from the World Health Organization and the United Nations. *International Psychogeriatrics, 21*(1), 69–77. https://doi.org/10.1017/S1041610208007527

Shah, A., & Bhandarkar, R. (2009). The relationship between general population suicide rates and educational attainment: A cross-national study. *Suicide & Life-Threatening Behavior, 39*(5), 463–470. https://doi.org/10.1521/suli.2009.39.5.463

Shah, A., & Chatterjee, S. (2008). Is there a relationship between elderly suicide rates and educational attainment? A cross-national study. *Aging & Mental Health, 12*(6), 795–799. https://doi.org/10.1080/13607860802427986

Shand, F., Duffy, L., & Torok, M. (2022). Can government responses to unemployment reduce the impact of unemployment on suicide? *Crisis, 43*(1), 59–66. https://doi.org/10.1027/0227-5910/a000750

Sharma, P. (2022). Impact of education on suicides in India. *Journal of Education Culture and Society, 13*(1), 419–428. https://doi.org/10.15503/jecs2022.1.419.428

Silva, T. L., Maranhão, T. A., Sousa, G. J. B., Silva, I. G. D., Lira, J. C. G., & Araujo, G. A. D. S. (2022). Spatial analysis of suicide in Northeastern Brazil and associated social factors. *Texto & Contexto-Enfermagem, 31*, e20210096. https://doi.org/10.1590/1980-265X-TCE-2021-0096

Skinner, A., Osgood, N. D., Occhipinti, J.-A., Song, Y. J. C., & Hickie, I. B. (2023). Unemployment and underemployment are causes of suicide. *Science Advances, 9*(28), eadg3758. https://doi.org/10.1126/sciadv.adg3758

Stack, S. (2021). Contributing factors to suicide: Political, social, cultural and economic. *Preventive Medicine, 152*(Pt 1), 106498. https://doi.org/10.1016/j.ypmed.2021.106498

Stark, C., Hopkins, P., Gibbs, D., Belbin, A., & Hay, A. (2007). Population density and suicide in Scotland. *Rural and Remote Health, 7*(3), 672. https://doi.org/10.22605/RRH672

Stuckler, D., Basu, S., Suhrcke, M., Coutts, A., & McKee, M. (2009). The public health effect of economic crises and alternative policy responses in Europe: An empirical analysis. *Lancet (London, England), 374*(9686), 315–323. https://doi.org/10.1016/S0140-6736(09)61124-7

Veisani, Y., & Khazaei, S. (2018). Inequality in self-immolation incidence according to HDI in Iran. *Burns: Journal of the International Society for Burn Injuries, 44*(3), 726–728. https://doi.org/10.1016/j.burns.2017.10.025

Vichi, M., Vitiello, B., Ghirini, S., & Pompili, M. (2020). Does population density moderate suicide risk? An Italian population study over the last 30 years. *European Psychiatry: The Journal of the Association of European Psychiatrists, 63*(1), e70. https://doi.org/10.1192/j.eurpsy.2020.69

Werneck, A. O., & Silva, D. R. (2020). Population density, depressive symptoms, and suicidal thoughts. *Brazilian Journal of Psychiatry, 42*(1), 105–106. https://doi.org/10.1590/1516-4446-2019-0541

World Health Organization. (2014). *Preventing suicide: A global imperative*. WHO. Retreived June 24, 2024, from https://apps.who.int/iris/handle/10665/131056

World Health Organization. (2021). *Suicide worldwide in 2019: Global health estimates*. WHO. Retreived September 15, 2021, from https://www.who.int/publications/i/item/9789240026643

Wu, A., Wang, J.-Y., & Jia, C.-X. (2015). Religion and completed suicide: A meta-analysis. *PLoS One, 10*(6), e0131715. https://doi.org/10.1371/journal.pone.0131715

Yamasaki, A., Araki, S., Sakai, R., Yokoyama, K., & Voorhees, A. S. (2008). Suicide mortality of young, middle-aged and elderly males and females in Japan for the years 1953–96: Time series analysis for the effects of unemployment, female labour force, young and aged population, primary industry and population density. *Industrial Health, 46*(6), 541–549. https://doi.org/10.2486/indhealth.46.541

Yang, Q., Hu, Y.-Q., Zeng, Z.-H., Liu, S.-J., Wu, T., & Zhang, G.-H. (2022). The relationship of family functioning and suicidal ideation among adolescents: The Mediating role of defeat and the moderating role of meaning in life. *International Journal of Environmental Research and Public Health, 19*(23), 15895. https://doi.org/10.3390/ijerph192315895

Zhai, H., Bai, B., Chen, L., Han, D., Wang, L., Qiao, Z., Qiu, X., Yang, X., & Yang, Y. (2015). Correlation between family environment and suicidal ideation in university students in China. *International Journal of Environmental Research and Public Health, 12*(2), Article 2. https://doi.org/10.3390/ijerph120201412

Zhu, J., Liu, H., Gao, R., Ding, L., Wang, J., Yang, Y., Zhou, D., & Li, Y. (2024). Understanding the educational inequalities in suicide attempts and their mediators: A Mendelian randomisation study. *General Psychiatry, 37*(1), e101369. https://doi.org/10.1136/gpsych-2023-101369

# Chapter 3
# Climate Change and Suicidal Behaviour

**Russell Kabir, Haniya Zehra Syed, and Divya Vinnakota**

**Abstract** This chapter examines the intricate relationship between climate change and suicidal behaviour, synthesizing emerging evidence on this critical public health issue. It explores how climate change impacts mental health through direct effects of temperature changes and extreme weather events, as well as indirect pathways such as economic disruption, displacement, and eco-anxiety. It highlights vulnerable populations, including farmers, rural communities, indigenous groups, and youth, who face disproportionate risks. The chapter also evaluates various intervention methods, ranging from community-based resilience programs to technological solutions, aimed at addressing climate-related mental health challenges and suicidal behaviour.

**Keywords** Climate change · Suicide · Suicidal behaviour · Eco-anxiety · Ecology

## 1 Introduction

Recent Global climate change is a major cause of threat to human existence on the earth (Kabir & Khan, 2016). Climate change, identified by prolonged changes in temperature and weather trends, has become a major global issue in the twenty-first century. Although its effects on the environment and economy are well-known, there is increasing worry over its impact on mental health, specifically its potential connection to suicidal behaviour. The Intergovernmental Panel on Climate Change

R. Kabir (✉) · H. Z. Syed
School of Allied Health and Social Care, Faculty of Health, Medicine and Social Care, Anglia Ruskin University, Chelmsford, Essex, UK
e-mail: russell.kabir@aru.ac.uk

H. Z. Syed
e-mail: Haniya.syed@aru.ac.uk

D. Vinnakota
School of Human and Health Sciences, University of Huddersfield, Huddersfield, UK
e-mail: divya.vinnakota@hud.ac.uk

 
S. M. Y. Arafat and S. K. Kar (eds.), *Ecological and Social Determinants of Suicidal Behavior*, South Asian Perspectives in Mental Health and Psychology,
https://doi.org/10.1007/978-981-96-4028-7_3

(IPCC, 2022) has pointed out that climate change is leading to more frequent and severe extreme weather events, higher sea levels, and altered precipitation patterns. These changes in the environment can have significant effects on both physical and mental well-being and health of humans.

Severe weather conditions related to climate change have also been connected to higher chances of suicide. In their 2015 study, Kõlves et al., systematically reviewed the connection between natural disasters and suicidal behaviours, discovering a rise in suicide rates after severe cyclones in Australia. In a similar manner, Carleton (2017) studied how climate variability affected suicide rates among farmers in India and found that drought events were linked to higher rates of suicide in this at-risk group. Kabir and Arafat (2017) reported that extreme climate conditions impact human health indirectly, decreasing food production, worsening malnutrition, affecting income sources, and education and this has severe mental health impacts on the people of Bangladesh.

The ways in which climate change is linked to suicidal behaviour are intricate and have many aspects. In their proposal, Page and Howard (2010) suggest that heat could affect the risk of suicide by directly impacting the brain physiologically, specifically affecting serotonin and other mood-regulating neurotransmitters. Studies have provided evidence that supports this hypothesis, as they reveal that suicide rates tend to peak during the warmer months, indicating a seasonal pattern (Petridou et al., 2002). The economic impacts of climate change could lead to a higher risk of suicide. Events influenced by the climate, such as droughts, floods, and storms, have the potential to cause crop losses, damage to property, and displacement, which can lead to financial difficulties and job loss—factors that are known to increase the risk of suicide (Norström & Grönqvist, 2015). Studies by Bryant and Garnham (2015), and Carleton (2017) have shown that the agricultural industry is especially at risk, as seen through connections between climate fluctuations and farmer suicides in India and Australia.

Numerous studies have recognized "eco-anxiety" or "climate anxiety" as a developing issue in mental health. According to Pihkala (2020), eco-anxiety is defined as a long-lasting fear of environmental catastrophe, leading to depression, anxiety, and possibly suicidal thoughts. Eco-anxiety is not an official clinical diagnosis, but it is becoming more acknowledged as a major source of stress, especially for young individuals (Hickman et al., 2021). The intersection of climate change and mental health also underscores concerns related to environmental justice. Marginalized groups such as Indigenous communities, low-income populations, and individuals in developing nations frequently experience unequal consequences of climate change and lack sufficient resources to manage its aftermath. This imbalance could worsen differences in mental health and raise the chances of suicide within these groups. With the worsening climate crisis, more research on its impact on mental health is urgently required. Obradovich et al. (2018) stress the significance of long-term studies in comprehending the lasting effects of climate change on mental health. Moreover, an increasing number of experts are advocating for the inclusion of mental health factors in plans to address and adapt to climate change (Berry et al., 2018). While the relationship between climate change and suicidal behaviour is complex and multifaceted, emerging evidence suggests a concerning association. This chapter is going to explore the possible implications of suicidal behaviour in relation to climate change.

## 2 Global Epidemiology of Suicide Attributable to Climate Change

Research conducted by Burke et al., (2018a, 2018b) examined information collected in the United States and Mexico over an extended period of time. For every 1 °C increase in monthly average temperature, suicide rates increased by 0.7% in the US and 2.1% in Mexico. Based on these results, scientists forecast that if global warming persists, there could be between 9,000 and 40,000 more suicides in the US and Mexico by 2050. A study by Heo et al. (2019) examined the relationship between ambient temperature and suicide rates across 50 U.S. states from 1999 to 2016. They found that a 1 °C increase in monthly average temperature was associated with a 0.7% increase in suicide rates. The effect was more pronounced in western states and during warmer months.

In India, where agriculture is a critical component of the economy, there is a significant correlation between climate-related factors and farmer suicides. In his research in 2017, Carleton discovered that if the temperature during the growing season goes above 20 °C, a rise of 1 °C in a single day would lead to an average increase of 70 annual suicides. The research suggests that the increase in temperatures in the past three decades has led to 59,300 suicides in India, contributing to 6.8% of the overall rise in the country's suicide rates.

Research conducted in Australia has concentrated on how drought affects suicide rates in rural areas. Hanigan et al. (2012) examined information from New South Wales spanning 38 years (1970–2007). It was discovered that rural male suicide rates rose by 15% as the drought index increased from the 30th to the 70th percentile of its historical range. The rise was even more notable for rural men between the ages of 30 and 49, with a 9% increase.

The Arctic's indigenous communities are especially at risk of suffering the consequences of climate change. Research conducted by Cunsolo Willox and colleagues in 2013 in Nunatsiavut, Canada, discovered that 45% of adults who were interviewed mentioned experiencing depression as a result of alterations in the environment, specifically affecting the land, ice, and weather. Although suicide rates are not being directly measured, this mental health effect indicates a higher likelihood of engaging in suicidal actions. Mohammanezhad et al. (2018) and Tom et al. (2024) identified pre-existing mental illness is a key determinant of suicide.

Risk of suicide related to climate change seems to differ based on age and gender. According to Hanigan et al. (2012), the effects of drought on suicide were strongest for rural men between the ages of 30 and 49 in Australia. Likewise, research conducted in Japan by Inoue et al. (2020) revealed that the suicide rate among males aged 65–74 rose by 3.3% with each 1 °C rise in daily maximum temperature. Farmers and those who work in agriculture appear to have a higher susceptibility to suicide risk associated with climate change.

Besides the results from India, research conducted by Bryant and Garnham (2015) in Australia discovered that economic pressure due to drought, when combined with traditional male beliefs of self-sufficiency, raises the likelihood of suicide among male farmers. Lower economic standing seems to heighten susceptibility to climate-related suicide risk. Research conducted by Kim et al. (2020) in South Korea discovered that the link between elevated temperatures and suicide was more pronounced in individuals with lower educational backgrounds and manual labourers. Rural populations are more vulnerable to climate-related suicide risk, particularly in relation to drought and agricultural impacts. However, urban populations are not immune. A study by Assunção and Chien (2016) in Taiwan found that suicide rates in urban areas increased by 4.8% for each 1 °C increase in daily mean temperature above 25 °C.

Seasonal patterns in the relationship between temperature and suicide rates. For example, Kim et al. (2014) found that in South Korea, suicide rates increased by 1.4% for each 1 °C increase in mean temperature, with the effect being strongest in the summer months. Extreme weather events also impact suicide rates. A study by Kessler et al. (2011) found that suicidal ideation and plans more than doubled in the aftermath of Hurricane Katrina, from 2.8% to 6.4%. Climate-induced displacement is an emerging concern for mental health and suicide risk. A study by Schwerdtle et al. (2018) highlighted that climate migrants face multiple stressors that can increase suicide risk, including loss of place, social disconnection, and economic instability. However, quantitative data on suicide rates among climate migrants is currently limited. Climate change may have unique impacts on youth mental health and suicide risk. A global survey by Hickman et al. (2021) found that 45% of young people (aged 16–25) reported that climate anxiety and distress affect their daily lives and functioning. While not directly linked to suicide, such chronic stress could potentially contribute to long-term suicide risk.

## 3 Unravelling the Relationship Between Climate Change and Suicidal Behaviour

The worsening impacts of climate change are gaining consideration globally, especially with its far-reaching effects on health and well-being. Climate change-induced mental health challenges have gained prominence as extreme weather events, rising temperatures, and environmental degradation continue to disrupt communities worldwide. Mental health impacts associated with climate change include depression, anxiety, post-traumatic stress disorder (PTSD), and suicidal behaviour (Cianconi et al., 2020).

The psychological impact of climate change can manifest in various ways. Heatwaves, for example, have been linked to increased aggression, impulsivity, and, consequently, suicide risk. Rising temperatures contributed to higher suicide rates in the United States and Mexico, suggesting that even small temperature increases can lead to thousands of additional suicides. Furthermore, extreme weather events like floods and droughts exacerbate stress by displacing people, disrupting communities, and creating long-term uncertainty (Burke et al., 2018a, 2018b). According to Hertzog et al., (2024), between heat range anomalies of 0 °C to 3 °C, adults and older adults were found to be vulnerable to the effects of temperature and increased suicide risks and out of the suicides reported from 2000–2009 in Australia, 0.5% were accredited to climate-change-induced heat anomalies (Hertzog et al., 2024).

## *3.1 Loss of Livelihood and Its Impact on Suicidal Behaviour*

One of the most significant ways in which climate change affects mental health is through its disruption of livelihoods. Many communities, particularly in low- and middle-income countries (LMICs), rely on agriculture, fisheries, and other climate-sensitive industries for their survival. When climate-related disasters such as droughts, floods, or hurricanes strike, they often result in crop failure, loss of income, and a deepening cycle of poverty. This can lead to significant psychological stress, feelings of hopelessness, and, in extreme cases, suicidal ideation (Clayton et al., 2017).

In India, the issue of farmer suicides has been particularly prominent. Erratic rainfall patterns, prolonged droughts, and the resulting agricultural losses have led to an alarming increase in suicides among farmers who face insurmountable financial debt and the pressure of providing for their families (Carleton, 2017). This phenomenon has also been observed in Australia, where drought-stricken rural communities have experienced spikes in suicide rates, particularly among men whose sense of identity and self-worth is tied to their role as providers (Hanigan et al., 2012). The intersection of economic distress and climate-induced environmental stressors creates a potent trigger for mental health crises, further highlighting the vulnerability of agricultural communities to both climate and mental health shocks.

## *3.2 Rising Sea Levels and Displacement*

Rising sea levels, one of the most visible consequences of climate change, threaten to displace millions of people living in coastal regions. The loss of homes, land, and infrastructure due to rising seas causes widespread displacement, often leading to forced migration. This process, referred to as climate-induced displacement, can have profound psychological impacts on affected populations, contributing to mental health issues, including suicidal behaviour (Palinkas & Wong, 2020).

In countries like Bangladesh, where large portions of the population live in low-lying coastal areas, the rising sea levels pose a severe threat. Displaced individuals often experience the loss of their homes and ancestral lands, which are tied to their cultural identity and sense of belonging. The psychological toll of displacement is compounded by the loss of social networks, and economic opportunities, and the uncertainty of finding new, stable living conditions (Wilkinson et al., 2019). Research has shown that displaced individuals and refugees are at higher risk of mental health disorders, including depression, anxiety, and suicidal behaviour (Talia et al., 2023). The disruption caused by displacement can also lead to social isolation and marginalization, further exacerbating the risk of suicide.

### *3.3 Spread of Diseases and Health-Related Stress*

Climate change has been directly linked to the spread of infectious diseases, particularly in regions where public health infrastructure is already weakened. As temperatures rise and weather patterns become more erratic, the habitats of disease vectors, such as mosquitoes, expand, leading to increased transmission of diseases like malaria, dengue fever, and Zika virus (McMicheal et al., 2006). The fear and anxiety surrounding the spread of these diseases can compound existing mental health challenges, leading to higher risks of suicidal behaviour.

During outbreaks of diseases linked to climate change, affected communities often experience heightened anxiety, isolation, and feelings of powerlessness. In addition, the fear of becoming infected can trigger panic and lead to increased social withdrawal, which in turn elevates the risk of depression and suicidal ideation. Vulnerable populations, such as the elderly, individuals with pre-existing health conditions, and those living in poverty, are particularly susceptible to both the physical and mental health impacts of climate-related diseases (Watts et al., 2018). In such settings, the combination of physical illness and psychological distress can lead to mental health crises, including suicide.

### *3.4 Fear of the Unknown: Eco-Anxiety and Climate Phobia*

Beyond the tangible effects of climate change, there is an emerging recognition of the psychological impact of the fear of future climate-related disasters. The concept of "eco-anxiety" has gained attention as individuals increasingly report feelings of helplessness, fear, and existential dread about the future of the planet (Clayton & Karazsia, 2020). Climate phobia, a term used to describe the intense fear of environmental collapse, is particularly prevalent among young people, who fear that their futures will be irrevocably harmed by climate change (Hickman et al., 2021).

Eco-anxiety is driven by constant exposure to distressing information about climate change, combined with the uncertainty of how severe the impacts will be. This chronic stress can have significant mental health consequences, including the development of depressive disorders and suicidal ideation. Individuals experiencing eco-anxiety often report a sense of powerlessness in the face of the climate crisis, as well as a feeling of being betrayed by governments and institutions that fail to take adequate action to mitigate climate change (Hickman et al., 2021). The psychological toll of living in constant fear of climate change is profound and can lead to serious mental health outcomes, including suicidal thoughts and behaviours.

### *3.5 Vulnerable Populations and Intersectional Effects*

The mental health impacts of climate change, including suicidal behaviour, are not evenly distributed. Vulnerable populations, including women, children, the elderly, indigenous communities, and those living in poverty, are disproportionately affected by climate-induced stressors. These groups often have fewer resources to cope with the impacts of climate change, and they are more likely to experience compounding stress from other social and economic challenges (Hayes et al., 2018).

Women, particularly those in rural and coastal regions, face unique vulnerabilities related to climate change. In many societies, women are responsible for securing their families' food, water, and energy. When these resources become scarce due to climate change, the psychological burden on women increases significantly, leading to higher rates of stress, anxiety, and depression (Tschakert & Machado, 2012). Moreover, women often have less access to mental health services and other forms of social support, further exacerbating their vulnerability to mental health crises, including suicidal behaviour.

Children and adolescents are also highly vulnerable to the mental health impacts of climate change. Young people are increasingly exposed to the realities of climate change through media, education, and personal experiences of environmental degradation. Many report feelings of anxiety, despair, and anger about the state of the planet and the lack of meaningful action to address climate change. Studies have shown that young people who experience eco-anxiety are at higher risk of developing mental health disorders, including depression and suicidal ideation (Hickman et al., 2021).

## 4 Climate Change Implications on Suicidal Behaviour

A study in New Zealand examined the relationship between temperature variation and suicide rates from 1988 to 2007. The researchers analysed three components of temperature variation: irregular, seasonal, and geographical. They found that irregular temperature increases were associated with a small rise in suicide rates (1.8% more suicides per 1 °C increase). Seasonal temperature variation showed little relationship with suicide rates. Geographical variation in temperature had a negative relationship with suicide rates when controlling for demographics. The conflicting effects of different types of temperature variation make it difficult to predict how climate change will impact future suicide rates (Williams et al., 2015). The connection between temperature and suicide is intricate and could involve several different mechanisms. Heat has the ability to impact brain function, and the neurotransmitter systems related to mood regulation (Page et al., 2012). Furthermore, elevated temperatures may interfere with sleeping schedules and lead to higher levels of irritation, which could worsen current mental health problems (Noelke et al., 2016).

Climate change is associated with an increase in the frequency and intensity of extreme weather events such as floods, hurricanes, and droughts (Kabir et al., 2014). These events can have profound impacts on mental health, including increased risk of suicide. For instance, floods have been associated with increased suicide rates in impacted communities. A 2006 study conducted by Kessler et al. discovered that residents in areas impacted by Hurricane Katrina experienced a notable rise in suicidal thoughts and intentions. In the same way, prolonged droughts have been linked to higher suicide rates in farming communities in nations such as India and Australia (Carleton, 2017; Hanigan et al., 2012). The ways in which extreme weather events are connected to suicide risk are complex and varied. Acute stress and trauma, loss of income and economic stress, displacement, and disturbance of social support networks are encompassed in this list (Berry et al., 2010; Kabir et al., 2016).

Albrecht et al. (2007) introduced the concept of "solastalgia" to explain the suffering brought on by environmental changes, especially within one's familiar surroundings. This idea has been associated with higher chances of mental health issues, such as thoughts of suicide, particularly in indigenous communities and individuals connected to the land (Cunsolo Willox et al., 2013). The impacts of climate change on economic and social systems can indirectly increase the risk of suicide. Changes in weather patterns can result in agricultural losses, which may cause financial strain and higher suicide risk for farmers (Berry et al., 2010). In a more general sense, economic disturbances caused by climate change can worsen inequality and social instability, which are recognized as risk factors for suicide (Fountoulakis et al., 2016).

## 5 Evaluation of Different Intervention Methods Focusing on Climate Change

Promoting healthy mental health is essential in treating the psychological distress brought on by climate change, given the possible rise in suicides and suicidal behaviour linked to global warming and climate change. People can benefit from enhancing their coping strategies and developing resilience to reduce elevated stress levels. Exercise, yoga, and most importantly raising awareness and providing people access to programs that assist them in managing their stress are all essential practices. An integrated community intervention was created to enhance practical disaster preparedness and foster mental health in Haiti, a nation vulnerable to climate change effects and prone to natural disasters (James et al., 2020). The manualized intervention included exercises that improved household readiness (e.g., creating an emergency action plan, and mapping community risks and resources) and promoted mental health literacy and coping skills (e.g., progressive muscle relaxation). The intervention participants reported higher intentions to provide mental health-focused assistance and fewer symptoms of anxiety, depression, and PTSD.

Climate change can trigger several mental health consequences such as PTSD, depression, anxiety, phobias, and sleep disorders, especially in more vulnerable groups such as children, older adults, and individuals with prior mental health problems (Breslau et al., 2008; Burke et al., 2018a, 2018b; Parker et al., 2016). Therefore, psychosocial and community resilience may play a significant role in reducing the suffering associated with climate change and natural disasters. Several interventions self-identified as initiatives to increase resilience. Following Super Typhoon Haiyan, the Philippines produced the six-module Katatagan intervention, which was evaluated in two different contexts (Hechanova et al. 2018; Hechanova et al., 2016). The intervention participants in Tacloban City, where the intervention was conducted by trained paraprofessionals, showed improvements in adaptive coping, individual resilience, and anxiety levels as compared to the control group (Hechanova et al. 2018). Health Futures Incorporated (HFI) conducted the intervention in the Samar Province as part of a mission trip. Compared to their baseline, the intervention participants showed improvements in all self-efficacy dimensions, as determined by a locally developed scale based on each Katatagan module. In both scenarios, benefits peaked just after the intervention and declined around the six-month follow-up.

A government-funded program called the Drought Mental Health Assistance Package (DMHAP) was put in place for the rural farming communities in New South Wales, Australia, who endure climate-related adversity (Hart et al., 2011; Tonna et al., 2009). DMHAP included early intervention (e.g., a rural telephone helpline, workshops for service network planning) and mental health promotion (e.g., resource booklet production, community mental health forums, mental health first aid training). The extended Rural Adversity Mental Health Program (RAMHP) provided targeted programs for priority groups, including as women, youth, older farmers, and Aboriginal communities, and expanded the number of dedicated drought mental health workers after receiving renewed funding. A rational emotive behaviour therapy (REBT) approach was evaluated in Nigeria, where floods are occurring more frequently due to climate change (Ede et al., 2022). Following an unfavourable triggering experience, participants in REBT, a brief therapy related to cognitive behavioural therapy (CBT), are encouraged to aggressively challenge irrational beliefs. Professional therapists provided 20 sessions of REBT to 49 flood victims who were suffering from clinical depression. The Hamilton Depression Scale revealed that the intervention group had significantly less symptoms of depression than the waiting control group.

Another resilience-building program, called Skills for Life Adjustment and Resilience (SOLAR), was tested in Tuvalu, a small island developing state (SIDS) that is susceptible to sea level rise (Gibson et al., 2021). Over the course of five days, 49 islanders who had been affected by Cyclone Pam and were exhibiting indications of mental illness took part in the group intervention led by a lay worker. The skills for healthy living, managing strong emotions, recovering from a disaster, accepting it, controlling worry and rumination, and upholding healthy relationships were all covered in this module. Participants' levels of psychological distress, PTSD symptoms, and functional impairment improved when compared to controls. Although benefits were diminished from the first post-intervention period, they were still present at the six-month follow-up. Furthermore, local government organizations can address suicidality brought on by climate change by increasing financial assistance and safety nets for particular groups of people, such as farmers and other agriculture workers who suffer from financial difficulties as a result of climate-related disasters (Kim, 2016). Aggressive measures to reduce greenhouse gas emissions will also help to lessen the likelihood of catastrophic climate events and mitigate the negative consequences of climate change on mental health (Cianconi et al., 2020). Early response programs, including setting aside public funds for mental health support following catastrophic events, are examples of further interventions.

During the 2017 floods in Bangladesh, a Red Cross Red Crescent humanitarian project was implemented to support river basin people' financial security and related psychological benefits (Gros et al., 2019). Prior to a flood peak, 1039 impoverished households received an unconditional cash transfer of BDT 5000 (equal to USD 60) based on a forecast. Intervention households were less likely than unsupported households to have experienced anxiety and depression continuously, as well as a lower likelihood of experiencing constant misery or unhappiness following the flood. A capacity building intervention was created in Ethiopia for pastoral communities facing difficulties with food shortages, shifting land, and increasingly severe droughts. The intervention comprised elements to enhance literacy and numeracy, create collective action groups, and motivate participants (Coppock et al., 2011). The distribution of donor funds for livestock trading and the encouragement of microenterprises were the specific macroeconomic components. According to the study, collective action groups led by 59 women were established, 11 of which received donor grants. Intervention participants in the Liben District who received donor grants in addition to capacity building after a significant drought scored much higher than their peers on study-defined mental health and well-being parameters.

The availability of mobile applications that provide users with mental health content can be a useful intervention technique in the current digital era. These kinds of accessible alternatives can be helpful to a large number of people, but in order to better serve a broad user base, it is crucial to make sure that these applications are customized to take into account various languages, cultural viewpoints, and geographic characteristics (Ramnath & Suri, 2021). In order to effectively meet the problems posed by climate change, mental health support may be made more accessible and efficient by utilizing technology and taking into account the diversity of requirements.

# 6 Conclusion

Climate change poses a significant and growing threat to mental health globally, with mounting evidence linking it to increased suicide risk. The relationship between climate change and suicidal behaviour is complex, involving direct impacts of temperature changes, extreme weather events, and indirect effects through economic disruption, displacement, and eco-anxiety. Vulnerable populations, including farmers, rural communities, indigenous groups, and youth, face disproportionate risks. While the global epidemiology of climate change-related suicide is still emerging, studies from various countries highlight concerning trends.

Addressing this challenge requires a multifaceted approach. Interventions ranging from community-based resilience programs to economic support for affected populations have shown promise. Mental health services must be integrated into climate change adaptation strategies, with a focus on accessibility and cultural appropriateness. Technological solutions, such as mobile mental health apps, offer potential for widespread support. However, these efforts must be coupled with aggressive measures to mitigate climate change itself. As the climate crisis intensifies, prioritizing mental health in climate policy and research is crucial for safeguarding vulnerable populations and building resilient communities in the face of environmental upheaval.

## References

Albrecht, G., Sartore, G. M., Connor, L., Higginbotham, N., Freeman, S., Kelly, B., & Pollard, G. (2007). Solastalgia: The distress caused by environmental change. *Australasian Psychiatry, 15*(supl), S95–S98. https://doi.org/10.1080/10398560701701288

Assunção, J., & Chein, F. (2016). Climate change and agricultural productivity in Brazil: Future perspectives. *Environment and Development Economics, 21*(5), 581–602.

Berry, H. L., Bowen, K., & Kjellstrom, T. (2010). Climate change and mental health: A causal pathways framework. *International Journal of Public Health, 55*(2), 123–132. https://doi.org/10.1007/s00038-009-0112-0

Berry, H. L., Waite, T. D., Dear, K. B., Capon, A. G., & Murray, V. (2018). The case for systems thinking about climate change and mental health. *Nature climate change, 8*(4), 282–290.

Breslau, N., Peterson, E. L., & Schultz, L. R. (2008). A second look at prior trauma and the posttraumatic stress disorder effects of subsequent trauma: A prospective epidemiological study. *Archives of General Psychiatry, 65*(4), 431–437. https://doi.org/10.1001/archpsyc.65.4.431

Bryant, L., & Garnham, B. (2015). The fallen hero: Masculinity, shame and farmer suicide in Australia. *Gender, Place & Culture, 22*(1), 67–82.

Burke, S. E., Sanson, A. V., & Van Hoorn, J. (2018). The psychological effects of climate change on children. *Current Psychiatry Reports, 20*, 1–8. https://doi.org/10.1007/s11920-018-0896-9

Burke, M., González, F., Baylis, P., Heft-Neal, S., Baysan, C., Basu, S., & Hsiang, S. (2018). Higher temperatures increase suicide rates in the United States and Mexico. *Nature Climate Change, 8*(8), 723–729. https://doi.org/10.1038/s41558-018-0222-x

Carleton, T. A. (2017). Crop-damaging temperatures increase suicide rates in India. *Proceedings of the National Academy of Sciences, 114*(33), 8746–8751. https://doi.org/10.1073/pnas.1701354114

Cianconi, P., Betrò, S., & Janiri, L. (2020). The impact of climate change on mental health: A systematic descriptive review. *Frontiers in Psychiatry, 11*, 490206. https://doi.org/10.3389/fpsyt.2020.00074

Clayton, S., Manning, C. M., Krygsman, K., & Speiser, M. (2017). Mental health and our changing climate: Impacts, implications, and guidance. *American Psychological Association, and ecoAmerica.*

Clayton, S., & Karazsia, B. T. (2020). Development and validation of a measure of climate change anxiety. *Journal of Environmental Psychology, 69*, 101434. https://doi.org/10.1016/j.jenvp.2020.101434

Coppock, D. L., Desta, S., Tezera, S., & Gebru, G. (2011). Capacity building helps pastoral women transform impoverished communities in Ethiopia. *Science, 334*(6061), 1394–1398. https://doi.org/10.1126/science.1211232

Cunsolo Willox, A., Harper, S. L., Ford, J. D., Edge, V. L., Landman, K., Houle, K., Blake, S., & Wolfrey, C. (2013). Climate change and mental health: an exploratory case study from Rigolet, Nunatsiavut, Canada. *Climatic Change, 121*(2), 255–270.https://doi.org/10.1007/s10584-013-0875-4

Ede, M. O., Adene, F. M., Okeke, C. I., Mezieobi, D. I., Isiwu, E. N., & Abdullahi, Y. (2022). The effect of rational emotive behaviour therapy on post-traumatic depression in flood victims. *Journal of Rational-Emotive & Cognitive-Behavior Therapy, 40*(1), 124–143. https://doi.org/10.1007/s10942-021-00401-7

Fountoulakis, K. N., Chatzikosta, I., Pastiadis, K., Zanis, P., Kawohl, W., Kerkhof, A. J., & Bech, P. (2016). Relationship of suicide rates with climate and economic variables in Europe during 2000–2012. *Annals of General Psychiatry, 15*(1), 19. https://doi.org/10.1186/s12991-016-0106-2

Gibson, K., Little, J., Cowlishaw, S., Ipitoa Toromon, T., Forbes, D., & O'Donnell, M. (2021). Piloting a scalable, post-trauma psychosocial intervention in Tuvalu: The Skills for Life Adjustment and Resilience (SOLAR) program. *European Journal of Psychotraumatology, 12*(1), 1948253. https://doi.org/10.1080/20008198.2021.1948253

Gros, C., Bailey, M., Schwager, S., Hassan, A., Zingg, R., Uddin, M. M., Shahjahan, M., Islam, H., Lux, S., Jaime, C., & de Perez, E. C. (2019). Household-level effects of providing forecast-based cash in anticipation of extreme weather events: Quasi-experimental evidence from humanitarian interventions in the 2017 floods in Bangladesh. *International Journal of Disaster Risk Reduction, 41*, 101275. https://doi.org/10.1016/j.ijdrr.2019.101275

Hanigan, I. C., Butler, C. D., Kokic, P. N., & Hutchinson, M. F. (2012). Suicide and drought in New South Wales, Australia, 1970–2007. *Proceedings of the National Academy of Sciences, 109*(35), 13950–13955. https://doi.org/10.1073/pnas.1112965109

Hart, C. R., Berry, H. L., & Tonna, A. M. (2011). Improving the mental health of rural New South Wales communities facing drought and other adversities. *Australian Journal of Rural Health, 19*(5), 231–238. https://doi.org/10.1111/j.1440-1584.2011.01225.x

Hayes, K., Blashki, G., Wiseman, J., Burke, S., & Reifels, L. (2018). Climate change and mental health: Risks, impacts and priority actions. *International Journal of Mental Health Systems, 12*(1), 28. https://doi.org/10.1186/s13033-018-0210-6

Hechanova, M. R. M., Waelde, L. C., & Ramos, P. A. P. (2016). Evaluation of a group-based resilience intervention for Typhoon Haiyan survivors. *Journal of Pacific Rim Psychology, 10*, e12. https://doi.org/10.1017/prp.2016.9

Hechanova, M. R., Docena, P. S., Alampay, L. P., Acosta, A., Porio, E. E., Melgar, I. E., & Berger, R. (2018). Evaluation of a resilience intervention for Filipino displaced survivors of Super Typhoon Haiyan. *Disaster Prevention and Management: An International Journal, 27*(3), 346–359. https://doi.org/10.1108/DPM-01-2018-0001

Heo, S., Bell, M. L., & Lee, J. T. (2019). Comparison of health risks by heat wave definition: Applicability of wet-bulb globe temperature for heat wave criteria. *Environmental research, 168*, 158–170.

Hertzog, L., Charlson, F., Tschakert, P., Morgan, G. G., Norman, R., Pereira, G., & Hanigan, I. C. (2024). Suicide deaths associated with climate change-induced heat anomalies in Australia: a time series regression analysis. *BMJ Mental Health, 27*(1). https://doi.org/10.1136/bmjment-2024-301131

Hickman, C., Marks, E., Pihkala, P., Clayton, S., Lewandowski, R. E., Mayall, E. E., Wray, B., Mellor, C., & van Susteren, L. (2021). Climate anxiety in children and young people and their beliefs about government responses to climate change: a global survey. *The Lancet Planetary Health, 5*(12), e863–e873. https://doi.org/10.1016/S2542-5196(21)00278-3

Inoue, T., Nunokawa, N., Kurisu, D., & Ogasawara, K. (2020). Particulate air pollution, birth outcomes, and infant mortality: Evidence from Japan's automobile emission control law of 1992. *SSM-Population Health, 11*, 100590.

IPCC. (2022). *Climate change 2022: Impacts, adaptation and vulnerability*. Contribution of Working Group II to the Sixth Assessment Report of the Intergovernmental Panel on Climate Change. Cambridge University Press.

James, L. E., Welton-Mitchell, C., Noel, J. R., & James, A. S. (2020). Integrating mental health and disaster preparedness in intervention: A randomized controlled trial with earthquake and flood-affected communities in Haiti. *Psychological Medicine, 50*(2), 342–352. https://doi.org/10.1017/S0033291719000163

Kabir, R., & Arafat, S. Y. (2017). Public health perspectives due to climate change in Bangladesh. *Birat Journal of Health Sciences, 2*(3), 316–317. https://doi.org/10.3126/bjhs.v2i3.18956

Kabir, R., & Khan, H. T. (2016). Climate change induced natural disasters impact on the health of the coastal people in Bangladesh. *International Journal of Perceptions in Public Health, 1*(1), 6–8.

Kabir, R., Khan, H. T., Ball, E., & Caldwell, K. (2014). Climate change and public health situations in the coastal areas of Bangladesh. *International Journal of Social Science Studies, 2*, 109. https://doi.org/10.11114/ijsss.v2i3.426

Kabir, R., Khan, H. T., Ball, E., & Caldwell, K. (2016). Climate change impact: The experience of the coastal areas of Bangladesh affected by cyclones Sidr and Aila. *Journal of Environmental and Public Health, 2016*(1), 9654753. https://doi.org/10.1155/2016/9654753

Kessler, R. (2011). Stormwater strategies: Cities prepare aging infrastructure for climate change.

Kim, E. J. (2016). The impacts of climate change on human health in the United States: A scientific assessment, by us global change research program. *Journal of the American Planning Association, 82*(4), 418–419.

Kim, K. H., Kabir, E., & Ara Jahan, S. (2014). A review of the consequences of global climate change on human health. *Journal of Environmental Science and Health, Part C, 32*(3), 299–318.

Kim, S., Kim, S. Y., Oh, J., Chae, Y., Park, J., Kim, D., & Kim, Y. M. (2020). Effects of the 2018 heat wave on health in the elderly: Implications for adaptation strategies to climate change. *Environmental Analysis, Health and Toxicology, 35*(4), e2020024.

Kõlves, K., Kõlves, K. E., & De Leo, D. (2015). Natural disasters and suicidal behaviours: A systematic literature review. *Journal of Affective Disorders, 172*, 215–225. https://doi.org/10.1016/j.jad.2012.07.037

McMicheal, A., Woodruff, R. & Hales, S., 2006. Climate change and human health: Present and future risks. *The Lancet, 367*(9513), 859–869. https://doi.org/10.1016/S0140-6736(06)68079-3

Mohammadnezhad, M., Konrote, A., & Kabir, R. (2018). Determinants of suicide in Pacific region and needs for considering equality amongst Pacific people: A systematic review. *Pacific Journal of Medical Sciences, 19*(1), 17–29.

Noelke, C., McGovern, M., Corsi, D. J., Jimenez, M. P., Stern, A., Wing, I. S., & Berkman, L. (2016). Increasing ambient temperature reduces emotional well-being. *Environmental Research, 151*, 124–129. https://doi.org/10.1016/j.envres.2016.06.045

Norström, T., & Grönqvist, H. (2015). The great recession, unemployment and suicide. *Journal of Epidemiology and Community Health, 69*(2), 110–116. https://doi.org/10.1136/jech-2014-204602

Obradovich, N., Migliorini, R., Paulus, M. P., & Rahwan, I. (2018). Empirical evidence of mental health risks posed by climate change. *Proceedings of the National Academy of Sciences, 115*(43), 10953–10958. https://doi.org/10.1073/pnas.1801528115

Page, L. A., & Howard, L. M. (2010). The impact of climate change on mental health (but will mental health be discussed at Copenhagen?). *Psychological Medicine, 40*(2), 177–180.

Page, L. A., Hajat, S., Kovats, R. S., & Howard, L. M. (2012). Temperature-related deaths in people with psychosis, dementia and substance misuse. *The British Journal of Psychiatry, 200*(6), 485–490.

Palinkas, L. A., & Wong, M. (2020). Global climate change and mental health. *Current Opinion in Psychology, 32*, 12–16. https://doi.org/10.1016/j.copsyc.2019.06.023

Parker, G., Lie, D., Siskind, D. J., Martin-Khan, M., Raphael, B., Crompton, D., & Kisely, S. (2016). Mental health implications for older adults after natural disasters—a systematic review and meta-analysis. *International Psychogeriatrics, 28*(1), 11–20. https://doi.org/10.1177/0004867415578344

Petridou, E., Papadopoulos, F. C., Frangakis, C. E., Skalkidou, A., & Trichopoulos, D. (2002). A role of sunshine in the triggering of suicide. *Epidemiology, 13*(1), 106–109.

Pihkala, P. (2020). Anxiety and the ecological crisis: An analysis of eco-anxiety and climate anxiety. *Sustainability, 12*(19), 7836. https://doi.org/10.3390/su12197836

Ramnath, S., & Suri, G. (2021). Managing depression in India: Opportunities for a targeted smartphone app. *International Journal of Social Psychiatry, 67*(8), 1035–1045. https://doi.org/10.1177/00207640211032253

Schwerdtle, P., Bowen, K., & McMichael, C. (2018). The health impacts of climate-related migration. *BMC medicine, 16*, 1–7.

Talia, M. (2023). Am I not your Tū/Akoi?: A Tuvaluan plea for survival in a time of climate emergency.

Tom, L. A., Syed, H. Z., & Kabir, R. (2024). Social factors in celebrity suicides: A content analysis of South Indian online news reports. *Asian Journal of Psychiatry and Mental Health, 1*(1). https://doi.org/10.62337/ajpmh.v1i1.4

Tonna, A., Kelly, B., Crockett, J., Greig, J., Buss, R., Roberts, R., & Wright, M. (2009). Improving the mental health of drought-affected communities: An Australian model. *Rural Society, 19*(4), 296–305. https://doi.org/10.5172/rsj.351.19.4.296

Tschakert, P., & Machado, M. (2012). Gender justics and rights in climate change adaptation: Opportunities and Pitfalls. *Ethics and Social Welfare, 6*(3), 275–289.

Watts, N., Amann, M., Arnell, N., Ayeb-Karlsson, S., Belesova, K., Berry, H., Bouley, T., Boykoff, M., Byass, P., Cai, W., Campbell-Lendrum, D., Chambers, J., Daly, M., Dasandi, N., Davies, M., Depoux, A., Dominguez-Salas, P., Drummond, P., Ekins, P., ... & Costello, A. (2018). The 2018 report of the Lancet Countdown on health and climate change: shaping the health of nations for centuries to come. *The Lancet, 392*(10163), 2479–2514. https://doi.org/10.1016/S0140-6736(18)32594-7

Wilkinson, A. J., Braggins, R., Steinbach, I., & Smith, J. (2019). Costs of switching to low global warming potential inhalers. An economic and carbon footprint analysis of NHS prescription data in England. *BMJ Open, 9*(10), e028763.

Williams, M. N., Hill, S. R., & Spicer, J. (2015). Will climate change increase or decrease suicide rates? The differing effects of geographical, seasonal, and irregular variation in temperature on suicide incidence. *Climatic Change, 130*(4), 519–528. https://doi.org/10.1007/s10584-015-1371-9

# Chapter 4
# Urbanization and Suicidal Behaviour

**Erika Pahuja, Ferose Azeez Ibrahim, and Praveen Pandey**

**Abstract** As cities continue to expand and evolve, it becomes imperative to examine the intricate relationship of urbanization and suicidal behaviour. The chapter delves into what urbanization entails, global urbanization trends, followed by a thorough exploration of theoretical perspectives. From Durkheim's seminal work to more recent frameworks like the Three Step Theory and concept of Urban Stress, we trace the evolution of thought connecting urban life to suicidal tendencies. Central to this discussion is an exhaustive examination of key urban factors influencing suicidal behaviours. These include social fragmentation, economic disparities, population density, and environmental stressors unique to urban living. A range of interventions, from community-based initiatives fostering social cohesion to environmental modifications and economic measures, are described. Alongside these, role of mental health services, leveraging technology and urban planning to create more supportive city environments, has been described rigorously. The chapter concludes by identifying critical gaps in the current research landscape, advocating for future studies that explore the nuanced dynamics of urbanization and suicidality. This comprehensive examination aims to inform policymakers, mental health professionals, and researchers about the complexities of urbanization and its implications for suicidal behaviour.

**Keywords** Urbanization · Suicide · Suicidal behaviour · Mental health

E. Pahuja
Specialty Trainee in General Adult and Old Age Psychiatry, North London NHS Foundation Trust, London, UK

F. A. Ibrahim (✉)
Specialty Trainee in General Adult Psychiatry, South-West London and St. Georges Mental Health Trust, London, UK
e-mail: ferose.dr@gmail.com

P. Pandey
Specialty Trainee in Child and Adolescent Psychiatry, East London NHS Foundation Trust, London, UK



S. M. Y. Arafat and S. K. Kar (eds.), *Ecological and Social Determinants of Suicidal Behavior*, South Asian Perspectives in Mental Health and Psychology,
https://doi.org/10.1007/978-981-96-4028-7_4

# 1 Urbanization

What is urbanization? Is there an established concept? Has urbanization affected the environment and health? Has there been an impact on mental health? While numerous questions about urbanization remain unresolved, there is a solid grasp of certain key aspects.

United Nations identifies Urbanization as a pivotal global trend of the twenty-first century, a transformative force that can be harnessed to enhance economic growth, productivity, and development (Urbanization | United Nations—CEB, 2024).

Throughout much of human history, majority of people globally resided in small, localized, close-knit communities. Over the recent decades, with mass migration of populations from rural to urban areas, this has changed dramatically, with more than half of the global population residing in the urban areas. It is important to note that a universally established definition of "urban areas" remains unestablished till date, and countries adopt their own national definition, and hence the concept and figures of "Urbanization" face criticism and discrepancies across various countries.

For instance:

India defines Urbanization as "Statutory places with a municipality, corporation, cantonment board, or notified town area committee and places satisfying all of the following three criteria: (1) 5,000 inhabitants or more; (2) at least 75 percent of the male working population engaged in non-agricultural pursuits; and (3) at least 400 inhabitants per square kilometer" (Ritchie et al., 2024), whereas the European Commission defines Urban centres (cities) as places with a minimum of 50,000 inhabitants plus a population density of at least 1500 people per square kilometer ($km^2$) or density of build-up area greater than 50%; Urban clusters (towns and suburbs) places with a minimum of 5,000 inhabitants plus a population density of at least 300 people per square kilometer ($km^2$) and Rural areas as places with fewer than 5,000 inhabitants (Ritchie et al., 2024).

Due to vast discrepancies in the definitions, the data also varies significantly, with 35% of Indian population residing in Urban areas (Urban Population (% of Total Population)—India | Data, 2024), whereas 75% of European population residing in urban areas (Urban Population (% of Total Population)—European Union | Data, 2024) in 2020. These discrepancies would understandably account for the discrepancies in catering the population needs in different countries, particularly to achieve the UN Sustainable Development Goals 11, by year 2030.

# 2 Global Urbanization Trend

As of 2024, more than half of the world's population resides in urban areas, with this proportion expected to increase to 68% by 2050 (Urban Health, 2021). In South Asia, particularly the Indian subcontinent, comprising countries such as India, Pakistan,

Bangladesh, and Sri Lanka, has experienced unprecedented urban expansion in recent decades, outpacing many other regions globally, with urban population increasing from 28% in 2001 to 36% in 2023 (Urban Population (% of Total Population)—India | Data, 2024). This rapid urbanization has brought about significant social, economic, and cultural changes, reshaping the fabric of society and presenting new challenges to public health and mental well-being.

## 3 Theoretical Perspectives Connecting Urbanization and Suicidality

### *3.1 Durkheim's Theory*

Emile Durkheim, French Sociologist, presented the Theory of Suicide in his classic literature, "Le Suicide". He defined Suicide as, "Suicide is applied to all cases of death resulting directly or indirectly from a positive or negative act of the victim himself, which he knows will produce this result" (Durkheim, 2005). However, this definition faced criticism, the first being, such foreknowledge varies significantly from one person or situation or another; and the second being, that while such practices may be widespread, they are ultimately individual in nature and are influenced by unique personal causes and consequences. Therefore emphasizing that they should be examined appropriately within psychology rather than sociology (Durkheim, 2005).

Durkheim actually never denied that suicide could be explained by psychological perspectives but insisted that it could also be manifestation of social *fact sui generis*. He attempted to derive sociological explanation of variations in social suicide rates, by postulating identical relations between societal or macro-level forces, integration and regulation- and suicide. When either is at extreme, the suicide rate is high.

**Integration**: Social integration is defined as the structure of social relationships surrounding an individual in their social groups or society at large, provides social support for individuals (Mueller et al., 2017).

**Regulation**: Moral regulation captures the guidance that a group or society's culture provides individuals through shared values, norms, etc., regarding what they should do and who they should be (Mueller et al., 2017).

Durkheim emphasized, in order to function optimally, a society needed to balance social integration and regulation, and extremes of either could affect the suicide rates. His theory summarized four types of suicide:

a. Egoistic suicide: It applies to those who are not strongly integrated into any social group, leading to extreme loneliness and high individualism. With limited social cohesion, compared to rural settings, people may experience isolation and loneliness, leading to increased rates of egoistic suicides (Mäkinen & Rojas, 2021)
b. Altruistic suicide: It is the opposite of egoistic suicide and applies to those who are susceptible to suicide stemming from their excessive integration into a group,

with suicide being the outgrowth of the integration. Strong group identities could encourage the behaviour (Mäkinen & Rojas, 2021)

c. Anomic suicide: It applies to those living in an unregulated society or social group, leading to a state of "normlessness". Durkheim believed that a sense of moral unity acted as a protective shield for group members, however, this protection is fragile and could change by societal changes or crises (Kar & Singh, 2023). Urban areas being more prone to such crises, with economic fluctuations, social instability, can cause feelings of hopelessness and despair, eventually leading to increased rates of anomic suicides (Mäkinen & Rojas, 2021)
d. Fatalistic suicide: It occurs as a result of over-regulation of society, wherein excessive norms and regulations create an oppressive and restrictive situation for an individual (Mäkinen & Rojas, 2021).

## *3.2 Maurice Halbwach's Theory*

Building on the foundation of Durkheim's theory and further refining his work, Halbwach's theory emphasized on societal causes of suicide, highlighting the increasing complexity of the modern society, which disrupts the social cohesion creating a sense of isolation, ultimately culminating in suicide. His study on suicide is perceived as a vindication of Durkheim's views by means of data unavailable to Durkheim. His work "The Causes of Suicide" (Halbwachs, 1978), even though began with an intent of apologia for Durkheim, has later been described as "*Il fait oeuvre positive et neuve*" (Coser, 1992). The divergence between urban and rural living, a notion which played pivotal role in Halbwach's work, was used to translate the distinctions between suicide rates in town and country. He demonstrated that rural milieus are generally more religiously inclined which acts as a protective factor against suicide. In addition to this, he argued that married life, children and in fact number of children provide immunity against suicide as they correlate with the frequency of interaction in domestic settings (Coser, 1992).

## *3.3 Strain Theory of Suicide (STS)*

Suicidal thoughts (ideation) can be triggered by significant life events, which may create conflicts, frustration, psychological pain, hopelessness and even desperation, and can be called psychological strains. The STS suggests that individuals with difficulties in sorting their psychological strains experience psychological torture and anger. The outward release of this anger leads to violence against others, whereas the inward release could lead to depression, anxiety or suicidal ideation (Zhang, 2019).

Durkheim's theory of anomie, a sociological concept, which means absence of social norms, became the basis of Strain Theory. The Strain Theory of Suicide demonstrates that psychological strain usually precedes a suicidal thought or determination.

During the state of normlessness, some people are motivated to expect great things in life and become vulnerable to greater frustration when these expectations remain unfulfilled, resulting in a type of strain (Agnew & White, 1992).

The STS defines four categories of strains: (Zhang, 2019).

a. Value Strain: occurs from at least two different social values.
b. Aspiration Strain: results from the large gap between aspiration and reality in life or the means to fulfil the aspiration.
c. Deprivation Strain: Arises from the relative deprivation including poverty, or people at social disadvantage.
d. Coping Strain. Arises from deficient coping skills during life crises.

The urban environment, with social and economic pressures, heightened competition, and often stark inequalities, can exacerbate the psychological strains. For instance, the obvious wealth disparity in urban areas may lead to deprivation strain, while the fast-paced, competitive urban lifestyle could contribute to coping strain (Zhang et al., 2011).

## *3.4 Three Step Theory of Suicide (3ST) and Interpersonal-Psychological Theory of Suicide (IPT)*

Three-Step Theory of Suicide (3ST) is proposed by Dr. Matthew K. Klonsky and Dr. Mark May (Klonsky & May, 2015) and Thomas Joiner proposed the Interpersonal-Psychological Theory of Suicide (IPT) (Joiner, 2005). Both these theories are being discussed together as they are closely related in providing psychological background to suicidal behaviour, with a specific emphasis on interpersonal factors.

Klonsky and May's Three Step Theory described three steps of progression from suicidal ideation to action: (Klonsky & May, 2015).

Step 1: Suicidal thoughts triggered by psychological pain and hopelessness.

Step 2: Considering suicide as an option when pain and hopelessness outweigh the connectedness.

Step 3: Attempting suicide when having the capacity to do so.

Joiner's IPT Theory describes three contributory factors to suicidal behaviour: (Joiner, 2005).

1. Thwarted Belongingness
2. Perceived Burdensomeness
3. Acquired Capability.

Urban environments, due to the accompanying stressors of economic hardships, social isolation, competitive environment could contribute to psychological pain eventually leading to development of feeling of hopelessness. Due to minimal or disrupted social cohesion, and lack of meaningful connections, people may feel isolated, hopeless and perceive themselves as a burden on their family/society. These complex emotions could contribute to development of suicidal thoughts, and alongside desensitization to pain due to exposure to violence, easy access to means like tall buildings, subways, trains, drug, and alcohol, could together increase vulnerability to self-harming behaviour.

### *3.5 Urban Stress*

Urban Stress is defined as state of bodily or mental tension developed through city living, or the physical, chemical, or emotional factors that give rise to that tension (Urban Stress—European Environment Agency, 2017). Urban life-related stressors include, but are not limited to, the poor-quality built environment, pollution, violence, overcrowding, crime and safety concerns, economic pressure, competitive and fast-paced lifestyle, social isolation, substance use, racism, and discrimination. Research has demonstrated that chronic exposure to such urban stressors may lead to depression amongst the dwellers (Hernandez et al., 2020).

## 4 Factors Contributing to the Impact of Urbanization on Suicidal Behaviour

### *4.1 Social Isolation and Social Fragmentation*

The relationship between social dynamics and suicide rates is not new and has been a subject of scholarly interest since Durkheim's groundbreaking work in the late nineteenth century (Durkheim, 2005). Social isolation and fragmentation are increasingly recognized as critical social determinants of suicide.

The concept of social fragmentation, while not precisely defined, generally refers to low levels of community integration often associated with high numbers of non-family households and high residential turnover. This phenomenon has become increasingly prominent in modern societies, particularly in rapidly changing contexts such as rural China (Li et al., 2016) and has been identified as a significant factor contributing to elevated suicide rates.

Social fragmentation extends beyond individual-level isolation to encompass broader societal changes that disrupt community cohesion. These changes can include increased mobility, urbanization, changing family structures, and the erosion of traditional social institutions. In the context of suicide research, social fragmentation is often operationalized through indicators such as high residential turnover, increased proportions of single-person households, and declining participation in community organizations.

Several studies have found strong associations between measures of social fragmentation and suicide rates. For instance, areas characterized by high levels of social fragmentation tend to have higher suicide rates, even after controlling for other socioeconomic factors. This relationship appears to be particularly pronounced in certain demographic groups, such as older adults and young people (Collings et al., 2009; Gunnell & Lewis, 2005; Hong & Knapp, 2013; Hooghe & Vanhoutte, 2011).

The mechanisms through which social fragmentation influences suicide risk are complex and multifaceted. At a fundamental level, fragmented communities may provide less social support and fewer resources for individuals struggling with mental health issues or life crises. The weakening of social norms and collective identity can also lead to a sense of alienation and purposelessness, which are known risk factors.

Moreover, social fragmentation can interact with other risk factors to create particularly vulnerable situations. For example, in communities experiencing rapid social change, traditional support systems may break down before new ones can be established, leaving individuals without adequate coping resources during times of stress.

Social isolation seems to be a broad, encompassing condition that stems from various social factors. Therefore, when evaluating suicidality, it is important to recognize social isolation as a multifaceted concept without a clear or fixed definition. Social isolation has emerged as a critical factor in the complex aetiology of suicide. This phenomenon encompasses not only physical separation from others but also perceived emotional disconnection and lack of social support.

This sociological perspective laid the foundation for understanding suicide not just as a result of individual psychological factors, but as a phenomenon deeply influenced by social context. Modern research has built upon this framework, examining how various forms of social isolation—from living alone to feeling alienated from one's community—can contribute to suicidal thoughts and behaviours. The interpersonal theory of suicide, described above, further emphasizes the role of social factors by proposing that the combination of perceived burdensomeness and thwarted belongingness, along with acquired capability, creates the conditions for suicidal behaviour.

Studies have consistently shown that individuals experiencing social isolation are at higher risk for suicidal ideation and attempts (Chen et al., 2020; Sainsbury, 1981; Trout, 1980). This relationship appears to be bidirectional, with social isolation both contributing to and resulting from mental health issues that increase suicide risk. The mechanisms through which social isolation influences suicidal behaviour are multifaceted, involving psychological, physiological, and societal factors. Psychologically, isolation can lead to feelings of loneliness, depression, and hopelessness. Physiologically, lack of social connection can affect stress responses, immune function, and overall physical health, further impacting mental well-being. At a societal level, the absence of strong social networks can deprive individuals of crucial support systems and resources that might otherwise help them navigate life's challenges.

The impact of social isolation on suicide risk varies across different demographic groups and contexts. For instance, older adults and adolescents may be particularly vulnerable to the effects of isolation. In older populations, factors such as retirement, loss of spouse, and reduced mobility can contribute to increased isolation and suicide risk (Fullen et al., 2021). Among adolescents, social media use and cyberbullying have introduced new dimensions to the relationship between isolation and suicidal behaviour. Additionally, certain occupations, living situations, and cultural contexts can exacerbate the risk associated with social isolation.

## 4.2 Economic Factors (Poverty, Unemployment, Income Inequality)

Urbanization has long been associated with various social and economic shifts, some of which contribute to an increased risk of suicide, particularly through the lens of economic deprivation. Satherley et al. (2022) stated that particular factors like increased concentration of low socioeconomic status, low social capital and social segregation play a significant role (Satherley et al., 2022). A study conducted in Australia, between 2004–2008, found that suicide rates in urban regions were positively associated with several indicators of deprivation- unemployment rate, median personal income, the number of tenant households in public housing (Law et al., 2014).

For instance, living in impoverished or deprived neighbourhoods is associated with a higher risk of developing mental health conditions compared to living in wealthier areas. The relationship between familial predisposition to mental illness and mental health was found to be stronger in more deprived neighbourhoods, with neighbourhood factors influencing urbanization effects, as seen in Turkey and India (Binbay et al., 2012; Subbaraman et al., 2014). People living in disadvantaged areas often face more challenges in building and maintaining supportive social connections, which can heighten their vulnerability to mental illness. This comparative economic stress, combined with the lack of social support and overwhelming living conditions, significantly heightens the risk factor for mental health deterioration and suicidal behaviour.

## 4.3 Population Density

Several epidemiological studies have shown a link between the population density of an area and the risk of suicide. Most research indicates that as population density decreases, suicide rates among males tend to rise. This inverse relationship has remained stable over the past 30 years and generally holds true regardless of age. This finding contrasts with reports of higher rates of mental health disorders in urban areas, suggesting that other factors—such as economic disadvantage, healthcare access, availability of firearms, and social isolation—may mediate this relationship. For females, however, no consistent link between population density and suicide has been observed, implying that men may be more affected by risk factors in areas with lower population density (Vichi et al., 2020).

## 4.4 Environmental Factors

There is increasing recognition that individuals' mental health can be affected by their physical and natural surroundings. Some prospective studies, using large samples, have shown protective links between exposure to greenspace and various mental health disorders. For example, in a large representative sample of urban adults in the United Kingdom, increase in residential greenspace was linked to a lower likelihood of developing major depressive disorder, even after accounting for factors like household and neighbourhood socioeconomic status (Sarkar et al., 2018).

A systematic review by Bolanis et al. concluded that there is an overwhelming body of evidence which indicates that greenspace exposure may protect the full range of suicide-related outcomes, including suicide mortality, self-harm, and suicidal thoughts, with potentially greater benefits seen in females (Bolanis et al., 2024).

## 4.5 Means of Suicide

Moving to urban areas often limits access to certain methods, like highly lethal pesticides. However, some methods are more closely associated with cities. For instance, jumping from heights is a common method in highly urbanized areas. In cities like Singapore and Hong Kong, where most people live in tall buildings, jumping is the most frequent method of suicide (Yip et al., 2021). Jumping from heights also varies by urbanization level in Taiwan (Yip et al., 2021) and is notably common among females in Luxembourg, where over 90% of the population lives in urban areas (Varnik et al., 2008).

Subway suicides are also prevalent in metropolitan areas. A review of subway suicides revealed that most people who attempt suicide this way are young males living alone with severe mental illness, often receiving treatment. Additionally, an increase in rail suicides has been noted near major psychiatric hospitals (Ratnayake et al., 2007).

A nationwide population study conducted in Taiwan by Chung et al., found that individuals who had lived in areas with higher levels of urbanization were more likely to use violent methods when committing suicide (Chung et al., 2008). Further a strong link has been found between violent suicides and severe mental illnesses like schizophrenia and major mood disorders (Appleby et al., 1997). There may be a tendency for people with mental illnesses to move to more urban areas, possibly due to the stigma associated with psychiatric conditions in conservative rural communities or to access better healthcare services in cities. Regarding lethality, the greater availability of medical services in urban areas means that individuals using less lethal methods may be more likely to survive. This could lead those who are determined to complete suicide to rely on more violent methods in cities (Judd et al., 2006).

### *4.6 Access and Utilization of Mental Health Services*

The rural–urban differences in suicidality may be a result of a lack of access to health care. There is evidence that those living in rural areas may be less likely to seek help and less likely to have a mental health-related diagnosis, which occurs in the context of health service use (Casant & Helbich, 2022). Those living in rural areas may be less likely to seek help due to distance to care or stigma. Another possible reason for urban–rural suicide disparities are related to the availability and quality of mental healthcare services (e.g., general practitioners, psychiatrists).

Urban environments, by contrast, often provide a more extensive network of mental health resources and support systems. The concentration of healthcare facilities, including hospitals, clinics, and specialized mental health centres, in urban areas allows for easier and more immediate access to professional help. This accessibility not only facilitates early intervention but also encourages regular follow-ups, which are crucial in managing mental health conditions and reducing suicide risk.

Moreover, urban settings typically offer a wider range of mental health professionals, including psychiatrists, psychologists, and counsellors. This diversity allows for more specialized care tailored to individual needs, potentially leading to more effective treatment outcomes. The presence of support groups and community mental health programmes in cities also contributes to creating a more supportive environment for those struggling with mental health issues.

The reduced stigma often associated with seeking mental health care in urban areas is another factor contributing to lower suicide rates. Urban populations tend to have more exposure to mental health awareness campaigns and educational initiatives, fostering a more open and accepting attitude towards mental health issues. This environment can encourage individuals to seek help without fear of judgment, leading to earlier interventions and better management of mental health conditions.

## 5 Interventions and Suicide Prevention Strategies

The above factors categorically indicate a strong connection between urbanization and suicidal behaviour, which warrants appropriate and timely interventions and prevention strategies. Despite multiple medical interventions, particularly treatment with anti-depressants, they haven't contributed to any significant reduction in the incidence of suicidal behaviour, but the above risk factors in urban areas have assumed a complex and challenging role, creating obstacles in implementing effective suicide prevention strategies.

A multifaceted approach involving community engagement, mental health services, environmental intervention, education, and policy initiatives appears to be a tangible solution to address the monstrous problem at hand.

## *5.1 Community-Based Approach*

When trying to address sensitive issues like suicide, it is imperative to identify where and how to begin. Communities play a massive role and have potential to contribute towards prevention of suicide and protection of their members by acting as a bridge between community needs, national policies and evidence-based interventions tailored to local circumstances (Preventing Suicide, 2019). Some countries have implemented multilevel community suicide prevention programmes and are observing synergistic effects when different activities and measures are implemented simultaneously (Harris et al., 2016). Suicide prevention strategies need a holistic approach and cannot be achieved by intervention of an individual or an institution alone but requires efforts from the whole community, by developing and demonstrating social cohesion and mass efforts to address the stigma. To begin with, it is of utmost importance to identify, target and support the most vulnerable population of the community.

### 5.1.1 Social Cohesion

Social Cohesion refers to a state of affairs concerning both the vertical and the horizontal interactions among members of society as characterized by a set of attitudes and norms that includes trust, a feeling of belonging and the readiness to engage and assist, as well as their behavioural manifestations (Orazani et al., 2023). Social cohesion is an attribute that applies to collectives/groups, not individuals, wherein there is absence of latent social conflict and presence of strong social bonds. A cohesive society is the one with stocks of social capital, which refers to features of social organization like trust, norms, and perceived reciprocity, etc. The social organizational approach views local communities and neighbourhoods as complex system of relations, kinship, friendship, networks (Orazani et al., 2023).

It has rightly been said "Our epidemic of loneliness and isolation has been an underappreciated public health crisis that has harmed individual and societal health, and our relationships are a source of healing and well-being hiding in plain sight" (Preventing Suicide through Social Connectedness, 2023). It is well established that both the objective condition of being alone and loneliness are strongly associated with suicide (Courtet, 2022), impact of which is widespread. This is where the role of social cohesion and connectedness comes in, where people engage amongst each other and create a sense of belonging, create meaningful relationships, are valued, and supported, leading to a community filled with resources (Preventing Suicide through Social Connectedness, 2023).

### 5.1.2 Stigma Reduction

Suicide is still considered a crime in around 20 countries across the world (Wu et al., 2022) and remains a stigma in most parts of the world, mainly low- and middle-income countries. Stigma is a denigrating trait, which reflects on the negative perception of society towards the stigmatized individual and involves labelling, stereotyping, loss of status, discrimination, and eventually social rejection. These plausible consequences act as an obstacle for seeking help not only from the community but also from the health care professionals.

Considering mental health and suicide are bred in the bone as a "stigmatized topic" in the wider community, which also interferes with implementation of suicide prevention steps, it is imperative that this is addressed by education, training and creating mass awareness.

Although educating and training gatekeepers (e.g., primary care physicians and health care workers) in identification and treatment of vulnerable or at-risk population, by conducting regular and periodic workshops, remains pertinent, but in order to address stigma, it is crucial that educating general public and addressing myths/stigma is initiated as early as with school goers. School-based awareness programmes, tailored in a way that they are acceptable to a particular community, can promote help-seeking behaviour and increase awareness of suicidal behaviour to encourage self-disclosure and prepare students and staff members to identify 'at-risk' peers (Kalafat & Elias, 1994).

Apart from educational institutes, various cultural and religious places, non-governmental organizations, and other stakeholders could contribute towards creating awareness about suicide and mental health, by organizing awareness campaigns. One such attempt to address this globally has been the organization of World Suicide Prevention Day (WSPD) by the International Association for Suicide Prevention, with World Health Organization (WHO) as a co-sponsor, every year on 10th September since 2003, wherein, the aim is to focus attention on the issue, reduce stigma and raise awareness among organizations, governments, and the public, giving a singular message that suicides are preventable (World Suicide Prevention Day, 2024).

## 5.2 *Environmental Intervention*

### 5.2.1 Urban Planning

As described above green spaces provide suicide risk buffering (Jiang et al., 2021), whereas it has been observed that unfavourable built environment could increase risks for successful suicide attempts (Wang et al., 2020). A systematic review conducted by Yi Gong et al. back in 2016 revealed urban environment has significant associations with psychological distress, including housing with deck access, neighbourhood quality, the amount of green space, land-use mix, industry activity and traffic volume (Gong et al., 2016).

Hence, better urban development with appropriate architectural amendments (sky view, street coverage) (Wang et al., 2020), with adequate green and blue spaces and other micro-environment (Gong et al., 2016) changes could contribute towards promoting psychological health and reducing suicide rates.

### 5.2.2 Means Restriction and Appropriate Legislative Measures

Availability to means of suicide is a known risk factor for suicide. The following explanations have been suggested as to how restricting physical access to means might contribute to preventing suicides:

Firstly, restricting access to means could delay the likely impulsive action and provide opportunity for the individual to take an alternative course like seeking help.

Secondly, it could provide the opportunity for others to intervene with the person, and

Lastly, even if the person carries out a suicidal act, the lethality of the method might have been reduced through a specific intervention (Hawton et al., 2024).

For instance, the introduction of a ban on a major highly hazardous pesticide in India resulted in reduction of pesticide related suicide (Arya et al., 2021), law prohibiting purchase, sale, transfer or possession of handguns by civilians in the District of Columbia resulted in 23% reduction in firearm suicide (Loftin et al., 1991), restricting the number of paracetamol that can be purchased on any occasion resulted in reduced size of paracetamol overdoses, and reduction in Paracetamol overdose suicides in England (Hawton et al., 2013), installing barriers or nets on bridges that have become hotspot for suicide have resulted in reduction of the particular site being used for the act (Hawton et al., 2024).

In addition to the above, physical barriers like sliding doors at train stations, restricting access to cliffs, structural modifications in multistorey buildings, restricting access to railway tracks, installing safety measures for ceiling fans, etc., could all contribute towards restricting means of suicide, and eventually suicide rates (Hawton et al., 2024).

It is evident from the above data that restricting means is an effective approach to suicide prevention, but at the same time, it is important to be mindful about possible alternative methods that could get highlighted when a particular method is addressed.

## *5.3 Safe Reporting of Suicide*

Internet and social media are extremely powerful tools to create awareness about methods of suicide, whether sought intentionally or accidentally. Media coverage provides cognitive ability about the means of suicide, leads to modelling, and is followed by increased suicide rates using the said method. For instance, the rate of suicide by charcoal burning in enclosed spaces dramatically increased in Hong Kong and Taiwan following a dramatic newspaper report (Liu et al., 2007), increase in suicides by hanging in both the USA and Australia following the widely publicized death of the film celebrity, Robin Williams (Fink et al., 2018; Pirkis et al., 2020).

Though it is recognized that media plays a crucial role in raising awareness about suicide being a public health concern, however, it remains the duty of the media personnel to report incidents responsibly and adhere to the national regulations, which can help minimize modelling.

## 5.4 Economic Measures

As stated above, socioeconomic conditions, including personal loss, and national downturns, are determinatives of suicide risk. Appropriate economic measures and policies with an aim to retain employment, enhance employment opportunities, financial compensation, debt management, work towards the reduction of poverty, and minimize the impact of economic upheavals in the country, with every appropriate stakeholder, like finance, labour, government, education, etc., playing suitable roles, could contribute towards the reduction of suicide rates (Sinyor et al., 2024).

## 5.5 Facilitating Access to Mental Health Services

Mental health services play a crucial role in preventing suicide, and particularly with the urban population being more prone to psychological distress, depression, and suicide, it is critical that easy, timely and professional support is available including crisis lines. Mental health services play a great role in identifying the risk factors and at-risk populations, provide assessment and treatment for mental health disorders, including drug and alcohol related disorders and psychosocial stressors.

Widespread access to mental health services also works towards increasing awareness and reduction of stigma related to mental disorders, encouraging people to seek support when needed. Incorporation of mental health training in curriculum for general practitioners, who are generally the first mode of contact for patients across the world, helps them identify high-risk patients, intervene appropriately, which could result in prevention of suicide.

Incorporation of 24hr crisis lines to provide immediate support for those experiencing suicidal thoughts and urges can provide an opportunity for professionals to intervene, support the individual and prevent the act. These is evidence to suggest that accessing crisis lines could result in reduction of immediate emotional distress and decrease suicidal thoughts.

With the advent of telepsychiatry, mental health care has become more accessible compared to traditional services, particularly in urban areas, and is mitigating the traditional constraints of having to travel, stigma, etc. One such large-scale effort is Tele manas, which was launched in India in 2022, seeks to leverage technology and provide comprehensive mental health services in an integrated fashion including both audio and video-based services (Ibrahim et al., 2020; Tele Manas, 2024). There is understandably immense potential in the world of digital psychiatry which can be harnessed to provide timely intervention for people who are experiencing suicide.

Urban areas have diverse population, including vulnerable groups who experience discrimination, such as refugees and migrants; indigenous peoples; lesbian, gay, bisexual, transgender, intersex (LGBTI) persons; and prisoners (Suicide Rates, 2024). Access to mental health services, who could provide tailored support for the said vulnerable group have the potential to meet the diverse needs of these groups and contribute towards the reduction of suicide rates in these high-risk communities.

## 6 Future Directions and Gaps in Research

To advance our understanding of the geographic variation in suicide rates, it is essential to identify and address existing gaps in research concerning the urban–rural divide. Several conceptual and methodological implications need to be considered for future studies.

Firstly, it is crucial for upcoming research to explore the urban–rural disparity through the lenses of age and socioeconomic factors. Previous studies have long recognized the differences in suicide rates between urban and rural areas, but age and socioeconomic status are critical confounding variables that can further influence these disparities. For instance, different age groups may experience varying levels of social isolation, access to mental health services, and economic opportunities, all of which can contribute to their risk of suicidality.

Furthermore, researchers must exercise caution when interpreting comparative results due to the methodological inconsistencies in how urban and rural areas are represented. The lack of consensus on the most effective way to define urbanity or rurality means that findings can differ significantly based on the criteria used for geographical delineation. Methodological approaches range from simple binary classifications—labelling areas as either urban or rural—to more refined stratifications that attempt to capture the continuum of urbanicity, which includes various community types from densely populated cities to sparsely populated rural areas. The complexity of defining urban and rural areas is further heightened by the diverse threshold values employed in these classifications, such as population density or geographic size. This lack of uniformity creates challenges in comparing studies and synthesizing findings across different research efforts. To enhance the comparability of research findings, it is imperative to adopt a more coherent framework for defining rurality and urbanicity.

From a theoretical standpoint, it is essential to further investigate the complexities of urban environments and their relationships with suicidality and self-harm. Recently, there has been a shift towards employing intersectional approaches in understanding these issues, which helps to highlight the multifaceted nature of risk factors. Rather than examining single social determinants, such as socioeconomic deprivation, intersectional frameworks consider the interplay of various social processes and environmental influences—such as access to social support, employment opportunities, and the presence of green spaces—on mental health outcomes.

By employing an intersectional approach, researchers can develop a more nuanced understanding of how these factors collectively influence suicidality and self-harm in urban contexts. This framework prioritizes the perspectives of those most affected by these issues, allowing for a deeper exploration of the unique challenges faced by individuals in different community settings.

Finally, future research should emphasize the importance of local community characteristics and how interactions with local environments, spaces, and communities modify risk factors for suicidality and self-harm. Understanding these dynamics can provide valuable insights into how to effectively address mental health challenges within both urban and rural populations. By considering the specific attributes of communities—such as the availability of mental health resources, community cohesion, and cultural attitudes toward mental health—researchers can identify targeted interventions that are better suited to the unique needs of individuals in varying geographic contexts. Overall, addressing these research gaps can lead to a more comprehensive understanding of the urban–rural divide in suicidality and inform effective strategies for prevention and intervention.

## 7 Conclusion

While urban areas typically offer improved access to mental health resources, they simultaneously introduce distinct pressures such as social disconnection, financial strain, and environmental stressors that may elevate suicide risk. The swift urbanization process, especially in developing nations, has thrust these concerns into the spotlight of public health discussions.

The research emphasizes the necessity of a diverse approach to urban suicide prevention. This strategy encompasses community-oriented initiatives to build social bonds and combat stigma, environmental adjustments to limit access to suicide means, economic policies to tackle poverty and disparity, and enhanced mental health service accessibility. Urban design's potential in fostering supportive and psychologically beneficial environments is identified as a key area for future focus.

The review exposes research gaps, calling for more refined and intersectional methodologies in urban suicide studies. Future research should aim to establish consistent definitions of urbanicity, delve into age-specific and socioeconomic aspects of urban–rural suicide differences, and explore the nuanced interactions between community features and individual risk factors.

As global urbanization continues, comprehending and tackling the specific challenges of urban suicide prevention becomes increasingly vital. This chapter stresses the importance of collaborative action among policymakers, urban designers, mental health experts, and community leaders to shape urban spaces that not only support life but also enhance mental health and resilience.

## References


Agnew, R., & White, H. R. (1992). An empirical test of general strain theory*. *Criminology, 30*(4), 475–500. https://doi.org/10.1111/j.1745-9125.1992.tb01113.x

Appleby, L., Shaw, J., & Amos, T. (1997). National confidential inquiry into suicide and homicide by people with mental illness. *The British Journal of Psychiatry, 170*(2), 101–102. https://doi.org/10.1192/bjp.170.2.101

Arya, V., Page, A., Gunnell, D., & Armstrong, G. (2021). Changes in method specific suicide following a national pesticide ban in India (2011–2014). *Journal of Affective Disorders, 278*, 592–600. https://doi.org/10.1016/j.jad.2020.09.085

Binbay, T., Drukker, M., Alptekin, K., Elbi, H., Tanık, F. A., Özkınay, F., Onay, H., Zağlı, N., & van Os, J. (2012). Evidence that the wider social environment moderates the association between familial liability and psychosis spectrum outcome. *Psychological Medicine, 42*(12), 2499–2510. https://doi.org/10.1017/S0033291712000700

Bolanis, D., Vergunst, F., Mavoa, S., Schmelefske, E., Khoury, B., Turecki, G., Orri, M., & Geoffroy, M.-C. (2024). Association between greenspace exposure and suicide-related outcomes across the lifespan: A systematic review. *Science of the Total Environment, 906*, 167451. https://doi.org/10.1016/j.scitotenv.2023.167451

Casant, J., & Helbich, M. (2022). Inequalities of suicide mortality across urban and rural areas: A literature review. *International Journal of Environmental Research and Public Health, 19*(5), Article 5. https://doi.org/10.3390/ijerph19052669

Chen, Z., Poon, K.-T., DeWall, C. N., & Jiang, T. (2020). Life lacks meaning without acceptance: Ostracism triggers suicidal thoughts. *Journal of Personality and Social Psychology, 119*(6), 1423–1443. https://doi.org/10.1037/pspi0000238

Chung, K.-H., Lee, H.-C., Kao, S., & Lin, H.-C. (2008). Urbanicity and methods of suicide: A nationwide population-based study. *Journal of Urban Health, 85*(1), 136–145. https://doi.org/10.1007/s11524-007-9238-7

Collings, S., Ivory, V., Blakely, T., & Atkinson, J. (2009). Are neighbourhood social fragmentation and suicide associated in New Zealand? A national multilevel cohort study. *Journal of Epidemiology & Community Health, 63*(12), 1035–1042. https://doi.org/10.1136/jech.2009.090985

Coser, L. (1992). On maurice halbwachs. *On Collective Memory*. https://www.academia.edu/download/47081834/Maurice_Halbwachs_On_Collective_Memory_1992.pdf

Courtet, P. (2022). Social cohesion, connection and prescription: Good ways for preventing suicide? *European Psychiatry, 65*(S1), S36–S36. https://doi.org/10.1192/j.eurpsy.2022.127

Durkheim, E. (2005). *Suicide* (0 ed.). Routledge. https://doi.org/10.4324/9780203994320

Fink, D. S., Santaella-Tenorio, J., & Keyes, K. M. (2018). Increase in suicides the months after the death of Robin Williams in the US. *PLoS ONE, 13*(2), e0191405. https://doi.org/10.1371/journal.pone.0191405

Fullen, M. C., Shannonhouse, L. R., Mize, M. C., & Miskis, C. (2021). Mental health distress in homebound older adults: Importance of the aging network. *Aging & Mental Health, 25*(8), 1580–1584. https://doi.org/10.1080/13607863.2020.1758920

Gong, Y., Palmer, S., Gallacher, J., Marsden, T., & Fone, D. (2016). A systematic review of the relationship between objective measurements of the urban environment and psychological distress. *Environment International, 96*, 48–57. https://doi.org/10.1016/j.envint.2016.08.019

Gunnell, D., & Lewis, G. (2005). Studying suicide from the life course perspective: Implications for prevention. *British Journal of Psychiatry, 187*(3), 206–208. https://doi.org/10.1192/bjp.187.3.206

Halbwachs, M. (1978). *The causes of suicide*. Free Press.

Harris, F. M., Maxwell, M., O'Connor, R., Coyne, J. C., Arensman, E., Coffey, C., Koburger, N., Gusmão, R., Costa, S., Székely, A., Cserhati, Z., McDaid, D., van Audenhove, C., & Hegerl, U. (2016). Exploring synergistic interactions and catalysts in complex interventions: Longitudinal, mixed methods case studies of an optimised multi-level suicide prevention intervention in four european countries (Ospi-Europe). *BMC Public Health, 16*(1), 268. https://doi.org/10.1186/s12889-016-2942-z

Hawton, K., Knipe, D., & Pirkis, J. (2024). Restriction of access to means used for suicide. *The Lancet Public Health, 9*(10), e796–e801. https://doi.org/10.1016/S2468-2667(24)00157-9

Hawton, K., Bergen, H., Simkin, S., Dodd, S., Pocock, P., Bernal, W., Gunnell, D., & Kapur, N. (2013). Long term effect of reduced pack sizes of paracetamol on poisoning deaths and liver transplant activity in England and Wales: Interrupted time series analyses. *BMJ, 346*. https://doi.org/10.1136/bmj.f403

Hernandez, D. C., Daundasekara, S. S., Zvolensky, M. J., Reitzel, L. R., Maria, D. S., Alexander, A. C., Kendzor, D. E., & Businelle, M. S. (2020). Urban stress indirectly influences psychological symptoms through its association with distress tolerance and perceived social support among adults experiencing homelessness. *International Journal of Environmental Research and Public Health, 17*(15), 5301. https://doi.org/10.3390/ijerph17155301

Hong, J., & Knapp, M. (2013). Geographical inequalities in suicide rates and area deprivation in South Korea. *The Journal of Mental Health Policy and Economics, 16*(3), 109–119.

Hooghe, M., & Vanhoutte, B. (2011). An ecological study of community-level correlates of suicide mortality rates in the Flemish region of Belgium, 1996–2005. *Suicide and Life-Threatening Behavior, 41*(4), 453–464. https://doi.org/10.1111/j.1943-278X.2011.00047.x

Ibrahim, F. A., Pahuja, E., Dinakaran, D., Manjunatha, N., Kumar, C. N., & Math, S. B. (2020). The future of telepsychiatry in India. *Indian Journal of Psychological Medicine, 42*(5_suppl), 112S-117S.

Jiang, B., Shen, K., Sullivan, W. C., Yang, Y., Liu, X., & Lu, Y. (2021). A natural experiment reveals impacts of built environment on suicide rate: Developing an environmental theory of suicide. *Science of the Total Environment, 776*, 145750. https://doi.org/10.1016/j.scitotenv.2021.145750

Joiner, T. (2005). *Why people die by suicide*. Harvard University Press.

Judd, F., Cooper, A.-M., Fraser, C., & Davis, J. (2006). Rural suicide—people or place effects? *Australian & New Zealand Journal of Psychiatry, 40*(3), 208–216. https://doi.org/10.1080/j.1440-1614.2006.01776.x

Kalafat, J., & Elias, M. (1994). An evaluation of a school-based suicide awareness intervention. *Suicide and Life-Threatening Behavior, 24*(3), 224–233. https://doi.org/10.1111/j.1943-278X.1994.tb00747.x

Kar, S. K., & Singh, S. (2023). Anomic suicides on rise during recently emerging crises: Revisiting Durkheim's model. *CNS Spectrums, 28*(6), 655–656. https://doi.org/10.1017/S1092852923002341

Klonsky, E. D., & May, A. M. (2015). The Three-Step Theory (3ST): A new theory of suicide rooted in the "ideation-to-action" framework. *International Journal of Cognitive Therapy, 8*(2), 114–129. https://doi.org/10.1521/ijct.2015.8.2.114

Law, C., Snider, A.-M., & De Leo, D. (2014). The influence of deprivation on suicide mortality in urban and rural Queensland: An ecological analysis. *Social Psychiatry and Psychiatric Epidemiology, 49*(12), 1919–1928. https://doi.org/10.1007/s00127-014-0905-1

Li, L. W., Xu, H., Zhang, Z., & Liu, J. (2016). An ecological study of social fragmentation, socioeconomic deprivation, and suicide in rural China: 2008–2010. *SSM—Population Health, 2*, 365–372. https://doi.org/10.1016/j.ssmph.2016.05.007

Liu, K. Y., Beautrais, A., Caine, E., Chan, K., Chao, A., Conwell, Y., Law, C., Lee, D., Li, P., & Yip, P. (2007). Charcoal burning suicides in Hong Kong and urban Taiwan: An illustration of

the impact of a novel suicide method on overall regional rates. *Journal of Epidemiology & Community Health, 61*(3), 248–253. https://doi.org/10.1136/jech.2006.048553
Loftin, C., McDowall, D., Wiersema, B., & Cottey, T. J. (1991). Effects of restrictive licensing of handguns on homicide and suicide in the district of Columbia. *New England Journal of Medicine, 325*(23), 1615–1620. https://doi.org/10.1056/NEJM199112053252305
Mäkinen, I. H., & Rojas, Y. (2021). Social theories of suicide. In D. Wasserman & C. Wasserman (Eds.), *Oxford textbook of suicidology and suicide prevention* (pp. 137–146). Oxford University Press. https://doi.org/10.1093/med/9780198834441.003.0019
Mueller, A. S., Abrutyn, S., & Osborne, M. (2017). Durkheim's "Suicide" in the Zombie Apocalypse. *Contexts, 16*(2), 44–49. https://doi.org/10.1177/1536504217714260
National Institute of Mental Health (2021, November 9). https://www.nimh.nih.gov/news/science-news/2021/researchers-find-disparities-in-suicide-risk-among-lesbian-gay-and-bisexual-adults
Orazani, S. N., Reynolds, K. J., & Osborne, H. (2023). What works and why in interventions to strengthen social cohesion: A systematic review. *Journal of Applied Social Psychology, 53*(10), 938–995. https://doi.org/10.1111/jasp.12990
Pirkis, J., Currier, D., Too, L. S., Bryant, M., Bartlett, S., Sinyor, M., & Spittal, M. J. (2020). Suicides in Australia following media reports of the death of Robin Williams. *Australian & New Zealand Journal of Psychiatry, 54*(1), 99–104. https://doi.org/10.1177/0004867419888297
Preventing Suicide Through Social Connectedness. (2023, September 13). https://www.army.mil/; https://www.army.mil/article/269920/preventing_suicide_through_social_connectedness
Preventing Suicide: A Community Engagement Toolkit. (2019). https://www.who.int/publications/i/item/9789241513791
Ratnayake, R., Links, P. S., & Eynan, R. (2007). Suicidal behaviour on subway systems: A review of the epidemiology. *Journal of Urban Health, 84*(6), 766–781. https://doi.org/10.1007/s11524-007-9211-5
Ritchie, H., Samborska, V., & Roser, M. (2024). *Urbanization*. Ourworldindata.Org. https://ourworldindata.org/urbanization
Sainsbury, P. (1981). Suicide in London: An Ecological Study, 1955. In J. Hayes & P. Nutman (Eds.), *Understanding the Unemployed: The Psychological Effects of Unemployment* (p. 55).
Sarkar, C., Webster, C., & Gallacher, J. (2018). Residential greenness and prevalence of major depressive disorders: A cross-sectional, observational, associational study of 94 879 adult UK Biobank participants. *The Lancet Planetary Health, 2*(4), e162–e173. https://doi.org/10.1016/S2542-5196(18)30051-2
Satherley, R.-M., Hazell, C. M., Jones, C. J., & Hanna, P. (2022). A systematic review of the effects of urban living on suicidality and self-harm in the UK and Ireland. *Journal of Urban Health, 99*(3), 385–408. https://doi.org/10.1007/s11524-022-00611-z
Sinyor, M., Silverman, M., Pirkis, J., & Hawton, K. (2024). The effect of economic downturn, financial hardship, unemployment, and relevant government responses on suicide. *The Lancet Public Health, 9*(10), e802–e806. https://doi.org/10.1016/S2468-2667(24)00152-X
Subbaraman, R., Nolan, L., Shitole, T., Sawant, K., Shitole, S., Sood, K., Nanarkar, M., Ghannam, J., Betancourt, T. S., Bloom, D. E., & Patil-Deshmukh, A. (2014). The psychological toll of slum living in Mumbai, India: A mixed methods study. *Social Science & Medicine, 119*, 155–169. https://doi.org/10.1016/j.socscimed.2014.08.021
Suicide Rates. (2024). https://www.who.int/data/gho/data/themes/mental-health/suicide-rates
Tele Manas. (2024). https://telemanas.mohfw.gov.in/home
Trout, D. L. (1980). The role of social isolation in suicide. *Suicide and Life-Threatening Behavior, 10*(1), 10–23. https://doi.org/10.1111/j.1943-278X.1980.tb00693.x
Urban Health. (2021, October 29). https://www.who.int/health-topics/urban-health#tab=tab_1
Urban Population (% of Total Population)—European Union | Data. (2024). https://data.worldbank.org/indicator/SP.URB.TOTL.IN.ZS?locations=EU
Urban Population (% of Total Population)—India | Data. (2024). https://data.worldbank.org/indicator/SP.URB.TOTL.IN.ZS?locations=IN

Urban Stress—European Environment Agency. (2017). https://www.eea.europa.eu/help/glossary/gemet-environmental-thesaurus/urban-stress

Urbanization | United Nations—CEB. (2024). https://unsceb.org/topics/urbanization

Varnik, A., Kolves, K., Van Der Feltz-Cornelis, C. M., Marusic, A., Oskarsson, H., Palmer, A., Reisch, T., Scheerder, G., Arensman, E., Aromaa, E., Giupponi, G., Gusmao, R., Maxwell, M., Pull, C., Szekely, A., Sola, V. P., & Hegerl, U. (2008). Suicide methods in Europe: A gender-specific analysis of countries participating in the "European Alliance Against Depression." *Journal of Epidemiology & Community Health, 62*(6), 545–551. https://doi.org/10.1136/jech.2007.065391

Vichi, M., Vitiello, B., Ghirini, S., & Pompili, M. (2020). Does population density moderate suicide risk? An Italian population study over the last 30 years. *European Psychiatry, 63*(1), e70. https://doi.org/10.1192/j.eurpsy.2020.69

Wang, P., Goggins, W. B., Zhang, X., Ren, C., & Lau, K.K.-L. (2020). Association of urban built environment and socioeconomic factors with suicide mortality in high-density cities: A case study of Hong Kong. *Science of the Total Environment, 739*, 139877. https://doi.org/10.1016/j.scitotenv.2020.139877

World Suicide Prevention Day 2024. (2024). https://www.who.int/campaigns/world-suicide-prevention-day/world-suicide-prevention-day-2024

Wu, K.C.-C., Cai, Z., Chang, Q., Chang, S.-S., Yip, P. S. F., & Chen, Y.-Y. (2022). Criminalisation of suicide and suicide rates: An ecological study of 171 countries in the world. *British Medical Journal Open, 12*(2), e049425. https://doi.org/10.1136/bmjopen-2021-049425

Yip, P., Guo, Y., Tang, L., & Chen, Y.-Y. (2021). Prevention of suicide by jumping: Experiences from Taipei City (Taiwan), Hong Kong, and Singapore. In D. Wasserman & C. Wasserman (Eds.), *Oxford Textbook of Suicidology and Suicide Prevention* (pp. 739–742). Oxford University Press. https://doi.org/10.1093/med/9780198834441.003.0083

Zhang, J. (2019). The strain theory of suicide. *Journal of Pacific Rim Psychology, 13*, e27. https://doi.org/10.1017/prp.2019.19

Zhang, J., Wieczorek, W. F., Conwell, Y., & Tu, X. M. (2011). Psychological strains and youth suicide in rural China. *Social Science & Medicine, 72*(12), 2003–2010. https://doi.org/10.1016/j.socscimed.2011.03.048

# Chapter 5
# Environmental Pollution and Suicidal Behavior

**Syeda Ayat-e-Zainab Ali, Tamkeen Saleem, and S. M. Yasir Arafat**

**Abstract** Suicide is a major public health issue globally. Although its widespread impact is undeniable, the risk factors are not yet fully understood, and attempts to accurately gauge risk have proven insufficient. There is a growing body of evidence that connects pollution in many forms—air, water, noise, soil, and chemical—to a number of mental health conditions, such as stress, anxiety, and depression, which are important risk factors for suicide. Furthermore, numerous demographic variables, including geography and meteorology, have a major impact on suicide. Hence, the data linking environmental pollutants to an increase in suicide rates is examined in this chapter. Additionally, it emphasizes the necessity for comprehensive public health strategies that address mental health and environmental issues.

**Keywords** Environmental pollution · Air pollution · Noise pollution · Chemical exposure · Meteorological factors · Geographical factors · Suicide · Suicidal behavior

## 1 Introduction

Suicide is a global public health issue. In 2016, it was responsible for 1.4% of all deaths worldwide. According to the World Health Organization, nearly 800,000 deaths were attributed to suicide in 2016, with over 79% of these occurrences happening in low- and middle-income countries (LMICs). Many more individuals

S. A.-Z. Ali (✉) · T. Saleem
Department of Clinical Psychology, Shifa Tameer-E- Millat University, Islamabad, Pakistan
e-mail: ayat.dcp@stmu.edu.pk

T. Saleem
e-mail: tamkeen.dcp@stmu.edu.pk

S. M. Y. Arafat
Department of Psychiatry, Bangladesh Specialized Hospital, Dhaka, Bangladesh
e-mail: arafatdmc62@gmail.com

 
S. M. Y. Arafat and S. K. Kar (eds.), *Ecological and Social Determinants of Suicidal Behavior*, South Asian Perspectives in Mental Health and Psychology,
https://doi.org/10.1007/978-981-96-4028-7_5

experience suicidal thoughts or attempt suicide. Despite the widespread impact of suicide, the underlying risk factors remain poorly understood.

Suicide represents a complex interplay of these elements, highlighting the need for continued research in this evolving field. Suicide risk assessment involves a range of factors at multiple levels. Individual-level factors include personal history of mental illness, previous non-fatal attempts, and socio-demographic factors. Social factors encompass issues like inadequate social connectedness and available health-related policies. Biological variables involve genetic constructs, epigenetic modifications, neurobiological factors, and metabolic influences. High-risk individuals often exhibit a combination of these clinical, psychological, sociological, and biological risk factors, with clinical and neurobiological aspects potentially playing a major role in suicidal behavior (Hawton & Van Heeringen, 2009; Turecki et al., 2019; Stone et al., 2017; Mann & Currier, 2010; Heeringen & Mann, 2014). Additionally, other psychological factors such as hopelessness are significant in those at higher, suggesting an intersection of both biological and non-biological factors (Costanza et al., 2020; Costanza et al., 2015; Galvao et al., 2018).

Historically, patterns in suicide rates have shown seasonal variations, peaking in corresponding spring and early summer in both Northern and Southern Hemispheres (Benard et al., 2015; Galvao et al., 2018). The wider variable of environment like meteorological issues, pollution of environmental ingredients, and geographical location are poorly explored but may influence or mediate these seasonal effects (Ajdacic-Gross et al., 2010; Woo et al., 2012).

A systematic review study suggests that bioclimatic factors, global geography, pollution, and seasonal changes may be potential suicide risk factors. Meteorological factors such as temperature, sunlight, and precipitation have close association with suicide rates. Higher exposure to sunlight is linked to an increased risk of suicidal behavior, while elevated temperatures were associated with a modest rise in suicide rates. Although precipitation was examined, the studies did not find significant associations with suicide risk. Additionally, the review covered air quality variables, noting that higher levels of air pollution and allergens were correlated with increased suicide rates and risk (Woo et al., 2012).

Most studies examining the link between pollution and suicidal behavior focused on individual-level variables (73.9%) instead of population-level factors (26.1%). Among the studies that investigated air pollutants, most found a notable relationship between at least one type of pollution and suicidal behavior. Similarly, studies also revealed that there is a significant relationship between high altitude and increased suicide rates (Asirdizer et al., 2018; Ha, & Tu, 2018; Sabic et al., 2019).

Given the increasing concern over rising suicide rates and the potential impact of environmental factors on public health outcomes, a comprehensive review of existing literature on relationship between environmental pollution and suicidal behavior is necessary. Understanding these modifiable or potentially modifiable risk factors is crucial for advancing understanding and prevention strategies.

## 2 Environmental Pollution and Suicidal Behavior

Several pollution factors have been linked to an increased risk of suicide, often through complex interactions with mental health. Here are some key pollution factors that research has associated with heightened suicide risk:

### *2.1 Air Pollution and Suicidality*

Along with many other factors, ambient air pollution has been proposed as a factor related to suicide rates (Casas et al., 2017; Gu et al., 2019; Sidorchuk et al., 2019). Evidence suggests that inflammation and oxidative stress caused by polluted air might be underlying mechanisms (Yao et al., 2015).

Exposure to nitrogen dioxide ($NO_2$), sulfur dioxide ($SO_2$), ozone ($O_3$), and particulate matter with aerodynamic diameters $\leq$ 2.5 μm or 10 μm ($PM_{2.5}$ or $PM_{10}$) is related to an increased risk of suicidal behavior (Bakian et al., 2015). A nation-wide study in Belgium found that short-term exposure to $PM_{10}$ and $O_3$ was linked to a higher suicidal risk, particularly during warm days (Casas et al., 2017). Another study revealed that long-term exposure to elevated levels of ambient air pollutants ($PM_1$, $PM_{2.5}$, $PM_{10}$, and $NO_2$) has been linked to an increased risk of suicidal ideation (SI) among adults in the rural areas of China. Notably, significant adverse outcomes on suicidal thought were noted among males, individuals who consume alcohol, those aged 36–64 years, and people with higher education levels (Luo et al., 2020).

### *2.2 Noise Pollution and Suicidal Behavior*

Noise induces the stress response through both direct and indirect pathways. The direct pathway involves hearing loss and damage to the inner ear, while the indirect pathway includes annoyance and sleep disturbances. These stress responses stimulate the hypothalamic-pituitary-adrenal (HPA) axis, leading to increased systemic inflammation, that can progress to neuroinflammation and subsequently result in heightened fear and anxiety.

A study in mice found that traffic noise led to hyperactivity of the HPA axis, which resulted in poorer performance on cognitive and motor tasks. Additionally, the study observed reductions in the size of the hippocampal formation, medial prefrontal cortex (mPFC), and amygdala, as well as decreased neuronal density in the mPFC and dentate gyrus (DG). While these findings suggest cognitive decline, the authors also noted that the mice exhibited anxiety-like behavior, linking the results to potential mental health issues. Additionally, it was observed depression-like behaviors, indicated by a decreased preference for sucrose and fewer crossings and rearings (standing on hind legs) (Jafari et al., 2018; Jafari et al., 2017). These experimental findings suggest a biological state has been related to anxiety- and depressive symptoms. However, further preclinical research is necessary to establish a strong correlation and elucidate the underlying mechanisms.

A Korean study with a sample size of 155,492 found that higher noise exposure during night was associated with elevated suicide risks. Study revealed younger adults with exposer to noise during night had a 32% higher mortality rate compared to the control group (HR: 1.3; 95% CI: 1–1.7). Hazard ratios were even higher for older adults and the risks were highest for those with at least one mental disorder (Min & Min, 2018). The National Cohort study of Switzerland investigated the link between source-specific transportation noise and suicide. The authors found that both road traffic and railway noise were associated with an increased risk of total suicides, with hazard ratios of 1.04 (95% CI 1.015–1.065) and 1.02 (95% CI 1.004–1.041), respectively, per 10 dB Lden. A study carried out in Spain indicated that short-term exposure to traffic noise is linked to increased emergency hospital admissions for anxiety, dementia, and suicides (Diaz et al., 2020).

### *2.3 Water Contamination and Suicidality*

Arsenic-contaminated drinking water (ACDW) is a significant global public health issue. Prior research indicated a potential link between ACDW consumption and an increased risk of depression (Rihmer et al., 2015). Arsenic, known for its high toxicity, adversely affects multiple systems, including the nervous system. In addition to epidemiological studies linking arsenic exposure with numerous physical disorders, there is evidence suggesting a connection between arsenic exposure and an increased risk of neuropsychiatric conditions such as anxiety and depression (Sen & Sarathi Biswas, 2012; Mukherjee et al., 2014).

Natural lithium can be mixed with water which has potential role in mood disorder and suicide prevention (Cade, 1949). Research indicates that high lithium level in potable water is related to reduced suicidal behavior (Araya et al., 2022; Fadaei, 2023).

## 3 Meteorological Factors and Suicidal Behavior

Recent analyses have identified that meteorological patterns can impact various human health and diseases, including migraine headache, cerebrovascular disease, multiple sclerosis, heart disease, asthma, and suicidal behavior. In a systematic study, Deisenhammer et al. (2003) found that there is relationship between the meteorological factors and suicidality by reviewing 27 studies.

### 3.1 Temperature and Suicide Rates

The biological mechanisms linking temperature to suicide remain poorly understood. Analyzing the effects of climate on human behavior is complicated by the intricate nature of both suicide and environmental factors.

Temperature has been found to be related to suicide rates. Recent increases in temperatures have been associated with a rise in suicides, particularly violent ones (Padhy et al., 2015). Higher temperatures have been significantly positively correlated with suicide attempts and violent suicide deaths (Preti & Miotto, 1998; Preti & Miotto, 2000), particularly in males revealed by two time-series analysis of national data on suicidal behavior between 1984 and 1995. However, another time-series analysis of the data between 1974 and 2003 identified a reverse relationship (Preti et al., 2007).

Suicidal behavior and other negative mental health outcomes are increasingly associated with the greenhouse effect, which is one of the factors contributing to climate change. The greenhouse effect is responsible for both rising global temperatures and extreme weather events like heatwaves and droughts. These occurrences have been shown to worsen stress, anxiety, and depression, especially among vulnerable populations (Watts et al., 2018). Studies reveal a robust association between elevated temperatures and a rise in suicide incidents. For example, Burke et al. (2018) showed that suicide rates increased by 2.1% in Mexico and by 0.7% in the United States for every 1 °C increase in the average monthly temperature. This shows that dealing with high heat can have a psychological toll that exacerbates mental health problems and increases thoughts of suicide.

To better understand the relationship one way is to understand it through biological perspective. The neurotransmitters such as dopamine, norepinephrine, and serotonin are crucial for mood regulation and body temperature control, thus, they play a role in this relationship. Specifically, temperature can affect the responsiveness and density of serotonin receptors (Tiihonen et al., 2017). Another proposition by Helama et al. (2013) reveals a potential link between psychiatric disorders and altered central nervous system transmission, with signals traveling from brown adipose tissue through the hypothalamus to the periaqueductal gray areas. Since these cerebral structures are involved in cognitive processes, their impaired function could contribute to more impulsive behaviors, including suicidality (Mann & Rizk, 2020). Another proposed mechanism is the effect of temperature on survival rates after a suicide attempt.

### 3.2 Seasonal Changes & Suicidal Behavior

Due to climate change, seasonal patterns are anticipated to shift. Studies have consistently identified seasonal trends in suicidal behavior (Diffenbaugh & Giorgi, 2012). Suicide rates peaked from late spring to early summer, regardless of local climate.

Similar trends have been observed in South Korea from 1992 to 2010 and findings indicated most of the patients experienced more suicide attempts in spring (Aguglia et al., 2016). A systematic review with 45 studies from 26 countries, covering over 2 million suicide deaths, confirmed notable seasonal variations, with peaks in spring and early summer, particularly in the northern hemisphere (Galvão et al., 2018). With global warming, these seasonal patterns may intensify, as increase in temperature throughout the year, especially in summer days, could further exacerbate the observed link between seasonal variation and suicidal behavior. Additionally, there may have associations certain types of mental illness that peaks in spring and summer (Reutfors et al., 2009).

While explaining the potential link, it is found that serotonin level is sensitive to climate factors, that may affect suicidality in different season (Brewerton et al., 2018). While another assumption can be considered. A longer duration of light during summer and spring may influence circadian rhythm and sleep–wake cycle that leads to poor impulse control and subsequently raised suicidal behavior. Warmer temperature during these seasons could be attributed to risk of suicidality (Gao et al., 2019).

## 4 Geographical Factors and Suicidal Behavior

Geography variables, such as altitude of residence, can also be a determinant for suicidal behavior. Research has indicated that suicide rates or risk tend to increase with higher altitude of residence (Asirdizer et al., 2018; Cornelius et al., 2021; Kious et al., 2018; Sabic et al., 2019).

Previous research has explored how topography, such as population density and elevation, influences suicide rates. They found that population density tends to be negatively correlated with suicide rates, while higher elevation is positively correlated (Brenner et al., 2011; DelMastro et al., 2011; Haws et al., 2009). Additionally, poor accessibility to social resources, like medical facilities, is also associated with higher suicide rates (Tondo et al., 2006).

Research on geographic division indicated that with the people living in the mountain division consistently showed the highest rates for both suicidal thoughts and suicide attempt. Individuals who had visited a mental health emergency department in the past year faced a heightened risk of SI, with an increase ranging from 28 to 65% across several divisions in the US. Geographic divisions had a significant impact on suicide attempt, with lower risks observed in the US (Xi et al., 2023).

## 5 Chemical or Biological Warfare Exposure and Suicidal Behavior

Chemical warfare (CW) is arguably one of the most lethal weapons that humanity has ever invented. Extremely poisonous synthetic chemicals known as CW agents can be distributed as a liquid, aerosol, gas, or as materials adsorbed to particles to form a powder. These CW materials affect humans in a way that is either fatal or incapacitating (Ganesan et al., 2010). Research conducted in Iraq among the Kurdish Halabja on 1988 gas attacks survivors demonstrates that exposure to chemical warfare agents (CWAs), especially sulfur mustard, was attributed to physical and mental health hazards. For example, people who are exposed to chemical warfare agents (CWAs) frequently have long-term lung, skin, and eye damage. They also succumb easily to suicidal thoughts, anxiety, and depression (Moradi et al., 2019).

Moreover, particularly in rural and agricultural populations, exposure to pesticides and fertilizers as well as other agricultural chemicals has been associated with an increase in suicide behavior. Toxic chemicals included in many chemical fertilizers can cause mental health issues such as anxiety, depression, and cognitive impairment over time. These diseases are known risk factors for suicide (Freire & Koifman, 2013). Specifically, it has been demonstrated that organophosphate pesticides, which are frequently used in agriculture, are neurotoxic and alter brain function, resulting in behavioral abnormalities and mood swings (Mew et al., 2017).

Significant psychological hazards are also posed by biological agents, despite their little research. Biological warfare can result in serious disease, terror, and disruption to society when germs or toxins are used. An unseen but frequently lethal threat can cause tension that can result in trauma and mental health concerns. It has been demonstrated that biological weapons like anthrax can cause both serious psychological discomfort and physical disease. Insomnia, anxiety, and sadness are common among assault survivors, and these are recognized risk factors for suicide thoughts and actions (Balali-Mood et al., 2013).

Suicidal behavior has been linked to an increase in mental health issues following nuclear radiation exposure. Populations impacted by nuclear accidents, like those at Chernobyl and Fukushima, experience long-term psychological effects. According to Havenaar et al. (1997), survivors of radiation exposure frequently suffer from severe anxiety, depression, and post-traumatic stress disorder (PTSD), which are disorders that are recognized to be risk factors for suicide. In addition to dislocation, loss of livelihood, and social shame, the dread of radiation's health effects can further worsen mental suffering, which in turn might lead to suicide related outcomes in certain cases.

According to a study conducted on survivors of the Chernobyl accident, individuals who were exposed to high radiation levels also had higher rates of depressive symptoms and suicidal thoughts (Loganovsky et al., 2008). Likewise, studies conducted following the Fukushima accident demonstrated that the psychological toll of radiation exposure, in conjunction with the post-disaster socio-economic conditions, markedly exacerbated the increase in suicide rates among impacted communities (Orui et al., 2018). Survivors' misery is exacerbated by the stigma associated with radiation exposure, fear of cancer, and feelings of powerlessness and loneliness.

## 6 Potential Gaps in the Research Related to Environmental Pollution and Suicidal Behavior

Suicide of one person cannot typically be attributed to a single event; rather, it is often influenced by a range of risk factors. Although there is considerable evidence that environmental conditions may heighten suicide risk, the exact nature of this relationship is still not fully quantified. There is still a dearth of research on the connection between environmental pollution and suicidality, and there are some significant gaps that need to be filled. Although certain research indicates a connection between air pollution, particularly particulate matter (PM2.5), and a higher risk of suicide, the underlying biological processes are still not well understood (Braithwaite et al., 2019). Few research has looked at long-term exposure and its psychological impacts, such as oxidative stress and neuroinflammation, which may be factors in the decline of mental health (Mingoti et al., 2022). Furthermore, not enough research has been done on the effects of other contaminants, such as heavy metals (Fu et al., 2023; Stack et al., 1994), contaminated water (Rihmer et al., 2015; Troiano et al., 2018), and noise pollution (Min & Min, 2018). While some case studies have documented the stress responses of individuals managing environmental contamination, there is a dearth of research on the psychosocial effects of residing on contaminated soil (Matthies et al., 2000). These pollutants have the potential to impair brain functioning, but it is yet unclear how they relate to mental health outcomes in general and suicide risk in particular.

Geographic and social differences in research are also clearly visible. The majority of investigations have been carried out in affluent nations with strong healthcare and air quality monitoring networks. Little is known about how pollution affects mental health in LMICs, where people may have less access to mental health treatments and frequently suffer higher pollution levels as a result of laxer environmental regulations (Bakian et al., 2015; Braithwaite et al., 2019; Kim et al., 2023).

A growing body of research indicates that natural outdoor settings, such as parks, grasslands, and woods, as well as blue spaces and areas along the shore, can improve mental health. How and to what degree these natural settings are linked to suicide mortality, however, is still a matter of much unknown (Helbich et al., 2018). Future research on an individual basis may validate the idea that taking environmental exposures into account can improve suicide prevention initiatives.

One further noteworthy research gap is the paucity of studies examining mediating factors that may interact with environmental stresses to increase the risk of suicide, such as socioeconomic inequality, unemployment, or a lack of social support. People who already have mental health issues or reside in low-income areas, for example, may be more susceptible to the negative impacts of pollution; however, this interaction is rarely studied. According to Bakian et al. (2015), incorporating these social and environmental aspects into research is essential to creating focused interventions.

## 7 Environmental Interventions and Suicide Prevention

There is now growing evidence that urbanization and environmental conditions function as background variables that may intensify, lessen, or initiate suicidal motives. Henceforth, managing the environment is a strategy for preventing suicide (Leenaars et al., 2000). Stengel suggested regulating the environment in the 1960s to lower the suicide rate. He pointed out that the detoxification of domestic gas—moving from high-CO coal gas to natural gas—might have lowered the suicide rate in the countries where the change had occurred (Leenaars et al., 2000; Stengel, 1964). Stengel's theory was validated by later studies conducted in England on the detoxification of home gas (Kreitman, 1976).

Additionally, Oliver and Hetzel in Australia showed a correlation between suicide rates and the availability of methods, or prescription drugs such as sedatives (Leenaars et al., 2000; Oliver & Hetzel, 1972). Restrictions on the sale and availability of very hazardous pesticides have significantly reduced the rate of suicide in nations like Sri Lanka, where ingesting pesticides is a prevalent means of suicide (Knipe et al., 2017). According to a review of studies on the impact of bans on highly toxic pesticides nationally, these bans are attributed to reduction of suicides due to pesticide ingestion. And in three of the six countries found decreases in overall suicide mortality (Gunnell et al., 2017). An interrupted time-series analysis in China revealed that the country's bans on paraquat in aqueous solution in 2016 and highly hazardous organophosphate pesticides in 2008 and 2006 respectively were accompanied by a 60.5% decline in the age-standardized suicide rate, which dropped from 6.50 per 100,000 people in 2006 to 2.56 per 100,000 people in 2018. The greatest notable reductions in pesticide-related suicides were in metropolitan areas (67.3%), among females (63.5%), and among those aged 15–44 (68.1%) (Yan et al., 2023). There may be 28,000 fewer suicides annually if highly hazardous pesticides are outlawed nationally in 14 countries. This strategy may also be a financially sensible way to prevent suicide in nations where the use of highly hazardous pesticides is common (Lee et al., 2021).

Incorporating physical alterations to the surroundings, like placing barriers atop bridges or other elevated areas, has also demonstrated remarkable efficacy. Installing safety nets and barriers on the Golden Gate Bridge in San Francisco is among the most well-known instances of this tactic (Whitmer & Woods, 2013). A meta-analysis encompassing nine research was carried out by Pirkis and colleagues (2013) to evaluate the efficacy of physical barriers. On average, it resulted in an 86% annual decrease in jumping suicides, with a corresponding 44% increase at neighboring locations, for a net reduction of 28% across all sites. It is important to acknowledge that these conclusions heavily depend on research with relatively low absolute suicide rates. As a result, the corresponding 95% confidence interval almost equally likely lies a decrease in suicides at nearby places as an increase in suicides (Pirkis et al., 2013). It is found overwhelmingly that physical barriers reduce suicides by jumping (Okolie et al., 2020). This effectiveness is demonstrated by the fact that the barriers don't need to be permanently replaced by other structures or techniques. When the barriers are tall enough to span the whole length of the bridge, the reduction is usually almost 100%. Furthermore, the cost-effectiveness of barrier construction may be shown in the large financial savings resulting from the decreased mortality rate, which greatly exceeds the cost of installation and maintenance. Moreover, the results of the recent study unequivocally demonstrate that physical obstacles are quite successful to prevent suicide by jumping, without substantial substitution of place and method (Merli & Costanza, 2024).

## 8 Conclusion

Environmental pollution is now seen as a major global health concern that aggravates psychological as well as physical ailments. Research on the connection between air, noise, water, chemical pollution, geographical and meteorological variables and suicide, is growing. Suicidal thoughts can result from both poor sleep and elevated stress levels, which have also been linked to noise pollution. Studies reveal that environmental factors including temperature, humidity, and seasonal variations can have a direct impact on an individual's behavior, and mental health. Due to factors like isolation, restricted access to mental health care, and socioeconomic difficulties, suicide rates in rural and isolated places are frequently greater than in urban areas. A higher risk of suicide may also result from environmental characteristics like high altitudes, which have been related to oxygen deprivation. Hence, it is crucial to comprehend the connection between environmental variables and suicidal behavior in order to create focused suicide prevention initiatives. Further, adapting mental health therapies to particular regions, temperatures, and seasons is essential to reducing the impact of environmental factors on suicide risk.

## References


Aguglia, A., Moncalvo, M., Solia, F., & Maina, G. (2016). Involuntary admissions in Italy: The impact of seasonality. *International Journal of Psychiatry in Clinical Practice, 20*(3), 232–238. https://doi.org/10.1080/13651501.2016.1214736

Ajdacic-Gross, V., Bopp, M., Ring, M., Gutzwiller, F., & Rossler, W. (2010). Seasonality in suicide—A review and search of new concepts for explaining the heterogeneous phenomena. *Social Science & Medicine, 71*(4), 657–666. https://doi.org/10.1016/j.socscimed.2010.05.030

Araya, P., Martínez, C., & Barros, J. (2022). Lithium in drinking water as a public policy for suicide prevention: Relevance and considerations. *Frontiers in Public Health, 10*. https://doi.org/10.3389/fpubh.2022.805774

Asirdizer, M., Kartal, E., Etli, Y., Tatlisumak, E., Gumus, O., Hekimoglu, Y., & Keskin, S. (2018). The effect of altitude and climate on suicide rates in Turkey. *Journal of Forensic and Legal Medicine, 54*, 91–95. https://doi.org/10.1016/j.jflm.2017.12.012

Bakian, A. V., Gates, A. J., & Boudreaux, M. H. (2015). Air pollution and suicide: A review of the literature. *Environmental Research, 143*, 196–207. https://doi.org/10.1016/j.envres.2015.09.010

Balali-Mood, M., Moshiri, M., & Etemad, L. (2013). Medical aspects of bio-terrorism. *Toxicon, 69*, 131–142. https://doi.org/10.1016/j.toxicon.2013.01.005

Benard, V., Geoffroy, P. A., & Bellivier, F. (2015). Saisons, rythmes circadiens, sommeil et vulnérabilité aux conduites suicidaires. *L'Encéphale, 41*(Suppl. 1), S29–S37. https://doi.org/10.1016/S0013-7006(15)30004-X

Braithwaite, I., Zhang, S., Kirkbride, J. B., Osborn, D. P., & Hayes, J. F. (2019). Air pollution (particulate matter) exposure and associations with depression, anxiety, bipolar, psychosis and suicide risk: A systematic review and meta-analysis. *Environmental Health Perspectives, 127*(12), 126002. https://doi.org/10.1289/EHP4595

Brenner, B., Cheng, D., Clark, S., & Camargo, C. A., Jr. (2011). Positive association between altitude and suicide in 2,584 US counties. *High Altitude Medicine & Biology, 12*(1), 31–35. https://doi.org/10.1089/ham.2010.1041

Brewerton, T. D., Putnam, K. T., Lewine, R. R. J., & Risch, S. C. (2018). Seasonality of cerebrospinal fluid monoamine metabolite concentrations and their associations with meteorological variables in humans. *Journal of Psychiatric Research, 99*, 76–82. https://doi.org/10.1016/j.jpsychires.2018.01.004

Burke, M., González, F., Baylis, P., Heft-Neal, S., Baysan, C., Basu, S., & Hsiang, S. (2018). Higher temperatures increase suicide rates in the United States and Mexico. *Nature Climate Change, 8*(8), 723–729. https://doi.org/10.1038/s41558-018-0222-x

Cade, J. F. J. (1949). Lithium salts in the treatment of psychotic excitement. *Medical Journal of Australia, 2*, 349–352. https://doi.org/10.5694/j.1326-5377.1949.tb66564.x

Casas, L., Rojas, C., & Rojas, S. (2017). Ambient air pollution and suicide: A systematic review. *Environmental Research, 156*, 527–538. https://doi.org/10.1016/j.envres.2017.03.010

Cornelius, S. L., Berry, T., Goodrich, A. J., Shiner, B., & Riblet, N. B. (2021). The effect of meteorological, pollution, and geographic exposures on death by suicide: A scoping review. *International Journal of Environmental Research and Public Health, 18*(15), 7809. https://doi.org/10.3390/ijerph18157809

Costanza, A., Amerio, A., Aguglia, A., Escelsior, A., Serafini, G., Berardelli, I., Pompili, M., & Amore, M. (2020). When sick brain and hopelessness meet: Some aspects of suicidality in the neurological patient. *CNS Neuroscience & Therapeutics, 19*(4), 257–263. https://doi.org/10.2174/1871527319666200611130804

Costanza, A., Baertschi, M., Weber, K., & Canuto, A. (2015). Neurological diseases and suicide: From neurobiology to hopelessness. *Revue Médicale Suisse, 11*(472), 402–405.

Deisenhammer, E. A., Kemmler, G., & Parson, P. (2003). Association of meteorological factors with suicide. *Acta Psychiatrica Scandinavica, 108*(6), 455–459. https://doi.org/10.1046/j.0001-690X.2003.00219.x

DelMastro, K., Hellem, T., Kim, N., Kondo, D., Sung, Y. H., & Renshaw, P. F. (2011). Incidence of major depressive episode correlates with elevation of substate region of residence. *Journal of Affective Disorders, 129*(1–3), 376–379. https://doi.org/10.1016/j.jad.2010.08.016

Diaz, J., Lopez-Bueno, J. A., Lopez-Ossorio, J. J., Gonzalez, J. L., Sanchez, F., & Linares, C. (2020). Short-term effects of traffic noise on suicides and emergency hospital admissions due to anxiety and depression in Madrid (Spain). *Science of The Total Environment, 710*, 136315. https://doi.org/10.1016/j.scitotenv.2019.136315

Diffenbaugh, N. S., & Giorgi, F. (2012). Climate change hotspots in the CMIP5 global climate model ensemble. *Climatic Change, 114*(3–4), 813–822. https://doi.org/10.1007/s10584-012-0570-x

Fadaei, A. (2023). An investigation into the association between suicide mortality rate and lithium levels in potable water: A review study. *International Clinical Psychopharmacology, 38*(2), 73–80. https://doi.org/10.1097/YIC.0000000000000432

Freire, C., & Koifman, S. (2013). Pesticides, depression and suicide: A systematic review of the epidemiological evidence. *International Journal of Hygiene and Environmental Health, 216*(4), 445–460. https://doi.org/10.1016/j.ijheh.2012.12.003

Fu, X., Li, H., Song, L., Cen, M., & Wu, J. (2023). Association of urinary heavy metals co-exposure and adult depression: Modification of physical activity. *Neurotoxicology, 95*, 117–126. https://doi.org/10.1016/j.neuro.2023.01.008

Galvão, P. V. M., Silva, H., & da Silva, C. M. F. P. (2018). Temporal distribution of suicide mortality: A systematic review. *Journal of Affective Disorders, 228*, 132–142. https://doi.org/10.1016/j.jad.2017.12.008

Ganesan, K., Raza, S. K., & Vijayaraghavan, R. (2010). Chemical warfare agents. *Journal of Pharmacy & Bioallied Sciences, 2*(3), 166–178. https://doi.org/10.4103/0975-7406.68498

Gao, J., Cheng, Q., Duan, J., Xu, Z., Bai, L., Zhang, Y., Zhang, H., Wang, S., Zhang, Z., Su, H., & Wang, J. (2019). Ambient temperature, sunlight duration, and suicide: A systematic review and meta-analysis. *Science of the Total Environment, 646*, 1021–1029. https://doi.org/10.1016/j.scitotenv.2018.07.315

Gu, J., Zheng, X., & Zhang, Z. (2019). Genetic and environmental factors influencing suicide: A review of epidemiologic studies. *Journal of Psychiatric Research, 115*, 70–85. https://doi.org/10.1016/j.jpsychires.2019.05.017

Gunnell, D., Knipe, D., Chang, S. S., Pearson, M., Konradsen, F., Lee, W. J., & Eddleston, M. (2017). Prevention of suicide with regulations aimed at restricting access to highly hazardous pesticides: A systematic review of the international evidence. *The Lancet global health, 5*(10), e1026–e1037. https://doi.org/10.1016/S2214-109X(17)30299-1

Ha, H., & Tu, W. (2018). An ecological study on the spatially varying relationship between county-level suicide rates and altitude in the United States. *International Journal of Environmental Research and Public Health, 15*(4), 671. https://doi.org/10.3390/ijerph15040671

Havenaar, J. M., Rumyantzeva, G. M., van den Brink, W., Poelijoe, N. W., Van den Bout, J., van Engeland, H., & Koeter, M. W. (1997). Long-term mental health effects of the Chernobyl disaster: An epidemiologic survey in two former Soviet regions. *American Journal of Psychiatry, 154*(11), 1605–1607. https://doi.org/10.1176/ajp.154.11.1605

Haws, C. A., Gray, D. D., Yurgelun-Todd, D. A., Moskos, M., Meyer, L. J., & Renshaw, P. F. (2009). The possible effect of altitude on regional variation in suicide rates. *Medical Hypotheses, 73*(4), 587–590. https://doi.org/10.1016/j.mehy.2009.05.007

Hawton, K., & van Heeringen, K. (2009). Suicide. *The Lancet, 373*(9659), 1372–1381. https://doi.org/10.1016/S0140-6736(09)60372-X

Van Heeringen, K., & Mann, J. J. (2014). The neurobiology of suicide. *The Lancet Psychiatry, 1*(1), 63–72. https://doi.org/10.1016/S2215-0366(14)70220-2

Helama, S., Holopainen, J., & Partonen, T. (2013). Temperature-associated suicide mortality: Contrasting roles of climatic warming and the suicide prevention program in Finland. *Environmental Health and Preventive Medicine, 18*(4), 349–355. https://doi.org/10.1007/s12199-013-0329-7

Helbich, M., de Beurs, D., Kwan, M. P., O'Connor, R. C., & Groenewegen, P. P. (2018). Natural environments and suicide mortality in the Netherlands: A cross-sectional, ecological study. *The Lancet. Planetary Health, 2*(3), e134–e139. https://doi.org/10.1016/S2542-5196(18)30033-0

Jafari, Z., Kolb, B. E., & Mohajerani, M. H. (2018). Chronic traffic noise stress accelerates brain impairment and cognitive decline in mice. *Experimental Neurology, 308*, 1–12. https://doi.org/10.1016/j.expneurol.2018.06.007

Jafari, Z., Faraji, J., Mirza Agha, B., Metz, G. A. S., Kolb, B. E., & Mohajerani, M. H. (2017). The adverse effects of auditory stress on mouse uterus receptivity and behavior. *Scientific Reports, 7*, 4720. https://doi.org/10.1038/s41598-017-04909-w

Kim, H. J., Kim, H. S., Kim, S., Hwang, J., Lee, H., Park, B., & Kim, B. (2023). Effects of vitamin D on associations between air pollution and mental health outcomes in Korean adults: Results from the Korea National Health and Nutrition Examination Survey (KNHANES). *Journal of Affective Disorders, 320*, 390–396. https://doi.org/10.1016/j.jad.2022.09.144

Kious, B. M., Kondo, D., & Renshaw, P. F. (2018). Living high and feeling low: Altitude, suicide, and depression. *Harvard Review of Psychiatry, 26*(1), 43–56. https://doi.org/10.1097/HRP.0000000000000158

Knipe, D. W., Gunnell, D., & Eddleston, M. (2017). Preventing deaths from pesticide self-poisoning—Learning from Sri Lanka's success. *The Lancet Global Health, 5*(7), e651–e652. https://doi.org/10.1016/S2214-109X(17)30208-5

Kreitman, N. (1976). The coal gas story. United Kingdom suicide rates, 1960–71. *Journal of Epidemiology & Community Health, 30*(2), 86–93.

Lee, Y. Y., Chisholm, D., Eddleston, M., Gunnell, D., Fleischmann, A., Konradsen, F., Bertram, M. Y., Mihalopoulos, C., Brown, R., Santomauro, D. F., Schess, J., & Van Ommeren, M. (2021). The cost-effectiveness of banning highly hazardous pesticides to prevent suicides due to pesticide self-ingestion across 14 countries: An economic modelling study. *The Lancet Global Health, 9*(3), e291–e300.

Leenaars, A., Cantor, C., Connolly, J., EchoHawk, M., Gailiene, D., He, Z. X., Kokorina, N., Lester, D., Lopatin, A. A., Rodriguez, M., Schlebusch, L., & Wenckstern, S. (2000). Controlling the environment to prevent suicide: International perspectives. *The Canadian Journal of Psychiatry, 45*(7), 639–644.

Loganovsky, K., Havenaar, J. M., Tintle, N. L., Guey, L. T., Kotov, R., & Bromet, E. J. (2008). The mental health of clean-up workers 18 years after the Chernobyl accident. *Psychological Medicine, 38*(4), 481–488. https://doi.org/10.1017/S0033291707002371

Luo, Z., Hou, Y., Chen, G., Wang, F., Tu, R., Dong, X., Wang, Y., Qiao, D., Liu, X., Liu, X., Hou, J., Mao, Z., Huo, W., Guo, Y., Li, S., & Wang, C. (2020). Long-term effects of ambient air pollutants on suicidal ideation in China: The Henan Rural Cohort Study. *Environmental Research, 188*, 109873. https://doi.org/10.1016/j.envres.2020.109873

Mann, J. J., & Currier, D. (2010). Stress, genetics, and epigenetic effects on the neurobiology of suicidal behavior and depression. *European Psychiatry, 25*(5), 268–271. https://doi.org/10.1016/j.eurpsy.2010.01.009

Mann, J. J., & Rizk, M. M. (2020). A brain-centric model of suicidal behavior. *American Journal of Psychiatry, 177*(10), 902–916. https://doi.org/10.1176/appi.ajp.2020.20081224

Matthies, E., Höger, R., & Guski, R. (2000). Living on polluted soil: Determinants of stress symptoms. *Environment and Behavior, 32*(2), 270–286.

Merli, R., & Costanza, A. (2024). Effectiveness of physical barriers to prevent suicide by jumping from high-risk bridges: From an integrative review to a northern Italian province's paradigm. *Preventive Medicine Reports, 42*, 102745. https://doi.org/10.1016/j.pmedr.2024.102745

Mew, E. J., Padmanathan, P., Konradsen, F., Eddleston, M., Chang, S. S., Phillips, M. R., & Gunnell, D. (2017). The global burden of fatal self-poisoning with pesticides 2006–15: Systematic review. *Journal of Affective Disorders, 219*, 93–104. https://doi.org/10.1016/j.jad.2017.05.002

Min, J.-Y., & Min, K.-B. (2018). Night noise exposure and risk of death by suicide in adults living in metropolitan areas. *Depression and Anxiety, 35*(9), 876–883. https://doi.org/10.1002/da.22789

Mingoti, M. E. D., Bertollo, A. G., Simões, J. L. B., Francisco, G. R., Bagatini, M. D., & Ignácio, Z. M. (2022). COVID-19, oxidative stress, and neuroinflammation in the depression route. *Journal of Molecular Neuroscience, 72*(6), 1166–1181. https://doi.org/10.1007/s12031-022-02004-y

Moradi, F., Söderberg, M., Moradi, F., Daka, B., Olin, A. C., & Lärstad, M. (2019). Health perspectives among Halabja's civilian survivors of sulfur mustard exposure with respiratory symptoms—A qualitative study. *PloS one, 14*(6), e0218648. https://doi.org/10.1371/journal.pone.0218648

Mukherjee, A. B., Singh, A., & Gupta, P. (2014). Arsenic exposure and neuropsychiatric disorders: A review. *Journal of Neurotoxicology and Neurological Disorders, 2*(1), 43–58. https://doi.org/10.1016/j.jnn.2014.03.002

Okolie, C., Wood, S., Hawton, K., Kandalama, U., Glendenning, A. C., Dennis, M., Price, S. F., Lloyd, K., & John, A. (2020). Means restriction for the prevention of suicide by jumping. *Cochrane Database Systematic Review, 25*(2), CD013543. https://doi.org/10.1002/14651858.cd013543

Oliver, R. G., & Hetzel, B. S. (1972). Rise and fall of suicide rates in Australia: Relation to sedative availability. *Medical Journal of Australia, 2*(17), 919–923.

Orui, M., Suzuki, Y., Maeda, M., & Yasumura, S. (2018). Suicide rates in evacuation areas after the Fukushima Daiichi nuclear disaster: A 5-year follow-up study in Fukushima prefecture. *Crisis: The Journal of Crisis Intervention and Suicide Prevention, 39*(5), 353–363. https://doi.org/10.1027/0227-5910/a000509

Padhy, S. K., Sarkar, S., Panigrahi, M., & Paul, S. (2015). Mental health effects of climate change. *Indian Journal of Occupational and Environmental Medicine, 19*(1), 3. https://doi.org/10.4103/0019-5278.156997

Pirkis, J., Spittal, M. J., Cox, G., Robinson, J., Cheung, Y. T. D., & Studdert, D. (2013). The effectiveness of structural interventions at suicide hotspots: A meta-analysis. *International Journal of Epidemiology, 42*(2), 541–548.

Preti, A., Lentini, G., & Maugeri, M. (2007). Global warming possibly linked to an enhanced risk of suicide: Data from Italy, 1974–2003. *Journal of Affective Disorders, 102*(1–3), 19–25. https://doi.org/10.1016/j.jad.2006.12.003

Preti, A., & Miotto, P. (1998). Seasonality in suicides: The influence of suicide method, gender, and age on suicide distribution in Italy. *Psychiatry Research, 81*(3), 219–231. https://doi.org/10.1016/S0165-1781(98)00099-7

Preti, A., & Miotto, P. (2000). Influence of method on seasonal distribution of attempted suicides in Italy. *Neuropsychobiology, 41*(1), 62–72. https://doi.org/10.1159/000026635

Reutfors, J., Ösby, U., Ekbom, A., Nordström, P., Jokinen, J., & Papadopoulos, F. C. (2009). Seasonality of suicide in Sweden: Relationship with psychiatric disorder. *Journal of Affective Disorders, 119*(1–3), 59–65. https://doi.org/10.1016/j.jad.2009.02.020

Rihmer, Z., Hal, M., Kapitány, B., Gonda, X., Vargha, M., & Döme, P. (2015). Preliminary investigation of the possible association between arsenic levels in drinking water and suicide mortality. *Journal of Affective Disorders, 182*, 23–25. https://doi.org/10.1016/j.jad.2015.04.042

Sabic, H., Kious, B. M., Boxer, D., Fitzgerald, C., Riley, C., Scholl, L., McGlade, E., Yurgelun-Todd, D., Renshaw, P. F., & Kondo, D. G. (2019). Effect of altitude on veteran suicide rates. *High Altitude Medicine & Biology, 20*(2), 171–177. https://doi.org/10.1089/ham.2018.0130

Sen, S., & Sarathi Biswas, R. (2012). The toxic effects of arsenic on the central nervous system: A review. *Journal of Neurotoxicology, 33*(1), 52–66. https://doi.org/10.1016/j.neuro.2012.01.003

Sidorchuk, A., Agerbo, E., & Sventek, R. (2019). Risk factors for suicide: A review. *World Psychiatry, 18*(1), 7–18. https://doi.org/10.1002/wps.20554

Stack, S., Gundlach, J., & Reeves, J. L. (1994). The heavy metal subculture and suicide. *Suicide and Life-Threatening Behavior, 24*(1), 15–23.

Stengel, E. (1964). *Suicide and attempted suicide.* Penguin Books.

Stone, D., Holland, K., Bartholow, B., Crosby, A., Davis, S., & Wilkins, N. (2017). *Preventing suicide: A technical package of policy, programs, and practices.* Centers for Disease Control and Prevention. https://www.cdc.gov/violenceprevention/pdf/suicideTechnicalPackage.pdf

Tiihonen, J., Halonen, P., Tiihonen, L., Kautiainen, H., Storvik, M., & Callaway, J. (2017). The association of ambient temperature and violent crime. *Scientific Reports, 7*, 6543. https://doi.org/10.1038/s41598-017-06720-z

Tondo, L., Albert, M. J., & Baldessarini, R. J. (2006). Suicide rates in relation to health care access in the United States: An ecological study. *Journal of Clinical Psychiatry, 67*(4), 517–523. https://doi.org/10.4088/JCP.v67n0404

Troiano, G., Mercurio, I., Melai, P., Lancia, M., Bacci, M., & Nante, N. (2018). Arsenic contamination in drinking water: Is there an association with suicide behavior?. *European Journal of Public Health, 28*(suppl_4), cky218–069. https://doi.org/10.1093/eurpub/cky218.069

Turecki, G., Brent, D. A., Gunnell, D., O'Connor, R. C., Oquendo, M. A., Pirkis, J., & Stanley, B. H. (2019). Suicide and suicide risk. *Nature Reviews Disease Primers, 5*(1), 74. https://doi.org/10.1038/s41572-019-0121-0

Watts, N., Amann, M., Arnell, N., Ayeb-Karlsson, S., Belesova, K., Berry, H., & Costello, A. (2018). The 2018 report of the Lancet Countdown on health and climate change: Shaping the health of nations for centuries to come. *The Lancet, 392*(10163), 2479–2514. https://doi.org/10.1016/S0140-6736(20)31196-X

Whitmer, D. A., & Woods, D. L. (2013). Analysis of the cost effectiveness of a suicide barrier on the Golden Gate Bridge. *Crisis, 34*(2), 71–146. https://doi.org/10.1027/0227-5910/a000179

Woo, J.-M., Okusaga, O., & Postolache, T. T. (2012). Seasonality of suicidal behavior. *International Journal of Environmental Research and Public Health, 9*(2), 531–547. https://doi.org/10.3390/ijerph9020531

Xi, W., Banerjee, S., Zima, B. T., Alexopoulos, G. S., Olfson, M., Xiao, Y., & Pathak, J. (2023). Effects of geography on risk for future suicidal ideation and attempts among children and youth. *AACAP Open, 1*(3), 206–217. https://doi.org/10.1016/j.jaacop.2023.07.002

Yan, Y., Jiang, Y., Liu, R., Eddleston, M., Tao, C., Page, A., & Liu, S. (2023). Impact of pesticide regulations on mortality from suicide by pesticide in China: An interrupted time series analysis. *Frontiers in psychiatry, 14*, 1189923. https://doi.org/10.3389/fpsyt.2023.1189923

Yao, X., Li, X., & Zhang, Y. (2015). The role of oxidative stress in air pollution-induced health effects: A systematic review. *Journal of Environmental Science and Health, Part C, 33*(1), 1–16. https://doi.org/10.1080/10590501.2014.979823

# Chapter 6
# Economic Environment, Recessions, and Suicidal Behaviour

**Aghdas Souresrafil, Mohammadreza Sheikhy-Chaman, Nasrin Abolhasan beigigallehzan, Mosleh Mirzaei, and Mohsen Rezaeian**

**Abstract** It is well known that suicide is one of the world's leading causes of death. Globally, the WHO's age-standardized 2019 suicide estimates show that the African region has the highest suicide rate at 11.2 per 100,000 population, followed by European region at 10.5 per 100,000 population. Prioritizing and designing targeted suicide prevention interventions and policies requires an understanding of the risk factors for suicidal behaviour. Socioeconomic conditions play a significant role in suicide. People who are economically disadvantaged, for instance in financial hardship and unemployment, are often more likely to attempt suicide, as suicide rates are higher in these groups. Suicide rates seem to decline with macro-policy interventions by governments to alleviate financial stress.

**Keywords** Economic environment · Macroeconomic · Recession · Suicide · Suicidal behaviour

---

A. Souresrafil
Department of Health Services and Health Promotion, School of Health, Occupational Environment Research Center, Rafsanjan University of Medical Sciences, Rafsanjan, Iran

M. Sheikhy-Chaman
Health Economics Policy Research Center, Tehran Medical Sciences, Islamic Azad University, Tehran, Iran

N. Abolhasan beigigallehzan
Health Management and Economics Research Center, Health Management Research InstituteIran University of Medical Sciences, Tehran, Iran

M. Mirzaei
Clinical Psychologist, Mental Health Research Center, Iran University of Medical Sciences and Health Services, Tehran, Iran

M. Rezaeian (✉)
Department of Epidemiology and Biostatistics, School of Health, Occupational Environment Research Center, Rafsanjan University of Medical Sciences, Rafsanjan, Iran
e-mail: m_rezaeian@rums.ac.ir



S. M. Y. Arafat and S. K. Kar (eds.), *Ecological and Social Determinants of Suicidal Behavior*, South Asian Perspectives in Mental Health and Psychology,
https://doi.org/10.1007/978-981-96-4028-7_6

## 1 Introduction

Suicide is a global public health concern that is preventable and results in the loss of 703,000 lives annually. The 17th most common cause of death in all age groups is suicide in 2019, in the same line, among people aged 15 to 29, itis the 4th most common cause of death (WHO, 2021). Almost 80% of suicide deaths around the world happen in low- and middle-income (LMIC) countries. Eight of the ten countries in the world with the highest suicide rates are also among these countries (Iemmi et al., 2016). A substantial economic cost is imposed on society as a result of suicide every year (Kinchin & Doran, 2017).

Suicide risk factors increase its likelihood. Multiple factors, including biological, psychological, sociocultural, and family-related factors can contribute to suicide risk (Senapati et al., 2024). The history and severity of mental disorders, history of attempted suicide, recent stressful life events, family history of suicide, and availability of access to lethal means are among main risk factors at individual level (Keyes et al., 2024). At ecological level, suicides are influenced by societal, economic, and cultural factors (Meda et al., 2022; Mostafazadeh-Bora et al., 2016). Various economic factors such as business cycles, unemployment, economic growth, and level of economic development affect suicide rates (Stack, 2021).

Economics has two important areas of study: Microeconomics and macroeconomics, which examine different aspects of the economy. According to K.E. Boulding, "Microeconomics is the study of particular households, individual prices, wages, incomes, individual industries, and particular commodities." In contrast, macroeconomics is that branch of economics which is concerned with the aggregates and averages of the whole economy (Salim & Literature, 2018). This chapter aims to examine the relationship between macroeconomic indicators and suicidal behaviour (for example, economic growth, income inequality, poverty, inflation, etc.). Through this chapter, social theories related to the macroeconomic environment in suicide, the comparison of suicide rates based on income groups classified by the World Bank, and the most common macroeconomic determinants of suicide will be discussed. Lastly, the relationship between government policies and suicidal behaviour reduction would be elaborated.

## 2 Suicide-Related Social Theories

The relationship between the economy and suicide is explained by three social theories (Rajkumar, 2023). They are known as (a) Durkheim's U-shaped theory, (b) Ginsberg's procyclical theory, and (c) Henry and Short's countercyclical theory (Lester, 2001). Different perspectives are proposed by each theory (Thibodeau & Lachaud, 2016). The economic crisis, unemployment, and changes in the level of social cohesiveness brought about by urbanization and immigration are some of the variables that sociological theories highlight as having a role in explaining suicidal behaviour (Pfeti & Miotto, 1999).

### 2.1 *Durkheim's Theory*

The investigation of the correlation between economic fluctuations and suicide mortality can be traced back to Durkheim's work from the late nineteenth century (1951) (Spaulding et al., 2010). According to Durkheim's theory, there is a curvilinear relationship between economic activities and suicide. A decline in social integration and social regulation, in Durkheim's view, is the root cause of the suicide (Lester, 2001).During periods of significant economic expansion or contraction, both social integration and social regulation may deteriorate, leading to heightened rates of suicidal behaviour (Yang, 1995).

### 2.2 *Henry and Short Theory*

Henry and Short's countercyclical theory, introduced in 1954. According to Henry and Short, there is a countercyclical relationship between suicide rate and the economic cycle, which implies that they should rise during recession and fall during expansion (Lester, 2001). It is based on the concept of desperation-aggression, which asserts that those in elevated economic positions may resort to suicide following the loss of their status during a recession (Asogwa & Onyezere, 2018).

### 2.3 *Gingsberg's Theory*

Based on Ginsberg's (1996) cycle theory, suicide is the direct consequence of an individual's dissatisfaction, which is directly correlated with the discrepancy between their actual reward and their aspiration level. In the event of a recession, the disparity between aspirations and rewards is reduced as the economy forces down business cycle, aspirations decrease more rapidly than rewards in the process. Consequently, there will be a decline in the suicide rate. As the economy expands, the prosperous economic environment prompts aspirations to rise at a quicker pace than rewards, resulting in suicide (Lester, 2001).

## 3 Regional Differences in Macroeconomic Indicators and Suicide Rates

In this part, suicide rates comparisons based on the classified groups of per capita gross national income by the World Bank have been considered (WBD, 2019). Figures 1, 2, and 3 illustrate the suicide rates trend per 100,000 individuals among male, female, and both genders in four income level categories of countries. In all groups, suicide rates decreased in 2019 compared to 2000. From lowest to highest, suicide rates per 100,000 population in low-income, upper-middle-income, low-middle-income, and high-income countries in 2019 were 6.05, 7.41, 9.08, and 14.59. In low-middle-income, high-income countries, the rate of suicides was higher than the world average (16.19). Higher-income and upper-middle-income countries had the greatest decline in the total suicide rate.

The number of deaths caused by suicide among men per 100,000 people in 2019 ranged from 8.78 in low-income countries to 10.20 in upper-middle-income countries

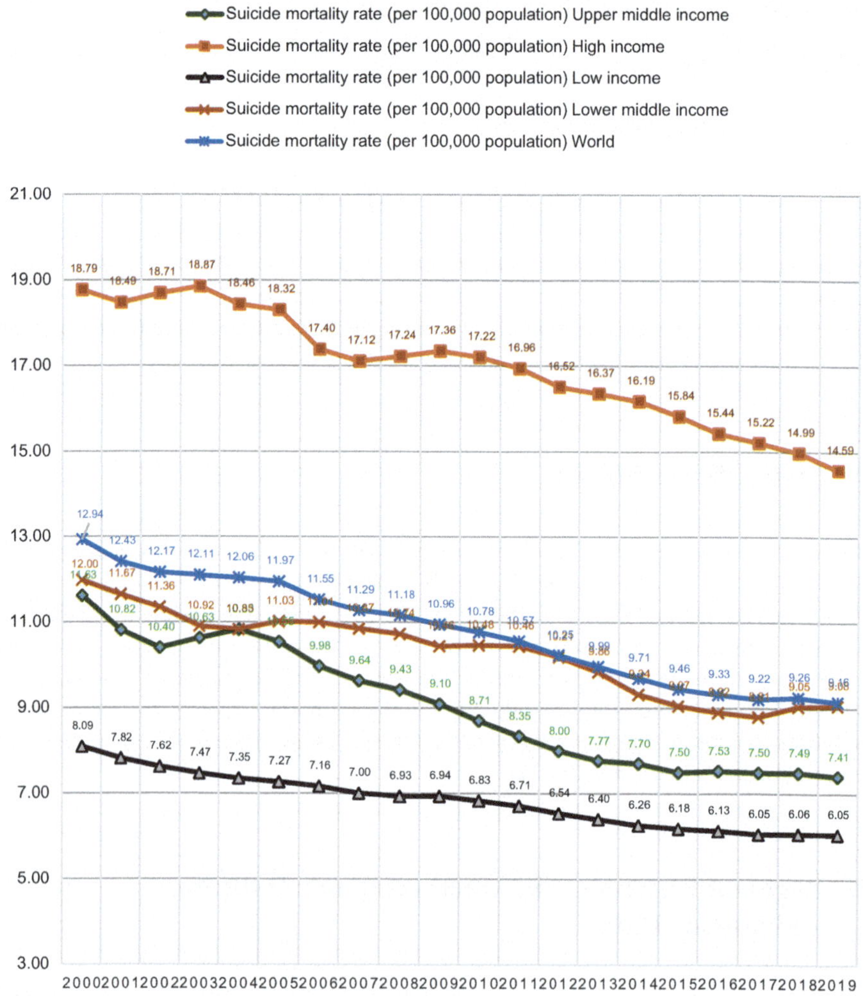


**Fig. 1** Suicide mortality rate (per 100,000 population) (Data from the database: World Bank Data, 2000–2019)

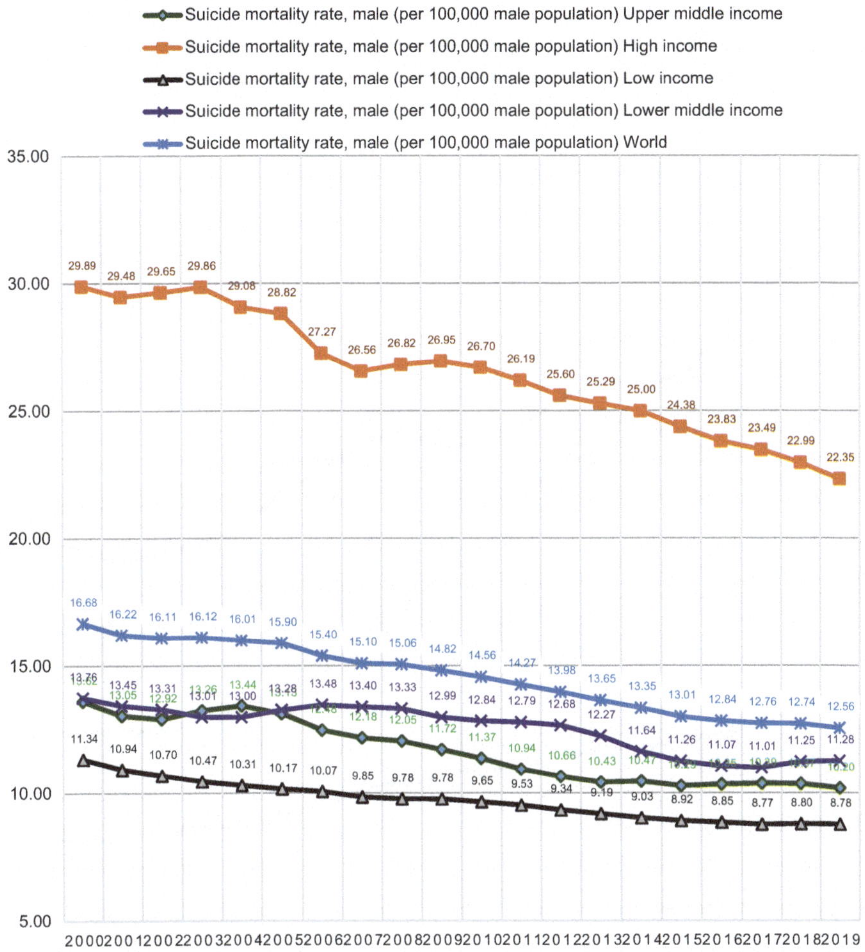


**Fig. 2** Suicide mortality rate, male (per 100,000 population) (Data from the database: World Bank Data, 2000–2019)

to 11.28 in low-middle-income countries to 22.35 in high-income countries. In low-middle-income and high-income countries, the suicide rate in men was higher than the world average (12.56). High-income countries experienced the greatest decline in male suicide rates.

The female suicide mortality rate per 100,000 population in 2019, from lowest to highest in low-income, upper-middle-income, low-middle-income, and high-income countries was 3.34, 4.51, 4.75, and 7.04. In countries with low-middle-income, high-income, females' suicide rates were higher than the world average (5.68). Countries with lower-middle-incomes had the steepest decline in suicide rates among women.

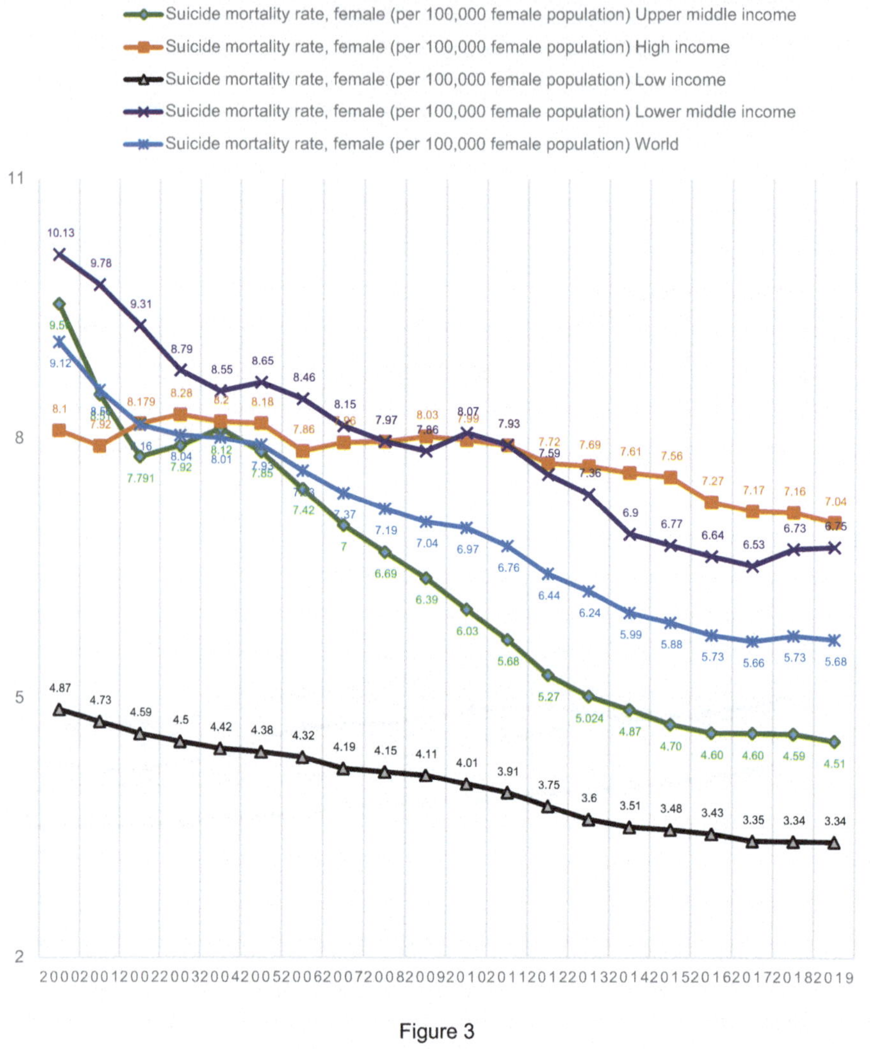


**Fig. 3** Suicide mortality rate, female (per 100,000 population) (Data from the database: World Bank Data, 2000–2019)

## 4 Economic determinants of Suicidal Behaviour

There are a variety of factors involved in suicide, including socioeconomic factors which play a significant role. Economic factors that contribute to suicide decisions include economic growth, unemployment, income inequality, poverty, economic recessions, economic uncertainty, inflation, and healthcare expenditures.

## *4.1 Economic Growth and Suicide Rates*

According to the economic growth definition, it is an increase in the capacity of a country to produce goods and services over time (Raisová & Ďurčová, 2014). The relationship between growth in Gross Domestic Product (GDP) and suicide rates has been extensively studied over the past few decades. A study by Meda et al. classified countries by income levels for each year (low, lower-middle, upper-middle, or higher) to examine the economy's effects on suicide rates. According to this study, despite significant differences between countries in the same income class (except for high-income countries), suicide rates are higher among men than women across all income classes. The GDP per capita has a small but significant effect on suicide rates globally. The effect is larger for low-income countries, where suicide rates decrease by almost 30% for every 1000 USD increase in GDP per capita, while suicide rates drop by 5% in lower-middle and upper-middle-income countries, and by 2% in high-income countries (Meda et al., 2022).

Blasco-Fontecilla et al. showed a variable correlation between purchasing power parity-adjusted GDP and suicide rates across 10 WHO regions. Their research found that Latin-American countries (lower-middle and upper-middle-income), South East Asian countries such as India, Western Pacific countries, including Japan, and high-income Asian countries, including China, had positively correlated GDP growth with suicide rates, whereas high-income and developing European countries had a negative correlation. This indicates that the impact of GDP growth on suicide rates can differ depending on the region's economic status (Blasco-Fontecilla et al., 2012).

A study focused on China, covering the period from 2004 to 2013, revealed a decline in suicide rates overall, which were negatively associated with GDP per capita. The data indicated that suicide rates vary by age, gender, and region, with the highest rates observed in rural areas and among males. It is estimated that the suicide rate declined by 0.498 times when GDP per capita increased by 2787 RMB (Yin, Xu, Shao, Li, & Wan, 2016). An increase in suicide rates was found during economic downturns in England and Wales after negative macroeconomic shocks. Among males, the impact was greater (Lepori et al., 2024). According to an econometrics model study covering 1994 to 2020, changes in GDP growth significantly influence suicide rates in the first year after the change. It seems that the impact of economic growth on suicide rates diminishes with time, highlighting the need to address the adverse health effects of economic fluctuations (Yang et al., 2023).

In a cross-national ecological study, a negative correlation was observed between GDP per capita with the suicide rate in women (Rajkumar, 2023). In a study of 15 European countries between 1970 and 1998, economic growth was shown to significantly affect suicide rates when accounting for country-specific time trends. This research highlighted the complexity of how economic factors impact suicide rates (Andrés, 2005). However, an analysis of data from 29 European countries revealed a strong correlation between suicide rates and most economic indices, though GDP per capita did not show a significant relationship with suicide rates (Fountoulakis et al., 2014).

Finally, in Japan, higher levels of real GDP per capita and economic growth generally leads to suicide rates reduction. This impact is more pronounced compared to other Organization for Economic Co-operation and Development (OECD) countries, with the study noting that suicide rates in Japan are more sensitive to economic factors than social factors. Variations were observed across different genders and age groups (Chen et al., 2009).

Based on the reviewed studies, there is a significant correlation between economic growth and suicide rates, particularly in high-income countries. Economic growth, however, has a different impact on suicide rates based on factors of region, gender, and socioeconomic status. As a result of these findings, it is essential to take into account economic indicators in public health strategies aimed at preventing suicide.

## 4.2 *Unemployment and Suicide Rates*

The unemployment rate is the percentage of the labour force that does not have a job but is available for and seeking employment (LFS, 2024). The link between unemployment and suicide rates is well-documented. Numerous studies consistently show that unemployment significantly increases the risk of suicide. For instance, Milner et al., through a systematic review and meta-analysis, found that long-term unemployment elevates the risk of suicide, particularly within the first five years. This review found that long-term unemployed people have a higher suicide and attempted suicide risk than those who are short-term unemployed, or the general population (Milner et al., 2013). Research analyzing data from 30 countries between 1960 and 2012 revealed that the Great Recession's impact on suicide rates was moderated by unemployment protection levels. Increased unemployment was associated with higher male suicide rates in most welfare regimes, except Scandinavian ones, and with female suicides in Eastern European countries (Norstrom & Gronqvist, 2015). Another meta-analysis, encompassing various countries, demonstrated that unemployment significantly increases the risk of suicidality, including suicide mortality, attempts, and ideation. There was a 1.97 odds ratio for suicidality in unemployed men. Suicide rates in women were higher when they were unemployed (OR = 1.87) (Amiri, 2021).

Laanani et al., using data from Western European countries between 2000 and 2010, found that a 10% increase in unemployment was associated with a 0.3% rise in suicide rates. Significant associations were noted in the Netherlands, the UK, and France, particularly during the 2008–2010 economic crisis. However, this relationship varied across countries and was inconsistent when considering the broader 'crisis effect,' indicating that while a statistical association exists, it is not uniformly causal (Laanani et al., 2015).

Results of the study by Meda et al. indicated that unemployment significantly impacts men's suicide rates more than females, especially in countries with high incomes (RR = 1.04) and high-middle-incomes (RR = 1.01). Suicide rates among women are not affected more by unemployment in low- and middle-income countries.

In some countries (e.g., Ethiopia and Guatemala) suicide rates among females are higher due to unemployment. Rising unemployment increases suicide rates in low-, lower-middle-, and upper-middle-income countries, particularly among middle-aged people (age 45–49) (Meda et al., 2022).

Analysis of monthly data from Australia between 2004 and 2016 revealed that both unemployment and underemployment significantly contributed to suicide rates. Approximately 9.5% of the 32,000 suicides during this period were related to labour underutilization, with 1575 suicides attributed to unemployment and 1496 to underemployment. To reduce suicide rates, economic policies aimed at achieving full employment are essential (Skinner et al., 2023).

In Japan, the trend of decreasing suicides reversed during the COVID-19 pandemic (2020–2022), with unemployment—especially long-term unemployment and dismissals—strongly linked to rising suicide rates. Short-term unemployment was associated with increased suicides among working-age women, while long-term unemployment correlated with higher suicide rates among working-age men (Matsumoto et al., 2023).

Altogether, research consistently demonstrates a strong link between unemployment and increased suicide rates across various populations and regions. Long-term unemployment, in particular, significantly raises suicide risks, with short-term unemployment also contributing notably in certain demographics. The impact of unemployment on suicide rates is influenced by factors such as unemployment duration and socioeconomic conditions. Effective interventions, including targeted economic policies and job creation, are essential for mitigating the adverse effects of unemployment on suicide rates.

### *4.3 Income Inequality and Suicide Rates*

Economic inequality is the variation in the distribution of assets, wealth, and income among individuals and/or populations. Also known as income disparity, wealth disparity, wealth and income differences, or wealth gap (OECD, 2018). In Numerous studies have examined the relationship between income inequality and suicide rates in a range of contexts and regions.

An ecological study examined the relationship between income inequality and suicide rates utilizing data from 1684 U.S. counties spanning 2012 to 2016. Traditional regression analyses found no significant overall association between income inequality and suicide rates after adjusting for age, race/ethnicity, gender, and unemployment. However, geographically weighted regression revealed significant spatial variations. In central U.S. counties, higher income inequality was associated with increased suicide rates, whereas in other regions, it was linked to decreased suicide rates. Research studies highlight the need to account for spatial differences in macroeconomic factors and public health outcomes when analyzing the impact of income inequality on suicide rates (Tran & Morrison, 2020).

Using rigorously controlled logistic regression models and various measures of inequality, another investigation in the United States identified that higher income inequality is associated with increased odds of suicide mortality. Specifically, reducing the Gini coefficient from the highest to lowest values observed across U.S. states could decrease the odds of suicide mortality by 20 to 55%. Lowering income inequality via policy actions could be a pluasible method of lowering suicide and alleviating the burden of suicide mortality (Irish, 2024).

In Brazil, data from 5507 municipalities between 2000 and 2011 revealed a positive association between income inequality, as measured by the Gini Index, and suicide rates (rate ratio RR: 1.055). This indicates that higher income inequality is linked to increased suicide rates in Brazil. Implementing social policies aimed at reducing income inequality could be an effective strategy for decreasing suicide rates, particularly in low and middle-income countries (Machado et al., 2015).

A recent study analysed youth suicide rates in high-income countries from 2000 to 2017, including Australia, Canada, France, Germany, Italy, Japan, Poland, the Republic of Korea, Spain, the UK, and the USA. It revealed increases in youth suicide rates in Australia, Canada, the UK, and the USA. These countries also exhibited higher levels of income inequality. The results suggest a correlation between rising youth suicide rates and higher income inequality, highlighting the potential importance of addressing income inequality in suicide prevention strategies (Padmanathan et al., 2020).

A population-based longitudinal study of Canadians aged 20 years or younger, using data from the Canadian Census Health and Environment Cohorts (2006–2019), explored the impact of income inequality on youth deaths. The study found that while income inequality was significantly associated with a higher risk of all-cause deaths and deaths of despair (including drug overdose and alcohol-related liver disease), the link to suicide was not statistically significant. These findings suggest that addressing economic disparities may play a key role in preventing premature mortality among young Canadians, although the direct relationship between income inequality and suicide rates remains inconclusive (Benny et al., 2022).

An ecological study was carried out in Iran aimed to ascertain the effects of income inequality, measured by the Gini coefficient, on suicide rates. Using data from the Iranian Urban and Rural Household Income and Expenditure Survey and the Iranian Forensic Medicine Organization, the researchers reported a Gini coefficient ranging from 0.2523 to 0.3755, with a mean of 0.3092. The analysis revealed a concentration index of −0.10, indicating a positive association between income inequality and suicide rates. Higher suicide rates were observed in provinces with greater income inequality. This study suggests that addressing income inequality could be crucial in understanding and mitigating suicide rates in Iran, and could serve as a starting point for investigating the sources of inequality in geographical areas and at the individual level in all provinces (Veisani et al., 2019).

Also, another survey in Iran discovered that income-related inequality in suicide across provinces was assessed by calculating the Gini coefficients for per capita income and suicide rates. The Gini coefficient for per capita income was 0.10, while for suicide rates, it was 0.34. A trivial decreasing trend in suicide rates was observed with increasing income quintiles, and the poorest-to-richest ratio in suicide rates was 2.01. The concentration index for suicide was −0.12, indicating a slight inverse relationship between income and suicide rates. This study suggests that lower-income might be a risk factor for completed suicide (Kazemi-Galougahi et al., 2018).

Based on the evidence presented, we can conclude that there is a complex and variable relationship between income inequality and suicide rates. Many studies from different countries and settings have demonstrated both positive and nuanced associations, which suggest that income inequality could be a key component of any strategies for preventing suicide across different countries and settings. Further research is needed to provide a better understanding of these dynamics to mitigate the impact of income disparities on suicide rates.

## *4.4 Economic Poverty and Suicide Rates*

The concept of economic poverty can be defined as a situation in which a household is unable to meet its basic needs due to insufficient financial resources. The definition of absolute poverty can be explained as a condition where a person needs the minimum amount of resources to survive. Relative poverty occurs when one compares one's poverty with that of others in the same social class (Mowafi & Khawaja, 2005).Examining the intricate connection between poverty and suicide rates is vital for implementing efficient intervention strategies. This topic has been explored through various studies using diverse methods, providing valuable perspectives.

A retrospective longitudinal cohort study examined the relationship between poverty and suicide risk among 558,147 older adults (aged 60–119 years) in South Korea over 12 years. The findings revealed that older adults in poverty had a significantly higher risk of suicide compared to their high-income counterparts, particularly among males and those aged 60–74. However, no significant association was found for females or individuals aged 75 and older. The study emphasizes the importance of tailoring suicide prevention efforts by income level, with a particular focus on older men in poverty (Choi et al., 2019).

Another longitudinal analysis using data from the Korean Welfare Panel Study data (2012–2018) examined the impact of relative deprivation on suicide risk among South Koreans who were aged 25 or older. The research found that higher levels of relative deprivation in income were significantly associated with increased odds of suicidal ideation and suicide planning or attempts. Notably, the effect was observed primarily in men. The study highlights that relative deprivation, beyond absolute income levels, is an important factor in suicide risk. These findings suggest that addressing income disparities could be an effective strategy for mitigating suicide risk, particularly in South Korea (Seponski et al., 2019).

Cross-sectional research compared attitudes toward suicide and suicidal thoughts across South Korean, Japanese, and American populations, focusing on attribution of poverty the highest prevalence of suicidal thoughts was found in South Korea, followed by Japan and the USA. In all three nations, individualistic attribution of poverty was linked to permissive attitudes toward suicide, which significantly affected the intensity of suicidal thoughts. The study suggests that poverty-related perceptions, particularly societal versus individualistic attributions, play a significant role in shaping attitudes toward suicide and suicide risk across different cultural contexts (Lee et al., 2021).

In Japan, examining data over 30 years, the results suggest that the relative poverty rate is associated with the suicide rate for both genders, with a particular impact on men. The findings highlight the need for organizations and professionals involved in suicide prevention to consider these results and formulate additional specific measures addressing economic concerns (Inoue et al., 2016).

A study focused on individuals between the age of 5 and 19 investigated the relationship between county-level poverty and pediatric suicide rates in the United States from 2007 to 2016. Throughout the study period, were identified within this age group. Suicide rates among these young people were correlated elevated levels of poverty at the county level. Specifically, counties with poverty levels of 10% or more exhibited progressively higher suicide rates compared to those with lower poverty levels. The association was notably strong for firearm suicides in high-poverty counties. These findings underline higher county-level poverty as a significant risk factor for pediatric suicide and highlight the need for targeted prevention strategies in impoverished communities (Hoffmann et al., 2020).

In another inquiry in the USA, employing data from 16 states between 2005 and 2011, it was pointed out that county-level poverty rates were strongly associated with suicide rates across both genders and all age groups. Poverty also had a notable impact on alcohol-involved suicides, particularly increasing risk for men aged 45–64 years, while showing a negative association for men aged 20–44 years. Population risk of suicide was most clearly associated with county-level poverty rates, highlighting that programmes addressing area poverty should be applied for reducing suicide risk (Kerr et al., 2017).

A study explored factors impacting suicide attempts among Cambodian women, revealing that 5.5% had previously attempted suicide. Analysis of qualitative data from 76 women identified four major themes, with poverty being a significant factor. Poverty was notably linked with increased suicide attempts, as financial constraints exacerbated issues such as untreated illness. Poverty is a major factor influencing suicide attempts. Considering these problems could have a significant impact on preventing suicide attempts in the future (Seponski et al., 2019).

A systematic review of the positive relationship between poverty and suicide in LMICs found that poverty, especially worse economic conditions, wealth decline, and unemployment, is linked to suicidal thoughts and behaviours (Iemmi et al., 2016). An ecological study by Muniyapillai et al. aimed to analyse socio-demographic risk factors and psychosocial stressors related to suicide. The researchers selected countries based on data from the World Health Organization, including the top ten countries with highest suicide rates and the ten nations with the lowest rates. The study observed that the poverty rate was not significantly associated with suicide rates. Suicide is a major public health concern, but global data on suicide is limited.

Further research is essential to better understand the factors influencing suicide rates universally (Muniyapillai et al., 2024).

According to the studies conducted in different global contexts, poverty appears to influence suicide risk in a variety of ways based on different age groups, genders, and cultural settings. The field of research on poverty-related suicide should be continued worldwide in order to provide cross-country comparisons to be able to minimize the risk of suicide due to poverty.

## 4.5 Recession and Suicide

The impact of recession on suicide should be analysed both from a microeconomic and macroeconomic point of view. A recession can be defined as a sustained decline in economic productivity, which at the macro level is measured by the national GDP and the rate of unemployment (Burns, 1946). As a result of the worldwide recession of the 1930s, which resulted in the loss of 30 million jobs worldwide and widespread social change, the importance of analyzing the effects of recessions on global health has become more evident since then (Bank, 2009; Oyesanya et al., 2015). According to the findings, recessions can have a variety of effects on the health indicators of a population in several ways, such as the change in suicide rates (Margerison-Zilko et al., 2016).

In every society, the suicide rate is a reflection of the psychological stress imposed on a large portion of the population. It has been shown in several studies that suicide rates tend to rise when the economy is in recession (El Ibrahimi et al., 2021; Oyesanya et al., 2015; Takeshima et al., 2015).

In a systematic review study, the evidence regarding economic recession and suicide was evaluated. According to the study, recession periods are known to increase the overall suicide rate. However, the study focused primarily on the relationship between recession and suicide in high-income countries in Europe and North America, and by recognizing this fact, the researchers emphasized the need for more research in low-income countries. Studies may have been affected by the use of different economic indicators to define economic recession. When multiple economic indicators are examined during this period, the most accurate assessment can be made. As an example, GDP is one of the most commonly used indicators when it comes to assessing the severity of recessions. As GDP does not provide information about wealth distribution, the lived experience of individuals may differ from what the GDP indicates. When comparing recession conditions among countries, these discrepancies can lead to bias (Oyesanya et al., 2015). Additionally, unemployment and debt have been considered in a number of studies as influencing factors impacting suicide during recession (Chang et al., 2013; Konieczna et al., 2022; Nordt et al., 2015; Reeves et al., 2014).

It was found in a study in 54 countries that the 2008 global economic crisis contributed to an estimated 4884 excess suicides, most of them occurring among men in American (more than six percent increase) and European (more than two percent increase) countries, whereas women in American countries experienced smaller magnitude increases of two to three percent. For women in European countries, there was no increase in suicide rates. There is evidence that the economic crisis had a greater effect on suicide rates in men than in women during the time of the recession. In Taiwan and Singapore, where the effects of the economic crisis were much smaller, such increases were not observed (Sinyor et al., 2024).

From 2014 to 2016, Brazil experienced a decline in GDP, indicating a prolonged recession. During this period, workers' average income and employment rate decreased (Figueiredo et al., 2022). Another study carried out in Brazil found that suicide rates are on the rise following the economic crisis in 2014. In terms of suicide standardized rates, the rate of suicide increased by 10% from 2010 to 2014, and by 11% from 2014 to 2017 (Machado et al., 2019). Further investigations indicated that suicide rates differed across different population groups in Brazil. As an example, the suicide mortality rate was higher among men than women (Figueiredo et al., 2022).

According to a study conducted in South Korea that examined suicide rates across different occupational groups, it was found that during the financial crisis at the beginning of 2009, the unemployment rate increased and continued until 2010. As a result, suicide rates, which had previously declined from 2005 to 2008, remained stable through the middle of 2009 and reached their highest historical peak in 2012. According to this study, rising unemployment has an impact on individual suicide rates, meaning that job losses or job insecurity will increase suicide rates as a result of rising unemployment. It was also shown in the study in South Korea that the suicide rate was significantly higher among employed individuals who lost their jobs than it was among unemployed individuals who had lost their jobs (Chan et al., 2014).

The relationship between recession and suicide has been reported in a variety of studies (Konieczna et al., 2022; Oyesanya et al., 2015; Reeves et al., 2014). In a study conducted during the 2008 financial crisis, suicide-related mortality was higher among men of working-age. As a result of rising unemployment and declining income, men experience greater psychological distress than women (Konieczna et al., 2022).

Sweden, Iceland, Finland, and Austria did not experience an upward trend in suicide rate during the global financial crisis. In fact, Finland even saw a decrease in suicide rate. There was no increase in suicide rates in Sweden, Iceland, Finland, or Austria during the global financial crisis. Suicide rates in Finland even decreased (Ásgeirsdóttir et al., 2020; Konieczna et al., 2022; Reeves et al., 2014). The study of How et al. found a strong correlation between recession, unemployment, and suicide. The occurrence of a recession leads to unemployment increasing, debt increasing, and individuals losing their assets, suffering from social isolation, and developing alcoholism, depression, and mental disorders. All these factors can lead to suicide attempts and death. Study results indicate that countries that provide social support to those with low incomes or who have lost income can minimize recessionary effects (Haw et al., 2015). For instance, during the 2008 financial crisis, Denmark did not see an increase in the suicide rate during that time. Denmark's effective measures in preventing suicide attempts and deaths were responsible for this trend. In this country, there is a social welfare system that provides a high level of social support to people with suicidal tendencies, as well as increased support for people with suicidal tendencies, which helps to prevent an unexpected rise in suicide rates (Konieczna et al., 2022).

Overall, there have been a variety of studies that have tracked the relationship between the recession and suicide across the globe in the last few years. Therefore, it is imperative that the government intervenes during such times to prevent the development of mental illnesses and suicide attempts, as well as providing appropriate healthcare services to the individuals.

### *4.6 Economic Uncertainty and Suicide*

As described by Milliken, uncertainty is characterized by the belief that one cannot predict something accurately due to a lack of confidence in one's own knowledge or abilities in the situation. Hence, uncertainty can be viewed as an environmental variable that affects an entire economy or business, rather than a problem or decision-making context that may be ambiguous, complex or risky (Sharma et al., 2020).

Economic uncertainty is a complex variable that has an impact on the health of society as a whole. Several studies have been conducted on this topic in the past. As De Bruin et al., (2020) examined the relationship between economic policy uncertainty (EPU) and suicide rate in 17 countries over a twenty-five year period (1990–2015), they found that economic uncertainty contributed to an increase in suicide rates (de Bruin et al., 2020). Similarly, Claveria et al., in a global study involving 183 countries, concluded that global EPU that is delayed by one year results in an increase in suicide rates. The study finds that when a global uncertainty shock occurs, its impact on suicide rate is not immediate, but is still influenced by other mediator variables. The analysis suggests that lagged economic uncertainty, unemployment, and economic growth all increase the risk of suicide. Africa and the Middle East are the regions where an increase in economic uncertainty has the greatest impact (Claveria, 2024).

A study by Eret al. extended the EPU index to include the World Uncertainty Index (WUI). The researchers examined the relationship between economic uncertainty and suicide rates across 141 countries between 2000 and 2019. An increase in economic uncertainty is directly related to an increase in suicide rates. In high-income countries, higher economic uncertainty was associated with a higher suicide rate. These findings did not hold true for countries with middle- and low-incomes (Er et al., 2023).

According to Abdo et al., economic uncertainty increases suicide rates among American men and women aged 15 to 24 and 55 to 64 (Abdou et al., 2022). Studying the relationship between dimensions of economic uncertainty and suicide rates in the UK revealed that economic uncertainty increased during the first year of the COVID-19 pandemic. According to the findings, women are more sensitive to uncertainty changes (Claveria et al., 2024). Vandoros' research also found a link between economic uncertainty and suicide rates. This study in England and Wales found that a spike in economic uncertainty affected suicides immediately, but short-lived. A one-day lag also has a positive effect, but subsequent days are unaffected. It appears that males are more affected than females (Vandoros et al., 2019). Similarly, Antonakakis et al. reported that rising EPU increases suicide-related deaths among young and elderly men in the United States, while females across all ages were found to be resilient to changes in economic policy uncertainty (Antonakakis & Gupta, 2017).

There has been speculation that one reason why studies have shown that higher suicide rates are associated with greater economic uncertainty in high-income countries may be because people in these countries have more to lose when uncertain times arise. The population of high-income countries is more aware of economic and social inequalities than the population of low-income countries. Economic uncertainty is a trigger for suicide contemplation (Er et al., 2023). Thus, reducing suicide rates in high-income countries can be achieved through the implementation of preventive policies before economic uncertainty occurs. In lower-income countries, the informal economy is more extensive, so people who lose their jobs can find work more easily. These countries have stronger family support networks during crises, while high-income countries tend to have weaker family support networks (Claveria et al., 2024).

In general, economic uncertainty is associated with an increase in suicide rates, particularly in high-income countries. The government is responsible for ensuring that there are financial and emotional support systems in place before entering periods of economic uncertainty so that suicide rates can be controlled.

## 4.7 *Inflation and Suicide*

An increase in general prices that is sustained and broad-based is considered inflation. According to Durkheim, social harms can arise from economic crises, and suicide is associated with macroeconomic indicators (Lester, 2001). According to an article published in 2001, inflation exerts a negative impact on the well-being of the average individual.

Inflation is another important economic factor that affects suicide rates. In addition, it impacts the daily lives, the purchasing power, and the country's consumer price index. A consumer's expectations of inflation results in a rise in prices and a decrease in the value of individual savings, which results in a loss of welfare (Beautrais & Mishara, 2008; Solano et al., 2012).

According to Sun & Zhang, in the United Kingdom from 1981 to 2011, inflation impacted suicide rates positively. In addition, suicide rates among groups older than 40 are significantly associated with unemployment and inflation rate, compared to younger groups (Sun & Zhang, 2016).

Iran experienced severe inflation from 2011 to 2021. The economic sanctions on Iran increased expected inflation and drove inflation higher than ever. During this period, suicide rates increased concurrently with deteriorating economic conditions and severe inflation (Jahani Dolatabad et al., 2023). The impact of inflation on suicide behaviours in Italy from 2001 to 2008 was investigated by Paola Solano et al. The study found a significant correlation between the rate of suicide attempts among individuals who were previously employed but now unemployed and the inflation rate. Nevertheless, there was no significant correlation between the inflation rate and suicide attempts among previously unemployed individuals (Solano et al., 2012).

In all, different studies have examined the effect of inflation on suicide rate alongside other economic indicators and found a positive correlation between intensified inflation and the rise in suicide rates, because the effects of inflation directly impact people's daily lives, and individuals can feel this negative impact on their lives. The effects of this pressure can range from suicide attempts to suicide deaths if not controlled through social support programmes and macroeconomic reforms.

## *4.8 Healthcare Spending and Suicide*

Spending on health reflects the final consumption of health services and goods, including public and private spending on medical services, goods, public health and prevention programmes, and administration, but excluding capital formation (OECD, 2015).There has been an increase in real healthcare costs for all OECD member countries over the last 20 years. Mental health is the third leading cause of disease burden in middle- and high-income countries. Despite that, the healthcare budget has only grown from 6.5% to 8.8% of GDP (Park et al., 2020).

Researchers argue that countries with a high suicide rate are often characterized by low healthcare expenditures, which generally correlate with a high suicide rate (Ferretti & Coluccia, 2009).One of the most important predictors of suicide rates is the state of the healthcare system (Máčel et al., 2023). Some studies have shown that in Western countries, individuals who attempt suicide often used medical care, particularly primary care, before their suicide (Da Cruz et al., 2011; Sohn et al., 2014).

Lange et al. study (2023) indicated that there is a decrease in the average suicide mortality rate among men in the American region with an increase in health expenditures per capita in the region (Lange et al., 2023). In Minoiu and Andres (2008), the share of health and welfare in total public spending was a strong indicator of suicide rates (Minoiu & Andrés, 2008). Most European countries with greater social welfare spending have lower male and female suicide rates (Yur'yev et al., 2012). However, state-level public mental health expenditures were found to be unpredictably related to state suicide rates in another analysis (Ross et al., 2012). The studies by Martin Máel et al., in the European Union and Johannessen et al., in Norway both conclude that there is no clear correlation between government healthcare spending and suicide rates (Johannessen et al., 2011; Máčel et al., 2023).

In all, more research is needed to examine the relationship between health expenditures and suicides. It is imperative for governments to allocate resources creatively and explore different methods to improve accessibility to healthcare services for people at risk.

## 5 Government Welfare Policies to Reduce Suicides

Even though economic factors have been linked to suicidal behaviours, relatively few research studies have examined the protective role of government policy interventions. In several studies, it has been found that government policies play a significant role in mediating the relationship between unemployment and suicide. A systematic review found a negative correlation between unemployment benefits and suicide rates (Shand et al., 2022). Research has shown that active unemployment policies and employment protection laws are beneficial in reducing suicide rates. Suicide among men has been reduced by these policies in particular (Mathieu et al., 2022).

Cylus et al. examined whether US state unemployment insurance programmes reduced the impact of economic recession on suicide. Study results indicate that unemployment benefits neutralize the impact of unemployment rates on suicide (Cylus et al., 2014). Similarly, in Japan, financial support was found to be inversely related to suicide mortality, indicating that poor economic conditions make financial support particularly essential (Okada et al., 2020).

In addition, two other studies found that each unit increase in the costs of the active labour market programme decreased suicide rates (Reeves et al., 2015; Stuckler et al., 2009). Another study found that a $1 increase in the mandatory minimum wage reduced suicide by 6% among people with low education (ages 18–64), while no effect was seen for those with college degrees. When unemployment was high, this relationship was stronger, and when unemployment was low, it decreased. Policies aimed at improving people's economic conditions can be protective, especially during recessions (Kaufman et al., 2020).

## 6 Conclusion

Suicide is a complex phenomenon caused by interaction between individual characteristics, social, cultural, and environmental factors, and is largely the result of a combination of factors. An important factor in suicidal behaviour is economic conditions. It is generally accepted that high GDP per capita and robust economic growth are associated with lower suicide rates, particularly in high-income countries. Suicide rates among youth can be correlated with income inequality, emphasizing the need to address income inequality in suicide prevention strategies. One of the most important predictors of suicide rates is the state of the health care system in the country. Macro-policy interventions by the government to reduce financial stress during rising unemployment appear to be beneficial in preventing suicides.

## References


Abdou, R., Cassells, D., Berrill, J., & Hanly, J. (2022). Revisiting the relationship between economic uncertainty and suicide: An alternative approach. *Social Science & Medicine, 306*, 115095.

Amiri, S. (2021). Unemployment and suicide mortality, suicide attempts, and suicide ideation: A meta-analysis. *International Journal of Mental Health, 51*(4), 294–318. https://doi.org/10.1080/00207411.2020.1859347

Andrés, A. R. (2005). Income inequality, unemployment, and suicide: A panel data analysis of 15 European countries. *Applied Economics, 37*(4), 439–451. https://doi.org/10.1080/0003684042000295304

Antonakakis, N., & Gupta, R. (2017). Is economic policy uncertainty related to suicide rates? Evidence from the United States. *Social Indicators Research, 133*(2), 543–560.

Ásgeirsdóttir, H. G., Valdimarsdóttir, U. A., Nyberg, U., Lund, S. H., Tomasson, G., Þorsteinsdóttir, Þ. K., Ásgeirsdóttir, T. L., & Hauksdóttir, A. (2020). Suicide rates in Iceland before and after the 2008 Global Recession: A nationwide population-based study. *European Journal of Public Health, 30*(6), 1102–1108.

Asogwa, E. U., & Onyezere, J. O. (2018). Economic recession in Nigeria: An important risk factor for suicide. *Archives of Business Research, 6*(11). https://doi.org/10.14738/abr.611.5544

Bank, W. (2009). *Global monitoring report 2009: A development emergency*. The World Bank.

Beautrais, A. L., & Mishara, B. L. (2008). World suicide prevention day:"think globally, plan nationally, act locally" (Vol. 29, pp. 59–63): Hogrefe & Huber Publishers.

Benny, C., Smith, B. T., Hyshka, E., Senthilselvan, A., Veugelers, P. J., & Pabayo, R. (2022). Investigating the association between income inequality in youth and deaths of despair in Canada: A population-based cohort study from 2006 to 2019. *J Epidemiol Community Health*. https://doi.org/10.1136/jech-2022-219630

Blasco-Fontecilla, H., Perez-Rodriguez, M. M., Garcia-Nieto, R., Fernandez-Navarro, P., Galfalvy, H., de Leon, J., & Baca-Garcia, E. (2012). Worldwide impact of economic cycles on suicide trends over 3 decades: Differences according to level of development. A mixed effect model study. *BMJ Open, 2*(3). https://doi.org/10.1136/bmjopen-2011-000785

Burns, A. (1946). *Measuring business cycles*. National Bureau of Economic Research.

Chan, C. H., Caine, E. D., You, S., Fu, K. W., Chang, S. S., & Yip, P. S. F. (2014). Suicide rates among working-age adults in South Korea before and after the 2008 economic crisis. *J Epidemiol Community Health, 68*(3), 246–252.

Chang, S. S., Stuckler, D., Yip, P., & Gunnell, D. (2013). Impact of 2008 global economic crisis on suicide: Time trend study in 54 countries. *Bmj, 347*, f5239. https://doi.org/10.1136/bmj.f5239

Chen, J., Choi, Y. J., & Sawada, Y. (2009). How is suicide different in Japan? *Japan and the World Economy, 21*(2), 140–150. https://doi.org/10.1016/j.japwor.2008.06.001

Choi, J. W., Kim, T. H., Shin, J., & Han, E. (2019). Poverty and suicide risk in older adults: A retrospective longitudinal cohort study. *International Journal of Geriatric Psychiatry, 34*(11), 1565–1571. https://doi.org/10.1002/gps.5166

Claveria, O., Soric, M., & Soric, P. (2024). Analysis of the impact of financial and labour uncertainty on suicide mortality in England. *Health Place, 89*, 103329. https://doi.org/10.1016/j.healthplace.2024.103329

Cylus, J., Glymour, M. M., & Avendano, M. (2014). Do generous unemployment benefit programs reduce suicide rates? A state fixed-effect analysis covering 1968–2008. *American Journal of Epidemiology, 180*(1), 45–52. https://doi.org/10.1093/aje/kwu106

Da Cruz, D., Pearson, A., Saini, P., Miles, C., While, D., Swinson, N., Williams, A., Shaw, J., Appleby, L., & Kapur, N. (2011). Emergency department contact prior to suicide in mental health patients. *Emergency Medicine Journal, 28*(6), 467–471. https://doi.org/10.1136/emj.2009.081869

de Bruin, A., Agyemang, A., & Chowdhury, M. I. H. (2020). New insights on suicide: Uncertainty and political conditions. *Applied Economics Letters, 27*(17), 1424–1429.

El Ibrahimi, S., Xiao, Y., Bergeron, C. D., Beckford, N. Y., Virgen, E. M., & Smith, M. L. (2021). Suicide distribution and trends among male older adults in the US, 1999–2018. *American Journal of Preventive Medicine, 60*(6), 802–811.

Er, S. T., Demir, E., & Sari, E. (2023). Suicide and economic uncertainty: New findings in a global setting. *SSM Population Health, 22*, 101387. https://doi.org/10.1016/j.ssmph.2023.101387

Ferretti, F., & Coluccia, A. (2009). Socio-economic factors and suicide rates in European Union countries. *Leg Med (Tokyo), 11*(Suppl 1), S92-94. https://doi.org/10.1016/j.legalmed.2009.01.014

Figueiredo, D., Sanchez-Villegas, P., Figueiredo, A. M., Moraes, R. M., Daponte-Codina, A., Schmidt Filho, R., & Vianna, R. P. T. (2022). Effects of the economic recession on suicide mortality in Brazil: Interrupted time series analysis. *Revista Brasileira de Enfermagem, 75*(Suppl 3), e20210778. https://doi.org/10.1590/0034-7167-2021-0778

Fountoulakis, K. N., Kawohl, W., Theodorakis, P. N., Kerkhof, A. J., Navickas, A., Hoschl, C., Lecic-Tosevski, D., Sorel, E., Rancans, E., Palova, E., Juckel, G., & Lopez-Ibor, J. (2014). Relationship of suicide rates to economic variables in Europe: 2000-2011. *The British Journal of Psychiatry, 205*(6), 486–496. https://doi.org/10.1192/bjp.bp.114.147454

Haw, C., Hawton, K., Gunnell, D., & Platt, S. (2015). Economic recession and suicidal behaviour: Possible mechanisms and ameliorating factors. *International Journal of Social Psychiatry, 61*(1), 73–81. https://doi.org/10.1177/0020764014536545

Hoffmann, J. A., Farrell, C. A., Monuteaux, M. C., Fleegler, E. W., & Lee, L. K. (2020). Association of pediatric suicide with county-level poverty in the United States, 2007–2016. *JAMA Pediatrics, 174*(3), 287–294. https://doi.org/10.1001/jamapediatrics.2019.5678

Iemmi, V., Bantjes, J., Coast, E., Channer, K., Leone, T., McDaid, D., Palfreyman, A., Stephens, B., & Lund, C. (2016). Suicide and poverty in low-income and middle-income countries: A systematic review. *Lancet Psychiatry, 3*(8), 774–783. https://doi.org/10.1016/S2215-0366(16)30066-9

Inoue, K., Fujita, Y., Takeshita, H., Abe, S., Fujihara, J., Ezoe, S., Sampei, M., Miyaoka, T., Horiguchi, J., Okazaki, Y., & Fukunaga, T. (2016). A long-term study of the association between the relative poverty rate and suicide rate in Japan. *Journal of Forensic Sciences, 61 Suppl 1*, S140–143. https://doi.org/10.1111/1556-4029.12998

Irish, A. J. (2024). State-level income inequality as a determinant of suicide mortality in the United States. *Social Work, 69*(4), 339–346. https://doi.org/10.1093/sw/swae035

Jahani Dolatabad, E., Ashayeri, T., & Shiri, M. (2023). Examining the relationship between macroeconomic indicators and suicide rates in the country's provinces: Secondary analysis of 2011–2021 statistics. *Strategic Research on Social Problems, 12*(3), 41–62.

Johannessen, H. A., Dieserud, G., Claussen, B., & Zahl, P. H. (2011). Changes in mental health services and suicide mortality in Norway: An ecological study. *BMC Health Services Research, 11*, 68. https://doi.org/10.1186/1472-6963-11-68

Kaufman, J. A., Salas-Hernández, L. K., Komro, K. A., & Livingston, M. D. (2020). Effects of increased minimum wages by unemployment rate on suicide in the USA. *Journal of Epidemiology and Community Health, 74*(3), 219. https://doi.org/10.1136/jech-2019-212981

Kazemi-Galougahi, M. H., Mansouri, A., Akbarpour, S., Bakhtiyari, M., Sartipi, M., & Moradzadeh, R. (2018). Income-related inequality in completed suicide across the provinces of Iran. *Epidemiol Health, 40*, e2018012. https://doi.org/10.4178/epih.e2018012

Kerr, W. C., Kaplan, M. S., Huguet, N., Caetano, R., Giesbrecht, N., & McFarland, B. H. (2017). Economic recession, alcohol, and suicide rates: Comparative effects of poverty, foreclosure, and job loss. *American Journal of Preventive Medicine, 52*(4), 469–475. https://doi.org/10.1016/j.amepre.2016.09.021

Keyes, K. M., Kandula, S., Martinez-Ales, G., Gimbrone, C., Joseph, V., Monnat, S., Rutherford, C., Olfson, M., Gould, M., & Shaman, J. (2024). Geographic variation, economic activity, and labor market characteristics in trajectories of suicide in the United States, 2008-2020. *American Journal of Epidemiology, 193*(2), 256–266. https://doi.org/10.1093/aje/kwad205

Kinchin, I., & Doran, C. M. (2017). The economic cost of suicide and non-fatal suicide behavior in the Australian workforce and the potential impact of a workplace suicide prevention strategy. *International Journal of Environmental Research and Public Health, 14*(4). https://doi.org/10.3390/ijerph14040347

Konieczna, A., Jakobsen, S. G., Larsen, C. P., & Christiansen, E. (2022). Recession and risk of suicide in Denmark during the 2009 global financial crisis: An ecological register-based study. *Scandinavian Journal of Public Health, 50*(5), 584–592. https://doi.org/10.1177/14034948211013270

Laanani, M., Ghosn, W., Jougla, E., & Rey, G. (2015). Impact of unemployment variations on suicide mortality in Western European countries (2000–2010). *J Epidemiol Community Health, 69*(2), 103–109. https://doi.org/10.1136/jech-2013-203624

Lange, S., Cayetano, C., Jiang, H., Tausch, A., & Oliveira e Souza, R. (2023). Contextual factors associated with country-level suicide mortality in the Americas, 2000–2019: A cross-sectional ecological study. *The Lancet Regional Health – Americas, 20*. https://doi.org/10.1016/j.lana.2023.100450

Lee, H., Park, C. H. K., Rhee, S. J., Kim, B., Lee, S. S., Ha, K., Baik, C. J., & Ahn, Y. M. (2021). The influence of poverty attribution on attitudes toward suicide and suicidal thought: A cross-national comparison between South Korean, Japanese, and American populations. *Comprehensive Psychiatry, 109*, 152259. https://doi.org/10.1016/j.comppsych.2021.152259

Lepori, G. M., Morgan, S., Assarian, B. A., & Mishra, T. (2024). Economic activity and suicides: Causal evidence from macroeconomic shocks in England and Wales. *Social Science & Medicine, 342*, 116538. https://doi.org/10.1016/j.socscimed.2023.116538

Lester, B. Y. (2001). Learnings from Durkheim and beyond: The economy and suicide. *Suicide and Life-Threatening Behavior, 31*(1), 15–31. https://doi.org/10.1521/suli.31.1.15.21306

LFS, I. L. O. (2024). Labour Force Statistics database (LFS). ILOSTAT. Accessed September 06, 2024. https://ilostat.ilo.org/data/

Máčel, M., Opelka, J., Němcová, H., & Labajová, A. (2023). *Impact of healthcare accessibility on suicide rates in the European Union: A cross-sectional correlation study.*

Machado, D. B., Pescarini, J. M., Araujo, L., & Barreto, M. L. (2019). Austerity policies in Brazil may affect violence related outcomes. *Ciência & Saúde Coletiva, 24*(12), 4385–4394. https://doi.org/10.1590/1413-812320182412.07422019

Machado, D. B., Rasella, D., & Dos Santos, D. N. (2015). Impact of income inequality and other social determinants on suicide rate in Brazil. *PLOS ONE, 10*(4), e0124934. https://doi.org/10.1371/journal.pone.0124934

Margerison-Zilko, C., Goldman-Mellor, S., Falconi, A., & Downing, J. (2016). Health impacts of the Great Recession: A critical review. *Current Epidemiology Reports, 3*(1), 81–91. https://doi.org/10.1007/s40471-016-0068-6

Mathieu, S., Treloar, A., Hawgood, J., Ross, V., & Kõlves, K. (2022). The role of unemployment, financial hardship, and economic recession on suicidal behaviors and interventions to mitigate their impact: A review. *Front Public Health, 10*, 907052. https://doi.org/10.3389/fpubh.2022.907052

Matsumoto, R., Motomura, E., & Okada, M. (2023). Impacts of complete unemployment rates disaggregated by reason and duration on suicide mortality from 2009–2022 in Japan. *Healthcare (Basel), 11*(20). https://doi.org/10.3390/healthcare11202806

Meda, N., Miola, A., Slongo, I., Zordan, M. A., & Sambataro, F. (2022). The impact of macroeconomic factors on suicide in 175 countries over 27 years. *Suicide and Life-Threatening Behavior, 52*(1), 49–58. https://doi.org/10.1111/sltb.12773

Milner, A., Page, A., & LaMontagne, A. D. (2013). Long-term unemployment and suicide: A systematic review and meta-analysis. *PLOS ONE, 8*(1), e51333. https://doi.org/10.1371/journal.pone.0051333

Minoiu, C., & Andrés, A. R. (2008). The effect of public spending on suicide: Evidence from U.S. state data. *The Journal of Socio-Economics, 37*(1), 237–261. https://doi.org/10.1016/j.socec.2006.09.001

Mostafazadeh-Bora, M., Zarghami, A., & Shahriari, M. (2016). Vital role of cultural and religious context on suicidal behavior. *Psychiatry & Clinical Neurosciences, 70*(12), 582–583. https://doi.org/10.1111/pcn.12458

Mowafi, M., & Khawaja, M. (2005). Poverty. *J Epidemiol Community Health, 59*(4), 260–264. https://doi.org/10.1136/jech.2004.022822

Muniyapillai, T., Kulothungan, K., Vignesh, K. N. J., Keerthi, C. S., Godwyn, S. R., Shivashankari, S. B., Bhonsle, S. R. B., Krishnakumar, S. P., & Suresh, S. D. (2024). Suicide and its risk factors - An ecological study. *Journal of Education and Health Promotion, 13*, 84. https://doi.org/10.4103/jehp.jehp_940_23

Nordt, C., Warnke, I., Seifritz, E., & Kawohl, W. (2015). Modelling suicide and unemployment: A longitudinal analysis covering 63 countries, 2000–11. *The Lancet Psychiatry, 2*(3), 239–245.

Norstrom, T., & Gronqvist, H. (2015). The Great Recession, unemployment and suicide. *J Epidemiol Community Health, 69*(2), 110–116. https://doi.org/10.1136/jech-2014-204602

OECD. (2015). Health expenditure per capita. In *Health at a Glance 2015: OECD Indicators*. OECD Publishing.

OECD. (2018). Income inequality (Publication no. https://doi.org/10.1787/459aa7f1-en). https://www.oecd-ilibrary.org/content/data/459aa7f1-en

Okada, M., Hasegawa, T., Kato, R., & Shiroyama, T. (2020). Analysing regional unemployment rates, GDP per capita and financial support for regional suicide prevention programme on suicide mortality in Japan using governmental statistical data. *BMJ Open, 10*(8), e037537. https://doi.org/10.1136/bmjopen-2020-037537

Oyesanya, M., Lopez-Morinigo, J., & Dutta, R. (2015). Systematic review of suicide in economic recession. *World Journal of Psychiatry, 5*(2), 243.

Padmanathan, P., Bould, H., Winstone, L., Moran, P., & Gunnell, D. (2020). Social media use, economic recession and income inequality in relation to trends in youth suicide in high-income countries: A time trends analysis. *Journal of Affective Disorders, 275*, 58–65. https://doi.org/10.1016/j.jad.2020.05.057

Park, D. S., Han, J., Torabi, M., & Forget, E. L. (2020). Managing mental health: Why we need to redress the balance between healthcare spending and social spending. *BMC Public Health, 20*(1), 393. https://doi.org/10.1186/s12889-020-08491-1

Pfeti, A., & Miotto, P. (1999). Social and economic influence on suicide: A study of the situation in Italy. *Archives of Suicide Research, 5*(2), 141–156. https://doi.org/10.1080/13811119908258324

Raisová, M., & Ďurčová, J. (2014). Economic growth-supply and demand perspective. *Procedia Economics and Finance, 15*, 184–191. https://doi.org/10.1016/s2212-5671(14)00476-6

Rajkumar, R. P. (2023). The association between nation-level social and economic indices and suicide rates: A pilot study. *Frontiers in Sociology, 8*, 1123284. https://doi.org/10.3389/fsoc.2023.1123284

Reeves, A., McKee, M., Gunnell, D., Chang, S. S., Basu, S., Barr, B., & Stuckler, D. (2015). Economic shocks, resilience, and male suicides in the Great Recession: Cross-national analysis of 20 EU countries. *The European Journal of Public Health, 25*(3), 404–409. https://doi.org/10.1093/eurpub/cku168

Reeves, A., McKee, M., & Stuckler, D. (2014). Economic suicides in the Great Recession in Europe and North America. *The British Journal of Psychiatry, 205*(3), 246–247. https://doi.org/10.1192/bjp.bp.114.144766

Ross, J. M., Yakovlev, P. A., & Carson, F. (2012). Does state spending on mental health lower suicide rates? *The Journal of Socio-Economics, 41*(4), 408–417. https://doi.org/10.1016/j.socec.2010.10.005

Salim, A. (2018). Macroeconomics and Microeconomics: An overview. *International Journal of Research in Humanities, Arts and Literature (IMPACT: IJRHAL), 6*(8), 119–124.

Senapati, R. E., Jena, S., Parida, J., Panda, A., Patra, P. K., Pati, S., Kaur, H., & Acharya, S. K. (2024). The patterns, trends and major risk factors of suicide among Indian adolescents – A scoping review. *BMC Psychiatry, 24*(1), 35. https://doi.org/10.1186/s12888-023-05447-8

Seponski, D. M., Somo, C. M., Kao, S., Lahar, C. J., Khann, S., & Schunert, T. (2019). Family, health, and poverty factors impacting suicide attempts in Cambodian women. *Crisis, 40*(2), 141–145. https://doi.org/10.1027/0227-5910/a000548

Shand, F., Duffy, L., & Torok, M. (2022). Can government responses to unemployment reduce the impact of unemployment on suicide? *Crisis, 43*(1), 59–66. https://doi.org/10.1027/0227-5910/a000750

Sharma, P., Leung, T. Y., Kingshott, R. P. J., Davcik, N. S., & Cardinali, S. (2020). Managing uncertainty during a global pandemic: An international business perspective. *Journal of Business Research, 116*, 188–192. https://doi.org/10.1016/j.jbusres.2020.05.026

Sinyor, M., Silverman, M., Pirkis, J., & Hawton, K. (2024). The effect of economic downturn, financial hardship, unemployment, and relevant government responses on suicide. *Lancet Public Health, 9*(10), e802–e806. https://doi.org/10.1016/S2468-2667(24)00152-X

Skinner, A., Osgood, N. D., Occhipinti, J. A., Song, Y. J. C., & Hickie, I. B. (2023). Unemployment and underemployment are causes of suicide. *Science Advances, 9*(28), eadg3758. https://doi.org/10.1126/sciadv.adg3758

Sohn, J., Cho, J., Moon, K. T., Suh, M., Ha, K. H., Kim, C., Shin, D. C., & Jung, S. H. (2014). Medical care expenditure in suicides from non-illness-related causes. *Journal of Preventive Medicine and Public Health, 47*(6), 327–335. https://doi.org/10.3961/jpmph.14.038

Solano, P., Pizzorno, E., Gallina, A. M., Mattei, C., Gabrielli, F., & Kayman, J. (2012). Employment status, inflation and suicidal behaviour: An analysis of a stratified sample in Italy. *International Journal of Social Psychiatry, 58*(5), 477–484. https://doi.org/10.1177/0020764011408651

Spaulding, J. A., Simpson, G., & Durkheim, E. (2010). *Suicide*: Simon and Schuster.

Stack, S. (2021). Contributing factors to suicide: Political, social, cultural and economic. *Preventive Medicine, 152*, 106498. https://doi.org/10.1016/j.ypmed.2021.106498

Stuckler, D., Basu, S., Suhrcke, M., Coutts, A., & McKee, M. (2009). The public health effect of economic crises and alternative policy responses in Europe: An empirical analysis. *The Lancet, 374*(9686), 315–323. https://doi.org/10.1016/S0140-6736(09)61124-7

Sun, B. Q., & Zhang, J. (2016). Economic and sociological correlates of suicides: Multilevel analysis of the time series data in the United Kingdom. *Journal Forensic Sciences, 61*(2), 345–351. https://doi.org/10.1111/1556-4029.13033

Takeshima, T., Yamauchi, T., Inagaki, M., Kodaka, M., Matsumoto, T., Kawano, K., Katsumata, Y., Fujimori, M., Hisanaga, A., & Takahashi, Y. (2015). Suicide prevention strategies in Japan: A 15-year review (1998–2013). *Journal of Public Health Policy, 36*, 52–66.

Thibodeau, L., & Lachaud, J. (2016). Impact of economic fluctuations on suicide mortality in Canada (1926–2008): Testing the Durkheim, Ginsberg, and Henry and Short theories. *Death Studies, 40*(5), 305–315. https://doi.org/10.1080/07481187.2015.1133727

Tran, F., & Morrison, C. (2020). Income inequality and suicide in the United States: A spatial analysis of 1684 U.S. counties using geographically weighted regression. *Spat Spatiotemporal Epidemiol, 34*, 100359. https://doi.org/10.1016/j.sste.2020.100359

Vandoros, S., Avendano, M., & Kawachi, I. (2019). The association between economic uncertainty and suicide in the short-run. *Social Science & Medicine, 220*, 403–410.

Veisani, Y., Delpisheh, A., Valizadeh, R., & Kikhavani, S. (2019). Income inequality by Gini-coefficient on suicide death in Iran: A review of national data. *Iranian Journal of Public Health, 48*(8), 1512–1517.

WBD, W. B. D. (2019). World Bank Country and Lending Groups. from https://datahelpdesk.worldbank.org/knowledgebase/articles/906519-world-bank-country-and-lending-groups

WHO, W. H. O. (2021). Geneva, Switzerland: Suicide Worldwide in 2019. Global Health Estimates.

Yang, B. (1995). The differential impact of the economy on suicide in the young and the elderly: The American experience. *Archives of Suicide Research, 1*(2), 111–120. https://doi.org/10.1080/13811119508258979

Yang, T. Y., Yang, Y. T., Chen, S. H., Lan, Y. T., & Peng, C. J. (2023). Dynamic effect of economic growth on the persistence of suicide rates. *Geospat Health, 18*(1). https://doi.org/10.4081/gh.2023.1201

Yin, H., Xu, L., Shao, Y., Li, L., & Wan, C. (2016). Relationship between suicide rate and economic growth and stock market in the People's Republic of China: 2004-2013. *Neuropsychiatric Disease and Treatment, 12*, 3119–3128. https://doi.org/10.2147/NDT.S116148

Yur'yev, A., Värnik, A., Värnik, P., Sisask, M., & Leppik, L. (2012). Role of social welfare in European suicide prevention. *International Journal of Social Welfare, 21*(1), 26–33. https://doi.org/10.1111/j.1468-2397.2010.00777.x

# Chapter 7
# War Trauma and Suicidal Behaviour

**Salahudeen Mirza, Nadine M. Melhem, James F. Leckman, and Murad M. Khan**

**Abstract** War-related traumatic experiences are globally prevalent. Traumatic stress plays a profound role in the development of suicide risk. In this chapter, we review the evidence linking war trauma to suicidal behaviour, with a focus on civilian populations which are relatively understudied as compared to veteran soldiers. We consider the specific aspects of war trauma as compared to other traumas, the documented associations between war trauma and suicidal thoughts and behaviours, refugees as a sub-population of special interest, the question of when suicide risk might emerge following war trauma, intervening mechanisms which may explain the associations, the powerful impacts of war trauma on children's development, and the implications for future research and practise. Taken together, this evidence base demonstrates that war trauma is profoundly disruptive and may contribute to further losses of life beyond the direct impacts of war-related violence. Public health efforts to reduce the burden of injuries and deaths related to suicidal behaviour must take into account the prevention of war and its related traumas.

**Keywords** War · War trauma · Armed conflict · Political violence · Traumatic stress · Refugee · Suicide prevention · Civilian · Terrorism

S. Mirza (✉) · J. F. Leckman
Child Study Centre, Yale School of Medicine, New Haven, CT, USA
e-mail: salahudeen.mirza@yale.edu

S. Mirza
Department of Psychiatry, Yale School of Medicine, New Haven, CT, USA

S. Mirza · N. M. Melhem
Department of Psychiatry, University of Pittsburgh School of Medicine, Pittsburgh, PA, USA

M. M. Khan
Brain and Mind Institute, Aga Khan University, Karachi, Sindh, Pakistan



S. M. Y. Arafat and S. K. Kar (eds.), *Ecological and Social Determinants of Suicidal Behavior*, South Asian Perspectives in Mental Health and Psychology,
https://doi.org/10.1007/978-981-96-4028-7_7

## 1 Background on War Trauma: Scope and Characteristics

War has in some way permeated much of human history. It has played a pivotal role in the establishment, development, and cessation of states and societies. Though much of war has remained consistent with time, the nature of its execution has dramatically changed. The twentieth century brought about "total war," radical advances in military technology, and a growing willingness and capability on the part of some countries to involve civilians when necessary. This can be seen clearly in the United States nuclear bombings of Hiroshima and Nagasaki, Japan, 1945, during the Second World War, in which over 200,000 Japanese, majority of civilians, are estimated to have been killed, with the survivors experiencing increased rates of disease and continued trauma which lasts to the present day (Douple et al., 2011; Yamada & Izumi, 2002).

The twentieth and twenty-first centuries also marked a growing shift toward "proxy wars," in which "uninvolved" countries provided major aid to those "involved" countries more directly involved in the fighting. Such was the case in Korea and Vietnam in the latter half of the twentieth century, proxy wars waged in Asia against the backdrop of the "Cold" War between the United States and the Soviet Union, which have culminated in over 2 million killed (Khorram-Manesh et al., 2021). The twenty-first century began with the "Global War on Terrorism," a constellation of wars led by the United States in the Middle East which continues in form today and stands at over 4.5 million dead and 38 million displaced (Watson Institute for International & Public Affairs, *Latest figures: Costs of war*, 2024). In 2023, there were 56 active state-based armed conflicts and 45 active one-sided conflicts ongoing worldwide (Kapadia, 2024). Wars which are attracting significant attention today and marked by significant mortality include the worsening of the Israel-Palestine conflict—standing at over 40,000 Palestinian civilians killed—and the worsening of the Russo-Ukrainian conflict—standing at over 30,000 Ukrainian civilians killed.

War is a profound source of trauma. Yet, the psychological impacts on civilians have often been understudied. In countries involved in wars yet wherein the populations are not directly exposed to war violence on the ground, the focus is often on veteran soldiers. Conversely, in those countries where civilians are living at constant threat of injury and death, there is a difficulty in establishing and maintaining the research infrastructure to carry out such studies. In this chapter, we review the available evidence on war trauma, with a specific focus on clarifying the contributions of war trauma among civilians to suicidal behaviour, an ultimate marker of psychological suffering.

## 2 Specific Aspects of War-Related Trauma as Compared to Other Traumas: Active Ingredients

Traumas, in whichever forms they come, hold much in common. When taking the definition proposed by the *American Psychiatric Association* in the 5th edition of the *Diagnostic and Statistical Manual of Mental Disorders* (DSM-5) (American Psychiatric Association, 2013), arguably the textbook authority on mental illness not just in the United States but throughout the world, traumatic events involve exposures, direct or indirect, to "death, threatened death, actual or threatened serious injury, or actual or threatened sexual violence." Clearly, the scope of what may be considered traumatic is broad. Exposure to potentially traumatic experiences is common (Knipscheer et al., 2020) but impacted individuals respond differently; when considering a given discrete or circumscribed chronic trauma, there is variability in how people do, with some continuing to suffer and others showing indications of resilience (Galatzer-Levy et al., 2018). However, the sequelae of early trauma can be buried deep within psychological and neurobiological circuits, with symptomatic manifestations appearing much later in life.

Traumas often co-occur. This is especially clear in the case of war. In civilian populations under assault, the significant threat of death will provoke traumatic stress (Holbrook et al., 2001). Direct physical injuries too can be traumatic both in the near- and long terms. Blast and other types of injuries can contribute to persistent chronic pain, psychological suffering, and impaired quality of life (Herrera-Escobar & Schneider, 2022). Witnessing of violence even in the absence of direct exposure alone can similarly have enduring and stressful effects (Zinzow et al., 2009). The fabric of routine life is completely destroyed in war. Workplaces, schools, higher education institutes, and community life centres are often obliterated. Uncertainty about the future, loss of loved ones, and grief all have their own traumatic impacts.

Psychological stress and physical health are closely intertwined. Poor sanitation conditions and limited access to nutritious foods and essential medications—often deliberately invoked by blockades—compromise physical health and breed psychological distress. When these circumstances are combined with overcrowding, which is often necessitated due to decreasing areas of safety, they also pave the way for infectious disease outbreaks, amplifying trauma (Marou et al., 2024). When medical facilities are not protected in bombardments, the treatment infrastructure suffers, compounding mental and physical health problems. These circumstances of threats to health coupled with the destruction of treatment infrastructures increase stress and trauma in vulnerable populations.

Coverage of war in the popular media may instil fear and provoke traumatic responses (Su et al., 2023). When war coverage involves graphic images, as it often does with increasingly uncensored footage courtesy of social media platforms, it may trigger even greater distress (Holman et al., 2024).

Importantly, the traumatic stress experienced during wartime is likely to be chronic and prolonged, as opposed to circumscribed in other cases of trauma. For example, individuals who are exposed to discrete traumas, such as a single episode of interpersonal violence, may experience post-traumatic stress related to that exposure. Individuals who are exposed to multiple, chronic, prolonged traumas also may experience post-traumatic stress, and its makeup may be more complex considering that the trauma was more extended and multi-faceted (Palic et al., 2016).

Seminal work on resilience implicated a shortlist of protective factors collectively known as "ordinary magic" due to their being part of normative (i.e., not extraordinary) adaptive processes in human development (Masten, 2014). These factors though derived with a focus on children provide a broader perspective on resilience under stress across developmental periods. Much of the shortlist focuses on support derived from interpersonal relationships and broader community systems, such as "caring family," "skilled parenting," "routines and rituals," and "well-functioning" schools and communities (Masten & Barnes, 2018). Access to these protective factors is compromised in war, facilitating greater traumatisation and potentially impairing the natural operation of resilience processes.

In summary, the trauma of war almost always has a powerful impact on an individual's mental health. The trauma of war pervades all aspects and domains of life; multiple forms of trauma build on and compound one another; the trauma is not circumscribed, being an every-day, all-day stress with no definite end in sight; protective resources are eroded, reducing buffers against trauma. This set of characteristics renders war trauma a "perfect storm" for the development of suicide risk.

## 3 Suicidal Behaviour is a Global Public Health Emergency

Suicide death is an ultimate and irreversible indication of psychological suffering. It is a global public health priority to prevent deaths by suicide. In 2019, the global toll of suicide deaths surpassed 700,000 (Suicide Worldwide in 2019, 2021). Over 75% of them occurred in lower- and middle-income countries (LMICs). LMICs are also the countries most affected by humanitarian crises including war and political violence.

Suicide is the fourth leading cause of death for ages 15–29 years, as well as 15–19 years (Suicide Worldwide in 2019, 2021). The World Health Organisation (WHO) Comprehensive Mental Health Action Plan 2013–2030 set a global target of one-third reduction in suicide death rate by 2030. The United Nations Sustainable Development Goals (SDGs) similarly include a global target of one-third reduction in mortality due to non-communicable diseases (including suicide death) by 2030. Though suicide death rates have been declining over the past two decades, they are not declining rapidly enough to reach these targets (Pirkis et al., 2024). Addressing the issue of suicide death requires concerted efforts across countries including prioritisation of LMICs.

Preventing suicide death on a global scale requires a public health-based approach (Pirkis et al., 2024). Central to this approach is a recognition that *social determinants of health*, such as trauma, play a major role in the development of suicidal behaviour.

Preventing death by suicide must require a combination of universal, selective, and indicated interventions (Pirkis et al., 2024). Universal interventions are aimed at decreasing risk and increasing protection among the entire population, not just those already showing an elevated risk for suicide. Selective interventions have similar aims, but they are focused on those who show signs of risk or predisposition to suicidal behaviour. Indicated interventions are more specialised and target those who are already showing signs of suicidal behaviour. An effective approach to suicide prevention recognises that each of these arms is needed, so as to capture individuals across the spectrum of risk within the population.

As we will show, war trauma is a highly relevant yet understudied target when considering lever points at which to engage suicide prevention and intervention strategies. Universal, selective, and indicated interventions all have a place when it comes to minimising the impacts of war trauma on suicide risk. Prior to considering these strategies, identifying the relationship between war trauma and suicide, the intervening mechanisms, and modifying characteristics, is crucial to developing an understanding of how vulnerable populations can best be supported.

## 4 Documented Associations Between War Trauma and Suicidal Behaviour

Traumatic experiences *en masse* are among the most robustly implicated risk factors in the development of suicidal behaviour, which is particularly significant given that there are very few such risk factors which are so well supported by the evidence base. Starting more broadly than war-specific trauma, traumatic stress, such as that demonstrated to meet a diagnosis of post-traumatic stress disorder (PTSD), is robustly associated with suicidal thoughts and behaviours. The meta-analytic evidence demonstrates that PTSD, across civilian and non-civilian populations, carries a relative risk (RR) of 2.09 for suicide death, RR of 4.05 for suicide attempt, and RR of 2.91 for suicidal ideation (Akbar et al., 2023). Similarly, a Swedish national cohort study of 3.1 million people linked medical diagnosis of PTSD to suicide death with a hazard ratio (HR) of 4.28, with a stronger association among women (Fox et al., 2021). Traumas during childhood, often captured by measurement of child abuse and neglect, are similarly highly and repeatedly implicated in suicide risk, with child abuse carrying odds ratio (OR) of 2.09 for suicide attempt and OR of 2.66 for suicidal ideation (Angelakis et al., 2019).

Historically, war was one of the earliest recognised sociological factors involved in suicide risk. However, the early conclusion was actually that war is protective, rather than a risk factor. In his 1897 seminal work on the social underpinnings of suicide, the French sociologist Emile Durkheim claimed, based on observations of empirical data from European countries such as Austria, Italy, Denmark, Saxony, France, and Germany, that suicide rates decrease during wartime (Durkheim, 2005). For example, war between Austria and Italy in 1866 led to decreases in suicide rates of

14% in both countries. Durkheim continued to argue that this decrease only occurs in "great national wars," which inspire popular passions and presumably increase societal integration, as opposed to "political wars," which do not rouse the people to band together to a similar extent. Among the great national wars, he listed the Franco-Prussian War (1870–71) as an example, while an example of a political war would be the Crimean War (1853–56)—with data, Durkheim somewhat convincingly showed that great national wars were more strongly associated with a decrease in suicide death rate, powering his theory that suicide is inversely related to societal integration. Further, decreases in suicide death rate were most pronounced in subregions within which the population was more closely engaged with the war, such as cities.

About 100 years later, a number of studies continued to replicate this basic pattern. When the armed forces size was used as a proxy for military involvement there was tentative evidence for an inverse association with suicide death rates from 1933 to 86 in the United States (Lester & Yang, 1991). Data from multiple (predominantly European) nations before, during, and after the First and Second World Wars demonstrated a decline in suicide rates during wartime whether the countries were officially participating in war or not (Lester, 1994). Data from France across 1826–1913 likewise showed lower suicide rates during periods of war as compared to peace (Lester, 1993). These conclusions have in some ways powered a continued assumption that war decreases suicides. We hope to show that this assumption is fundamentally misguided, or at least incomplete. Indeed, others already have to some extent, such as one argument that war does not increase societal integration for all, and may even prompt expectations of exclusion for some vulnerable groups—leading to some subgroup increases in suicide death rates (van Tubergen & Ultee, 2006). We aim to go further in arguing that if anything, war actually increases suicide risk in some subgroups based on exposure and characteristics of the affected subgroups.

A fundamental distinction must be made between a country's involvement in war and the people's experiences of war *trauma*. In these early studies, the relationship between war and suicide was assessed at the population level: "war" as an exposure was operationalised as the time period during which the country was involved in war, and suicide was coarsely captured in national suicide death rates. The nature of war has substantially changed since Durkheim's time. For one, exposure of civilians to war-related violence is more common today. In the time leading to Durkheim's analysis, "total war" and the killing of civilians were less rampant. Though the impacts of war could still reverberate through the population of a warring country, the violence did not have the reach that it does today. This also increases the scope of civilian traumatisation possible in a present-day war. Proxy wars, enabled by advances in military technology such as long-range missiles, can involve the total traumatisation of one "warring" civilian population while minimal impact to another. For example, during the United States War on Iraq (2003–2011) upward of 200,000 Iraqi civilians were killed on Iraqi soil, as compared to no American civilians on United States soil. Durkheim's analysis, aside from being confined to the time in which he conducted them, did not capture the experiences of those directly exposed to violent terror, as the majority of civilians included in his studies likely did not experience direct exposures to wartime violence. They also do not capture the variability inherent in these exposures—that the severity of exposures may vary within a population, and that the variability of these exposures may be meaningfully related to mental health outcomes within the affected population.

Additionally, focusing only on national suicide death rates to some extent washes out some of the heterogeneity expected if we purport that not all members of the population of a warring country are equally affected by war trauma. Finally, Durkheim's analyses and many others focused predominantly on high-income European countries. However, the countries most impacted by the violence and destruction of war are LMICs, and LMICs also bear the burden of global suicide deaths. These countries for a variety of reasons have been almost completely underrepresented in the research to date, but as we will describe in some studies below there is still some data from them to paint a picture which contrasts with depicting war as protective.

We also revisit Durkheim's analysis of the mechanisms underlying war's supposed protective effects. Does war really promote societal integration, as Durkheim argued in the case of "great national wars"—those which rally the people and bring them together for a common cause? We argue that in the present day, the great national war is dead. If such wars are defined by their bringing together of society, we have seen nothing but the opposite in recent years. A starting point is to consider the response to war in higher-income countries such as the United States. The War in Vietnam (1955–75) brought about nationwide protests; division arose over the issue of withdrawal of troops during the War in Afghanistan (2001–2021); and American public support is waning for the Russo-Ukrainian War (2014–) and the Israeli War on Gaza (2023–), with large-scale protests over American involvement in the latter war. Also, compared to the wars which Durkheim studied, modern wars have a particularly strong colonial-imperial character—they are uneven, and one country often bears the brunt of the suffering in terms of violence and deaths. We cannot expect that societal integration will increase in all belligerent countries. Civil wars and other internal humanitarian crises—which prevail especially in LMICs—similarly divide, instead of unite, the people. A comprehensive and recent review of the literature suggests that war harms social cohesion (Fiedler, 2023).

We searched the literature for studies which focussed on civilians exposed to war and associations with suicidal thoughts and behaviours. Below we present some powerful and compelling studies which further our understanding of war's impacts at a more granular level.

In Lebanon (an LMIC), civil war in 1975–1989 resulted in injury to about 15% of the population, and wider-spread exposure to trauma. Drawing on data from 2002 to 2003, over 10 years post-war, Karam and colleagues studied the associations among ten specific war exposures and suicidal ideation, plans, and attempts, among a sample of 2857 adults randomly selected to be nationally representative of the population of Lebanon (Karam et al., 2012). Suicidal ideation, plans, and attempts were most likely to emerge post-war (ORs = 2.4–4.0), as opposed to pre-war or peri-war. Further, being a civilian in a terror region during the war was significantly associated with subsequent onset of suicidal ideation (OR = 3.1) and suicide attempt (OR = 4.0), and witnessing atrocities was significantly associated with subsequent onset of suicide attempt (OR = 3.0). The association between impulse-control disorders and suicide attempt was strengthened among individuals exposed to these war-related experiences.

In the former Yugoslavia, war during the 1990s involved substantial harms to civilians. Drawing on data from 2005 to 2006, Jankovic and colleagues studied the relationship between war traumatic events and suicidality, when adjusting for other significant risk factors, among a sample of 3313 randomly sampled adult residents of five Balkan countries (four LMICs) and 854 refugees in three Western European countries, all originally from the former Yugoslavia (Jankovic et al., 2013). In the main sample, the number of potentially traumatic war events (total possible 24; the average was 4.2) was significantly associated with suicidal ideation and/or plans and/or attempt (aOR = 1.1). When war traumatic events were considered individually, war-related imprisonment (4% of main sample) was significantly associated with suicidal ideation and/or plans and/or attempt (aOR = 3.0). These associations remained significant in the refugee sample (19% of the refugee sample endorsed war-related imprisonment).

In Ukraine (an LMIC), Russian invasion beginning in 2014 led to a war that did not affect geographical regions evenly in the early phase. The Donetsk region in eastern Ukraine was affected, while the Kirovograd region in central Ukraine was unaffected, powering a study of the impact of war exposures on adolescent suicide risk based on the variability in exposures. Drawing on data from 2016 to 2017, Sourander and colleagues studied the relationship between region (war-affected versus unaffected) and war trauma exposure with suicidality and/or self-harm among a sample of 2752 (1449 war-affected) Ukrainian adolescents recruited from public schools (Sourander et al., 2024). Girls (aOR = 2.3) and boys (aOR = 1.4) in the war-affected region showed higher rates of suicidality and/or self-harm. In more demarcated analyses focussing on suicide attempt, suicidal ideation, and self-harm separately, girls in the war-affected region showed higher rates of all three (aORs 1.6–2.6), while boys in the war-affected region showed higher rates of suicidal ideation (aOR = 1.7). Among adolescents living in the war-affected region, the number of war trauma exposures was associated with suicidality and/or self-harm, with adolescents endorsing 5 + exposures showing the strongest risk (aOR = 3.2). When considering specific exposures, the highest odds were for being a victim of violence or used as a human shield (aOR = 3.4), finding it difficult to adapt to a new location (aOR = 2.6), and experiencing forced separation from parents or family members (aOR = 2.5).

In Eastern Uganda (an LMIC), various forms of civil conflicts have been ongoing, including killings, torture, displacement, and major disruptions to the social fabric of life. Kinyanda and colleagues studied the relationship between war-related psychosocial factors and lifetime suicide attempt among a sample of 1560 randomly selected adults from four subcounties of war-affected Eastern Uganda (Kinyanda et al., 2013). Sexual torture was significantly associated with suicide attempt in males (12% of males had sexual torture, OR = 2.49) and females (19% of females had sexual torture, OR = 1.92). When other predictors were included in a multivariate model, sexual torture became nonsignificant, which led the authors to include that the effects of sexual torture on suicide attempt may be indirect through their impacts on psychological, medical, and psychosocial processes.

## 5 Refugees as a Sub-Population of Special Interest

Refugees are a special sub-population of individuals impacted by war who have physically left the original conflict zone for other destinations, though these destinations themselves are not always completely safe havens. Refugees experience a complex combination of traumatic stressors, including traumatic experiences during war and prior to migration as well as stressors associated with the migration and resettlement. The pressures of acculturation and adaptation to a novel context may compound earlier traumas. However, their mental health may also benefit from targeted systems of support, facilitating resilience after trauma. Being physically removed from war zones may provide better opportunities for the operation of adaptive resilience processes, though of course trauma has enduring effects.

Though there are a number of studies characterising suicidal thoughts and behaviours and refugees and displaced peoples more broadly, a systematic review of 77 studies found that only 8 identified studies compared the refugee groups to the host population (Cogo et al., 2022). Importantly, the majority of studies focussed on this topic were concerned with suicidal ideation, as opposed to suicide attempt or suicide death. The evidence tentatively suggested that refugees granted asylum may show lower rates of suicidal behaviour. But at the same time, those living in camps or seeking asylum showed concerning signs of higher risk. Asylum-seeking reflects those who are seeking refugee status but have not yet been granted it; these individuals experience high uncertainty and distress. Meta-analysis of 11 studies estimated the prevalence of 21% for suicidal ideation and 0.6% for suicide attempt among refugees and asylum-seekers (Haase et al., 2022). Though these estimates were not directly compared with general population in the same study, comparison to the literature suggests higher burden of suicidal ideation in refugees and asylum-seekers.

Large nationwide cohort studies add to the picture of refugee mental health, and focussing on some specific results is helpful. In one study, three nationwide cohorts of about 5 million Swedish-born and refugee individuals (mostly from Muslim-Majority Countries) each were followed up for 4–9 years (Amin et al., 2021). Refugees showed a lower rate of suicide attempt overall (HR = 0.82) though some subgroups such as those from Iran showed higher risk (HR = 1.66). They also tended to show a lower rate of suicide deaths though this effect was less convincing (HR = 0.64). A follow-up study of all Swedish individuals treated for suicide attempt in specialised healthcare settings (upward of 85,000 suicide attempters) found that refugees utilised less specialised healthcare than the Swedish-born population prior to and following the suicide attempt, possibly presenting one explanatory mechanism or at least an interventional target (Amin et al., 2021). In a Dutch population study focused on asylum-seekers (as opposed to those granted refugee status) versus the Dutch population collectively followed up over 79 million person-years, asylum-seekers showed higher rates of suicide death (rate ratio = 2.00) and self-harm behaviour (rate ratio = 1.42) compared to the Dutch population, but in males only (Goosen et al., 2011). Asylum procedure and transfer between centres were noted as a source of stress related to self-harm behaviour in nearly 40% of cases.

Palestinian refugees have been displaced within their own communities under Israeli occupation and often placed in camps in neighbouring countries which are also struggling with their own humanitarian challenges. Though they are technically considered "refugees" they may be different in important ways from other refugees who arrive in comparatively higher-income countries such as those refugees who re-settled in Sweden and appear to be "protected." Prior to the onset of the new war in 2023, Itani and colleagues studied the prevalence and associated characteristics of suicidal ideation and planning among 14,303 Palestinian middle school students living in occupied Palestinian territory or United Nations Relief and Works Agency (UNRWA) refugee camps (Itani et al., 2017). The Palestinian middle school students showed a 26% prevalence of suicidal ideation and/or planning, a higher rate than other countries in the region. This high prevalence is concerning and suggests that refugee children in this region who are likely exposed to continuing trauma are a high priority. To our knowledge, further study has not been possible after the onset of the ongoing war on Gaza, and suicide prevention must be an even higher priority now considering the mass traumatisation of the already vulnerable Palestinian people.

More evidence on refugee and asylum-seeking populations is needed to better understand the evolution of war trauma's impacts on suicide risk. For example, what aspects of the resettlement process can be targeted to maximise the protection of these clearly vulnerable populations? Why do refugees overall—at least in higher-income countries—appear to show a lower risk of suicidal behaviour despite their high burden of trauma? It could be that those individuals who are able to attain refugee status are different in some ways from those who stay behind (Elshahat et al., 2022). Also, becoming a refugee may come with support systems that facilitate resilience. Regardless, trauma-informed care and an awareness of suicide prevention strategies is a necessity when dealing with refugee populations.

## 6 Timescale of War Trauma's Sequelae

It is worth asking, if war trauma does increase the risk for suicidal behaviour, when does that risk eventuate? We have already noted that in one study (Karam et al., 2012), the emergence of suicidal thoughts and behaviours was mostly tied to post-war as opposed to peri-war period, at least according to retrospective recall. Could it be possible that the drive to survive against external threats to life in the midst of an active war zone supersedes suicidal urges, such that they only express themselves later? Overall, there has been a paucity of studies overall which have been able to systematically explore this question with sound data. Most studies that we have explored are only able to reach participants years after the traumatic exposures, so the onset point of suicidal thoughts and behaviours is unclear. When assessment and measurement are compromised during wartime, good data collection and risk ascertainment may only be possible sometime later. Though, in some studies which we covered the research teams were able to capture populations who were actively living through war trauma, showing concurrent links to suicide risk (Kinyanda et al., 2013; Sourander et al., 2024). Similarly, a review of reviews found a high burden of mental health problems in individuals *presently* living in conflict zones—though suicide was not an explicit focus (Carpiniello, 2023).

Moving beyond the measurement limitations inherent in wartime, could there still be cases in which the negative sequelae only show themselves later? In one systematic review of 42 populations under study for the development of PTSD, 29 populations showed delayed-onset PTSD symptom trajectories (Bonde et al., 2022). Individuals with more severe exposures to trauma were more likely to show these delayed-onset trajectories. In peacekeeping soldiers, retrospective recall of warzone exposures increased from post-deployment to follow-up 1–3 years later, suggesting that symptoms may become worse with time (Roemer et al., 1998). Perhaps populations exposed to war trauma may include subgroups who also show delayed onsets of more problematic profiles, including delayed expression of suicidal behaviour. It will take more focused and rigorous research to better clarify the time-scale evolution of risk development. In the meantime, though, early identification, prevention, and intervention strategies are the best way to interrupt the development of suicidal behaviour before it is too late—perhaps even if there are no explicit signs at the time of assessment.

## 7 Mechanisms by Which War Trauma May Elevate Suicide Risk

Various theories of suicide provide space for the consideration of the effects of war trauma. Within the framework of the Interpersonal Theory (IPT) of Suicide (Van Orden et al., 2010), traumatic experiences may drive suicide risk by promoting social alienation (thwarted belongingness: "*I am alone*") and leading individuals to feel less wanted or valuable (perceived burdensomeness: "*I am a burden*"). Further, they may facilitate the acquired capability for suicide, consisting of an increased tolerance of pain and a reduced fear of death. People exposed to war violence are exposed to a greater burden of "painful and provocative experiences," and as they encounter death and the concept of death more often this may reduce its unfamiliarity and the associated fear.

Consultation of the Three-Step Theory (3ST) of Suicide (Klonsky et al., 2021) similarly reveals pathways by which war trauma may pave the way for suicide risk. Within the 3ST, suicidal desires emerge from pain and hopelessness (1) and the triumph of pain over connectedness (2), with culmination in suicide attempt if there is the capability for suicide (3). People traumatised by war suffer from psychological and physical pain and hopelessness (1); often lose family, friends, and communities which provide them with connectedness, including when they are able to flee to a different location (2); and as described in context of the IPT, they may show greater acquired capability for suicide (3).

Another theory, the Integrated Motivational-Volitional (IMV) Model of Suicidal Behaviour (O'Connor & Kirtley, 2018), stratifies the development of suicidal behaviour into three stages: pre-motivational phase (background), motivational phase (ideation/intention formation), and volitional phase (behavioural enaction). Aspects of war trauma which may promote movement along this trajectory include the exposure to adverse events (pre-motivational), development of social and cognitive problems (motivational), and acquired capability (volitional). In the classical stress-diathesis paradigm (van Heeringen, 2012), in which suicide risk is purported to arise from an interplay between more enduring risk factors and stressful activators, war traumatic experiences could fit in both as diatheses and stressors. Chronically traumatic experiences earlier or even later in life could embed themselves as diatheses by their impacts on developing neurocognitive, socio-emotional, and biological systems, increasing trait vulnerability; war traumas as states could also activate risk on top of pre-existing diatheses.

Biological aspects of stress response have received significant attention as possible mediators of the effects of trauma on suicide risk. The hypothalamic–pituitary–adrenal (HPA) axis is a neuroendocrine system often studied as a physiological indication of stress response and exposure (Gunnar & Quevedo, 2008). Activation of the HPA axis begins with registration of threat in the brain, which cascades downward with the ultimate production of cortisol by the adrenal glands (Smith & Vale, 2006). Peripheral cortisol levels typically rise in response to psychological stressors. Cortisol has some helpful effects in energy mobilisation, and sufficient activation of the HPA axis is necessary for an adaptive stress response. However, prolonged high levels of cortisol can be physiologically damaging.

In adults exposed to war, hair cortisol concentrations (HCCs) were elevated (Etwel et al., 2014; Fischer et al., 2017; Steudte et al., 2011). In Syrian refugee children, HCCs were elevated in those with more war-related traumatic exposures (strongest in older children), but they decreased with time elapsed since the exposures (Smeeth et al., 2023). Urinary cortisol levels were decreased in adult survivors of the Holocaust with PTSD (Yehuda et al., 1995). Over time, urinary cortisol levels increased in those whose PTSD symptoms improved (Yehuda et al., 2007). Overall, there also appear to be decreases in peripheral cortisol levels in the offspring of Holocaust survivors with PTSD, suggesting a transgenerational impact of war trauma (Yehuda & Bierer, 2008).

A history of suicide attempt has been associated with decreased salivary cortisol response to psychological stress (Melhem et al., 2016). Further, an innovative study used hair cortisol concentrations as a proxy for cortisol levels prior to suicide attempt, finding evidence that cortisol levels were decreased before the attempt was made (Melhem et al., 2017). Taken together, there is at the least a compelling role for the HPA axis in the pathophysiology of war traumatic stress, though it is less clear from the individual studies considered if there is any consistent effect mediating the relationship between war trauma and suicide risk. To better understand this potential relationship, more studies are needed assessing aspects of war traumatic stress, HPA axis physiology, and suicidal thoughts and behaviours together.

Epigenetic alterations, in which patterns of gene expression are enduringly modified by early life experiences, are often under focus (McGowan & Szyf, 2010). Epigenetic changes may be one mechanism by which early adverse experiences get "under the skin" to propagate the impact of trauma. In early studies where childhood abuse was the traumatic exposure, the glucocorticoid receptor (*NR3C1*) promoter, a key gene in the HPA axis, was more methylated in hippocampus of suicide decedents with history of childhood abuse as opposed to suicide decedents without history of childhood abuse, concomitant with increased gene expression (McGowan et al., 2009). This study kickstarted a number of studies considering the epigenetics of trauma and suicide, but we have been unable to identify any rigorous studies which carefully measure war traumatic exposures, indices of epigenetic modifications such as DNA methylation, and suicidal thoughts and behaviours. This too is a gap in the literature for better understanding of the underlying biological mechanisms.

However, at the time of publishing this chapter, we did identify a novel study focussed on buccal cell DNA methylation changes associated with germline, prenatal, and direct exposures to violence across three generations of Syrian refugees (Mulligan et al., 2025). Violence exposures included the 1980 Hama city massacre and the 2011 Syrian uprising and conflicts. Epigenome-wide association study of methylation at >850,000 CpG genomic sites revealed 14 CpG sites associated with germline exposures and 21 CpG sites associated with direct exposures to war-related violence. Results supported a dose-response relationship of higher trauma burden being associated with larger-magnitude changes in DNA methylation at the implicated CpG sites. Children exposed to war-related violence pre-natally also showed an accelerated pattern of biological aging. These results importantly provide strong evidence for biological impacts of war-related violence exposures and further that they can cascade across generations. However, the question remains whether these peripheral DNA methylation changes impact brain functioning or contribute to mental health problems including suicide risk. Aside from the paucity of molecular genetic studies, we did not identify any neuro-imaging studies focussed on the impacts of war trauma on brain structure and function in civilians. This understanding would also be critical to refining an understanding of mechanism; though neuro-imaging studies abound in veteran populations, the nature of the trauma may not parallel that in civilians.

## 8 War Trauma as an Assault on Children's Development: Relation to a Lifespan Developmental Perspective on Suicide Risk

Though all lose in war, children are the biggest losers (Bürgin et al., 2022). The assaults of war on children's development lay the seeds for a lifetime of dysfunction. Early developmental trauma is a robust risk factor for suicidal behaviour (Vidal-Ribas et al., 2024). Indeed, a lifespan perspective on suicide risk includes the understanding that the pathways to suicide begin early in (and sometimes even prior to) life. Early adverse experiences can have "sleeper effects" that persist years later (Holmes, 2013). When considering that in most cases, the civilian populations in countries directly affected by war-related violence are predominantly made up of youth, the urgency of documenting and disseminating the psychiatric and public health consequences of war trauma as a developmentally toxic stressor is clear. Interrupting pathways of risk early on is also paramount.

There is very limited research on war trauma in childhood and later suicide risk. Our primary call then is to increase the number of studies focussed on this area. Some youth-focused studies were covered earlier. How could childhood war trauma contribute to the risk of suicide? As we have mentioned, childhood is a sensitive time. The brain is plastic, and further, the early experiences within relationships play a foundational role in the establishment of the self and basic formation of self-regulation. Environmental unpredictability and danger can also compromise neurocognitive development. One study found that refugee children exposed to war trauma showed increased sustained attention to threat (Michalek et al., 2022), which could start them on a path toward suicide risk. When children are directly involved in war violence as child soldiers, they may experience especially complex traumatic experiences related to personal engagement in violence, maltreatment, and stigma (Betancourt et al., 2020; Kohrt et al., 2008). The extent to which these experiences lead them to feel hopeless, alone, or burdensome must be controlled to prevent the development of suicide risk. Targeting former child soldiers to improve family and community connections as well as reduce stigmatisation may be essential to promoting their mental health (Betancourt et al., 2020).

War traumatic exposures can harm children even when they are not direct. The children of refugee parents with PTSD themselves show a higher risk for psychiatric disorders; this association exists even when the children are not refugees themselves (Back Nielsen et al., 2019). This might suggest that strategies to support war-affected parents' own mental health are essential to prevent the transgenerational negative sequelae of war trauma. The three-generation epigenetic study of Syrian refugee families provides further evidence for transgenerational consequences of war trauma stretching back all the way to the experiences of grandparents (Mulligan et al., 2025). Further, coverage of war in the media can be exceptionally distressing for children (Pfefferbaum et al., 2020). Increasing awareness of the potentially harmful impacts of media coverage of war for children, parental engagement in children's media consumption, and referral options for children experiencing distress may be helpful ways to prevent this distress from increasing more serious risk.

Multi-level, resilience-oriented trauma prevention, and intervention approaches are essential to promoting child development in war-affected populations. As highlighted in a recent editorial in the *European Child and Adolescent Psychiatry (*Bürgin et al., 2022*)*, the impact of war and forced displacement not only has an immediate negative impact, but it can lead to PTSD, anxiety, and depressive disorders. This is especially true when the child is separated from their parents and other family members. Ideally, the children and their families should receive evidence-based interventions as soon as possible. Sadly, war-exposed parents often show less warmth and more harshness toward their children (Eltanamly et al., 2021).

One of the authors (J.L.F.) provides insight based on collaborative efforts to global peace-building, with a focus on early childhood development. These strategies, though not explicitly indicated for suicide prevention, may help ameliorate risk and promote better mental health, providing protective buffers against suicide. Despite the tragic realities of the current conflicts in the Middle East, some members of Palestinian and Israeli communities have created organisations that bring together individuals from both sides of the divide. One of these organisations is the Parents Circle—Families Forum. All of the members of this organisation have lost an immediate family member to the ongoing conflict. An organisation that brings together individuals who have fought on both sides of the divide in Israel and Palestine is Combatants for Peace (PfP). PfP is a grassroots movement that works to end the occupation of the West Bank and Gaza and to bring peace, equality and freedom to their homeland. Women Wage Peace is the largest grassroots peace movement in Israel. Last but not least, there is an Italian NGO—Empowerment and Resilience for Children Everywhere—that brings together child and adolescent mental health professionals from both sides of the divide to conduct training programs for their colleagues to benefit the children affected by the ongoing conflict.

An international organisation devoted to building a more peaceful world is the Early Childhood Peace Consortium (ECPC), where "all children are the stars of today and leaders of tomorrow." The ECPC is a global consortium of United Nations agencies, NGOs, academia, and practitioners focused on sharing scientific and practice-based evidence on how investment in early childhood development (ECD) can contribute to sustainable peace, social cohesion, and social justice. They recognise that investing in ECD can be a powerful and cost-effective strategy for reducing violence, poverty, and exclusion and for building peaceful societies across the world (Britto et al., 2021; Leckman et al., 2021).

## 9 The Way Forward and Shorter-Term and Longer-Term Strategies to Bolster Resilience in Wartime Contexts

Considering that war is a complex issue which researchers may only dream of fully preventing, there must be a set of strategies which at the least ameliorate its impacts. We have already integrated some of these points throughout the Chapter but presenting them together may be helpful. To the extent that researchers, politicians, and other bodies are able to document and disseminate the harmful impacts of war on suicide risk, they should continue to do so. There is a pressing need for more detailed and rigorous studies exploring the associations between forms of war trauma and suicide risk as well as the intervening mechanisms. This gap is especially apparent when focusing on civilians as opposed to veterans—as we have done so in this Chapter. Though research in general on mechanisms is lacking, there is especially a lack of research on biological mechanisms which may be helpful. We are also lacking compelling information on interventions which may work to reduce suicide risk in war-traumatised populations, such as randomised controlled trials.

Coverage of war in the media should be carefully controlled to prevent further distress and traumatisation. Though it may be difficult to screen for mental health concerns in populations living in active war zones, this should be a high priority of humanitarian agencies. Refugees should similarly be regularly assessed for signs of suicide risk and not assumed to be protected against the development of suicidal behaviour. Evidence that suicidal behaviour may emerge in the post-war period warrants close follow-up even in situations where the direct exposure to war trauma is waning.

Children and youth must be prioritised in responses to minimise the impacts of trauma considering the strong associations of early life trauma with suicide risk. As has been revealed in studies of resilience, supporting the normative adaptive processes which operate in recovery from adversity may be sufficient (Masten, 2014). This would include promoting children's connections with supporting figures and nurturing their development of self-regulation skills.

Universal, selective, and indicated interventions all may have a role to play (Pirkis et al., 2024). Universal strategies may include efforts to promote mental health in the general war-affected population. They can borrow from strategies in other contexts, such as the development of social safety nets and means restrictions, and the prevention of continued trauma such as by some strategies outlined above. Selective strategies might include targeting of war-affected individuals who show concerningly high burdens of trauma and other markers of risk for suicidal behaviour such as lacking social connections, endorsement of suicidal ideation or hopelessness, and signs of capability. These interventions may aspire to address aspects of distress and minimise trauma as well as provide counselling to reduce co-morbid mental health concerns. Indicated interventions focussed on those at the highest risk for suicide death as well as those who have engaged in self-harm might integrate trauma-informed care practises and continue efforts to address trauma burden while also providing suicide-specific treatments to the extent that they are available.

LMICs are of particular focus considering that they bear the brunt of both war trauma and suicide deaths yet they are deprived of surveillance and treatment infrastructure when compared to higher-income countries. National suicide prevention strategies should consider the impact of war trauma and strategies to reduce the burden of violence.

## 10 Conclusion: Addressing War Trauma Must be Part of a Global Suicide Prevention Strategy

In this chapter, we reviewed evidence that war trauma must be considered as a source of suicidal behaviour risk. When considering efforts around the world to reduce deaths by suicide, we are committing a great mistake if we do not consider the impact of war, especially in LMICs. This is yet another reason, of many reasons, to advocate for peacebuilding and the reduction of armed conflicts. It is also a call for suicide prevention and intervention delivery to war-affected individuals and communities. Finally, our review suggests numerous areas where research is lacking. Having a more complete knowledge base on the impact of civilian war trauma on suicidal behaviour will be essential to moving these efforts beyond documentation to policy-making, prevention, and intervention.

## References


Akbar, R., Arya, V., Conroy, E., Wilcox, H. C., & Page, A. (2023). Posttraumatic stress disorder and risk of suicidal behavior: A systematic review and meta-analysis. *Suicide & Life-Threatening Behavior, 53*(1), 163–184. https://doi.org/10.1111/sltb.12931

American Psychiatric Association. (2013). Diagnostic and statistical manual of mental disorders (5th ed.). https://doi.org/10.1176/appi.books.9780890425596

Amin, R., Helgesson, M., Runeson, B., Tinghög, P., Mehlum, L., Qin, P., Holmes, E. A., & Mittendorfer-Rutz, E. (2021). Suicide attempt and suicide in refugees in Sweden - A nationwide population-based cohort study. *Psychological Medicine, 51*(2), 254–263. https://doi.org/10.1017/S0033291719003167

Amin, R., Rahman, S., Tinghög, P., Helgesson, M., Runeson, B., Björkenstam, E., Qin, P., Mehlum, L., Holmes, E. A., & Mittendorfer-Rutz, E. (2021). Healthcare use before and after suicide attempt in refugees and Swedish-born individuals. *Social Psychiatry and Psychiatric Epidemiology, 56*(2), 325–338. https://doi.org/10.1007/s00127-020-01902-z

Angelakis, I., Gillespie, E. L., & Panagioti, M. (2019). Childhood maltreatment and adult suicidality: A comprehensive systematic review with meta-analysis. *Psychological Medicine, 49*(07), 1057–1078. https://doi.org/10.1017/s0033291718003823

Back Nielsen, M., Carlsson, J., Køster Rimvall, M., Petersen, J. H., & Norredam, M. (2019). Risk of childhood psychiatric disorders in children of refugee parents with post-traumatic stress disorder: A nationwide, register-based, cohort study. *The Lancet Public Health, 4*(7), e353–e359. https://doi.org/10.1016/S2468-2667(19)30077-5

Betancourt, T. S., Thomson, D. L., Brennan, R. T., Antonaccio, C. M., Gilman, S. E., & VanderWeele, T. J. (2020). Stigma and acceptance of Sierra Leone's child soldiers: A prospective longitudinal study of adult mental health and social functioning. *Journal of the American Academy of Child and Adolescent Psychiatry, 59*(6), 715–726. https://doi.org/10.1016/j.jaac.2019.05.026

Bonde, J. P. E., Jensen, J. H., Smid, G. E., Flachs, E. M., Elklit, A., Mors, O., & Videbech, P. (2022). Time course of symptoms in posttraumatic stress disorder with delayed expression: A systematic review. *Acta Psychiatrica Scandinavica, 145*(2), 116–131. https://doi.org/10.1111/acps.13372

Britto, P. R., Hanöz-Penney, S., Ponguta, L. A., Sunar, D., Issa, G., Hein, S. D., do Rosário, M. C., Almuneef, M. A., Korucu, I., Togo, Y., Kurbonov, J., Choibekov, N., Phan, H. T. T., Fallon, N. S., Artukoğlu, B. B., Hartl, F. J., Salah, R., Fitzpatrick, S., Connolly, P., & Leckman, J. F. (2021). Pathways to a more peaceful and sustainable world: The transformative power of children in families. *Development and Psychopathology, 33*(2), 409–420. https://doi.org/10.1017/S0954579420000681

Bürgin, D., Anagnostopoulos, D., Vitiello, B., Sukale, T., Schmid, M., & Fegert, J. M. (2022). Impact of war and forced displacement on children's mental health-multilevel, needs-oriented, and trauma-informed approaches. *European Child & Adolescent Psychiatry, 31*(6), 845–853. https://doi.org/10.1007/s00787-022-01974-z

Carpiniello, B. (2023). The mental health costs of armed conflicts-A review of systematic reviews conducted on refugees, asylum-seekers and people living in war zones. *International Journal of Environmental Research and Public Health, 20*(4). https://doi.org/10.3390/ijerph20042840

Cogo, E., Murray, M., Villanueva, G., Hamel, C., Garner, P., Senior, S. L., & Henschke, N. (2022). Suicide rates and suicidal behaviour in displaced people: A systematic review. *PloS One, 17*(3), e0263797. https://doi.org/10.1371/journal.pone.0263797

Douple, E. B., Mabuchi, K., Cullings, H. M., Preston, D. L., Kodama, K., Shimizu, Y., Fujiwara, S., & Shore, R. E. (2011). Long-term radiation-related health effects in a unique human population: Lessons learned from the atomic bomb survivors of Hiroshima and Nagasaki. *Disaster Medicine and Public Health Preparedness, 5 Suppl 1*(0 1), S122–S133. https://doi.org/10.1001/dmp.2011.21

Durkheim, E. (2005). *Suicide: A Study in Sociology* (2nd ed.). Routledge. https://doi.org/10.4324/9780203994320

Elshahat, S., Moffat, T., & Newbold, K. B. (2022). Understanding the healthy immigrant effect in the context of mental health challenges: A systematic critical review. *Journal of Immigrant and Minority Health, 24*(6), 1564–1579. https://doi.org/10.1007/s10903-021-01313-5

Eltanamly, H., Leijten, P., Jak, S., & Overbeek, G. (2021). Parenting in times of war: A meta-analysis and qualitative synthesis of war exposure, parenting, and child adjustment. *Trauma, Violence & Abuse, 22*(1), 147–160. https://doi.org/10.1177/1524838019833001

Etwel, F., Russell, E., Rieder, M. J., Van Uum, S. H., & Koren, G. (2014). Hair cortisol as a biomarker of stress in the 2011 Libyan war. *Clinical and Investigative Medicine. Medecine Clinique et Experimentale, 37*(6), E403–E408. https://doi.org/10.25011/cim.v37i6.22245

Fiedler, C. (2023). What do we know about How armed conflict affects social cohesion? A review of the empirical literature. *International Studies Review, 25*(3), viad030. https://doi.org/10.1093/isr/viad030

Fischer, S., Duncko, R., Hatch, S. L., Papadopoulos, A., Goodwin, L., Frissa, S., Hotopf, M., & Cleare, A. J. (2017). Sociodemographic, lifestyle, and psychosocial determinants of hair cortisol in a South London community sample. *Psychoneuroendocrinology, 76*, 144–153. https://doi.org/10.1016/j.psyneuen.2016.11.011

Fox, V., Dalman, C., Dal, H., Hollander, A.-C., Kirkbride, J. B., & Pitman, A. (2021). Suicide risk in people with post-traumatic stress disorder: A cohort study of 3.1 million people in Sweden. *Journal of Affective Disorders, 279*, 609–616. https://doi.org/10.1016/j.jad.2020.10.009

Galatzer-Levy, I. R., Huang, S. H., & Bonanno, G. A. (2018). Trajectories of resilience and dysfunction following potential trauma: A review and statistical evaluation. *Clinical Psychology Review, 63*, 41–55. https://doi.org/10.1016/j.cpr.2018.05.008

Goosen, S., Kunst, A. E., Stronks, K., van Oostrum, I. E. A., Uitenbroek, D. G., & Kerkhof, A. J. F. M. (2011). Suicide death and hospital-treated suicidal behaviour in asylum seekers in the

Netherlands: A national registry-based study. *BMC Public Health, 11*(1), 484. https://doi.org/10.1186/1471-2458-11-484
Gunnar, M. R., & Quevedo, K. M. (2008). Early care experiences and HPA axis regulation in children: A mechanism for later trauma vulnerability. *Progress in Brain Research, 167*, 137–149. https://doi.org/10.1016/S0079-6123(07)67010-1
Haase, E., Schönfelder, A., Nesterko, Y., & Glaesmer, H. (2022). Prevalence of suicidal ideation and suicide attempts among refugees: A meta-analysis. *BMC Public Health, 22*(1), 635. https://doi.org/10.1186/s12889-022-13029-8
Herrera-Escobar, J. P., & Schneider, J. C. (2022). From survival to survivorship — Framing traumatic injury as a chronic condition. *The New England Journal of Medicine, 387*(7), 581–583. https://doi.org/10.1056/nejmp2205162
Holbrook, T. L., Hoyt, D. B., Stein, M. B., & Sieber, W. J. (2001). Perceived threat to life predicts posttraumatic stress disorder after major trauma: Risk factors and functional outcome. *The Journal of Trauma, 51*(2), 287–292; discussion 292–293. https://doi.org/10.1097/00005373-200108000-00010
Holman, E. A., Garfin, D. R., & Silver, R. C. (2024). It matters what you see: Graphic media images of war and terror may amplify distress. *Proceedings of the National Academy of Sciences of the United States of America, 121*(29), e2318465121. https://doi.org/10.1073/pnas.2318465121
Holmes, M. R. (2013). The sleeper effect of intimate partner violence exposure: Long-term consequences on young children's aggressive behavior. *Journal of Child Psychology and Psychiatry, and Allied Disciplines, 54*(9), 986–995. https://doi.org/10.1111/jcpp.12071
Itani, T., Jacobsen, K. H., & Kraemer, A. (2017). Suicidal ideation and planning among Palestinian middle school students living in Gaza Strip, West Bank, and United Nations Relief and Works Agency (UNRWA) camps. *International Journal of Pediatrics & Adolescent Medicine, 4*(2), 54–60. https://doi.org/10.1016/j.ijpam.2017.03.003
Jankovic, J., Bremner, S., Bogic, M., Lecic-Tosevski, D., Ajdukovic, D., Franciskovic, T., Galeazzi, G. M., Kucukalic, A., Morina, N., Popovski, M., Schützwohl, M., & Priebe, S. (2013). Trauma and suicidality in war affected communities. *European Psychiatry: The Journal of the Association of European Psychiatrists, 28*(8), 514–520. https://doi.org/10.1016/j.eurpsy.2012.06.001
Kapadia, F. (2024). The value of peace: A public health of consequence, January 2024. *American Journal of Public Health, 114*(1), 15–16. https://doi.org/10.2105/AJPH.2023.307522
Karam, E. G., Salamoun, M. M., Mneimneh, Z. N., Fayyad, J. A., Karam, A. N., Hajjar, R., Dimassi, H., Nock, M. K., & Kessler, R. C. (2012). War and first onset of suicidality: The role of mental disorders. *Psychological Medicine, 42*(10), 2109–2118. https://doi.org/10.1017/S0033291712000268
Khorram-Manesh, A., Burkle, F. M., Goniewicz, K., & Robinson, Y. (2021). Estimating the number of civilian casualties in modern armed conflicts-A systematic review. *Frontiers in Public Health, 9*, 765261. https://doi.org/10.3389/fpubh.2021.765261
Kinyanda, E., Weiss, H. A., Mungherera, M., Onyango-Mangen, P., Ngabirano, E., Kajungu, R., Kagugube, J., Muhwezi, W., Muron, J., & Patel, V. (2013). Prevalence and risk factors of attempted suicide in adult war-affected population of eastern Uganda. *Crisis, 34*(5), 314–323. https://doi.org/10.1027/0227-5910/a000196
Klonsky, E. D., Pachkowski, M. C., Shahnaz, A., & May, A. M. (2021). The three-step theory of suicide: Description, evidence, and some useful points of clarification. *Preventive Medicine, 152*(Pt 1), 106549. https://doi.org/10.1016/j.ypmed.2021.106549
Knipscheer, J., Sleijpen, M., Frank, L., de Graaf, R., Kleber, R., Ten Have, M., & Dückers, M. (2020). Prevalence of potentially traumatic events, other life events and subsequent reactions indicative for posttraumatic stress disorder in the Netherlands: A general population study based on the Trauma Screening Questionnaire. *International Journal of Environmental Research and Public Health, 17*(5), 1725. https://doi.org/10.3390/ijerph17051725
Kohrt, B. A., Jordans, M. J. D., Tol, W. A., Speckman, R. A., Maharjan, S. M., Worthman, C. M., & Komproe, I. H. (2008). Comparison of mental health between former child soldiers and

children never conscripted by armed groups in Nepal. *JAMA: The Journal of the American Medical Association, 300*(6), 691–702. https://doi.org/10.1001/jama.300.6.691

Leckman, J. F., Ponguta, L. A., Pavarini, G., Hein, S. D., McCarthy, M. F., Staiti, H., Hanöz-Penney, S., Rubinstein, J., Pruett, K. D., Yazgan, M. Y., Fallon, N. S., Hartl, F. J., Ziv, M., Salah, R., Britto, P. R., Fitzpatrick, S., & Panter-Brick, C. (2021). Love and peace across generations: Biobehavioral systems and global partnerships. *Comprehensive Psychoneuroendocrinology, 8*(100092), 100092. https://doi.org/10.1016/j.cpnec.2021.100092

Lester, D. (1993). The effect of war on suicide rates. A study of France from 1826 to 1913. *European Archives of Psychiatry and Clinical Neuroscience, 242*(4), 248–249. https://doi.org/10.1007/bf02189971

Lester, D. (1994). Suicide rates before, during and after the world wars. *European Psychiatry: The Journal of the Association of European Psychiatrists, 9*(5), 262–264. https://doi.org/10.1017/s092493380000362x

Lester, D., & Yang, B. J. (1991). Association between war and suicide and homicide. *Psychological Reports, 68*(3 Pt 1), 1030. https://doi.org/10.2466/pr0.1991.68.3.1030

Marou, V., Vardavas, C. I., Aslanoglou, K., Nikitara, K., Plyta, Z., Leonardi-Bee, J., Atkins, K., Condell, O., Lamb, F., & Suk, J. E. (2024). The impact of conflict on infectious disease: A systematic literature review. *Conflict and Health, 18*(1), 27. https://doi.org/10.1186/s13031-023-00568-z

Masten, A. S. (2014). *Ordinary magic: Resilience in development*. Guilford Publications. https://books.google.com/books/about/Ordinary_Magic.html?id=9VD3AwAAQBAJ

Masten, A. S., & Barnes, A. J. (2018). Resilience in children: Developmental perspectives. *Children (Basel, Switzerland), 5*(7). https://doi.org/10.3390/children5070098

McGowan, P. O., Sasaki, A., D'Alessio, A. C., Dymov, S., Labonté, B., Szyf, M., Turecki, G., & Meaney, M. J. (2009). Epigenetic regulation of the glucocorticoid receptor in human brain associates with childhood abuse. *Nature Neuroscience, 12*(3), 342–348. https://doi.org/10.1038/nn.2270

McGowan, P. O., & Szyf, M. (2010). The epigenetics of social adversity in early life: Implications for mental health outcomes. *Neurobiology of Disease, 39*(1), 66–72. https://doi.org/10.1016/j.nbd.2009.12.026

Melhem, N. M., Keilp, J. G., Porta, G., Oquendo, M. A., Burke, A., Stanley, B., Cooper, T. B., Mann, J. J., & Brent, D. A. (2016). Blunted HPA axis activity in suicide attempters compared to those at high risk for suicidal behavior. *Neuropsychopharmacology: Official Publication of the American College of Neuropsychopharmacology, 41*(6), 1447–1456. https://doi.org/10.1038/npp.2015.309

Melhem, N. M., Munroe, S., Marsland, A., Gray, K., Brent, D., Porta, G., Douaihy, A., Laudenslager, M. L., DePietro, F., Diler, R., Driscoll, H., & Gopalan, P. (2017). Blunted HPA axis activity prior to suicide attempt and increased inflammation in attempters. *Psychoneuroendocrinology, 77*, 284–294. https://doi.org/10.1016/j.psyneuen.2017.01.001

Michalek, J., Lisi, M., Binetti, N., Ozkaya, S., Hadfield, K., Dajani, R., & Mareschal, I. (2022). War-related trauma linked to increased sustained attention to threat in children. *Child Development, 93*(4), 900–909. https://doi.org/10.1111/cdev.13739

Mulligan, C. J., Quinn, E. B., Hamadmad, D., Dutton, C. L., Nevell, L., Binder, A. M., Panter-Brick, C., & Dajani, R. (2025). Epigenetic signatures of intergenerational exposure to violence in three generations of Syrian refugees. *Scientific Reports, 15*(1), 5945. https://doi.org/10.1038/s41598-025-89818-z

O'Connor, R. C., & Kirtley, O. J. (2018). The integrated motivational-volitional model of suicidal behaviour. *Philosophical Transactions of the Royal Society of London. Series B, Biological Sciences, 373*(1754). https://doi.org/10.1098/rstb.2017.0268

Palic, S., Zerach, G., Shevlin, M., Zeligman, Z., Elklit, A., & Solomon, Z. (2016). Evidence of complex posttraumatic stress disorder (CPTSD) across populations with prolonged trauma of varying interpersonal intensity and ages of exposure. *Psychiatry Research, 246*, 692–699. https://doi.org/10.1016/j.psychres.2016.10.062

Pfefferbaum, B., Tucker, P., Varma, V., Varma, Y., Nitiéma, P., & Newman, E. (2020). Children's reactions to media coverage of war. *Current Psychiatry Reports, 22*(8), 42. https://doi.org/10.1007/s11920-020-01165-0

Pirkis, J., Dandona, R., Silverman, M., Khan, M., & Hawton, K. (2024). Preventing suicide: A public health approach to a global problem. *The Lancet. Public Health, 0*(0). https://doi.org/10.1016/S2468-2667(24)00149-X

Roemer, L., Litz, B. T., Orsillo, S. M., Ehlich, P. J., & Friedman, M. J. (1998). Increases in retrospective accounts of war-zone exposure over time: The role of PTSD symptom severity. *Journal of Traumatic Stress, 11*(3), 597–605. https://doi.org/10.1023/A:1024469116047

Smeeth, D., McEwen, F. S., Popham, C. M., Karam, E. G., Fayyad, J., Saab, D., Rieder, M. J., Elzagallaai, A. A., van Uum, S., & Pluess, M. (2023). War exposure, post-traumatic stress symptoms and hair cortisol concentrations in Syrian refugee children. *Molecular Psychiatry, 28*(2), 647–656. https://doi.org/10.1038/s41380-022-01859-2

Smith, S. M., & Vale, W. W. (2006). The role of the hypothalamic-pituitary-adrenal axis in neuroendocrine responses to stress. *Dialogues in Clinical Neuroscience, 8*(4), 383–395. https://www.ncbi.nlm.nih.gov/pubmed/17290797

Sourander, A., Silwal, S., Osokina, O., Hinkka-Yli-Salomäki, S., Hodes, M., & Skokauskas, N. (2024). Suicidality and self-harm behavior of adolescents during the early phase of the war in Ukraine. *Journal of the American Academy of Child and Adolescent Psychiatry*. https://doi.org/10.1016/j.jaac.2024.03.015

Steudte, S., Kolassa, I.-T., Stalder, T., Pfeiffer, A., Kirschbaum, C., & Elbert, T. (2011). Increased cortisol concentrations in hair of severely traumatized Ugandan individuals with PTSD. *Psychoneuroendocrinology, 36*(8), 1193–1200. https://doi.org/10.1016/j.psyneuen.2011.02.012

Suicide worldwide in 2019. (2021). *World Health Organization*. https://www.who.int/publications/i/item/9789240026643

Su, Z., McDonnell, D., Cheshmehzangi, A., Bentley, B. L., Ahmad, J., Šegalo, S., da Veiga, C. P., & Xiang, Y.-T. (2023). Media-induced war trauma amid conflicts in Ukraine. *Perspectives on Psychological Science: A Journal of the Association for Psychological Science, 18*(4), 908–911. https://doi.org/10.1177/17456916221109609

van Heeringen, K. (2012). Stress–diathesis model of suicidal behavior. In *The Neurobiological Basis of Suicide*. CRC Press/Taylor & Francis. https://www.ncbi.nlm.nih.gov/books/NBK107203/

Van Orden, K. A., Witte, T. K., Cukrowicz, K. C., Braithwaite, S., Selby, E. A., & Joiner, T. E., Jr. (2010). The interpersonal theory of suicide. *Psychological Review, 117*(2), 575. https://doi.org/10.1037/a0018697

van Tubergen, F., & Ultee, W. (2006). Political integration, war and suicide: The dutch paradox? *International Sociology: Journal of the International Sociological Association, 21*(2), 221–236. https://doi.org/10.1177/0268580906061377

Vidal-Ribas, P., Govender, T., Yu, J., Livinski, A. A., Haynie, D. L., & Gilman, S. E. (2024). The developmental origins of suicide mortality: A systematic review of longitudinal studies. *European Child & Adolescent Psychiatry, 33*(7), 2083–2110. https://doi.org/10.1007/s00787-022-02092-6

Watson Institute for International & Public Affairs. (2024). *Latest figures: Costs of war*. The Costs of War. https://watson.brown.edu/costsofwar/figures

Yamada, M., & Izumi, S. (2002). Psychiatric sequelae in atomic bomb survivors in Hiroshima and Nagasaki two decades after the explosions. *Social Psychiatry and Psychiatric Epidemiology, 37*(9), 409–415. https://doi.org/10.1007/s00127-002-0572-5

Yehuda, R., & Bierer, L. M. (2008). Transgenerational transmission of cortisol and PTSD risk. *Progress in Brain Research, 167*, 121–135. https://doi.org/10.1016/S0079-6123(07)67009-5

Yehuda, R., Kahana, B., Binder-Brynes, K., Southwick, S. M., Mason, J. W., & Giller, E. L. (1995). Low urinary cortisol excretion in Holocaust survivors with posttraumatic stress disorder. *The American Journal of Psychiatry, 152*(7), 982–986. https://doi.org/10.1176/ajp.152.7.982

Yehuda, R., Morris, A., Labinsky, E., Zemelman, S., & Schmeidler, J. (2007). Ten-year follow-up study of cortisol levels in aging holocaust survivors with and without PTSD. *Journal of Traumatic Stress, 20*(5), 757–761. https://doi.org/10.1002/jts.20228

Zinzow, H. M., Ruggiero, K. J., Resnick, H., Hanson, R., Smith, D., Saunders, B., & Kilpatrick, D. (2009). Prevalence and mental health correlates of witnessed parental and community violence in a national sample of adolescents. *Journal of Child Psychology and Psychiatry, and Allied Disciplines, 50*(4), 441–450. https://doi.org/10.1111/j.1469-7610.2008.02004.x

# Chapter 8
# Religion, Spirituality, and Suicidal Behavior

**David Lester and Mahboubeh Dadfar**

**Abstract** A review of research on the impact of religion and spirituality on suicidal behavior clearly shows that, in most countries, religiosity and religious homogeneity reduce suicidal behavior both at the societal level and for individuals. However, countries with different majority religions also differ in social and economic ways which makes interpretation of the differences in suicide rates difficult. There are exceptions in countries where religion is not in line with government policies. Intrinsic religiosity (e.g., adherence to beliefs, and the practice of religious rituals) is more of a protective factor against suicidality than extrinsic religiosity (e.g., the side benefits of social interaction).

**Keywords** Religion · Spirituality · Suicidal behavior · Suicide · Suicidal thoughts

## 1 Introduction

Although mental and behavioral disorders such as suicide in many cases have personal and family roots, studies have shown that these problems are intertwined with economic and social factors (Knapp & Wong, 2020; Lester & Dadfar, 2022a, 2022b). Suicidal behavior can be best understood using a comprehensive approach (Chelmardi et al., 2023). In a study in Iran, Sezavar et al. (2023) found that the socio-economic variables such as divorce rates, crime rates, income inequality, and economic instability have a positive impact on suicide rates, while employment and the age structure of the population (e.g., the proportion of those aged 50–69) have

D. Lester (✉)
Stockton University, Galloway, NJ, USA
e-mail: david.lester@stockton.edu

M. Dadfar
School of Behavioral Sciences and Mental Health, Iran University of Medical Sciences, Tehran, Iran
e-mail: dadfar.m@iums.ac.ir

 
S. M. Y. Arafat and S. K. Kar (eds.), *Ecological and Social Determinants of Suicidal Behavior*, South Asian Perspectives in Mental Health and Psychology,
https://doi.org/10.1007/978-981-96-4028-7_8

a negative effect on suicide. Another important factor affecting suicide rates is religion. Turecki and Brent (2016) indicated that religiosity is a social factor that impacts on risk of suicide and suicidal behavior resulting in a decreased risk of suicide and suicidality.

One of the enduring topics in suicidology ever since Durkheim's book on suicide in 1897 has been the impact of religion on suicide (Durkheim, 1897). Indeed, sociologists have viewed Durkheim's assertion that Roman Catholic countries have lower suicide rates than Protestant countries as *Durkheim's one law* (Merton, 1967; Pope & Danigelis, 1981). Most of the research on this topic has focused on European countries, where countries with Roman Catholic majorities do indeed appear to have lower suicide rates than countries with Protestant majorities. More recently, it has been noted that countries with Muslim majorities have very low suicide rates, but this may be a result in part of the socio-economic status of Muslim-majority countries and the accuracy of mortality statistics (Arafat et al., 2022).

There are three ways in which religion may impact suicide. First, in Durkheim's theory, religion's impact is from the social integration that religion creates. People go to places of religious worship and interact with others, often making friends. Religions also involve activities outside of worship, such as festivals and fund-raising activities. This great social network makes finding support, especially in time of crisis, easier to obtain. Secondly, religions lead to shared beliefs. The greater uniformity of Catholic beliefs as compared to the fractured Protestant religions results in greater social regulation for Catholics. Thirdly, some of the beliefs, such as a belief in life after death, make life on earth more tolerable. Indeed, most religions make suicide a sin in order to prevent people dying by suicide to get the better life that they expect after death.

In this chapter, we will first examine national differences in suicide rates and explore how these might be related to religious variables. Then we will examine the association between religion on suicidal behavior at the individual level, examining more specific aspects of religion (such as attendance at religious services) and also the impact of religion on less lethal forms of suicidal behavior such as non-fatal suicide attempts and suicidal ideation.

## 2 National Differences in Suicide Rates

Most of the research on national differences in suicide rates was conducted in the twentieth century. Lester (1996) attempted to get suicide rates for as many countries as possible for 1970 and 1980 and created a research sample of 63 countries, although African and Middle Eastern countries were under-represented. Lester studied 66 variables and used two data sources for the percentage of Christians, Catholics, and Muslims. The correlations with suicide rates for the two data sources are shown in Table 1.

**Table 1** Correlations between suicide rates and percentage of different religious groups in 63 countries (from Lester, 1996)

| Suicide rate and percentage of religious | | |
|---|---|---|
| % Christians | +0.12 | +0.08 |
| % Catholics | −0.15 | – |
| % Muslims | −0.30* | −0.33* |

* statistically significant $p < 0.05$

These results confirmed the lower suicide rate in Islamic countries. However, as noted above, countries with different majority religions do have different socio-economic characteristics and different standards for collecting accurate mortality data.

With a reduced variable list of 22 variables, Lester (1996) then identified six factors (clusters) of variables, and the three religion variables loaded by themselves on one factor. This factor score was not associated with the suicide rates of the countries, indicating that other variables (such as female labor force participation and the percentage of elderly) were more powerful predictors of national suicide rates.

## *2.1 Catholics Versus Protestants*

For the Christian denominations (Catholics, Baptists, and Protestants), the highest suicide rates are found among for Protestants and the lowest rates are found for Catholics and evangelical Baptists (Panczak et al., 2013). Differences for some European countries are shown in Table 1. Several hypotheses have been proposed for these differences including the degree of participation in religious activities, leading to an expanded social network (Pescosolido & Georgianna, 1989) and less involvement in risky activities such as alcohol consumption. However, in the Western countries, coroners and medical examiners in Catholic countries are more likely to hide suicides (by classifying suicides as accidental or natural deaths) than coroners and medical examiners in Protestant countries (Cantor et al., 1997).

However, it has been noted that the differences between Catholic and Protestant countries differed more after the Second World War than before. The lower suicide rate in Catholic countries was much greater after the war, while economic development was less in Catholic countries after the war (Pope & Danigelis, 1981). Table 2 presents average suicide rates in the twentieth century for some European countries.

The association between religion and suicide can be extended to religious beliefs. Lester (1992) obtained data from national surveys in 12 European countries and the USA and found that a greater extent of belief in both life after death and in God was related to the lower suicide rates in the countries.

There are, of course, other religious sects in Western countries. For example, Kunz (1987) found no higher rate of suicide among Mormons in Utah as compared to residents with other religions. No studies have appeared on Jehovah's Witnesses,

**Table 2** Average suicide rates by country, 1919–1972 (from Pope & Danigelis, 1981)

| Protestant | Average suicide rates | Catholic | Average suicide rates |
|---|---|---|---|
| Denmark | 19.5 | Austria | 28.0 |
| Finland | 18.6 | Belgium | 15.0 |
| Iceland | 9.3 | Ireland | 2.7 |
| Norway | 6.9 | Italy | 7.1 |
| Sweden | 17.0 | Luxembourg | 12.7 |
| | | Portugal | 9.0 |
| | | Spain | 5.3 |
| Mean | 14.3 | Mean | 11.4 |

but unpublished studies have appeared on attempted suicides among Seventh Day Adventists (Trivino, 2000).

## 2.2 *Muslim-Majority Countries*

More recently, suicide rates have been collected and studied for Muslim-majority countries (e.g., Arafat et al., 2022, 2024; Lester, 2006). Lew et al. (2022) collected suicide rates for 46 Muslim countries, and 11 had a higher suicide rate above the global rate in 2019. In terms of region, Islamic countries in the Sub-Saharan area revealed the highest weighted average age-standardized suicide rate of 10.02 (per 100,000 per year) while South-eastern Asia recorded the lowest rate (2.58). The estimated suicide rates ranged from 1.09 in Afghanistan to 18.05 in Kazakhstan.

It is of interest to note that, while studies in Europe have focused on the different Christian sects, research on Muslim countries have ignored Shia versus Sunni differences. In the first study of this variable, Zeyrek-Rios et al. (2022) found that the presence of Shariah rule in 46 Muslim-majority countries was related to the lower estimated suicide rates, as was the proportion of Muslims in the population (see Table 3).

## 2.3 *Religious Homogeneity*

Ellison et al. (1997) argued that religious homogeneity (the extent to which the inhabitants of a country are attached and committed to a single religion) would be a more appropriate variable for sociological studies of societal rates of suicide. The residents of a country with less religious homogeneity would be exposed to more alternatives to and criticisms of their own religion and, therefore, have less confidence in the validity of their religious beliefs. In a test of their hypothesis,

**Table 3** Predicting suicide rates in Islamic countries

| Pearson correlations | Suicide rate | Male/female suicide rate ratio |
|---|---|---|
| Suicide rate | | −0.10 |
| Population | −0.15 | −0.05 |
| Percentage of Muslim | −0.18 | $-0.32^{*}$ |
| HDI | $-0.51^{***}$ | $+0.50^{***}$ |
| Percentage of Shia | −0.20 | +0.13 |
| Shariah rule | $-0.3^{*}$ | −0.04 |
| *Regressions (β)* | | |
| Population | −0.04 | +0.01 |
| Percentage of Muslim | $-0.26^{*}$ | −0.23# |
| HDI | $-0.52^{***}$ | $+0.45^{**}$ |
| Percentage of Shia | −0.02 | +0.04 |
| Shariah rule | $-0.3^{*}$ | −0.04 |
| $R^2$ | 0.46 | 0.30 |

* Significant in a backward multiple regression; HDI is the Human Development Index; $^{*}p < 0.05$; $^{**}p < 0.01$; $^{***}p < 0.001$

Ellison et al. studied 296 small regions in the United States and found that religious homogeneity was strongly associated, negatively, with the suicide rates. The more religious homogeneity, the lower the suicide rates.

In Iran, there is complete religious homogeneity (a religious monopoly) but Islam is divided into two main religions (e.g., Shia and Sunni). In a study of regions within Iran, Taleban (2022) found that the regions with more religious homogeneity had higher suicide rates.

## 2.4 Studies of Individuals

Does religion protect people from suicidal behavior? Religiosity and spirituality are typically measured by psychological inventories, for example, religiosity (e.g., Abdel-Khalek, 2017) and spirituality (Hall & Edwards, 2022). A review of the research revealed that 84% of studies identified lower rates of suicidal behavior among more religious people (Koenig et al., 2001), but some articles indicated no association between religiosity and suicidal behavior (e.g., Dadfar et al., 2023a; Eshun, 2003).

# 3 Religiosity

Lester (2017) reviewed research on whether self-reported measures of religiosity were protective for suicidality. He noted that scores on Francis's measure of religiosity (Francis, 1992) were negatively related to the non-fatal suicidal behavior (suicidal ideation and attempts), a protective effect. For example, in a sample of college students, Lester and Francis (1993) found that those with higher religiosity scores less often had past and current suicidal ideation even after controls for depression and locus of control.

It has been reported that intrinsic religiosity (e.g., adherence to the beliefs of the religion) was negatively associated with non-lethal suicidal behaviors, again a protective effect, but not extrinsic religiosity (e.g., the social aspects of religious involvement). Lester and Walker (2017) found the association of intrinsic religiosity with current suicidal ideation had limitations. In a sample of college students, they found that intrinsic religiosity protected against current suicidal ideation for women but not for men and for European American students but not for African American students.

## *3.1 Muslim Countries*

Most of this research on religiosity and suicidal behavior has been conducted on Western samples, but Dadfar et al. (2021a, 2021b) revealed that scores on a measure of religiosity were negatively related to suicidality in a sample of Iranian psychiatric outpatients, but not in a sample of university employees. Another study revealed that religiosity was negatively related to suicidal thought in both Kuwaiti and American students (Abdel-Khalek & Lester, 2007). In both countries, religiosity was positively associated with self-ratings of mental and physical health.

Most people who die by suicide do not have deep religious beliefs, and there is no spiritual connection with God in their life plan. A person who believes in God and the Day of Judgment does not easily give up when faced with problems and frustrations because if they follow God's orders, God will reward them (Atoofi et al., 2021; Dadfar et al., 2023b).

Many people are afraid of dying by suicide based on their belief that suicide is a sin. Therefore, strengthening religious beliefs can prevent the occurrence of suicide or attempted suicide. Askari et al. (2019) found that religious and spiritual beliefs can play an important role in reducing the occurrence of suicidal behavior by helping individuals to cope with unpleasant events, develop a positive attitude, and increase their hope and self-esteem.

Suicide and self-destructive behaviors are strictly prohibited and forbidden in Islam religion, and those who do it will not receive God's mercy. Strengthening the relationship with God, as well as promoting hope, anger control, patience, and perseverance, can prevent suicidal behavior (Wiki Feqh, 2024). The role of Islamic beliefs in the meaning of life (such as life as a gift, repentance, hope, optimism, patience, trust, life after death, and connection with God) and the collective rituals in Islam and the accompanying religious networks of social support are very effective in preventing suicide. Religiosity has a great influence in suicidal behavior in both personal and social dimensions (Elmi & Shaverani, 2013). The individual dimension includes depression, alcohol use and unhealthy sexual relationships, and also a belief in repentance, the blessings of life, hope, optimism, patience, trust, remembrance of death, and the promise of a hereafter. The social dimension includes religious activity as in, for example, Islamic group rituals such as Ramadan fasting, Friday prayers, congregational prayers, and Hajj, as well as religious social support networks such as group rituals in Mosques and religious social associations.

## 4 Spirituality

In a study of Canadians, Rasic et al. (2009) asked respondents whether spiritual values played an important role in their lives and their frequency of worship attendance. Religious participation was related to decreased odds of a suicide attempt and suicidal ideation. However, social support was more important for predicting suicidal ideation than was spirituality.

Lester (2012) explored the relevance of different aspects of spirituality and religiosity on suicidal behavior in college students. A history of suicidal ideation was positively associated with a measure of intrinsic religiosity but not with extrinsic aspects. Suicidal ideation was also positively associated with the awareness aspect of religiosity (e.g., "I have a sense of how God is working in my life") and the instability aspect (e.g., "My emotional connection with God is unstable") but not with the grandiosity aspect (e.g., "God recognizes that I am more spiritual than most people") or the impression management aspect (e.g., "I am always in a worshipful mood when I go to church") aspects.

The role of spirituality in impacting suicidal behavior has been examined in relation to recent important worldwide issues. For example, Mahamid et al. (2023) studied a sample of Palestinians living in the West Bank who are experiencing stressors on a daily basis resulting from the Israeli military attacks on Gaza and attacks by Israeli settlers on the West Bank. Mahamid et al. found that suicidal ideation correlated positively with post-traumatic stress symptoms and negatively with social support and spirituality. A path analysis suggested that social support, spirituality, and mindfulness mediated the relationship between post-traumatic stress symptoms and suicidal thoughts.

Upenieks (2022) studied suicidal ideation resulting from the COVID-19 pandemic (declared by the WHO in March 2020). In a 2021 national survey of Americans, struggles with religion and spirituality were associated with suicidal ideation. Spirituality struggles were assessed by beliefs in divine control and religious attendance and, the higher this index of spirituality struggles, the greater likelihood of suicidal ideation in the prior year. Belief in divine control lessened the likelihood of suicidal ideation.

Aryapooran and Shibani (2021) found that attachment to God, spiritual well-being and psychological resilience, and training based on these variables were associated with a reduction in suicidal thoughts in students during epidemics such as COVID-19. With wars taking place in many countries, suicidal behavior in soldiers and veterans is of concern. Rubenstein et al. (2021) followed up American veterans for 7 years and found that organized religious activity lessened the incidence of post-traumatic stress disorder and suicidal ideation, whereas private religious activities did not do so.

In Dutch and Belgian adults, Huijs et al. (2024) found that spirituality was associated with well-being and mental distress. Studies conducted in Iran showed that religious and spiritual well-being has an important role in coping with psychosocial problems such as suicide (Abdolahrezaee et al., 2020; Atoofi et al., 2019; Dadfar et al., 2021a, 2021b; Shirzad et al., 2020).

Akwash (2017) suggested that, in the present era, the process of integrating psychology with religion is expanding, and psychology can be based on the teachings of religion with the aim of creating harmony and balance in the individual through the relationship between the mind and the soul as in, for example, a spiritual psychotherapy intervention program called "Rebuild your life" proposed by Paukert et al. (2009). In a sample of psychiatric inpatients, Friedrich-Killinger (2020) found that psychotherapy achieved better results if religion was central to the client's life and was incorporated into the therapeutic process.

The effectiveness of spiritual interventions has been shown in several studies. For example, it has been found to reduce suicidal thoughts (Gholandoz & Sardary, 2019) and to ameliorate death distress (Dadfar et al. 2023c; Sharifi et al., 2023a, 2023b, 2024). In a meta-analysis of the effect of religiosity and spirituality on the treatment of psychoses in Iranian patients, Safara et al. (2019) reported a strong effect in 34.4% of the studies, a medium effect in 31.4%, and a weak effect in 34%.

## 5 What if Religion is Stigmatized?

Zhang et al. (2024) explored whether religious beliefs and religiosity remain positively associated with both physical and mental health in China where the status of religious believers is low and they often suffer from discrimination. For example, during the Cultural Revolution (1966–1976), religious sites were sometimes destroyed. China identifies five religions (Buddhism, Catholicism, Daoism, Islam, and Protestantism) and some 10% of the population have religious beliefs. Using a Chinese national database, Zhang et al. found significant negative correlations between having a religious belief and physical and mental health, the opposite to research findings in Western countries.

## 6 Conclusions

This review of research on the impact of religion and spirituality on suicidal behavior clearly shows that, in most countries, religiosity and religious homogeneity reduce suicidal behavior both at the societal level and for individuals. The impact at the societal level is consistently found except for countries where religion is discouraged and religious individuals are discriminated against, for example, China. It is noteworthy that much of this research has been carried out in Muslim countries and not only in WEIRD (Western, Educated, Industrialized, Rich, and Democratic) countries.

Religions have particular beliefs (intrinsic religiosity) and also involve social and interpersonal activities (extrinsic religiosity), and research has shown that intrinsic religiosity and spirituality have a beneficial impact on reducing suicidal behavior in individuals (both suicidal ideation and suicidal acts). It has been suggested that religious beliefs and spirituality could be incorporated into counseling for suicidal individuals to better help them withstand the stressors and hassles of daily life.

## References

Abdel-Khalek, A. M. (2017). The construction and validation of the Arabic Scale of Intrinsic Religiosity (ASIR). *Psychology and Behavioral Science: International Journal, 4*(4), Article 555644. https://doi.org/10.19080/PBSIJ.2017.04.555644

Abdel-Khalek, A. M., & Lester, D. (2007). Religiosity, health, and psychopathology in two cultures. *Mental Health, Religion & Culture, 10*, 537–550. https://doi.org/10.1080/13674670601166505

Abdolahrezaee, N., Khanmohammadi, A., Dadfar, M., Rashedi, V., & Behnam, L. (2020). Prediction of hope, physical health, and mental health by mediating variable of religious spiritual well-being in elderly. *Mental Health, Religion & Culture, 23*(10), 928–940. https://doi.org/10.1080/13674676.2020.1819220

Akwash, F. B. A. (2017). Psychotherapy and religion. *International Journal for Psychotherapy in Africa, 2*(1), 94–115. https://ezenwaohaetorc.org/journals/index.php/IJPA/article/view/937/0

Arafat, S. M. Y., Marthoenis, M., Khan, M. M., & Rezaeian, M. (2022). Association between suicide rate and human development index, income, and the political system in 46 Muslim-majority countries: An ecological study. *European Journal of Investigation in Health, Psychology and Education, 12*(7), 754–764. https://doi.org/10.3390/ejihpe12070055

Arafat, S. M. Y., Rezaeian, M., & Khan, M. M. (2024). Suicidal behavior in Islamic countries: An overview. In S. M. Y. Arafat, M. Rezaeian, M. M. Khan (Eds.), *Suicidal behavior in Muslim majority countries*. Springer, Singapore. https://doi.org/10.1007/978-981-97-2519-9_1

Aryapooran, S., & Shibani, H. (2021). Suicidal thoughts in students during Covid-19: Role of attachment to God, spiritual well-being and psychological resilience. *Culture in Islamic University, 11*(3), 465–486. https://doi.org/10.22034/ciu.2021.1140

Askari, S., Ghafarzadegan, R., & Ghorbani, A. (2019, March 10–12). *Role of religion and spirituality on the rate of suicide and providing appropriate solutions to achieve mental peace*. Paper presented in the National conference on suicide and related behaviors, Zanjan University of Medical Sciences, Rouzbeh International Conference Center. Tehran, Iran. https://eprints.arums.ac.ir/4972/#:~:text=Roleofreligionandspiritualityontherateofsuicideandprovidingappropriatesolutionstoachievementalpeace

Atoofi, M. K., Dadfar, M., & Turan, Y. (2021). The Farsi version of the belief in a day of judgment scale: Development of a brief version. *Mental Health, Religion & Culture, 24*(3), 231–234. https://doi.org/10.1080/13674676.2020.1737923

Atoofi, M. K., Dadfar, M., Turan, Y., & Behnam, L. (2019). Multidimensional Inventory for Religious Spiritual Well-Being (MI RSWB 48): Validation with Iranian psychiatric outpatients. *Mental Health, Religion & Culture, 22*(10), 1011–1020. https://doi.org/10.1080/13674676.2019.1652892

Cantor, C. H., Leenaars, A. A., & Lester, D. (1997). Under-reporting of suicide in Ireland 1960–1989. *Archives of Suicide Research, 3*, 5–12. https://doi.org/10.1023/A:1009699126206

Chelmardi, A. R. K., Rashid, S., Dadfar, M., & Lester, D. (2023). Understanding suicidal behavior using a comprehensive approach. *Illness, Crisis & Loss, 31*(2), 228–243. https://doi.org/10.1177/10541373211051058

Dadfar, M., Atoofi, M. K., & Rezaei, A. (2023b). Effectiveness of religious spiritual integrated therapy (RSIT) for reduction of death distress in the Iranian outpatients with generalized anxiety disorder (GAD). *Mankind Quarterly, 63*(3), 427–442. https://doi.org/10.46469/mq.2023.63.3.4

Dadfar, M., Gunn III, J. F., & Lester, D. (2023a). The suicidal Behavior questionnaire-revised (SBQ-R): Validation in Iranian psychiatric outpatients. *Suicide Studies, 4*(2), 4–14. https://www.researchgate.net/publication/366673562_Suicide_Studies_2023_42

Dadfar, M., Lester, D., & Abdel-Khalek, A. (2021). Religiosity, happiness and suicidal behavior. *Mental Health, Religion & Culture, 24*, 128–141. https://doi.org/10.1080/13674676.2020.1767554

Dadfar, M., Lester, D., Turan, Y., & Beshai, J. A. (2023c). Belief in a day of judgment and locus of control in university students from three nations: Iran, Turkey and the USA. *Mental Health, Religion & Culture, 26*)5(, 431–442. https://doi.org/10.1080/13674676.2022.2047912

Dadfar, M., Lester, D., Turan, Y., Beshai, J. A., & Unterrainer, H.-F. (2021). Religious spiritual well-being: Results from Muslim Iranian clinical and non-clinical samples by age, sex and group. *Journal of Religion, Spirituality & Aging, 33*(1), 16–37. https://doi.org/10.1080/15528030.2020.1818161

Durkheim, E. (1897). *Le Suicide*. Felix Alcan. https://en.wikipedia.org/wiki/Le_Suicid%C3%A9

Ellison, C., Burr, J., & McCall, P. (1997). Suicide homogeneity and metropolitan suicide rates. *Social Forces, 76*, 273–299. https://doi.org/10.1093/sf/76.1.273

Elmi, G., & Shaverani, M. (2013). Function of Islamic beliefs and rituals in reducing suicide. *The Mirror of Knowledge, 10*(32), 163–189. https://ensani.ir/fa/article/309395/functionofIslamicbeliefsandritualsinreducingsuicide

Eshun, S. (2003). Sociocultural determinants of suicide ideation. *Suicide & Life-Threatening Behavior, 33*, 165–171. https://doi.org/10.1521/suli.33.2.165.22779

Francis, L. J. (1992). Reliability and validity of the Francis Scale of Attitudes toward Christianity (adult). *Panorama, 4,* 17–19. https://scholar.google.com/scholar_lookup?title=Reliability+and+validity+of+the+Francis+Scale+of+Attitude+Towards+Christianity+%28adult%29&author=L.+J.+Francis&publication_year=1992&journal=Panorama&pages=17-19

Friedrich-Killinger, S. (2020). Centrality of religiosity as a resource for therapy outcome? *Journal of Religions, 11*(4), 1–16. https://doi.org/10.3390/re/11040155

Gholandoz, P. M., & Sardary, B. (2019). The effectiveness of positive psychology training with emphasis on religious doctrines on reducing students' high-risk behaviors with suicidal thoughts. *Journal of Positive Psychology, 6*(3), 51–68. https://doi.org/10.22108/ppls.2021.122201.1907

Hall, T. W., & Edwards, K. J. (2022). The Spiritual Assessment Inventory: A theistic model and measure for assessing spiritual development. *Journal of the Scientific Study of Religion, 41*(2), 341–357. https://doi.org/10.1111/1468-5906.00121

Huijs, T., Braam, A. W., Kruizinga, R., Jacobs, N., Reijnders, J., & Simons, M. (2024). Spirituality as a predictor of well-being, mental distress or both: A four-week follow-up study in a sample of Dutch and Belgian adults. *Religions, 15*, 179. https://doi.org/10.3390/rel15020179

Knapp, M., & Wong, G. (2020). Economics and mental health: The current scenario. *World Psychiatry, 19*(1), 3–14. https://doi.org/10.1002/wps.20692

Koenig, H. G., McCullough, M., & Larson, D. B. (2001). *Handbook of religion and health*. Oxford University Press. https://academic.oup.com/book/50224

Kunz, P. R. (1987). Religion and suicide. *Dialogue Journal, 20*, 115–117. https://www.dialoguejournal.com/…/sbi/articles/Dialogue_…PDFfile

Lester, D. (1992). Religiosity, suicide and homicide: A cross-national examination. *Psychological Reports, 71*(3_suppl), 1282–1282. https://doi.org/10.2466/pr0.1992.71.3f.1282

Lester, D. (1996). *Patterns of suicide and homicide in the world*. Nova Science. https://psycnet.apa.org/record/1997-97576-000

Lester, D. (2006). Suicide and Islam. *Archives of Suicide Research, 10(1)*, 77–97. https://doi.org/10.1080/13811110500318489

Lester, D. (2012). Spirituality and religiosity as predictors of depression and suicidal ideation. *Psychological Reports, 110*(1), 247–250. https://doi.org/10.12466/02.12.PR0.110.1.247-250

Lester, D. (2017). Does religiosity predict suicidal behavior? *Religions, 8*(11), 238. https://doi.org/10.3390/rel8110238

Lester, D., & Dadfar, M. (2022a). Do the Dark Triad traits protect against depression and suicidal ideation? *Mankind Quarterly, 62*(3), 522–533. https://doi.org/10.46469/mq.2022.62.3.7

Lester, D., & Dadfar, M. (2022b). Sociotropy, autonomy, depression, and suicidality. *Suicide Studies, 3*(4), 2–10. https://www.researchgate.net/publication/359146221_Suicide_Studies_2022_34

Lester, D., & Francis, L. J. (1993). Is religiosity related to suicidal ideation after personality and mood are taken into account? *Personality & Individual Differences, 15*, 591–592. https://doi.org/10.1016/0191-8869(93)90342-Z

Lester, D., & Walker, R. L. (2017). Religiosity is a protective factor for suicidal ideation in European American students but not in African American students. *Omega—Journal of Death and Dying, 74*, 295–303. https://doi.org/10.1177/0030222815598452

Lew, B., Lester, D., Kõlves, K., Yip, P. S. F., Chen, Y-Y., Chen, W. S., Hasan, M. T., Koenig, H. G., Wang, Z. Z., Fariduddin, M. N., Zeyrek-Rios, E. Y., Chan, C. M. H., Idzwan, F., Fitriana, M., Dolo, H., Gonultas, B., Dadfar, M., Davoudi, M., Abdel-Khalek, A. M., … Ibrahim, N. (2022). An analysis of age-standardized suicide rates in Muslim-majority countries in 2000–2019. *BMC Public Health, 22*(1), 882. https://doi.org/10.1186/s12889-022-13101-3

Mahamid, F., Bdier, D., Jabr, S., & Hinnawi, Z. (2023). The association between posttraumatic stress symptoms and suicidal ideations among Palestinians. *Cambridge Prisms: Global Mental Health, 10*(e48), 1–8. https://doi.org/10.1017/gmh.2023.41

Merton, R. K. (1967). *On theoretical sociology*. Free Press. https://archive.org/details/ontheoreticalsoc00mert

Panczak, R., Spoerri, A., Zwahlen, M., Bopp, M., Gutzwiller, F., & Egger, M. (2013). Religion and suicide in patients with mental illness or cancer. *Suicide & Life-Threatening Behavior, 43*, 213–222. https://doi.org/10.1111/sltb.12009

Paukert, A. L., Phillips, L., Cully, J. A., Loboprabhu, S. M., Lomax, J. W., & Stanley, M. A. (2009). Integration of religion into cognitive-behavioral therapy for geriatric anxiety and depression. *Journal of Psychiatric Practice, 15*(2), 103–112. https://doi.org/10.1097/01.pra.0000348363.88676.4d

Pescosolido, B. A., & Georgianna, S. (1989). Durkheim, suicide, and religion: Toward a network theory of suicide. *American Sociological Review, 54*, 33–48. https://doi.org/10.2307/2095660

Pope, W., & Danigelis, N. (1981). Sociology's "one law." *Social Forces, 60*, 495–516. https://doi.org/10.1093/sf/60.2.495

Rasic, D. T., Beli, S. L., Elias, B., Katz, L. Y., Enns, M., Sareen, J., & Swampy Cree Suicide Prevention Team. (2009). Spirituality, religion and suicidal behavior in a nationally representative sample. *Journal of Affective Disorders, 114*, 32–40. https://doi.org/10.1016/j.jad.2008.08.007

Rubenstein, A., Koenig, H. G., Marin, D. B., Sharma, V., Harpaz-Rotem, I., & Pietrzak, R. H. (2021). Religion, spirituality, and risk for incident posttraumatic stress disorder, suicidal ideation, and hazardous drinking in U.S. military veterans: A 7-year, nationally representative, prospective cohort study. *Journal of Affective Disorders, 295*, 1110–1117. https://doi.org/10.1016/j.jad.2021.08.128

Safara, M., Balali-Dehkordi, N., & Sadidpour, S.S. (2019). A meta-analysis of the effect of religiosity and spirituality on treatment of psychotic-clinical disorders (2003–2013). *Research in Religion and Health, 5*(3), 124–136. https://api.semanticscholar.org/CorpusID:210374423

Sezavar, F., Firoozy, M., & Sezavar, M. (2023). The effect of economic and social factors on the suicidal behavior of society in Iran (with emphasis on risk and economic instability). *Social Welfare Quarterly, 23*(90), 53–88. http://refahj.uswr.ac.ir/article-1-4183-fa.html

Sharifi, M., Koenig, H. G., Dadfar, M., Turan, Y., & Gorbani, A. R. (2024). The effectiveness of spirituality-centered cognitive therapy on body image, sexual function, illness perception and intrusive thoughts in women after mastectomy. *Religions, 15*(5), 578. https://doi.org/10.3390/rel15050578

Sharifi, M., Saeidi, S., Al Zaben, F.N., Dadfar, M., & Turan, Y. (2023a). The effectiveness of spiritual group therapy on resilience in mothers of children with learning disabilities. *Mankind Quarterly, 64*(1), 165–178. https://doi.org/10.46469/mq.2023.64.1.11

Sharifi, M., Saeidi, S., Koenig, H.G., Dadfar, M., & Turan, Y. (2023b). The effect of integrated religious cognitive behavioral therapy (ICBT) on psychological symptoms in women with breast cancer. *Mankind Quarterly, 63*(4), 617–635. https://doi.org/10.46469/mq.2023.63.4.4

Shirzad, F., Dadfar, M., & Atoofi, M. K. (2020). Spirituality in Iran: From theory to clinical practice. *Mental Health, Religion & Culture, 23*(7), 653–656. https://doi.org/10.1080/13674676.2019.1674796

Taleban, M. R. (2022). Empirical study on the relationship between religious homogeneity and suicide in Iran. *Iranian Journal of Sociology, 23*(1), 131–147. https://www.noormags.ir/view/fa/articlepage/2025102/

Trivino, J. E. (2000). Characteristics of Hispanic Seventh-day Adventist adolescents who attempted suicide. *Dissertation Abstracts, 60*(12B), 6351. https://doi.org/10.32597/dissertations/739/

Turecki, G., & Brent, D. A. (2016). Suicide and suicidal behaviour. *Lancet, 387*(10024), 1227–1239. https://doi.org/10.1016/S0140-6736(15)00234-2

Upenieks, L. (2022). Religious/spiritual struggles and suicidal ideation in the COVID-19 era: Does the belief in divine control and religious attendance matter? *Psychology of Religion & Spirituality, 14*(3), 338–350. https://doi.org/10.1037/rel0000467

Wiki Feqh. (2024). *Suicide*. https://fa.wikifeqh.ir

Zeyrek-Rios, E. Y., Lester, D., & Lew, B. (2022). The variation of suicide rates in Muslim nations: the impact of Shariah Rule and Shia/Sunni proportion. *Suicide Studies, 3*(4), 72–74. https://www.researchgate.net/publication/359146221_Suicide_Studies_2022_34

Zhang, J., Zhao, L., & Lester, D. (2024). Religion, religiosity and health in China. *Suicide Studies, 5*(3), 64–73. https://www.researchgate.net/publication/359146221_Suicide_Studies_2024_53

# Chapter 9
# Pandemics and Suicidal Behaviour

**Vikas Menon, Natarajan Varadharajan, and Ragul Ganesh**

**Abstract** The recent COVID-19 pandemic has brought the issue of mental health and suicide to the forefront; indeed, experts have described it as a 'perfect storm', implying the role of the pandemic in driving suicidal behaviours. However, an association between the two is neither novel nor unfounded. In this chapter, we provide an overview of the historical trends in the relationship between viral disease outbreaks and suicide rates, pandemic-related risk factors that may drive suicide risk, impact on special populations, and prevention strategies. Finally, we end with a discussion on challenges in suicide research during pandemics. It is hoped that the chapter will provide useful insights for informing practice, policy, and preparedness to handle suicide and mental health, more broadly, during future viral disease outbreaks.

**Keywords** Pandemics · Viral diseases · COVID-19 · Suicide · Suicide prevention · Suicide risk factors

## 1 Introduction

Suicide is a major global public health issue. Worldwide, more than 700,000 people take their own lives annually with devastating familial, social, and economic consequences. In recognition of its growing burden, global target 3.2 of the World Health Organization's (WHO's) Comprehensive Mental Health Action Plan 2013–2030 aims to reduce the burden of suicide by one-third by 2030 (World Health Organization, 2021a).

Historically, limited evidence suggests that viral disease outbreaks have been associated with an increased suicide rate, particularly in its later stages (Leaune et al., 2020). Measures used to contain the pandemic, such as isolation, quarantine,

V. Menon (✉) · N. Varadharajan · R. Ganesh
Department of Psychiatry, Jawaharlal Institute of Postgraduate Medical Education and Research (JIPMER), Puducherry, India
e-mail: drvmenon@gmail.com

 
S. M. Y. Arafat and S. K. Kar (eds.), *Ecological and Social Determinants of Suicidal Behavior*, South Asian Perspectives in Mental Health and Psychology,
https://doi.org/10.1007/978-981-96-4028-7_9

and lockdown, may impact routines and livelihoods of people promoting loneliness, interpersonal problems, loss of wages, depression, anxiety, insomnia, substance use, self-harm, and suicidal behaviour (Cohen et al., 2024; Kumar & Nayar, 2021). All these, coupled with a lack of access to regular sources of support and coping, may cause difficulties in adjustment. A large body of evidence points to worsening mental health during the COVID-19 pandemic, compared to the pre-pandemic period (Breslau et al., 2021; Pierce et al., 2020).

For similar reasons, an increase in suicide rates in the general population has been noted in both pandemics as well as epidemics, such as the 2003 Severe Acute Respiratory Syndrome (SARS) in Hong Kong (Chan et al., 2006; Cheung et al., 2008), 1918 influenza outbreak in the United States (Wasserman, 1992), 1889–1894 Russian influenza outbreak in Europe (Smith, 1995), and the 2013–2016 Ebola outbreak in Guinea (Keita et al., 2017). In all these studies, the impact on suicide rates outlasted the period of the infection rise, underscoring the need to strengthen health systems and orient policy responses towards suicide prevention in the wake of infectious disease outbreaks.

Further, the longer-term impact of the pandemic on mental health and suicide may be disproportionately high in low-and-middle-income countries (LAMICs) where the existing health infrastructure is overloaded, health inequity is widespread, treatment gap for mental health and suicide is considerable, and social security support is meagre. However, there is scarce evidence on the long-term impact of infectious disease outbreaks on suicide rates in LAMICs. The available literature is not representative and largely overlooks key issues such as gender perspectives.

In this context, the present chapter aims to provide an overview of the key risk factors for suicidal behaviour during infectious pandemics, with a focus on at-risk populations. We specifically discuss the impact of the pandemic on suicide rates and trends to inform prevention activities. Finally, we discuss challenges in suicide research during a pandemic. The information provided in this chapter is likely to be of interest to clinicians, academics, research regulatory bodies, and policymakers.

## 2 Risk Factors for Suicidal Behaviour During the Pandemic

Pandemics disrupt the normal lives of individuals. While psychosocial factors remain largely the same, they impact suicidal behaviour to varying degrees in different pandemics across time (Mukhtar & Candilis, 2022). The recent COVID-19 pandemic and its effect on suicide mortality have been described as a perfect storm, bringing about considerable changes to the individual and society in terms of economic, psychosocial, and health-related factors compared to the earlier pandemics (Reger et al., 2020). Most risk factors outlined below can be understood in the framework of the biopsychosocial perspective (Menon et al., 2020) and through the lens of suicide theories by Joiner (Van Orden et al., 2010), Durkheim (Taylor, 1982), three-step (Klonsky & May, 2015), and social stress theories (Rubinstein, 1986) (Box 1 and Table 1).

**Box 1: Risk Factors Associated with Suicidal Behaviours During the Pandemic**

1. **Demographic factors**
   1.1 Age—younger or older
   1.2 Vocation—health care professional
2. **Socioeconomic factors**
   2.1 Economic factors (financial loss, unemployment)
   2.2 Social isolation
3. **Illness related factors**
   3.1 Anxiety symptoms
   3.2 Patients with chronic illness
   3.3 Sleep-related issues (poor sleep quality and nightmares)
   3.4 Pre-existing psychiatric disorder/prior history of suicide
   3.5 Substance use
4. **Psychological and social factors**
   4.1 Access to means
   4.2 Pandemic-related experiences (lockdown, quarantine, fear of contracting illness)
   4.3 Experiences of lockdown/quarantine
   4.4 Irresponsible media reporting of suicides during the pandemic
   4.5 Loneliness
   4.6 Low resilience
   4.7 Relationship difficulties

## 3 Demographic Factors

### *3.1 Age*

#### 3.1.1 Adolescents

Adolescents are considered a vulnerable group, with suicide being the fourth largest cause of death worldwide. In comparison to adults, adolescents are more prone to experiencing anxiety, depressive symptoms, and insomnia, along with suicidal thoughts and behaviour. This could be attributed to feelings of loneliness and heightened exposure to media coverage of suicides during pandemic times (Barberis et al., 2022; Murata et al., 2021).

**Table 1** Theories of suicide and their link with risk factors for suicide during a pandemic

| Theory of suicide | Association with suicide risk factors during a pandemic |
|---|---|
| **Durkheim's theory** (Taylor, 1982)<br>Suicide is influenced by the social relationships within a group or a class of individuals and it depends on the degree of social integration and social regulation | |
| Egoistic suicide (minimal social integration)<br>Altruistic suicide (excessive social integration)<br>Anomic suicide (minimal social regulation)<br>Fatalistic suicide (excessive social regulation) | Pandemic-related experiences (lockdown, quarantine, social isolation) lead to a lack of belonging and connectedness with society<br>Healthcare workers due to fear of spreading infection to family<br>Socioeconomic factors (financial loss, unemployment, loss of loved ones) especially those with chronic illness)<br>Pandemic-related experiences (lockdown, quarantine, social isolation) can also lead to a sense of entrapment with no hope for a future without suffering |
| **Interpersonal theory** (Van Orden et al., 2010)<br>Perceived burdensomeness<br>Thwarted belongingness | Socioeconomic factors (financial loss, unemployment, loss of loved ones) especially those with chronic illness)<br>Pandemic-related experiences (lockdown, quarantine, social isolation) lead to a lack of belonging and connectedness with society |
| **Three-step theory** (Klonsky & May, 2015)<br>Pain, hopelessness, connection, suicide capability | Pandemic-related experiences, economic factors resulting in distress leading to a feeling of being left alone or entrapment |
| **Biopsychosocial theory** (Menon et al., 2020)<br>Biological<br>Psychological<br>Social | Role of inflammation by neurotrophic virus increasing vulnerability to suicide<br>Low resilience, pandemic-related experiences, personality-related factors (intolerance to uncertainty), isolation<br>Socioeconomic factors, irresponsible media reporting |

### 3.1.2 Older Adults

The older adult population is often associated with medical comorbidities such as cardiovascular disorders, diabetes, and cancer. During pandemics, their perceived burdens can increase due to social isolation, lack of domestic help, self-neglect, existential issues, loneliness, and difficulty in accessing adequate medical care, making them a vulnerable group that may exhibit more suicidal behaviour (Wand et al., 2020) (Chan et al., 2006; Cheung et al., 2008; Martínez-Alés et al., 2023; Na et al., 2021). Furthermore, when they are not participating in decision-making during pandemics, their autonomy, self-esteem, and mobility are affected. (Banerjee, 2020) Particularly during the SARS epidemic, an increase in older adult suicides was observed among females (Chan et al., 2006; Cheung et al., 2008).

### 3.2 *Vocation—Healthcare Professionals*

Healthcare personnel, including physicians, nursing staff, and other allied professionals involved in patient care, are under immense pressure due to concerns about infection. They also face challenges such as isolating themselves from family or the fear of spreading the virus to them, shortages of manpower when colleagues become sick, lack of protective gear, and overwhelmed facilities, all of which contribute to significant burnout and work-related stress. Being the backbone of any nation's pandemic response, they are a vulnerable population that is more likely to experience anxiety, insomnia, and depression symptoms, particularly during unusual pandemics. This raises their risk of contemplating suicide. (Krishnamoorthy et al., 2020; Reger et al., 2020; Zhou et al., 2020). During the COVID-19 pandemic, many people faced the threat of eviction from their homes, which added to their psychological distress, leading to a cycle of social isolation and disconnection (Logie & Turan, 2020).

## 4 Socioeconomic Factors

As outlined earlier, suicide and related behaviour are complex. Hence, applying the biopsychosocial approach is important to understand it from a sociological perspective, as suggested by Durkheim (Menon et al., 2021). Psychosocial factors played a major role in suicide-related behaviour and ideations emerging during widespread outbreaks (Leaune et al., 2020).

### 4.1 *Economic Factors*

The financial impact of any pandemic is huge because of unemployment from layoffs, loss of business, cancelled events, debts, and fear of losing housing (Elbogen et al., 2021), which results in varying degrees of suicidal behaviours (Barberis et al., 2022.; Du et al., 2023; Reger et al., 2020). This impact becomes more pronounced in low and middle-income countries where many small-scale industries and migrant and daily wage workers are affected (Banerjee et al., 2021; Gunnell et al., 2020).

### 4.2 *Social Isolation*

The objective sense of being alone is referred to as social isolation. During pandemics and epidemics, quarantine and restriction protocols become mandatory, particularly in regions with high mortality rates. This disrupts individuals' normal routines and social connections, leading to significant distress. Those at a high risk of infection and mortality are more likely to be isolated from loved ones and may experience suicidal ideation (Biagioli et al., 2021; Chan et al., 2006; Du et al., 2023; Yip et al., 2010). The lack of social integration can engender feelings of entrapment and detachment from social networks, particularly among migrants, potentially leading to anomic suicide (Menon et al., 2021).

This is also consistent with Joiner's interpersonal theory of suicide, which states that thwarted belongingness increases suicide risk (Van Orden et al., 2010). Reduced access to religious and community groups during pandemics may further increase feelings of social isolation, leading to more suicidal ideation (Reger et al., 2020).

# 5 Illness-Related Factors

Older adult individuals and those with chronic medical conditions like cancer form a vulnerable population who are always at heightened risk of any infection (Biagioli et al., 2021; Cheung et al., 2008; Ernst et al., 2022). Medical and psychiatric complications arising from flu, HIV, and COVID-19 also increase the suicide risk (Mukhtar & Candilis, 2022).

## *5.1 Anxiety*

Fear of contracting/stigma due to the infection, experiences of infection and distress due to uncertainty, social isolation, loss of loved ones, and financial issues faced by individuals heightens the anxiety states or predisposes them to anxiety disorder (either exacerbating pre-existing or new onset). This has been one of the critical risk factors predisposing to suicidal ideations (Allan et al., 2021; Du et al., 2023). Especially during COVID-19, there was extensive coverage 24*7 on news channels related to the mortality and risk of infection, which increased the risk of anxiety among the public (Garfin et al., 2020).

## *5.2 Sleep Quality*

Sleep is an essential component for normal emotional well-being and functioning. Sleep disturbances and frequent nightmares have been related independently to suicidal ideations (Guo et al., 2024). Both were extensively reported during the pandemic (Gupta et al., 2020; Krishnamoorthy et al., 2020) and were found to be associated with suicidal-related behaviour (Bolstad et al., 2024; Du et al., 2023). A recent study with data from 11 countries found that the frequency of nightmares increased during the pandemic by 4.5% when compared to before, and it was associated with an increased likelihood of suicidal ideations (Bolstad et al., 2024). The anxiety of contracting the infection was also correlated with the severity of insomnia (Killgore et al., 2020; Sher, 2020).

### *5.3 Pre-existing Mental Disorders*

Pre-existing mental illnesses, particularly depressive disorders, appear to be a significant risk factor for suicide conduct during pandemics. The psychological burden in these people is increased by limited access to mental health facilities, grieving over loved ones lost, social disengagement, social isolation, and loneliness, in addition to financial difficulties (Barlattani et al., 2023; Berardelli et al., 2021; Na et al., 2021). Individuals who had previously attempted suicide were shown to be more vulnerable during the pandemic. (Du et al., 2023). Among others, those with obsessive–compulsive, anxiety, and eating disorders experienced worsening of the illness, predisposing them to suicidal-related behaviour (Barberis et al., 2022). Also, peak mental health problems may be evident in the aftermath of a pandemic (Gunnell et al., 2020).

### *5.4 Substance Use*

Substance use, like alcohol intake, has been a well-known risk factor associated with suicidality (Ferrari et al., 2014). Multiple studies have found that alcohol consumption, particularly among heavy drinkers and cannabis users in middle-aged and older individuals, has elevated the risk of suicide-related behaviour during the recent COVID-19 pandemic (Geda et al., 2022; Varin et al., 2023). However, contextual factors operate due to different restrictions and policies across countries. Suicide rates increased in Australia and India (Sohi et al., 2022), where alcohol consumption declined and alcohol sales were prohibited during the early stages of the COVID-19 pandemic (Shoib et al., 2022).

The sudden and complete restriction imposed in countries like India led to a surge in suicides. Alcohol users experienced extreme despair due to withdrawal symptoms, and increasing suicidal behaviour (Ahmed et al., 2020; Syed & Griffiths, 2020).

## 6 Psychological and Physical Factors

In addition to those who already have mental health conditions, people with psychological problems such as low self-esteem and loneliness are another vulnerable population that is more likely to attempt suicide (Almaghrebi, 2021; Du et al., 2023).

## 6.1 Access to Means

Another significant modifiable risk factor to consider is easy access to means like firearms and pesticides. Research has shown that the sales of these items tend to increase during pandemics, which can contribute to heightened risk factors for individuals (Gunnell et al., 2020; Reger et al., 2020).

## 6.2 Pandemic-Related Experiences

The COVID-19/SARS pandemic and the associated experiences of lockdown, quarantine, and the fear of contracting the illness can lead to suicide-related behaviours in vulnerable individuals such as adolescents, health workers, and older adults (Cheung et al., 2008; Du et al., 2023; Ernst et al., 2022; Gracia et al., 2021; Yip et al., 2010). Besides this, COVID-19 infection causes significant neurobiological changes, leading to neuropsychiatric manifestations later; therefore, recovered COVID-19 survivors are at an elevated risk of suicide (Sher, 2020).

Drawing from Durkheim's sociological perspective, it is imperative to recognize that the apprehension surrounding the contraction of infection and the subsequent transmission to one's family may cultivate a sense of fatalism, potentially inciting acts of altruistic self-harm (Menon et al., 2021).

## 6.3 Irresponsible Media Reporting of Suicides During the Pandemic

Research suggests that irresponsible media reporting predisposes or precipitates suicidal behaviour, referred to as the 'Werther effect' (Niederkrotenthaler et al., 2020). Extensive media coverage of suicide can increase anxiety in the general population, too (Garfin et al., 2020; Gunnell et al., 2020; Kar et al., 2021). Repeated celebrity suicides during the pandemic and the extensive coverage in television and print media like newspapers (Kar et al., 2020), which do not adhere to the WHO-recommended guidelines for responsible media reporting of suicides, trigger imitative suicides. Multiple lines of research along these lines point towards the role of irresponsible media reporting towards suicide (Ganesh et al., 2022; Kar et al., 2021; Menon et al., 2021).

### *6.4 Loneliness*

Loneliness, a modifiable risk factor, is the subjective feeling of being alone (Allan et al., 2021; Antonelli-Salgado et al., 2021; Du et al., 2023), particularly in high-risk individuals (older adults and those with chronic illnesses like cancer who are elevated risk of contracting the infection) predisposed to suicidal ideation (Antonelli-Salgado et al., 2021; Ernst et al., 2022). Feelings of social detachment stemming from loneliness have the potential to precipitate egoistic suicide (Mueller et al., 2021).

### *6.5 Low Resilience*

Resilience is a psychological construct that determines how an individual copes with adversity. Those with low resilience are at increased risk of developing suicide-related behaviours (four-fold) independent of age, sex, marital, and employment status. This risk increased further when they had pre-existing mental illnesses like major depressive disorder (Llistosella et al., 2022).

### *6.6 Relationship Difficulties*

Reports of maltreatment, domestic abuse, and relationship issues have significantly increased throughout the COVID-19 pandemic. The implementation of COVID-19 restriction protocols exacerbated these issues, leading to a rise in suicidal ideation among affected individuals. Particularly concerning is the situation of families with pre-existing marital disharmony and violence, as they are now forced to cohabit for extended periods due to lockdowns and other restrictions. This prolonged proximity has heightened these families' challenges, potentially leading to further negative outcomes (Barberis et al., 2022; Blum et al., 2024; Knowles et al., 2022).

## 7 Suicidal Behaviour During the Pandemic in Special Populations

A pandemic can create a disproportionate impact on vulnerable populations, including children and adolescents, patients with mental illness, women, older adults and other vulnerable groups like the LGBTQ community and migrants (Table 2).

**Table 2** Risk factors for suicide during a pandemic in special population

| Population | Risk factors |
|---|---|
| Child and adolescent | Disruption in schooling, depression, substance use, family history of suicidal behaviour, increased time spent on media related to the pandemic |
| Older adults | Loneliness, pre-existing psychiatric illness, medical comorbidities, perceived health concerns |
| Healthcare workers | Work-related stress, fear of contagion, history of psychiatric illness, prior suicide attempts, living alone, substance use, poor working conditions, having infected family members, changes in work patterns |
| Women | Loneliness, economic challenges, maltreatment, domestic violence, feeling like a burden, lack of meaningful social connections |

## 7.1 Children and Adolescents

Adolescents were more likely to report suicidal ideation or behaviour compared to adults. Depression and loneliness were identified as significant contributors to the increased rates of suicidal behaviours among children and adolescents during the pandemic. During the pandemic, children and adolescents experienced significant disruptions in their daily activities. Factors such as remote schooling, potential illness, and economic shutdowns exacerbated these mental health challenges, further elevating the risk of suicidality.

The pandemic also exacerbated various risk factors for mental illness among this population, including excessive screen time, minimal physical activity, a rise in domestic violence, worsening parental mental health, increased parental substance use, financial instability, and the loss of family members.

Adolescent girls were found to be particularly affected by these changes (Gracia et al., 2021). The most common method of suicide among this age group was hanging (Schnitzer et al., 2023). Studies examining suicidal behaviour among college students during the pandemic have identified several key risk factors. These include substance abuse, poor sleep quality, a personal or family history of suicidal behaviours, and the presence of internalizing symptoms such as anxiety and depression (Nomura et al., 2021a, 2021b).

Approximately three-fourths of suicides among young people occurred within a month of lockdown measures being implemented. Higher social media exposure, especially the information related to the pandemic, predicts suicidal behaviour in adolescents (Murata et al., 2021). The psychological distress, which is already widespread due to the pandemic, could worsen without sufficient family support.

## 7.2 Older Adults

Older adults are also at increased risk of mental health issues during the pandemic due to age-related changes to the immune system, which would make it harder for them to cope with the infection and disease. Studies reported that loneliness and disconnectedness could contribute to an excess rate of suicides among older adults (Cheung et al., 2008). Findings from other studies highlighted that those with a history of psychiatric disorders and those with significant health concerns were at a heightened risk of suicidal behaviours during the pandemic (Louie et al., 2021; Winkler et al., 2020).

The population over 60 years of age is particularly at risk, as evidenced by elevated COVID-19 peritraumatic distress scores, rendering them more susceptible to adverse psychological outcomes. Among older adults, the prevalence of peritraumatic distress was significantly higher in those residing in rural areas, living alone, with comorbidities, or with poor self-rated health status compared to others (Fadila et al., 2022).

The combination of heightened stress from life events and existing psychological distress is a significant predictor of suicidal risk, with a moderate correlation observed between stress levels and suicidal ideation.

## 7.3 Healthcare Workers

Healthcare workers (HCWs) are vulnerable to adverse psychological outcomes during a pandemic due to their high risk of exposure. The heightened risk among HCWs can exacerbate during the pandemic due to burnout, reduced connectedness with family and friends, and bearing witness to the human toll of the pandemic.

A study evaluating press media reports of healthcare worker suicides identified stress related to work and fear of contagion as the most common causes of suicidal behaviour during the pandemic (Jahan et al., 2021). A previous history of psychiatric illness, prior suicide attempts, living alone, poor physical health, single or separated marital status, and substance use are factors that aggravate suicidal tendencies in HCWs (García-Iglesias et al., 2022). Additional contributing factors include economic concerns, poor working conditions, having infected family members, changes in work patterns, and experiencing discrimination from society due to the fear of exposure.

Additionally, operational difficulties such as insufficient personal protective equipment, increased patient loads, decision-making pressures, high patient mortality, extended shifts, and reallocation from usual services have further impacted HCWs' mental well-being (Mahalingam et al., 2022). HCWs are particularly vulnerable to fatal suicide attempts due to their access to potent medications and their knowledge of effective dosages.

## 7.4 *Patients with Psychiatric Disorders*

Patients with severe mental illness are at higher risk of suicidality compared to those without psychiatric disorders. A study conducted in psychiatry hospitals found that those who are at a younger age, with a family history of suicide attempts, severe depressive symptoms and inpatient status, were at higher risk of suicidality (Li et al., 2022).

The implementation of strict lockdown measures had a negative psychological impact on psychiatric inpatients (Hao et al., 2020). A study involving 312 participants diagnosed with eating disorders revealed that the severity of their psychopathology intensified during the lockdown phase of the pandemic, and the symptoms persisted even during the post-lockdown phase. However, suicidal ideations were predominantly reported only during the lockdown period (Monteleone et al., 2021).

## 7.5 *Women*

Research has identified loneliness and economic challenges as contributing factors (Reger et al., 2020) for suicidal behaviour. However, other studies reported an overall rise in suicide rates, regardless of age or employment status (Kikuchi et al., 2023) among women. The literature also emphasizes the role of maltreatment, domestic violence, relationship issues, and financial hardships in exacerbating suicidal tendencies (Knowles et al., 2022). Additional factors, such as feeling like a burden, lack of meaningful social connections, and social isolation, have been consistently reported in those with suicidal behaviour (Crasta et al., 2020; Han et al., 2021).

## 7.6 *Others*

There was a significant worsening of depressive symptoms, with rates considerably higher than pre-COVID levels among the marginalized groups. Studies in transgender and gender-diverse individuals found worsening in self-harm ideation due to factors such as financial difficulty, feeling unsafe and undue delay in planned surgeries like gender-affirming surgery (Zwickl et al., 2023).

Migrants faced significant challenges in accessing the mental healthcare services. They were at risk of isolation and separation from their support networks. Their work was severely impacted due to the informal nature of the jobs. A study conducted in Qatar found that younger age, current feelings of hopelessness, and prior self-harm attempts were strongly associated with suicidal behaviour migrants (AlAbdulla et al., 2022).

# 8 Impact of the pandemic on Trends in Suicidal Behaviour

## *8.1 Influenza Pandemic*

First investigated during the Great Influenza pandemic (also known as the Spanish Flu) of 1918–1920, the impact of the pandemic on suicide and related behaviours revealed that increasing social distancing increased suicide rates independently of influenza mortality rate (Stack & Rockett, 2021; Wasserman, 1992).

However, a time-series analysis study by Rück et al. (2021) (Sweden) of various influenza pandemics (1910–1978 yearly data) failed to reveal any short-term or long-term association between death rates due to influenza or suicide. Interestingly, another study using similar data from studies done in the USA disputes that the flu pandemic had led to a decrease in suicide rates (Gaddy, 2021).

## *8.2 COVID-19 Pandemic*

Only one study examined the rate of psychiatric admissions in University Psychiatric Hospital Vrapče, Zagreb, between 1919 and 1920 and found no significant rise in psychiatric admissions during the Influenza and the COVID-19 pandemic. However, a difference was observed in specific diagnostic categories. This study found that during COVID-19, the biggest decline of psychiatric admissions was observed for the affective disorders group, closely followed by schizophrenia spectrum disorders.

In contrast, during the Spanish flu, the psychogenic disorder group had the biggest decline, followed by schizophrenia spectrum disorders, with an increase in affective disorder patients (Vukojević et al., 2021). This pattern is unlikely to be attributed to the restriction of travel alone. Although it's observed that mental health issues problems might increase, not necessarily to a clinically diagnosable stage. The significance of these findings is not well understood.

As previously discussed, any pandemic disrupts individuals' normal lives, causing significant distress due to various psychosocial and economic factors and predisposing them to suicide. During viral outbreaks other than COVID-19, psychosocial factors have been linked to suicide. However, there is only weak evidence for an increase in suicide rates. Even during the COVID-19 pandemic, there was a significant surge in research reports related to suicide. Similar to previous pandemics, trends in suicidal behaviour (such as ideations, attempts, and deaths) have not been as significant as expected (Tandon, 2021).

A study evaluated news reports from 56 online media publications during the COVID-19 pandemic (March to May 2020) and found that there was a 67.7% increase compared to the corresponding previous year (March to May 2019) before the pandemic. Hanging was the most common method employed for suicide followed by poisoning and jumping in front of a train. Also, there was a significant increase in suicides by hanging with a decrease in poisoning and jumping in front of trains compared to the period before the pandemic. This observed trend could reflect the increase in suicidal behaviour in the community or the increase in sensational media reporting of suicide (Kar et al., 2021; Pathare et al., 2020).

In terms of demographics, older individuals, married, men, employed, and having poor physical and mental health were at increased suicide risk compared to the pre-pandemic times (Kar et al., 2021; Pathare et al., 2020). Based on the meta-analysis by Pathirathna et al. (2022), the total number of suicidal attempts and deaths during the COVID-19 pandemic were 12,746 and 33,345, respectively. Due to the different timelines of data collection throughout the pandemic and limited data availability from certain studies, obtaining a combined estimate is challenging (Pathirathna et al., 2022).

The evidence on trends in suicidal behaviour during a pandemic is conflicting and depends on the socio-demographic and economic status of the country. A systematic review of 18 studies found that 22.2% reported an increasing trend in suicidal attempts, 11.1% showed a decreasing trend, and one study reported no change. For suicidal deaths, 16.7% of studies reported an increasing trend, 5.6% reported a decreasing trend, and 16.7% reported no change (Pathirathna et al., 2022). One study even reported a decreasing trend of suicidal deaths during the crisis, which increased after the crisis had passed (Nomura et al, 2021a, 2021b).

An earlier review assessing suicide mortality in 21 high- and upper-middle-income countries during the early pandemic also failed to find a consistent rise in suicide rates. Nine countries, including Japan, New Zealand, South Korea, the United States, Australia, Canada, Chile, Ecuador, and Germany, experienced a decrease in regional suicides, whereas no rate change was noted in other countries (Pirkis et al., 2021). New evidence from a recent living systematic review indicates that there is a lack of clear association between the COVID-19 pandemic and an increase in suicidal behaviour. However, concerning trends have been observed in Nepal and Japan (John et al., 2021). It is conceivable that the shared distress experienced across societies has led to a 'coming together' effect among certain individuals and communities, potentially bolstering resilience and hope (Sinyor et al., 2022).

## 9 Prevention

World Health Organization (WHO) developed various initiatives, such as a series of messages to improve psychosocial well-being targeting different groups such as adults, children, and healthcare workers.

The LIVE LIFE framework encapsulates the core components of a strategic approach to suicide prevention (World Health Organization, 2021b). It establishes the foundational elements for suicide prevention, representing leadership, interventions, vision, and evaluation. The LIFE pillars include critical interventions such as reducing access to the means of suicide, improving media reporting, equipping young people with essential life skills, and ensuring early identification and management.

## 9.1 Universal Interventions

Suicide prevention necessitates a comprehensive strategy that targets the entire population through universal measures. Active policies addressing employment, such as job search assistance, training programs, and subsidized employment, have positively affected health and quality of life. At the national level, increased government investment in active labour market policies has been linked to a reduction in the impact of unemployment on suicide rates.

There were various initiatives in India by the Government and other institutions to address the mental health challenges (Rangaswamy et al., 2022). To reduce the burden of mental illness, the Indian government has incorporated mental health services into the package of services provided under Comprehensive Primary Health Care through the Ayushman Bharat initiative. The MOHFW provided a toll-free helpline, videos, and advisories on coping with stress, yoga, and meditation during the pandemic. Various guidelines were released, such as Minding Our Minds, Mental Health Support for Healthcare Workers Guidelines, and Managing Mental Illness in Hospitals.

Hanging, firearms, poisoning/overdose, and jumping from heights are among the most frequently reported suicide methods (Cano-Montalbán & Quevedo-Blasco, 2017). To reduce the risk of suicide, access to these lethal means is often restricted through various strategies. These include limiting the size of medication packs, designing safer environments—particularly in hospitals—by reducing potential suspension points for hanging, enforcing stricter firearm regulations, installing barriers and safety nets at known jumping sites, and controlling access to highly lethal pesticides.

During the pandemic, it is crucial to reinforce policies that restrict access to suicidal means. For instance, stockpiling medications and pesticides due to fears of shortages may increase risks (Motamed-Jahromi et al., 2021), and governments at both national and regional levels should monitor the sales of these potentially lethal items. Temporary restrictions on the quantity of medications purchased per person could be implemented alongside public awareness campaigns and policies that ensure the safe storage of drugs and pesticides.

Reduction of substance use, including alcohol through treatment and national policies were shown to decrease suicide rates. Psychosocial issues during the pandemic can influence an increase in substance use, which in turn could aggravate the risk of suicidal behaviour (Norström & Rossow, 2016). WHO, along with other government bodies, raised awareness regarding the negative consequences of alcohol and other substance use during the pandemic.

Responsible media coverage plays a critical role in preventing suicidal behaviours among readers (Sisask & Värnik, 2012). Critical practices include avoiding the sensationalization or normalization of suicide, limiting detailed descriptions of methods and locations, and refraining from displaying photos or videos related to suicide. Additionally, media outlets should provide information on the effectiveness of suicide prevention strategies and resources for seeking help.

During the pandemic, it is especially important to consider the implications of reporting on suicide, particularly when the content is pandemic-related. Journalists must be made aware of and adhere to existing WHO guidelines for responsible media coverage of suicide, with particular emphasis on pandemic-related content (World Health Organization, 2023). The increased time individuals spend consuming media during crisis events has been associated with heightened distress, making it crucial to recommend limiting media exposure during such periods to mitigate adverse effects.

## 9.2 Selective Interventions

Interventions such as the 'Living with the Times' toolkit were developed to support the mental health and psychosocial well-being of older adults. The toolkit had key messages in the form of posters that could be easily used to have guided conversations and taking care of older adults.

The pandemic presents unique challenges to suicide prevention efforts, particularly as many trained gatekeepers, such as frontline responders, are primarily occupied with addressing the needs of those affected by the virus (Grover et al., 2020). Additionally, lockdown measures have made it difficult for members of the general population to engage with individuals at risk of suicide. Emerging at-risk populations, such as first responders, healthcare workers, and individuals bereaved by COVID-19, should also be prioritized while planning intervention strategies.

In response, various organizations have intensified efforts to train a broad range of key individuals, including teachers, first responders, community volunteers, and students, to identify and support suicidal individuals during the pandemic. To ensure both safety from infection and broad participation, these training programs could be conducted online, allowing for continued education and the involvement of a more significant number of volunteers (Nozawa et al., 2022).

## 9.3 Indicated Interventions

Indicated preventive strategies for individuals exhibiting suicidal behaviour should emphasize the availability and implementation of pharmacological and psychological treatments for mental disorders, ensuring continuity of care through enhanced follow-up and the expanded use of telemedicine and other digital health platforms. NIMHANS released comprehensive guidance on mental healthcare during COVID-19 for general medical and specialized mental health settings.

Online capacity building through the iGOT-Diksha platform was initiated for Training health workers in providing psychosocial support. Telemedicine platforms such as eSanjeevani OPD were launched to allow patients to consult doctors remotely, and people also showed interest in using such innovative telemedicine programs (Ganesh et al., 2022).

**Table 3** Interventions for suicide prevention during the pandemic

| Universal intervention | Selective intervention | Indicated intervention |
|---|---|---|
| • Addressing unemployment, poverty, and social inequities<br>• Ensuring broad access to mental health services<br>• Promoting responsible media practices that highlight available support resources;<br>• Curbing alcohol consumption<br>• Limiting access to lethal means of suicide | • Interventions for vulnerable groups<br>• Gatekeeper training | • Treatment of mental illness<br>• Continuity of care<br>• Telepsychiatry |

The national tele-mental health program, Tele-Manas Program, was initiated to address mental health issues nationwide. These initiatives aimed to provide comprehensive mental health support during the pandemic, utilizing digital platforms and community outreach.

The COVID-19 pandemic has highlighted the need to increase resources for preventive activities at the community level. Table 3 summarizes various interventions for suicide prevention during the pandemic. Many governments worldwide increased the funds for welfare measures and focused on improving mental healthcare accessibility after the pandemic. Governments have also implemented various measures, including telemedicine services, to address the closure of traditional mental health services and enact legislative amendments to support telepsychiatry. These initiatives extended mental healthcare access to populations in remote areas, thereby overcoming restrictions on movement and ensuring continued support for those in need.

## 10 Conclusion

Limited evidence links pandemics and viral disease outbreaks with increased suicidal behaviour in the population. A range of demographic, socio-economic, physical and mental illness-related, and psychological factors may confer increased vulnerability to suicide during a pandemic. Sub-populations such as children, older adults, patients with mental illness, and the marginalized sections of society are disproportionately impacted by the pandemic, leading to an increased risk of suicide. Given this scenario, and given the impact of pandemics on suicide trends and rates, there is a need for a coordinated, collaborative, multi-sectoral approach to suicide prevention during pandemics. These approaches, while anchored in evidence, must also reflect local priorities to have the maximum uptake and impact.

## References

Ahmed, S., Khaium, M. O., & Tazmeem, F. (2020). COVID-19 lockdown in India triggers a rapid rise in suicides due to the alcohol withdrawal symptoms: Evidence from media reports. *The International Journal of Social Psychiatry, 66*(8), 827–829. https://doi.org/10.1177/0020764020938809

AlAbdulla, M., Reagu, S. M., Hassan, M. H. M. O., Elhassan, N. M., Sayed, S., Makki, I., Elzain, M., Wadoo, O., & Kumar, R. (2022). Suicidal behavior in a migrant majority population and impact on trends during the early Covid-19 period: A cross sectional study in Qatar. *Discover Psychology, 2*(1), 28. https://doi.org/10.1007/s44202-022-00040-8

Allan, N. P., Volarov, M., Koscinski, B., Pizzonia, K. L., Potter, K., Accorso, C., Saulnier, K. G., Ashrafioun, L., Stecker, T., Suhr, J., & Allan, D. M. (2021). Lonely, anxious, and uncertain: Critical risk factors for suicidal desire during the COVID-19 pandemic. *Psychiatry Research, 304*, 114144. https://doi.org/10.1016/j.psychres.2021.114144

Almaghrebi, A. H. (2021). Risk factors for attempting suicide during the COVID-19 lockdown: Identification of the high-risk groups. *Journal of Taibah University Medical Sciences, 16*(4), 605–611. https://doi.org/10.1016/j.jtumed.2021.04.010

Antonelli-Salgado, T., Monteiro, G. M. C., Marcon, G., Roza, T. H., Zimerman, A., Hoffmann, M. S., Cao, B., Hauck, S., Brunoni, A. R., & Passos, I. C. (2021). Loneliness, but not social distancing, is associated with the incidence of suicidal ideation during the COVID-19 outbreak: A longitudinal study. *Journal of Affective Disorders, 290*, 52–60. https://doi.org/10.1016/j.jad.2021.04.044

Banerjee, D. (2020). 'Age and ageism in COVID-19': Elderly mental health-care vulnerabilities and needs. *Asian Journal of Psychiatry, 51*, 102154. https://doi.org/10.1016/j.ajp.2020.102154

Banerjee, D., Kosagisharaf, J. R., & Sathyanarayana Rao, T. S. (2021). 'The dual pandemic' of suicide and COVID-19: A biopsychosocial narrative of risks and prevention. *Psychiatry Research, 295*, 113577. https://doi.org/10.1016/j.psychres.2020.113577

Barberis, N., Cannavò, M., Cuzzocrea, F., & Verrastro, V. (2022). Suicidal behaviours during Covid-19 pandemic: A review. *Clinical Neuropsychiatry, 19*(2), 84–96. https://doi.org/10.36131/cnfioritieditore20220202

Barlattani, T., D'Amelio, C., Capelli, F., Mantenuto, S., Rossi, R., Socci, V., Stratta, P., Di Stefano, R., Rossi, A., & Pacitti, F. (2023). Suicide and COVID-19: A rapid scoping review. *Annals of General Psychiatry, 22*, 10. https://doi.org/10.1186/s12991-023-00441-6

Berardelli, I., Sarubbi, S., Rogante, E., Cifrodelli, M., Erbuto, D., Innamorati, M., Lester, D., & Pompili, M. (2021). The impact of the COVID-19 pandemic on suicide ideation and suicide attempts in a sample of psychiatric inpatients. *Psychiatry Research, 303*, 114072. https://doi.org/10.1016/j.psychres.2021.114072

Biagioli, V., Albanesi, B., Belloni, S., Piredda, A., & Caruso, R. (2021). Living with cancer in the COVID-19 pandemic: An Italian survey on self-isolation at home. *European Journal of Cancer Care, 30*(2), e13385. https://doi.org/10.1111/ecc.13385

Blum, Y., Akhavan, S., Rogers, M. L., Astudillo-García, C. I., Çinka, E., Kantas Yilmaz, F., Peper-Nascimento, J., Streb, J., Chistopolskaya, K., Cohen, L. J., Dudeck, M., Lutz, M., Lee, M.-B., Husain, M. I., Kuśmirek, O., Valvassori, S. S., You, S., Menon, V., Galynker, I., & Barzilay, S. (2024). The role of interpersonal stressors and connectedness in acute suicide risk and the suicide crisis syndrome during the COVID-19 pandemic. *Journal of Affective Disorders, 354*, 19–25. https://doi.org/10.1016/j.jad.2024.02.087

Bolstad, C. J., Holzinger, B., Scarpelli, S., De Gennaro, L., Yordanova, J., Koumanova, S., Mota-Rolim, S., Benedict, C., Bjorvatn, B., Chan, N. Y., Chung, F., Dauvilliers, Y., Espie, C. A., Inoue, Y., Korman, M., Koscec Bjelajac, A., Landtblom, A.-M., Matsui, K., Merikanto, I., … Nadorff, M. R. (2024). Nightmare frequency is a risk factor for suicidal ideation during the COVID-19 pandemic. *Journal of Sleep Research*, e14165. https://doi.org/10.1111/jsr.14165

Breslau, J., Finucane, M. L., Locker, A. R., Baird, M. D., Roth, E. A., & Collins, R. L. (2021). A longitudinal study of psychological distress in the United States before and during the COVID-19 pandemic. *Preventive Medicine, 143*, 106362. https://doi.org/10.1016/j.ypmed.2020.106362

Cano-Montalbán, I., & Quevedo-Blasco, R. (2017). Sociodemographic variables most associated with suicidal behaviour and suicide methods in Europe and America. A systematic review. *European Journal of Psychology Applied to Legal Context, 10*(1), 15–25. https://doi.org/10.5093/ejpalc2018a2

Chan, S. M. S., Chiu, F. K. H., Lam, C. W. L., Leung, P. Y. V., & Conwell, Y. (2006). Elderly suicide and the 2003 SARS epidemic in Hong Kong. *International Journal of Geriatric Psychiatry, 21*(2), 113–118. https://doi.org/10.1002/gps.1432

Cheung, Y. T., Chau, P. H., & Yip, P. S. F. (2008). A revisit on older adults suicides and Severe Acute Respiratory Syndrome (SARS) epidemic in Hong Kong. *International Journal of Geriatric Psychiatry, 23*(12), 1231–1238. https://doi.org/10.1002/gps.2056

Cohen, L. J., Liang, Y., Peterkin, D., McGibbon, K., Rappa, F., Rogers, M. L., You, S., Chistopolskaya, K., Enikolopov, S., Barzilay, S., Menon, V., Husain, M. I., Dudeck, M., Streb, J., Çinka, E., Yilmaz, F. K., Kuśmirek, O., Valvassori, S. S., Blum, Y., & Galynker, I. (2024). Relationship between severity and length of exposure to COVID-19 parameters and resulting government responses and the suicide crisis syndrome (SCS). *Disaster Medicine and Public Health Preparedness, 18*, e68. https://doi.org/10.1017/dmp.2023.235

Crasta, D., Daks, J. S., & Rogge, R. D. (2020). Modeling suicide risk among parents during the COVID-19 pandemic: Psychological inflexibility exacerbates the impact of COVID-19 stressors on interpersonal risk factors for suicide. *Journal of Contextual Behavioral Science, 18*, 117–127. https://doi.org/10.1016/j.jcbs.2020.09.003

Du, W., Jia, Y. J., Hu, F. H., Ge, M. W., Cheng, Y. J., Qu, X., & Chen, H. L. (2023). Prevalence of suicidal ideation and correlated risk factors during the COVID-19 pandemic: A meta-analysis of 113 studies from 31 countries. *Journal of Psychiatric Research, 166*, 147–168. https://doi.org/10.1016/j.jpsychires.2023.07.040

Elbogen, E. B., Lanier, M., Blakey, S. M., Wagner, H. R., & Tsai, J. (2021). Suicidal ideation and thoughts of self-harm during the COVID-19 pandemic: The role of COVID-19-related stress, social isolation, and financial strain. *Depression and Anxiety, 38*(7), 739–748. https://doi.org/10.1002/da.23162

Ernst, M., Beutel, M. E., & Brähler, E. (2022). Cancer as a risk factor for distress and its interactions with sociodemographic variables in the context of the first wave of the COVID-19 pandemic in Germany. *Scientific Reports, 12*, 2021. https://doi.org/10.1038/s41598-022-06016-x

Fadila, D. E. S., Ibrahim, F. M., & El-Gilany, A.-H. (2022). Psychological distress among older adults during COVID-19 pandemic: Prevalence and associated factors. *Geriatric Nursing (New York, N.Y.), 43*, 265. https://doi.org/10.1016/j.gerinurse.2021.12.006

Ferrari, A. J., Norman, R. E., Freedman, G., Baxter, A. J., Pirkis, J. E., Harris, M. G., Page, A., Carnahan, E., Degenhardt, L., Vos, T., & Whiteford, H. A. (2014). The burden attributable to mental and substance use disorders as risk factors for suicide: Findings from the global burden of disease study 2010. *PLoS ONE, 9*(4), e91936. https://doi.org/10.1371/journal.pone.0091936

Gaddy, H. G. (2021). Social distancing and influenza mortality in 1918 did not increase suicide rates in the United States. *SSM—Population Health, 16*, 100944. https://doi.org/10.1016/j.ssmph.2021.100944

Ganesh, R., Deb, K. S., & Subbiah, A. (2022). Technology and medical care in India: Growth of telehealth awareness during the COVID-19 pandemic. *The Journal of the Association of Physicians of India, 70*(10), 11–12. https://doi.org/10.5005/japi-11001-0111

García-Iglesias, J. J., Gómez-Salgado, J., Fernández-Carrasco, F. J., Rodríguez-Díaz, L., Vázquez-Lara, J. M., Prieto-Callejero, B., & Allande-Cussó, R. (2022). Suicidal ideation and suicide attempts in healthcare professionals during the COVID-19 pandemic: A systematic review. *Frontiers in Public Health, 10*, 1043216. https://doi.org/10.3389/fpubh.2022.1043216

Garfin, D. R., Silver, R. C., & Holman, E. A. (2020). The novel coronavirus (COVID-2019) outbreak: Amplification of public health consequences by media exposure. *Health Psychology : Official*

*Journal of the Division of Health Psychology, American Psychological Association, 39*(5), 355–357. https://doi.org/10.1037/hea0000875

Geda, N., Feng, C., & Peters, B. (2022). Suicidal ideation among Canadian adults during the COVID-19 pandemic: The role of psychosocial factors and substance use behaviours. *BMC Psychiatry, 22*(1), 711. https://doi.org/10.1186/s12888-022-04353-9

Gracia, R., Pamias, M., Mortier, P., Alonso, J., Pérez, V., & Palao, D. (2021). Is the COVID-19 pandemic a risk factor for suicide attempts in adolescent girls? *Journal of Affective Disorders, 292*, 139–141. https://doi.org/10.1016/j.jad.2021.05.044

Grover, S., Mehra, A., Sahoo, S., Avasthi, A., Tripathi, A., D'Souza, A., Saha, G., Jagadhisha, A., Gowda, M., Vaishnav, M., Singh, O., Dalal, P. K., & Kumar, P. (2020). State of mental health services in various training centers in India during the lockdown and COVID-19 pandemic. *Indian Journal of Psychiatry, 62*(4), 363–369. https://doi.org/10.4103/psychiatry.IndianJPsychiatry_567_20

Gunnell, D., Appleby, L., Arensman, E., Hawton, K., John, A., Kapur, N., Khan, M., O'Connor, R. C., & Pirkis, J. (2020). Suicide risk and prevention during the COVID-19 pandemic. *The Lancet. Psychiatry, 7*(6), 468–471. https://doi.org/10.1016/S2215-0366(20)30171-1

Guo, Z., Han, X., Kong, T., Wu, Y., Kang, Y., Liu, Y., & Wang, F. (2024). The mediation effects of nightmares and depression between insomnia and suicidal ideation in young adults. *Scientific Reports, 14*(1), 9577. https://doi.org/10.1038/s41598-024-58774-5

Gupta, R., Grover, S., Basu, A., Krishnan, V., Tripathi, A., Subramanyam, A., Nischal, A., Hussain, A., Mehra, A., Ambekar, A., Saha, G., Mishra, K. K., Bathla, M., Jagiwala, M., Manjunatha, N., Nebhinani, N., Gaur, N., Kumar, N., Dalal, P. K., … Avasthi, A. (2020). Changes in sleep pattern and sleep quality during COVID-19 lockdown. *Indian Journal of Psychiatry, 62*(4), 370–378. https://doi.org/10.4103/psychiatry.IndianJPsychiatry_523_20

Han, Y., Jang, J., Cho, E., & Choi, K.-H. (2021). Investigating how individual differences influence responses to the COVID-19 crisis: The role of maladaptive and five-factor personality traits. *Personality and Individual Differences, 176*, 110786. https://doi.org/10.1016/j.paid.2021.110786

Hao, F., Tan, W., Jiang, L., Zhang, L., Zhao, X., Zou, Y., Hu, Y., Luo, X., Jiang, X., McIntyre, R. S., Tran, B., Sun, J., Zhang, Z., Ho, R., Ho, C., & Tam, W. (2020). Do psychiatric patients experience more psychiatric symptoms during COVID-19 pandemic and lockdown? A case-control study with service and research implications for immunopsychiatry. *Brain, Behavior, and Immunity, 87*, 100–106. https://doi.org/10.1016/j.bbi.2020.04.069

Jahan, I., Ullah, I., Griffiths, M. D., & Mamun, M. A. (2021). COVID-19 suicide and its causative factors among the healthcare professionals: Case study evidence from press reports. *Perspectives in Psychiatric Care, 57*(4), 1707–1711. https://doi.org/10.1111/ppc.12739

John, A., Eyles, E., Webb, R. T., Okolie, C., Schmidt, L., Arensman, E., Hawton, K., O'Connor, R. C., Kapur, N., Moran, P., O'Neill, S., McGuiness, L. A., Olorisade, B. K., Dekel, D., Macleod-Hall, C., Cheng, H.-Y., Higgins, J. P. T., & Gunnell, D. (2021). The impact of the COVID-19 pandemic on self-harm and suicidal behaviour: Update of living systematic review. *F1000Research, 9*, 1097. https://doi.org/10.12688/f1000research.25522.2

Kar, S. K., Menon, V., Arafat, S. M. Y., & Kabir, R. (2020). Research in Mental Health During the COVID-19 pandemic: Quality versus quantity. *Sultan Qaboos University Medical Journal [SQUMJ], 20*(4), e406–407. https://doi.org/10.18295/squmj.2020.20.04.024

Kar, S. K., Menon, V., Arafat, S. M. Y., Rai, S., Kaliamoorthy, C., Akter, H., Shukla, S., Sharma, N., Roy, D., & Sridhar, V. K. (2021). Impact of COVID-19 pandemic related lockdown on suicide: Analysis of newspaper reports during pre-lockdown and lockdown period in Bangladesh and India. *Asian Journal of Psychiatry, 60*, 102649. https://doi.org/10.1016/j.ajp.2021.102649

Keita, M. M., Taverne, B., Sy Savané, S., March, L., Doukoure, M., Sow, M. S., Touré, A., Etard, J. F., Barry, M., Delaporte, E., & PostEboGui Study Group. (2017). Depressive symptoms among survivors of Ebola virus disease in Conakry (Guinea): Preliminary results of the PostEboGui cohort. *BMC Psychiatry, 17*(1), 127. https://doi.org/10.1186/s12888-017-1280-8

Kikuchi, K., Anzai, T., & Takahashi, K. (2023). The unusual increase in suicides among women in Japan during the COVID-19 pandemic: A time-series analysis until October 2021. *Journal of Epidemiology, 33*(1), 45–51. https://doi.org/10.2188/jea.JE20220186

Killgore, W. D. S., Cloonan, S. A., Taylor, E. C., Fernandez, F., Grandner, M. A., & Dailey, N. S. (2020). Suicidal ideation during the COVID-19 pandemic: The role of insomnia. *Psychiatry Research, 290*, 113134. https://doi.org/10.1016/j.psychres.2020.113134

Klonsky, E. D., & May, A. M. (2015). The Three-Step Theory (3ST): A New Theory of Suicide Rooted in the "Ideation-to-Action" Framework. *International Journal of Cognitive Therapy, 8*(2), 114–129. https://doi.org/10.1521/ijct.2015.8.2.114

Knowles, J. R. P., Gray, N. S., O'Connor, C., Pink, J., Simkiss, N. J., & Snowden, R. J. (2022). The role of hope and resilience in protecting against suicidal thoughts and behaviors during the COVID-19 pandemic. *Archives of Suicide Research: Official Journal of the International Academy for Suicide Research, 26*(3), 1487–1504. https://doi.org/10.1080/13811118.2021.1923599

Krishnamoorthy, Y., Nagarajan, R., Saya, G. K., & Menon, V. (2020). Prevalence of psychological morbidities among general population, healthcare workers and COVID-19 patients amidst the COVID-19 pandemic: A systematic review and meta-analysis. *Psychiatry Research, 293*, 113382. https://doi.org/10.1016/j.psychres.2020.113382

Kumar, A., & Nayar, K. R. (2021). COVID 19 and its mental health consequences. *Journal of Mental Health (Abingdon, England), 30*(1), 1–2. https://doi.org/10.1080/09638237.2020.1757052

Leaune, E., Samuel, M., Oh, H., Poulet, E., & Brunelin, J. (2020). Suicidal behaviors and ideation during emerging viral disease outbreaks before the COVID-19 pandemic: A systematic rapid review. *Preventive Medicine, 141*, 106264. https://doi.org/10.1016/j.ypmed.2020.106264

Li, Y.-C., Bai, W., Cai, H., Wu, Y., Zhang, L., Ding, Y.-H., Yang, J.-J., Du, X., Zeng, Z.-T., Lu, C.-M., Feng, K.-X., Mi, W.-F., Zhang, L., Liu, H.-Z., Balbuena, L., Cheung, T., Su, Z., An, F.-R., & Xiang, Y.-T. (2022). Suicidality in clinically stable bipolar disorder and schizophrenia patients during the COVID-19 pandemic. *Translational Psychiatry, 12*, 303. https://doi.org/10.1038/s41398-022-02045-2

Llistosella, M., Castellvi, P., Miranda-Mendizabal, A., Recoder, S., Calbo, E., Casajuana-Closas, M., Leiva, D., Manolov, R., Matilla-Santander, N., & Forero, C. G. (2022). Low resilience was a risk factor of mental health problems during the COVID-19 pandemic but not in individuals exposed to COVID-19: A cohort study in Spanish adult general population. *International Journal of Environmental Research and Public Health, 19*(22), 15398. https://doi.org/10.3390/ijerph192215398

Logie, C. H., & Turan, J. M. (2020). How do we balance tensions between COVID-19 public health responses and stigma mitigation? Learning from HIV research. *AIDS and Behavior, 24*(7), 2003–2006. https://doi.org/10.1007/s10461-020-02856-8

Louie, L. L. C., Chan, W. C., & Cheng, C. P. W. (2021). Suicidal risk in older patients with depression during COVID-19 pandemic: A case control study. *East Asian Archives of Psychiatry: Official Journal of the Hong Kong College of Psychiatrists = Dong Ya Jing Shen Ke Xue Zhi: Xianggang Jing Shen Ke Yi Xue Yuan Qi Kan, 31*(1), 3–8. https://doi.org/10.12809/eaap2055

Mahalingam, K., Surbhi, Balaji, A., Ganesh, R., Daniel, R. A., Aggarwal, R., Soni, K. D., Singh, A. K., Khanna, P., Gupta, V., & Trikha, A. (2022). Is it a challenging task to work with personal protective equipment in a COVID-19 ICU: Findings from a hospital-based cross-sectional study from north India. *Journal of Family Medicine and Primary Care, 11*(5), 1935–1942. https://doi.org/10.4103/jfmpc.jfmpc_1937_21

Martínez-Alés, G., López-Cuadrado, T., Morrison, C., Keyes, K., & Susser, E. (2023). The impact of the COVID-19 pandemic on suicide mortality in Spain: Differences by sex and age. *Journal of Affective Disorders, 329*, 315–323. https://doi.org/10.1016/j.jad.2023.02.115

Menon, V., Padhy, S. K., & Pattnaik, J. I. (2020). Two to tango: Deconstructing the COVID-19 and suicidality conundrum from a biopsychosocial perspective. *Asian Journal of Psychiatry, 54*, 102400. https://doi.org/10.1016/j.ajp.2020.102400

Menon, V., Padhy, S. K., & Pattnaik, J. I. (2021). COVID-19 pandemic and suicidality: Durkheim revisited. *Australian & New Zealand Journal of Psychiatry, 55*(3), 324–324. https://doi.org/10.1177/0004867420957085

Monteleone, A. M., Marciello, F., Cascino, G., Abbate-Daga, G., Anselmetti, S., Baiano, M., Balestrieri, M., Barone, E., Bertelli, S., Carpiniello, B., Castellini, G., Corrivetti, G., De giorgi, S., Favaro, A., Gramaglia, C., Marzola, E., Meneguzzo, P., Monaco, F., Oriani, M. G., … Monteleone, P. (2021). The impact of COVID-19 lockdown and of the following "re-opening" period on specific and general psychopathology in people with Eating Disorders: The emergent role of internalizing symptoms. *Journal of Affective Disorders, 285*, 77–83. https://doi.org/10.1016/j.jad.2021.02.037

Motamed-Jahromi, M., Meshkani, Z., Mosavi-Negad, S. M., Momenabadi, V., & Ahmadzadeh, M. S. (2021). Factors affecting panic buying during COVID-19 outbreak and strategies: A scoping review. *Iranian Journal of Public Health, 50*(12), 2473–2485. https://doi.org/10.18502/ijph.v50i12.7929

Mueller, A. S., Abrutyn, S., Pescosolido, B., & Diefendorf, S. (2021). The social roots of suicide: Theorizing how the external social world matters to suicide and suicide prevention. *Frontiers in Psychology, 12*, 621569. https://doi.org/10.3389/fpsyg.2021.621569

Mukhtar, F., & Candilis, P. (2022). Pandemics and suicide risk. *The Journal of Nervous and Mental Disease, 210*(10), 799–807. https://doi.org/10.1097/NMD.0000000000001536

Murata, S., Rezeppa, T., Thoma, B., Marengo, L., Krancevich, K., Chiyka, E., Hayes, B., Goodfriend, E., Deal, M., Zhong, Y., Brummit, B., Coury, T., Riston, S., Brent, D. A., & Melhem, N. M. (2021). The psychiatric sequelae of the COVID-19 pandemic in adolescents, adults, and health care workers. *Depression and Anxiety, 38*(2), 233–246. https://doi.org/10.1002/da.23120

Na, P. J., Tsai, J., Hill, M. L., Nichter, B., Norman, S. B., Southwick, S. M., & Pietrzak, R. H. (2021). Prevalence, risk and protective factors associated with suicidal ideation during the COVID-19 pandemic in U.S. military veterans with pre-existing psychiatric conditions. *Journal of Psychiatric Research, 137*, 351–359. https://doi.org/10.1016/j.jpsychires.2021.03.021

Niederkrotenthaler, T., Braun, M., Pirkis, J., Till, B., Stack, S., Sinyor, M., Tran, U. S., Voracek, M., Cheng, Q., Arendt, F., Scherr, S., Yip, P. S. F., & Spittal, M. J. (2020). Association between suicide reporting in the media and suicide: Systematic review and meta-analysis. *BMJ (Clinical research ed.), 368*, m575. https://doi.org/10.1136/bmj.m575

Nomura, K., Minamizono, S., Maeda, E., Kim, R., Iwata, T., Hirayama, J., Ono, K., Fushimi, M., Goto, T., Mishima, K., & Yamamoto, F. (2021a). Cross-sectional survey of depressive symptoms and suicide-related ideation at a Japanese national university during the COVID-19 stay-home order. *Environmental Health and Preventive Medicine, 26*, 30. https://doi.org/10.1186/s12199-021-00953-1

Nomura, S., Kawashima, T., Harada, N., Yoneoka, D., Tanoue, Y., Eguchi, A., Gilmour, S., Kawamura, Y., & Hashizume, M. (2021b). Trends in suicide in Japan by gender during the COVID-19 pandemic, through December 2020. *Psychiatry Research, 300*, 113913. https://doi.org/10.1016/j.psychres.2020.113622

Norström, T., & Rossow, I. (2016). Alcohol consumption as a risk factor for suicidal behavior: A systematic review of associations at the individual and at the population level. *Archives of Suicide Research: Official Journal of the International Academy for Suicide Research, 20*(4), 489–506. https://doi.org/10.1080/13811118.2016.1158678

Nozawa, K., Ishii, A., Asaoka, H., Iwanaga, M., Kumakura, Y., Oyabu, Y., Shinozaki, T., Imamura, K., Kawakami, N., & Miyamoto, Y. (2022). Effectiveness of an online peer gatekeeper training program for postsecondary students on suicide prevention in Japan: Protocol for a randomized controlled trial. *JMIR Research Protocols, 11*(4), e34832. https://doi.org/10.2196/34832

Pathare, S., Vijayakumar, L., Fernandes, T. N., Shastri, M., Kapoor, A., Pandit, D., Lohumi, I., Ray, S., Kulkarni, A., & Korde, P. (2020). Analysis of news media reports of suicides and attempted suicides during the COVID-19 lockdown in India. *International Journal of Mental Health Systems, 14*(1), 88. https://doi.org/10.1186/s13033-020-00422-2

Pathirathna, M. L., Nandasena, H. M. R. K. G., Atapattu, A. M. M. P., & Weerasekara, I. (2022). Impact of the COVID-19 pandemic on suicidal attempts and death rates: A systematic review. *BMC Psychiatry, 22*(1), 506. https://doi.org/10.1186/s12888-022-04158-w

Pierce, M., Hope, H., Ford, T., Hatch, S., Hotopf, M., John, A., Kontopantelis, E., Webb, R., Wessely, S., McManus, S., & Abel, K. M. (2020). Mental health before and during the COVID-19 pandemic: A longitudinal probability sample survey of the UK population. *The Lancet. Psychiatry, 7*(10), 883–892. https://doi.org/10.1016/S2215-0366(20)30308-4

Pirkis, J., John, A., Shin, S., DelPozo-Banos, M., Arya, V., Analuisa-Aguilar, P., Appleby, L., Arensman, E., Bantjes, J., Baran, A., Bertolote, J. M., Borges, G., Brečić, P., Caine, E., Castelpietra, G., Chang, S.-S., Colchester, D., Crompton, D., Curkovic, M., … Spittal, M. J. (2021). Suicide trends in the early months of the COVID-19 pandemic: An interrupted time-series analysis of preliminary data from 21 countries. *The Lancet Psychiatry, 8*(7), 579–588. https://doi.org/10.1016/S2215-0366(21)00091-2

Rangaswamy, T., Grover, S., Tyagi, V., & Bhan, A. (2022). How did the mental health care system in India respond to COVID 19 pandemic? *Schizophrenia Bulletin Open, 3*(1), sgac043. https://doi.org/10.1093/schizbullopen/sgac043

Reger, M. A., Stanley, I. H., & Joiner, T. E. (2020). Suicide mortality and coronavirus disease 2019—A perfect storm? *JAMA Psychiatry, 77*(11), 1093–1094. https://doi.org/10.1001/jamapsychiatry.2020.1060

Rubinstein, D. H. (1986). A stress-diathesis theory of suicide. *Suicide & Life-Threatening Behavior, 16*(2), 182–197. https://doi.org/10.1111/j.1943-278x.1986.tb00351.x

Rück, C., Mataix-Cols, D., Malki, K., Adler, M., Flygare, O., Runeson, B., & Sidorchuk, A. (2021). Swedish nationwide time series analysis of influenza and suicide deaths from 1910 to 1978. *British Medical Journal Open, 11*(7), e049302. https://doi.org/10.1136/bmjopen-2021-049302

Schnitzer, P. G., Dykstra, H., & Collier, A. (2023). The COVID-19 pandemic and youth suicide: 2020–2021. *Pediatrics, 151*(3), e2022058716. https://doi.org/10.1542/peds.2022-058716

Sher, L. (2020). COVID-19, anxiety, sleep disturbances and suicide. *Sleep Medicine, 70*, 124. https://doi.org/10.1016/j.sleep.2020.04.019

Shoib, S., Gaitán Buitrago, J. E. T., Shuja, K. H., Aqeel, M., de Filippis, R., Abbas, J., Ullah, I., & Arafat, S. M. Y. (2022). Suicidal behavior sociocultural factors in developing countries during COVID-19. *L'encephale, 48*(1), 78–82. https://doi.org/10.1016/j.encep.2021.06.011

Sinyor, M., Knipe, D., Borges, G., Ueda, M., Pirkis, J., Phillips, M. R., & Gunnell, D. (2022). Suicide risk and prevention during the COVID-19 pandemic: One year on. *Archives of Suicide Research, 26*(4), 1944–1949. https://doi.org/10.1080/13811118.2021.1955784

Sisask, M., & Värnik, A. (2012). Media roles in suicide prevention: A systematic review. *International Journal of Environmental Research and Public Health, 9*(1), 123–138. https://doi.org/10.3390/ijerph9010123

Smith, F. B. (1995). The Russian influenza in the United Kingdom, 1889–1894. *Social History of Medicine: The Journal of the Society for the Social History of Medicine, 8*(1), 55–73. https://doi.org/10.1093/shm/8.1.55

Sohi, I., Chrystoja, B. R., Rehm, J., Wells, S., Monteiro, M., Ali, S., & Shield, K. D. (2022). Changes in alcohol use during the COVID-19 pandemic and previous pandemics: A systematic review. *Alcoholism, Clinical and Experimental Research, 46*(4), 498–513. https://doi.org/10.1111/acer.14792

Stack, S., & Rockett, I. R. H. (2021). Social distancing predicts suicide rates: Analysis of the 1918 flu pandemic in 43 large cities, research note. *Suicide & Life-Threatening Behavior, 51*(5), 833–835. https://doi.org/10.1111/sltb.12729

Syed, N. K., & Griffiths, M. D. (2020). Nationwide suicides due to alcohol withdrawal symptoms during COVID-19 pandemic: A review of cases from media reports. *Journal of Psychiatric Research, 130*, 289–291. https://doi.org/10.1016/j.jpsychires.2020.08.021

Tandon, R. (2021). COVID-19 and suicide: Just the facts. Key learnings and guidance for action. *Asian Journal of Psychiatry, 60*, 102695. https://doi.org/10.1016/j.ajp.2021.102695

Taylor, S. (1982). *Durkheim and the study of suicide.*

Van Orden, K. A., Witte, T. K., Cukrowicz, K. C., Braithwaite, S. R., Selby, E. A., & Joiner, T. E., Jr. (2010). The interpersonal theory of suicide. *Psychological Review, 117*(2), 575–600. https://doi.org/10.1037/a0018697

Varin, M., Liu, L., Gabrys, R., Gariepy, G., MacEachern, K. H., & Weeks, M. (2023). Increased alcohol use, heavy episodic drinking, and suicide ideation during the COVID-19 pandemic in Canada. *Revue Canadienne De Sante Publique* [*Canadian Journal of Public Health*], *114*(1), 33–43. https://doi.org/10.17269/s41997-022-00689-7

Vukojević, J., Đuran, N., Žaja, N., Sušac, J., Šekerija, M., & Savić, A. (2021). 100 Years apart: Psychiatric admissions during Spanish flu and COVID-19 pandemic. *Psychiatry Research, 303*, 114071. https://doi.org/10.1016/j.psychres.2021.114071

Wand, A. P. F., Zhong, B.-L., Chiu, H. F. K., Draper, B., & De Leo, D. (2020). COVID-19: The implications for suicide in older adults. *International Psychogeriatrics*, 1–6. https://doi.org/10.1017/S1041610220000770

Wasserman, I. M. (1992). The impact of epidemic, war, prohibition and media on suicide: United States, 1910–1920. *Suicide & Life-Threatening Behavior, 22*(2), 240–254. https://doi.org/10.1111/j.1943-278X.1992.tb00231.x

Winkler, P., Formanek, T., Mlada, K., Kagstrom, A., Mohrova, Z., Mohr, P., & Csemy, L. (2020). Increase in prevalence of current mental disorders in the context of COVID-19: Analysis of repeated nationwide cross-sectional surveys. *Epidemiology and Psychiatric Sciences, 29*, e173. https://doi.org/10.1017/S2045796020000888

World Health Organization. (2021a). *Comprehensive mental health action plan 2013–2030*. https://www.who.int/publications/i/item/9789240031029

World Health Organization. (2021b). *LIVE LIFE: An implementation guide for suicide prevention in countries*. https://www.who.int/publications/i/item/9789240026629

World Health Organization. (2023). *Preventing suicide: A resource for media professionals, 2023 update*. World Health Organization.

Yip, P. S. F., Cheung, Y. T., Chau, P. H., & Law, Y. W. (2010). The impact of epidemic outbreak. *Crisis, 31*(2), 86–92. https://doi.org/10.1027/0227-5910/a000015

Zhou, Y., Wang, W., Sun, Y., Qian, W., Liu, Z., Wang, R., Qi, L., Yang, J., Song, X., Zhou, X., Zeng, L., Liu, T., Li, Z., & Zhang, X. (2020). The prevalence and risk factors of psychological disturbances of frontline medical staff in china under the COVID-19 epidemic: Workload should be concerned. *Journal of Affective Disorders, 277*, 510–514. https://doi.org/10.1016/j.jad.2020.08.059

Zwickl, S., Angus, L. M., Qi, A. W. F., Ginger, A., Eshin, K., Cook, T., Leemaqz, S. Y., Dowers, E., Zajac, J. D., & Cheung, A. S. (2023). The impact of the first three months of the COVID-19 pandemic on the Australian trans community. *International Journal of Transgender Health*. https://doi.org/10.1080/26895269.2021.1890659

# Chapter 10
# Politics and Suicide

**David Lester and Mahboubeh Dadfar**

**Abstract** One of the contributing factors to suicidal behavior is politics. This essay will examine the political aspects of suicide and how the national and local political climate impacts suicide rates, including voting preferences, conservative versus liberal governments, the role of colonialism, and the impact of armed conflict and civil war. A social justice-oriented political approach may prevent suicide and, certainly, liberal governments can formulate national strategies for suicide prevention.

**Keywords** Economy · Governance · Policymaking · Voting · Colonialization · Political protests · Political action · Social justice · Suicide · Suicide prevention

## 1 Introduction

One of the contributing factors to suicide is politics (Michelsen, 2015; Stack, 2021). For example, political violence can impact suicide rates (Standish, 2020), while liberal governments can develop national suicide prevention plans to prevent suicide from a social justice perspective (Button, 2016; White & Morris, 2019). A recent example of this is the establish of a toll-free three-digit suicide prevention telephone number in the United States (988). Hjelmeland and Knizek (2017) argued that ideology, politics, power, and vested interests (such as national psychiatric associations) continue to promote the notion that 90% of suicides have psychiatric disorders which is the cause of those deaths. They argue that there is no basis for this claim and, furthermore, such a claim impedes suicide prevention. National and global events, as well as political decisions, can increase despair and helplessness in the general

D. Lester (✉)
Stockton University, Galloway, NJ, USA
e-mail: david.lester@stockton.edu

M. Dadfar
School of Behavioral Sciences and Mental Health, Iran University of Medical Sciences, Tehran, Iran
e-mail: dadfar.m@iums.ac.ir



S. M. Y. Arafat and S. K. Kar (eds.), *Ecological and Social Determinants of Suicidal Behavior*, South Asian Perspectives in Mental Health and Psychology,
https://doi.org/10.1007/978-981-96-4028-7_10

population, thereby increasing the prevalence of suicidal thoughts and behavior. This puts a special responsibility at the national level on policymakers and government officials (Poursharifi, 2024). Let us first examine the impact on suicidal behavior of economic variables that are under the control of governments.

## 2 The HDI and the Misery Index

Governments have a tremendous impact, of course, on the economy and, therefore, the status of their constituents. The Human Development Index (HDI) is a combination of three factors: health and long life; educational opportunities achievements; and appropriate living standards, variables that are impacted by government policies. The relationship between the HDI and suicide rate has been investigated in different countries, and the results have shown that, at least in some underdeveloped countries, there is a strong relationship between the HDI and suicide mortality (Arafat et al., 2022; Khazaei et al., 2017). In a study of 85 countries, Shah (2009, 2010) found that elderly suicide rates were related to the HDI, but in a curvilinear way, an inverted U-shaped function, indicating that elderly suicide rates were higher at intermediate levels of the HDI.

There are three very important rates in the economy: the economic growth rate, the unemployment rate, and the inflation rate. Among them, unemployment and inflation rates are more important for people because they experience increases and decreases of unemployment and inflation daily, and changes in these rates can have a great impact on their lives. The Misery Index (MI) is the sum of the unemployment rate and the inflation rate (after transformation to comparable statistics), and Yang and Lester (1992, 1999) found that this was strongly associated with the suicide rate in a time-series analysis in the United State for the period 1939–1986 (Pearson $r = 0.77$). Poursharifi (2024) found that there was also a strong relationship between the suicide rate and the MI in Iran. Based on this, it is necessary to focus on improving the HDI and reducing the MI in order to prevent suicide in Iran and in other countries.

However, paying attention to economic issues should not let us ignore cultural and personal issues. Regarding suicide rates in Iran, Nourinia (2024) noted that there are many factors influencing suicide, and they interact at three levels, and his analysis applies to all countries.

(1) Micro-level factors are personal issues, interpersonal relationships, and the mental states of the individual. However, these factors are impacted by the complex processes of collective life and government policies. Policymakers often focus on issues such as acute depression, acute psychosis, romantic failure, poverty, family quarrels, lack of job success, disgrace, and shame, thereby reducing suicide to an individual problem that they do not have to deal with.
(2) Middle-level factors include issues related to organizational and institutional relationships which are created by the individuals' position in society, positions such as social class This position defines both the individuals' interpretation of

themselves and their life and the extent of their benefits. This position defines the possible options for social life and provides access to ways and means of achieving economic and social goals, and these factors such as educational opportunities and job-training programs. At this level, occasional politicians accept that, if special attention is paid to these issues, some people would not have turned to suicide. For example, if a person has an unpleasant job situation with conditions difficult to endure and discrimination, this person may decide to die by suicide as the only way to escape from that situation. People need to have access to well-paid employment and benefits and, if not, the opportunity to seek alternative employment.

(3) Macro-level factors and issues arise from the general atmosphere governing the society, in which individuals have no say, and which are caused by societal processes, the social system, and the political system at the macro level, especially policies and programs established by the political system which open up, close or limit opportunities in the society. Individuals can participate at this level by voting for particular political parties in local and national elections. In the United States, for example, Republican policies typically favor the wealthy while Democratic policies favor the lower social classes.

Governments should act to maintain human dignity and create an open civil space to promote social and political participation by the people whom they govern and to maintain citizenship rights. Those counseling suicide individuals typically focus on the micro-level because they are unable to have any impact at the middle- and macro levels since this is a responsibility of governments.

## 3 Politics at the National Level: Political Stability and Instability

### *3.1 Comparing Countries*

Countries vary in how politically stable they are. The unstable events range from cabinets resigning to civil war. Feierabend and Feierabend (1966) rated countries for their degree of political stability. Using their data for a sample of 36 countries with available data, Lester (1973) found that the total suicide rate and the suicide rates for males and for females were not associated with the ratings of political instability.[1] Interestingly, the homicide rate was positively associated with the index of political instability. The more unstable countries had higher homicide rates.

[1] Lester did not report which countries were in the sample.

## 3.2 Presidential Elections in the United States

The political atmosphere can also be unstable in a country when there is an election at the national level and, in addition, when the ruling party loses the election and a new government from a different political party takes over. Andress and Corey (1976) studied suicide rates in California and Riverside County in California for the period 1960–1974. Suicide rates rose in the years preceding years with Presidential elections and declined in the years after the election. Suicide rates were also high in the year (1973) of the Watergate scandal[2] and declined in the year that President Nixon resigned.[3]

Classen and Dunn (2010) explored whether the outcome of Presidential elections in the United States had an impact on the suicide rate. For the period 1981–2005, they found that the suicide rates in the states that supported the winning candidate were higher in the year of the election than in states that supported the losing candidate, for both males and females. This difference dissipates in the following year. Classen and Dunn speculated that the negative impact of supporting the loser increases social integration, much as natural disasters and wars seem to do, and, therefore, results in a decrease in suicides in line with Durkheim's (1897) theory that social integration is associated with a lower suicide rate.

## 3.3 The Impact of Conservative Versus Liberal Governments

Page et al. (2002) studied the impact of the political views of the government on suicide rates in Australia which has a two-party system: social democrats and conservatives. At the state level for the period 1901–1998, Page et al. found that, when both the governments at the Federal and in New South Wales (one of the provinces of Australia) were conservative, the relative risks of suicide for men in Australia and in New South Wales and for women in New South Wales (but not in Australia as a whole) were higher than when both governments were social democrats.

Blakely and Collins (2002) saw this result as stemming from a tendency under conservative governments to encourage individualism and a reluctance of conservative governments to promote beneficial public policies for the middle and lower social classes, resulting in an increase in anomie in the citizens which, in turn, increases the suicide rate according to Durkheim (1897). However, Lester (2024) found that the available research on countries suggests that countries whose residents obtain higher scores on measures of individualism tend to have lower suicide rates. Furthermore, Blakely and Collins argued that the results presented by Page et al. were not

---

[2] When the offices of the Democrats in the Watergate Building were broken into.

[3] Research has been inconsistent on whether suicide rates change during the years of Presidential elections in the United States in general, whether or not the ruling party wins or loses (Boor, 1981; Wasserman, 1983).

convincing, especially since there could be other societal factors influencing both suicide rates and voter preferences, thereby leading to a spurious association.

More broadly, Voracek et al. (2003) studied Austria's 121 districts and found that higher suicide rates in 1988–1994 predicted swings in the elections (losses) for the ruling political parties in the 1995–1999 elections. Voracek et al. speculated that the aftermath of suicides might produce socially and politically alienated survivors of the suicides who shape swings towards opposition parties in subsequent general elections.

Political beliefs can also impact government policies and suicide rates. For example, in the United States, conservatives and liberals have different views on policies concerning firearms, with the conservatives favoring fewer restrictions. Butterworth and Anestis (2019) asked a sample of owners of firearms about their opinion about safety measures for firearms (such as safe storage of firearms). They found that conservative views regarding social issues predicted greater opposition to imposing safety measures for firearms for others (but not for themselves). However, conservative views about the economy were not associated with attitudes toward safety measures for firearms.

In a study of political opinions in the residents of countries, Fernquist (1995) studied nine western European countries for the period 1975–1989 and found that support for European political integration by the majority of the population (i.e., the European Union) was negatively associated with elderly suicide rates. On the other hand, Steeg et al. (2020) found that counties, where the vote by the British for leaving the European Union was greater, had higher suicide rates. Overall, therefore, support for political integration lowers the suicide rate, while support for political disintegration raises the suicide rate.

## 4 Government Efforts to Prevent Suicide

Lezine (2018) reviewed legislation relevant to preventing suicide by the American Congress and Senate. Programs were proposed and passed both under Democratic and Republican Presidents, and most received unanimous support in both houses. Only one of the four proposals did not receive unanimous support, with a few Republicans opposing it. Lezine also looked at state proposals to prevent suicide. Once Lezine took into account the number of years that one party controlled the state legislature, Republican legislators proposed and passed more state plans for preventing suicide.

## 5 Physician-Assisted Suicide

One area in which political opinions play a role is in the legalization of physician-assisted suicide. For example, at the present time in the United States, California, Colorado, District of Columbia, Hawaii, Montana, Maine, New Jersey,

New Mexico, Oregon, Vermont, and Washington have passed legislations to make physician-assisted suicide available if certain conditions are met. There are, of course, strong opinions supporting physician-assisted suicide (e.g., Szasz, 2002) and strong opinions opposing it (e.g., Hendin, 1996). In the United States, Republicans are more likely to be what is termed *pro-life* and, therefore, more likely to oppose physician-assisted suicide, than are Democrats.

## 6 The Impact of Colonialization

Many indigenous tribes appear to have had very few suicides prior to colonialization by Western countries, but their rates of suicide after colonialization are often very high. Shahtahmasebi (2016) noted this change in suicidal behavior for the indigenous Maoris in New Zealand. The impact of colonialism on the indigenous people and, specifically, on suicide, often arouses strong anger even today. As Tisha and Polanco (2022) have written "Our intent is to argue, specifically from the perspective of coloniality and our racialized, gendered, and monetized bodies, that suicide is rather an extension of modernity's colonial genocide" (p. 120). In line with this, Wexler (2009) argued that ongoing residual colonialization accounts, in part, for the suicides of young native Alaskans.

## 7 Suicide as a Political Protest

Protesting tyranny has a long history, and individuals occasionally die by suicide (without harming others) to protest government policies (Coleman, 1987). Thich Quang Duc, a 66-year-old Buddhist monk died by self-burning in South Vietnam on June 11, 1963 to protest the policies oppressing the Buddhists by the President. Norman Morrison, 31 years old, set fire to himself on November 2, 1965, outside the Pentagon to protest the Vietnam War. Jan Palach, a 20-year-old student, died by self-burning in Prague on January 16, 1969 protesting the Soviet invasion of Czechoslovakia. In recent years, self-immolation has become a common form of political protest (Crosby et al., 1977), most recently in Tibet.

## 8 Civil Conflict

Some countries occasionally experience severe conflict within the country. This can have a large impact on suicidal behavior.

### *8.1 The Impact of Armed Conflict*

Armed conflict and civil war often result in suicide terrorism these days in which an individual kills himself or herself, at the same time killing the enemy forces or civilians (see, Taylor & Ryan, 1988). Lester (2020) has reviewed research and theory on suicide terrorists and suicide terrorism and argued that this behavior is a form of suicide, but it is important to note here that Islam does not consider such acts as suicides but rather as martyrdom. For example, Abdel-Khalek (2004) argued that suicide terrorism by Palestinians was not altruistic suicide but rather *martyrdom,* and martyrdom is not the same suicide.[4]

At the individual level of analysis, Abdeen et al. (2018) collected data from Palestinian students from schools in the West Bank and East Jerusalem in Israel. They were asked about their exposure to armed conflict using the *Subjective Threat from Armed Conflict Events (STACE)* scale (Harel-Fisch et al., 2010) which asked questions about exposure to armed conflicts as a result of the Israeli military and settler incursions in the prior 12 months. Along with a large number of other variables (such as abuse, bullying, and family support), exposure to armed conflict predicted both attempted suicide and suicidal ideation in the previous year.

## 9 Conclusions

To what extent should political theory and political action focus on suicide? Button and Marsh (2020; see also Button, 2016) argued that suicide is, in part, a response to social conditions that impair a dignified existence for people. For example, as we have seen above, at the societal level, the unemployment rate often predicts the suicide rate. Button and Marsh discussed the impact of societal issues such as inequality, intergenerational poverty, racism, sexism, and homophobia which impact suicidal behavior and which, in themselves, should be of concern to governments. Therefore, if a society is concerned about suicide in its citizens, then tackling unemployment has a secondary motivation. Governments should, therefore, work toward removing those conditions that impair human existence which, of course, is a liberal political view.

As an illustration of this issue, Kondo and Oh (2010) noted that suicide presumed to be caused by overwork (known as *karoshi* in Japan) rose dramatically in Japan after 1999 during the economic crises there. In 2009, the ruling government regime changed, and the Democratic party governed. This democratic government then expanded the unemployment insurance program, tightened regulations concerning

[4] Suicide is proscribed by the Koran. However, the Islamic commanders of the suicide terrorists do not consider the acts to be suicide, but rather martyrdom or self-sacrifice in the service of Allah. This attitude may be necessary to persuade individuals to become suicide terrorists, but the behavior is clearly suicidal. For an analysis of how the concept of martyrdom and jihad has changed over time, see Acosta (2010).

temporary employment, and improved the safety net for poor families. Governments can, and should, act to prevent suicide.

## References

Abdeen, Z., Brunstein-Klomek, A., Nakash, O., Shibli, N., Nagar, M., Agha, H., Hallaq, S., Kanat-Maymon, Y., Juerges, H., Levav, I., & Qasrawi, R. (2018). The association between political violence and the connection between bullying and suicidality among Palestinian youth. *Suicide & Life-Threatening Behavior, 48*(1), 95–104. https://doi.org/10.1111/sltb.12338

Abdel-Khalek, A. M. (2004). Neither altruistic suicide, nor terrorism, but martyrdom: A Muslim perspective. *Archives of Suicide Research, 8*, 99–103. https://doi.org/10.1080/13811110490243840

Acosta, A. T. (2010). The suicide bomber as Sunni Shi'i hybrid. *Middle East Quarterly, 17*(3), 13–20. https://www.researchgate.net/publication/291978633_The_suicide_bomber_as_Sunni-Shi'i_hybrid

Andress, V. R., & Corey, D. M. (1976). Regional suicide rates as a function of national political change. *Psychological Reports, 39*(3), 955–958. https://doi.org/10.2466/pr0.1976.39.3.955

Arafat, S. M. Y., Marthoenis, M., Khan, M. M., & Rezaeian, M. (2022). Association between suicide rate and human development index, income, and the political system in 46 Muslim-majority countries: An ecological study. *European Journal of Investigation in Health, Psychology and Education, 12*(7), 754–764. https://doi.org/10.3390/ejihpe12070055

Blakely, T., & Collins, S. (2002). Is there a causal association between suicide rates and the political leanings of government? *Journal of Epidemiology & Community Health, 56*(10), 772. https://doi.org/10.1136/jech.56.10.722

Boor, M. (1981). Effects of United States presidential elections on suicide and other causes of death. *American Sociological Review, 46*(5), 616–618. PMID: 11630823.

Butterworth, S. E., & Anestis, M. D. (2019). Political beliefs, region of residence, and openness to firearm means safety measures to prevent suicide. *Archives of Suicide Research, 23*(4), 616–633. https://doi.org/10.1080/13811118.2018.1486250

Button, M. E. (2016). Suicide and social justice: Toward a political approach to suicide. *Political Research Quarterly, 69*(2), 270–280. https://doi.org/10.1177/1065912916636689

Button, M. E., & Marsh, I. (Eds.). (2020). *Suicide and social justice: New perspectives on the politics of suicide and suicide prevention*. Routledge. https://doi.org/10.4324/9780429460494

Classen, T. J., & Dunn, R. A. (2010). The politics of hope and despair: The effect of presidential election outcomes on suicide rates. *Social Science Quarterly, 91*(3), 593–612. http://www.jstor.org/stable/42956420

Coleman, L. (1987). *Suicide clusters*. Faber & Faber. https://books.google.com/books/about/Suicide_Clusters.html?id=8eIDAQAAIAAJ

Crosby, K., Rhee, J. O., & Holland, J. (1977). Suicide by fire: a contemporary method of political protest *International Journal of Social Psychiatry, 23*(1), 60–69. https://doi.org/10.1177/002076407702300111

Durkheim, E. (1897). *Le suicide*. Felix Alcan. https://archive.org/details/lesuicidetudede00durkgoog

Feierabend, I. K., & Feierabend, R. L. (1966). Aggressive behaviors within politics, 1948–1962: A cross-national study 1. *Journal of Conflict Resolution, 10*(3), 249–271. https://doi.org/10.1177/002200276601000301

Fernquist, R. M. (1995). Elderly suicide in western Europe 1975–1989. *Omega, 32*, 39–48. https://doi.org/10.2190/b3kq-fxyx-wr7b-yp6w

Harel-Fisch, Y., Radwan, Q., Walsh, S. D., Laufer, A., Amitai, G., Fogel-Grinvald, H., & Abdeen, Z. (2010). Psychosocial outcomes related to subjective threat from armed conflict events (STACE):

Findings from the Israeli-Palestinian cross-cultural HBSC study. *Child Abuse & Neglect, 34*(9), 623–638. https://doi.org/10.1016/j.chiabu.2009.12.007

Hendin, H. (1996). *Seduced by death: doctors, patients, and assisted suicide.* W.W. Norton. https://archive.org/details/seducedbydeathdo0000hend

Hjelmeland, H., & Knizek, B. L. (2017). Suicide and mental disorders: A discourse of politics, power, and vested interests. *Death Studies, 41*(8), 481–492. https://doi.org/10.1080/07481187.2017.1332905

Khazaei, S., Armanmehr, V., Nematollahi, S., Rezaeian, S., & Khazaei, S. (2017). Suicide rate in relation to the Human Development Index and other health related factors: A global ecological study from 91 countries. *Journal of Epidemiology and Global Health, 7*(2), 131–134. https://doi.org/10.1016/j.jegh.2016.12.002

Kondo, N., & Oh, J. (2010). Suicide and karoshi (death from overwork) during the recent economic crises in Japan: The impacts, mechanisms and political responses. *Journal of Epidemiology & Community Health, 64*(8), 649–650. https://doi.org/10.1136/jech.2009.090787

Lester, D. (1973). National homicide and suicide rates as a function of political stability. *Psychological Reports, 33*(1), 298. https://doi.org/10.2466/pr0.1973.33.1.298

Lester, D. (2020). *Suicide terrorists and terrorism.* Nova. https://doi.org/10.52305/zfun3821

Lester, D. (2024). Collectivism-individualism and suicide. *Suicide Studies, 5*(3), 124–132. https://www.researchgate.net/publication/

Lezine, D.A. (2018). U.S. political parties and support for suicide prevention. *Suicide & Life-Threatening Behavior, 48*(2), 199–203. https://doi.org/10.1111/sltb.12350

Michelsen, N. (2015). *Politics and suicide: The philosophy of political self-destruction* (1st ed.). Routledge, Taylor & Francis. https://www.taylorfrancis.com/.../politics-suicide-nicholas-michelsen

Nourinia, H. (2024, April 28). *Levels of suicide analysis in Iran.* https://www.khabaronline.ir/news/1900455/

Page, A., Morrell, S., & Taylor, R. (2002). Suicide and political regime in New South Wales and Australia during the 20th century. *Journal of Epidemiology & Community Health, 56*(10), 766–772. https://doi.org/10.1136/jech.56.10.766

Poursharifi, H. (2024). *Suicide prevention in Iran: challenges and solutions.* https://iranpa.org

Shah, A. (2009). The relationship between elderly suicide rates and the human development index. *International Psychogeriatrics, 21*(1), 69–77. https://doi.org/10.1017/s1041610208007527

Shah, A. (2010). A replication of the relationship between elderly suicide rates and the human development index in a cross-national study. *International Psychogeriatrics, 22*(5), 727–732. https://doi.org/10.1017/s1041610210001110

Shahtahmasebi, S. (2016). Politics and suicide prevention in indigenous populations. In J. Merrick (Ed.), *Public health: Some international aspects* (pp. 189–195). Nova. https://novapublishers.com/shop/public

Stack, S. (2021). Contributing factors to suicide: Political, social, cultural and economic. *Preventive Medicine, 152*(1), #106498. https://doi.org/10.1016/j.ypmed.2021.106498

Standish, K. (2020). Social, cultural and political violence. In *Suicide through a peacebuilding lens.* Palgrave Macmillan. https://doi.org/10.1007/978-981-13-9737-0_6

Steeg, S., Webb, R. T., Ibrahim, S., Appleby, L., & Kapur, N. (2020). Suicide rates and voting choice in the UK's 2016 national Brexit referendum on European Union membership. *British Journal of Psychology Open, 6*, e57. https://doi.org/10.1192/bjo.2020.32

Szasz, T. (2002). *Fatal freedom.* Syracuse University Press. https://archive.org/details/fatalfreedomethi00szas

Taylor, M., & Ryan, H. (1988). Fanaticism, political suicide and terrorism. *Terrorism, Violence, 11*, 91–111. https://doi.org/10.1080/10576108808435703

Tisha, X., & Polanco, M. (2022). An autopsy of the coloniality of suicide. *Health, 26*(1), 120–135. https://doi.org/10.1177/13634593211038517

Voracek, M., Formann, A. K., Fülöp, G., & Sonneck, G. (2003). Suicide and general elections in Austria. *Journal of Affective Disorders, 74*, 257–266. https://doi.org/10.1016/s0165-0327(02)00018-6
Wasserman, I. M. (1983). Political business cycles, presidential elections, and suicide and mortality patterns. *American Sociological Review, 48*(5), 711–720.
Wexler, L. (2009). Identifying colonial discourses in Inupiat young people's narratives as a way to understand the no future of Inupiat youth suicide. *American Indian & Alaskan Native Mental Health Research, 16*(1), 1–24. https://doi.org/10.5820/aian.1601.2009.1
White, J., & Morris, J. (2019). Re-thinking ethics and politics in suicide prevention: Bringing narrative ideas into dialogue with critical suicide studies. *International Journal of Environmental Research and Public Health, 16*(18), 3236. https://doi.org/10.3390/ijerph16183236
Yang, B., & Lester, D. (1992). The misery index and an index of misery. *Atlantic Economic Journal, 20*(3), 98. https://doi.org/10.1007/bf02300179
Yang, B., & Lester, D. (1999). The misery index and suicide. *Psychological Reports, 84*(3, Pt 2), 1086. https://doi.org/10.2466/PR0.84.3.1086-1086

# Chapter 11
# War Crisis and Protest Suicide

**S. M. Yasir Arafat, Sujita Kumar Kar, and Mohsen Rezaeian**

**Abstract** Suicide is a global public health challenge with multifactorial risk factors. Along with psychiatric risk factors, socio-politico-environmental factors affect suicidal behavior among general populations. Protest suicide is a rare type of suicide attributed to socio-politico-environmental issues like war, oppression, and human rights violations which first noted on June 11, 1963. War protest suicide is an extremely rare and special form of suicide noted protesting the Vietnam and Israel-Palestine wars. So far, it has been noted in the Western countries and considered as a Western Phenomenon. Based on Durkheim's category, war protest suicide is considered as an altruistic form of suicide. The classic war protest suicide reveals adult male without an identified mental disorder, suicide by self-burning at important public places showing their disapproval of war and appealing for change. This chapter discusses the dimensions of protest suicide with special consideration for war protest suicide.

**Keywords** Protest suicide · Political suicide · War · Self-burning · Crisis and suicide

## 1 Introduction

Social unrest is not uncommon in history. Some unrest is prevalent somewhere in this world at any given time, keeping some individuals under significant distress. War is the oldest and a classic example of social unrest (Rezaeian, 2015) affecting human

S. M. Y. Arafat (✉)
Department of Psychiatry, Bangladesh Specialized Hospital, Dhaka, Bangladesh
e-mail: arafatdmc62@gmail.com

S. K. Kar
Department of Psychiatry, King George's Medical University, Lucknow, India

M. Rezaeian
Department of Epidemiology and Biostatistics, School of Health, Occupational Environment Research Center, Rafsanjan University of Medical Sciences, Rafsanjan, Iran



S. M. Y. Arafat and S. K. Kar (eds.), *Ecological and Social Determinants of Suicidal Behavior*, South Asian Perspectives in Mental Health and Psychology,
https://doi.org/10.1007/978-981-96-4028-7_11

life in various ways. About 191 million deaths happened due to war-related injuries in twentieth century; 50% of the deaths were civilians (Rezaeian, 2015). However, the public health impact of war is grossly under-estimated and under-studied (Rezaeian, 2020). At the same time, there is concern about the under-reporting and manipulation of death and wounded numbers by the parties involved in the war (Rezaeian, 2009). Therefore, trustworthy data is a challenging issue while assessing the public health impact of wars.

Wars affect health, socioeconomic conditions, and environment of the regions involved. In addition to deaths and physical injury, wars affect physical and mental health across the countries. Low- and middle-income countries (LMICs) of Africa and Middle East are more affected by wars than high-income countries (Rezaeian, 2015, 2021). Among the regions, Middle East is hotspot for war over the decades. At the same time countries of North America, Western Europe, Japan, and Middle East are spending the extensive amount on military expenditure (Rezaeian, 2021).

The ongoing war crises (Ukraine-Russia, Israel-Palestine) are having a significant impact on people who are direct victims of this crisis (being injured, displaced, abused, and deprived of essential facilities). Additionally, people who witness the humanitarian crisis in different corners of the world through press and social media, also experience significant distress. Individuals, organizations, and agencies attempt to reduce the unrest by showing their distress to a larger mass in the form of protest in various forms. Sometimes, the protest takes extreme forms leading to killing oneself. Protest suicide is an extreme form of displacement of distress (anger) towards self as a response to unacceptable social unrest.

Aaron Bushnell, 25-year-old active duty-member of the US Air Force, poured gasoline on his body in front of the Israeli embassy in Washington and set fire on February 25, 2024 Sunday afternoon (Donegan, 2024). He was live-streaming the event on Twitch by his mobile and explaining his considerations behind the attempt where he mentioned his disappointment due to the ongoing genocide in Palestine. He shouted repeatedly mentioning "Free Palestine!".

Another attempt of fire setting on oneself after dousing gasoline was noted on December 2023 outside the Israeli consulate in Atlanta, Georgia, USA. A Palestinian flag was found nearby the place. The detailed identification of the protester was not revealed (Reuters, 2023). These very recent cases are classic examples of war protest suicide to convey distress concerning the humanitarian crisis that arose because of the ongoing Israel-Palestine war (Donegan, 2024; Reuters, 2023). This chapter, therefore, discusses the dimensions of protest suicide with special consideration for war protest suicide.

## 2 Characteristics of Protest Suicide

Historically, protest suicide has been noted all over the world (Crosby et al., 1977). It has been considered for persuasive technique for expected change and a social action instead of personal events (Jorgensen-Earp, 1987; Spehr & Dixon, 2014).

It is more commonly noticed in LMICs (Nooraeen & Croarkin, 2023). Among the methods (burning, hanging, poising), self-burning is the commonest method of protest suicide (Kim, 2019; Nooraeen & Croarkin, 2023). Social oppression, human rights suppression, political interest, family and living problems, demand fulfillment, and workplace injustices are the commonly identified risk factors (Arafat et al., 2024; Canetto & Rezaeian, 2020; Kim, 2019; Nooraeen & Croarkin, 2023).

Usually, the intention is mentioned beforehand, attempts happen in publicly important places, and attempts happen in absence of mental disorder in case of public protest suicide (Arafat et al., 2024; Biggs, 2013; Crosby et al., 1977). It can also be influenced as socio-cultural learning (Biggs, 2013; Spehr & Dixon, 2014). It can be revealed in various forms like political vs non-political; public vs personal; and individual vs group (Fig. 1).

On the basis of the stimulus, it can be sociopolitical like war, social oppression, and human rights violations. It can be non-political when the stimulus is related to personal gains like protest of property grabbing, job regularization, and loan repayment. Based on persuasion for change, it can be public or private. When the suicide intends to pursue greater changes beneficial to all like cessation of war, it turns into public attempt. When persuasion for changes is expected at personal level, it turns into personal attempt. Based on the number of persons involved in the event, it can be single or it can be performed in group with common interest. When a single person attempts, it is an individual event and when more than one person with the common interest attempts, it is a group event.

Once performed protest suicide activates emotional responses in multiple domains of society in various levels (Lahiri, 2014). In this time of modern technology, it disseminates swiftly among the populations across the countries. Usually the events get media attention with videos or with at least a photo of self-burn. It can ignite or reinforce protest among the community people related to the stimulus and protesting the ongoing practice.

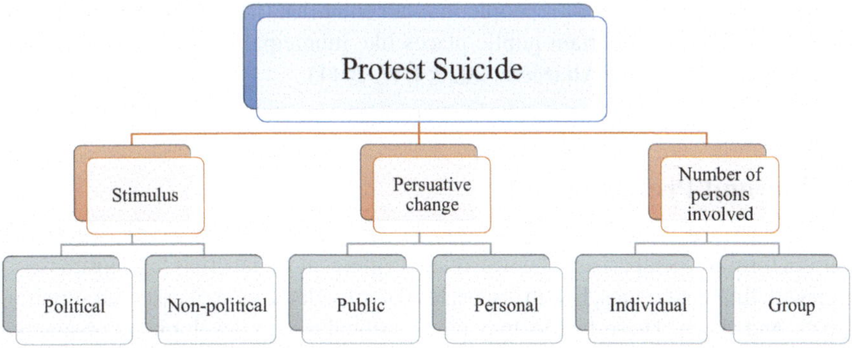


**Fig. 1** Different types of protest suicide

## 3 History and Evolution of Protest Suicide

The first documented political protest suicide was found on June 11, 1963 in South Vietnam when a Buddhist monk named Thich Quang Ducset set fire on himself and died in a public square for protesting some policies of the Government (Crosby et al., 1977) which was covered by David Halbarstam, an American journalist (Biggs, 2005). After the event, several similar suicides were repeated among the monks for protesting the same policies. Thich Quang's death resulted in huge protest against religious oppression in South Vietnam under Ngo Dinh Diem regime. The event ignites further protests and further protest suicide attempts (additional three monks and one nun) against the Government and consequently the USA withdrew its support for Diem regime. Later, Diem was ousted by military coup in November 1963 (Biggs, 2005). The case of Quang's protest suicide facilitated the events of protests in Vietnam.

The famous case of Mohamed Bouazizi (December 17, 2010), a 26-year-old male, has received global attention and led to the "Arab Spring". He put fire on himself to protest the confiscation of his scales that turns into a revolution (Lageman, 2020). Mohamed Bouazizi was a street vendor selling fruits and vegetables in Tunisia. In the morning of December 17, 2010, the law-enforcing authority confiscated his cart and wires as he had no formal permit to do the work (Lageman, 2020). Then attempted to make complains to the governor in Sidi Bouzid. He was refused to make it and frustrated. Subsequently, he set fire on himself outside the governor's office (Britannica, 2024). There were allegations of bribery by the police from Mohamed Bouazizi due to his illegal vendorship at street. He died on January 04, 2011 and by this time, protest had started demanding corrupted and authoritarian regime of Ben Ali who was in power since 1987 (Britannica, 2024). On January 14 Ben Ali had to resign and fled due to the protest of the people of Tunisia. Then, Egyptians started to protest against Hosni Mubarak in Cairo, Alexandria and other cities of Egypt. Subsequently, protest started in Bahrain (Tahrir Square), Libya, Syria, and Yemen. Modeling the death of Mohamed Bouazizi, dozens of people in Arab countries (from Morocco to Yemen) burnt themselves at important public places like municipal buildings, parliaments, and presidential palaces (Aljazeera, 2020; DW, 2011).

## 4 War and Protest Suicide

War is a form of social crisis. The war-related emergent social crisis has close association with financial issues, health issues, loss of jobs, disruption of essential supplies, threats, and abuse. These factors may play a critical role in development of suicidal behavior. The theory of suicide proposed by *Emile Durkheim* largely explains several possible explanations to the suicidal behavior during war. War may result in loss of social support system and may also produce social isolation, which may increase the risk of suicide (Motillon-Toudic et al., 2022). Loss of social cohesiveness, disruption in the social integrity, fall in social economy, substance abuse, and violence-physical abuse are well-known influencers of suicidal behavior (Kołodziej-Sarzyńska et al., 2019). During the war, these social crises are common, which might trigger the suicidal behavior. Health may be affected due to lack of social support, social attachment and other activities of social integration, resulting in development of suicidal behavior (Berkman et al., 2000; Kushner & Sterk, 2005; Na et al., 2022).

The protest suicide during the war might result from loss of social identity and feeling disintegrated from the mainstream society. The loss of purpose of life in the society during war may trigger anomic suicide (Kar & Singh, 2023). Protest suicides during times of social crisis might result from too much of social integration resulting in altruistic suicide (Stack, 2004). Too much of taking social responsibility during the time of war crisis may trigger suicidal behavior in an individual. In the other way, protest suicide attempt may happen to initiate the change for the society to stop war which is considered as altruistic form of suicide.

The protest suicide by *Aaron Bushnell* received mixed reactions in public as well as media (Donegan, 2024; Fernández, 2024; Geoghegan et al., 2024; Mehmood, 2024; Plerre, 2024; Stanton, 2024). It raises concerns of mental health services and suicide contagion. It again reminded the potential challenges of preventing protest suicides. When suicide happens with respect to any protest which involves the interest of a larger mass, it sets an example for other involved individuals to adopt such an extreme step as a solution for crisis. So, glorifying such incidents in media or social media (Biggs, 2013) may increase the risk of copycat suicide in society.

A similar attempt was noted protesting the in the Vietnam War in November 1965, by *Norman Morrison*, a 32-year-old man by setting fire on himself at Pentagon in Washington (Crosby et al., 1977). Another 22-year-old male, *Roger LaPorte*, died by self-burning in front of the United Nations Headquarters in New-York after eight days of the index case. At least three citizens of USA died by self-immolation during the Vietnam War protesting the war (Andriolo, 2006).

In 1969, a series of political protests by self-immolation was found for Soviet Union's invasion of Czechoslovakia (Crosby et al., 1977). It started with the self-immolation of *Jan Palach* (January 16, 1969), a 20-year-old male student of history poured gasoline on himself and set fire at Wenceslas Square in the New Town of Prague (Andriolo, 2006; Kauppinen, forthcoming). He died on January 19, 1969 due to burn. In the following months of Jan Palach's, several similar attempts (Jan Zajíc, a student in Prague; Josef Hlavatý, a brewery worker in Pilsen; Miroslav Malinka, a construction worker in Brno; and Evžen Plocek, a reform communist in Jihlava (Radio Prague International, 2019). No supporting information is available of having mental disorder among the deceased and all the suicides happened by self-burning. The events got attention in global media and disseminated swiftly in the community.

These classic war protest suicides reveal adult males without an identified mental disorder, suicide by self-burning at important public places showing their disapproval of war and appealing for change (Crosby et al., 1977; Spehr & Dixon, 2014). So far, it has been noted in the Western countries and considered as a Western Phenomenon (Taylor & Ryan, 1988). This may be explained by our previous discussion that Western countries are the major expenders in military (Rezaeian, 2021).

Based on Durkheim's category considering the two dimensions mentioned social integration and moral regulation, war protest suicide is considered as an altruistic form of suicide when people die by suicide for others (Durkheim, 1897/2002). Protest suicides pose challenges in multiple dimensions in regards to its prevention as the events are sporadic, rare, and planed; attributable factors are related to greater social context, lack of psychiatric morbidity, and strong media attention and dissemination.

## 5 Conclusion

War protest suicide is an extremely rare and special form of suicidal behavior classically noted as a Western Phenomenon and considered as an altruistic form of suicide. The classic war protest suicide reveals adult males without an identified mental disorder, suicide by self-burning at important public place showing their disapproval of war and appealing for change. Further studies are warranted to explore the phenomenon and prevent the risk factors of such suicide i.e., war.

## References


Aljazeera. (2020). *What is the Arab Spring, and how did it start?*. https://www.aljazeera.com/news/2020/12/17/what-is-the-arab-spring-and-how-did-it-start (accessed on July 03, 2024)

Andriolo, K. (2006). The twice-killed: Imagining protest suicide. *American Anthropologist, 108*(1), 100–113. https://doi.org/10.1525/aa.2006.108.1.100

Arafat, S. Y., Kar, S. K., Parvin, S., & Kabir R. (2024). Protest suicide in South Asia: Cases and literature review. *South East Asian Journal of Suicide Prevention, 1*(1). https://seajsp.qvjournal.com/index.php/about/article/view/5

Berkman, L. F., Glass, T., Brissette, I., & Seeman, T. E. (2000). From social integration to health: Durkheim in the new millennium. *Social Science & Medicine (1982), 51*(6), 843–857. https://doi.org/10.1016/s0277-9536(00)00065-4

Biggs, M. (2005). Dying without killing: Self-immolations, 1963–2002. In *Making sense of suicide missions* (pp.173–208).

Biggs, M. (2013). How repertoires evolve: The diffusion of suicide protest in the Twentieth Century. *Mobilization: An International Quarterly,* 18(4), 407–428. https://doi.org/10.17813/maiq.18.4.njnu779530x55082

Britannica. (2024). Mohamed Bouazizi. https://www.britannica.com/biography/Mohamed-Bouazizi (accessed on July 02, 2024).

Canetto, S. S., &Rezaeian, M. (2020). Protest suicide among Muslim women: A human rights perspective. In M. E. Button & I. Marsh (Eds.), *Suicide and social justice: New perspectives on the politics of suicide and suicide prevention* (pp. 102–121). Routledge/Taylor & Francis Group. https://doi.org/10.4324/9780429460494-7

Crosby, K., Rhee, J. O., & Holland, J. (1977). Suicide by fire: A contemporary method of political protest. *The International Journal of Social Psychiatry, 23*(1), 60–69. https://doi.org/10.1177/002076407702300111

Durkheim, É. (1897/2002). *Suicide: A study in sociology*. Taylor & Francis Group.

Donegan, M. (2024, February 28). Aaron Bushnell set himself on fire outside an Israeli embassy. It is our loss he is no longer with us. *The Guardian*. Available at: https://www.theguardian.com/commentisfree/2024/feb/28/aaron-bushnell-self-immolation-gaza-israel (accessed on 17 June 2024).

DW. (2011). *Political suicide*. https://www.dw.com/en/death-by-fire-self-immolation-in-the-arab-world/a-14898706 (accessed on July 03, 2024).

Fernández, B. (2024). *Suicide vs genocide: Rest in power, Aaron Bushnell*. Available at: https://www.aljazeera.com/opinions/2024/2/26/suicide-vs-genocide-rest-in-power-aaron-bushnell (accessed on 17 June 2024).

Geoghegan, T., Epstein, K., & Wendling, M. (2024, February 26). *Aaron Bushnell: US airman dies after setting himself on fire outside Israeli embassy in Washington*. Available at: https://www.bbc.com/news/world-us-canada-68405119 (accessed on 17 June 2024).

Jorgensen-Earp, C. R. (1987). "Toys of desperation" suicide as protest rhetoric. *Southern Speech Communication Journal, 53*(1), 80–96. https://doi.org/10.1080/10417948709372714

Kar, S. K., & Singh, S. (2023). Anomic suicides on rise during recently emerging crises: Revisiting Durkheim's model. *CNS Spectrums, 28*(6), 655–656. https://doi.org/10.1017/S1092852923002341

Kauppinen, A. (forthcoming). Suicide as protest. In M. Cholbi& P. Stellino (Eds.), *Oxford handbook of the philosophy of suicide*. Oxford University Press.

Kim, S.-C. (2019). The trajectory of protest suicide in South Korea, 1970–2015. *Journal of Contemporary Asia*, 1–26. https://doi.org/10.1080/00472336.2019.1607889

Kołodziej-Sarzyńska, M., Majewska, M., Juchnowicz, D., & Karakuła-Juchnowicz, H. (2019). Risk factors of suicide with reference to the theory of social integration by Émile Durkheim. *Psychiatria Polska, 53*(4), 865–881. https://doi.org/10.12740/PP/92217

Kushner, H. I., & Sterk, C. E. (2005). The limits of social capital: Durkheim, suicide, and social cohesion. *American Journal of Public Health, 95*(7), 1139–1143. https://doi.org/10.2105/AJPH.2004.053314

Lageman, T. (2020). *Remembering Mohamed Bouazizi: The man who sparked the Arab Spring*. Alzazira. https://www.aljazeera.com/features/2020/12/17/remembering-mohamed-bouazizi-his-death-triggered-the-arab (accessed on June 17, 2024).

Lahiri, S. (2014). Choosing to die: Suicide bombing and suicide protest in South Asia. *Terrorism and Political Violence, 27*(2), 268–288. https://doi.org/10.1080/09546553.2013.8063

Mehmood, J. (2024). *Aaron Bushnell and Islam's stance on suicide and self-immolation*. Available at: https://www.alhakam.org/aaron-bushnell-and-islams-stance-on-suicide-and-self-immolation/ (accessed on 17 June 2024).

Motillon-Toudic, C., Walter, M., Séguin, M., Carrier, J. D., Berrouiguet, S., & Lemey, C. (2022). Social isolation and suicide risk: Literature review and perspectives. *European Psychiatry, 65*(1), e65. https://doi.org/10.1192/j.eurpsy.2022.2320

Na, P. J., Bommersbach, T., Pietrzak, R. H., & Rhee, T. G. (2022). Durkheim's theory of social integration and suicide revisited: Is it diversity of social networks or perceived strength of social support that matters? *The Journal of Clinical Psychiatry, 84*(1), 22m14477. https://doi.org/10.4088/JCP.22m14477

Nooraeen, S., & Croarkin, P. E. (2023). Protest suicide: Considerations for psychiatrists and psychologists. *Frontiers in Psychiatry, 14*, 1213420. https://doi.org/10.3389/fpsyt.2023.1213420

Plerre, J. (2024). *A postscript and postmortem on the suicide of Aaron Bushnell | Psychology Today New Zealand*. Available at: https://www.psychologytoday.com/nz/blog/psych-unseen/202403/a-postscript-and-postmortem-on-the-suicide-of-aaron-bushnell (accessed on 17 June 2024).

Radio Prague International. (2019). *Czech martyr Jan Palach's enduring legacy, 50 years after his self-immolation*. https://english.radio.cz/czech-martyr-jan-palachs-enduring-legacy-50-years-after-his-self-immolation-8141155 (accessed on July 02, 2024).

Rezaeian, M. (2009). A review on the most important consequences of wars and armed conflicts. *Middle East Journal of Business, 4*, 7–9.

Rezaeian, M. (2015). War epidemiology: an urgent plea. *Epidemiology (Cambridge, Mass.), 26*(1), e10–e11. https://doi.org/10.1097/EDE.0000000000000209

Rezaeian, M. (2020). "War epidemiology" versus "peace epidemiology": A personal view. *Archives of Iranian Medicine, 23*(4Suppl1), S38–S42. https://doi.org/10.34172/aim.2020.s8

Rezaeian, M. (2021). Illustrating wars and armed conflicts from a different perspective: Who suffer and who invest the most? *Middle East Journal of Business, 6*(1), 12–14.

Reuters. (2023). *Protester self-immolates outside Israeli consulate in Atlanta.* https://www.reuters.com/world/us/protester-self-immolates-outside-israeli-consulate-atlanta-2023-12-01/ (accessed on July 02, 2024).

Spehr, S., & Dixon, J. (2014). Protest suicide: A systematic model with heuristic archetypes. *Journal for the Theory of Social Behaviour, 44*(3), 368–388.

Stack, S. (2004). Emile Durkheim and altruistic suicide. *Archives of Suicide Research, 8*(1), 9–22. https://doi.org/10.1080/13811110490243741

Stanton, A. (2024). *Aaron Bushnell called a 'hero' for pro-Palestinian self-immolation.* Available at: https://www.newsweek.com/aaron-bushnell-called-hero-pro-palestinian-self-immolation-1873454 (accessed on 17 June 2024).

Taylor, M., & Ryan, H. (1988). Fanaticism, political suicide and terrorism. *Terrorism, 11*(2), 91–111. https://doi.org/10.1080/10576108808435703

# Chapter 12
# Media's Influence on Suicidal Behavior

**Arya Thirumeni, Lekshmi Vimala, R. Dhanasekara Pandian, and Anish V. Cherian**

**Abstract** Suicide is a complex global health issue, with over 700,000 deaths annually. Media portrayals of suicide can significantly influence suicidal behavior. This chapter explores the multifaceted relationship between media and suicide, examining the influence of various media forms, including traditional media, social media, television, and film. It discusses the Werther and Papageno effects, highlighting the potential for media to trigger copycat suicides or, conversely, promote help-seeking behaviors. The chapter also analyzes the mechanisms through which media influences suicidal behavior, including social cognitive theory, priming theory, cultivation theory, and newer models like algorithmic influence and digital echo chambers. It emphasizes the role of media in suicide prevention, advocating for responsible reporting, media literacy, and collaboration among stakeholders. The chapter provides an overview of media guidelines, ethical considerations, and the latest recommendations from the World Health Organization (WHO). It also explores policy measures, public education strategies, and the potential of AI and technology in suicide prevention. By promoting responsible media portrayals and fostering media literacy, we can harness the power of media to mitigate suicidal behavior and promote mental well-being.

**Keywords** Suicide prevention · Suicide contagion · Media reporting · Media literacy · WHO guidelines

A. Thirumeni · R. D. Pandian · A. V. Cherian
Department of Psychiatric Social Work, National Institute of Mental Health and Neurosciences (NIMHANS), Bengaluru, India

L. Vimala (✉)
Mental Health Practitioner, Kerala, India
e-mail: lekshmivimala@gmail.com



S. M. Y. Arafat and S. K. Kar (eds.), *Ecological and Social Determinants of Suicidal Behavior*, South Asian Perspectives in Mental Health and Psychology,
https://doi.org/10.1007/978-981-96-4028-7_12

## 1 Introduction

Media plays a pivotal role in shaping public perceptions, behaviors, and attitudes toward sensitive issues such as suicide. With the rise of digital platforms, the way suicide is reported and discussed has evolved, becoming more immediate and far-reaching. Historically, newspapers and television were the main sources of information on suicide, but the rapid spread of content on social media has created both opportunities and risks (Phillips, 1974; Pirkis et al., 2019).

Suicide is a multifaceted issue that requires an understanding of the psychological, social, cultural, and environmental factors involved. Media coverage can either contribute to suicide contagion or help prevent it by promoting mental health education and specific treatments (Vijayakumar, 2016). The influence of media on suicidal behavior has been studied extensively, particularly in relation to the Werther effect, where sensationalized reporting leads to suicide contagion (Phillips, 1974). However, the Papageno effect shows that responsible media portrayals focusing on help-seeking behaviors can prevent suicides (Niederkrotenthaler et al., 2010).

Research has shown that media reporting plays a critical role in influencing suicidal behavior. For example, a study in Bangladesh highlighted how media coverage sensationalizes suicide reporting as opposed to spreading information on education and awareness related to suicide (Arafat et al., 2020). Studies from China and Japan have demonstrated that irresponsible media reporting can increase the likelihood of copycat suicides, especially following high-profile celebrity deaths (Chen et al., 2013; Ueda et al., 2017).

The digital age has amplified the impact of media on suicide. Social media platforms facilitate the rapid dissemination of both harmful and helpful content, but their unregulated nature often allows harmful content to spread unchecked (Naslund et al., 2016). In countries like India and Bangladesh, where mental health resources are often limited and stigma around suicide remains high, media plays a key role in either perpetuating harmful behaviors or providing a lifeline through awareness and education (Arafat et al., 2019; Ganesh et al., 2020).

Media coverage of suicide presents both risks and opportunities: it can contribute to suicide contagion or help prevent it by educating the public and promoting mental health resources. Understanding how media influences suicidal behavior is critical for designing effective suicide prevention strategies, particularly in LMICs, where mental health services are often inadequate (Vijayakumar, 2016; WHO, 2023).

## 2 Types of Media and Their Effects on Human Behavior

How suicide is presented before the various forms of media influence public behavior and attitude varies. Historically, traditional media like newspapers and television have been sources through which people learn about suicide. Digital platforms and social media have led to tremendous extensions in the media's power and influence and, with it, bring both challenges and opportunities in terms of managing the presentation of suicide.

## *2.1 Newspaper Reporting of Suicide*

The reportage of suicide cases by newspapers has, over time, defined public perception toward suicide. Most of the early and prevailing studies on media influence responded to sensationalism in reporting suicide cases in newspapers. As a general principle, sensationalism reporting is very vivid in describing how suicide occurred, where suicide occurred, and other personal aspects of the suicide victim. These reports usually create romanticized or heroic images of a suicide that might create the impression that it is a theatrical act in response to personal problems.

It could be argued that one of the first recorded cases of media-induced suicide contagion was presented in the publishing of Johann Wolfgang von Goethe's novel entitled The Sorrows of Young Werther in 1774. The plot was centered on the character who, after being beleaguered by unrequited love, ended his life, and in the well-documented description of his suicide, the wave of imitative suicides swept across Europe. This developed into a phenomenon later named the Werther Effect, wherein it was observed that young men imitated the protagonist's appearance with the same attire and followed similar methods in committing suicide (Phillips, 1974).

Since the Werther Effect, hundreds of studies have confirmed the phenomenon, especially about newspaper reportage and the actual influence on suicide rates. Analyses done in Austria during the 1980s and 1990s confirmed that scandalous reportage had a harmful impact. An apparent rise in subway suicides in Vienna was identified as specifically attributable to sensationalized attention, such as graphic accounts of the victims and their actions. In reply, the Austrian government worked with media sources to formulate guidelines for responsible reporting, including avoiding explicit details and focusing on preventive measures. After their formulation and implementation, the suicide rates significantly declined in the city (Etzersdorfer & Sonneck, 1998).

Although the interventions have been successful, sensationalist reporting remains to this day, and the plague is affecting most parts of the world. That sensationalism, driven by the craving for dramatic headlines and higher readership, continues to challenge the fall in contagion effects associated with suicidal reporting. Responsible reporting can, however, minimize the risks. For example, studies suggested that when the articles report suicide as a preventable tragedy and provide details regarding how to avail facilities of mental health services, then the contagion effect will be reduced (Niederkrotenthaler et al., 2010).

## 2.2 The Papageno Effect

The Papageno Effect is the counterpoint to the Werther Effect in that media can provide a protective influence by focusing on stories of survivors of suicidal crises. Indeed, the concept is named after a character in Mozart's The Magic Flute, who, through interventions made by his friends, does not succeed in his suicide attempt. According to Niederkrotenthaler et al. (2010),when media focus on coping strategies and help-seeking behavior, then it prevents suicides.

This impact has been observed in the findings of studies whose media reportage was focused on healing, psychiatric treatment, and assistance networks. For example, when newspapers and television shows carry interviews with individuals who have had suicidal thoughts but sought treatment and got better, suicide rates tend to decline. Such a message that suicide is not the only alternative and help is available can speak to persons in crisis.

Good examples of the Papageno effect can be seen in mental health advocacy campaigns on social media. Social media, especially Instagram and Twitter, is often shared with stories of recovery and resilience, often supported by mental health experts and organizations. Millions of people can reach out to this form of platform and get a tidbit of hope and information on where to get help.

## 2.3 Social Media and Suicide

Social media has brought in a new paradigm in the discussion and depiction of suicide. The user-generated content in social media is less controlled than professionally edited content in other traditional media. Thus, social media would pose risks and opportunities for suicide prevention alike.

On one side, social media can act as an advocacy vehicle for good mental health discussions and peer support. These sites include but are not limited to Twitter, Facebook, and Instagram, which launch campaigns related to different kinds of psychological health disorders and support preventive measures against suicide. The hashtag #HereForYou on Instagram has created room to freely discuss mental health issues and reach services to cope with such disorders (Naslund et al., 2016). Peer support communities on any platform like Reddit can help share their personal experiences with mental health and provide advice and encouragement to people with similar mental health issues.

Conversely, social media enables the proliferation of malicious content. Pro-suicide forums, for instance, have been associated with clusters of suicidal behaviors, especially among young people and those in the age bracket of adolescents to young adults. The nature of the content is often glamorized, encouraging participants to engage in self-harm behaviors. A notorious example of this kind of phenomenon is the "Blue Whale Challenge," a viral social media spectacle that possibly urged young people to accomplish a series of dangerous tasks, ending with suicide. Although the degree to which the challenge influenced any real individuals is disputed, several suicides of teenagers around the world have been traced to the challenge (Mukhra et al., 2019).

The fast dissemination of content on social media hinders content moderation. Some Internet companies have used algorithms and content moderation tools to flag such content but cannot regulate their sheer volumes. In addition, platforms like Reddit, which allow users anonymity, will only exacerbate the harmful and unchallenged spread of pro-suicide messages.

## 2.4 *Television and Movie Portrayals of Suicide*

For an extended period, suicide has been viewed through television shows and films that often exaggerate and sensationalize it. The reported cases of suicide might attract the interest of people, but they can also lead to dangerous behavior when such portrayals are not handled responsibly. A very recent example can be seen in the Netflix series 13 Reasons Why, which tells the story of the suicide of a teenage girl who leaves tapes behind to explain why she took such a drastic measure. At its release, the show opened a debate on its portrayal of suicide and what effect it might have on viewers.

Several studies have investigated the effect that 13 Reasons Why had on suicide rates. In one case, it was noted that following its release, the suicide rate of U.S. young people aged 10–17 years increased by 28.9% during the month following its release (Bridge et al., 2020). Some critics at the time of the program's airing pointed out that the graphic presentation of the self-inflicted death of the principal character and not giving much focus to the existence of mental health care could incite susceptible people to try the very same things they witnessed on television. Some also criticized the show as it portrayed suicide as a way of attention and control over other people's lives, which would give a deadly message to susceptible viewers.

However, the potential negative impact of television and film on suicide prevention may be neutralized by the appropriate handling of the theme. The appropriate portrayal of suicide in films such as The Skeleton Twins and It's Kind of a Funny Story presents a message of therapy, support systems, and recovery. These movies reveal the elaborate struggles of psychological issues without romanticizing suicide, thus offering viewers a new perspective on the issue. Research has indicated that if the media focuses on recovery and services available to care for mental health, there is a decrease in the risk of contagion (Pirkis et al., 2006).

## 2.5 *Celebrity Suicides-Global Phenomenon*

Celebrity suicides, particularly those celebrities being either popular or famous public figures, represent a hot media agenda. For instance, every celebrity death by suicide receives extensive media coverage; this kind of media reporting has its impact on public health.

One of the best-known incidents is that of actor Robin Williams in 2014. Suicide rates in the United States increased around 10% in the months after Williams' death, with notable increases in suicides by asphyxiation, which is how Williams died (Fink et al., 2018). The vivid media coverage of Williams' suicide, including the modality and his struggles, apparently accounts for much of this increase in suicide rates.

One of the determining factors that has a bearing on the general reactions of the public is how the media has reacted to and handled celebrity suicides. The focus of attention when it first emerged as news was mainly on the tragic death of a talented individual and the circumstances leading to such a death, which arguably glorified the act and could even incite imitation. On the contrary, when the media focus their attention and attention on access to mental health resources for preventing suicide, suicide contagion is less likely to happen (Zalsman et al., 2016). Media guidelines provide aspects, with the World Health Organization as well recommending limiting details of the method applied in suicides to preventive measures while providing resources on mental health (World Health Organization, 2023).

Celebrity suicides also open space for public debate over issues related to mental health if their coverage includes expert commentaries or advice on how to seek help. A good example from India regarding such cases is immediately after the suicide of renowned personalities like Sushant Singh Rajput, when depression, substance abuse, and other related matters also begin to dominate public discourses. This kind of awareness can make more people seek help and reduce the stigma associated with mental health issues. However, the media reporting of the event was found to be highly polarizing and clickbait (Ganesh et al., 2020; Menon et al., 2022). The media face the biggest challenge of finding a balance so as not to sensationalize but to create awareness instead.

## 3 Mechanisms of Media Influence on Suicidal Behavior

Through contemporary research, it has been discussed how the mechanisms work through which media impacts suicidal behaviors. The earlier traditional theories, like Werther and Papageno's effects, describe how media can be viewed to directly contribute to suicide contagion or act as a protective factor. Digital Echo Chambers and Algorithmic Influence are the newer mechanisms that are explored in this domain, which investigates how social media and digital platforms influence suicidal behaviors.

## 3.1 Social Cognitive Theory

Albert Bandura's Social Cognitive Theory posits that human behavior is learned from one's environment, and people learn from others through social interaction and observation, especially from mass media and other influences in their surroundings. Such portrayals of suicide in ways that make individuals feel suicide would be a viable means to alleviate the hassle of life may trigger imitation among vulnerable individuals (Bandura, 1986). The theory is applicable when relating the impact of the media's portrayal of suicide on susceptible youth, particularly adolescents and young adults.

On the other hand, this theory also throws light on the fact that if the media depicts more positive information instead of romanticizing suicide and encourages how suicide is avoidable by seeking help, showcasing people surviving their problems, it can have a positive impact on people.

## 3.2 Priming Theory

According to the priming theory, exposure to particular media content activates people's thoughts and behaviors. The more suicide appears in the media and is sensationalized and graphic, the more likely it primes individuals with such orientation to think more about suicide, which increases their chance of acting out suicidal behavior (Berkowitz, 1984).

For example, repeated exposure to news reports and social media can easily make ideation accessible in the minds of depressed or mentally challenged individuals through exposure to suicidal content. This activation of cognition makes it very probable to attempt suicide if the media elaborates on the method to commit the suicidal act or if it presents death as the only solution to awful problems.

Thus, prevention of priming effects would depend upon media coverage of stories or events of suicides. Avoiding dramatic reporting about suicide and instead reporting about prevention and support decreases the chance of cognitive activation related to suicidal behavior.

## 3.3 Cultivation Theory

The Cultivation Theory proposed by George Gerbner suggests that extended exposure to mass media content can shape an individual with a very different understanding of reality (Gerbner, 1969). Repeatedly having suicide appear as one of the most common responses to difficulties in films, television shows, and news may lead one to believe that suicide is one of the more common or even inevitable reactions to the hardships of life (Gerbner, 1976; Stack, 2003). This theory is particularly relevant in today's media environment with regards to content on suicide. At times, it becomes widely available not only from the traditional media but also from social platforms such as YouTube, Instagram, and TikTok. Continuous exposure to such content can normalize the behavior, especially for impressionable viewers who might already feel isolated or hopeless (Pirkis et al., 2016).

On the other side of the spectrum, if media platforms were to continue reporting suicide as an avoidable tragedy and focus on the available resources and support, it would aid in creating a perception change within society and lead away from the risk of suicide contagion (Gould et al., 2014). In doing so, more hopeful and supportive media narratives can be encouraged in suicide prevention efforts (Cheng et al., 2007).

## *3.4 Newer Mechanisms of Media Influence*

In addition to traditional theories, newer models have emerged to explain how digital platforms and social media algorithms influence suicidal behavior.

### 3.4.1 Digital Echo Chambers and Algorithmic Influence

Algorithms on social media personalize whatever users view as per the browsing behavior and interaction on the platforms. This would result in digital echo chambers: repeated engagement with the same kind of content, which can sustain the negative thought pattern. Vulnerable individuals may be trapped in those echo chambers as they tend to re-engage themselves with content regarding suicide or self-harm (Cinelli et al., 2021).

Algorithms designed to engage users also pose the risk of exposing vulnerable users to content that exacerbates their distress. For example, if a person has interacted with posts regarding depression or suicide on Instagram, then he would be fed more relevant content on the same topics, thus sustaining the cycle that fuels depression.

### 3.4.2 Cognitive Behavioral Cybernetic Model

This is a model that integrates the nature of CBT with cybernetics, suggesting that digital environments such as social media must be considered as systems in the regulation of behavior through feedback loops. The presence of suicide-related content, for instance, in these environments encourages faulty patterns and, therefore, increases suicidal ideation in the individual (Heffer & Willoughby, 2019).

The model suggests that regulation of online spaces is important for avoiding constant exposure of vulnerable individuals to deleterious content. Various digital interventions, including mental health chatbots, AI-driven content moderation, etc., can at least disrupt these feedback loops and give positive reinforcement to most people.

### 3.4.3 Networked Narrative Theory

The way personal stories are put out and received has changed with the advent of social media. Networked Narrative Theory suggests that the very same feature that allows such user-generated content to go viral also creates new risks but also introduces new opportunities for suicide prevention (Gibbs et al., 2015).

What is worthwhile to point out, though, is that when stories of suicide are circulated around on platforms like Twitter or Instagram, they may continue the stated suicidal behavior (if the stories glorify or sensationalize suicide) or help prevent it (if the stories focus more on recovery and support). The networked nature of social media enables rapid dissemination with effects dependent upon how the narrative is framed.

## 4 The Role of Media in Suicide Prevention

Suicide and its associated behaviors pose significant challenges to the health services and public policy initiatives across the globe, and with its complex nature, it is difficult to ascertain all the risk factors which could make a person susceptible to an attempt (Turecki et al., 2019). Hence it is imperative to also simultaneously promote the protective factors to successfully curb the rates of suicide, and in this context, media can play a major part (Vijayakumar, 2016).

While media can be an agent of contagion, it equally has a tremendous scope to perform the role of savior in the context of suicide by heightening awareness about mental health and extending support and stories of recovery. If leading and guidance are proper and if reporting is conducted responsibly, then media houses can take the attention of media from sensationalism toward education and prevention, thus reducing the chance of suicide contagion. This chapter demonstrates the various ways media can be an instrument for suicide prevention.

### *4.1 Mass Media as an Advocacy Tool for Mental Health*

Mass media plays a pivotal role in suicide prevention by raising awareness, reducing stigma, and encouraging help-seeking behavior. In India, social media campaigns like #SPEAK have initiated open discussions on mental health, promoting early intervention and reducing stigma (Latha et al., 2020). In Bangladesh, Arafat's research highlights how responsible media reporting can shift public perceptions of suicide and encourage help-seeking (Arafat, 2019). In U.S., collaborations between media and mental health organizations, such as the National Suicide Prevention Lifeline and ABC, have demonstrated success by increasing calls to suicide prevention hotlines (Pirkis et al., 2006). Digital platforms like Instagram's #HereForYou campaign and YouTube's mental health collaborations have also contributed by providing crisis support tools directly through their platforms, engaging younger audiences. These initiatives demonstrate the powerful role of mass media in normalizing mental health conversations and advocating for suicide prevention globally.

## *4.2 Positive Narratives and Peer Support*

Positive news reports may minimize the rate of suicide, especially when hope and recovery seem to be guaranteed with the firm projection of the availability of support. The existence of some people who have managed to emerge from the problems and have indeed sought help can aid others facing such problems. The positives in which media portrayals give a clue to the success stories of mental health interventions and the role that social support plays will convince a victim to seek solutions instead of suicide.

In fact, the Papageno Effect is one of the major mechanisms by which positive media narratives prevent suicide. Highlighting the stories of people who had successfully overcome suicidal ideation through support from friends, family, or mental health professionals, the media may offer alternative solutions to the victims in crisis. It helps viewers realize that there is still hope left for them.

Peer support networks, particularly those that already exist in digital communities, help individuals maintain their well-being and make practical recommendations to individuals experiencing mental health-related challenges. Online peer support groups have been shown to reduce feelings of loneliness and provide individuals with the needed impetus to seek clinical intervention; these findings have been supported by a number of researchers, such as Naslund et al. (2016).

Another area of expanded scope is in the form of digital intervention, such as mental health chatbots and crisis counseling apps. For instance, an app like Talkspace or BetterHelp allows users to get connected with licensed therapists through messaging or video calls. The digital tools help supplement traditional mental health services by offering flexible, on-demand support, especially for younger people who are more comfortable using technology for communication.

An example of this trend toward the utilization of media as a force for good in suicide prevention is the integration of positive stories into the content and the facilitation of peer support through digital networks. It may be the case that focusing on the preventability of the issue and pushing forward that help is available can contribute to the reduction of stigma around mental health issues and encourage people to seek help.

# 5 Media Guidelines and Ethical Considerations

Given the media's significant influence on suicidal behavior, organizations like the World Health Organization (WHO), Press Council of India (PCI), Samaritans (UK), and Mindframe (Australia) have developed guidelines to encourage responsible reporting of suicide. These guidelines aim to reduce the risk of suicide contagion and promote awareness and prevention without sensationalism (Samaritans, 2022; World Health Organization, 2023). However, in the rapidly evolving digital age, content often spreads quickly, bypassing traditional checks (Pirkis & Blood, 2001).

## *5.1 WHO and Other Guidelines*

The **WHO** guidelines advise against sensationalizing suicide, sharing specific details of the method, or glamorizing the act. Instead, media outlets are encouraged to focus on prevention, available mental health resources, and crisis helplines (World Health Organization, 2023). The guidelines also discourage oversimplification of suicide causes and advocate for using non-stigmatizing language like "died by suicide." By adhering to these standards, media professionals can help reduce the risk of imitation and guide those in crisis toward therapeutic resources (World Health Organization, 2023).

The **Press Council of India (PCI)** guidelines align with WHO's, urging the media to avoid sensationalist headlines and protect the privacy of the deceased and their families. PCI advises avoiding graphic details and considering the impact of reporting on suicide survivors, particularly family members (PCI, 2022).

The **Samaritans Guidelines** recommend focusing on mental health and recovery rather than the act of suicide itself. They discourage speculation on motives, which can oversimplify complex issues, and promote sensitive language, such as "died by suicide." Including support resources is also emphasized (Samaritans, 2022).

The **Mindframe Guidelines** in Australia advise against glamorizing suicide, particularly among young people. These guidelines stress cultural sensitivity, especially when reporting on Indigenous communities, and discourage the use of images or depictions of the method of suicide (Mindframe, 2023).

Other organizations, such as the American Foundation for Suicide Prevention (AFSP) and the Centers for Disease Control and Prevention (CDC), support similar guidelines. They recommend avoiding repetitive coverage, especially following high-profile suicides, and including expert insights to educate the public on the complexities of suicide and mental health (AFSP, 2022; Stone et al., 2017). These standards concur with the recommendations of WHO but also provide media professionals with further guidelines on best practices, for instance, not to cover repeatedly the same story, particularly in crucial periods following the suicide of an admired celebrity or a widely publicized one. A good suggestion is to include statements from experts who deal with mental health in any report, which might enlighten the public on the sophisticated matters of suicide and,' in general, mental issues.

## 5.2 Challenges in Implementation Guidelines

Although there are defined guidelines, ensuring systematic adherence to recommendations through media outlets remains a challenge. One significant challenge faced by media operators is the competitive nature of the media industry. Success in this industry often relies on sensationalism and dramatic stories to attract viewers and increase revenue, which can result in violations of media guidelines, especially in the case of high-profile or celebrity suicides (Sisask & Värnik, 2012). The pressure to deliver attention-grabbing content, even when it conflicts with responsible reporting, remains a pervasive issue.

Additionally, the rise of digital journalism and social networking further complicates the implementation of media guidelines. With the rapid spread of information across digital media, many news stories are published with minimal editorial review. User-generated content such as blogs, social networking posts, and amateur videos often go viral, amplifying sensationalism and misinformation about suicide (Burnap et al., 2015). Platforms like YouTube, TikTok, and Twitter enable widespread content sharing, but these platforms often lack robust tools for content moderation, leading to an overwhelming volume of suicide-related posts (Arendt et al., 2019).

Another challenge is the global reach of digital media, where content created in one country is easily accessed by audiences in other regions with different cultural attitudes toward suicide. For example, coverage of celebrity suicides in the United States may be consumed by audiences in countries where suicide is heavily stigmatized, increasing the risk of suicide contagion in areas with limited mental health support and poor suicide prevention literacy (Arafat et al., 2021).

Efforts to address these challenges include the development of AI-based content moderation tools. These tools aim to automatically flag and remove harmful self-harm-related content from digital platforms. However, these tools are not without flaws and continue to spark debates regarding the ethics of using artificial intelligence to moderate sensitive content (Ransing et al., 2021). Additionally, while guidelines provide the foundation for responsible reporting, media professionals must be educated on the complexities of suicide, mental health, and the profound impact their reporting can have on real-world behaviors (Niederkrotenthaler et al., 2020).

## 5.3 Case Studies on Effective and Ineffective Reporting

Many case studies describe what's been happening in the real world, that is, the effects of responsible and irresponsible reporting on media outlets and in suicide.

An international example of effective reporting was put in place in Austria, where subway suicides in Vienna during the 1980s triggered heavily reduced suicide rates after being dealt with by the media responsibly. The Austrian government consulted with a fair number of media houses after years of sensationalized reporting, including various details on how each of the suicides were carried out. The media agreed not to describe suicide vividly and made efforts to give more information regarding available mental health resources instead. After launching these guidelines, subway suicides considerably went down in Vienna, thus demonstrating that responsible reporting in the media could effectively reduce suicide contagion.

On the other hand, the media's story of Kurt Cobain's suicide, the Nirvana leader in 1994, is a cautionary tale of irresponsible reporting. The tremendous amount of media attention over Cobain's death, including even graphic details in which he killed himself and idealization of the struggles he faced, contributed to a spurt in Seattle suicides of identified young men who took after him. This creates an awareness of the risk of suicide glorification in media reports and implementing ethical practices to circumvent suicide contagion (Stack, 2005).

## 6 Way Forward: Policy Measures, Media Literacy, and Joint Efforts

As media coverage has a huge impact on suicidal behavior, it's high time to take measures that can reduce the damage as well as responsible reporting. It calls for all sectors, including governments, media professionals, mental health organizations, and the public, to work in unison. Because media landscapes continue changing with the advent of digital online media, there is a growing need to address challenges in light of rapid developments in the area of content distribution as well as the globalization of media coverage. The following section highlights key areas of concern within the role of the media regarding suicide prevention, particularly with regard to policy initiatives, public education, and cross-sector collaboration.

### *6.1 Policy Initiations: Improving Media Guidelines*

Governments and regulatory bodies of the media will, therefore, be at the forefront of ensuring that suicide accounts are reported based on set ethical standards. While the World Health Organization and others, make recommendations on responsible reporting, this is largely left to voluntary compliance among most media houses. Policy interventions can, therefore, fill the gap by setting enforceable rules to hold specific media houses responsible for irresponsible reports that may lead to suicide contagion.

Another step would be to include media reporting guidelines in national suicide prevention strategies. Governments may engage mental health organizations and media regulatory bodies to allow for the incorporation of suicide reporting into the broader public health policy. Austria is a case in point, whereby collaboration between the government and media houses led to the development and implementation of a responsible reporting guideline, thus successfully reducing the suicide rates (Etzersdorfer & Sonneck, 1998). In the same vein, other nations may see it as useful to embrace suicide reporting guidelines in their national mental health policies, from which there would be more significant awareness and consciousness within respective media houses on such specific guidelines.

Besides the above national policies, there is an increased need for international cooperation with regard to the nature of digital media that involves the whole world. Content with suicide can mushroom across borders within seconds, hence the cultural aspect of controlling its influence in different cultural settings. International Organizations, such as the United Nations and WHO, can really play a critical role in establishing international standards for reporting suicide cases in the media. Such firms can partner with social media sites and online news sources to make suggestions for universal standards that will transcend various countries and cultures to ensure a comprehensive approach to suicide prevention through media reporting.

Governments and media houses can also adopt incentives and punishments for their effective implementation. Media houses that consistently adhere to responsible reportage guidelines should be accorded certain recognitions or awards that hint at their respect for ethical journalism. Similarly, those harboring sensational or injurious reporting should attract penalties such as fines or public condemnation. This will encourage the media houses to think more about the health of the public than sensationalism and will fashion a much more responsible and compassionate media landscape.

## *6.2 Media Literacy and Public Education*

Media literacy among the public is essential in reducing the destructive impact of irresponsible suicide reporting. Media literacy refers to one's ability to analyze and evaluate media messages, thus enabling an individual to understand how these messages influence behavior and perceptions (Potter, 2018). Concerning suicide reporting, media literacy could empower individuals to detect sensationalism and seek accurate information on mental health and suicide (Pirkis et al., 2019).

Public education campaigns should be integrated into school curricula, community programs, and digital media. These campaigns can help citizens critically understand media messages, become alert to exaggerated reporting, and be aware of suicide contagion. Such programs can empower the public to respond critically to harmful media representations of suicide and encourage individuals to seek help from competent professionals (Stack, 2003).

Schools can implement programs targeting the most affected age groups, such as adolescents. These programs can train students on the portrayal of suicide in the media, the importance of mental health providers, and how to support friends in a suicidal crisis (Zenere & Lazarus, 2009). Schools can collaborate with mental health professionals to connect students exhibiting suicidal behavior due to media exposure with counseling intervention and suicide prevention resources.

Digital spaces like YouTube and Instagram may offer solutions for enhancing media literacy by partnering with mental health organizations to provide critical educational content (Arendt, 2019). Platforms can feature videos, infographics, and articles teaching users how to critically assess suicide-related content and where to seek help if they or someone they know is suicidal. By leveraging digital media's strengths, these platforms can make media literacy more accessible to younger audiences, who are more likely to consume online content (Carrotte et al., 2021).

Media literacy programs should also target journalists and content creators by providing training for responsible suicide reporting (Niederkrotenthaler et al., 2020). Journalism schools and media organizations can update their curricula to include mental health issues and ethical suicide reporting guidelines (Goldsmith et al., 2002). Practical tools for journalists could include framing stories in a manner that avoids sensationalism, prioritizes public health, and emphasizes prevention and support.

### *6.3 Collaboration Among Stakeholders*

The media's influence on suicidal behavior must be addressed with collaborative efforts from media professionals, mental health experts, policymakers, and the public at large. If these stakeholders join forces, suicide reporting guidelines will be more widely understood, implemented, and adopted by media outlets (Niederkrotenthaler et al., 2020). Such collaborations between media houses and mental health experts can foster cooperation. The media can consult with mental health professionals to ensure that stories are told in a way that protects against suicide contagion while raising awareness about available mental health resources (Tatum et al., 2010). In return, media professionals can use their platforms to promote the work of mental health organizations, thereby raising awareness about suicide prevention and promoting help-seeking behaviors (Pirkis et al., 2017).

In addition to partnering with mental health professionals, the media should collaborate extensively with policymakers to ensure that suicide reporting becomes part of broader public health strategies. Policymakers can help establish regulations that encourage responsible reporting, while media professionals can advocate for national awareness of mental health in public life (Rathnayake et al., 2020). Through such collaboration, all-rounded suicide prevention policies can be developed that include the role of media reporting and the availability of mental health services.

Collaboration is also needed within communities. Local media outlets can partner with community organizations, schools, and healthcare providers to raise awareness about suicide prevention and mental health services (Gould et al., 2014). These collaborations could result in community-based initiatives, such as suicide prevention workshops, public forums on mental health, and support groups for those affected by suicide. As mental health advocates and media professionals work together, it is hoped that supportive environments will emerge within communities.

Finally, online social media platforms have a responsibility to contribute to the formation of public suicide discourse. Major social media sites, such as Facebook, Twitter, and YouTube, must commit resources to enhance content moderation systems by flagging and removing harmful content related to suicide (Arendt et al., 2019). These platforms can also collaborate with mental health organizations to create digital tools that allow users to connect directly with helplines or mental health professionals. This initiative would demonstrate that companies are making efforts to protect their users, contributing significantly to global suicide prevention efforts (Ransing et al., 2021).

## 6.4 The Role of A.I. and Technology in Suicide Prevention

With the rise of artificial intelligence (A.I.) and machine learning, there are new opportunities for using technology to monitor and prevent suicide-related content from spreading across digital platforms. AI-driven content moderation tools can automatically detect and flag harmful content, such as pro-suicide messages or graphic depictions of suicide, reducing the risk of contagion (Glen, 2020). Additionally, they can help detect patterns of behavior that may indicate suicide risk, allowing intervention by providing focused support or mental health resources to a relevant platform (O'Dea et al., 2021). AI-based models have also been proposed to assist in responsible media reporting of suicides, ensuring that such content is handled sensitively to prevent harmful effects like contagion or sensationalism (Ransing et al., 2021).

Beyond content moderation, A.I. can be used to design personalized interventions in mental health. For instance, an AI-powered chatbot can offer instant access to a user seeking crisis counseling, allowing immediate support in real-time for a person contemplating suicide. These chatbots can initiate conversations about the user's mental health, provide coping strategies, and assist in getting professional help if required (Fitzpatrick et al., 2017). Solutions like these can complement established services by offering easily accessible, on-demand assistance to individuals facing a crisis.

However, AI has ethical implications for suicide prevention that mainly center on privacy and security. There needs to be a consideration of crafting tools for consent and privacy to protect sensitive data regarding mental health (Vayena et al., 2018). Moreover, clear guidelines must be established to ensure that AI-driven interventions are monitored appropriately and do not replace human intervention entirely (Rajpurkar et al., 2020).

# 7 Conclusion

The connection between media and suicidal behavior is complex, both as a risk and as an opportunity for the interruption of suicides. Although irresponsible reporting may be responsible for suicide contagion, media can also engage in positive roles regarding raising mental health issues awareness, promoting recovery stories, and providing resources to those in crises. After all, with the even more rapid evolution of media in the new digital era, it is paramount that ethical reporting, along with media literacy and collaboration among stakeholders, are emphasized to promote a media landscape that supports mental well-being.

Moving forward, governments, media organizations, and mental health professionals must work together to enforce guidelines that prevent the glorification or sensationalization of suicide. Public education efforts should focus on improving media literacy, empowering individuals to assess media messages and seek help when needed critically. By promoting a team approach to suicide prevention, we can minimize the negative consequences of irresponsible media portrayals and help ensure that media is used as a force for good in working to mitigate one of the most pressing public health issues of our time.

# References

American Foundation for Suicide Prevention. *Safe reporting guidelines for media.* https://afsp.org/safereporting/

American Foundation for Suicide Prevention. (2022). Recommendations for reporting on suicide.

Andreassen, C. S., Pallesen, S., & Griffiths, M. D. (2016). The relationship between addictive use of social media, narcissism, and self-esteem: Findings from a large national survey. *Addictive Behaviors, 64*, 287–293. https://doi.org/10.1016/j.addbeh.2016.03.006

Arafat, S. Y. (2019). Current challenges of suicide and future directions of management in Bangladesh: A systematic review. *Global Psychiatry, 2*(1), 09–20. https://doi.org/10.2478/gp-2019-0001

Arafat, S. Y., Mali, B., & Akter, H. (2020). Do Bangladeshi newspapers educate public while reporting suicide? A year round observation from content analysis of six national newspapers. *Asian Journal of Psychiatry, 48*, 101920. https://doi.org/10.1016/j.ajp.2019.101920

Arafat, S. M. Y., Menon, V., & Kar, S. K. (2021). Media and suicide prevention in Southeast Asia: Challenges and directions. *Journal of Public Health (Oxford, England), 43*(1), e123–e124. https://doi.org/10.1093/pubmed/fdaa084

Arendt, F., Scherr, S., & Romer, D. (2019). Effects of exposure to self-harm on social media: Evidence from a two-wave panel study among young adults. *New Media & Society, 21*(11–12), 2422–2442.

Bandura, A. (1986). *Social foundations of thought and action: A social cognitive theory*. Prentice-Hall.

Berkowitz, L. (1984). Some effects of thoughts on anti- and prosocial influences of media events: A cognitive-neoassociation analysis. *Psychological Bulletin, 95*(3), 410–427. https://doi.org/10.1037/0033-2909.95.3.410

Bridge, J. A., Greenhouse, J. B., Ruch, D., Stevens, J., Ackerman, J., Sheftall, A. H., & Campo, J. V. (2020). Association between the release of Netflix's 13 reasons why and suicide rates in the

United States: An interrupted time series analysis. *Journal of the American Academy of Child & Adolescent Psychiatry, 59*(2), 236–243.

Burnap, P., Colombo, W., & Scourfield, J. (2015, August). Machine classification and analysis of suicide-related communication on twitter. In *Proceedings of the 26th ACM Conference on Hypertext & Social Media* (pp. 75–84).

Carrotte, E. R., Webb, M., Flego, A., Vincent, B., Heath, J., & Blanchard, M. (2021). Acceptability, safety, and resonance of the pilot digital suicide prevention campaign "better off with you": Qualitative study. *JMIR Formative Research, 5*(3), e23892.

Chen, Y. Y., Chen, F., Gunnell, D., & Yip, P. S. (2013). The impact of media reporting on the emergence of charcoal burning suicide in Taiwan. *PLoS ONE, 8*(1), e55000. https://doi.org/10.1371/journal.pone.0055000

Cheng, A. T., Hawton, K., Chen, T. H., Yen, A. M., Chang, J. C., Chong, M. Y., Liu, C. Y., Lee, Y., Teng, P. R., & Chen, L. C. (2007). The influence of media reporting of a celebrity suicide on suicidal behavior in patients with a history of depressive disorder. *Journal of Affective Disorders, 103*(1–3), 69–75.

Cinelli, M., Quattrociocchi, W., Galeazzi, A., Valensise, C. M., Brugnoli, E., Schmidt, A. L., & Scala, A. (2021). The echo chamber effect on social media. *Proceedings of the National Academy of Sciences, 118*(9), e2023301118. https://doi.org/10.1073/pnas.2023301118

Etzersdorfer, E., & Sonneck, G. (1998). Preventing suicide by influencing mass-media reporting: The Viennese experience 1980–1996. *Archives of Suicide Research, 4*(1), 67–74.

Fink, D. S., Santaella-Tenorio, J., & Keyes, K. M. (2018). Increase in suicides the months after the death of Robin Williams in the U.S. *PLoS ONE, 13*(2), e0191405.

Fitzpatrick, K. K., Darcy, A., & Vierhile, M. (2017). Delivering cognitive behavioral therapy to young adults with symptoms of depression and anxiety through a smartphone application: A randomized controlled trial. *Journal of Medical Internet Research, 19*(5), e114. https://doi.org/10.2196/jmir.7402

Ganesh, R., Singh, S., Mishra, R., & Sagar, R. (2020). The quality of online media reporting of celebrity suicide in India and its association with subsequent online suicide-related search behavior among the general population: An infodemiology study. *Asian Journal of Psychiatry, 53*, 102380. https://doi.org/10.1016/j.ajp.2020.102380

Gerbner, G. (1969). Toward "cultural indicators": The analysis of mass mediated public message systems. *AV Communication Review, 17*, 137–148. https://doi.org/10.1007/BF02769102

Gerbner, G. (1976). Living with television: The violence profile. *Journal of Communication, 26*(2), 172–194. https://doi.org/10.1111/j.1460-2466.1976.tb01397.x

Gibbs, M., Meese, J., Arnold, M., Nansen, B., & Carter, M. (2015). #Funeral and Instagram: Death, social media, and platform vernacular. *Information, Communication & Society, 18*(3), 255–268. https://doi.org/10.1080/1369118X.2014.987152

Goldsmith, S. K., Pellmar, T. C., Kleinman, A. M., & Bunney, W. E. (2002). *Reducing suicide: A national imperative*. The National Academies Press. https://doi.org/10.17226/10398

Gould, M. S., Kleinman, M. H., Lake, A. M., Forman, J., & Midle, J. B. (2014). Newspaper coverage of suicide and initiation of suicide clusters in teenagers in the USA, 1988–96: A retrospective, population-based, case-control study. *The Lancet Psychiatry, 1*(1), 34–43. https://doi.org/10.1016/S2215-0366(14)70225-1

Heffer, T., Good, M., Daly, O., MacDonell, E., & Willoughby, T. (2019). The longitudinal association between social-media use and depressive symptoms among adolescents and young adults: An empirical reply to Twenge et al. (2018). *Clinical Psychological Science, 7*(3), 462–470.

Latha, K., Meena, K. S., Pravitha, M. R., Dasgupta, M., & Chaturvedi, S. K. (2020). Effective use of social media platforms for promotion of mental health awareness. *Journal of Education and Health Promotion, 9*(1), 124. https://doi.org/10.4103/jehp.jehp_90_20

Lingel, J. (2017). *Digital countercultures and the struggle for community*. MIT Press.

Menon, V., Kar, S. K., & Varadharajan, N. (2022). Quality of media reporting following a celebrity suicide in India. *Journal of Public Health, 44*(1), e133–e140. https://doi.org/10.1093/pubmed/fdab154

Mindframe. Reporting suicide and mental illness: A resource for media professionals. https://mindframe.org.au

Mukhra, R., Baryah, N., Krishan, K., & Kanchan, T. (2019). 'Blue Whale Challenge': A game or crime? *Science and Engineering Ethics, 25*, 285–291.

Naslund, J. A., Aschbrenner, K. A., Marsch, L. A., & Bartels, S. J. (2016). The future of mental health care: Peer-to-peer support and social media. *Epidemiology and Psychiatric Sciences, 25*(2), 113–122. https://doi.org/10.1017/S2045796015001067

Niederkrotenthaler, T., Braun, M., Pirkis, J., Till, B., Stack, S., Sinyor, M., & Arendt, F. (2020). Association between suicide reporting in the media and suicide: Systematic review and meta-analysis. *The BMJ, 368*, m575. https://doi.org/10.1136/bmj.m575

Niederkrotenthaler, T., Voracek, M., Herberth, A., Till, B., Strauss, M., Etzersdorfer, E., & Sonneck, G. (2010). Role of media reports in completed and prevented suicide: Werther v. Papageno effects. *British Journal of Psychiatry, 197*(3), 234–243. https://doi.org/10.1192/bjp.bp.109.074633

O'Dea, B., Ciarrochi, J., & Christensen, H. (2021). Detecting and responding to suicide risk: The role of social media and mental health platforms. *Journal of Affective Disorders, 280*, 352–359. https://doi.org/10.1016/j.jad.2020.11.018

Phillips, D. P. (1974). The influence of suggestion on suicide: Substantive and theoretical implications of the Werther effect. *American Sociological Review, 39*(3), 340–354. https://doi.org/10.2307/2094294

Pirkis, J., & Blood, R. W. (2001). Suicide and the media: Part I. Reportage in nonfictional media. *Crisis: The Journal of Crisis Intervention and Suicide Prevention, 22*(4), 146.

Pirkis, J., Blood, R. W., Beautrais, A., Burgess, P., & Skehan, J. (2017). Media guidelines on the reporting of suicide. *Crisis: The Journal of Crisis Intervention and Suicide Prevention, 27*(2), 82–87. https://doi.org/10.1027/0227-5910.27.2.82

Pirkis, J. E., Burgess, P. M., Francis, C., Blood, R. W., & Jolley, D. J. (2006). The relationship between media reporting of suicide and actual suicide in Australia. *Social Science & Medicine, 62*(11), 2874–2886.

Pirkis, J., Mok, K., Robinson, J., & Nordentoft, M. (2016). Media influences on suicidal thoughts and behaviors. In *The international handbook of suicide prevention* (pp. 743–757).

Pirkis, J., Rossetto, A., Nicholas, A., Ftanou, M., Robinson, J., & Reavley, N. (2019). Suicide prevention media campaigns: A systematic literature review. *Health Communication, 34*(4), 402–414.

Potter, W. J. (2018). *Media literacy*. Sage publications.

Press Council of India. (2022). Guidelines for reporting on suicide. https://presscouncil.nic.in/WriteReadData/Pdf/Norms2022.pdf

Ransing, R., Menon, V., Kar, S. K., & Arafat, S. M. (2021). Artificial intelligence-based models for augmenting media reporting of suicide: Challenges and opportunities. *Global Psychiatry Archives, 4*(2), 123–129.

Rajpurkar, P., Irvin, J., Zhu, K., Yang, B., Mehta, H., Duan, T., ... & Ng, A. Y. (2017). CheXNet: Radiologist-level pneumonia detection on chest X-rays with deep learning. arXiv preprint arXiv:1711.05225.

Rathnayake, S., Jayasundara, L. D., & Kottegoda, S. (2020). The role of policymakers and media in promoting mental health awareness and responsible reporting. *Journal of Public Health Policy, 41*(4), 550–561. https://doi.org/10.1057/s41271-020-00228-7

Samaritans. (2022). Media guidelines for reporting suicide. https://www.samaritans.org/media-centre/media-guidelines-reporting-suicide

Sisask, M., & Värnik, A. (2012). Media roles in suicide prevention: A systematic review. *International Journal of Environmental Research and Public Health, 9*(1), 123–138. https://doi.org/10.3390/ijerph9010123

Stack, S. (2003). Media coverage as a risk factor in suicide. *Journal of Epidemiology & Community Health, 57*(4), 238–240. https://doi.org/10.1136/jech.57.4.238

Stack, S. (2005). Suicide in the media: A quantitative review of studies based on nonfictional stories. *Suicide and Life-Threatening Behavior, 35*(2), 121–133.

Stone, Deborah M. et al. (2017). Preventing suicide : A technical package of policies, programs, and practice.

Tatum, J. L., Clayton, R. H., & Ramchand, R. (2010). Preventing suicide contagion: The role of media and the importance of responsible reporting. *Journal of Mental Health, 19*(2), 101–109. https://doi.org/10.3109/09638230903578053

Turecki, G., Brent, D. A., Gunnell, D., O'Connor, R. C., Oquendo, M. A., Pirkis, J., & Stanley, B. H. (2019). Suicide and suicide risk. *Nature Reviews Disease Primers, 5*(1), 74.

Ueda, M., Mori, K., Matsubayashi, T., & Sawada, Y. (2017). Tweeting celebrity suicides: Users' reaction to prominent suicide deaths on Twitter and subsequent increases in actual suicides. *Social Science & Medicine, 189*, 158–166. https://doi.org/10.1016/j.socscimed.2017.07.021

Vayena, E., Blasimme, A., & Cohen, I. G. (2018). Machine learning in medicine: addressing ethical challenges. *PLoS medicine, 15*(11), e1002689.

Vijayakumar, L. (2016). Suicide in women. *Indian Journal of Psychiatry, 58*(S2), S233–S238. https://doi.org/10.4103/0019-5545.161484

World Health Organization. (2023). Preventing suicide: A resource for media professionals (Update 2023). https://www.who.int/publications/i/item/9789240076846

Zalsman, G., Hawton, K., Wasserman, D., van Heeringen, K., Arensman, E., Sarchiapone, M., & Balazs, J. (2016). Suicide prevention strategies revisited: A 10-year systematic review. *The Lancet Psychiatry, 3*(7), 646–659. https://doi.org/10.1016/S2215-0366(16)30030-X

Zenere, F. J., & Lazarus, P. J. (2009). The decline in youth suicide in an urban, multicultural public school system following the introduction of a suicide prevention and intervention program. *Suicide and Life-Threatening Behavior, 39*(6), 644–653. https://doi.org/10.1111/j.1943-278X.1997.tb00518.x

# Chapter 13
# Nutrition, Mental Health, and Suicidal Behavior

**Ramdas Ransing, Nikhita Das, Rashmi Agarwalla, and Limalemla Jamir**

**Abstract** Suicide and suicidal behavior are complex health conditions. The various factors such as psychological, social, and biological are associated with suicide and suicidal behavior. Despite its potential significance, only few studies have explored the relationship between nutrition and suicidal behavior. Studies have consistently shown that nutritional deficiencies are prevalent among persons with mental disorders, who are also at increased risk of suicidal behavior. This chapter explores the complex interplay between nutrition and suicidal behavior, the underlying mechanisms, and discussion on potential prevention and treatment strategies. The chapter concludes by highlighting critical areas for future research in suicide and nutrition.

**Keywords** Suicide · Nutrients · Prevention · Management · Suicidal behavior

## 1 Introduction

Suicide is a public health concern and it is one of the leading causes of age-standardized years of life lost. It has been ranked as 5th leading cause of mortality in the youth in almost all regions (Naghavi, 2019). Studies have reported psychological, environmental, biological, and social factors for suicide. Significant risk factors for suicidal behavior include drinking alcohol, smoking, and engaging in risky sexual behaviors (Franklin et al., 2017; Turecki et al., 2019). Suicide has been described as a multifaceted construct in relation to psychiatric symptoms, medical conditions, and lifestyle risk factors (Park et al., 2018; Tousignant et al., 2011; Zhang et al., 2010). Suicides have tremendous impact on the family and friends. The web of causation

R. Ransing (✉) · N. Das
Department of Psychiatry, Clinical Neurosciences, and Addiction Medicine, All India Institute of Medical Sciences, Guwahati, Assam, India
e-mail: ramdas_ransing123@yahoo.co.in

R. Agarwalla · L. Jamir
Department of Community and Family Medicine, All India Institute of Medical Sciences, Guwahati, Assam, India



S. M. Y. Arafat and S. K. Kar (eds.), *Ecological and Social Determinants of Suicidal Behavior*, South Asian Perspectives in Mental Health and Psychology,
https://doi.org/10.1007/978-981-96-4028-7_13

of suicide ideation and behavior needs to be understood well in order to prevent it. Recently, considerable attention has been paid to the concept of life satisfaction and well-being as psychosocial indicators of mental health. It has been hypothesized that life satisfaction and meaning in life can help people overcome adversity. Factors associated with optimal well-being and life satisfaction included prudent lifestyle behaviors such as healthy eating (Bray & Gunnell, 2006).

One area of importance is dietary patterns and their association with depressive symptoms and suicidal ideation. There is evidence that dietary behaviors like consumption of empty calories, junk food, and fast food are associated with suicidal tendencies in adolescents and young adults (Berardelli et al., 2018; Jacob et al., 2020; Lee et al., 2019). For example, a large-scale study from 32 countries showed a significant positive association between fast food consumption and suicide attempts (pooled odds ratio [OR], 1.31) in 26 countries (Jacob et al., 2020). On the other hand, the consumption of fruits and vegetables decreases behavioral problems. In fact, the consistent intake of one to three servings of fruit and the consumption of 2 green vegetables is significant in decreasing the risk of depression (Bryant, 2018).

The various dimensions of health fail to include nutrition as one of the important components of health, especially affecting mental health. Correcting dietary intake is possible because diet is a modifiable habit. Once someone modifies his or her dietary intake, a healthy eating pattern should remain across the entire lifespan. In the past few decades, a lot of progress has been made to identify public health strategies for the prevention of mental health and suicide. Although the approach to suicide has always involved clinical aspects, especially the assessment and the treatment of depression, it seems necessary to consider risk factors like dietary habits that can be identified and modified through specific lifestyle interventions (Bryant, 2018).

## 2 Nutrition and Suicide Behavior: Relationship, and Underlying Mechanism

Nutrients such as omega-3 fatty acids, B vitamins, and minerals (e.g., magnesium, zinc, iron), regulate the mood and suicide behavior. The mechanisms underlying the relationship between poor nutrition and suicide behavior is still unclear. However, it involves a complex interplay of biological, psychological, and social factors. The exploration of these mechanisms is essential for developing the suicide prevention strategies. Although studies are limited, we briefly discussed the role of various nutrients in mental disorder, suicide, and suicide behavior.

## 2.1 Role of Amino Acids (AA)

The underlying cause of suicide or suicidal behavior is a disturbance in neurotransmitters such as serotonin, dopamine, epinephrine, and norepinephrine. Nutritional intake of certain AAs affects the synthesis of these neurotransmitters.

Dopamine is synthesized from phenylalanine, and epinephrine and norepinephrine are produced from dopamine. The level of phenylalanine was reduced in patients with MDD relative to control (Teraishi et al., 2018). Low levels of tryptophan, tyrosine, methionine, phenylalanine, phenylalanine, tyramine, GABA, and kynurenine are associated with MDD (Parker & Brotchie, 2011). Conversely, concentrations of isoleucine, valine, and leucine increased in patients with MDD (Fellendorf et al., 2019). A low level of L-histidine has been reported in a patient with anxiety and MDD since L-histidine regulates neurotransmitters (Solís Arce et al., 2021).

Tryptophan is the precursor of serotonin, and the recommended daily dose of tryptophan is 300 mg per day. A previous study found that in 15 patients with a history of MDD, consuming a tryptophan-free drink worsened their depressive symptoms, while adding tryptophan improved their mood (Khanna et al., 2019).

Glycine, an excitatory amino acid and N-methyl-d-aspartate receptor modulator, was significantly elevated in serum samples from veterans reporting suicidal ideation (Szabo et al., 2014).

## 2.2 Role of Fatty Acid

Omega-3 fatty acid contribute to the fluidity of cell membranes and the production of neurotransmitters such as serotonin (Thurfah et al., 2022). The antidepressant effects of n-3 polyunsaturated fatty acids (PUFAs) may be contributed to antioxidant properties, adjustment of serotonin, modulation of proinflammatory cytokines, and Brain derived neurotrophic factor (BDNF) (Huang et al., 2021). Low level of omega-3 fatty acids is associated with an increased risk of depression and suicidal ideation (Freeman et al., 2006). In addition, patients with depression have low level of saturated fatty acid, eicosapentaenoic acid (EPA), Docosahexaenoic acid (DHA), and n-3 PUFA than controls (Lin et al., 2010; Szczesniak et al., 2016). The content of n-3 PUFAs in plasma is inversely related to the risk of mental disorders including the suicide risk.

A lack of fish and seafood consumption has been linked to a greater incidence of depression (Nabavi et al., 2017). Dietary administration of omega-3 may protect from depression, and administration of omega 3 has been established to improve and ameliorate symptoms of depression in clinical studies (Chang et al., 2020).

## 2.3 Role of Vitamins

The adequate levels of B vitamins are essential for the synthesis of neurotransmitters. Vitamin B6 (pyridoxine) affects the neurotransmitter systems such as serotonergic, adrenergic, and glutamatergic systems (Mansour, 2022). Vitamins B9 and B12 participate in the synthesis of monoamines and other vital methylation reactions in the central nervous system (Gilbody et al., 2007). In addition, B3 (nicotinamide) is neuroprotective and antioxidant at low dose. The deficiency of vitamins B6, B9, and B12 prevents the transformation of homocysteine into methionine, leading to hyperhomocysteinemia that is associated with cytotoxicity, oxidative stress, apoptosis, and ultimately depression (Sangle et al., 2020).

Higher consumption of dietary B vitamins was related to a lower incidence of anxiety, depression, and stress symptoms (Mahdavifar et al., 2021). Low levels of B vitamins (Folate and B12) are associated with depression, and risk of suicide (Coppen & Bolander-Gouaille, 2005; Freeman et al., 2006). Vitamin D protects the brain from the reduction of serotonin and dopamine (Cass et al., 2006). Low levels of vitamin D, or hypovitaminosis D, have been linked to an increased susceptibility to depression (Hoang et al., 2011).

## 2.4 Role of Minerals

Minerals (magnesium, zinc, selenium, iron) are essential for neurotransmitter function and mood regulations. Zinc is required for neuromodulation and regulation of neurotransmitters systems (e.g., dopaminergic, glutaminergic, and serotonergic systems) (Yi et al., 2011). It also increases the expression of Brain derived neurotropic factor (Bitanihirwe & Cunningham, 2009). Deficiencies in minerals like magnesium and zinc have been linked to mood disturbances and an elevated risk of suicide (Wang et al., 2018). A meta-analysis indicated that dietary consumption of iron and zinc was connected to a lower incidence of depression (Li et al., 2017). Magnesium deficiency has been implicated in disruption of the hypothalamic–pituitary–adrenal (HPA), which is implicated in the pathogenesis of depression and anxiety disorders (Sartori et al., 2012). A systematic review found that magnesium intake is inversely correlated with depressive symptoms, suggesting a beneficial effect of magnesium in treating MDD (Derom et al., 2013).

## 2.5 Role of Diet and Macronutrients

A diet inadequate in essential micronutrients and macronutrients is more likely impair the cognitive function, leading to impairments in emotional regulation, executive function, and decision-making capacity (Mansour, 2022). Also, the individual with poor nutritional habits may experience lower self-esteem and self-worth. Diet in high processed food or sugars can contribute to mood swings and instability (Akbaraly et al., 2009). Such Instability can worsen the feelings of hopelessness, increasing the risk of stress, anxiety, and suicidal ideations.

### *2.6 Role of Social Factors Related to Nutrition*

Social factors also play a crucial role in the relationship between poor nutrition and suicidal behavior. Low socio-economic status significantly influences access to nutritious foods (Sánchez-Villegas et al., 2013). This can create a cycle of poor health and increased vulnerability to mental health disorders, including depression and anxiety, which are linked to suicidal ideation. Thus, the link between poor nutrition to suicidal behavior are multifaceted, involving biological, psychological, and social dimensions. Thus, nutrition-based suicide prevention strategies should have focus on addressing these dimensions.

### *2.7 Role of Infection Related to Nutrition*

The neurotropic protozoan parasite *Toxoplasma gondii* has been linked to suicidal behavior (Alvarado-Esquivel et al., 2021). Individuals at increased risk comprise those with a history of chronic alcohol consumption, inadequate nutrition and immunocompromised status. Following the initial infection with Toxoplasma gondii, plasma antibody levels remain elevated for life. The *T. gondii* seropositivity has been linked with suicidal behavior, anxiety, and depression (Arling et al., 2009). The underlying mechanism of suicidal behavior in individuals with toxoplasmosis involves both direct effects on neuronal function and immune-mediated alterations in dopamine and serotonin synthesis.

## 3 Nutrition as a Personalized Intervention for Suicide or Suicide Behavior

Though, the evidence is still unclear, the diet and nutritional interventions has potential to reduce suicide risk and suicidal behavior. Thus, the diet and nutritional intervention may be used for prevention and treatment of suicide or suicidal behavior and mental disorders. Omega-3 fatty acids supplementation are effective in reducing the depression and anxiety (Ransing et al., 2022). The Mediterranean diet rich in fruits, vegetables, whole grains, legumes, and healthy fats has been linked to lower rates of depression and anxiety (Sánchez-Villegas et al., 2013). The dietary items included in this diet are anti-inflammatory. In contrast, Western diet which are high in processed foods, carbohydrates, and saturated fats have been associated with increased rates of depression and anxiety. Also, western diet is associated with poorer mental health outcomes (Akbaraly et al., 2009). Thus, promoting the healthier dietary patterns can potentially reduce the prevalence of mental health issues, including suicidal behavior.

Addressing the nutritional deficiencies in patients with mental disorders is crucial for reducing the suicide risk. Nutritional assessments should be conducted in patients with mental disorders or at risk of suicide to identify and address these nutritional deficiencies.

## 4 Public Health Approaches for Suicide Prevention Due to Poor Nutrition

Addressing suicide risk stemming from poor nutrition requires a structured approach that encompasses various levels of prevention: primordial, primary, secondary, and tertiary (Fig. 1). Each level targets specific aspects of poor nutrition and its impact on mental health, aiming to reduce the risk of suicidal ideation. A multi-level approach is essential for preventing suicide due to malnutrition. By focusing on structured prevention strategies, communities can effectively address the complex relationship between nutrition and mental health. Public awareness initiatives must be culturally sensitive and designed to engage diverse populations while ensuring access to necessary resources. Collaboration among healthcare providers, policymakers, and community organizations is crucial for implementing these strategies successfully.

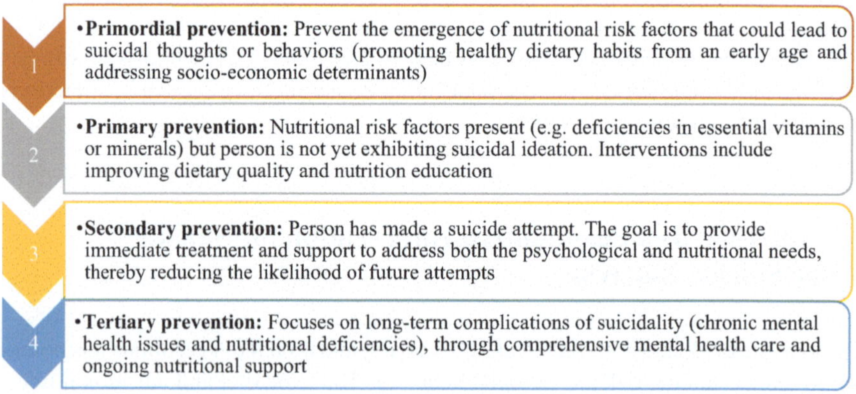


**Fig. 1** Levels of prevention in the context of suicide due to nutritional problems

## 4.1 Primordial Prevention

Primordial prevention strategies aimed at preventing the emergence of risk factors related to malnutrition that could lead to suicidal ideation focus on public awareness campaigns, community engagement initiatives, and policy advocacy. Public awareness campaigns educate communities about the critical role of nutrition in mental health, highlighting the risks associated with malnutrition and its potential link to suicide. Community engagement initiatives promote healthy eating habits through activities such as community gardens, cooking classes, and nutritional workshops in schools and local organizations, fostering a culture of health and well-being. Additionally, policy advocacy plays a crucial role in supporting legislation that enhances food security and improves access to nutritious foods, particularly in underserved areas. By addressing these foundational aspects of nutrition and mental health, these strategies work together to create an environment that mitigates the risk factors associated with malnutrition and promotes overall psychological well-being (Berg et al., 2020).

Examples from India:

- *Poshan Abhiyan* Initiative: Focuses on nutrition education highlighting the risks associated with malnutrition. This initiative aims to improve nutritional outcomes and well-being for children, pregnant women, and breastfeeding mothers across India.
- Mid-Day Meal Scheme: Provides nutritious meals to government school children and serves as a platform for nutritional education, social equity and addressing foundational issues of hunger and low literacy in vulnerable populations (*School Education|Government of India, Ministry of Education*, n.d.).
- National Food Security Act (NFSA): The national policy improves food security and access to nutritious foods particularly in underserved areas, thereby addressing the root causes of malnutrition that can lead to mental health issues.

## 4.2 Primary Prevention

To effectively reduce the incidence of malnutrition-related mental health issues before they manifest, a multifaceted approach focusing on primary prevention is essential. By addressing nutritional deficiencies early, we can enhance overall mental well-being and prevent the onset of related disorders. Nutritional education programs and micronutrient supplementation programs such as Integrated Child Development Services in India should be implemented efficiently to target at-risk populations, such as low-income families and adolescents, emphasizing the importance of balanced diets rich in essential nutrients like iron, omega-3 fatty acids, and vitamin B12. These programs can enhance knowledge and promote healthier eating habits, ultimately improving nutritional status and mental well-being (Xu et al., 2021).

Additionally, screening for nutritional deficiencies in schools and community health settings can help identify individuals at risk of malnutrition early on, allowing for timely interventions before symptoms develop (Majamanda et al., 2014). Follow-up interventions can then be tailored to meet individual needs. Providing screenings in community health settings allows for broader outreach and ensures that vulnerable populations receive necessary assessments. This proactive approach enables healthcare providers to recommend dietary changes or supplements and even screen for mental health issues early on.

Food fortification is essential in addressing micronutrient deficiencies that impact mental health and reduce suicide risk. By adding vitamins and minerals like iron, vitamin D, and B vitamins to staple foods, these programs help prevent deficiencies linked to mood disorders. Research shows that adequate micronutrient levels are associated with improved mental health outcomes, including reduced suicidal thoughts. Thus, food fortification enhances nutritional status and serves as a vital strategy for improving mental well-being and preventing suicide.

Finally, ensuring access to nutritional resources is crucial for providing vulnerable populations with healthy food options, thereby supporting their overall health and reducing the likelihood of mental health issues related to poor nutrition as food insecurity significantly increases mental stress and suicide risk (Brown et al., 2022). The uncertainty of food availability creates chronic stress, worsening psychological distress, and suicidal thoughts. Therefore, expanding meal programs provides immediate access to healthy foods for those in need, with local farms and grocery stores collaborating to supply fresh produce. Additionally, mobile food pantries can effectively reach underserved areas, ensuring that all community members have access to nutritious meals. Collaborating with local nonprofits and community organizations further enhances resource distribution and builds a strong support network for families facing food insecurity.

## *4.3 Secondary Prevention*

Secondary prevention focuses on identifying and addressing existing nutritional deficiencies that may contribute to suicidal thoughts or behaviors. Eating disorders like anorexia nervosa and bulimia nervosa significantly elevate the risk of suicide due to the severe emotional distress they cause (Myers, 2020). Key strategies to mitigate this risk include establishing crisis intervention services for immediate medical management of nutritional disorders and mental health support, creating support groups for individuals to share experiences related to nutrition and mental health, and integrating nutritional assessments into mental health care protocols. This comprehensive approach addresses both nutritional needs and mental health issues simultaneously, leading to improved outcomes and reduced suicide risk (Smith et al., 2018).

Additionally, farmers are a critical demographic in India's suicide and food security issues. Over the past decade, the agricultural sector has reported more than 112,000 suicides, with 11,290 farmers and farm laborers taking their own lives in

2022—a 3.7% increase from the previous year (Haridas et al., 2022). Key factors include poverty, economic distress, rising input costs, high debt levels, and climate change impacts like erratic rainfall leading to crop failures. Social stigma around mental health further complicates the issue. Addressing these challenges requires a comprehensive approach that includes improved agricultural policies, financial support for farmers, and integrating mental health services with nutritional support programs to enhance resilience and well-being (Memdani et al., 2024).

### 4.4 Tertiary Prevention

Tertiary prevention focuses on managing the consequences of severe malnutrition on mental health, including suicidal ideation. Key strategies include developing rehabilitation programs aimed at restoring nutritional health while addressing underlying mental health issues or disorders such as anorexia nervosa, bulimia through therapy. Establishing long-term support systems is also essential, providing ongoing monitoring and regular check-ins for individuals recovering from malnutrition-related crises.

For instance, Nutritional Rehabilitation Centers (NRCs) are specialized facilities designed to treat severely malnourished children, especially those with medical complications. These centers provide medical treatment alongside nutritional rehabilitation for children suffering from severe acute malnutrition (SAM) (Katole et al., 2022). They also emphasize family involvement, engaging families in the treatment process and educating them about nutrition and mental health. Family-based interventions encourage caregivers to support their loved ones in achieving nutritional goals while fostering a supportive environment. The impact of NRCs extends beyond physical recovery; they also address psychological aspects, helping to reduce the risk of mental health issues that can lead to suicidal thoughts.

In addition, education on self-care practices related to nutrition and mental health management can empower individuals at risk of suicide due to malnutrition, ensuring they have the tools needed for long-term recovery.

## 5 Conclusion

Although, the relationship between nutrition and suicide is still in its infancy, the role of nutrients in mental disorders are being explored with some favorable research findings. Research indicates that various nutrients can modulate biomarkers and molecular mechanisms underlying mental illnesses and suicide risk, providing opportunities to use nutrition as one of the preventive or treatment approach. The underlying mechanisms of nutritional therapies in suicide or suicidal behavior are not yet fully understood and warrant future research through well-designed studies.

Further, across the world there is a significant lack of linkage between nutrition-focused programs and mental health initiatives, which hampers comprehensive health outcomes. Despite the recognition that food insecurity and nutritional deficiencies are closely associated with poor mental health, evidenced by studies linking inadequate nutrition to increased risks of depression and anxiety, there is need to integrate nutrition focused programs with mental health programs. For instance in India, while *Poshan Abhiyan* aims to combat malnutrition and *Anemia Mukt Bharat* targets iron deficiency, neither program systematically addresses the psychological impacts of malnutrition or incorporates mental health screenings and interventions. This disconnect is particularly concerning given that deficiencies in essential nutrients like iron, omega-3 fatty acids, and vitamin B12 have been shown to exacerbate mental health issues, potentially leading to suicidal ideation. Consequently, a more integrated approach that combines nutritional support with mental health services is essential for effectively addressing the intertwined challenges of malnutrition and mental well-being across the world including India.

## References

Akbaraly, T. N., Brunner, E. J., Ferrie, J. E., Marmot, M. G., Kivimaki, M., & Singh-Manoux, A. (2009). Dietary pattern and depressive symptoms in middle age. *The British Journal of Psychiatry: THe Journal of Mental Science, 195*(5), 408–413. https://doi.org/10.1192/bjp.bp.108.058925

Alvarado-Esquivel, C., Estrada-Martínez, S., Pérez-Álamos, A. R., Beristain-García, I., Alvarado-Félix, Á. O., Alvarado-Félix, G. A., & Sifuentes-Álvarez, A. (2021). Toxoplasma gondii infection and suicidal behavior in people with alcohol consumption. *Pathogens (Basel, Switzerland), 10*(6), 734. https://doi.org/10.3390/pathogens10060734

Arling, T. A., Yolken, R. H., Lapidus, M., Langenberg, P., Dickerson, F. B., Zimmerman, S. A., Balis, T., Cabassa, J. A., Scrandis, D. A., Tonelli, L. H., & Postolache, T. T. (2009). Toxoplasma gondii antibody titers and history of suicide attempts in patients with recurrent mood disorders. *The Journal of Nervous and Mental Disease, 197*(12), 905–908. https://doi.org/10.1097/NMD.0b013e3181c29a23

Berardelli, I., Corigliano, V., Hawkins, M., Comparelli, A., Erbuto, D., & Pompili, M. (2018). Lifestyle interventions and prevention of suicide. *Frontiers in Psychiatry, 9*, 567. https://doi.org/10.3389/fpsyt.2018.00567

Berg, E., Wilhelm, K., & Handley, T. (2020). Should we increase the focus on diet when considering associations between lifestyle habits and deliberate self-harm? *BMC Psychiatry, 20*(1), 560. https://doi.org/10.1186/s12888-020-02950-0

Bitanihirwe, B. K. Y., & Cunningham, M. G. (2009). Zinc: The brain's dark horse. *Synapse (New York, N. Y.), 63*(11), 1029–1049. https://doi.org/10.1002/syn.20683

Bray, I., & Gunnell, D. (2006). Suicide rates, life satisfaction and happiness as markers for population mental health. *Social Psychiatry and Psychiatric Epidemiology, 41*(5), 333–337. https://doi.org/10.1007/s00127-006-0049-z

Brown, A. D., Seligman, H., Sliwa, S., Barnidge, E., Krupsky, K. L., Demissie, Z., & Liese, A. D. (2022). Food insecurity and suicidal behaviors among US high school students. *The Journal of School Health, 92*(9), 898–906. https://doi.org/10.1111/josh.13199

Bryant, Z. J. (2018). *Association of dietary intake with suicidal ideation or suicide attempts in adolescents*. Walden Dissertations and Doctoral Studies. 5681. https://scholarworks.waldenu.edu/dissertations/5681

Cass, W. A., Smith, M. P., & Peters, L. E. (2006). Calcitriol protects against the dopamine- and serotonin-depleting effects of neurotoxic doses of methamphetamine. *Annals of the New York Academy of Sciences, 1074*(1), 261–271. https://doi.org/10.1196/annals.1369.023

Chang, J.P.-C., Chang, S.-S., Yang, H.-T., Chen, H.-T., Chien, Y.-C., Yang, B., Su, H., & Su, K.-P. (2020). Omega-3 polyunsaturated fatty acids in cardiovascular diseases comorbid major depressive disorder—Results from a randomized controlled trial. *Brain, Behavior, and Immunity, 85*, 14–20. https://doi.org/10.1016/j.bbi.2019.03.012

Coppen, A., & Bolander-Gouaille, C. (2005). Treatment of depression: Time to consider folic acid and vitamin B12. *Journal of Psychopharmacology (Oxford, England), 19*(1), 59–65. https://doi.org/10.1177/0269881105048899

Derom, M.-L., Sayón-Orea, C., Martínez-Ortega, J. M., & Martínez-González, M. A. (2013). Magnesium and depression: A systematic review. *Nutritional Neuroscience, 16*(5), 191–206. https://doi.org/10.1179/1476830512Y.0000000044

Fellendorf, F. T., Platzer, M., Pilz, R., Rieger, A., Kapfhammer, H.-P., Mangge, H., Dalkner, N., Zelzer, S., Meinitzer, A., Birner, A., Bengesser, S. A., Queissner, R., Hamm, C., Hartleb, R., & Reininghaus, E. Z. (2019). Branched-chain amino acids are associated with metabolic parameters in bipolar disorder. *The World Journal of Biological Psychiatry, 20*(10), 821–826. https://doi.org/10.1080/15622975.2018.1487077

Franklin, J. C., Ribeiro, J. D., Fox, K. R., Bentley, K. H., Kleiman, E. M., Huang, X., Musacchio, K. M., Jaroszewski, A. C., Chang, B. P., & Nock, M. K. (2017). Risk factors for suicidal thoughts and behaviors: A meta-analysis of 50 years of research. *Psychological Bulletin, 143*(2), 187–232. https://doi.org/10.1037/bul0000084

Freeman, M. P., Hibbeln, J. R., Wisner, K. L., Davis, J. M., Mischoulon, D., Peet, M., Keck, P. E., Marangell, L. B., Richardson, A. J., Lake, J., & Stoll, A. L. (2006). Omega-3 fatty acids: Evidence basis for treatment and future research in psychiatry. *The Journal of Clinical Psychiatry, 67*(12), 1954–1967. https://doi.org/10.4088/jcp.v67n1217

Gilbody, S., Lightfoot, T., & Sheldon, T. (2007). Is low folate a risk factor for depression? A meta-analysis and exploration of heterogeneity. *Journal of Epidemiology & Community Health, 61*(7), 631–637. https://doi.org/10.1136/jech.2006.050385

Haridas, S., Ramaswamy, J., Natarajan, T., & Nedungadi, P. (2022). Micronutrient interventions among vulnerable population over a decade: A systematic review on Indian perspective. *Health Promotion Perspectives, 12*(2), 151–162. https://doi.org/10.34172/hpp.2022.19

Hoang, M. T., DeFina, L. F., Willis, B. L., Leonard, D. S., Weiner, M. F., & Brown, E. S. (2011). Association between low serum 25-hydroxyvitamin D and depression in a large sample of healthy adults: The cooper center longitudinal study. *Mayo Clinic Proceedings, 86*(11), 1050–1055. https://doi.org/10.4065/mcp.2011.0208

Huang, T., Balasubramanian, R., Yao, Y., Clish, C. B., Shadyab, A. H., Liu, B., Tworoger, S. S., Rexrode, K. M., Manson, J. E., Kubzansky, L. D., & Hankinson, S. E. (2021). Associations of depression status with plasma levels of candidate lipid and amino acid metabolites: A meta-analysis of individual data from three independent samples of US postmenopausal women. *Molecular Psychiatry, 26*(7), 3315–3327. https://doi.org/10.1038/s41380-020-00870-9

Jacob, L., Stubbs, B., Firth, J., Smith, L., Haro, J. M., & Koyanagi, A. (2020). Fast food consumption and suicide attempts among adolescents aged 12–15 years from 32 countries. *Journal of Affective Disorders, 266*, 63–70. https://doi.org/10.1016/j.jad.2020.01.130

Katole, A., Naik, G., Kujur, A., & Kumar, M. (2022). Performance appraisal of nutritional rehabilitation centers in Central India: A retrospective facility-based descriptive study. *Indian Journal of Community Medicine: Official Publication of Indian Association of Preventive & Social Medicine, 47*(2), 272–276. https://doi.org/10.4103/ijcm.ijcm_776_21

Khanna, P., Chattu, V., & Aeri, B. (2019). Nutritional aspects of depression in adolescents—A systematic review. *International Journal of Preventive Medicine, 10*(1), 42. https://doi.org/10.4103/ijpvm.IJPVM_400_18

Lee, H. J., Kim, C. H., Han, I., & Kim, S. H. (2019). Emotional state according to breakfast consumption in 62276 South Korean Adolescents. *Iranian Journal of Pediatrics, In Press* (In Press). https://doi.org/10.5812/ijp.92193

Li, Z., Li, B., Song, X., & Zhang, D. (2017). Dietary zinc and iron intake and risk of depression: A meta-analysis. *Psychiatry Research, 251*, 41–47. https://doi.org/10.1016/j.psychres.2017.02.006

Lin, P.-Y., Huang, S.-Y., & Su, K.-P. (2010). A meta-analytic review of polyunsaturated fatty acid compositions in patients with depression. *Biological Psychiatry, 68*(2), 140–147. https://doi.org/10.1016/j.biopsych.2010.03.018

Mahdavifar, B., Hosseinzadeh, M., Salehi-Abargouei, A., Mirzaei, M., & Vafa, M. (2021). Dietary intake of B vitamins and their association with depression, anxiety, and stress symptoms: A cross-sectional, population-based survey. *Journal of Affective Disorders, 288*, 92–98. https://doi.org/10.1016/j.jad.2021.03.055

Majamanda, J., Maureen, D., Munkhondia, T. M., & Carrier, J. (2014). The effectiveness of community-based nutrition education on the nutrition status of under-five children in developing countries. A systematic review. *Malawi Medical Journal: The Journal of Medical Association of Malawi, 26*(4), 115–118.

Mansour, H. M. (2022). Nutrition and psychiatric disorders: focus on schizophrenia. In *Nutrition and Psychiatric Disorders* (pp. 313–368). Springer, Singapore. https://doi.org/10.1007/978-981-19-5021-6_15

Memdani, L., Memdani, A., & Memdani, A. (2024). Farmers' suicides in India: A qualitative study of Andhra Pradesh (AP) and Telangana States of India. *Indian Journal of Community Medicine: Official Publication of Indian Association of Preventive & Social Medicine, 49*(4), 629–632. https://doi.org/10.4103/ijcm.ijcm_206_22

Myers, C. A. (2020). Food insecurity and psychological distress: A review of the recent literature. *Current Nutrition Reports, 9*(2), 107–118. https://doi.org/10.1007/s13668-020-00309-1

Nabavi, S. M., Daglia, M., Braidy, N., & Nabavi, S. F. (2017). Natural products, micronutrients, and nutraceuticals for the treatment of depression: A short review. *Nutritional Neuroscience, 20*(3), 180–194. https://doi.org/10.1080/1028415X.2015.1103461

Naghavi, M. (2019). Global, regional, and national burden of suicide mortality 1990 to 2016: Systematic analysis for the global burden of disease study 2016. *BMJ, l94*. https://doi.org/10.1136/bmj.l94

Park, S., Lee, Y., Youn, T., Kim, B. S., Park, J. I., Kim, H., Lee, H. C., & Hong, J. P. (2018). Association between level of suicide risk, characteristics of suicide attempts, and mental disorders among suicide attempters. *BMC Public Health, 18*(1), 477. https://doi.org/10.1186/s12889-018-5387-8

Parker, G., & Brotchie, H. (2011). Mood effects of the amino acids tryptophan and tyrosine: 'Food for Thought' III. *Acta Psychiatrica Scandinavica, 124*(6), 417–426. https://doi.org/10.1111/j.1600-0447.2011.01706.x

Ransing, R., Menon, V., Kar, S. K., de Filippis, R., & Mohamed, W. (2022). Nutrition and depression. In *Nutrition and Psychiatric Disorders* (pp. 139–169). Springer Nature Singapore Singapore.

Sánchez-Villegas, A., Martínez-González, M. A., Estruch, R., Salas-Salvadó, J., Corella, D., Covas, M. I., Arós, F., Romaguera, D., Gómez-Gracia, E., Lapetra, J., Pintó, X., Martínez, J. A., Lamuela-Raventós, R. M., Ros, E., Gea, A., Wärnberg, J., & Serra-Majem, L. (2013). Mediterranean dietary pattern and depression: The PREDIMED randomized trial. *BMC Medicine, 11*, 208. https://doi.org/10.1186/1741-7015-11-208

Sangle, P., Sandhu, O., Aftab, Z., Anthony, A. T., & Khan, S. (2020). Vitamin B12 supplementation: Preventing onset and improving prognosis of depression. *Cureus*. https://doi.org/10.7759/cureus.11169

Sartori, S. B., Whittle, N., Hetzenauer, A., & Singewald, N. (2012). Magnesium deficiency induces anxiety and HPA axis dysregulation: Modulation by therapeutic drug treatment. *Neuropharmacology, 62*(1), 304–312. https://doi.org/10.1016/j.neuropharm.2011.07.027

*School Education|Government of India, Ministry of Education.* (n.d.). Retrieved October 14, 2024, from https://www.education.gov.in/mid-day-meal

Smith, A. R., Zuromski, K. L., & Dodd, D. R. (2018). Eating disorders and suicidality: What we know, what we don't know, and suggestions for future research. *Current Opinion in Psychology, 22*, 63–67. https://doi.org/10.1016/j.copsyc.2017.08.023

Solís Arce, J. S., Warren, S. S., Meriggi, N. F., Scacco, A., McMurry, N., Voors, M., Syunyaev, G., Malik, A. A., Aboutajdine, S., Adeojo, O., Anigo, D., Armand, A., Asad, S., Atyera, M., Augsburg, B., Awasthi, M., Ayesiga, G. E., Bancalari, A., Björkman Nyqvist, M., Omer, S. B., et al. (2021). COVID-19 vaccine acceptance and hesitancy in low- and middle-income countries. *Nature Medicine*. https://doi.org/10.1038/s41591-021-01454-y

Szabo, S. T., Kilts, J. D., Naylor, J. C., Youssef, N. A., Strauss, J. L., Morey, R. A., Brancu, M., Hamer, R. M., Bradford, D. W., VA Mid-Atlantic MIRECC Work Group, & Marx, C. E. (2014). Amino acids as biomarker candidates for suicidality in male OEF/OIF veterans: Relevance to NMDA receptor modulation and nitric oxide signaling. *Military Medicine, 179*(5), 486–491. https://doi.org/10.7205/MILMED-D-13-00337

Szczesniak, O., Hestad, K. A., Hanssen, J. F., & Rudi, K. (2016). Isovaleric acid in stool correlates with human depression. *Nutritional Neuroscience, 19*(7), 279–283. https://doi.org/10.1179/1476830515Y.0000000007

Teraishi, T., Kajiwara, M., Hori, H., Sasayama, D., Hidese, S., Matsuo, J., Ishida, I., Kajiwara, Y., Ozeki, Y., Ota, M., Hattori, K., Higuchi, T., & Kunugi, H. (2018). 13C-phenylalanine breath test and serum biopterin in schizophrenia, bipolar disorder and major depressive disorder. *Journal of Psychiatric Research, 99*, 142–150. https://doi.org/10.1016/j.jpsychires.2018.01.019

Thurfah, J. N., Christine, null, Bagaskhara, P. P., Alfian, S. D., & Puspitasari, I. M. (2022). Dietary supplementations and depression. *Journal of Multidisciplinary Healthcare, 15*, 1121–1141. https://doi.org/10.2147/JMDH.S360029

Tousignant, M., Pouliot, L., Routhier, D., Vrakas, G., McGirr, A., & Turecki, G. (2011). Suicide, schizophrenia, and schizoid-type psychosis: Role of life events and childhood factors. *Suicide & Life-Threatening Behavior, 41*(1), 66–78. https://doi.org/10.1111/j.1943-278X.2010.00002.x

Turecki, G., Brent, D. A., Gunnell, D., O'Connor, R. C., Oquendo, M. A., Pirkis, J., & Stanley, B. H. (2019). Suicide and suicide risk. *Nature Reviews. Disease Primers, 5*(1), 74. https://doi.org/10.1038/s41572-019-0121-0

Wang, J., Um, P., Dickerman, B. A., & Liu, J. (2018). Zinc, magnesium, selenium and depression: A review of the evidence, potential mechanisms and implications. *Nutrients, 10*(5), 584. https://doi.org/10.3390/nu10050584

Xu, Y. Y., Sawadogo-Lewis, T., King, S. E., Mitchell, A., & Roberton, T. (2021). Integrating nutrition into the education sector in low- and middle-income countries: A framework for a win–win collaboration. *Maternal & Child Nutrition, 17*(3), e13156. https://doi.org/10.1111/mcn.13156

Yi, L.-T., Xu, H.-L., Feng, J., Zhan, X., Zhou, L.-P., & Cui, C.-C. (2011). Involvement of monoaminergic systems in the antidepressant-like effect of nobiletin. *Physiology & Behavior, 102*(1), 1–6. https://doi.org/10.1016/j.physbeh.2010.10.008

Zhang, J., Xiao, S., & Zhou, L. (2010). Mental disorders and suicide among young rural Chinese: A case-control psychological autopsy study. *The American Journal of Psychiatry, 167*(7), 773–781. https://doi.org/10.1176/appi.ajp.2010.09101476

# Chapter 14
# Sports and Suicidal Behavior

**Rizwana Amin, Nisma Merdad, and Muhammad Ali Asadullah**

**Abstract** Suicidal behavior has become one of the most important global concerns for professionals in various industries including sports. This chapter has outlined several antecedents of suicidal behavior recognizing the increasing suicidal tendencies among sports professionals. These antecedents of suicidal behaviors can be categorized as physical, psychological, social, individual, and organizational level factors. The physical suicidal antecedents include injuries, mental health, and physical and substance abuse. The psychological antecedents include performance pressure and anxiety, identity and self-worth perceptions, and isolation and stigma. The social factors include cultural expectations and masculinity, media influence, and community support and resources. The individual-level antecedents of suicidal behavior include personality, coping strategies, and trauma and adverse experiences. Organizational factors include effective coaching, economic support, psychological counseling, health facilities, food, and dietary support, transparent hiring mechanisms, grievance handling platforms, and infrastructure. At the end, this chapter outlines some preventive measures which can be taken to overcome the issue of suicidal tendencies among athletes. This chapter concludes with the need for policy reforms and future research to overcome the issue of suicidal tendencies of sports professionals.

**Keywords** Suicide · Sports · Suicidal tendencies · Sports professionals · Athletes

---

R. Amin (✉) · N. Merdad
Psychology Department, Effat University, KSA, Jeddah, Saudi Arabia
e-mail: riamin@effatuniversity.edu.sa

N. Merdad
e-mail: nmerdad@effatuniversity.edu.sa

M. A. Asadullah
College of Business Administration, University of Khorfakkan, Sharjah, United Arab Emirates
e-mail: Muhammad.Asadullah@ukf.ac.ae

 
S. M. Y. Arafat and S. K. Kar (eds.), *Ecological and Social Determinants of Suicidal Behavior*, South Asian Perspectives in Mental Health and Psychology,
https://doi.org/10.1007/978-981-96-4028-7_14

## 1 Suicidal Behavior: An Overview

Suicide has attracted significant attention from public healthcare policymakers across the globe for being a leading cause of death, particularly among young adults aged 15–29 (Bertuccio et al., 2024). According to the World Health Organization (WHO), almost 800,000 people die by suicide each year, while numerous individuals attempt to take their own lives (Lovero et al., 2023). This issue affects individuals across various socioeconomic, geographical, and demographic backgrounds, emphasizing the need for comprehensive attention and support (Stack, 2021). Suicidal behavior begins with suicidal ideation (such as thinking or planning suicide), passes through the phase of suicide attempts (non-fatal, self-directed behavior with the intent to die), and ends with suicide resulting in death from self-harm (Reece, 2022; Sher & Oquendo, 2023). Suicidal behavior is a very complex but multifaceted phenomenon originating from an interplay between biological (such as mental health conditions including depression, anxiety, and substance use disorders), social (such as relationship issues and significant life changes), and/or economic factors (de Beurs et al., 2023). These factors negatively influence the mental health of an individual leading to extreme depression, bipolar disorder, and substance use disorders which drive individuals toward suicidal behavior (Moller et al., 2022). Warning signs of suicidal behavior may include talking about wanting to die, withdrawing from social interactions, giving away belongings, or exhibiting extreme mood swings (Kedar, 2021). Despite all, triggers of suicidal behavior include intense emotional or physical pain, a pervasive sense of hopelessness, or overwhelming life stressors like relationship problems or financial difficulties (Bloch-Elkouby et al., 2022).

## 2 Sports, Mental Health, and Suicidal Behavior

With the growing recognition of sports participation in mental well-being (Piñeiro-Cossio et al., 2021), scholarly and societal interest in comprehending the relationship between sports, mental health, and suicidal behavior has gained considerable attention (Schinke et al., 2022). For instance, some recent studies (Marquez et al., 2020; Martín-Rodríguez et al., 2024) have demonstrated that sports positively impact mental health by providing purpose, and social connection, boosting mood and overall well-being while relieving stress, depression, and anxiety simultaneously. Sports discipline individuals and enhance their resilience and emotional equilibrium strengthening mental health (Larsen et al., 2021). However, the sports industry also characterizes some unique mental health challenges (such as competitiveness, a high-pressure environment, fear of failure, and the intense focus on performance (Ramalingam, 2023) which pose intense psychological and emotional demands (Barnes et al., 2021) and drive sports professionals to suicidal behavior (de Oliveira Camilo et al., 2024). Sportsmen may feel emotionally burdened by the pressure to meet personal or external expectations and may feel isolated (Hilpisch et al., 2024). Further, the mental health struggles of athletes may also remain hidden (Pereira Vargas et al., 2024) as athletes may be hesitant to seek psychological help to avoid the stigma (Walton et al., 2024). Consequently, mental health issues may remain unaddressed, and the risk of suicidal behavior increases (Ryan & Oquendo, 2020).

## 3 Sports and Suicidal Behavior: Historical Accounts

The issue of suicide among athletes has brought attention to the mental health challenges faced in the sports world. Several high-profile cases illustrate the risk factors associated with competition, pressure, and public scrutiny. One well-known tragedy is that of NFL player Junior Seau, who allegedly died by suicide in 2012 (Hunt, 2022). Despite his success as a celebrated linebacker, Seau struggled with the effects of concussions and the immense pressure of professional sports. His death sparked discussions about the potential impact of brain injuries and mental health issues in contact sports. Another notable incident involves professional wrestler Chris Benoit, who, in 2007, reportedly killed his wife and son before taking his own life. Benoit had a reputation for his intense personality, which was coupled with high demands in his profession. Autopsies revealed significant neurological damage, raising concerns about the mental health implications of injuries and lifestyle choices in wrestling ("Study Suggests Brain Damage May Have Affected Benoit—ESPN," 2007). In 2013, The case of Olympic silver medalist Clara Hughes, who has openly discussed her battles with depression, underscores the unique pressures faced by competitive athletes ("Clara Hughes Talks About Her Battle with Depression," 2011). Although she survived a suicide attempt, her story highlights the stigma surrounding mental health in sports and the need for athletes to feel comfortable seeking help. These cases reveal common risk factors linked to suicide in sports, such as pressure to perform, public scrutiny, and injuries that may lead to mental health challenges.

## 4 Role of Competitive Sports Events on Suicidal Behavior

The mega sports events (such as the Olympics, FIFA World Cup, and Asian Games) significantly influence the behaviors of both the audience as well as the athletes (Müller & Gaffney, 2018). The outcome of the event, emotional connection with the team members and the fans, camaraderie, and shared happiness are some commonly known challenges of athletes' mental health struggles (He, 2024). Athletes lacking such opportunities may become more vulnerable to suicidal tendencies (Statuta, 2023). Particularly, the feelings of failure, disappointment, and sadness triggered by a loss can exacerbate pre-existing mental health problems, especially if they are already dealing with depression or anxiety (Chang et al., 2020; Runacres et al., 2021). Even, in some cases, major losses can lead to an increase in suicide rates, particularly among those who strongly identify with the team (Batty et al., 2023; McLoughlin et al., 2021). The phenomenon of suicide during major sporting events is not isolated but reflects broader societal issues related to mental health stigma and the lack of adequate support systems for individuals in distress (Arafat & Hossain, 2018).

Sports events can be categorized as global sports events, regional competitions, and local or national competitions. The intensity of suicidal tendencies may increase as an athlete moves from national to regional and then to global events, yet the suicidal tendency may persist in all cases. Athletes participating in global sports, such as the Olympics and World Cup, experience increased suicidal tendencies for a variety of reasons including amplified pressures, uncertainty, and routine disruptions (Elliott, 2024), social media scrutiny, harsh criticism, and a heightened sense of inadequacy. The pressure to constantly excel, win, or set new records compounds these emotions, leaving athletes emotionally drained (Wagner, 2018). Studies suggest that external pressures, added to the already intense demands of elite sports, heighten the risk of depression and suicidal ideation among athletes (Kühnle, 2020). The fear of letting down their nation, sponsors, or even fans, becomes a heavy burden to bear, making it critical for these athletes to have robust mental health support systems. Proactively addressing mental health challenges, offering access to therapy, and providing avenues for stress relief are essential steps to safeguard their well-being during challenging times (Gustafsson et al., 2023; Parveen et al., 2024; Walton et al., 2024).

Regional sports events, such as the Asian Games, demonstrate cultural pride and serve as the stage where national pride is intensely tied to athletic performance (Lenger & Schumacher, 2015). Hence, emotions for securing medals and bringing honor to the homeland can become overwhelming in athletes participating in international competitions like the Olympics (Penfold, 2019). Athletes often feel that success equates to national glory, while failure is met with deep personal and societal disappointment (Afremow, 2015). After the 2002 Asian Games, for instance, several athletes who did not meet performance expectations expressed suicidal thoughts, and one heartbreaking case ended in death (Kee et al., 2016). The emotional rollercoaster that athletes experience can deplete their mental health resources for which coping with persisting disappointment could become challenging (Bloom, 2021). The local or national sports events may have a similar influence on young athletes for whom these competitions pave their way toward larger aspirations, such as qualifying for the Olympics or breaking into professional leagues (Harrison, 2020). Career uncertainty, financial pressures, and the ever-present threat of injury cast a shadow over their ambitions, creating an atmosphere of anxiety that permeates training and competition (Fitzgerald, 2020; Haugen, 2022; Parveen et al., 2024).

## 5 Risk Factors of Suicidal Behavior in Sports

The rising concern over suicidal behavior among athletes is becoming increasingly alarming. As the intensity and competitiveness of professional sports increase, athletes face unique pressures that can lead to severe mental health challenges, sometimes resulting in suicidal thoughts and actions (Kedar, 2021). Unlike the general population, athletes encounter a complex mix of stressors, including psychological pressure to perform and the physical demands related to their identities and career success (Parveen et al., 2024; Walton et al., 2024). Consequently, suicidal behavior among athletes is a multifaceted issue influenced by a combination of physical, psychological, organizational, individual, and societal factors (Table 1). This chapter offers insights into these elements to better understand the drivers of suicidal intent among athletes.

### *5.1 Physical Risk Factors*

Physical health is essential for participation in sports, as athletes must maintain their fitness to be eligible. While physical fitness supports mental well-being, athletes are also vulnerable to injuries from the demands of their sport. Injuries are closely linked to mental health, as they can lead to psychological distress and feelings of disconnection during recovery. Athletes often face long recuperation periods that may contribute to increased depression and anxiety. Research indicates that those with significant injuries that threaten their careers are at a higher risk for mental health issues, including suicidal thoughts (Hays, 2021). The emotional toll can lead to an identity crisis and anxiety related to recovery and re-injury potential (Gustafsson et al., 2018). Physical and substance abuse are critical issues in sports. Physical abuse includes sexual harassment, bullying, and punishment, as highlighted by various documented cases. Substance abuse, in contrast, may involve athletes using drugs to cope with pain or emotional distress, including performance-enhancing drugs and recreational substances. This behavior can worsen mental health issues and elevate the risk of suicide (Didymus & Backhouse, 2020). Studies show a bidirectional relationship; substance abuse can lead to suicidal thoughts, and those with such thoughts may turn to drugs or alcohol to escape (Haugen, 2022; Li et al., 2021).

### *5.2 Psychological Risk Factors*

Psychological factors are a key component in understanding the mental health challenges that can lead to suicidal behavior in athletes (Chang et al., 2020). Sportsmen, particularly those in highly competitive environments, face relentless pressure to

**Table 1** Risk factors for suicide behaviors in sports

| Risk factors | Specific factors | Description |
|---|---|---|
| Physical risk factors | Injuries | Physical injuries can lead to psychological distress and feelings of isolation, increasing the risk of suicidal thoughts |
| | Mental health issues | Mental health challenges often arise from injuries and can significantly impact athletes' well-being |
| | Substance abuse | Athletes may use substances to cope with physical or emotional pain, creating a bidirectional relationship with suicidal ideation |
| | Physical abuse | Experiences of bullying or harassment can contribute to emotional distress, impacting mental health |
| Psychological risk factors | Performance pressure and anxiety | High expectations from coaches and public scrutiny can lead to overwhelming stress and feelings of inadequacy |
| | Identity and self-worth | Career-threatening injuries can disrupt identity and self-worth, contributing to depression and suicidal thoughts |
| | Isolation and stigma | The stigma around mental health issues can prevent athletes from seeking help, leading to feelings of loneliness |
| Social risk factors | Cultural expectations and masculinity | Societal norms around masculinity can discourage male athletes from seeking help, heightening feelings of shame |
| | Media influence | Both traditional and social media can amplify pressures and criticism, leading to emotional distress among athletes |
| | Community support and resources | Lack of adequate support and mental health resources can contribute to feelings of helplessness among athletes |
| Individual-level risk factors | Personality traits | Certain traits, like perfectionism and high neuroticism, can increase vulnerability to mental health issues |

(continued)

**Table 1** (continued)

| Risk factors | Specific factors | Description |
|---|---|---|
| | Coping approach | Effective coping strategies can protect against suicidal thoughts, while maladaptive strategies can increase risk |
| | Trauma and adverse experiences | A history of trauma can resurface under stress, leading to increased anxiety and depression |

perform at peak levels, which may result in overwhelming stress, anxiety, and inadequacy feelings (Gustafsson et al., 2018).

### 5.2.1 Performance Pressure and Anxiety

Performance pressure is one of the primary psychological risk factors provoking suicidal thoughts among athletes. Sportsmen and athletes, especially at elite levels, are often subjected to high expectations from coaches, sponsors, and fans. The fear of failure to perform as well as actual poor performances both trigger negative thoughts. Athletes may internalize their performance outcomes as reflections of their self-worth (Gustafsson et al., 2018). When they fail to meet these expectations, feelings of inadequacy can arise, leading to a downward spiral of depression (Kühnle, 2020). Social media platforms can amplify criticism and public scrutiny where athletes feel like they are being monitored through a microscope. The resulting anxiety can become overwhelming, making it difficult for athletes to function both in and out of their sport (Gill, 2023). This is also one of the reasons that the return plan of the losing team is kept confidential in various countries to avoid public assault.

### 5.2.2 Identity and Self-worth

Identity and self-worth are other important psychological factors tied to suicidal behavior in athletes. These factors indicate psychological face setbacks (Messner, 2018) which aggravate the feelings of purposelessness, despair, and emotional void among athletes and put them at risk of suicidal behavior. Research shows that athletes who suffer from career-threatening injuries often experience significantly higher rates of depression and suicidal thoughts, as the reality of losing their athletic career can be emotionally devastating. The combination of a fractured identity and an uncertain future makes these athletes particularly vulnerable to mental health struggles (Edwards, 2023; Timpka et al., 2022).

### 5.2.3 Isolation and Stigma

Isolation triggered by the fear of stigma is one of the most important psychosocial factors provoking suicidal tendencies among athletes. Sportsmen are often expected to demonstrate psychological strength to cope with emotional labor either by suppressing their emotions or by displaying emotions that are not genuine (Bloom, 2021). This environment characterizing emotional labor may prevent them from expressing their vulnerabilities for seeking psychological or physical support. The stigma surrounding mental health issues is particularly pronounced in competitive sports, where admitting to struggles can be seen as a weakness (Pike, 2018). Moreover, the individualistic nature of some sports, like tennis or gymnastics, can compound feelings of loneliness. Unlike team sports, where athletes may find support from teammates, individual athletes often face their challenges alone, making them more susceptible to feelings of isolation and hopelessness (McKenzie, 2018).

## *5.3 Social Risk Factors*

The broader societal context plays a critical role in shaping the mental health landscape for athletes. Various societal pressures can significantly impact an athlete's well-being. Some critical social factors influencing the mental health and suicidal tendencies of sportsmen include cultural expectations and masculinity, public and social media influence, and community support.

### 5.3.1 Cultural Expectations and Masculinity

Masculinity represents the social role expectation that emerges as one of the traditional factors that emphasize toughness, resilience, and emotional stoicism in sportsmen (Smith, 2024). This cultural framework discourages male sportsmen from expressing vulnerability or seeking help for mental health issues. As a result, male athletes may be less likely to reach out for support when they encounter emotional or psychological challenges. The pressure to conform to these societal expectations can lead to feelings of shame and isolation, heightening the risk of suicidal thoughts and behaviors (Ramaeker et al., 2019). On the other hand, female athletes may experience a stream of public criticism in some cultures prohibiting the participation of women in public events including sports.

### 5.3.2 Media Influence

Media has two important facets including public media like news channels and magazines and social media platforms such as YouTube, Twitter, WhatsApp, Facebook, and others. Irrespective of their nature, both types of media create an equal amount of pressure on sportsmen and cause psychological distress. The media's portrayal of sports and sportsmen can further exacerbate mental health issues. The sensationalism surrounding athletic performances, especially failures, can be detrimental. Sportsmen may feel immense pressure to live up to public expectations and may experience significant emotional distress following a loss or poor performance (Souter et al., 2018). Social media can amplify these pressures, providing a platform for criticism and negative commentary. Sportsmen often face harsh judgment from fans and pundits creating an environment where they feel constantly evaluated. This scrutiny can lead to anxiety and depression, particularly when athletes experience disappointment from their supporters for their high standards (Hayes et al., 2019).

### 5.3.3 Community Support and Resources

The availability of mental health resources and community support is crucial in mitigating the risk factors associated with suicidal behavior. Unfortunately, many sportsmen may find that sports organizations do not provide adequate mental health support. In some cases, the focus on physical performance can overshadow the importance of mental well-being. Without access to mental health resources, athletes may struggle to cope with their emotional challenges. This lack of support can contribute to feelings of helplessness, increasing the risk of suicidal thoughts and actions (Schinke et al., 2018). Public sentiments also demonstrate the presence of community support and the availability of emotional resources. The athletes failing to win sports events may also fail to win public support and emotional resources.

## *5.4 Individual-Level Risk Factors*

Suicidal tendencies can also vary from individual to individual. Personality is one of the most important individual-level factors influencing the mental health and suicidal tendencies of athletes.

### 5.4.1 Personality Traits

Researchers have identified over 1,400 personality traits, both positive and negative, that develop during early life stages and can become fixed. Athletes with strong personality traits are better equipped to cope with the psychosocial, economic, and skill-related demands of their sport. Conversely, athletes lacking key traits, such as resilience, confidence, and optimism, may be more vulnerable to psychological distress and suicidal tendencies. Specific traits, like perfectionism, can increase mental health challenges by heightening anxiety and fear of failure. Additionally, athletes prone to overthinking may face increased stress and depression, which can lead to suicidal thoughts (Kang & Gong, 2024). Those with high levels of neuroticism often struggle with emotional regulation, experiencing intense anxiety and depression. These traits can amplify the psychological pressures faced by athletes and contribute to a higher risk of suicidal behavior (Chang et al., 2020).

### 5.4.2 Coping Approach

Effective coping strategies demonstrate the strong capabilities of athletes to manage their stress and adversity. Sportsmen and/or athletes who use effective coping strategies, such as problem-solving skills, emotional regulation, and social support, are generally better equipped to handle the pressures of their sport (Leprince et al., 2018). Conversely, those who rely on maladaptive coping strategies, such as avoidance or substance use, may be at a higher risk for developing mental health issues and suicidal thoughts (Haugen, 2022). Life transitions, such as moving from amateur to professional status or retiring from sports, can also trigger significant emotional upheaval. These transitions often come with increased pressures and uncertainties, leading to feelings of loss and despair. Sportsmen and athletes who struggle to adapt to these changes may experience heightened vulnerability to suicidal behavior (Li et al., 2021).

### 5.4.3 Trauma and Adverse Experiences

Personal history plays a significant role in an athlete's mental health. Athletes with a history of trauma related to adverse childhood experiences, abuse, or other significant life stressors may carry psychological burdens that affect their performance and overall well-being. Hence the personality history of sportsmen may resurface during high-stress situations, contributing to their anxiety and depression (Copeland et al., 2024). Furthermore, the cumulative effect of stressors in an athlete's life—both inside and outside of their sport—can lead to a sense of overwhelm. Athletes who lack adequate support systems may find it challenging to cope with these stressors, increasing their risk of suicidal thoughts and behaviors (Rowan et al., 2023).

## *5.5 Organizational-Level Risk Factors*

Various organizational factors also prove suicidal tendencies among the athletes. Such factors may include the provision of effective coaching services, economic support, psychological counseling, health facilities, food, and dietary support, transparent hiring mechanisms, grievance handling platforms, and infrastructure. These factors may directly or indirectly influence the mental health of sportsmen and provoke suicidal intentions.

# 6 Preventive Roles of Sports in Suicide Risk

In recent years, an increasing body of research has highlighted the significant role sports can play in protecting against suicide risk, particularly among young people. Sports participation offers a buffer against suicidal thoughts and behaviors, thanks largely to the psychological and social benefits that regular involvement can provide. A pivotal longitudinal study by Taliaferro et al. (2011) revealed a meaningful link between consistent sports involvement and reduced suicidal ideation and attempts among adolescents. This chapter compiled a list of factors contributing to suicidal tendencies among athletes despite their sustained sports participation over time. These factors assimilate to the findings of a systematic literature review conducted by Huo (2024) emphasizing the protective nature of physical activities against suicidal outcomes. This chapter identified these factors drawing on the findings of various studies that underscore the positive impact of sports on mental health and social connectivity.

## *6.1 Stress Management Programs*

Various public and private initiatives can be taken at the organizational level to manage the stress of athletes. Stress has become a universal challenge for adolescents and young adults today. Engaging in physical activity is one of the most effective ways to manage stress (Grasdalsmoen et al., 2020). Well-structured sports activities can promise a reduction in high-risk behaviors including suicide (Çetinkaya & Kirtepe, 2018) by allowing individuals to develop skills necessary for handling life's challenges. Teamwork and shared experiences may also enhance the ability of athletes to cope with stress and build resilience. Participating in these activities can provide a sense of belonging, making it easier for them to address challenges. Informal relationships such as friendships with team members (Eather et al., 2023; Eime et al., 2013) can also positively influence psychological health. These relationships often serve as a valuable source of support during difficult times, contributing to overall well-being. Incorporating sports into public policy could provide beneficial mental health outcomes for youth and young adults. By promoting physical education programs and increasing access to sporting activities, we can help individuals utilize the stress-relieving benefits of sports. This approach not only enhances mood and well-being but also supports the development of resilience needed to navigate the pressures of modern life, positioning sports as a meaningful resource in the conversation around suicide risk.

### 6.2 *Support Program for Young Athletes*

Youth is one of the most prominent classes entering the sports industry. The preventive measures taken at the organizational level that support youth in coping with suicidal thoughts can prove very effective. For instance, adolescents involved in team sports report lower levels of suicidal thoughts (Eime et al., 2013). These supportive relationships are especially significant in the face of external stressors such as cyberbullying or social marginalization. Similarly, inclusive sports environments play a crucial role in the inclusion of various socially deprived groups and those experiencing cyber bullying (LaRocca, 2023; Rodelli et al., 2018). An inclusive environment may foster a sense of acceptance and community to combat feelings of isolation and alienation and develop resilience to better navigate the challenges of a sports career. Overall, the characteristics of an inclusive sports environment may contribute to a decrease in suicidal ideation (Lester, 2014; Park et al., 2020). Further, the confidence, discipline, and teamwork skills developed through sports participation equip students with valuable tools for managing emotional stress and positive mental health outcomes.

## 7 Implications for Public Policy and Future Research

This chapter recommends that effective stress management programs for youth, transparent hiring and performance evaluation mechanisms, psychological support mechanisms, public education initiatives to increase community support for athletes competing national level, and effective human resource management policies may prove effective in regulating the suicidal tendencies of athletes. The measures taken to regulate the physical, social, psychological, individual, and organizational factors need significant attention from policymakers at the level of the sports industry as well as the public policymakers. By promoting access to sports facilities and organized activities, policymakers can address some inequities that limit participation, such as socio-economic barriers. Ensuring that all young people can engage in sports will help embed these protective benefits across society.

Further research should continue to unravel the nuanced mechanisms through which sports mitigate suicide risk. Particularly, various case investigations, intervention studies, and field survey studies may be encouraged through mutual involvement of academic and sports industry professionals. Some research grant schemes could encourage significant research attention at the national and global level to identify various solutions to reduce suicidal tendencies in sports professionals. Exploring personalized sports interventions that address specific needs of marginalized communities can offer deeper insights into effective prevention strategies. Additionally, examining the long-term effects of regular sports involvement on mental health across various life stages may yield valuable information for developing comprehensive support systems.

# 8 Summary

This chapter explains that sports, which are generally viewed as a means to promote physical fitness and mental well-being, characterize various pressures such as competition, performance expectations, and the fear of failure, which can disturb the mental health of sports professionals and put them at the risk of suicide. It has organized existing research on suicidal behavior to identify several risk factors that may expose athletes to suicidal tendencies. These antecedents of suicidal behaviors can be categorized as physical, psychological, social, individual, and organizational level factors. This chapter has also proposed some strategies to overcome these risk factors which include a supportive environment, stress management programs, and programs designed to ensure essential support for young athletes. By prioritizing sports in educational and public policy contexts, communities can effectively harness sports as a preventive measure against suicide, paving the way for healthier, more connected futures.

## References


Afremow, J. (2015). *The champion's mind: How great athletes think, train, and thrive.* Rodale Books.

Arafat, S. M. Y., & Hossain, M. S. (2018). Suicide during international sports events (football World Cup-2018). *Asian Journal of Psychiatry, 36*, 92–93. https://doi.org/10.1016/j.ajp.2018.07.004

Barnes, F. B., Fletcher, D., & Neely, K. C. (2021). Stress-related growth in elite sport performers: Qualitative differentiators in psychosocial mechanisms. *The Sport Psychologist, 35*(4), 293–304. https://doi.org/10.1123/tsp.2020-0015

Batty, G. D., Frank, P., Kujala, U. M., Sarna, S. J., & Kaprio, J. (2023). Suicide and depression in former contact sports participants: Population-based cohort study, systematic review, and meta-analysis. *EClinicalMedicine, 60.* https://doi.org/10.1016/j.eclinm.2023.102026

Bertuccio, P., Amerio, A., Grande, E., La Vecchia, C., Costanza, A., Aguglia, A., Berardelli, I., Serafini, G., Amore, M., Pompili, M., & Odone, A. (2024). Global trends in youth suicide from 1990 to 2020: An analysis of data from the WHO mortality database. *EClinicalMedicine, 70.* https://doi.org/10.1016/j.eclinm.2024.102506

de Beurs, D., de Winter, R. F. P., Helbich, M., & Bockting, C. (2023). Suicidal behavior from a complex system perspective: Individual, dynamical, and contextual. In *Suicide Risk Assessment and Prevention* (pp. 1281–1294). Springer International Publishing. https://doi.org/10.1007/978-3-030-41319-4_35-1

Bloom, G. (2021). *Keeping your head in the game: Untold stories of the highs and lows of a life in sport.* Penguin UK.

Bloch-Elkouby, S., Yanez, N., Chennapragada, L., Richards, J., Cohen, L., & Galynker, I. (2022). The narrative crisis model of suicide: A novel and empirically grounded diathesis-stress model of suicide. In *Suicide risk assessment and prevention* (pp. 1–16). Springer International Publishing. https://doi.org/10.1007/978-3-030-41319-4_14-1

Chang, C. J., Putukian, M., Aerni, G., Diamond, A. B., Hong, E. S., Ingram, Y. M., Reardon, C. L., & Wolanin, A. T. (2020). Mental health issues and psychological factors in athletes: Detection, management, effect on performance, and prevention: American medical society for sports medicine position statement. *Clinical Journal of Sport Medicine, 30*(2), e61–e87. https://doi.org/10.1097/JSM.0000000000000817

Çetinkaya, T., & Kırtepe, A. (2018). The investigation of attitudes to cope with stress in terms of different variables of physical education and sports students. *Turkish Journal of Sport and Exercise, 20*(2), 74–80. https://doi.org/10.15314/tsed.426322

Copeland, C., Reynolds, A., & Ackley, J. (2024). Is it Hard Out Here for a Player?: Understanding the relationship between adverse childhood experiences and athletic identity among college student athletes. *Journal of Intercollegiate Sport, 17*(2). https://doi.org/10.17161/jis.v17i2.20761

Didymus, F. F., & Backhouse, S. H. (2020). Coping by doping? A qualitative inquiry into permitted and prohibited substance use in competitive rugby. *Psychology of Sport and Exercise, 49*, 101680. https://doi.org/10.1016/j.psychsport.2020.101680

Eather, N., Wade, L., Pankowiak, A., & Eime, R. (2023). The impact of sports participation on mental health and social outcomes in adults: A systematic review and the 'Mental Health through Sport' conceptual model. *Systematic Reviews, 12*(1), 102. https://doi.org/10.1186/s13643-023-02264-8

Edwards, C. (2023). Mental health emergencies in athletes. In *Sport and mental health: From research to everyday practice* (pp. 69–78). Springer International Publishing.

Eime, R., Young, J., Harvey, J., Charity, M., & Payne, W. (2013). A systematic review of the psychological and social benefits of participation in sport for children and adolescents: Informing development of a conceptual model of health through sport. *International Journal of Behavioral Nutrition and Physical Activity, 10*(1), 1–21. https://doi.org/10.1186/1479-5868-10-98

Elliott, R. (2024). *Mental health and sport: Supporting elite athletes*. Taylor & Francis.

Fitzgerald, M. (2020). The comeback quotient: A get-real guide to building mental fitness in sport and life. VeloPress. https://www.simonandschuster.com/books/The-Comeback-Quotient/Matt-Fitzgerald/9781948007160

Gill, R. (2023). *Perfect: Feeling Judged on Social Media*. John Wiley & Sons. https://doi.org/10.1002/9781119593921

Grasdalsmoen, M., Eriksen, H., Lønning, K., & Sivertsen, B. (2020). Physical exercise, mental health problems, and suicide attempts in university students. *BMC Psychiatry, 20*(1), 1–11. https://doi.org/10.1186/s12888-020-02583-3

Gustafsson, H., Davis, P., & Davis, L. (2023). Fear of failure in athletes: Fanning the fire of sport desire or burning out? In *Routledge International Handbook of Failure* (pp. 53–66). Routledge.

Gustafsson, H., Madigan, D. J., & Lundkvist, E. (2018). Burnout in athletes. In *Handbuch Stressregulation und Sport* (pp. 489–504). https://doi.org/10.1007/978-3-662-49322-9_24

Harrison, M. (2020). *Personal Next: What We Can Learn from Elite Athletes Navigating Career Transition*. LifeTree Media.

Haugen, E. (2022). Athlete mental health & psychological impact of sport injury. *Operative Techniques in Sports Medicine, 30*(1), 150898. https://doi.org/10.1016/j.otsm.2022.150898

Hays, K. F. (2021). *Integrating exercise, sports, movement, and mind: Therapeutic unity*. Routledge.

Hayes, M., Filo, K., Riot, C., & Geurin, A. (2019). Athlete perceptions of social media benefits and challenges during major sport events. *International Journal of Sport Communication, 12*(4), 449–481. https://doi.org/10.1123/ijsc.2019-0062

He, M. (2024). Sports identification in situational problem-solving: A framework for understanding fans' communicative behaviors in sports crises. *Communication & Sport*, 21674795241271191. https://doi.org/10.1177/21674795241271191

Hilpisch, C., Krüger, K., Raab, M., Wiese, L., Zentgraf, K., & Mutz, M. (2024). Burnout symptoms in elite athletes: Assessing the role of effort–reward imbalance, support, and emotions. *International Review for the Sociology of Sport*, 1–21. https://doi.org/10.1177/10126902241248767

Huo, M. (2024). Can sports participation be a protective factor against suicide-related outcomes in adolescents: A systematic review. *Frontiers in Psychology, 15*, 1341795. https://doi.org/10.3389/fpsyg.2024.1341795

Hunt, M. (2012, May 5). Suicides are more trauma for NFL. *Milwaukee Journal Sentinel*. https://archive.jsonline.com/sports/nfl-players-suicides-raise-troubling-questions-bs594s3-150110275.html

Kedar, T. (2021). Suicide and suicide risk factors: A literature review. *Asian Journal of Nursing Education and Research, 11*(3), 441–446. https://doi.org/10.52711/2349-2996.2021.00107

Kang, W., & Gong, C. (2024). Exploring potential mediating mechanisms between maladaptive perfectionism and athlete burnout based on multi-theory perspectives. *Frontiers in Psychology, 15*, 1416281. https://doi.org/10.3389/fpsyg.2024.1416281

Kee, Y. H., Fry, J. M., Wang, J. C. K., Chong, Y. W., & Li, C. (2016). Silver lining in winning silver: An exploratory study of supporters' reactions and coping on social media towards Lee Chong Wei's London Olympics defeat. *Asia Pacific Journal of Sport and Social Science, 5*(1), 1–15. https://doi.org/10.1080/21640599.2016.1145938

Kühnle, F. (2020). Sad stories for a better future: Narratives and functions of depression stories in elite athletes' autobiographies. *European Journal for Sport and Society, 17*(3), 196–213. https://doi.org/10.1080/16138171.2020.1792074

LaRocca, D., James, K. A., Rosenberg, S., Ma, M., & Brooks-Russell, A. (2023). Team sports participation, depression, and suicidal ideation in lesbian, gay, bisexual, transgender, and questioning adolescents. *Psychology in the Schools, 60*, 902–911. https://doi.org/10.1002/pits.22792

Larsen, C., Moesch, K., Durand-Bush, N., & Henriksen, K. (Eds.). (2021). *Mental health in elite sport: Applied perspectives from across the globe*. Routledge.

Lenger, A., & Schumacher, F. (2015). The social functions of sport: A theoretical approach to the interplay of emerging powers, national identity, and global sport events. In *Globalistics and Globalization Studies: Global Transformations and Global Future* (pp. 231–248). https://www.sociostudies.org/almanac/articles/the_social_functions_of_sport-_a_theoretical_approach_to_the_interplay_of_emerging_powers-_national_/

Lester, D. (2014). Participation in sports teams and suicidal behavior: An analysis of the 1995 National College Health Risk Behavior Survey. *Perceptual and Motor Skills, 119*(1), 38–41. https://doi.org/10.2466/06.15.pms.119c13z5

Leprince, C., D'Arripe-Longueville, F., & Doron, J. (2018). Coping in teams: Exploring athletes' communal coping strategies to deal with shared stressors. *Frontiers in Psychology, 9*, 1908. https://doi.org/10.3389/fpsyg.2018.01908

Li, X., Chi, G., Taylor, A., Chen, S. T., Memon, A. R., Zhang, Y., Song, Y., Li, J., Luo, X., & Zou, L. (2021). Lifestyle behaviors and suicide-related behaviors in adolescents: Cross-sectional study using the 2019 YRBS data. *Frontiers in Public Health, 9*, 766972. https://doi.org/10.3389/fpubh.2021.766972

Lovero, K. L., Dos Santos, P. F., Come, A. X., Wainberg, M. L., & Oquendo, M. A. (2023). Suicide in global mental health. *Current Psychiatry Reports, 25*(6), 255–262. https://doi.org/10.1007/s11920-023-01423-x

Müller, M., & Gaffney, C. (2018). Comparing the urban impacts of the FIFA World Cup and Olympic Games from 2010 to 2016. *Journal of Sport and Social Issues, 42*(4), 247–269. https://doi.org/10.1177/0193723518771830

Marquez, D. X., Aguiñaga, S., Vásquez, P. M., Conroy, D. E., Erickson, K. I., Hillman, C. H., & Powell, K. E. (2020). A systematic review of physical activity and quality of life and well-being. *Translational Behavioral Medicine, 10*(5), 1098–1109. https://doi.org/10.1093/tbm/ibz198

Martín-Rodríguez, A., et al. (2024). Sporting mind: The interplay of physical activity and psychological health. *Sports, 12*(1), 37. https://doi.org/10.3390/sports12010037

McKenzie, A. I. (2018). Me or We? The Effect of Team and Individual Sports Activity on Executive Functioning. https://ir.lib.uwo.ca/psych_uht/34

Messner, M. (1987). The meaning of success: The athletic experience and the development of male identity. In *The Making of Masculinities* (Routledge Revivals) (pp. 193–209). https://doi.org/10.4324/9781315738505-12

McLoughlin, E., Fletcher, D., Slavich, G. M., Arnold, R., & Moore, L. J. (2021). Cumulative lifetime stress exposure, depression, anxiety, and well-being in elite athletes: A mixed-method study. *Psychology of Sport and Exercise, 52*, 101823. https://doi.org/10.1016/j.psychsport.2020.101823

Moller, C. I., Davey, C. G., Badcock, P. B., Wrobel, A. L., Cao, A., Murrihy, S., Sharmin, S., & Cotton, S. M. (2022). Correlates of suicidality in young people with depressive disorders: A systematic review. *Australian & New Zealand Journal of Psychiatry, 56*(8), 910–948. https://doi.org/10.1177/00048674221086498

de Oliveira Camilo, J. A., Almeida, J. C. S., & Galán, C. H. (2024). El suicidio en el Contexto del Deporte de Élite: una Síntesis Meta-etnográfica. *Retos: nuevas tendencias en educación física, deporte y recreación, 54*, 633–641. https://doi.org/10.47197/retos.v54.103459

Parveen, M., Sultan, S., & Yunus, A. (2024). Lived experiences of shame: An exploratory study of women in sports. *Journal of Development and Social Sciences, 5*(3), 242–253. https://doi.org/10.47205/jdss.2024(5-III)21

Park, S., Park, S., Jang, S., Oh, G., & Oh, I. (2020). The neglected role of physical education participation on suicidal ideation and stress in high school adolescents from South Korea. *International Journal of Environmental Research and Public Health, 17*(8), 2838. https://doi.org/10.3390/ijerph17082838

Penfold, T. (2019). National identity and sporting mega-events in Brazil. *Sport in Society, 22*(3), 384–398. https://doi.org/10.1080/17430437.2018.1490266

Pereira Vargas, M. L. F., Papathomas, A., Williams, T. L., Kinnafick, F. E., & Rhodes, P. (2024). Diverse paradigms and stories: Mapping 'mental illness' in athletes through meta-study. *International Review of Sport and Exercise Psychology, 17*(1), 343–369. https://doi.org/10.1080/1750984X.2021.2001840

Pike, E. C. J. (2018). Mental illness stigma. In M. Atkinson (Ed.), *Sport, Mental Illness, and Sociology* (pp. 9–22). Emerald Publishing Limited. https://doi.org/10.1108/S1476-285420180000011002

Piñeiro-Cossio, J., Fernández-Martínez, A., Nuviala, A., & Pérez-Ordás, R. (2021). Psychological well-being in physical education and school sports: A systematic review. *International Journal of Environmental Research and Public Health, 18*(3), 864. https://doi.org/10.3390/ijerph18030864

Ramalingam, B. (2023). *Upshift: Turning pressure into performance and crisis into creativity.* Flatiron Books.

Ramaeker, J., & Petrie, T. A. (2019). "Man up!": Exploring intersections of sport participation, masculinity, psychological distress, and help-seeking attitudes and intentions. *Psychology of Men & Masculinities, 20*(4), 515–523. https://doi.org/10.1037/men0000198

Ryan, E. P., & Oquendo, M. A. (2020). Suicide risk assessment and prevention: Challenges and opportunities. *Focus, 18*(2), 88–99. https://doi.org/10.1176/appi.focus.20200011

Reece, V. E. (2022). Understanding suicidal thought: A qualitative descriptive generic study. Northcentral University.

Rodelli, M., Bourdeaudhuij, I., Dumon, E., Portzky, G., & DeSmet, A. (2018). Which healthy lifestyle factors are associated with a lower risk of suicidal ideation among adolescents faced with cyberbullying? *Preventive Medicine, 113*, 32–40. https://doi.org/10.1016/j.ypmed.2018.05.002

Rowan, M., Sarafin, S. R., Willoughby, K., & McManama O'Brien, K. H. (2023). Mental health concerns in athletes. *Psychological considerations in the young athlete: A multidisciplinary approach* (pp. 21–58). Springer International Publishing.

Runacres, A., Mackintosh, K. A., & McNarry, M. A. (2021). Health consequences of an elite sporting career: Long-term detriment or long-term gain? A meta-analysis of 165,000 former athletes. *Sports Medicine, 51*, 289–301. https://doi.org/10.1007/s40279-020-01379-5

Schinke, R. J., Giffin, C., Cosh, S., Douglas, K., Rhind, D., Harwood, C., Si, G., & Papaiounnou, A. (2022). International society of sport psychology position stand: Mental health through occupational health and safety in high performance sport. *International Journal of Sport and Exercise Psychology, 20*(6), 1711–1733. https://doi.org/10.1080/1612197X.2021.1992857

Schinke, R. J., Stambulova, N. B., Si, G., & Moore, Z. (2018). International society of sport psychology position stand: Athletes' mental health, performance, and development. *International Journal of Sport and Exercise Psychology, 16*(6), 622–639. https://doi.org/10.1080/1612197X.2017.1295557

Sher, L., & Oquendo, M. A. (2023). Suicide: An overview for clinicians. *Medical Clinics, 107*(1), 119–130. https://doi.org/10.1016/j.mcna.2022.03.008

Smith, N. B. (2024). Emotional stoicism and affective masculinities in Chad Harbach's The Art of Fielding. *NORMA, 19*(2), 96–110. https://doi.org/10.1080/18902138.2024.2327737

Stack, S. (2021). Contributing factors to suicide: Political, social, cultural and economic. *Preventive Medicine, 152*, 106498. https://doi.org/10.1016/j.ypmed.2021.106498

Statuta, S. M. (Ed.). (2023). *Mental health considerations in the athlete, an issue of Clinics in Sports Medicine, E-Book* (Vol. 43, No. 1). Elsevier Health Sciences.

Souter, G., Lewis, R., & Serrant, L. (2018). Men, mental health and elite sport: A narrative review. *Sports Medicine—Open, 4*(1), 57. https://doi.org/10.1186/s40798-018-0175-7

Taliaferro, L., Eisenberg, M., Johnson, K., Nelson, T., & Neumark-Sztainer, D. (2011). Sport participation during adolescence and suicide ideation and attempts. *International Journal of Adolescent Medicine and Health, 23*(1), 3–10. https://doi.org/10.1515/ijamh.2011.002

Timpka, T., Dahlström, Ö., Fagher, K., Adami, P. E., Andersson, C., Jacobsson, J., Svedin, C. G., & Bermon, S. (2022). Vulnerability and stressors on the pathway to depression in a global cohort of young athletics (track and field) athletes. *Scientific Reports, 12*(1), 7901. https://doi.org/10.1038/s41598-022-12145-0

Walton, C. C., Purcell, R., Pilkington, V., Hall, K., Kenttä, G., Vella, S., & Rice, S. M. (2024). Psychological safety for mental health in elite sport: A theoretically informed model. *Sports Medicine, 54*(3), 557–564. https://doi.org/10.1007/s40279-023-01912-2

Wagner, U. (2018). Agency constraints and possibilities: Athletes maneuvering between the logics of community, market, profession and corporation in their quest for individual sponsorships. *International Review for the Sociology of Sport, 53*(2), 213–233. https://doi.org/10.1177/1012690216643953

# Chapter 15
# Suicidal Behavior in Marginalized Populations (Indigenous Peoples, Sexual and Gender Minorities, Refugee and Migrant Populations)

**Ching Sin Siau, Muhamad Nur Fariduddin, Norhayati Ibrahim, Pei Boon Ooi, and Caryn Mei Hsien Chan**

**Abstract** In this chapter we explore the intersection of marginalization and suicidal behaviors across three key groups: Indigenous Peoples, sexual and gender minorities, as well as refugee and migrant populations. It draws on various theoretical frameworks, such as Joiner's Interpersonal Theory of Suicide, the three-step theory of suicide, and minority stress models, to help explain the heightened vulnerability to suicidal ideation and behaviors that we see within marginalized populations. Focusing on Indigenous Peoples, in this chapter we address the historical, structural, and cultural factors that contribute to elevated suicide rates in this group, emphasizing the role of colonial legacies, limited access to healthcare, and ongoing discrimination. The chapter further investigates sexual and gender minority populations, whose experiences of minority stress, internalized stigma, and societal rejection exacerbate mental health challenges. This in turn leads to increased prevalence of suicidal ideation and suicide attempts. Lastly, the chapter examines refugee and migrant populations, highlighting how pre- and post-migration stressors, such as trauma, displacement, and exclusion from host societies, elevate suicide risk.

**Keywords** Suicide · Marginalized · Behaviors · Indigenous peoples · Sexual and gender minorities · Refugee and migrant populations

C. S. Siau · C. M. H. Chan
Centre for Community Health Studies, Faculty of Health Sciences, Universiti Kebangsaan Malaysia, Kuala Lumpur, Malaysia

M. N. Fariduddin (✉)
Faculty of Education, Universiti Teknologi MARA, Bandar Puncak Alam, Selangor, Malaysia
e-mail: fariduddin@uitm.edu.my

N. Ibrahim
Centre for Healthy Ageing and Wellness (H-CARE), Faculty of Health Sciences, Universiti Kebangsaan Malaysia, Kuala Lumpur, Malaysia

P. B. Ooi
School of Medical and Life Sciences, Sunway University, Petaling Jaya, Selangor, Malaysia



S. M. Y. Arafat and S. K. Kar (eds.), *Ecological and Social Determinants of Suicidal Behavior*, South Asian Perspectives in Mental Health and Psychology,
https://doi.org/10.1007/978-981-96-4028-7_15

## 1 Introduction: Conceptualizing Marginality and Suicidal Behaviors

Mano Yogalingam, 23, was a Tamil asylum seeker arriving in Australia from Sri Lanka in 2013. Ten years later, he had died by suicide. According to the Tamil Refugee Council, a contributing factor to his decision to end his life was due to living on a bridging visa. This meant Mr. Mano would have lived in a limbo of uncertainty over his future, despite contributing to the community and economy of the country (Immigration Policy, 2024). Mr. Mano is one among countless individuals whose mental health had suffered due to their status of being an individual in the marginalized community, and had chosen to end their lives by suicide.

Marginalization has been defined as "the process through which persons are peripheralized based on their identities, associations, experiences, and environment" (Hall et al., 1994, p. 25). Marginalization refers to a condition where an individual or group suffers from disparities and inequities due to social, economic, and political factors such as through inadequate education, employment, income, and access to social and health services (Havranek et al., 2015). These are collectively known as social determinants of health. The concern arises when these resources are inequitably distributed across subgroups within nationality, race, gender, socioeconomic status, sexual orientation, and other sociopolitical categories (Heidenreich et al., 2011), resulting in certain disadvantaged subgroups suffering from worse health outcomes and a higher burden of disease compared with other groups (Baah et al., 2019).

Being marginalized negatively impacts mental health and increases vulnerability to suicide and suicidal behaviors. A few theories have been employed to conceptualize the relationship between marginalization and suicidality, such as Joiner's *Interpersonal Theory of Suicide (IPTS)*, the three-step theory of suicide (3ST), the minority stress theory, and socioecological models of suicide (Joiner, 2005; Klonsky & May, 2015; Meyer et al., 2021; Shepherd et al., 2023; Van Orden et al., 2010). A core similarity in these theories is the interdependence between the individual's personal wellbeing and a meaningful presence and participation in the surrounding world. Concepts such as "belongingness" in the IPTS and "connectedness" in the 3ST are used to depict such relationships.

Based on the IPTS conceptualization, marginalized individuals may suffer from a sense of thwarted belongingness, in which they feel lonely and experience a lack of social support due to their marginalized identity, relationships, or environments. To compound the lack of belonging, marginalized individuals may further perceive that they are a burden to those around them and therefore were expendable to society, giving rise to suicidal ideation (Shepherd et al., 2023). In the 3ST conceptualization, an individual's sense of connectedness, which encompasses connections to one's life meaning and social environment including work and hobbies, may be protective against suicide desire (Klonsky & May, 2015). The lack of such connectedness, compounded by pain and hopelessness, may lead to serious suicidal ideation.

Moreover, marginalized individuals are often minority groups who may experience more minority stress from distal stressors such as violence, bullying, and prejudice from majority groups, and proximal stressors such as internalized stigma, and these are associated with higher levels or frequency of suicidal ideation and suicide attempts (Ferlatte et al., 2015; Meyer et al., 2021). From the socioecological viewpoint, marginality may be due to an individual's limited access to resources or discrimination from interpersonal, community, and larger sociopolitical environments and cultural milieu (Callo-Concha et al., 2014). Intersectionality, or having more than one marginalized identity, have been associated with worse mental health and suicidality outcomes (Forrest et al., 2023; Shepherd et al., 2023).

In this chapter, the relationship between marginalized status and suicidal behaviors will be further discussed in the following groups: (1) Indigenous Peoples; (2) sexual and gender minorities; and (3) refugee and migrant populations.

## 2 Indigenous Peoples

According to the United Nations, there is no one definition for Indigenous Peoples as Article 33 of the United Nations Declaration on the Rights of Indigenous Peoples (UNDRIP) defers the rights of deciding definitions of Indigenous identities to the Indigenous Peoples themselves (WHO, 2024a, 2024b). The World Bank characterizes Indigenous Peoples as distinct social and cultural groups that share collective ancestral ties to the lands and natural resources where they live, occupy, or from which they have been displaced (World Bank, 2024). The United Nations estimates that 6% of the global population comprises Indigenous People, and a majority are from Asia and the Pacific (WHO, 2024a, 2024b).

Indigenous Peoples have a shared colonial past, and continue to carry the burden of prejudice and discrimination from other groups (González et al., 2022). As a result of challenges in health resource accessibility, availability, acceptability, and quality through historical and structural marginalization (WHO, 2024a, 2024b), they continue to face challenges in mental health and high suicide rates. A meta-analysis on suicide and suicidal behaviors in ethnic minorities found that Indigenous Peoples have 2.8 higher suicide risk ratio, and a pooled suicide rate of 23.2 per 100,000 population; most of the studies reviewed were from high-income countries (Troya et al., 2022). Another review of suicide mortality in Indigenous Peoples globally found a wide range of suicide rates (Pollock et al., 2018). For example, suicide rate was 123 per 100,000 in the Philippines Palawan communities and 0.4 per 100,000 in Malaysia (Ali et al., 2014; Jollant et al., 2014). These differences could be due to cultural and historical differences between Indigenous groups, such as historical and current state-sanctioned discrimination and abuse (Pollock et al., 2018), and also methodological differences across studies. For example, Ali et al.'s (2014) study data were based on deaths certified by medical officers, which could yield a biased rate in Indigenous populations specifically given their health access barriers.

Suicide rates in certain Indigenous Peoples have increased exponentially (Pollock et al., 2018). These increases may be comparable to increases in non-Indigenous populations, such as in Australia, the US, and Brazil (excepting Indigenous Peoples from Amazonas and Mato Grosso do Sul states) (de Araujo et al., 2023; Nguyen et al., 2023). Among Inuit, the rates increased from 2.4 (year 1901–1930) (Bjerregard & Larsen, 2015) to a peak of 121 per 100,000 during 1985–1989 (Seidler et al., 2023). Among Aborigines and Torres Strait Islanders in Northern Territory, Australia, the suicide rates were 6.1 and 50.4 per 100,000 population in 1981 and 2002, respectively (Measey et al., 2006). In other peoples, especially in small populations, the suicide rates tended to fluctuate yearly (Pollock et al., 2018).

In terms of suicidal behaviors, a number of studies have found higher prevalence in ideation and attempt in youth compared to other age groups (Armstrong et al., 2019; Dickson et al., 2019). The prevalence among Aboriginal and Torres Strait Islander youth had been recorded to be between 9.1 and 46% (Dickson et al., 2019). A study found that Indigenous post-secondary students in Canada had higher odds of reporting self-harm, serious suicidal ideation, and suicide attempt compared to their non-Indigenous peers (Hop Wo et al., 2020). Data from the Australian Longitudinal Study on Male Health (Ten to Men) found that recent suicidal ideation and lifetime suicide attempt were 17.6% and 17.0%, respectively, in Indigenous Peoples, which is two and three times higher than their non-Indigenous counterparts (Armstrong et al., 2017). In an Indigenous sample in Panama, the prevalence of suicidal ideation was 22.9% (Walker et al., 2019).

Several demographic factors have been implicated as contributing to differing suicide rates and suicidal behaviors in Indigenous populations. Suicide in Indigenous People seemed to disproportionately affect the younger age group. Pollock et al.'s (2018) review reported that 89% of the studies recorded the age group of less than 30 years old to have the highest suicide rate. A review of suicidal behavior risk factors among American Indian and Alaska Native peoples, however, found mixed results, where some studies reported suicidal behaviors to be more prevalent in youth, while others found no significant differences (Fetter et al., 2023). With regard to sex, males had higher suicide rates, while females had higher suicide attempts and suicidal ideation in Indigenous Peoples generally (Pollock et al., 2018). A study comparing Indigenous and non-Indigenous off-reserve adults in Canada found that socioeconomic factors explained a large proportion in the variation in suicidal behaviors between these populations. Controlling for socioeconomic factors reduced disparities in lifetime suicidal ideation by 10.2% and suicide plan by 5.8% in the Indigenous group (Hajizadeh et al., 2021).

Minority stress-related factors, such as discrimination, was a significant factor in Aboriginal and Torres Strait Islander people's suicidal ideation. Discrimination accounted for approximately 15.3% of the relationship between their Indigenous status and suicidal thoughts (Haregu et al., 2022). Previous generation familial experience with Indian Residential School (IRS) system in Canadian Indigenous Peoples on-reserve was also associated with higher lifetime suicidal ideation and suicide attempt (McQuaid et al., 2017). In another study on Sámi in Norway, focus group discussions revealed themes of distal minority stress in the form of discrimination from the majority society, stigma about mental health problems within the Sámi culture, and systemic disparities created by unequal treatment in mental health care. Proximal minority stress was present in self-stigma from a need to be strong based on Sámi cultural norms, leading to reluctance to divulge mental health needs and suicidality (Stoor et al., 2019).

Interventions to prevent suicide and mitigate suicidal behaviors among Indigenous Peoples have been carried out mainly in the West, with emphasis on culturally guided, community-based interventions being designed and carried out (Harlow & Clough, 2014; Redvers et al., 2015). Examples of intervention strategies included educational and mental health literacy activities, gatekeeper training, and community-based prevention (Clifford et al., 2013; Stoor et al., 2021). Restriction of alcohol availability through prohibition laws were effective in reducing suicide rates and risks (Berman, 2014; Wood & Grunewald, 2006). A concern regarding most interventional studies were high risk of bias and a lack of methodological rigor in study design (Leske et al., 2020).

## 3 Sexual and Gender Minorities (SGM)

The World Health Organization (2024a, 2024b) recognizes the diversity of people in terms of sexual orientation, gender identity, expression, and sex characteristics (SOGIESC). People who identify as sexual and gender minority (SGM), or lesbian, gay, bisexual, transgender, intersex, or queer (LGBTIQ+), are marginalized and experience elevated suicide rates and suicidal behaviors. Marginalization of SGM individuals may originate from distal or proximal minority stress, such as victimization by others (Ibrahim et al., 2022) or internal stigma preoccupation (Elmer et al., 2022). This marginalization also leads to difficulties or hesitancy in accessing health care despite being more at-risk of being exposed to discriminatory and violent actions (WHO, 2024a, 2024b). The experience of minority stress has been linked to suicidal ideation and suicide attempt in this population (de Lange et al., 2022). Data from the National Violent Death Reporting System (NVDRS) in the US estimated that 24% of suicide deaths in 12- to 14-year-olds, and 8% of 25- to 29-year-olds were LGBT (Ream, 2019).

Suicidal thoughts, plans, and attempts were more prevalent among lesbian, gay, and bisexual adults across nearly all age and racial/ethnic groups compared to their heterosexual counterparts (Ramchand et al., 2022). In sexual minority adults, lifetime prevalence of suicide attempt was 11% and 20% in population- and community-based surveys, respectively (Hottes et al., 2016). Among SGM youth, suicide attempt was 3.5 times higher than non-SGM youth, with odds ratios of 5.87, 4.87, and 3.71 in transgender, bisexual, and homosexual youth, respectively (Di Giacomo et al., 2018). Compared with cisgender youth, gender minority youth had more than two times the odds of past-year suicidal ideation and suicide attempt (Jackman et al., 2021). Another study found that suicidal ideation was 28% and suicide attempt was 14.8% in gender non-confirming youths up to 25 years old (Surace et al., 2021). Between 2008 to 2018, past-30-day suicidal ideation increased significantly in all SGM subgroups, except for transgender and unsure/questioning university students (Kerr et al., 2024). Another study uncovered significant differences in suicide risk across SGM subgroups in college students. For example, pansexual students were 33% higher odds of endorsing more than two suicide risks (Horwitz et al., 2020).

Various factors have been identified as contributing to higher suicidal behaviors in the SGM population. Among Australian LGBT suicide decedents, psychological autopsy revealed a higher lack of acceptance from family members, poor self-acceptance due to internalized stigma, more negative feelings regarding one's own sexuality or gender, dissatisfaction with one's appearance, higher physical and sexual abuse experiences, higher physical aggression, and greater incidence of mental health disorders, compared to living controls (Skerrett et al., 2016).

With regard to suicidal ideation, a machine learning analysis revealed the top ten associated factors in Canadian LGBTQI2S+ individuals, as follows: seeking assistance from healthcare professionals for mental health or substance use concerns since the pandemic began, current self-assessed mental health condition, experiencing insults from parents or adults during childhood, having ever encountered messages that identifying as LGBTQI2S+ is abnormal, age in years, feelings of depression in the past week, a lifetime diagnosis of mental illness, a lifetime diagnosis of depressive disorder, feelings of sadness in the past week, and having ever feigned being straight or cisgender for acceptance (Kundu et al., 2022). Protective factors against suicidal ideation and behavior in SGM youth were alliances for gender and sexuality, curricula that are inclusive of LGBTQ+ topics, school policies that affirm LGBTQ+ identities, familial support, peer support, and mental health resources (Gorse, 2022). Suicidal ideation was higher among those who were more religious in a university sample in the US (Dyer, 2022).

Based on these findings, mitigation and intervention measures against the high prevalence of suicide and suicidal behaviors in the SGM population are important. A recent review revealed that most interventions for LGBTQ+ individuals rarely targeted suicidal ideation and behaviors, but had instead focused on mitigating minority stress and other correlates of suicidality (Chang et al., 2024). In another review, suicidal outcomes were different for sexual and gender minorities, pointing to different needs in these two populations. For example, public health initiatives, school programs, and psychosocial interventions were effective to mitigate suicidal behaviors in sexual and gender minorities (Melvin et al., 2024). More recently, digital health interventions (e.g., videos and mobile applications), mainly with the purpose of reducing suicidal thoughts and behaviors and increasing help-seeking in SGM have shown preliminary feasibility and effectiveness (Paudel et al., 2024).

## 4 Refugees and Migrant Populations

According to the WHO, there are currently about 281 million international migrants worldwide (WHO, 2024b). About 122.6 million people have experienced forcible displacement, which includes refugees (37.9 million), asylum seekers (8 million), and internally displaced persons (68.3 million), while 5.8 million are in need of international protection (The United Nations High Commissioner for Refugees [UNHCR],

2024). One million children are born into refugee status, while there are a total of 35 million children who suffered from forcible displacement (WHO, 2024b).

Refugees and migrant persons are marginalized people, as being removed from their land of origin may expose them to political, economic, and social exclusion, and this exclusion leaves them vulnerable to further exploitation and inequity. These people may also suffer from worse mental health conditions as the reasons for their refugee and migrant statuses are usually due to unavoidable and potentially traumatic circumstances, in economic hardship, insecurity, limited access to essential services, conflicts, environmental degradation, and natural disasters (Mesa-Vieira et al., 2022; WHO, 2024b). It is telling that 65% of all refugees originated from five countries characterized by war, conflicts, and economic hardship: Syrian Arab Republic, Venezuela, Ukraine, and Afghanistan (UNHCR, 2024).

Refugees and migrant persons suffer from higher rates or prevalence of suicide death and suicidal behaviors compared to those who are living in their host countries (Bevione et al., 2024; Forte et al., 2018), even though a Swedish study indicated being refugees and migrant persons have lower risk of suicide (Hollander et al., 2020). A meta-review of systematic reviews and meta-analyses estimated suicide rates, stratified according to country income category, to be 14.78, 16, and 290 per 100,000 refugees per year in high-income, upper middle-income, and low-income countries, respectively (Bevione et al., 2024). Suicidal behaviors were estimated to be 16% for suicidal ideation, 6% for attempted suicide, and 4% for suicide plan in a meta-analysis of 51 studies (Amiri, 2022). Based on Bevione et al.'s (2024) meta-review according to host country income, a much more varied prevalence of suicidal behaviors was obtained, with suicide attempt prevalence at 0.82% in high- and higher middle-income countries and 1.21% at low- and lower middle-income countries, and suicidal ideation prevalence at 7.5% (high-income countries), 23.8% (upper middle-income countries), 7.9% (lower middle-income countries), and 12.9% (low-income countries).

Refugees may have higher suicide rate and suicidal behavior levels due to a host of pre-migration and post-migration stressors (Keyes, 2000). For example, among Afghan refugees, depressive and posttraumatic symptomatology may have occurred due to witnessing atrocities, losing family members, and enduring stressful escape and transit experiences (Alemi et al., 2014). A study in Germany showed that 30% of refugees who have recently arrived at the host country had suicidal ideation, and suicidal ideation was associated with those of younger age, with experience of sexual violence, had spent a longer time in transit, and had posttraumatic stress and depressive symptoms (Nesterko et al., 2022). Among Eritrian refugees in Ethiopia in a refugee camp, those with exposure to trauma and having posttraumatic stress disorder had higher odds of having suicidal ideation and attempts (Gebremeskel et al., 2022a, 2022b). The current status of the refugee may also affect their suicidality. For example, refugees who are granted asylum have lower suicidality than their host country counterparts, while those who are living in camps had higher risks (Cogo et al., 2022).

While migrant workers may leave their countries more voluntarily than refugees, they can still experience stressors specific to their displaced status, leading to higher suicidal behaviors. For example, a study among Latino immigrants in Spain and the US found that immigration stressors, posttraumatic stress, trauma exposure, and depression were associated with higher odds of 30-day suicidal ideation (Fortuna et al., 2016). Migrants may also occupy a lower socioeconomic status, leading to higher probabilities of being discriminated against and exploited, heightening risk levels of suicide, such as was found in a study on Filipino home care workers in Israel (Ayalon, 2012). Another study on Bhutanese resettled refugees in Arizona, US found that isolation and increased burdensomeness were associated with employment-related stressors, the pressure of providing for their families, illiteracy, family conflicts, and separation from family members (Ellis et al., 2015). Suicidality may be more pronounced in first generation migrants, compared with second generation migrants, as was shown in a study in Germany, where first generation migrants reported higher suicidal ideation compared to non-migrants, whereas there was no significant difference in second generation migrants (Beutel et al., 2016). Interestingly, there are mixed findings on the level of acculturation and suicidality in refugee and migrant populations. In what is called the acculturation paradox, Latinx immigrants who were more acculturated faced a higher risk of suicide-related outcomes. However, this paradox did not apply for Asian immigrants, in which an opposite trend was observed (Lee et al., 2024).

Interventions to prevent suicidal behaviors in refugee and migrant populations are lacking. In a review, of the eight studies conducted, none of the studies were conclusively effective in reducing suicidality. However, most of the eight studies used multiple synergistic strategies, which were deemed to be most promising (Haroz et al., 2020). Apart from intervening directly with refugee and migrants, providing gatekeeper training for health providers in identifying and intervening with suicide risk is important (Ingram et al., 2022; Procter et al., 2021).

## 5 Limitations and Future Directions

Several limitations exist for studies regarding the marginalized and suicidal behaviors. First, most of the studies were conducted in high-income countries, leading to a dearth of information on those from lower and middle-income countries, where a majority of suicide deaths occurred. A second limitation is in the high risk of bias in intervention studies, and reliance on self-report data as an outcome measure, rather than objective data from other sources. Reliable data on suicide rate and suicidal behavior prevalence in these populations may be lacking, due to legal, political, socioeconomic barriers, and intersecting stigmatization against marginality and suicidal behaviors.

Future studies should continue to emphasize agenda setting to include the representation and voice of the marginalized, in co-designing fundamental and applied studies involving marginalized groups (Pratt, 2019). In addition, methodological rigor should be emphasized to reduce bias in studies, including high-quality and multilevel intervention studies to prevent suicidal behaviors in these populations and intersecting marginalized identities. Suicide surveillance systems that are sensitive to ensuring comprehensive data collection on suicide rates and trends in these populations should be devised. Legal, political, and socioeconomic barriers to health care utilization in these populations should be identified and mitigated.

## 6 Conclusions

Suicide and suicidal behaviors in marginalized populations are high, and are increasing in various subpopulations. Theories specific to suicide, such as the interpersonal theory of suicide and three-step theory of suicide, and wider socioecological theories and minority stress theory have been proposed to conceptualize risk and protective factors associated with suicidal behaviors in marginalized peoples. Interventions for suicide prevention are mostly conducted in high-income countries. There is a need to address suicide and suicidal behaviors in marginalized populations to ensure equitable health outcomes.

## References

Alemi, Q., James, S., Cruz, R., Zepeda, V., & Racadio, M. (2014). Psychological distress in Afghan refugees: A mixed-method systematic review. *Journal of Immigrant and Minority Health, 16*, 1247–1261. https://doi.org/10.1007/s10903-013-9861-1

Ali, N. H., Zainun, K. A., Bahar, N., Haniff, J., Hamid, A. M., Bujang, M. A. H., Mahmood, M. S., & NSRM Study Group. (2014). Pattern of suicides in 2009: Data from the National Suicide Registry Malaysia. *Asia-Pacific Psychiatry, 6*(2), 217–225. https://doi.org/10.1111/j.1758-5872.2012.00227.x

Amiri, S. (2022). Prevalence of suicide in immigrants/refugees: A systematic review and meta-analysis. *Archives of Suicide Research, 26*(2), 370–405. https://doi.org/10.1080/13811118.2020.1802379

Armstrong, G., Pirkis, J., Arabena, K., Currier, D., Spittal, M. J., & Jorm, A. F. (2017). Suicidal behaviour in Indigenous compared to non-Indigenous males in urban and regional Australia: Prevalence data suggest disparities increase across age groups. *Australian & New Zealand Journal of Psychiatry, 51*(12), 1240–1248. https://doi.org/10.1177/00048674177040

Ayalon, L. (2012). Suicidal and depressive symptoms in Filipino home care workers in Israel. *Journal of Cross-Cultural Gerontology, 27*, 51–63. https://doi.org/10.1007/s10823-011-9156-8

Baah, F. O., Teitelman, A. M., & Riegel, B. (2019). Marginalization: Conceptualizing patient vulnerabilities in the framework of social determinants of health—An integrative review. *Nursing Inquiry, 26*(1), e12268. https://doi.org/10.1111/nin.12268

Berman, M. (2014). Suicide among young Alaska Native men: Community risk factors and alcohol control. *American Journal of Public Health, 104*(S3), S329–S335. https://doi.org/10.2105/AJPH.2013.301503

Beutel, M. E., Jünger, C., Klein, E. M., Wild, P., Lackner, K. J., Blettner, M., Banerjee, M., Michal, M., Wiltink, J., & Brähler, E. (2016). Depression, anxiety and suicidal ideation among 1st and 2nd generation migrants-results from the Gutenberg health study. *BMC Psychiatry, 16*, 1–10. https://doi.org/10.1186/s12888-016-0995-2

Bevione, F., Panero, M., Abbate-Daga, G., Cossu, G., Carta, M. G., & Preti, A. (2024). Risk of suicide and suicidal behavior in refugees. A meta-review of current systematic reviews and meta-analyses. *Journal of Psychiatric Research.* https://doi.org/10.1016/j.jpsychires.2024.07.024

Bjerregaard, P., & Larsen, C. V. L. (2015). Time trend by region of suicides and suicidal thoughts among Greenland Inuit. *International Journal of Circumpolar Health, 74*(1), 26053. https://doi.org/10.3402/ijch.v74.26053

Callo-Concha, D., Sommer, J. H., Kleemann, J., Gatzweiler, F. W., & Denich, M. (2014). Marginality from a socio-ecological perspective. In *Marginality: Addressing the Nexus of poverty, exclusion and ecology* (pp. 57–65). https://doi.org/10.1007/978-94-007-7061-4_4

Chang, C. J., Livingston, N. A., Rashkovsky, K. T., Harper, K. L., Kuehn, K. S., Khalifian, C., Harned, M. S., Tucker, R. P., & Depp, C. A. (2024). A scoping review of suicide prevention interventions for lesbian, gay, bisexual, transgender, queer, and other sexual and gender minority individuals. *LGBT Health.* https://doi.org/10.1089/lgbt.2023.0262

Clifford, A. C., Doran, C. M., & Tsey, K. (2013). A systematic review of suicide prevention interventions targeting indigenous peoples in Australia, United States, Canada and New Zealand. *BMC Public Health, 13*, 1–11. https://doi.org/10.1186/1471-2458-13-463

Cogo, E., Murray, M., Villanueva, G., Hamel, C., Garner, P., Senior, S. L., & Henschke, N. (2022). Suicide rates and suicidal behaviour in displaced people: A systematic review. *PLoS ONE, 17*(3), e0263797. https://doi.org/10.1371/journal.pone.0263797

de Araujo, J. A. P., Fialho, É., Alves, F. J. O., Cardoso, A. M., Orellana, J. D. Y., Naslund, J. A., Barreto, M. L., Patel, V., & Machado, D. B. (2023). Suicide among Indigenous peoples in Brazil from 2000 to 2020: A descriptive study. *The Lancet Regional Health–Americas, 26*. https://doi.org/10.1016/j.lana.2023.100591

de Lange, J., Baams, L., van Bergen, D. D., Bos, H. M., & Bosker, R. J. (2022). Minority stress and suicidal ideation and suicide attempts among LGBT adolescents and young adults: A meta-analysis. *LGBT Health, 9*(4), 222–237. https://doi.org/10.1089/lgbt.2021.0106

Di Giacomo, E., Krausz, M., Colmegna, F., Aspesi, F., & Clerici, M. (2018). Estimating the risk of attempted suicide among sexual minority youths: a systematic review and meta-analysis. *JAMA Pediatrics, 172*(12), 1145–1152. https://doi.org/10.1001/jamapediatrics.2018.2731

Dickson, J. M., Cruise, K., McCall, C. A., & Taylor, P. J. (2019). A systematic review of the antecedents and prevalence of suicide, self-harm and suicide ideation in Australian Aboriginal and Torres Strait Islander youth. *International Journal of Environmental Research and Public Health, 16*(17), 3154. https://doi.org/10.3390/ijerph16173154

Dyer, W. J. (2022). Refining research on the intersection between sexual orientation, suicide, and religiosity. *Psychology of Religion and Spirituality, 14*(2), 179. https://doi.org/10.1037/rel0000451

Ellis, B. H., Lankau, E. W., Ao, T., Benson, M. A., Miller, A. B., Shetty, S., Lopes Cardozo, B., Geltman, P. L., & Cochran, J. (2015). Understanding Bhutanese refugee suicide through the interpersonal-psychological theory of suicidal behavior. *American Journal of Orthopsychiatry, 85*(1), 43–55. https://doi.org/10.1037/ort0000028

Elmer, E. M., van Tilburg, T., & Fokkema, T. (2022). Minority stress and loneliness in a global sample of sexual minority adults: The roles of social anxiety, social inhibition, and community involvement. *Archives of Sexual Behavior, 51*(4), 2269–2298. https://doi.org/10.1007/s10508-021-02132-3

Ferlatte, O., Dulai, J., Hottes, T. S., Trussler, T., & Marchand, R. (2015). Suicide related ideation and behavior among Canadian gay and bisexual men: A syndemic analysis. *BMC Public Health, 15*, 1–9. https://doi.org/10.1186/s12889-015-1961-5

Fetter, A. K., Wiglesworth, A., Rey, L. F., Azarani, M., Chicken, M. L. P., Young, A. R., Riegelman, A., & Gone, J. P. (2023). Risk factors for suicidal behaviors in American Indian and Alaska Native peoples: A systematic review. *Clinical Psychological Science, 11*(3), 528–551. https://doi.org/10.1177/21677026221126732

Forrest, L. N., Beccia, A. L., Exten, C., Gehman, S., & Ansell, E. B. (2023). Intersectional prevalence of suicide ideation, plan, and attempt based on gender, sexual orientation, race and ethnicity, and rurality. *JAMA Psychiatry, 80*(10), 1037–1046. https://doi.org/10.1001/jamapsychiatry.2023.2295

Forte, A., Trobia, F., Gualtieri, F., Lamis, D. A., Cardamone, G., Giallonardo, V., Fiorillo, A., Girardi, P., & Pompili, M. (2018). Suicide risk among immigrants and ethnic minorities: a literature overview. *International Journal of Environmental Research and Public Health, 15*(7), 1438. https://doi.org/10.3390/ijerph15071438

Fortuna, L. R., Alvarez, K., Ortiz, Z. R., Wang, Y., Alegría, X. M., Cook, B. L., & Alegria, M. (2016). Mental health, migration stressors and suicidal ideation among Latino immigrants in Spain and the United States. *European Psychiatry, 36*, 15–22. https://doi.org/10.1016/j.eurpsy.2016.03.001

Gebremeskel, T. G., Berhe, M., & Tesfa Berhe, E. (2022). Suicide attempts among adult Eritrean refugees in Tigray, Ethiopia: prevalence and associated factors. *Risk Management and Healthcare Policy*, 133–140. https://doi.org/10.2147/RMHP.S311335

Gebremeskel, T. G., Berhe, M., Tesfahunegn, T. B., Gesesew, H. A., & Ward, P. R. (2022). Prevalence and factors associated with suicidal ideation among adult Eritrean refugees in Northern Ethiopia. *Frontiers in Public Health, 10*, 841848. https://doi.org/10.3389/fpubh.2022.841848

González, R., Carvacho, H., & Jiménez-Moya, G. (2022). Psychology and indigenous people. *Annual Review of Psychology, 73*(1), 431–459. https://doi.org/10.1146/annurev-psych-012921-045304

Gorse, M. (2022). Risk and protective factors to LGBTQ+ youth suicide: A review of the literature. *Child and Adolescent Social Work Journal, 39*(1), 17–28. https://doi.org/10.1007/s10560-020-00710-3

Hall, J. M., Stevens, P. E., & Meleis, A. I. (1994). Marginalization: A guiding concept for valuing diversity in nursing knowledge development. *Advances in Nursing Science, 16*(4), 23–41. https://doi.org/10.1097/00012272-199406000-00005

Hajizadeh, M., Hu, M., Asada, Y., & Bombay, A. (2021). Explaining the gaps in psychological distress and suicidal behaviours between non-Indigenous and Indigenous adults living off-reserve in Canada: A cross-sectional study. *Canadian Medical Association Open Access Journal, 9*(1), E215–E223. https://doi.org/10.9778/cmajo.20200177

Haregu, T., Jorm, A. F., Paradies, Y., Leckning, B., Young, J. T., & Armstrong, G. (2022). Discrimination experienced by Aboriginal and Torres Strait Islander males in Australia: Associations with suicidal thoughts and depressive symptoms. *Australian & New Zealand Journal of Psychiatry, 56*(6), 657–666. https://doi.org/10.1177/00048674211031168

Harlow, A. F., & Clough, A. (2014). A systematic review of evaluated suicide prevention programs targeting indigenous youth. *Crisis, 35*(5), 310–321. https://doi.org/10.1027/0227-5910/a000265

Haroz, E. E., Decker, E., Lee, C., Bolton, P., Spiegel, P., & Ventevogel, P. (2020). Evidence for suicide prevention strategies with populations in displacement: A systematic review. *Intervention Journal of Mental Health and Psychosocial Support in Conflict Affected Areas, 18*(1), 37–44. https://doi.org/10.4103/INTV.INTV_10_19

Havranek, E. P., Mujahid, M. S., Barr, D. A., Blair, I. V., Cohen, M. S., Cruz-Flores, S., Davey-Smith, G., Dennison-Himmelfarb, C. R., Lauer, M. S., Lockwood, D. W., & Prevention, C. E. (2015). Social determinants of risk and outcomes for cardiovascular disease: A scientific statement from the American heart association. *Circulation, 132*(9), 873–898. https://doi.org/10.1161/CIR.0000000000000228

Heidenreich, P., Trogdon, J., & Khavjou, M. (2011). AHA policy statement: Forecasting the future of cardiovasular disease in the United States. *Circulation, 123*, 933–944. https://doi.org/10.1161/CIR.0b013e31820a55f5

Hollander, A. C., Pitman, A., Sjöqvist, H., Lewis, G., Magnusson, C., Kirkbride, J. B., & Dalman, C. (2020). Suicide risk among refugees compared with non-refugee migrants and the Swedish-born majority population. *The British Journal of Psychiatry, 217*(6), 686–692. https://doi.org/10.1192/bjp.2019.220

Hop Wo, N. K., Anderson, K. K., Wylie, L., & MacDougall, A. (2020). The prevalence of distress, depression, anxiety, and substance use issues among Indigenous post-secondary students in Canada. *Transcultural Psychiatry, 57*(2), 263–274. https://doi.org/10.1177/1363461519861824

Horwitz, A. G., Berona, J., Busby, D. R., Eisenberg, D., Zheng, K., Pistorello, J., Albucher, R., Coryell, W., Favorite, T., Walloch, J. C., & King, C. A. (2020). Variation in suicide risk among subgroups of sexual and gender minority college students. *Suicide and Life-Threatening Behavior, 50*(5), 1041–1053. https://doi.org/10.1111/sltb.12637

Hottes, T. S., Bogaert, L., Rhodes, A. E., Brennan, D. J., & Gesink, D. (2016). Lifetime prevalence of suicide attempts among sexual minority adults by study sampling strategies: A systematic review and meta-analysis. *American Journal of Public Health, 106*(5), e1–e12. https://doi.org/10.2105/AJPH.2016.303088

Ibrahim, N., Aen, M., Amit, N., Said, Z., & Siau, C. S. (2022). Victimisation, depression and suicidal ideation among lesbian, gay and bisexual adults in Malaysia. The *Malaysian Journal of Medical Sciences: MJMS, 29*(4), 120. https://doi.org/10.21315/mjms2022.29.4.11

Immigration Policy. (2024, August 28). Grief and shock in Melbourne after Tamil asylum seeker dies by self-immolation. *Australia Broadcasting Corporation.* Retrieved from https://www.abc.net.au/news/2024-08-28/tamil-asylum-seeker-self-immolates-melbourne-protest/104281638

Ingram, J., Lyford, B., McAtamney, A., & Fitzpatrick, S. (2022). Preventing suicide in refugees and asylum seekers: A rapid literature review examining the role of suicide prevention training for health and support staff. *International Journal of Mental Health Systems, 16*(1), 24. https://doi.org/10.1186/s13033-022-00534-x

Jackman, K. B., Caceres, B. A., Kreuze, E. J., & Bockting, W. O. (2021). Suicidality among gender minority youth: Analysis of 2017 Youth Risk Behavior Survey data. *Archives of Suicide Research, 25*(2), 208–223. https://doi.org/10.1080/13811118.2019.1678539

Jollant, F., Malafosse, A., Docto, R., & Macdonald, C. (2014). A pocket of very high suicide rates in a non-violent, egalitarian and cooperative population of South-East Asia. *Psychological Medicine, 44*(11), 2323–2329. https://doi.org/10.1017/S0033291713003176

Kerr, D. C., Bae, H., & Dermody, S. S. (2024). Trends and disparities in suicidal thoughts and behaviors and mental health symptoms among sexual and gender minority college students in the US, 2008–2018. *Psychology of Sexual Orientation and Gender Diversity, 11*(2), 305. https://doi.org/10.1037/sgd0000599

Keyes, E. F. (2000). Mental health status in refugees: An integrative review of current research. *Issues in Mental Health Nursing, 21*(4), 397–410. https://doi.org/10.1080/016128400248013

Klonsky, E. D., & May, A. M. (2015). The three-step theory (3ST): A new theory of suicide rooted in the "ideation-to-action" framework. *International Journal of Cognitive Therapy, 8*(2), 114–129. https://doi.org/10.1521/ijct.2015.8.2.114

Kundu, A., Fu, R., Grace, D., Logie, C., Abramovich, A., Baskerville, B., Yager, C., Schwartz, R., Mitsakakis, N., Planinac, L., & Chaiton, M. (2022). Correlates of past year suicidal thoughts among sexual and gender minority young adults: A machine learning analysis. *Journal of Psychiatric Research, 152*, 269–277. https://doi.org/10.1016/j.jpsychires.2022.06.013

Lee, C. S., Sirin, S. R., Choi, E., & Sin, E. J. (2024). Meta-Analysis of acculturation and suicide-related outcomes: A test of the immigrant paradox. *Journal of Racial and Ethnic Health Disparities, 11*(2), 913–927. https://doi.org/10.1007/s40615-023-01572-y

Leske, S., Paul, E., Gibson, M., Little, B., Wenitong, M., & Kolves, K. (2020). Global systematic review of the effects of suicide prevention interventions in Indigenous peoples. *Journal of Epidemiology and Community Health, 74*(12), 1050–1055. https://doi.org/10.1136/jech-2019-212368

McQuaid, R. J., Bombay, A., McInnis, O. A., Humeny, C., Matheson, K., & Anisman, H. (2017). Suicide ideation and attempts among First Nations peoples living on-reserve in Canada: The intergenerational and cumulative effects of Indian residential schools. *The Canadian Journal of Psychiatry, 62*(6), 422–430. https://doi.org/10.1177/07067437177020

Measey, M. A. L., Li, S. Q., Parker, R., & Wang, Z. (2006). Suicide in the Northern Territory, 1981–2002. *Medical Journal of Australia, 185*(6), 315–319. https://doi.org/10.5694/j.1326-5377.2006.tb00585.x

Melvin, G. A., Tatnell, R., Bush, R., Pepping, C. A., Clancy, E. M., Zanetti, N., James, L., & Staiger, P. K. (2024). A scoping review of suicide prevention initiatives for sexual and gender minority people. *Psychology of Sexual Orientation and Gender Diversity.* https://doi.org/10.1037/sgd0000721

Mesa-Vieira, C., Haas, A. D., Buitrago-Garcia, D., Roa-Diaz, Z. M., Minder, B., Gamba, M., Salvador, D., Gomez, D., Lewis, M., Gonzalez-Jaramillo, W. C., Pahud de Mortanges, A., Buttia, C., Muka, T., Trujillo, N., & Franco, O. H. (2022). Mental health of migrants with pre-migration exposure to armed conflict: A systematic review and meta-analysis. *Lancet Public Health, 7*, e469–e481. https://doi.org/10.1016/S2468-2667(22)00061-5

Meyer, I. H., Russell, S. T., Hammack, P. L., Frost, D. M., & Wilson, B. (2021). Minority stress, distress, and suicide attempts in three cohorts of sexual minority adults: A U.S. probability sample. *PLoS One, 16*(3), 0246827. https://doi.org/10.1371/journal.pone.0246827

Nesterko, Y., Haase, E., Schönfelder, A., & Glaesmer, H. (2022). Suicidal ideation among recently arrived refugees in Germany. *BMC Psychiatry, 22*(1), 183. https://doi.org/10.1186/s12888-022-03844-z

Nguyen, T., Ullah, S., Looi, J. C., Allison, S., Mulder, R., & Bastiampillai, T. (2023). Indigenous suicide rates in the United States, Australia and New Zealand between 2006 and 2019. *Australian & New Zealand Journal of Psychiatry, 57*(10), 1324–1330. https://doi.org/10.1177/00048674231167327

Paudel, K., Gautam, K., Bhandari, P., Shah, S., Wickersham, J. A., Acharya, B., Sapkota, S., Adhikari, S. K., Baral, P.P., Shrestha, A., & Shrestha, R. (2024). Digital health interventions for suicide prevention among LGBTQ: A narrative review. *Health Prospect: Journal of Public Health, 23*(1), 1–10.https://doi.org/10.3126/hprospect.v23i1.62795

Pollock, N. J., Naicker, K., Loro, A., Mulay, S., & Colman, I. (2018). Global incidence of suicide among Indigenous peoples: A systematic review. *BMC Medicine, 16*, 1–17. https://doi.org/10.1186/s12916-018-1115-6

Pratt, B. (2019). Inclusion of marginalized groups and communities in global health research priority-setting. *Journal of Empirical Research on Human Research Ethics, 14*(2), 169–181. https://doi.org/10.1177/1556264619833858

Procter, N., Posselt, M., Ferguson, M., McIntyre, H., Kenny, M. A., Curtis, R., Loughhead, M., Clement, N., & Mau, V. (2021). An evaluation of suicide prevention education for people working with refugees and asylum seekers. *Crisis.* https://doi.org/10.1027/0227-5910/a000777

Ramchand, R., Schuler, M. S., Schoenbaum, M., Colpe, L., & Ayer, L. (2022). Suicidality among sexual minority adults: Gender, age, and race/ethnicity differences. *American Journal of Preventive Medicine, 62*(2), 193–202. https://doi.org/10.1016/j.amepre.2021.07.012

Ream, G. L. (2019). What's unique about lesbian, gay, bisexual, and transgender (LGBT) youth and young adult suicides? Findings from the National Violent Death Reporting System. *Journal of Adolescent Health, 64*(5), 602–607. https://doi.org/10.1016/j.jadohealth.2018.10.303

Redvers, J., Bjerregaard, P., Eriksen, H., Fanian, S., Healey, G., Hiratsuka, V., Jong, M., Larsen, C. V. L., Linton, J., Pollock, N., Silviken, A., & Chatwood, S. (2015). A scoping review of Indigenous suicide prevention in circumpolar regions. *International Journal of Circumpolar Health, 74*(1), 27509. https://doi.org/10.3402/ijch.v74.27509

Seidler, I. K., Tolstrup, J. S., Bjerregaard, P., et al. (2023). Time trends and geographical patterns in suicide among Greenland Inuit. *BMC Psychiatry, 23*, 187. https://doi.org/10.1186/s12888-023-04675-2

Shepherd, B. F., Kelly, L. M., Brochu, P. M., Wolff, J. C., & Swenson, L. P. (2023). An examination of theory-based suicidal ideation risk factors in college students with multiple marginalized identities. *American Journal of Orthopsychiatry, 93*(2), 107. https://doi.org/10.1037/ort0000666

Skerrett, D. M., Kõlves, K., & De Leo, D. (2016). Factors related to suicide in LGBT populations. *Crisis, 37*(5), 361–369. https://doi.org/10.1027/0227-5910/a000423

Stoor, J. P. A., Berntsen, G., Hjelmeland, H., & Silviken, A. (2019). "If you do not birget [manage] then you don't belong here": A qualitative focus group study on the cultural meanings of suicide among Indigenous Sámi in arctic Norway. *International Journal of Circumpolar Health, 78*(1), 1565861. https://doi.org/10.1080/22423982.2019.1565861

Stoor, J. P. A., Eriksen, H. A., & Silviken, A. C. (2021). Mapping suicide prevention initiatives targeting Indigenous Sámi in Nordic countries. *BMC Public Health, 21*, 1–11. https://doi.org/10.1186/s12889-021-12111-x

Surace, T., Fusar-Poli, L., Vozza, L., Cavone, V., Arcidiacono, C., Mammano, R., Basile, L., Rodolico, A., Bisicchia, P., Caponnetto, P., & Aguglia, E. (2021). Lifetime prevalence of suicidal ideation and suicidal behaviors in gender non-conforming youths: A meta-analysis. *European Child & Adolescent Psychiatry, 30*, 1147–1161. https://doi.org/10.1007/s00787-020-01508-5

Troya, M. I., Spittal, M. J., Pendrous, R., Crowley, G., Gorton, H. C., Russell, K., Byrne, S., Musgrove, R., Hannah-Swain, S., Kapur, N., & Knipe, D. (2022). Suicide rates amongst individuals from ethnic minority backgrounds: A systematic review and meta-analysis. *EClinicalMedicine, 47*. https://doi.org/10.1016/j.eclinm.2022.101399

UNHCR. (2024). Refugee Data Finder. Retrieved from https://www.unhcr.org/refugee-statistics

Van Orden, K. A., Witte, T. K., Cukrowicz, K. C., Braithwaite, S. R., Selby, E. A., & Joiner, T. E., Jr. (2010). The interpersonal theory of suicide. *Psychological Review, 117*(2), 575. https://doi.org/10.1037/a0018697

Walker, R. J., Campbell, J. A., Dawson, A. Z., & Egede, L. E. (2019). Prevalence of psychological distress, depression and suicidal ideation in an indigenous population in Panamá. *Social Psychiatry and Psychiatric Epidemiology, 54*, 1199–1207. https://doi.org/10.1007/s00127-019-01719-5

Wood, D. S., & Gruenewald, P. J. (2006). Local alcohol prohibition, police presence and serious injury in isolated Alaska Native villages. *Addiction, 101*(3), 393–403. https://doi.org/10.1111/j.1360-0443.2006.01347.x

WHO. (2024a). Improving LGBTQI health and well-being with consideration for SOGIESC. Retrieved from https://www.who.int/activities/improving-lgbtqi-health-and-well--being-with-consideration-for-sogiesc

WHO. (2024b). Frequently asked questions on the health and rights of Indigenous Peoples. Retrieved from https://www.who.int/initiatives/global-plan-of-action-for-health-of-indigenous-peoples/frequently-asked-questions-on-the-health-and-rights-of-indigenous-peoples

# Chapter 16
# Suicidal Behavior Among Prisoners

**Pawan Sharma, Swarndeep Singh, and Arghya Pal**

**Abstract** Suicide is a major public health concern and a global phenomenon among all groups of people. There is a higher prevalence of suicidal ideations, suicide attempts, and deaths by suicide among incarcerated individuals as compared to the general population. This contributes to a major burden of morbidity and mortality among the prisoners worldwide. It is seen that the interplay between the pre-existing vulnerabilities, exacerbated by prison-specific stressors, which may culminate in the risk of suicide becoming action (i.e., the transition from ideations to suicidal attempt) in this already vulnerable population. This problem is compounded by a lack of resources especially in low- and middle-income countries. The management and prevention of suicide among prisoners through the implementation of targeted interventions aimed at high-risk prisoners in combination with universal strategies that help promote the mental health and well-being of all the people in prisons are urgently needed. There is also a need for policy development at the global level that can be implemented in all prisons worldwide to guide governments and various stakeholders in achieving this. In this chapter, we discuss the epidemiology, risk factors, theoretical models, and special considerations to keep in mind while planning management and prevention strategies for suicide among prisoners.

**Keywords** Suicide · Self-harm · Prison-specific stressors · Mental health · Suicide prevention

---

P. Sharma (✉)
Department of Psychiatry, Patan Academy of Health Sciences, School of Medicine, Lalitpur, Nepal
e-mail: pawansharma@pahs.edu.np

S. Singh
Department of Psychiatry, Vardhman Mahavir Medical College (VMMC) & Safdarjung Hospital, New Delhi, India

A. Pal
Department of Psychiatry, All India Institute of Medical Sciences, Kalyani, West Bengal, India

 
S. M. Y. Arafat and S. K. Kar (eds.), *Ecological and Social Determinants of Suicidal Behavior*, South Asian Perspectives in Mental Health and Psychology,
https://doi.org/10.1007/978-981-96-4028-7_16

## 1 Introduction

Suicide is a major public health concern and occurs throughout the lifespan. Globally, it has been estimated by the World Health Organization that more than 7 lakh people die by suicide every year (or one in every 100 deaths was by suicide), and suicide was the third leading cause of death among 15–29-year-olds globally in 2021 (WHO, 2024). Though suicide and self-harm are intensely individual experiences but are also affected by societal factors (Knipe et al., 2022). Different population groups have varied risks of suicide. The risk is higher among the most vulnerable and disadvantaged members of society like people suffering from mental health disorders and criminal offenders in prison (Fazel & Runeson, 2020). The rate of suicide among prisoners is higher than the general population and is regarded as an international public health challenge (Fazel et al., 2017). A study done in 24 high-income countries between 2013 and 2017 showed that the rates of suicide among male prisoners were 3–8 times higher than the general population, whereas the rate of suicide among female prisoners was more than 10 times higher (Fazel et al., 2017). There have been reports of suicide among prisoners in the Southeast Asian region, however, there is a paucity of literature on this regard (Arafat et al., 2024). Suicide and suicidal behavior among the prison population warrants immediate concern, and its prevention should be regarded as an international priority. In this chapter, we aim to discuss the epidemiology, risk factors, different theoretical models, and management as well as prevention of suicide among the prison population.

## 2 Epidemiology

An ecological study conducted in 12 countries with 861 deaths (810 male), showed that the crude relative rates of suicide were at least three times higher than the general population (Fazel et al., 2011). Another study on 3906 prison suicides reported in 24 countries between 2011 and 2014 showed that the rates of suicide in prison varied from 23 per 100,000 prisoners in the USA, to 180 per 100,000 prisoners in Norway. This rate was well above that reported in the general population. However, the rates were not significantly different in male and female prisoners (Fazel et al., 2017). A registry-based study from Norway showed that suicide was the leading cause (53%) of death in prison. Most number of suicides were by men (93.5%), and most common modalities were hanging strangulation, and suffocation (Bukten & Stavseth, 2021). A study from New Zealand among 1212 adults (1093 men) incarcerated across 13 prisons showed that one-third (34.6%) of participants had a lifetime history of suicidal ideation. Among them, 55.6% attempted suicide (i.e., 19.2% of all prisoners) at some point (Favril et al., 2020a). The National Crime Records Bureau report of India states that rates of suicide in Indian prisons have doubled over 20 years, from 12·12 per 100,000 people (2001) to 24·23 per 100,000 people (2019); and this was 2.3 times higher than the general population rate as of the year 2019 (Gowda et al., 2021).

A systematic review and meta-analysis of 20 studies from 20 countries comprising 19,882 individuals (6.5% women) showed a pooled prevalence of suicide attempts during incarceration to be 8.6% in men and 12.2% in women (Favril et al., 2022). A national clinical survey of 2-year sample of self-inflicted deaths in prisoners from the UK showed that among 72 deaths: 85 (49%) were of prisoners on remand; 55 (32%) occurred within 7 days of reception into prison. The commonest method was hanging or self-strangulation (92%) (Shaw et al., 2004). A rapid review of 35 studies in low- and middle-income countries showed the prevalence of suicidal ideation ranging from 2.3% to 14.9% among prisoners, which was higher compared to the general population in those regions. However, this prevalence was lower as compared to high-income countries. Female prisoners had a higher prevalence than male prisoners (Hill et al., 2022). The prevalence of suicide behavior among the prisoners of South East Asia varies widely and most of the countries do not have exact statistics. It is a suicide-dense area with 29% of total suicides of world i.e., higher than the global rate and higher than Western countries; we can assume same is true for the prison population (Arafat et al., 2024).

## 3 Risk Factors

Suicidal behavior among people in prisons is likely to be an outcome of the complex interplay between pre-existing individual vulnerabilities and prison-specific factors following the individual's incarceration or prison confinement. The available research has suggested that several different factors related to these two broad themes or constructs, either exclusively or in combination with each other, are likely to be responsible for causing suicidal ideation, attempted suicides, and suicidal deaths in the prison population. A systematic review and meta-analysis analyzed 77 studies from 27 countries (total of 35,351 suicides) to identify key risk factors for suicide among people in prisons (Zhong et al., 2021). Among individual-specific risk factors, the most significant ones included current suicidal ideation during imprisonment, a history of suicide attempts, and a current psychiatric diagnosis. Prison-specific risk factors included being in a single cell, lack of social visits, remand status, serving life sentences, and conviction for violent offenses, especially homicide. Also, a recent systematic review assessed 36 risk factors for suicide attempts among prisoners and reported suicidal ideation, a history of self-harm, and markers of psychiatric disorders as the most significant ones. Furthermore, prison-environment-related factors such as being subjected to solitary confinement, experiences of victimization, and inadequate social support while in prison were significantly associated with increased suicide attempts (Favril et al., 2022).

## 3.1 Pre-Existing Vulnerabilities

At the time of arrival in prison, individuals are more likely to have a positive past or present history of mental health issues. Research suggests even the new prisoners have reported a significantly higher prevalence of a history of mental illnesses, substance use disorders, traumatic life events, and prior suicidal ideations or behaviors as compared to the general population. A recent meta-analysis estimated the one-year pooled prevalence rates of different psychiatric disorders in prisoners across 13 low- and middle-income countries: psychosis—6.2%; major depression—16.0%; alcohol use disorders—3.8%, and drug use disorders—5.1% (Baranyi et al., 2019). Furthermore, another recent umbrella review confirmed significantly higher rates of psychiatric morbidity among prisoners compared to the general population (Favril et al., 2024). These conditions are strong risk factors for suicide due to the increased likelihood of these prisoners experiencing hopelessness, impulsivity, and impaired reality testing or judgment.

Research conducted across different countries and institutional settings has consistently shown that prisoners with psychiatric disorders, such as depression, bipolar disorder, schizophrenia, and personality disorders, especially borderline and antisocial personality disorders, are at a significantly higher risk of suicide (Fazel et al., 2016). Moreover, prisoners with concurrent substance use disorder and mental illness (also known as dual diagnosis) constitute a particularly more vulnerable group, having a significantly higher risk of engaging in impulsive and self-destructive behaviors including suicide attempts. Finally, a history of trauma, including childhood maltreatment or abuse and exposure to interpersonal violence, is another critical pre-existing vulnerability factor that puts the prisoner at a markedly increased risk of engaging in self-injurious behaviors including suicide attempts (Angelakis et al., 2020). Thus, there is a need to conduct a systematic risk assessment of all prisoners upon arrival to screen for pre-existing vulnerabilities or individual-level risk factors for suicidal behaviors.

## 3.2 Prison Stressors

The prison settings introduce an individual to several unique stressors, which can exacerbate pre-existing vulnerabilities or even precipitate suicidal behaviors in prisoners who may never have suffered from any prior mental health issues. Thus, the initial time period immediately following the incarceration of an individual in prison has been described as a "critical period" in the available literature due to newly admitted prisoners being at exceptionally high risk for suicidal behaviors (Pratt et al., 2006). This could be because of several reasons, such as the shock of being imprisoned, fear due to uncertainty about life in prison, and extreme adjustment issues in acclimatizing to the prison environment. According to available literature

(Humber et al., 2011), several prison-environment-related factors have been associated with an increased risk of suicide. These include overcrowding, lack of privacy, bullying by fellow inmates, solitary confinement, loss of individual freedoms (e.g., restricted mobility, sleep or meal timings, etc.), and fear of physical or sexual assault. Most noticeably, solitary confinement has been reported to produce grave negative psychological effects on an individual, and can even precipitate a "suicide crisis" in a significant proportion of prisoners. Research suggests that prisoners subjected to solitary confinement were at about seven times higher risk of attempting suicide as compared to the general prison population (Haney, 2018). Lastly, inadequate or poor access to mental health care and support services in prisons often leads to under- and inadequate treatment of mental health conditions among prisoners and an increased risk of suicidal behaviors. Most prisons worldwide lack sufficient resources to provide comprehensive mental health care services, hence relying more on punishment-oriented approaches (i.e., custodial care) rather than evidence-based therapeutic approaches (i.e., medical care). This problem is likely even more acute in resource-poor settings across several low- and middle-income countries.

### *3.3 Combined Stressors*

The risk of suicide could possibly increase manifolds as a result of the complex interaction between the individuals' pre-existing vulnerabilities and newly introduced environment-related stressors among people in prisons. For example, a prisoner having a pre-existing history of childhood sexual abuse, when exposed to various kinds of prison stressors such as solitary confinement, bullying, or institutional neglect, is likely to experience a compounded effect. This increases the likelihood of overwhelming his or her ability to effectively cope with them. This has been described as "double jeopardy" since pre-imprisonment psychological vulnerabilities of an individual interact with the harsh prison life environment to create a marked degree of distress and puts him/ her at an increased risk of suicide (Rabe, 2012). This combined effect is even more pronounced in prisoners with severe mental illnesses who are subjected to extreme prison stressors such as rigorous imprisonment or isolation. Research has suggested that prisoners with mental health disorders including substance use (Kaba et al., 2014), when subjected to solitary confinement, have a significantly higher risk of doing suicide. Increased feelings of hopelessness, helplessness, and entrapment in them could explain this elevated suicide risk. Most of these prison stressors are cumulative, which gradually results in overwhelming the incarcerated individuals' ability to cope with them over a period of time, pushing some prisoners towards suicidal acts as a way of escaping from their unbearable reality.

### 3.4 *Factors Predisposing Ideations to Action*

While many prisoners develop suicidal ideations either fleetingly for a brief period, often preceding some immediate stressor, or persistently for long periods of time, only a fraction of them progress to suicidal attempts or completed suicide in prison. A better understanding of the various factors that could be responsible for this transition from suicidal ideations to actual suicidal behaviors is of vital importance in both risk stratifications to direct often limited mental health resources towards those in the maximum need of them and developing effective preventive strategies to prevent suicide in the prison population. Factors that usually predispose people to act on their suicidal ideations include easy access to lethal means, high trait impulsivity, perceived or actual lack of social support, feelings of being trapped, or perceived burdensomeness on their loved ones. This holds equally well for both the general and prison populations. A systematic review suggested that among factors related to the prison environment, access to lethal means (e.g., hanging points, sharp objects) was a significant factor in facilitating the transition from ideation to action (Marzano et al., 2016). This, coupled with the more frequent impulsive nature of suicidal behavior among prisoners compared to the general population and a relative lack of mental health interventions focusing on building coping skills and problem-solving abilities of prisoners, has been reported to increase the risk of actual suicide in prisons.

Further studies exploring the influence of the prison environment on suicidal ideation and behavior suggest that factors associated with suicidal thoughts are distinct from those influencing the prisoner's transition to an actual suicidal attempt. For instance, (Favril et al., 2020b) identified the following factors to be significantly associated with suicide attempts among prisoners with suicidal ideation: a history of violent offenses, drug use while incarcerated, exposure to others' suicidal behavior, and a lifetime history of non-suicidal self-injury. Although markers of psychiatric disorders and certain aspects related to the prison environment were associated with an increased risk of having suicidal ideation, they were not associated with progression to suicide attempts.

## 4 Theoretical Models Explaining Suicidal Behavior in Prisoners

Several theoretical models provide frameworks for understanding the multifactorial nature of suicidal behavior among prisoners, integrating the aforementioned risk factors:

## 4.1 Interpersonal-Psychological Theory of Suicide

This theory suggests that suicide occurs in the presence of perceived burdensomeness, thwarted belongingness, and an acquired capability for self-harm. In the prison context, individuals may feel isolated and disconnected from their usual social support systems, and being confined might reinforce their feelings of being a burden on their loved ones and society in general. Finally, repeated exposure to violence, threats, and self-harm behaviors by other inmates within the prisons can diminish the fear of death in an individual, increasing their capability for actually acting on one's suicidal thoughts (Mandracchia & Smith, 2015).

## 4.2 Cry for Help Model

This model suggests that suicidal behavior among prisoners may be a means to communicate their distress or a desperate cry for help, particularly in socio-cultural settings where emotional expression or mental health issues are usually stigmatized or ignored. Research has also suggested that self-harm and suicidal behaviors in prisoners are sometimes employed as strategies to gain attention, alleviate perceived injustices, and secure a transfer to safer or more supportive settings (Dear et al., 2000).

## 4.3 Stress-Vulnerability Model

This model suggests an interaction between the individual's inherent predisposition or vulnerability (e.g., high impulsivity) and subsequent environmental stressors following their incarnation or confinement into prison as the critical factors required for precipitating suicidal behaviors. Research conducted among people in prisons has also provided supporting evidence for this model. For instance, cognitive deficits and impulsivity among prisoners coupled with prison-environment-related stressors such as confinement or loss of privileges have been reported to precipitate suicidal behaviors in them (Scott et al., 2023).

## 4.4 Escape Theory

This theory suggests that suicide could be seen as a means of escape from a perceived intolerable situation by an individual. In prison settings, this usually manifests as an escape from the guilt of one's crime, severe interpersonal conflicts, or chronic psychological pain due to life-long confinement or loss of privileges enjoyed by an individual before imprisonment (Liebling & Arnold, 2004).

Overall research suggests that the perception of being a burden to others coupled with feelings of entrapment following incarceration are most relevant for suicidal behaviors in prison settings. Prisoners who perceive themselves as a burden on their loved ones or society in general, coupled with experiencing a sense of inescapable distress within the prison, have been reported to be at high risk for engaging in actual suicidal behaviors (Rivlin et al., 2013). Lastly, the absence of protective factors, such as the presence of supportive relationships or meaningful engagement in activities inside prison, has also been suggested to be an important factor responsible for the progression from suicidal thoughts to actual attempts in an individual. By integrating the knowledge gained from the above-mentioned theoretical models of suicide and empirical evidence on risk factors predicting suicidal behaviors in prison settings, we can develop and implement effective multifaceted preventive strategies and therapeutic interventions targeting suicidal behaviors among prisoners.

## 5 Special Considerations in Management

From the review of risk factors as detailed above, two important considerations need to be appreciated while addressing the problem of suicide in incarcerated individuals. Though these considerations are primarily in the context of suicidal behavior in prison, it will still be prudent to consider them in the context of other high-risk situations like psychiatric inpatient wards or refugee camps (Favril, 2021).

### *5.1 Interaction of the Vulnerable to an Intimidating Situation*

It is imperative to state that the prison is an intimidating institution for most people. Though in Indian context it has been renamed as correctional home, "intimidation" still plays an important role in that approach. Overall, the stay in prison is associated with higher perception of social isolation, trauma, and bullying (Marzano et al., 2016). Furthermore, results of multiple studies have suggested that individuals who attempt suicide in prison tend to have a more negative experience in prison than other individuals who have not attempted suicide (Blaauw et al., 2001; Marzano et al., 2016; Rivlin et al., 2013). Evidence has also suggested that the rates of psychological morbidity like depression, hopelessness, impulsivity, aggression and decrease in self-esteem are usually higher in suicide attempters than non-attempters (Rivlin et al., 2013). Hence, it can be conceptualized that suicidality in prison is a culmination of the interaction of pre-existing or emerging vulnerabilities of the individual with a daunting institutional environment.

### *5.2 Distinguishing Measures Towards Suicidal Thoughts and Behavior*

The premise of this consideration is derived from the fact that suicidality and its outcome in any individual in any setting is usually multifactorial. Moreover, suicidality in the context of prison often tends to follow a trajectory of initial presentation as a thought and progressing to behavior and attempts with deepening resolve in terms of lethality and intent. From the perspective of interventions, this allows us to devise distinct interventions for the various stages of suicidality. The strategies to counter the predisposing vulnerabilities and immediate precipitating factors need to be discrete. Evidence also urges us to customize the approaches to focus on distinct outcomes (thoughts or behavior) and their causes (individual or environmental) (Klonsky et al., 2021).

### *5.3 Understanding the Effect of Social Restriction in Prison*

In a prison, the mobility of an individual is obviously curbed. Being in a closed and restricted space can be beneficial in terms of the prevention of suicide by implementing stricter supervision of the individual. On the other hand, this deprivation can also worsen the mental health issues of the person and can lead to an increase in suicidality. This can pose a dilemma to the managing team. There will be a need to customize the approach according to the available expertise and local resource allocation (Hofstra et al., 2020).

## 6 Prevention Strategies

In alignment with the emerging evidence of a multifactorial causative model to suicide in prison, the prevention strategies also need to be multipronged. The strategies to prevent suicide among prisoners can be outlined as follows:

### *6.1 Early Identification*

One of the most robust methods to intervene is to screen for individuals at risk of suicide. In order to identify the at-risk individuals early, the screening should be introduced both early and preferably at the time of intake and also should be repeated periodically and should not just be limited to be a one-off exercise (Marzano et al., 2016). The various factors that can lead to a higher risk in an individual has been shown in the following (Box 1):

**Box 1: Common factors leading to a higher risk of suicide**

| |
|---|
| First intake in prison |
| Long sentence |
| Media coverage of case or a suicide by a fellow inmate |
| Breakdown in relationship or loss of relatives |
| Change in their status under the law or penitentiary conditions |
| Solitary confinement |
| History of suffering from assault or intimidation in the prison |
| Language barriers |
| History of mental health issues or past attempts |

Various guidelines encourage the use of structured screening tools for this purpose (WHO, 2000). Gould et al. had conducted a systematic review of the various screening tools that are available for use in this population (Gould et al., 2018). The review acknowledged the lack of a screening tool with good psychometric properties that can be used across socio-cultural boundaries. However, the review identified the Viennese Instrument for Suicidality in Correctional Institutions and the Dutch screening tool to be better-performing tools in this regard (Frottier et al., 2008) (Hausam et al., 2024). The review comprised eight tools which mostly originated from Canada and European countries and had no representation from any Asian countries.

## 6.2 *Observation of High-Risk Individuals*

Once an at-risk individual is identified, a multisectoral collaboration should be formed to protect the life of the individual. This collaboration should be built on clear guidelines to the various stakeholders involved and should assume the responsibility of placing the individual under observation, monitoring, and treating the person. Such collaboration will also require a flow of information across sectors, though clear guidelines need to be framed regarding issues regarding confidentiality and how much is to be shared to various stakeholders and under what circumstances (Slade & Forrester, 2015).

The immediate step after identifying an at-risk individual is to place him under observation. Further guidelines on observation can be as follows (Fig. 1):

Once these measures have been implemented and the initial risk is neutralized, mental health services and psychosocial care should be offered to the subject.

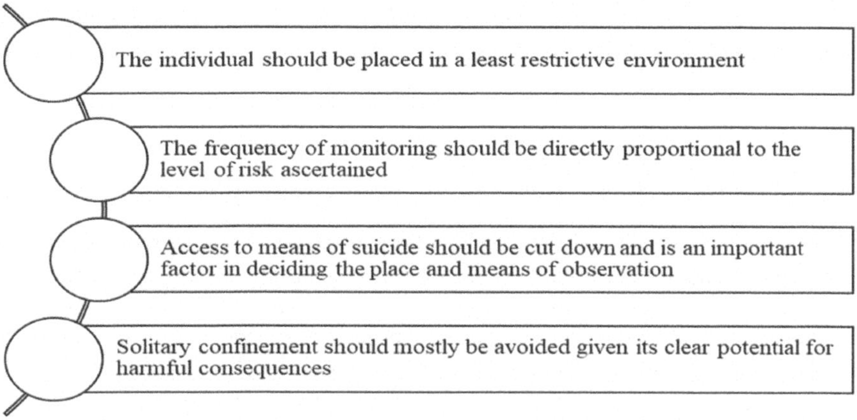


**Fig. 1** Principles of placing a high-risk individual under observation

### *6.3 Alignment of Specialized Mental Health Services*

It is to be appreciated that incarcerated subjects have high unmet clinical needs (Jakobowitz et al., 2017). The Nelson Mandela Rules for the protection of rights of persons deprived of liberty details the minimum international standard of healthcare that should be available in a prison, which has been accepted by the United Nations. It clearly states that the levels of healthcare available in the prison should be at par with that available in the community. This has also been stated by other experts of the field (Bolton et al., 2015; Fazel et al., 2016). To achieve that, appropriate resources in terms of manpower and infrastructure should be present.

Yoon et al. conducted a meta-analysis and systematic review of the various randomized controlled trials using psychotherapeutic measures among prisoners. The review consisted of data from 37 studies and found that the largest evidence base is for cognitive behavioral therapy and mindfulness-based therapies, though the effect size is modest (Yoon et al., 2017). However, the benefits were also short-lasting and tended to wane out at 3 and 6 months follow-up. Though this study did not find any significant difference in the outcome of individual and group therapies, another study by Johnson et al. found group interpersonal therapy to be more cost-effective than individual therapy (Johnson et al., 2019). The evidence surrounding trauma-focused interventions has also been encouraging in at least two systematic reviews and has been successful in mitigating the symptoms of post-traumatic stress disorder in the prisoners. These therapies were also successfully delivered in the prison setting. However, lack of a comparison group hampered the sample size in the meta-analysis (Bartlett et al., 2015) (Malik et al., 2023).

Experts in the field have also expressed interest in the efficacy of self-administered digital psychotherapeutic interventions and brief interventions (e.g., safety planning), since they have been encouraging options in the general population. However, whether they can also be translated into practice for prison inmates is a matter of further research (Favril, 2021) (Marzano et al., 2016).

## 6.4 Creating "Healthy Prisons"

Till now, most of the interventions that have been talked about should be considered as primary or secondary prevention. However, it will be prudent to invest in primordial prevention and create a 'healthy prison', so that suicidality can be addressed at the very nascent stage. The concept of a healthy prison is to create an institution, where the targeted interventions for at-risk individuals are complemented by strategies targeted to all the inmates of the prison to promote physical and mental well-being. The strategies include provision for purposeful activity and social support. The examples of such endeavors can be exposure to education, vocational skills, recreation and physical exercise. Research conducted on such measures has reported an increase in cognitive performance and a decrease in suicidal ideations in the subjects following exposure to purposeful activity (Stephenson et al., 2021). As a part of the supportive measure, proponents have also advocated for means of maintaining meaningful relationships with the family members with appropriate provisions of online meetings and also parole for physical encounters.

Finally, another concept that has gained popularity in this aspect has been the development of a peer-based support scheme, where there is access of interacting with trained peers (Bagnall et al., 2015) (Ludlow et al., 2015). In the review by Bagnall et al., which included both quantitative and qualitative assessments and consisted of fifty-seven studies, showed that peer education interventions resulted in a decrease in risky behavior and had a positive effect on the inmates (Bagnall et al., 2015). There has been remarkable qualitative research on the experience of suicide survivors in the prison, which showed that subjects appreciated that being able to talk to others and the feeling of being listened can be helpful in averting suicides in prison (Borrill et al., 2005) (Suto & Arnaut, 2010) The concept of healthy prison has been elaborated in Fig. 2.

## 6.5 Dealing with the Aftermath

Like has been the experience in the community setting, despite the best efforts, there can be instances of completed suicide in the prison settings. Roulston et al. conducted a scoping review on the lived experiences of the staff and close relatives of persons who had committed suicide in the prison (Roulston et al., 2021). The themes that arose from the review were the distress for the family members stemmed from the fact that the bad news of completed suicide was provided to them in an inaccurate and untimely manner. For the staff, the prominent approach was of avoidance, to prevent contamination of their personal and family spheres. The review identified certain

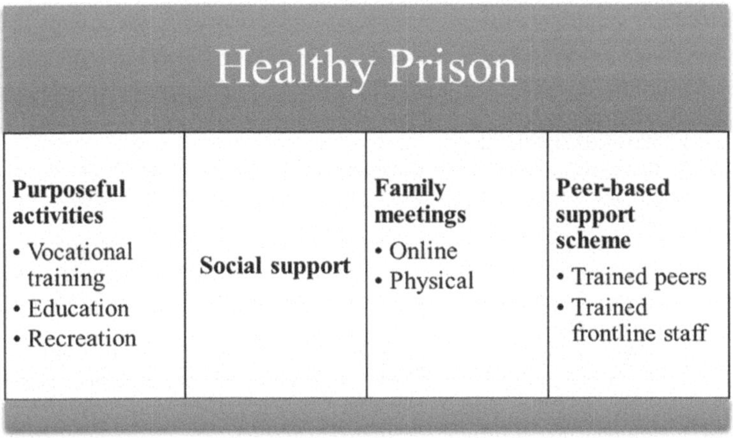


**Fig. 2** Outline for creating 'healthy prisons'

areas where there was a need for more investment of efforts, which included unmet advocacy, care of bereaved family members, long-term social care of the affected families, and psychosocial support, counseling, and supervision of the staff involved in the immediate care of the attempters.

## 7 Conclusion

Suicide is a major public health concern throughout the world in all population groups. But the prevalence and risk of suicide are exponentially high among the vulnerable groups like prison population. This is the combined result of pre-existing individual vulnerabilities among the incarcerated individuals and prison-specific factors. The factors like easy access to lethal means, high trait impulsivity, perceived or actual lack of social support, feelings of being trapped, or perceived burdensomeness predispose people to act on their suicidal ideations. Hence, to prevent this untoward event there should be provision for timely identification of suicide risk, observation of prisoners at high-risk, provision of specialized mental health services, and creating a supportive prison environment. There is a need for better understanding of this phenomena in the prison population especially in the LMICs where it is understudied. Considering the scarcity of resources in this part of the world, it is essential that research also aims to translate needs into a contextualized, culture specific and deliverable service mode. There is also a need for policy development at the international level that can be implemented in all prisons worldwide.

## References


Angelakis, I., Austin, J. L., & Gooding, P. (2020). Childhood maltreatment and suicide attempts in prisoners: A systematic meta-analytic review. *Psychological Medicine, 50*(1), 1–10. https://doi.org/10.1017/S0033291719002848

Arafat, S. M. Y., Kar, S. K., Abhayanayake, C., Sharma, P., & Marthoenis, M. (2024). Prison mental health in South-East Asia: A narrative review. *Brain and Behavior, 14*(8), e70004. https://doi.org/10.1002/brb3.70004

Bagnall, A. M., South, J., Hulme, C., Woodall, J., Vinall-Collier, K., Raine, G., Kinsella, K., Dixey, R., Harris, L., & Wright, N. M. (2015). A systematic review of the effectiveness and cost-effectiveness of peer education and peer support in prisons. *BMC Public Health, 15*(1), 290. https://doi.org/10.1186/s12889-015-1584-x

Baranyi, G., Scholl, C., Fazel, S., Patel, V., Priebe, S., & Mundt, A. P. (2019). Severe mental illness and substance use disorders in prisoners in low-income and middle-income countries: A systematic review and meta-analysis of prevalence studies. *The Lancet Global Health, 7*(4), e461–e471. https://doi.org/10.1016/S2214-109X(18)30539-4

Bartlett, A., Jhanji, E., White, S., Anne Harty, M., Scammell, J., & Allen, S. (2015). Interventions with women offenders: A systematic review and meta-analysis of mental health gain. *The Journal of Forensic Psychiatry & Psychology, 26*(2), 133–165. https://doi.org/10.1080/14789949.2014.981563

Blaauw, E., Kerkhof, A., Winkel, F., & Sheridan, L. (2001). Identifying suicide risk in penal institutions in the Netherlands. *The British Journal of Forensic Practice, 3*(4), 22–28. https://doi.org/10.1108/14636646200100024

Bolton, J. M., Gunnell, D., & Turecki, G. (2015). Suicide risk assessment and intervention in people with mental illness. *BMJ (Clinical Research Ed.), 351*, h4978. https://doi.org/10.1136/bmj.h4978

Borrill, J., Snow, L., Medlicott, D., Teers, R., & Paton, J. (2005). Learning from 'near misses': Interviews with women who survived an incident of severe self-harm in prison. *The Howard Journal of Criminal Justice, 44*(1), 57–69. https://doi.org/10.1111/j.1468-2311.2005.00355.x

Bukten, A., & Stavseth, M. R. (2021). Suicide in prison and after release: A 17-year national cohort study. *European Journal of Epidemiology, 36*(10), 1075–1083. https://doi.org/10.1007/s10654-021-00782-0

Dear, G. E., Thompson, D. M., & Hills, A. M. (2000). Self-harm in prison: Manipulators can also be suicide attempters. *Criminal Justice and Behavior, 27*(2), 160–175. https://doi.org/10.1177/0093854800027002002

Favril, L. (2021). Epidemiology, risk factors, and prevention of suicidal thoughts and behaviour in prisons: A literature review. *Psychologica Belgica, 61*(1), 341–355. https://doi.org/10.5334/pb.1072

Favril, L., Indig, D., Gear, C., & Wilhelm, K. (2020a). Mental disorders and risk of suicide attempt in prisoners. *Social Psychiatry and Psychiatric Epidemiology, 55*(9), 1145–1155. https://doi.org/10.1007/s00127-020-01851-7

Favril, L., O'Connor, R. C., Hawton, K., & Vander Laenen, F. (2020b). Factors associated with the transition from suicidal ideation to suicide attempt in prison. *European Psychiatry: The Journal of the Association of European Psychiatrists, 63*(1), e101. https://doi.org/10.1192/j.eurpsy.2020.101

Favril, L., Rich, J. D., Hard, J., & Fazel, S. (2024). Mental and physical health morbidity among people in prisons: An umbrella review. *The Lancet Public Health, 9*(4), e250–e260. https://doi.org/10.1016/S2468-2667(24)00023-9

Favril, L., Shaw, J., & Fazel, S. (2022). Prevalence and risk factors for suicide attempts in prison. *Clinical Psychology Review, 97*, 102190. https://doi.org/10.1016/j.cpr.2022.102190

Fazel, S., & Runeson, B. (2020). Suicide. *New England Journal of Medicine, 382*(3), 266–274. https://doi.org/10.1056/NEJMra1902944

Fazel, S., Grann, M., Kling, B., & Hawton, K. (2011). Prison suicide in 12 countries: An ecological study of 861 suicides during 2003–2007. *Social Psychiatry and Psychiatric Epidemiology, 46*(3), 191–195. https://doi.org/10.1007/s00127-010-0184-4

Fazel, S., Hayes, A. J., Bartellas, K., Clerici, M., & Trestman, R. (2016). Mental health of prisoners: Prevalence, adverse outcomes, and interventions. *The Lancet Psychiatry, 3*(9), 871–881. https://doi.org/10.1016/S2215-0366(16)30142-0

Fazel, S., Ramesh, T., & Hawton, K. (2017). Suicide in prisons: An international study of prevalence and contributory factors. *The Lancet Psychiatry, 4*(12), 946–952. https://doi.org/10.1016/S2215-0366(17)30430-3

Frottier, P., König, F., Matschnig, T., Seyringer, M. E., & Frühwald, S. (2008). VISCI–Viennese instrument for suicidality in correctional institutions. *Psychiatrische Praxis, 35*(1), 21–27. https://doi.org/10.1055/s-2007-970884

Gould, C., McGeorge, T., & Slade, K. (2018). Suicide screening tools for use in incarcerated offenders: A systematic review. *Archives of Suicide Research: Official Journal of the International Academy for Suicide Research, 22*(3), 345–364. https://doi.org/10.1080/13811118.2017.1334611

Gowda, G. S., Shadakshari, D., Vajawat, B., Reddi, V. S. K., Math, S. B., & Murthy, P. (2021). Suicide in Indian prisons. *The Lancet Psychiatry, 8*(8), e19. https://doi.org/10.1016/S2215-0366(21)00233-9

Haney, C. (2018). The psychological effects of solitary confinement: A systematic critique. *Crime and Justice, 47*, 365–416. https://doi.org/10.1086/696041

Hausam, J., Calvano, D., & Opitz-Welke, A. (2024). Comparison of two suicide screening instruments for identifying high-risk individuals in prison. *Frontiers in Psychiatry, 15* https://doi.org/10.3389/fpsyt.2024.1362928

Hill, K., Wainwright, V., Stevenson, C., Senior, J., Robinson, C., & Shaw, J. (2022). Prevalence of mental health and suicide risk in prisons in low- and middle-income countries: A rapid review. *The Journal of Forensic Psychiatry & Psychology, 33*(1), 37–52. https://doi.org/10.1080/14789949.2021.2016891

Hofstra, E., van Nieuwenhuizen, C., Bakker, M., Özgül, D., Elfeddali, I., de Jong, S. J., & van der Feltz-Cornelis, C. M. (2020). Effectiveness of suicide prevention interventions: A systematic review and meta-analysis. *General Hospital Psychiatry, 63*, 127–140. https://doi.org/10.1016/j.genhosppsych.2019.04.011

Humber, N., Hayes, A., Senior, J., Fahy, T., & Shaw, J. (2011). Identifying, monitoring and managing prisoners at risk of self-harm/suicide in England and Wales. *Journal of Forensic Psychiatry & Psychology, 22*(1), 22–51. https://doi.org/10.1080/14789949.2010.518245

Jakobowitz, S., Bebbington, P., McKenzie, N., Iveson, R., Duffield, G., Kerr, M., & Killaspy, H. (2017). Assessing needs for psychiatric treatment in prisoners: 2. Met and unmet need. *Social Psychiatry and Psychiatric Epidemiology, 52*(2), 231–240. https://doi.org/10.1007/s00127-016-1313-5

Johnson, J. E., Stout, R. L., Miller, T. R., Zlotnick, C., Cerbo, L. A., Andrade, J. T., Nargiso, J., Bonner, J., & Wiltsey-Stirman, S. (2019). Randomized cost-effectiveness trial of group interpersonal psychotherapy (IPT) for prisoners with major depression. *Journal of Consulting and Clinical Psychology, 87*(4), 392–406. https://doi.org/10.1037/ccp0000379

Kaba, F., Lewis, A., Glowa-Kollisch, S., Hadler, J., Lee, D., Alper, H., Selling, D., MacDonald, R., Solimo, A., Parsons, A., & Venters, H. (2014). Solitary confinement and risk of self-harm among jail inmates. *American Journal of Public Health, 104*(3), 442–447. https://doi.org/10.2105/AJPH.2013.301742

Klonsky, E. D., Pachkowski, M. C., Shahnaz, A., & May, A. M. (2021). The three-step theory of suicide: Description, evidence, and some useful points of clarification. *Preventive Medicine, 152*(Pt 1), 106549. https://doi.org/10.1016/j.ypmed.2021.106549

Knipe, D., Padmanathan, P., Newton-Howes, G., Chan, L. F., & Kapur, N. (2022). Suicide and self-harm. *The Lancet, 399*(10338), 1903–1916. https://doi.org/10.1016/S0140-6736(22)00173-8

Liebling, A., & Arnold, H. (2004). *Prisons and their moral performance: A study of values, quality, and prison life*. Oxford University Press.
Ludlow, A., Schmidt, B., Akoensi, T., Liebling, A., Giacomantonio, C., & Sutherland, A. (2015). Self-inflicted deaths in NOMS' custody amongst 18–24 year olds: Staff experience, knowledge and views.
Malik, N., Facer-Irwin, E., Dickson, H., Bird, A., & MacManus, D. (2023). The effectiveness of trauma-focused interventions in prison settings: A systematic review and meta-analysis. *Trauma, Violence & Abuse, 24*(2), 844–857. https://doi.org/10.1177/15248380211043890
Mandracchia, J. T., & Smith, P. N. (2015). The interpersonal theory of suicide applied to male prisoners. *Suicide & Life-Threatening Behavior, 45*(3), 293–301. https://doi.org/10.1111/sltb.12132
Marzano, L., Hawton, K., Rivlin, A., Smith, E. N., Piper, M., & Fazel, S. (2016). Prevention of suicidal behavior in prisons. *Crisis, 37*(5), 323–334. https://doi.org/10.1027/0227-5910/a000394
Pratt, D., Piper, M., Appleby, L., Webb, R., & Shaw, J. (2006). Suicide in recently released prisoners: A population-based cohort study. *The Lancet, 368*(9530), 119–123. https://doi.org/10.1016/S0140-6736(06)69002-8
Rabe, K. (2012). Prison structure, inmate mortality and suicide risk in Europe. *International Journal of Law and Psychiatry, 35*(3), 222–230. https://doi.org/10.1016/j.ijlp.2012.02.012
Rivlin, A., Hawton, K., Marzano, L., & Fazel, S. (2013). Psychosocial characteristics and social networks of suicidal prisoners: Towards a model of suicidal behaviour in detention. *PLoS ONE, 8*(7), e68944. https://doi.org/10.1371/journal.pone.0068944
Roulston, A., McKeaveney, C., Anderson, M., McCloskey, P., & Butler, M. (2021). Deaths in prison custody: A scoping review of the experiences of staff and bereaved relatives. *British Journal of Social Work, 51*(1), 223–245. https://doi.org/10.1093/bjsw/bcaa095
Scott, R., Aboud, A., & Smith, T. (2023). Using the stress–vulnerability model to better understand suicide in prison populations. *Psychiatry, Psychology and Law, 30*(3), 299–333. https://doi.org/10.1080/13218719.2021.2013340
Shaw, J., Baker, D., Hunt, I. M., Moloney, A., & Appleby, L. (2004). Suicide by prisoners: National clinical survey. *The British Journal of Psychiatry, 184*(3), 263–267. https://doi.org/10.1192/bjp.184.3.263
Slade, K., & Forrester, A. (2015). Shifting the paradigm of prison suicide prevention through enhanced multi-agency integration and cultural change. *The Journal of Forensic Psychiatry & Psychology, 26*(6), 737–758. https://doi.org/10.1080/14789949.2015.1062997
Stephenson, T., Leaman, J., O'Moore, É., Tran, A., & Plugge, E. (2021). Time out of cell and time in purposeful activity and adverse mental health outcomes amongst people in prison: A literature review. *International Journal of Prisoner Health, 17*(1), 54–68. https://doi.org/10.1108/ijph-06-2020-0037
Suto, I., & Arnaut, G. L. Y. (2010). Suicide in prison: A qualitative study. *The Prison Journal, 90*(3), 288–312. https://doi.org/10.1177/0032885510373499
WHO. (2000). Preventing suicide in jails and prisons. Retrieved from September 14, 2024, https://www.who.int/publications/i/item/9789241595506
WHO. (2024). Suicide. Retrieved from September 05, 2024, https://www.who.int/news-room/fact-sheets/detail/suicide
Yoon, I. A., Slade, K., & Fazel, S. (2017). Outcomes of psychological therapies for prisoners with mental health problems: A systematic review and meta-analysis. *Journal of Consulting and Clinical Psychology, 85*(8), 783–802. https://doi.org/10.1037/ccp0000214
Zhong, S., Senior, M., Yu, R., Perry, A., Hawton, K., Shaw, J., & Fazel, S. (2021). Risk factors for suicide in prisons: A systematic review and meta-analysis. *The Lancet Public Health, 6*(3), e164–e174. https://doi.org/10.1016/S2468-2667(20)30233-4

# Chapter 17
# Social Views About Assisted Suicide, Euthanasia, Physician-Assisted Suicide, and Positions of Various Organisations and Countries

**Matilda Burton and Nilamadhab Kar**

**Abstract** Euthanasia and assisted suicide in their various forms remain a heated and polarising debate. There is global variance in the legalisation of forms of assisted dying; with it being legalized in some form in some countries, and staunchly prohibited in others. As legal status varies from country to country, so do religious and social views; within some countries, there is entrenched opposition to the premise of assisted dying, whereas in others it has become increasingly socially acceptable; and in some countries generalised acceptance of euthanasia is the majority viewpoint. Religious and historical perspectives can be used as a lens to explain and understand these varying social views. This chapter provides the religious, historical, legal, and ethical perspectives related to assisted dying.

**Keywords** Assisted suicide · Euthanasia · Law · Physician-assisted suicide · Religion · Society

## 1 Introduction

Throughout the course of human history, and more intensely in the last few decades, assisted dying in its various forms has been a tempestuous and polarising topic. Within the medical community, the topic is becoming increasingly relevant as medical advances continue, and our attitudes towards the rights of those at the end of their life evolve. Today, euthanasia, or physician-assisted dying (EPAS) is legalized in

M. Burton · N. Kar (✉)
Black Country Healthcare NHS Foundation Trust, Wolverhampton, UK
e-mail: n.kar@nhs.net

N. Kar
University of Wolverhampton, Wolverhampton, UK

Sri Sri University, Cuttack, Odisha, India



S. M. Y. Arafat and S. K. Kar (eds.), *Ecological and Social Determinants of Suicidal Behavior*, South Asian Perspectives in Mental Health and Psychology,
https://doi.org/10.1007/978-981-96-4028-7_17

some form in certain countries; in others, it remains illegal and resolutely taboo for various cultural and religious reasons. Enduring concerns regarding EPAS remain, both regarding the theoretical process mandated in legislation, and how EPAS would be practically carried out.

This chapter explores the distinct three variances: assisted suicide, euthanasia, and physician-assisted suicide, mainly focusing on EPAS. A commentary on the historical and religious understandings of EPAS within different societies is discussed; to provide an understanding of the varying social views across cultures and how they have formed; and the various legal and ethical challenges that exist.

## *1.1 Definitions*

There are various related terms and it is prudent to describe them in the beginning (Table 1). Within the literature, there is often a distinction between 'active', and 'passive' euthanasia; the difference being that passive euthanasia may involve a person not intervening to prevent another person's death, and active euthanasia involves the direct hastening of a person's death through a lethal dose of medication or other means (Fontalis et al., 2018). This chapter primarily focuses on physician-assisted suicide.

**Table 1** Description of various terms related to EPAS

| | |
|---|---|
| Euthanasia | Voluntary active euthanasia is the act of intentionally ending another person's life, at their capacitous and voluntary request. This is usually done through a doctor administering medication (Mroz et al. 2021). |
| Non-voluntary euthanasia | Non-voluntary euthanasia involves the facilitating of someone's death without their consent; in situations where informed and purposeful consent is not possible, such as the patient being in a comatose state. Involuntary euthanasia would represent the facilitation of death against a patient's will (Mroz et al. 2021). |
| Assisted suicide | When a person intentionally aids another person's death, by providing them with the means to do so, or assisting them in the process in a manner that the suicide would not have been possible without the external person's involvement (Fontalis et al. 2018). |
| Physician-assisted suicide | Physician-assisted suicide is defined as a physician intentionally facilitating a person's death by providing the means to do so, such as issuing a prescription for lethal medication, at the person's voluntary and capacitous request. In this case, the action of ending life is done by the patient, who is given the medication by the physician (Fontalis et al. 2018). |

## 2 Religious Views on EPAS

There are variances across the major religions in theological perspectives that may explain how EPAS may be accepted or rejected by followers of each religion. The prominence of ideas linked to EPAS across religious texts is discussed; with a view to understanding how prevailing religious beliefs may have informed social views and explain the position of various countries' differing legal approach.

Within Christianity, although EPAS is not mentioned within the Bible, there are several core themes throughout scripture that relevant theological arguments derive from and can be used as a lens to understand religious approaches to EPAS. Within several passages of the Bible, God issues direct, clear instructions that the taking of life is prohibited; and mandates punishment for doing so. Humans are described as being made in God's image; and so, there is a unique sanctity ascribed to human life which adamantly opposes the ending of it (Stempsey, 1997). The very framework of the Bible ascribes God as the creator, and sustainer of life—and to end life should happen only at God's command. Suffering on earth is viewed as temporary and inevitable; and occurs along the path to a suffering-free eternal life in Heaven after death (Grove et al., 2022). Keeping this core idea in mind, although EPAS is not directly referenced, there is strong implied theological opposition throughout the entirety of the Bible. In consistency with these views, the main branches of Christianity—Catholic, Protestant, and Eastern Orthodox—are united in opposing EPAS. This then serves to form the majority views of Christianity's constituent followers.

In Islam, although the Quran does not directly discuss EPAS, there are several consistent themes that contribute to formulating an interpretation that strongly opposes EPAS, considering it to be a form of murder (Sobotková, 2019). As within Christianity, Allah is the sole creator and sustainer of life; he determines everything, including the timing of a person's death (Madadin, 2020)—and so the philosophy of Islam is focused towards saving and prolonging life. EPAS is therefore almost universally condemned as a form of murder by Islamic scholars; and opposition tends to form the majority viewpoint of the religion's followers. As such, it is not legalised in any Muslim-majority countries (Grove et al., 2022).

In the Hindu view, the soul along with the influence of karma of continues after death, to the next life, in multiple cycles of birth and death. Suicide is considered as bad karma that affects the soul's spiritual progress, and is generally prohibited in Hinduism. Within the polytheistic, pantheistic or monistic belief and cultural systems of Hinduism, there is no distinct dominant view on EPAS; and Hindu philosophies both for and against EPAS exist. Ideas that may oppose EPAS are that Hinduism has, universally, maintained a resolute philosophy of respect for all living things, with strong opposition against the act of killing and violence—a principle of paramount importance known as ahimsa (Grove et al., 2022). However, considering the diversity of Hindu philosophies, specific discussions or studies related to EPAS amongst Hindus in general population are rather scarce (Chakraborty et al., 2017). Hindu belief systems leave space for more nuanced and diverse reflection regarding EPAS.

EPAS is a complex topic within Judaism. A central tenant of *halakha,* Jewish Law, is the sanctity of human life. There is a widespread perception that *halakha* instructs that a dying person's life should be extended at all costs, a duty that is held by those who can offer aid to the suffering person, such as a doctor. There is, however, no clear consensus throughout the theological and spiritual discourse as to whether this is a universal, unrelenting principle. In addition to a duty to preserve life, there is also a recognised duty to alleviate suffering; and within The Talmud, there is an assertion that extreme suffering can often be worse than death. The balance of the obligation to alleviate suffering, while prolonging life, has formed the basis of the decision of some authorities to rule that while withholding life-prolonging treatment can be permitted; removing treatment that would imminently cause a patient's death is forbidden. In this way, 'passive' euthanasia is widely accepted (Linzer, 2013). This is reflected within Israeli law; in which passive euthanasia is accepted through the Terminally Ill Patient Law of 2005 (Jotkowitz & Glick, 2009).

Karma and rebirth are central to Buddhist philosophy; suffering is part of life; such as death in the cycle of rebirths. Buddhism aims to find liberation from suffering, but not through death; in that regard, EPAS will not be able to alleviate suffering and will merely delay it to a subsequent life (Grove et al., 2022). Buddhism advocates towards attaining peaceful deaths (Upasen et al., 2022). Within cultural Buddhism, there is a qualified acceptance of certain forms of self-harm; certain motivations for suicide such as altruism, and self-immolation as a form of political protest (Kelly, 2011). Buddhist philosophy condemns harm to living things and mandates compassion as an important virtue. In healthcare, this manifests as aiming to obtain a peaceful death—a goal that influences decision-making (McCormick, 2013).

Although various theological perspectives on EPAS have been discussed based on religious texts, it must be acknowledged that religious affiliations do not necessarily determine a person's individual moral stance (Dorji et al., 2020). However, across the major worldwide religions, there are recurring themes that form the basis of moral views that may oppose EPAS, such as suffering on Earth being part of the journey to a better future after death. It is important that legislation considers and represents the views of those who hold religious-based objections to EPAS.

## 3 Historical Accounts

The origins of the word 'euthanasia' have initially been credited to the Roman historian Suetonius, who in his writings described how Emperor Augustus died 'quickly and without suffering' in the arms of his wife, Livia (Letellier, 2003), and 'experienced the euthanasia he had wished for'. The word was interpreted to mean a 'good' death—one without the terminal suffering often evoked when considering a person's death. The term euthanasia was later used in a medical context by Francis Bacon, a philosopher, to describe a situation in which a physician held a responsibility to 'alleviate the physical sufferings of the body' to facilitate a pain-free, happy death for their patient. Karl Marx further developed on Bacon's ideas and theorised that a doctor had an inextricable moral duty to ease the suffering of death, bringing this duty within the medical realm of responsibility (Nyman et al., 1996).

Euthanasia is first referenced in practice in ancient Greek and Roman texts, although the practice of taking human life was condemned by dominating Hippocratic principles. Throughout later human history, euthanasia continued to be practised within various forms with customs such as suffocation, removing people from their sick beds to be placed outside, and swiftly removing a pillow from a person's head—which was thought to hasten death (Stolberg, 2007). Despite the endurance of the practice through the centuries, in Judeo-Christian tradition, EPAS has long been strongly opposed, and this view gained prominence as Christianity grew. Although within different cultures this resolute approach has not persisted through time; for example, in Japan, suicide is not traditionally viewed as a sin, and in some situations can be dignified, and even honourable (Otani, 2010).

Within Britain, amongst medical scholars in the early 1800s, morphine and chloroform were proposed as treatments to 'treat the pains of death' and widely used for this purpose; however, this was not with a goal of accelerating death, rather relieving the symptoms of dying. The contemporary euthanasia debate was ignited in 1870 by a proposal by Samuel Williams, a schoolteacher, who suggested the usage of chloroform to patients to hasten their death, with the goal of achieving a 'quick and painless death' (Brenna, 2021). This proposal achieved both widespread acclaim and opposition; however medical doctors largely did not participate in the discussion, which remained philosophical in nature (Brenna, 2021).

The first attempt to legalise EPAS within the United States came in 1906, when within the General Assembly of Ohio, a bill was proposed that proposed allowing the deliberate administration of anaesthetic to cause a patient's death—if they were of sound mind, and suffering from either a fatal injury, an irrevocable illness, or great physical pain (Appel, 2004). This bill was inspired by Anna Sophina Hall; a leading figure in the euthanasia movement who had dedicated herself to the cause after watching her mother suffer a prolonged death from liver cancer. The bill was rejected; however, it represented a shift in societal views (Appel, 2004).

The debate surrounding EPAS intensified in Britain in the 1930s; when the Voluntary Euthanasia Legalisation Society was founded—later renamed, and today known as *Dignity in Dying*. The society called for the legalisation of EPAS which resulted in proposed legislation reaching the House of Lords, although it did not progress further. In 1936, King George V died; although at the time kept a secret, his death was caused by a fatal dose of morphine, deliberately given by his physician, to hasten his death as he suffered from cardiorespiratory failure (Ramsay, 1994).

Some countries have a challenging historical past with euthanasia, where widespread discomfort around the practice remains pervasive. For example, in Germany during the period of the Nazi government, euthanasia programmes with eugenic ideals were created. In 1933, many doctors had an active role in these euthanasia programmes. It was reported that, an estimated 200,000 to 300,000 people were killed under the guise of 'mercy killing'—deemed to be 'unfit' due to physical or mental disability. The atrocities in this period to some are sobering examples of the importance of ensuring any EPAS legislation protects the patient and reinforces their right to make the decision (Grodin et al., 2018). This period created an unfortunate public association of euthanasia with eugenics and Nazi ideology, which marred public debate for several years.

## 4 Current Status in Different Countries

Within this section, the legality of EPAS across different countries is discussed, with notable examples being highlighted. As of writing, EPAS (*active* euthanasia) is legal in the Netherlands, Belgium, Luxembourg, Columbia, Canada, Switzerland, Spain, New Zealand, some territories of Australia, and within eleven American states (Emanuel et al., 2016). Passive euthanasia—that is to say, the refusal or withdrawal of life-saving treatment, is either legislated for or not explicitly banned in most countries. An example of this is India, in which the Supreme Court legalized passive euthanasia in 2011 in a landmark judgement (Sinha et al., 2012), although this specific judgement gave no specific instruction and was not practically applicable. A further judgement in 2018 and 2023 helped to develop the criteria for passive euthanasia: that the patient must be able to consent (via a living will) and must be terminally ill or in a vegetative state (Shekhawat et al., 2023). The decision to allow passive euthanasia, in individual cases, would be scrutinised by an independent medical board, consisting of doctors with more than five years of experience. Despite the development of the law's clarity, in 2023 there had been no reported case of passive euthanasia in India (Supreme Court of India & Delhi High Court, 2024).

Only a handful of countries, Russia being an example, outlaw even passive euthanasia (Shestak & Dyachenko, 2020). In general, Western Europe is experiencing a surge of support for legislation of EPAS; whereas within Eastern and Central Europe, support is decreasing (Emanuel et al., 2016). EPAS laws, and support, vary across Asia. In Japan, there is a developing legal framework for implementing EPAS, which is not currently ratified in law. China similarly has a legal 'grey area' in which there is no clear law explicitly dictating the legality of passive euthanasia (active euthanasia remains equivalent to homicide in Chinese law), and so there is ambiguity and uncertainty in situations where passive euthanasia may be considered (Weng et al., 2011). There is, as of the time of writing, no Asian country with EPAS legislation. In countries with theocratic governments and populations of a majority practicing religious background, EPAS is explicitly banned; rather unsurprisingly when considering the prominent religious arguments that have previously been discussed. Opposition to EPAS is often deeply entrenched within religious societies; again, because of the vast theological perspectives that condemn the practice. In Ireland, EPAS is illegal—a reflection of the largely Catholic population—and staunchly forbidden under the guidelines of the Irish Medical Council. EPAS is however, the subject of debate more recently, due to the proposal of a bill in the Irish parliament, which may indicate a slow transition of society to harbour more favourable views (Clarke et al., 2021).

As wider society becomes more versed in understanding their own health, and interactions with doctors become less paternalistic and more mutualistic, there is a greater emphasis on patient choice, across all societies. Shared care is supported across all branches of medicine; the patient comes to a decision jointly with their medical team, as opposed to the past days of absolute medical authority. A patient's right to self-determination has formed some of the more prominent supportive arguments for EPAS in more recent times; replacing the 'intolerable suffering argument'—that patients with incurable diagnoses are often described as experiencing 'intolerable suffering' as their disease progresses; and as the cause of their suffering is their illness, the only effective proposed way to end their suffering is death. The 'intolerable suffering' supportive argument has, in some ways, faded; replaced by the 'control' argument, that a person should have the ability to control the end of their life (Randall & Downie, 2010).

In the UK, assisting a person's suicide is a prosecutable offence under the 1961 Suicide Act; however, this law is rarely enacted, and arrests are vanishingly rare. In 2021, an Assisted Dying Bill was introduced into the House of Lords; that proposes that terminally ill patients with a prognosis of less than six months should be given the ability to opt for a medically assisted death (UK Parliament, 2021). The bill is awaiting its second reading, after which it is largely expected to progress. The potential of the introduction of EPAS is therefore hotly anticipated in the UK.

### *4.1 The Netherlands*

The system within the Netherlands has served as a 'model' for other countries. The Netherlands was the first country to legalise EPAS; beginning with official tolerance in 1985, and then progressing to full legalisation in 2002 (der Heide et al., 2005). Since the law's conception, cases of EPAS have continually risen annually (Groenewoud et al., 2021). This law broadly allows EPAS in fixed circumstances: if the person is suffering 'unbearably without hope' from either a physical or mental condition (Roehr, 2021). They must also be competent to make the decision; and any request must involve two doctors to certify the appropriateness of the request. There are a certain number of criteria to be met: that the suffering of the patient has no realistic prospect of improvement, that their request for EPAS is enduring and not transient, and that the patient has been fully made aware of their options and possible alternative treatments (Janssen, 2002).

Despite the implementation of the law, it has been suggested within the literature that the legislation did not lead to an increase in EPAS cases in the Netherlands; it just provided a regulated and proper framework for them to happen (Onwuteaka-Philipsen et al., 2012). From this perspective, any increase in reported EPAS cases is not as a result of the legislation's implementation, but deaths that would have occurred without it In 2016, 4% of all deaths in the Netherlands were recorded as being due to EPAS (Pascoe, 2017).

## 5 Bioethical Debate

> 'Neither will I administer a poison to
> anybody when asked to do so, nor will
> I suggest such a course' -
> The Hippocratic Oath (Ahlzen, 2020)

The role of the doctor has been inextricably associated with Hippocrate's mandate that a doctor should 'first do no harm'; although interestingly this phrase was not present within the original Hippocratic Oath but is widely misremembered and assumed to have been (Hajar, 2017). The Hippocratic Oath contains a deontology-based philosophy: that the doctor's duty to their patient must be to take care of the ill with selflessness, dedication, and enduring compassion—and their ultimate duty is to cause no harm (Tännsjö, 2005).

Deontology, as an ethical theory, defines a person's action as right or wrong depending on the morality of the action itself, regardless of the consequences of the action. Using Hippocrate's framework, we can take the duty of a doctor to be to cause no harm, and to treat their patient—regardless of the consequences of the action. The duty of a doctor to cause no harm is where the ambiguity and differing interpretations may lie. In the context of EPAS, active euthanasia would be prohibited using a deontological perspective (Tännsjö, 2005) if the death was the *intention* of the action. Deontological arguments therefore do not support active EPAS legislation, but there may be circumstances in which EPAS may be accepted if death was not the intended action, but a consequence—for example, prescribing a lethal dose of morphine with the ostensible intention of relieving intractable pain (Alexander & Moore, 2020).

Beneficence asserts that a doctor's moral obligation is to act in a manner that does 'good', and that benefits the patient maximally. The concept of beneficence can be applied to EPAS in either supportive or critical arguments. Some would suggest that, using the ideas of beneficence, a doctor should be motivated towards preserving life above all else; with a focus on relieving the symptoms of a patient's suffering, rather than ending their life. Others would suggest that beneficence requires the doctor to support the autonomy of their patient, and that they must act to relieve their suffering. Promotion of a patient's autonomy may also contradict beneficence; if a doctor is the arbiter of what action would benefit a patient the most, they may believe that ending a patient's life would not be the action that benefitted them the most (Benedict et al., 1998) while the patient may disagree. An autonomy-based approach to EPAS would be morally justifiable if a person with full decision-making capacity has independently, autonomously made the decision to end their life—however, an autonomy-based approach would also mean that *any* person (who does not necessarily have an untreatable condition) should be able to request it, and that their motives would not be scrutinised or applied to an objective standard before approval (Braun, 2022). One benefit of an autonomy-based approach is that, firstly, the emphasis of the decision and act is placed with the patient, rather than the doctor.

Additionally, it avoids the expressivist objection: that, in EPAS systems, EPAS is often available to a specific group of patients. This may externally suggest that any person with these conditions has a life not worth living, which unquestionably is not a belief shared by everyone living with the conditions. The expressivist objection to EPAS has been a core argument against its legislation; representing the concerns of many disabled people that their lives would be judged not worth living (Braun, 2022).

Lastly, virtue ethics will be discussed in the context of euthanasia. Virtue ethics is a philosophy that asserts that an action is morally acceptable based on the intent, and moral character, of the actor. If their intent is virtuous, then regardless of the consequences of the action, their action was morally justifiable. In this context, EPAS may be acceptable if the intention of the doctor facilitating the death is to relieve the suffering of their patient and to honour their wishes. Of course, this argument would therefore ascribe strict protocol and processes to EPAS; in that, a doctor administering lethal medication or facilitating a patient's death was acting virtuously (Begley, 2008) and with no malintent or ulterior motives.

## 6 Position of Different Organisations

There are various voluntary organisations that represent views across the spectrum of either support or criticism of EPAS. 'Dignity in Dying' is a prominent British organisation dedicated to campaigning for greater autonomy in end-of-life care, with the resolute belief that an option of a pain-free, peaceful death should be an option for everyone, with stringent legal safeguards and protective mechanisms in place. The organisation is resolutely secular; and not aligned with any political or cultural affiliations. The group was established in 1935; and its membership was reported to be formed of 25,000 active members by 2010 (Dignity in Dying, 2016). As British society becomes more secular, and religious values are less strongly associated with legislation, views towards EPAS have softened. Humanists UK is another organisation that, while not solely advocating for the legalisation of EPAS, represents members who support secular humanism. As part of this ethos, EPAS is viewed through the frame of supporting an 'open society', a philosophical proposal of a society in which individual liberty and agencies are supported by government policy and the state healthcare system (Humanists UK, 2024).

The World Federation of Right-to-Die Societies represents an international federation of voluntary organisations that advocate for access to EPAS. It was founded in 1980 and represents 60 Right-to-Die Societies from across the world, representing 30 countries as of 2020 (World Federation of Right to Die Societies, 2020). As part of their campaigning, the 'World Right to Die Day' was established, which is annually celebrated on November the 2nd, ostensibly to raise awareness of the topic and promote further discussion.

From a global perspective, Exit International is an eminent not-for-profit organisation that supports EPAS. It has met controversy over the years; namely, through the publication of the 'The Peaceful Pill Handbook', a book that provides information on euthanasia and assisted suicide (not physician-assisted suicide), targeted towards those who are considering ending their lives (Nitschke & Stewart, 2006). The book describes various methods, and rates them based on scales of peacefulness and reliability. It has been criticised for its recommendation of the internet as a source of purchasing lethal drugs, such as sodium nitrite (Stephenson et al., 2022).

There are voluntary organisations that campaign against the legalisation of EPAS; Care Not Killing is a prominent organisation based in the United Kingdom that opposes EPAS. Their goals are focused instead on improving palliative care and ensuring existing laws that prohibit EPAS are strengthened. Their rationale is based on several arguments; mainly that if EPAS was legalised, vulnerable people would be at risk of coercion and pressure to end their lives, and that if people are 'properly cared for' they would not request EPAS (Care Not Killing, 2009)—a suggestion that when patients receive adequate symptomatic treatment for their condition, they would not consider EPAS.

## *6.1 Professional Bodies*

It is important to appreciate the spectrum of opinions held by medical professionals, as within a system that legalises EPAS, they will be the enactors of the procedure. The views represented by medical practitioners are broad in nature; as they represent the ethics of the individual, there is no uniform opinion—however, the stance of professional bodies needs further discussion.

In a 2009 postal survey of 3733 medical practitioners practicing in England, it was found that the majority of the doctors surveyed displayed opposition to the legalisation of EPAS. Strikingly, palliative specialists were particularly noted to be opposed. Religious beliefs were cited as reasons for personal opposition to legalisation. Additionally, reservations were expressed regarding the practicality of implementing a system in a way that safeguards the most vulnerable in society (Seale, 2009), with fear legislation would have inadequate safeguards. A 2012 systematic review that included 15 studies later again identified that the majority of UK doctors were opposed to EPAS. Major themes identified were, religious affiliations, but also scepticism about adequate safeguards, and the concern that the provision of palliative care may be affected (McCormack et al., 2012). Traditionally, palliative medicine doctors are unlikely to support EPAS. In 2019 Royal College of Physicians (RCP) put a vote to their members regarding their policy on EPAS—ultimately the vote resulted in the college moving to adopt a neutral stance. Most (80%) of palliative medicine doctors voted to maintain a position of opposition (BBC News, 2019)—a significant finding as this group of doctors would spend the most time with terminally ill patients, and likely be expected to be most involved in EPAS if it were legalised.

Although these studies reflect a greater hesitancy within the medical profession to support EPAS when compared to the public, this is not necessarily the same across all disciplines of medicine. A study that utilised structured interviews with general practitioners (GPs) in the UK found that those who had not personally witnessed terminal suffering were against EPAS legalisation; however, those who had felt EPAS could be justified in certain situations. The prominent themes in this study were again apprehensions of the potential for harm; but also, a desire to respect a patient's autonomy and right to self-determination (Hussain & White, 2009). Having personal experience of witnessing terminal, intractable suffering has often been reported as a potential causative factor for having sympathetic views towards EPAS (Jewell, 2009).

It is clear, there is no uniform consensus amongst medical practitioners, and the decision to either support or oppose EPAS appears inextricably associated with a person's personal experience and religious views. Amongst the wider public, however, there is evidence within the literature that there is a tendency for the public to support the legalisation of EPAS. A 2019 cross-sectional study that used questionnaires to assess the views and perceptions of the UK public regarding EPAS legislation found that 70% of respondents thought EPAS should be legalised; and a further 62% supported the involvement of doctors in cases of assisted dying (Pentaris & Jacobs, 2020). It is clear then, that there is a level of disconnect between the views of the doctors of the UK, and the UK public at large.

Good Medical Practice, a guideline by the UK regulatory body the General Medical Council (GMC), in its beginning statement, instructs a doctor that they must 'Make the care of your patient your first concern' and act in their 'best interests' when providing care (Breen et al., 2010); ultimately issuing guidance that defines the central role of a doctor as acting in their patient's best interests. This unwavering notion of aiming for a patient's best interests is where nuance can be found; what are a patient's best interests, and by which parameters can they be measured? The GMC instructs doctors that they should not aim for a 'serious adverse outcome' (of which death is included) in their treatment recommendations; a stance that implicitly opposes EPAS.

The British Medical Association (BMA) the foremost trade union representing doctors in the UK, in 2021 changed their policy regarding EPAS. While previously they had taken an opposing stance, their updated position is one of neutrality (BMA, 2021). Despite this change, however, they are resolute in advocating for doctors who voice their concerns regarding EPAS and the potential role of the doctor in implementing it. In terms of the guidance the BMA offers to its members, their stance is that a patient's 'best interests' must include 'clinical improvement'; that is to say, improvement in relation to their health circumstances and well-being (British Medical Association, 2009). This term, again, is open to interpretation: many would argue that ending terminal suffering would represent a clear improvement of a patient's well-being, and by extension represent their best interests.

There are differing views in professional bodies abroad. In America, both the American Medical Association and the American College of Physicians are unanimous in vehement opposition to the legalisation of EPAS (Fontalis et al., 2018). This opposition within professional bodies is also found within countries where EPAS is not only not legalised, but realistically not likely to be implemented in the next few years, such as those countries that have a high proportion of religious citizens. In the

Netherlands, where EPAS is legalised, doctors are reminded by their professional body that they are not obligated to honour requests to perform euthanasia. However, when they do decide to accept a patient's request, there are strict criteria to be met (KNM, 2017). Passive euthanasia which is 'withholding or withdrawing treatment necessary to maintain life' has received legal sanction in India following a landmark ruling by the Supreme Court (Gupta & Bansal, 2023). Following this the Government of India has suggested the draft guidelines for passive euthanasia for doctors, to 'consider' withdrawing life support in terminally ill patients; however, the Indian Medical Association (IMA) has reservations; although the proportion of doctors favouring euthanasia is growing in India (Shekhawat et al., 2023). There has been further work by The Indian Council of Medical Research in defining 'do not attempt CPR, withholding life-sustaining treatment, withdrawing life-sustaining treatment, euthanasia, active shortening of the dying process, physician-assisted suicide', etc. in the Indian sociocultural context (Salins et al., 2018).

## *6.2 Dignitas and 'Suicide Tourism'*

Dignitas is a nonprofit organisation based in Sweden that provides EPAS services. The term Dignitas has become synonymous with the EPAS debate. By the end of 2020, Dignitas had helped 3248 people to end their lives (Dignitas, 2020). Dignitas has the motto 'To live with dignity, to die with dignity', with a mission statement of improving choice in care at the end of one's life. Dignitas has proved to be a polarising organisation and has been the subject of much criticism. One of these is that Dignitas promotes 'suicide tourism'; in that people from countries in which EPAS is not legal, travel to Dignitas with the intention of ending their life. In 2023, it was reported that 40 UK citizens travelled to Dignitas to end their lives (Waple, 2024). Assisting a suicide remains a criminal offence in the UK; as such, anyone who travels with a person who goes to Dignitas to end their life is at risk of arrest and prosecution (Bird, 2022). Although in practice, those who are arrested rarely are prosecuted—there have been just four cases of prosecution of assisted suicide in the UK (CPS, 2019), the legal ramifications are still a threat for anyone who facilitated a person's death, be that through travelling with them, or supporting the travel plans. Proponents of EPAS point to 'suicide tourism' as evidence that the current law is failing patients in the UK; in that clearly, those who seek a physician-assisted death have the means to achieve it by travelling abroad, and a ban does not universally stop this from happening, as seen by the continued numbers of UK citizens who do make this decision.

## 7 Challenges

To discuss some of the challenges an EPAS system would face, we can consider some of the challenges seen within the Netherlands. Although EPAS is strongly supported amongst Dutch society; it has not come without controversial cases. There have been cases reported of young Dutch citizens who have been granted euthanasia on the grounds of intolerable suffering with no prospect of improvement (as is mandated by law), due to psychiatric conditions such as chronic depression, anxiety, and personality disorder that are thought to be refractory to treatment (Pressly, 2018; Sherwood, 2024). These cases fuel debate, as to some, the ending of the life of physically healthy young individuals appeared irreconcilable with ideas of their best interest; while for others, the cases exhibit the right to self-determination and ultimate autonomy that EPAS campaigners promote. Psychiatric conditions meet the criteria for EPAS just as physical health conditions; as long as the approving doctor is satisfied the patient meets the strict criteria (van Veen et al., 2022).

It is clear that an EPAS system needs stringent safeguards and regulations. Many of the challenges in its implementation is ensuring that those who are most vulnerable in society are not harmed by an EPAS system, as has been the subject of debate in countries where EPAS is legalised. A group of patients with clear vulnerability is patients with a dementia diagnosis, who ultimately may lose their ability to have the mental capacity to consent to EPAS as their disease progresses. In patients with significant cognitive impairment, who lack the mental capacity to request significant medical procedures, there will always be complex debate—which intensifies when EPAS is the decision involved. In the Netherlands, only 30–40% of surveyed GPs would oblige a request for EPAS for a patient with dementia; this is compared to 60% of the public who would consider it to be acceptable (Brinkman-Stoppelenburg et al., 2020). This displays a level of discord between the attitudes of the public and the medical professionals in the Netherlands, and a clear uncertainty and reluctance in the medical profession. Many concerns focus on the ability of the doctor to ascertain that a patient is suffering unbearably in this instance, if a patient has lost the ability to meaningfully communicate. Even with the presence of a written advance directive, a doctor may question how they could determine the patient was competent and had the mental capacity at the time of writing the directive.

## 8 EPAS and Suicide Prevention

One suggestion of the opposing debate of legalising EPAS is that it may undermine suicide prevention efforts; and that the availability of EPAS may make it more acceptable to end one's life and increase the incidence of deaths caused by suicide. Concerns of turning EPAS as a method of dealing with suicidal intent associated with psychiatric illnesses are not new (Hendin, 1995). There is even a suggestion, and concern, that a patient may utilise the healthcare system as their method; and that their request for EPAS is the result of a symptom of psychiatric illness. This is a serious emerging issue world-wide (Sprung et al., 2018) and in spite of safeguards built into the legal and procedural framework there is a possibility of EPAS being inappropriately used.

Suicidality is a recognised symptom of psychiatric illness; and one that would be prominent in patients that have significantly severe disease, who may also fit the criteria for EPAS. Suicidal tendencies and behaviour can fluctuate over time; and there is ample empirical evidence to suggest that they can be treated successfully (Mehlum et al., 2020). Patients with personality disorders are often likely to display suicidality and are at increased risk of suicide (Mehlum et al., 2020). In the Netherlands, psychiatric conditions that have no meaningful prospect of recovery qualify a person to be considered for EPAS (Sherwood, 2024). Considering the suffering of psychiatric illness could be as severe as the physical illnesses, the contrast of commitment of psychiatry to prevent suicide and the physician-assisted suicide creates a moral and philosophical dilemma, which needs further debate, and appropriate standards of evaluation of suffering in physical and mental illnesses (Kious & Battin, 2019).

A 2021 systematic review suggested that the characteristics of patients who request EPAS for psychiatric conditions were very similar to those who die by suicide: with self-harm being a consistent trend (Calati et al., 2020). Alternatively, there have been claims that having accessible EPAS may reduce the incidence of self-initiated deaths—from both suicide and EPAS combined. However, a 2022 systematic review of six studies that examined deaths in areas that had legalised EPAS indicated that there were higher rates of self-initiated death (both EPAS and suicide) in countries that had legalised EPAS (Doherty et al., 2022), showing that deaths by suicide do not decrease if an EPAS pathway is available, as some would suggest. An explanation could be that a socially accepted, legalised system may lower the personal threshold of an individual to consider ending their own life, leading to a generalised increase in self-initiated deaths. Similar studies have also demonstrated that self-initiated deaths have shown an increase in cases amongst older women in countries with legalised EPAS, a population group who are epidemiologically more vulnerable to depression (Doherty et al., 2022). This indicates an unmet suicide prevention need within these populations and a suggestion that patients suffering from suicidal ideation may be more vulnerable in a system where EPAS is legalised. As, clearly, certain psychiatric disorders will result in suicidality as a core symptom, and there is the possibility that the healthcare system could then be used as an instrument for those with suicidal ideation.

As the acceptance of EPAS grows in the countries and more countries legalize it, another concern that will affect psychiatrists. There will be requests for psychiatrists to assist medical, surgical and palliative colleagues in differentiating this end-of-life practice from suicide as many of these patients would have cognitions of hopelessness and possibly depressive and other psychiatric disorders. There is a suggestion to consider the change in terminology to medical aid in dying (MAID) from physician-assisted suicide; with specific indicators to distinguish MAID from suicide (Bostwick et al., 2024). However, it still remains a complex issue which may affect suicide prevention efforts in specific groups of patients.

## 9 Conclusion

There is a global discrepancy in the acceptance of EPAS. In some countries, it will likely remain prohibited and socially unacceptable for years to come; with the laws in these countries reflecting the entrenched social opposition that is often rooted in religious affiliation. In countries where EPAS has been legalised, support is often attributed to a generalised increase in support for patient autonomy, and an increasing reluctance to encounter the 'terminal suffering' that has haunted the human experience of death for so long. The idea of a 'good death' that EPAS aims to achieve is certainly the intention; however, concerns remain from medical professionals, the disabled community, and voluntary organisations regarding its impact on those who are amongst the most vulnerable in our society. It is clear that, over the next few years, it is likely there will be even more countries adopting a permissive legal stance towards EPAS. With this, the need to ensure that the system has stringent criteria and appropriate regulation is of paramount importance. Future research needs may be focused on the intersection between psychiatric patients and EPAS requests, and how EPAS can be safely implemented while maintaining stringent safeguards.

## References

Ahlzen, R. (2020). Suffering, authenticity, and physician assisted suicide. *Medicine, Health Care and Philosophy, 23*, 353–359. https://doi.org/10.1007/s11019-019-09929-z

Alexander, L., & Moore, M. (2020). *Deontological ethics*. https://plato.stanford.edu/entries/ethics-deontological/

Appel, J. M. (2004). A duty to kill? A duty to die? Rethinking the euthanasia controversy of 1906. *Bulletin of the History of Medicine, 78*, 610–634. https://doi.org/10.1353/bhm.2004.0106

BBC News. (2019). *Assisted dying: Doctors' group adopts neutral position*. https://www.bbc.co.uk/news/health-47641766 [accessed 09 April 2025].

British Medical Association (2009). *The ethics of caring for older people*. Blackwell.

Begley, A. M. (2008). Guilty but good: Defending voluntary active euthanasia from a virtue perspective. *Nursing Ethics, 15*, 434–445. https://doi.org/10.1177/0969733008090514

Benedict, S., Pierce, A. G., & Sweeney, S. (1998). Historical, ethical, and legal aspects of assisted suicide. *Journal of the Association of Nurses in AIDS Care, 9*, 34–44. https://doi.org/10.1016/s1055-3290(98)80059-9

Bird, N. (2022). Assisted dying: "I was arrested for taking someone to dignitas." *BBC news*. https://www.bbc.co.uk/news/uk-wales-63599107

BMA. (2021). *BMA moves to neutral stance on assisted dying*. https://www.bma.org.uk/news-and-opinion/bma-moves-to-neutral-stance-on-assisted-dying

Bostwick, J. M., Pabst Battin, M., Cohen, L., & Strouse, T. B. (2024). Words matter: Why distinguishing medical aid in dying from suicide should matter to a consultation-liaison psychiatrist. *Journal of the Academy of Consultation-Liaison Psychiatry, 65*(4), 388–395. https://doi.org/10.1016/j.jaclp.2024.04.003

Braun, E. (2022). An autonomy-based approach to assisted suicide: A way to avoid the expressivist objection against assisted dying laws. *Journal of Medical Ethics, 49*, medethics-2022–108375. https://doi.org/10.1136/jme-2022-108375

Breen, K., Cordner, S., Thomson, C., & Plueckhahn, V. (2010). *Good medical practice: Professionalism*. Cambridge University Press.

Brenna, C. T. A. (2021). Regulating death: A brief history of medical assistance in dying. *Indian Journal of Palliative Care*, 1–4. https://doi.org/10.25259/ijpc_426_20
Brinkman-Stoppelenburg, A., Evenblij, K., Pasman, H. R. W., van Delden, J. J. M., Onwuteaka-Philipsen, B. D., & van der Heide, A. (2020). Physicians' and public attitudes toward euthanasia in people with advanced dementia. *Journal of the American Geriatrics Society, 68*, 2319–2328. https://doi.org/10.1111/jgs.16692
Calati, R., Olié, E., Dassa, D., Gramaglia, C., Guillaume, S., Madeddu, F., & Courtet, P. (2020). Euthanasia and assisted suicide in psychiatric patients: A systematic review of the literature. *Journal of Psychiatric Research, 135*. https://doi.org/10.1016/j.jpsychires.2020.12.006
Care Not Killing. (2009). *About us—care not killing—promoting care, opposing euthanasia—care not killing*. https://www.carenotkilling.org.uk/about/
Chakraborty, R., El-Jawahri, A. R., Litzow, M. R., Syrjala, K. L., Parnes, A. D., & Hashmi, S. K. A. (2017). Systematic review of religious beliefs about major end-of-life issues in the five major world religions. *Palliative and Supportive Care, 15*(5), 609–622. https://doi.org/10.1017/S1478951516001061
Clarke, C., Cannon, M., Skokauskas, N., & Twomey, P. (2021). The debate about physician assisted suicide and euthanasia in Ireland—implications for psychiatry. *International Journal of Law and Psychiatry, 79*, 101747. https://doi.org/10.1016/j.ijlp.2021.101747
CPS. (2019). *Assisted suicide*. The Crown Prosecution Service. https://www.cps.gov.uk/publication/assisted-suicide
der Heide, A., Onwuteaka-Philipsen, B. D., van Delden, J., & Gevers, J. K. M. (2005). Fourth evaluation of the law on the review of termination of life on request and assisted suicide (euthanasia act). *PubMed, 149*, 2187–2189.
Dignitas. (2020). *Statistics*. http://www.dignitas.ch/index.php?option=com_content&view=article&id=32&Itemid=72&lang=en
Dignity in Dying. (2016). *Dignity in dying—join the campaign*. https://www.dignityindying.org.uk/
Doherty, A. M., Axe, C. J., & Jones, D. A. (2022). Investigating the relationship between euthanasia and/or assisted suicide and rates of non-assisted suicide: Systematic review. *BJPsych Open, 8*. https://doi.org/10.1192/bjo.2022.71
Dorji, N., Lapierre, S., & Dransart, D. A. C. (2020). Perception of medical assistance in dying among Asian Buddhists living in Montreal, Canada. *OMEGA—Journal of Death and Dying, 85*(3), 003022282094864. https://doi.org/10.1177/0030222820948645
Emanuel, E. J., Onwuteaka-Philipsen, B. D., Urwin, J. W., & Cohen, J. (2016). Attitudes and practices of euthanasia and physician-assisted suicide in the United States, Canada, and Europe. *JAMA, 316*(1), 79–90. https://doi.org/10.1001/jama.2016.8499
Fontalis, A., Prousali, E., & Kulkarni, K. (2018). Euthanasia and assisted dying: What is the current position and what are the key arguments informing the debate? *Journal of the Royal Society of Medicine, 111*, 407–413. https://doi.org/10.1177/0141076818803452
Grodin, M. A., Miller, E. L., & Kelly, J. I. (2018). The Nazi physicians as leaders in eugenics and "euthanasia": Lessons for today. *American Journal of Public Health, 108*, 53–57. https://doi.org/10.2105/ajph.2017.304120
Groenewoud, A. S., Atsma, F., Arvin, M., Westert, G. P., & Boer, T. A. (2021). Euthanasia in the Netherlands: A claims data cross-sectional study of geographical variation. *BMJ Support Palliat Care*. bmjspcare-2020-002573. https://doi.org/10.1136/bmjspcare-2020-002573
Grove, G., Lovell, M., & Best, M. (2022). Perspectives of major world religions regarding euthanasia and assisted suicide: A comparative analysis. *Journal of Religion and Health, 61*. https://doi.org/10.1007/s10943-022-01498-5
Gupta, A. K., & Bansal, D. (2023). Euthanasia—review and update through the lens of a psychiatrist. *Industrial Psychiatry Journal, 32*(1), 15–18. https://doi.org/10.4103/ipj.ipj_259_21
Hajar, R. (2017). The physician's oath: Historical perspectives. *Heart Views, 18*, 154–159. https://doi.org/10.4103/heartviews.heartviews_131_17

Hendin, H. (1995). Assisted suicide, euthanasia, and suicide prevention: The implications of the Dutch experience. *Suicide Life Threat Behavior Spring, 25*(1), 193–204. https://doi.org/10.1111/j.1943-278X.1995.tb00403.x

Humanists UK. (2024). *A humanist view of society*. https://humanists.uk/campaigns/humanist-view-of-society/

Hussain, T., & White, P. (2009). GPs' views on the practice of physician-assisted suicide and their role in proposed UK legalisation: A qualitative study. *The British Journal of General Practice, 59*, 844–849. https://doi.org/10.3399/bjgp09X472908

Janssen, A. (2002). The new regulation of voluntary euthanasia and medically assisted suicide in the Netherlands. *International Journal of Law, Policy and the Family, 16*, 260–269. https://doi.org/10.1093/lawfam/16.2.260

Jewell, D. (2009). Our debt to those who are dying: The UK medical establishment should reconsider its stance on assisted suicide. *British Journal of General Practice, 59*, 809–810. https://doi.org/10.3399/bjgp09x472863

Jotkowitz, A. B., Glick, S. (2009). The Israeli terminally ill patient law of 2005. *Journal of Palliative Care, 25*(4), 284–8. PMID: 20131585. https://pubmed.ncbi.nlm.nih.gov/20131585/

Kelly, B. D. (2011). Self-immolation, suicide and self-harm in Buddhist and Western traditions. *Transcultural Psychiatry, 48*(3), 299–317. https://doi.org/10.1177/1363461511402869

Kious, B. M., & Battin, M. P. (2019). Physician aid-in-dying and suicide prevention in psychiatry: A moral crisis? *American Journal of Bioethics, 19*(10), 29–39. https://doi.org/10.1080/15265161.2019.1653397

KNM. (2017). *Euthanasia in the Netherlands*. https://www.knmg.nl/actueel/nieuws/nieuwsbericht/euthanasia-in-the-netherlands

Letellier, P. (2003). History and definition of a word. In *Euthanasia : Ethical and human aspects* (pp. 13–24). Council of Europe.

Linzer, D. (2013). Treatment of terminally ill patients according to Jewish law. *AMA Journal of Ethics, 15*, 1081–1087. https://doi.org/10.1001/virtualmentor.2013.15.12.msoc2-1312

Madadin, M. (2020). The Islamic perspective on physician-assisted suicide and euthanasia. *Medicine, Science and the Law, 60*, 278–286. https://doi.org/10.1177/0025802420934241

McCormack, R., Clifford, M., Conroy, M. (2012). Attitudes of UK doctors towards euthanasia and physician-assisted suicide: A systematic literature review. *Palliative Medicine, 26*(1), 23–33. https://doi.org/10.1177/0269216310397688

McCormick, A. J. (2013). Buddhist ethics and end-of-life care decisions. *Journal of Social Work in End-of-Life & Palliative Care, 9*(2–3), 209–225. https://doi.org/10.1080/15524256.2013.794060

Mehlum, L., Schmahl, C., Berens, A., Doering, S., Hutsebaut, J., Kaera, A., Kramer, U., Moran, P. A., Renneberg, B., Ribaudi, J. S., Simonsen, S., Swales, M., Taubner, S., & di Giacomo, E. (2020). Euthanasia and assisted suicide in patients with personality disorders: A review of current practice and challenges. *Borderline Personality Disorder and Emotion Dysregulation, 7*(1). https://doi.org/10.1186/s40479-020-00131-9

Mroz, S., Dierickx, S., Deliens, L., Cohen, J., & Chambaere, K. (2021). Assisted dying around the world: A status quaestionis. *Annals of Palliative Medicine, 9*, 57. https://doi.org/10.21037/apm-20-637

Nitschke, P., & Stewart, F. (2006). *The peaceful pill handbook*. Exit International US Ltd.

Nyman, D. J., Eidelman, L. A., & Sprung, C. L. (1996). Euthanasia. *Critical Care Clinics, 12*, 85–96. https://doi.org/10.1016/s0749-0704(05)70216-5

Onwuteaka-Philipsen, B. D., Brinkman-Stoppelenburg, A., Penning, C., de Jong-Krul, G. J. F., van Delden, J. J. M., & van der Heide, A. (2012). Trends in end-of-life practices before and after the enactment of the euthanasia law in the Netherlands from 1990 to 2010: A repeated cross-sectional survey. *The Lancet, 380*, 908–915. https://doi.org/10.1016/s0140-6736(12)61034-4

Otani, I. (2010). "Good manner of dying" as a normative concept: "Autocide","granny dumping" and discussions on euthanasia/death with dignity in Japan. *International Journal of Japanese Sociology, 19*, 49–63. https://doi.org/10.1111/j.1475-6781.2010.01136.x

Pascoe, R. (2017). Number of official cases of euthanasia rise 10% in the Netherlands. *DutchNews.Nl.* https://www.dutchnews.nl/2017/04/number-of-official-cases-of-euthanasia-rise-10-in-the-netherlands/

Pentaris, P., & Jacobs, L. (2020). UK public's views and perceptions about the legalisation of assisted dying and assisted suicide. *OMEGA—Journal of Death and Dying, 86*, 003022282094725. https://doi.org/10.1177/0030222820947254

Pressly, L. (2018). *The troubled 29-year-old helped to die by Dutch doctors.* BBC News. https://www.bbc.co.uk/news/stories-45117163

Ramsay, J. H. R. (1994). A king, a doctor, and a convenient death. *BMJ, 308*, 1445. https://doi.org/10.1136/bmj.308.6941.1445

Randall, F., & Downie, R. (2010). Assisted suicide and voluntary euthanasia: Role contradictions for physicians. *Clinical Medicine, 10*, 323–325. https://doi.org/10.7861/clinmedicine.10-4-323

Roehr, B. (2021). Assisted dying around the world. *BMJ, 374*, 22. https://doi.org/10.1136/bmj.n2200

Salins, N., Gursahani, R., Mathur, R., Iyer, S., Macaden, S., Simha, N., Mani, R. K., & Rajagopal, M. R. (2018). Definition of terms used in limitation of treatment and providing palliative care at the end of life: The Indian council of medical research commission report. *Indian Journal of Critical Care Medicine, 22*(4), 249–262. https://doi.org/10.4103/ijccm.IJCCM_165_18

Seale, C. (2009). Legalisation of euthanasia or physician-assisted suicide: Survey of doctors' attitudes. *Palliative Medicine, 23*, 205–212. https://doi.org/10.1177/0269216308102041

Shekhawat, R. S., Kanchan, T., Saraf, A., Ateriya, N., Meshram, V. P., & Setia, P. (2023). Knowledge, attitude and practices (KAP) of medical professionals on euthanasia: A study from a tertiary care centre in India. *Cureus, 15*. https://doi.org/10.7759/cureus.34788

Sherwood, H. (2024). Dutch woman, 29, granted euthanasia approval on grounds of mental suffering. *The Guardian.* https://www.theguardian.com/society/article/2024/may/16/dutch-woman-euthanasia-approval-grounds-of-mental-suffering

Shestak, V., & Dyachenko, M. (2020). *On certain aspects of legal regulation of euthanasia in Russian and foreign criminal law.* https://papers.ssrn.com/sol3/papers.cfm?abstract_id=3613800

Sinha, V., Sarkhel, S., & Basu, S. (2012). Euthanasia: An Indian perspective. *Indian Journal of Psychiatry, 54*, 177. https://doi.org/10.4103/0019-5545.99537

Sobotková, V. (2019). Boundaries of life and death from the viewpoint of Shi'i Islamic jurisprudence and the consequences in the field of Islamic bioethics. *Religio, 27*, 269–290. https://journals.phil.muni.cz/religio/article/view/23262

Sprung, C. L., Somerville, M. A., Radbruch, L., Collet, N. S., Duttge, G., Piva, J. P., Antonelli, M., Sulmasy, D. P., Lemmens, W., Ely, E.W. (2018, October). Physician-assisted suicide and euthanasia: Emerging issues from a global perspective. *Indian Journal of Palliative Care, 33*(4), 197–203.

Stempsey, W. E. (1997). End-of-life decisions: Christian perspectives. *Christian Bioethics, 3*, 249–261. https://doi.org/10.1093/cb/3.3.249

Stephenson, L., Wills, S., van den Heuvel, C., Humphries, M., & Byard, R. W. (2022). Increasing use of sodium nitrite in suicides—an emerging trend. *Forensic Science, Medicine and Pathology.* https://doi.org/10.1007/s12024-022-00471-8

Stolberg, M. (2007). Active euthanasia in pre-modern society, 1500–1800: Learned debates and popular practices. *Social History of Medicine, 20*, 205–221. https://doi.org/10.1093/shm/hkm034

Supreme Court of India and Delhi High Court. (2024). *Validity of euthanasia in India: Constitutional and legal approach.* https://www.lexology.com/library/detail.aspx?g=247c8c66-b3ed-4179-bfe1-7df289a0cde5

Tännsjö, T. (2005). Moral dimensions. *BMJ, 331*, 689–691. https://doi.org/10.1136/bmj.331.7518.689

UK Parliament. (2021). *Assisted dying bill [HL]—parliamentary bills—UK parliament.* https://bills.parliament.uk/bills/2875

Upasen, R., Thanasilp, S., Akkayagorn, L., Chimluang, J., Tantitrakul, W., Doutrich, D. L., & Saengpanya, W. (2022). Death acceptance process in Thai Buddhist patients with life-limiting cancer: A grounded theory. *Global Qualitative Nursing Research, 9*, 23333936221111810. https://doi.org/10.1177/23333936221111809

van Veen, S. M. P., Widdershoven, G. A. M., Beekman, A. T. F., & Evans, N. (2022). Physician assisted death for psychiatric suffering: Experiences in the Netherlands. *Frontiers in Psychiatry, 13*, 895387. https://doi.org/10.3389/fpsyt.2022.895387

Waple, K. (2024). Assisted dying: Family shares experience of dignitas. Accessed on October 03, 2024, https://www.bbc.com/news/articles/ced3ngwp3g5o

Weng, L., Joynt, G. M., Lee, A., et al. (2011). Attitudes towards ethical problems in critical care medicine: The Chinese perspective. *Intensive Care Medicine, 37*(4), 655–664.

World Federation of Right to Die Societies. (2020). *Member organizations—the world federation of right to die societies.* https://wfrtds.org/member-organizations/

# Chapter 18
# Suicide-Promoting Groups and Sites

**Rubina Jahan and Md. Ashiquir Rahaman**

**Abstract** The emergence of suicide-promoting groups and sites poses a critical public health concern; however, there is a notable lack of comprehensive research on these entities at a global level. Given that young people, particularly adolescents, constitute a significant portion of online platform users and that suicide rates are alarmingly high within this demographic, it is crucial to examine these intersections. Such understanding is essential for designing and implementing effective suicide prevention initiatives that can address the unique vulnerabilities of this population. This chapter investigates the types of suicide-promoting sites and groups, targeted demographics, and associated risk factors, along with the grooming strategies employed to engage users. Additionally, it highlights the psychosocial and cultural factors that contribute to these issues, as well as the legal protocols, ethical practices, and limitations surrounding them. Ultimately, the chapter advocates for enhanced prevention and intervention strategies to address the growing concerns associated with these entities.

**Keywords** Mental health · Suicide · Suicide-promoting sites · Risk factors · Suicide prevention

## 1 Overview

In today's world, internet has become an integral part, accessible to people from all walks of life. It is now the go-to place for information, entertainment, and social connections, serving as a primary source for addressing personal needs, including mental health support. People often turn to online communities and groups to seek

R. Jahan (✉)
SAJIDA Foundation, Dhaka, Bangladesh
e-mail: rumirj@gmail.com

Md. A. Rahaman
Department of Clinical Psychology, University of Dhaka, Dhaka, Bangladesh



S. M. Y. Arafat and S. K. Kar (eds.), *Ecological and Social Determinants of Suicidal Behavior*, South Asian Perspectives in Mental Health and Psychology,
https://doi.org/10.1007/978-981-96-4028-7_18

validation, share experiences, and find comfort in dealing with mental health challenges, especially in the case of self-harm and suicide. Since these topics are often seen as taboo in society, and individuals fear being shamed or judged, vulnerable people frequently seek refuge in anonymous online platforms where they can find validation, advice, and a sense of community. Unfortunately, this anonymity can also create spaces where harmful behaviors are encouraged, leading to the growth of suicide-promoting groups and sites. These platforms, rather than offering support, can foster dangerous environments making it crucial to raise awareness about their impact and promote safer, healthier alternatives for those in need of mental health support.

## *1.1 Suicide-Promoting Sites and Groups*

Suicide-promoting groups and sites are often referred to as "pro-suicide" platforms, which have become a significant concern and area of study in the field of mental health. These sites are defined as online spaces that provide step-by-step guides for attempting suicide, encourage the act of taking one's life, or foster suicidal thoughts through their content or community discussions (Stabin, 2013). Varying in purpose and structure, these sites and groups often glorify or romanticize suicide, offering harmful advice, sharing dangerous content, and even promoting self-destructive behavior among vulnerable users. The anonymity and vast reach of the internet have allowed such spaces to thrive, posing a serious threat to those struggling with mental health issues. Therefore, understanding the impact of these online communities is critical for prevention efforts, as they can directly influence real-life behavior and contribute to the rising suicide rates in certain demographics.

## *1.2 Types of Suicide-Promoting Groups*

Suicide-promoting sites and groups vary significantly in content, purpose, and the ways they engage with vulnerable individuals (Fig. 1). With the rapid advancement of technology and the increasing accessibility of the internet, the risks have multiplied, offering a wider variety of platforms for harmful content to thrive. Social media, anonymous forums, entertainment content, and even dark web communities now provide multiple avenues for such groups to operate, making it easier for vulnerable individuals to encounter these dangerous spaces. This technological expansion has not only increased the reach of these harmful communities but also made them harder to monitor and regulate.

Pro-suicide content is not confined to dedicated pro-suicide websites. It can appear in chat rooms, message boards, blogs, and almost any platform that permits open information sharing. Below are some common types:

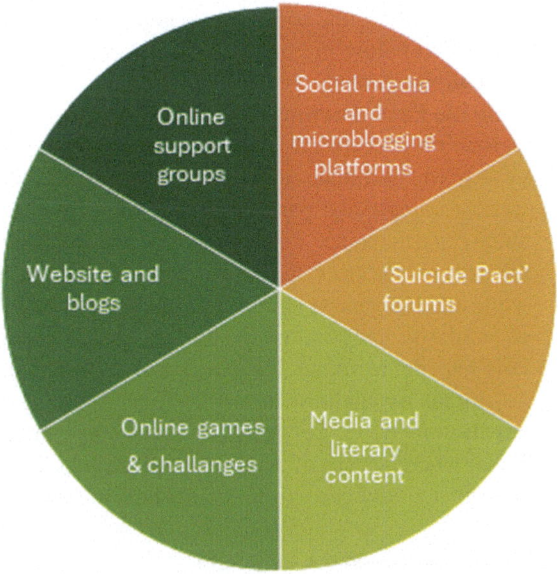


**Fig. 1** Various types of suicide-promoting groups and sites

- **Social Media and Microblogging Platforms**

  Social media encompasses various applications, websites, and blogs that allow individuals worldwide to connect over the internet for chatting, content sharing, video calls, and a range of other user functionalities (Stephenson et al., 2021). Recent research highlights a correlation between higher internet usage and increased suicide rates in the general population (Shah, 2010). Social media and microblogging platforms are numerous and have profound effects on vulnerable populations. Firstly, there are many private chatrooms, pages, and blog sites on popular platforms like Facebook, Instagram, TikTok, WeChat, Snapchat, Telegram, and Tumblr have a history of leading users to communities that glorify self-harm or provide detailed accounts of suicidal ideation, enabling an environment that normalizes these feelings (Stabin, 2013). Study found that young adults frequently cited online forums as sources of suicide stories and that exposure to these stories was associated with increased suicidal thoughts (Dunlop et al., 2011).

  Secondly, these platforms can indirectly contribute to suicidal behavior by permitting individuals to join as support systems without adequate oversight. Many such platforms that facilitate user interactions do not implement comprehensive content moderation, allowing the unmonitored sharing of graphics, images, and methodical information related to suicide. This lack of oversight enables harmful content to proliferate within these communities, significantly increasing the risk for vulnerable users. Moreover, the absence of clear safety protocols and ethical guidelines further exacerbates this issue, creating an environment where dangerous information can circulate unchecked (Robinson et al., 2015).

Consequently, while social media holds the potential for positive engagement, its unchecked nature presents substantial challenges for mental health and suicide prevention efforts.

- **"Suicide Pact" Forums**

  Suicide pact forums are online platforms where individuals connect anonymously to coordinate joint suicides (Rajagopal, 2004). Often found on the dark web or unregulated parts of the internet, these forums foster emotional bonds among participants, reinforcing suicidal ideation and commitment to follow through on the pact. Some encourage in-person meetings to carry out the act, while others focus on virtual coordination. These forums create a dangerous sense of solidarity, presenting suicide as a shared experience, which can be particularly harmful to vulnerable individuals seeking belonging. The anonymity makes it difficult for authorities to intervene, allowing these communities to operate largely unnoticed. Between 2003 and 2005, there were incidents in Japan and Korea where groups of young individuals who met through suicide pact websites coordinated and carried out their plans to end their lives together (BBC, 2004, 2010).

- **Online Games and Challenges**

  Online Game Challenges refer to dangerous and manipulative platforms that engage individuals, often teenagers, in harmful tasks, sometimes culminating in suicide. A prominent example is the *"Blue Whale Challenge,"* which reportedly originated in Russia and gained global attention for allegedly involving a 50-day sequence of escalating tasks, ultimately pushing participants to take their own lives (BBC, 2017). These platforms prey on vulnerable individuals, manipulating their emotions and creating a sense of isolation, fear, or obligation to complete the challenge, often functioning as pressure groups. The anonymous and decentralized nature of such platforms presents significant challenges for law enforcement and mental health professionals. Their difficulty to track allows these "suicide challenges" to spread across regions quickly and without timely intervention.

- **Media and Literary Content**

  Research has consistently shown that media depictions of suicide, particularly those that normalize, glamorize, or desensitize the issue, can lead to imitative behavior. This phenomenon, known as the *"Werther effect"* or *"suicide contagion,"* is well-documented outside of online contexts as well (Niederkrotenthaler et al., 2010). One prominent example is *13 Reasons Why*, a novel by Jay Asher that gained immense popularity after its adaptation into a Netflix series, which tells the story of a high school student, Hannah Baker, who leaves behind a series of tapes detailing the reasons for her suicide. Studies have identified a concerning correlation between the release of the Netflix series and a spike in suicide rates among U.S. youth aged 10–19. Following the show's release in April 2017, researchers documented a nearly 29% increase in suicide rates for this age group, with boys being particularly affected (Niederkrotenthaler et al., 2019). The study also noted an increase in social media attention during the same period, reinforcing concerns about media contagion—where suicide-related content can influence vulnerable viewers and lead to actual suicidal behavior (Niederkrotenthaler et al., 2019; NIH,

2019). Mental health professionals also argue that the novel glamorizes suicide by portraying it as a form of revenge or a solution to emotional pain. Such portrayals could influence vulnerable readers, particularly adolescents, in harmful ways and potentially lead to copycat suicides.

Regarding other media, like movies or shows such as *Suicide Squad*, although not directly linked to a significant increase in suicides, the glamorization or trivialization of suicide in popular culture has long raised ethical concerns. Mental health professionals stress the importance of responsibly portraying sensitive subjects like suicide to prevent harmful effects, especially on impressionable young audiences. As studies have revealed a strong link between widely publicized suicides and subsequent increases in suicide rates, underscoring the dangers of these narratives in popular media (Sisask & Värnik, 2012).

## 2 What Is "Suicide Tourism"

The concept of suicide tourism first emerged in the literature in the late 1900s. Broadly, it refers to individuals traveling to countries or jurisdictions where physician-assisted suicide or euthanasia is legally permitted to end their lives (Yu et al., 2020). This phenomenon has been notably observed in countries like Switzerland, the Netherlands, and Mexico. For example, organizations such as Dignitas in Switzerland provide assistance in ending life under strict conditions (Gauthier et al., 2015), while in Mexico, liquid pentobarbital, a drug commonly used for euthanizing pets, has attracted individuals seeking a painless and peaceful death (Emmott, 2008). Though various reasons exist for suicide tourism, the notable motivations are incurable illnesses like neurological and rheumatic diseases, chronic pain, or diminished quality of life due to age or disability (Gauthier et al., 2015; Hurst & Mauron, 2003). Suicide tourism gained popularity through a combination of cultural, literary, and media influences. For example, Akihabara Forest in Japan became infamous as a suicide hotspot, largely due to its portrayal in Wataru Tsurumi's 1993 book The Complete Manual of Suicide, which explicitly recommended it as an ideal place to end one's life (Salazar, 2022). The forest's reputation spread globally as media reports on the increasing number of suicides there amplified its grim appeal (Pretto, 2021). While some countries, such as Switzerland, the Netherlands, and Belgium, allow euthanasia or physician-assisted suicide under strict criteria, many other nations consider it illegal, forcing individuals in prohibitive regions to seek alternatives abroad (Gauthier et al., 2015; Sperling, 2019). Therefore, the phenomenon raises significant ethical concerns. One argument suggests that allowing non-residents access to assisted suicide services commodifies death, turning it into a transaction (Lerner & Caplan, 2015). Conversely, proponents argue that the right to die with dignity should not be constrained by geographical boundaries, emphasizing personal autonomy and the relief of suffering (George, 1994). However, from a societal perspective, concerns have been raised about vulnerable individuals feeling coerced or pressured to end their lives due to inadequate support systems, financial burdens, or lack of access to quality care (Gamondi et al., 2013). Despite these ethical complexities, suicide tourism continues to grow. The intersection of legal, ethical, and medical perspectives makes this issue a critical concern for policymakers, raising important questions about the future of assisted suicide legislation on a global scale.

## 3 Understanding the Dynamics of These Groups and Sites

### *3.1 Affected Demographics and Risk Factors*

In the past two decades, social media has significantly reshaped global social interactions, with young people and teenagers emerging as the most active and frequent users (Anderson & Jiang, 2018). This demographic is particularly susceptible to the influence of social media on behavior, morals, education, and mental health. A 2019 Pew Research Center survey of nearly 750 teens aged 13–17 in the United States revealed that 45% of respondents are online almost constantly, with 97% engaging on platforms like TikTok, YouTube, Facebook, Instagram, and Snapchat (Orben, 2020). Research indicates that suicidal behavior in younger individuals is more susceptible to the influence of online content compared to older populations (Dobson, 1999).

Globally, suicide remains the second leading cause of death among adolescents and young adults, particularly those aged 15–29 (WHO, 2014). In regions like South Asia, socioeconomic factors exacerbate the risk, as lower-income individuals often turn to online platforms in the absence of formal mental health services (Patel & Kleinman, 2003). Experts have expressed concerns over the role of social media and text messaging in contributing to anxiety, depression, and lowered self-esteem among youth. A survey by the Royal Society for Public Health in the UK, involving 14- to 24-year-olds, found that platforms like Snapchat, Facebook, Twitter, and Instagram were associated with increased feelings of depression, anxiety, poor body image, and loneliness (Jan et al., 2017).

The presence of pro-suicide content on the internet is a significant concern for parents of adolescents and young children, who, having grown up in the digital age, are highly skilled at accessing information online from an early age. Adolescents exhibit a higher prevalence of risk-taking behaviors, including substance abuse, reckless driving, and non-suicidal self-harm each of which serves as a potential risk factor for suicide attempts (Joiner, 2005).

This demonstrates the dangerous cycle between young people's use of online social network platforms and their heightened vulnerability to emotional and psychological crises, creating fertile ground for suicide-promoting groups and sites to exploit. The combination of high social media engagement and underlying mental health struggles makes this demographic particularly vulnerable to harmful online influences.

### *3.2 Grooming and Manipulation Tactics Used by Such Groups/Sites*

Suicide-promoting groups and sites often employ grooming and manipulation tactics that target vulnerable individuals, particularly those struggling with emotional distress (Fig. 2). These tactics typically start by offering a sense of community and understanding, appealing to individuals who feel isolated or misunderstood (Baumeister, 1990). These online communities present themselves as caring and supportive, gradually normalizing suicidal ideation and presenting suicide as an acceptable or even rational solution to their problems (Joiner, 2005). A key component of these tactics is emotional manipulation, where individuals are encouraged to keep their engagement with the group secret, which further isolates them from outside support systems.

Additionally, these platforms use desensitization techniques, where individuals are gradually exposed to increasingly harmful content, such as detailed descriptions or images of suicide methods. This process not only lowers their emotional barriers but also makes the idea of self-harm seem normalized or even inevitable. Even if individuals realize the dangerous trajectory, they are often deeply embedded in the group, making it difficult to escape the manipulative environment. The grooming process preys on emotional vulnerability, reinforcing suicidal thoughts while cutting off avenues for real support and intervention.

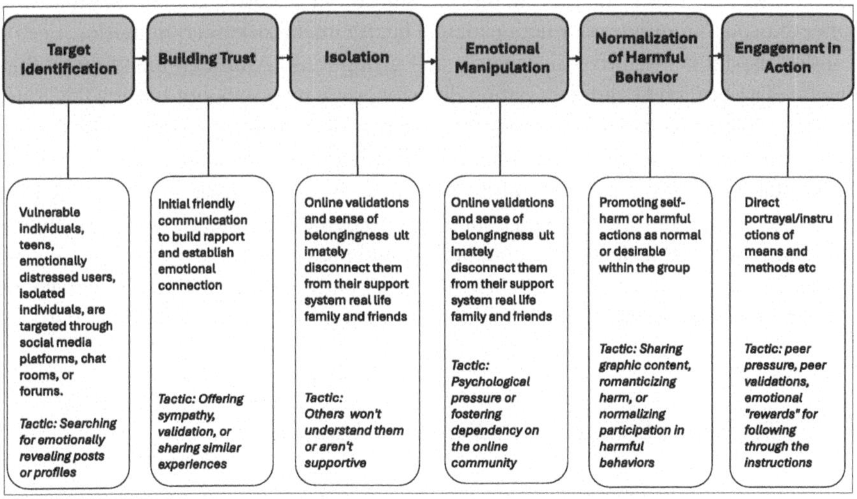


**Fig. 2** Grooming and manipulation tactics used by such online groups/sites

## 4 Psychosocial and Cultural Determinants of Suicide-Promoting Sites and Groups

In today's world, the rise of suicide-promoting websites, social media groups, and online platforms reflects a concerning intersection of psychological, sociocultural, and economic factors. While the internet can offer community and belonging, some platforms normalize or encourage suicidal behavior. Understanding why individuals are drawn to these spaces requires exploring the underlying psychosocial and cultural drivers.

### *4.1 Psychology of Engaging in These Platforms*

Individuals experiencing distress and suicidal ideation are psychologically vulnerable, which may draw them to suicide-promoting online platforms. These individuals often seek an outlet for their despair, finding appeal in the content and community these platforms offer. Research shows that people with suicidal thoughts frequently search for suicide-related information online for both emotional and informational purposes, including methods and others' experiences (Bell et al., 2018; Mok et al., 2016). One strong psychological aspect that drives individuals to engage in these platforms is the search for validation. These platforms provide a space where shared experiences can normalize suicidal thoughts, reinforcing negative coping mechanisms rather than encouraging constructive mental health interventions (Baumeister, 1990). Another aspect is cognitive dissonance and groupthink. Although many know that suicide is a permanent and devastating decision, they may seek out forums that validate their internal conflict. Once they become part of such groups, groupthink (Janis, 1972) often emerges, where the collective reinforcement of suicidal ideation within the community eliminates dissenting opinions. Another factor is the anonymity offered by these platforms, which contributes to deindividuation (Zimbardo, 1969). This anonymity reduces social accountability and increases the likelihood of individuals engaging in behavior they might avoid in person, creating an environment where suicidal ideation can thrive without external intervention (Davidson et al., 2020).

### *4.2 The Role of Social Isolation and Alienation*

Social isolation has long been recognized as a risk factor for suicide (Motillon-Toudic et al., 2022). In today's digital age, social isolation may be exacerbated by over-reliance on online communication, where relationships are more superficial and transient. Suicide-promoting platforms exploit these feelings, offering a space where users can communicate without judgment, albeit often in ways that reinforce their alienation. These groups serve as a community for individuals who feel isolated in their offline lives, but the interactions are often negative, reinforcing suicidal thoughts instead of fostering resilience (Minkkinen et al., 2017). This phenomenon, where individuals with shared negative experiences bond over their struggles, creates a paradoxical situation where a sense of community fosters self-destructive behavior.

### 4.3 Impact of Stigma, Discrimination, and Insufficient Support System

Mental health-related stigma plays a central role in why individuals may turn to online spaces rather than seeking professional help. In many cultures, discussing mental health issues like depression or suicidal ideation is taboo, leading individuals to hide their struggles and discourage them from seeking help (Ahad et al., 2023). As a result, those experiencing suicidal thoughts may turn to online platforms where they can express themselves without fear of judgment. Besides, marginalized groups, including lesbian, gay, bisexual, and transgender (LGBT) individuals, and racial, ethnic, and religious minorities, often face discrimination that exacerbates mental health challenges. These groups experience higher levels of depression and suicidal ideation, with fewer resources or safe spaces to seek help. In such scenarios, the isolation stemming from discrimination leads to further entrenchment in online spaces that validate negative emotions. The absence of culturally congruent mental health services leaves marginalized individuals feeling unsupported, increasing their susceptibility to harmful online content.

### 4.4 Economic and Sociocultural Factors

Economic stress is a major factor in suicidal behavior, often leading to hopelessness and suicidal ideation (Mathieu et al., 2022). Due to financial constraints, people are increasingly reaching out to online support, leading them to uncensored platforms, including those that promote suicide. Those facing financial hardship may seek escape in suicide-promoting platforms. Cultural norms that emphasize self-reliance, masculinity, or honor can prevent individuals from seeking mental health support. In many Asian cultures, for example, the concept of "saving face" discourages admitting vulnerability during a crisis (Kramer et al., 2002). Cultural pressures around honor and success may drive individuals to these online groups, where distorted support encourages viewing suicide to preserve dignity or escape overwhelming stress.

# 5 Legal and Ethical Consideration

The rise of the internet has significantly transformed how individuals, communities, and organizations communicate and share information, including topics related to mental health and suicide. However, the emergence of suicide-promoting websites and online communities presents substantial legal and ethical challenges. In this section, we will illustrate the legal framework regulating these sites, focusing on issues related to freedom of speech, internet privacy, and jurisdictional limitations. We will then explore the ethical considerations in regulating online content and present case studies highlighting legal actions taken against such sites.

## *5.1 Legal Framework in Regulating Suicide-Promoting Sites and Groups*

- **Freedom of Speech**

  Freedom of speech is a fundamental principle practiced in many democratic societies, providing individuals the right to express their thoughts and opinions without censorship. However, this right is not absolute, particularly when it intersects with public health concerns, including the promotion of self-harm and suicide. In this context, maintaining a delicate balance between protecting free expression and preventing harm must be prioritized (Mishara & Weisstub, 2024).

  There has been an argument that while individuals have the right to discuss suicide, promoting it can lead to counterproductive consequences. For instance, Section 230 of the Communications Decency Act in the United States provides immunity to online platforms for user-generated content, complicating efforts to regulate harmful speech (Goodman & Whittington, 2019). This legal framework protects platforms from liability for the content shared by their users, often allowing suicide-promoting groups to operate without oversight. Conversely, in countries like Germany and Australia, restrictions and regulations exist regarding harmful content. The German Criminal Code prohibits the dissemination of materials that encourage suicide, reflecting a more interventionist approach to public health (Göken & Zwießler, 2022). In this context, courts have ruled that promoting suicide does not fall under the protective umbrella of free speech, especially when it poses a threat to vulnerable individuals. However, many Low- and Middle-Income Countries (LMICs), including Bangladesh, lack clear protocols for regulating harmful online content. The absence of comprehensive regulations makes at-risk populations in these countries more vulnerable to suicide.
- **Internet Privacy**

  Internet privacy presents another legal consideration in regulating suicide-promoting sites. Users often seek anonymity when discussing sensitive topics like suicidal thoughts. While this anonymity can provide a safe space for individuals to express themselves, it also complicates efforts to identify and intervene in cases of imminent risk. Laws such as the General Data Protection Regulation (GDPR) in the European Union emphasize user privacy, which can limit authorities' ability to monitor online content or intervene in potentially harmful situations (Hoofnagle et al., 2019). The GDPR directs that user data be collected and processed transparently, yet the sensitive nature of discussions surrounding suicide may prevent individuals from disclosing their identities, further complicating regulatory efforts (Hoofnagle et al., 2019).

- **Jurisdiction Limitations**
  Jurisdictional issues present substantial challenges in regulating suicide-promoting sites, particularly in our interconnected digital world. Many platforms host content that is accessible across borders, complicating the enforcement of local laws. For instance, a website based in one country may attract users from multiple jurisdictions, each with its own legal standards regarding harmful content. The Convention on Cybercrime, also known as the Budapest Convention on Cybercrime, attempts to address these challenges by promoting international cooperation in combating cybercrime, including content that promotes self-harm and suicide (Tosoni, 2018). However, the application of these laws remains inconsistent. In practice, local authorities may find it difficult to pursue legal action against sites operating outside their jurisdiction.

## 5.2 *Ethical Issues in Regulating Sites and Groups*

The ethical considerations surrounding the regulation of suicide-promoting sites are complex and multifaceted. The regulatory bodies must navigate the fine line between protecting individuals from harm and respecting their autonomy. Several ethical issues arise in this context:

- **Autonomy vs. Protection**
  Individuals experiencing suicidal ideation often seek out online communities where they can find solace and understanding. Regulating these spaces may be perceived as an intrusion on personal space. Such regulations could inadvertently push vulnerable individuals further into isolation, where they may not receive the support they need (Daine et al., 2013). Conversely, the obligation to protect vulnerable individuals from potential harm raises ethical questions about the extent of intervention. Therefore, the ethical challenge lies in determining when and how to intervene without compromising individuals' rights to seek community and share experiences.
- **Harm Reduction vs. Censorship**
  Another ethical dilemma involves the balance between harm reduction and censorship. Efforts to regulate suicide-promoting content may lead to accusations of censorship, potentially dismantling valuable discussions about mental health that could be beneficial for individuals seeking support (Celedonia et al., 2021).

Thus, the ethical imperative may be to create safe spaces for dialogue while simultaneously monitoring for harmful content that could lead to suicide.

### *5.3 Case Studies: Legal Actions Taken Against Suicide-Promoting Sites in Australia*

In 2006, Australia became the first country to criminalize pro-suicide websites. However, this move sparked heated debate on free speech, but it demonstrated the government's commitment to preventing access to harmful platforms (Pirkis et al., 2009). Critics argue that the law may overreach by criminalizing a broad range of behaviors, unnecessarily violating the autonomy of individuals seeking to end their lives and facing jurisdictional limitations that leave foreign websites largely unaffected. On the other hand, supporters contend that the law can restrict access to domestic pro-suicide websites and raise public awareness about suicide-related content on the internet. Additionally, the law can encourage community efforts to prevent suicide and reinforce societal norms against the promotion of suicidal behavior.

In 2015, the Australian government initiated the eSafety Commissioner, a regulatory body responsible for overseeing online safety, including content related to suicide and self-harm (eSafety Commissioner, 2015). The Commissioner has the authority to issue removal notices for harmful content, reflecting a proactive stance on regulating online spaces. The eSafety Commissioner collaborates with platforms to facilitate the removal of harmful material while promoting mental health resources and support services. In June 2021, the Australian Government enacted the Online Safety Act 2021, granting the eSafety Commissioner enhanced powers to better protect Australians from the most severe forms of online harm (Online Safety Act, 2021).

In 2019, Ross and Debbie Cameron's 22-year-old son tragically took his own life, allegedly encouraged by members of a specific U.S.-based website (Bridges, 2022). A 2021 investigation by The New York Times revealed that 45 people worldwide had died by suicide after visiting that website (Barbaro, 2021). In response, Ross and Debbie Cameron tirelessly advocated for action, leading to the temporary blocking of the website in Australia. However, the website later resurfaced under a different URL. Following a thorough analysis by the Australian police and the eSafety Commissioner, a decision was made to permanently block the site across Australia. Despite this, the website's representatives claimed that the Australian government's actions were an infringement on free speech and privacy. This regulatory approach underscores an ethical commitment to protecting vulnerable individuals while maintaining a balance with the need for open dialogue about mental health.

# 6 Prevention and Intervention Strategies

## *6.1 Support System for the Individuals at Risk*

Social, familial, and communal support systems play a critical role in protecting individuals at risk of self-harm, suicide, or any mental health crisis (Iohan-Barak & Orbach, 2021). Research shows that individuals with strong, positive relationships with family members, friends, or their community are less likely to engage in self-harm or experience suicidal ideation (Puuskari et al., 2017). This is because such support systems foster a sense of belonging, emotional validation, and practical assistance, which significantly reduce feelings of isolation, a known risk factor for suicidal behavior (Joiner, 2005). Additionally, a sense of connection to parents, peers, and a positive school climate serves as a strong protective factor against emotional distress and suicidal behavior (Foster et al., 2017).

However, individuals who lack access to these supportive systems may turn to online groups or websites, which, while offering some form of connection, can exacerbate their vulnerability. Therefore, governments, healthcare providers, and communities must work collaboratively to create environments where individuals have access to robust social networks. This can be achieved through mental health awareness programs, the development of community-based support groups, and the integration of family and community involvement in treatment plans for at-risk individuals. Schools, workplaces, and local organizations can also play a proactive role by developing peer support programs and promoting open dialogues around mental health. Strengthening these support networks provides immediate help and builds long-term resilience, reducing the risk of individuals turning to harmful online spaces.

## *6.2 Increased Accountability*

Accountability is essential to ensure that online platforms take responsibility for the content they host. Given the potential for harm, both legal and ethical accountability mechanisms should be established to hold websites, social media platforms, and other online spaces responsible for promoting or failing to address content related to self-harm and suicide. Governmental and policy-level initiatives play a crucial role in this effort. For example, the United Kingdom's Online Safety Act 2023 aims to impose stricter requirements on social media platforms to prevent the spread of harmful content, including posts that glorify self-harm (The Online Safety Act, 2023). Under the act, platforms are held accountable for failing to promptly remove such content, with significant penalties for non-compliance. In addition to legislative measures, platforms must adopt stronger internal accountability policies. Many social media companies have introduced community standards that explicitly prohibit the promotion of suicide and self-harm, incorporating mechanisms for flagging and removing harmful content. These platforms often provide periodic reports on the number of harmful posts removed to ensure transparency.

### 6.3 Content Moderation Policies of Groups/Sites

To make the internet a safer space and prevent behaviors encouraging suicide, often provoked by certain websites and online groups, regular content moderation is essential. Achieving effective moderation requires both human oversight and automated systems to ensure rigorous filtering of harmful content without much delay (Marsoof et al., 2023). Human moderators are crucial for detecting subtle and contextual cases of harmful content that automated systems may overlook. Trained moderators can evaluate content within its broader context and intervene when necessary. However, relying solely on human moderation is impractical due to the vast amount of content generated daily and the emotional toll of reviewing distressing material. Continuous training and supervision for moderators are vital to maintaining the effectiveness of this approach. In parallel, automated moderation tools, particularly those powered by artificial intelligence (AI), can help identify patterns in language and behavior that signal suicidal ideation or the promotion of suicide. For example, Facebook's suicide detection algorithms analyze posts, comments, and messages to identify individuals at risk for suicidal behavior, flagging their content for review and recommending necessary preventive actions. However, there are several ethical and legal concerns associated with this approach (Celedonia et al., 2021).

### 6.4 Role of Artificial Intelligence (AI) in Combatting Suicide Promotion

AI plays an increasingly critical role in combatting the promotion of suicide on online platforms. Through machine learning algorithms, AI systems can monitor vast amounts of content, detect patterns linked to suicidal ideation, and support early intervention efforts. These algorithms are trained on large datasets to identify linguistic cues and behavioral patterns that suggest suicidal tendencies. Factors such as tone, phrases, keywords, language, and post frequency are analyzed to pinpoint users who may be at risk. Studies show that machine learning models can predict suicidal behavior with reasonable accuracy when trained on relevant datasets (Lee & Pak, 2022). Platforms like Facebook and Twitter use AI-driven systems that flag potentially harmful content for human moderators, who can then initiate appropriate interventions. AI can also be employed for predictive analytics, enabling platforms to identify at-risk individuals even before they seek out harmful communities. By analyzing users' online behavior over time, these predictive models can detect mood shifts, increased isolation, or frequent interaction with harmful content, which are early indicators of suicidal ideation or behavior. However, this approach raises ethical and legal concerns, as it involves analyzing users' social media activity, often without their knowledge or explicit consent (Celedonia et al., 2021).

### *6.5 Role of Mental Health Professionals and Crisis Intervention Services*

Mental health professionals can play a key role in reducing suicide risk for individuals exposed to suicide-promoting websites through crisis intervention. They can provide direct support and collaborate with online platforms to offer integrated crisis services. Many platforms, such as Google, Facebook, and Instagram, have partnered with mental health organizations to offer timely interventions. For example, Google displays the National Suicide Prevention Lifeline when users search for suicide-related content. Facebook and Instagram connect users with resources from organizations like the Crisis Text Line and National Suicide Prevention Lifeline, offering support or contacting emergency services if needed. Crisis services, such as Kaan Pete Roi, The Trevor Project, and Crisis Text Line, provide immediate assistance to individuals in distress, often reaching them at critical moments. Moreover, studies show that engaging with crisis services via online platforms can significantly reduce the likelihood of suicidal behavior (da Silva et al., 2015; He et al., 2022), highlighting the importance of collaboration between online platforms and mental health services.

## 7 Conclusion

A deeper understanding of the complexities surrounding suicide-promoting sites and groups is essential for developing effective prevention and intervention strategies. Focused research efforts on specific cultural contexts are imperative, as these dynamics vary significantly across regions. This chapter calls for strengthened legal frameworks and ethical guidelines to regulate such content, alongside community-based mental health interventions. And support systems. Ultimately, addressing this issue requires a coordinated effort involving policymakers, digital platforms, and mental health professionals to mitigate the substantial risks posed by these platforms.

## References


Ahad, A., Sanchez-Gonzalez, M., & Junquera, P. (2023). Understanding and addressing mental health stigma across cultures for improving psychiatric care: A narrative review. *Cureus, 15*(5), e39549. https://doi.org/10.7759/cureus.39549

Anderson, M., & Jiang, J. (2018). *Teens, social media & technology 2018*. Pew Research Center. Retrieved September 23, 2024 from https://apo.org.au/node/175701

Barbaro, M. (2021). Kids are dying. How are these sites still allowed? *The New York Times*. https://www.nytimes.com/2021/12/09/podcasts/the-daily/suicide-investigation.html?

Baumeister, R. F. (1990). Suicide as escape from self. *Psychological Review, 97*(1), 90. https://doi.org/10.1037/0033-295x.97.1.90

BBC. (2004). *Why are suicide pacts on the rise in Japan?* BBC News. Retrieved September 23, 2024 from http://news.bbc.co.uk/2/hi/talking_point/3737072.stm

BBC. (2010). *'Secretive world' of suicide websites*. BBC News. Retrieved September 23, 2024 from https://www.bbc.com/news/uk-11387910

BBC. (2017). *Blue Whale: What is the truth behind an online 'suicide challenge'?* . BBC News. Retrieved September 23, 2024 from https://www.bbc.com/news/world-39729819

Bell, J., Mok, K., Gardiner, E., & Pirkis, J. (2018). Suicide-related internet use among suicidal young people in the UK: Characteristics of users, effects of use, and barriers to offline help-seeking. *Archives of Suicide Research, 22*(2), 263–277. https://doi.org/10.1080/13811118.2017.1334609

Bridges, A. (2022). *Pro-suicide website blocks access to Australians after families speak out*. ABC News. Retrieved Setember 25, 2024 from https://www.abc.net.au/news/2022-11-21/pro-suicide-website-blocks-australians-after-families-speak-out/101680284

Celedonia, K. L., Corrales Compagnucci, M., Minssen, T., & Lowery Wilson, M. (2021). Legal, ethical, and wider implications of suicide risk detection systems in social media platforms. *Journal of Law and the Biosciences, 8*(1), lsab021. https://doi.org/10.1093/jlb/lsab021

Daine, K., Hawton, K., Singaravelu, V., Stewart, A., Simkin, S., & Montgomery, P. (2013). The power of the web: A systematic review of studies of the influence of the internet on self-harm and suicide in young people. *PLoS ONE, 8*(10), e77555. https://doi.org/10.1371/journal.pone.0077555

da Silva, J. A., Siegmund, G., & Bredemeier, J. (2015). Crisis interventions in online psychological counseling. *Trends Psychiatry Psychother, 37*(4), 171–182. https://doi.org/10.1590/2237-6089-2014-0026

Davidson, S. S., Bradshaw Hoppock, A., Rohmeyer, R. A., Keebler, J., & Frederick, C. M. (2020). *Deindividuation in anonymous social media: Does anonymous social media lead to an increase in non-normative behavior?*

Dobson, R. (1999). Internet sites may encourage suicide. *BMJ, 319*(7206), 337. https://doi.org/10.1136/bmj.319.7206.337

Dunlop, S. M., More, E., & Romer, D. (2011). Where do youth learn about suicides on the Internet, and what influence does this have on suicidal ideation? *Journal of Child Psychology and Psychiatry, 52*(10), 1073–1080. https://doi.org/10.1111/j.1469-7610.2011.02416.x

Emmott, R. (2008). *Euthanasia tourists snap up pet shop drug in Mexico*. Reuters. https://www.reuters.com/article/lifestyle/euthanasia-tourists-snap-up-pet-shop-drug-in-mexico-idUSN03299458/

*eSafety Commissioner*. (2015). Australian Government. Retrieved September 25, 2024 from https://www.esafety.gov.au/

Foster, C. E., Horwitz, A., Thomas, A., Opperman, K., Gipson, P., Burnside, A., Stone, D. M., & King, C. A. (2017). Connectedness to family, school, peers, and community in socially vulnerable adolescents. *Children and Youth Services Review, 81*, 321–331. https://doi.org/10.1016/j.childyouth.2017.08.011

Gamondi, C., Pott, M., & Payne, S. (2013). Families' experiences with patients who died after assisted suicide: A retrospective interview study in southern Switzerland. *Annals of Oncology, 24*(6), 1639–1644. https://doi.org/10.1093/annonc/mdt033

Gauthier, S., Mausbach, J., Reisch, T., & Bartsch, C. (2015). Suicide tourism: A pilot study on the Swiss phenomenon. *Journal of Medical Ethics, 41*(8), 611–617. https://doi.org/10.1136/medethics-2014-102091

George, R. P. (1994). Life's dominion: An argument about abortion, euthanasia, and individual freedom. By Ronald Dworkin. New York: Alfred A. Knopf, 1993. 273 p. $23.00. *American Political Science Review, 88*(2), 444–446. https://doi.org/10.2307/2944721

Göken, H., & Zwießler, F. (2022). Assisted suicide in Germany: The landmark ruling of the German Federal Constitutional Court of February 26, 2020. *German Law Journal, 23*(4), 661–671. https://doi.org/10.1017/glj.2022.34

Goodman, E. P., & Whittington, R. (2019). *Section 230 of the Communications Decency Act and the future of online speech*. Rutgers Law School Legal Studies Research Paper Series. Электронный ресурс: https://papers.ssrn.com/sol3/papers.cfm. https://www.gmfus.org/sites/default/files/Goodman%2520%2520Whittington%2520-%2520Section%2520230%2520paper%2520-%25209%2520Aug.pdf

He, C., Chang, S., Lu, Y., Zhang, H., Zhou, H., Guo, Y., & Gao, B. L. (2022). Effects of online psychological crisis intervention for frontline nurses in COVID-19 pandemic. *Front Psychiatry, 13*, 937573. https://doi.org/10.3389/fpsyt.2022.937573

Hoofnagle, C. J., Van Der Sloot, B., & Borgesius, F. Z. (2019). The European Union general data protection regulation: What it is and what it means. *Information & Communications Technology Law, 28*(1), 65–98. https://doi.org/10.1080/13600834.2019.1573501

Hurst, S. A., & Mauron, A. (2003). Assisted suicide and euthanasia in Switzerland: Allowing a role for non-physicians. *BMJ, 326*(7383), 271–273. https://doi.org/10.1136/bmj.326.7383.271

Iohan-Barak, M., & Orbach, I. (2021). Psychopathology and risk factors for suicide in the young. In D. Wasserman (Ed.), *Oxford textbook of suicidology and suicide prevention* (2nd ed., pp. 557–572). https://doi.org/10.1093/med/9780198834441.003.0066

Janis, I. L. (1972). *Victims of groupthink: A psychological study of foreign-policy decisions and fiascoes*. Houghton Mifflin.

Jan, M., Soomro, S., & Ahmad, N. (2017). Impact of social media on self-esteem. *European Scientific Journal, 13*(23), 329–341. https://doi.org/10.19044/esj.2017.v13n23p329

Joiner, T. E. (2005). *Why people die by suicide*. Harvard University Press.

Kramer, E. J., Kwong, K., Lee, E., & Chung, H. (2002). Cultural factors influencing the mental health of Asian Americans. *Western Journal of Medicine, 176*(4), 227.

Lee, J., & Pak, T. Y. (2022). Machine learning prediction of suicidal ideation, planning, and attempt among Korean adults: A population-based study. *SSM Population Health, 19*, 101231. https://doi.org/10.1016/j.ssmph.2022.101231

Lerner, B. H., & Caplan, A. L. (2015). Euthanasia in Belgium and the Netherlands: On a slippery slope? *JAMA Internal Medicine, 175*(10), 1640–1641. https://doi.org/10.1001/jamainternmed.2015.4086

Marsoof, A., Luco, A., Tan, H., & Joty, S. (2023). Content-filtering AI systems–limitations, challenges and regulatory approaches. *Information & Communications Technology Law, 32*(1), 64–101. https://doi.org/10.1080/13600834.2022.2078395

Mathieu, S., Treloar, A., Hawgood, J., Ross, V., & Kõlves, K. (2022). The role of unemployment, financial hardship, and economic recession on suicidal behaviors and interventions to mitigate their impact: A review. *Frontiers in Public Health, 10*, 907052. https://doi.org/10.3389/fpubh.2022.907052

Minkkinen, J., Oksanen, A., Kaakinen, M., Keipi, T., & Räsänen, P. (2017). Victimization and exposure to pro-self-harm and pro-suicide websites: A cross-national study. *Suicide and Life-Threatening Behavior, 47*(1), 14–26. https://doi.org/10.1111/sltb.12258

Mishara, B. L., & Weisstub, D. N. (2024). *Practical ethics in suicide: Research, policy and clinical decision-making*. Cambridge University Press.

Mok, K., Ross, A. M., Jorm, A. F., & Pirkis, J. (2016). An analysis of the content and availability of information on suicide methods online. *Journal of Consumer Health on the Internet, 20*(1–2), 41–51. https://doi.org/10.1080/15398285.2016.1167579

Motillon-Toudic, C., Walter, M., Séguin, M., Carrier, J.-D., Berrouiguet, S., & Lemey, C. (2022). Social isolation and suicide risk: Literature review and perspectives. *European Psychiatry, 65*(1), e65. https://doi.org/10.1192/j.eurpsy.2022.2320

Niederkrotenthaler, T., Stack, S., Till, B., Sinyor, M., Pirkis, J., Garcia, D., et al. (2019). Association of increased youth suicides in the United States with the release of 13 Reasons Why. *JAMA Psychiatry, 76*(9), 933–940. https://doi.org/10.1001/jamapsychiatry.2019.0922

Niederkrotenthaler, T., Voracek, M., Herberth, A., Till, B., Strauss, M., Etzersdorfer, E., Eisenwort, B., & Sonneck, G. (2010). Role of media reports in completed and prevented suicide: Werther v. Papageno effects. *The British Journal of Psychiatry, 197*(3), 234–243. https://doi.org/10.1192/bjp.bp.109.074633

NIH. (2019). *Release of '13 Reasons Why' associated with increase in youth suicide rates.* Intramural Research Program. https://irp.nih.gov/news-and-events/in-the-news/release-of-13-reasons-why-associated-with-increase-in-youth-suicide-rates

*Online Safety Act 2021.* Australian Government. Retrieved September 25, 2024 from https://www.legislation.gov.au/C2021A00076/latest/text

*The Online Safety Act 2023.* United Kingdom. Retrieved Septemmber 25, 2024 from https://www.gov.uk/government/publications/online-safety-act-explainer/online-safety-act-explainer#:~:text=The%20Online%20Safety%20Act%202023,users'%20safety%20on%20their%20platforms

Orben, A. (2020). Teenagers, screens and social media: A narrative review of reviews and key studies. *Social Psychiatry and Psychiatric Epidemiology, 55*(4), 407–414. https://doi.org/10.1007/s00127-019-01825-4

Patel, V., & Kleinman, A. (2003). Poverty and common mental disorders in developing countries. *Bulletin of the World Health Organization, 81*, 609–615.

Pirkis, J., Neal, L., Dare, A., Blood, R. W., & Studdert, D. (2009). Legal bans on pro-suicide web sites: An early retrospective from Australia. *Suicide and Life-Threatening Behavior, 39*(2), 190–193. https://doi.org/10.1521/suli.2009.39.2.190

Pretto, R. (2021). *Aokigahara. A dark tourism spot in Japan.* Travel Tomorrow. https://traveltomorrow.com/aokigahara-a-dark-tourism-spot-in-japan/

Puuskari, V., Aalto-Setälä, T., Komulainen, E., & Marttunen, M. (2017). Suicidal ideation, suicide attempts, and psychological distress among intoxicated adolescents in the pediatric emergency department. *Nordic Journal of Psychiatry, 72*(2), 137–144. https://doi.org/10.1080/08039488.2017.1400099

Rajagopal, S. (2004). *Suicide pacts and the internet* (Vol. 329, pp. 1298–1299). British Medical Journal Publishing Group.

Robinson, J., Rodrigues, M., Fisher, S., Bailey, E., & Herrman, H. (2015). Social media and suicide prevention: Findings from a stakeholder survey. *Shanghai Archives of Psychiatry, 27*(1), 27. https://doi.org/10.11919/j.issn.1002-0829.214133

Salazar, G. M. (2022). Macabre tourism in Japan Case study Aokigahara Forest and Nagoro Village. *Journal of Global Tourism Research, 7*(2), 151–156. https://doi.org/10.37020/jgtr.7.2_151

Shah, A. (2010). The relationship between general population suicide rates and the Internet: A cross-national study. *Suicide and Life-Threatening Behavior, 40*(2), 146–150. https://doi.org/10.1521/suli.2010.40.2.146

Sisask, M., & Värnik, A. (2012). Media roles in suicide prevention: A systematic review. *International Journal of Environmental Research and Public Health, 9*(1), 123–138. https://doi.org/10.3390/ijerph9010123

Sperling, D. (2019). *Suicide tourism: Understanding the legal, philosophical, and socio-political dimensions.* Oxford University Press. https://doi.org/10.1093/oso/9780198825456.001.0001

Stabin, D. (2013). *Suicide promotion online: Frequency of access by high risk individuals.* Masters Theses. 1111. https://thekeep.eiu.edu/theses/1111/

Stephenson, A., Cohen, G. A., Beller, Y., & Greenbaum, D. (2021, August 18). Suicide prevention technologies and social media platforms: Legal, social and ethical implications. *Social and Ethical Implications.* https://doi.org/10.2139/ssrn.4194066

Tosoni, L. (2018). Rethinking privacy in the Council of Europe's Convention on Cybercrime. *Computer Law & Security Review, 34*(6), 1197–1214. https://doi.org/10.1016/j.clsr.2018.08.004

WHO. (2014). *Preventing suicide: A global imperative.* World Health Organization. Retrieved September 23, 2024 from https://iris.who.int/bitstream/handle/10665/131056/9789241564779_eng.pdf?sequence=1

Yu, C.-E., Wen, J., & Meng, F. (2020). Defining physician-assisted suicide tourism and travel. *Journal of Hospitality & Tourism Research, 44*(4), 694–703. https://doi.org/10.1177/1096348019899437

Zimbardo, P. (1969). *The human choice: Individuation, reason, and order versus deindividuation, impulse, and chaos.* Nebraska Symposium on Motivation/University of Nebraska Press.

# Chapter 19
# The Impact of Laws on Suicide

**David Lester and Mahboubeh Dadfar**

**Abstract** This chapter reviews the status of laws in countries around the world criminalizing suicide and attempted suicide and efforts to change these laws. The trend is for suicidal behavior to be decriminalized. The impact of laws and government regulations concerning the methods used by those dying by suicide is reviewed and found, in many instances, to reduce the use of those methods for suicide and, sometimes, to reduce the total suicide rate by all methods, for example, restricting access to firearms and switching domestic gas from coal gas to natural gas.

**Keywords** Decriminalization · Criminalization · Ethics · Euthanasia · Law · Legislation · Suicide · Politics · Psychology

## 1 Introduction

The law and legal issues, both at the national level and at the local level, can have a major impact on suicidal behavior. For example, in countries where attempting suicide is a criminal offense, suicidal people may be placed in prison. In countries or provinces within a country where physician-assisted suicide is legal, some suicidal people can find help in their decision to die by suicide. In this chapter, we will explore these issues and their impact on suicidal behavior.

D. Lester (✉)
Stockton University, Galloway, NJ, USA
e-mail: david.lester@stockton.edu

M. Dadfar
School of Behavioral Sciences and Mental Health, Iran University of Medical Sciences, Tehran, Iran
e-mail: dadfar.m@iums.ac.ir

 
S. M. Y. Arafat and S. K. Kar (eds.), *Ecological and Social Determinants of Suicidal Behavior*, South Asian Perspectives in Mental Health and Psychology,
https://doi.org/10.1007/978-981-96-4028-7_19

## 2 The Direct Effects of Laws

The only time when national laws about suicide were coded was by Lester (2002b) using information supplied by the American embassies in countries.[1] Of course, laws have changed since then, but Lester pointed out the severity of laws on suicide in 2002 and formed a Guttman Scale[2] (Table 1).

## 3 Decriminalizing Suicide

In many countries, suicide is a criminal act. What happens when countries decriminalize suicide? Canada decriminalized suicide in 1972, and Lester (1992) found that there was no impact on suicidality. New Zealand decriminalized suicide in 1961, and Lester (1993) found that the suicide rate did not change significantly after this action. Lester (2002a) looked at 7 countries, including Canada and New Zealand, and added England and Wales, Finland, Hong Kong, Ireland, and Sweden. Comparing the suicide rates for the five years before decriminalization and the five years afterward for all 7 countries combined, the suicide rate rose from 9.7 per 100,000 per year to 11.2, a significant increase. Lester did note that this increase might be result of coroners and medical examiners classifying suicide more accurately after the decriminalization.

Stemming from Islamic ethics and teaching, suicide is not considered to be a crime in Iran. Being an accessory[3] or aide in suicide is also not considered to be a crime, and no punishment is imposed for this. Therefore, suicide is not an issue for the courts of Iran. Punishment has been imposed only for computer crimes that lead to accessory in suicide (Beigi, 2019; Mirzaie, 2020). In Iran, computer crimes regarding suicide involve inviting/inciting/encouraging people to die by suicide through computer and telecommunication systems or data carriers.

A dead person cannot be punished. A person who kills himself has lost his highest asset, which is his life, and there is no way to punish him. If someone attempts suicide in a public place, he or she may endanger others or disrupt public order, and so punishment is possible and appropriate. However, in Iran, attempted suicide by soldiers and other military persons is criminalized.

---

[1] Makinen (1997) coded laws in European countries for aiding and abetting suicide.

[2] A **Guttman scale**, cumulative scaling, or scalogram analysis is formulated with components that can be ordered in a hierarchical manner.

[3] Accessory to a crime is defined as someone who cooperates and is involved in committing criminal behavior through incitement, deception and trickery, facilitating the occurrence of crime, and providing means for the crime.

**Table 1** Coding national laws on suicide in 2002 (from Lester, 2002b)

| Nation | Completed suicide | Attempted suicide | Assisted suicide |
|---|---|---|---|
| Sri Lanka | np | Crime (1) | Crime (death) |
| Bahamas | np | Misdemeanor | Crime (life) |
| Brunei | np | Crime | Crime (life) |
| Cyprus | np | Misdemeanor | Felony (life) |
| Grenada | np | Misdemeanor (2) | Crime (15) |
| Ghana | np | Misdemeanor | Felony (10+) |
| Singapore | np | Crime (1) | Crime (10) |
| Zambia | np | Crime | Crime |
| Gambia | np | Misdemeanor | Crime |
| Costa Rica | np | np/psychiatric | Crime (5) |
| Israel | np | np/psychiatric | Felony (20) |
| Canada | np | np | Crime (14) |
| New Zealand | np | np | Crime (14) |
| Italy | np | np | Crime (12) |
| Mexico | np | np | Crime (7) |
| El Salvador | np | np | Crime (5) |
| Hungary | np | np | Felony (5 |
| Lithuania | np | np | crime (5) |
| Poland | np | np | Crime (5) |
| Slovenia | np | np | Crime (5) |
| Switzerland | np | np | Crime (5) |
| Tunisia | np | np | Crime (5) |
| Surinam | np | np | Crime (3) |
| Armenia | np | np | Crime |
| Denmark | np | np | Crime |
| Germany | np | np | Crime |
| Japan | np | np | Crime |
| Norway | np | np | Crime |
| Slovakia | np | np | Crime |
| South Africa | np | np | Crime |
| Luxembourg | np | np | Not legally regimented |
| Portugal | np | np | No information |
| Malta | No information | No information? | Crime (death) |

np = no penalty; maximum penalty in years is given in parentheses

## 4 State Laws About Suicide

Lester (1988) looked at 8 aspects of state laws for the 48 continental states of the United States in 1980: (1) criminal penalties for attempted suicide, (2) criminal penalties for aiding another in suicide or forming a suicide pacts, (3) permitting the use of reasonable force to prevent an individual from suicidal behavior, (4) criminal penalties for knowing of a suicide but failing to inform the authorities, (5) allowing individuals to decline extra-ordinary life-support measures in certain issues, (6) limiting insurers from withholding life insurance payments after a suicide, (7) statutes about workmen's compensation after a suicide, and (8) abolishing forfeiture of property and assets after a suicide. None of these elements of state laws were significantly associated with state suicide rates, and when combined to form a single score for strictness, they explained only 19% of the variance in the suicide rates.

## 5 Criminalizing Attempted Suicide

Does criminalizing attempted suicide have any impact on suicide rates? Lew et al. (2022) compared the suicide rates in 20 countries with criminalized suicide attempt against the global rate of suicide and to a comparison group of 20 countries where suicide attempt is not criminalized, matched with geographical location and majority religion. There was a wide variation in the suicide rates of the countries where suicide attempt is criminalized, from 1.7 per 100,000 per year (Brunei) in 2000 to 25.8 (Guyana). The mean suicide rate of the countries which criminalized suicide attempt was lower than the mean suicide rate of the 20 comparison countries over the 20 years (for example, in 2000, 10.7 versus 17.2), but the average annual percentage decrease in the suicide rate was greater in the countries where attempted suicide was not criminalized. As always, we must remember that, where suicidal behavior is criminalized, legal officials may result in an undercount of suicides.

## 6 Decriminalization of Attempted Suicide

Harsh treatment of suicides and attempted suicides has been a usual approach throughout history, and it has also been prevalent today. Persons with suicidal behavior are still being persecuted in some countries of the world. However, criminalizing and punishing people who have hurt themselves, perhaps as a "cry for help," may not necessarily work as deterrent (Farberow & Shneidman, 1961). However, in order to change these legal structures, more is involved than just changing phrases in a statute . Reform requires a long and enduring process of social evolution and modification. Recently, some countries have repealed laws that have disproportionate penalties.

Kahn and Lester (2013) described efforts in India, Ghana, and Singapore to decriminalize attempted suicide. These countries can no longer justify the reasons for maintaining to enforcing the criminalization of suicide. Each country's creation of the law started with British colonial rule, but the United Kingdom itself has decriminalized suicide and attempted suicide long ago. Today, many other countries recognize that persons with suicidal behavior need psychiatric services, social support, and compassion, rather than criminal punishment.

Changes have occurred in India and Singapore but will likely face problems in Ghana. Ghana lacks specific supports (which, at the present time, only NGOs can provide) and has a diverse population with a lot of ethnicities. Because strategies are successful in one country does not mean that these approaches will be successful in others.

## 7 Indirect Effects of Laws and Government Regulations

In many cases, laws and government regulations can have an impact on suicide indirectly. For example, in 1989, Iceland permitted the sale of extra-strong beer (5% alcohol). This was followed by an increase in sales of beer and a decrease in sales of spirits. Lester (1999) found that this change was followed by a decrease in the suicide rate.

### *7.1 Gun Control Laws*

#### 7.1.1 The United States

The impact of laws restricting access to firearms on suicide has been studied extensively (Lester, 2019). The first study, by Lester and Murrell (1980), used a coding of American state handgun control laws in 1968 and found that states with stricter handgun control laws had lower suicide rates in 1969–1971, and this association was also found for the suicide rate of all age groups. Yang and Lester (1991) also found that the strictness of handgun control laws was negatively related to the firearm suicide rate and the total suicide rate, suggesting that suicidal people do not switch to other methods for suicide if handguns are less available.

More recently, Anestis et al. (2015) studied the impact of three state laws (permit to buy a handgun, registration of handguns, license to own a handgun) on suicide rates in 2010. States with any of these three laws had lower firearm suicide rates and lower overall suicide rates, also indicating no switching of methods when handgun laws were in place, as well as a lower percentage of suicides using firearms.

### 7.1.2 Other Countries

Canada strengthened its gun control laws (Bill C-51) in 1977. In an early study, Mundt (1990) indicated that this new law did not have an impact on suicide rates. Lester and Leenaars (1994) examined the period of 1969–1985 and found that the proportion of suicides using guns decreased after passage of the law, as did the firearm suicide rate. However, the suicide rate by all other methods increased suggesting that suicidal individuals switched methods for suicide. Leenaars and Lester (1997) found that the impact of the gun control law on suicide was found only for those under the age of 65.

Austria passed stricter gun control laws in 1997, raising the minimum age for purchase to 21 and instituting checks on safe storage. Kapusta et al. (2007) found a decrease in the firearm suicide rate after this change in laws, and this was found for all sex-by-age groups except women over the age of 64 and youths under the age of 20.

New Zealand toughened firearm laws in 1992, requiring licenses to own a gun, passing a test on basic regulations for gun ownership, and police approval of gun purchases. After the passage of the law, the firearm suicide rate dropped by 46%. The proportion of suicides using firearms also dropped, but there was no change in the overall suicide rate (Beautrais et al., 2006).

In Iran, there are strict laws regarding the carrying, using, and trafficking of weapons, and not everyone can obtain them easily. Firearms are available only to the military, law enforcement, and armed security personnel, except in special cases where people can obtain a license to carry weapons (Weapons Trafficking and Carrying Act, 2024).

## 7.2 *Fencing in Bridges*

Local governments are often persuaded to fence in bridges from which people jump to their deaths. Typically, the number of suicides from a fenced-in bridge declines, but often suicides from other bridges in the area increase. However, Pelletier (2007) assessed suicide by jumping from the Memorial Bridge, Maine, before and after putting in safety fences in 1983. Between 1960 and 1982, there were 14 suicides versus none afterward (between 1984 and 2005) by jumping from the bridge. During these same two periods, there were nine and nine suicides by jumping from high places in Augusta (other than from the mentioned bridge) indicating that those who might have jumped from the bridge did not jump from other high places.

Beautrais (2001) took advantage of a decision by a town council somewhere in Australia or New Zealand to remove safety fences from a bridge because (i) they were unsightly, (ii) they disrupted rescue efforts, and (iii) they did not prevent suicide. In the four-year periods before and after the removal of the fences, the number of suicides increased from 3 to 15, with estimated rates of 0.29 before the removal of the fences, rising to 1.29 per 100,000 per year afterward.

### 7.3 *Restricting Sales of Paracetamol (Acetaminophen) and Pesticides*

Occasionally, governments have restricted the sales of potentially lethal medications, such as barbiturates, which did not require a prescription. For example, it became common in England to use paracetamol for attempting suicide, resulting in occasional deaths. (In addition, paracetamol can cause severe liver damage.) In an effort to reduce the use of paracetamol for suicidal behavior, the government ordered that tablets could be sold only in packets containing fewer numbers of pills and had to be enclosed in plastic blisters which slowed people down in their endeavor to obtain a large number of pills for an overdose.

Hawton et al. (2001) studied the impact of these moves on the use of paracetamol and salicylates for suicidal behavior. In the year following this move, deaths from suicide using paracetamol decreased by 21% and the number from salicylates by 48%. Liver transplants after overdosing with paracetamol decreased by 66%. The number of non-fatal suicide attempts using paracetamol decreased by 11%.

Gunnell et al. (2017) reviewed research on the impact of restricting access to pesticides or banning extremely hazardous pesticides and found that these restrictions and bans reduced the use of pesticides for suicide. In some countries, the impact was also a reduction in the overall suicide rate. There have also been programs to promote safe storage of pesticides (and in some countries, firearms), but these programs appear to be less effective in reducing their use for suicide (Pearson et al., 2017).

### 7.4 *Domestic Gas and Car Exhaust*

In order to improve the environment, governments encouraged and then ordered a switch from domestic gas (which is highly toxic) to natural gas for home use and the use of catalytic converters to decrease the carbon monoxide in car exhaust, both of which were popular methods for suicide before detoxification.

In the United States, the percentage of carbon monoxide in car exhaust was 8.5% before 1968 and 3.0% in the 1970s (Landers, 1981). The number of people dying by suicide in the United States did not change over that period, but the percentage of suicides using car exhaust declined from 9.9% in 1965 to 7.1% in 1979 (Clarke & Lester, 1986, 1989). This suggests that suicidal people simply switched methods for their suicides.

Regarding the detoxification of domestic gas, Lester (1995) found that, in three countries where domestic gas was a popular method for suicide (Northern Ireland, Scotland, and Switzerland) the overall suicide rate declined after detoxification. In three countries where domestic gas was not a popular method for suicide (Japan, the Netherlands, and the United States), the overall suicide rate increased after detoxification. For a fuller discussion of the impact of making a method for suicide less available, see Clarke and Lester (1989) and Lester (2009).

## 8 Assisted Suicide

Assisted suicide, and especially physician-assisted suicide, was considered by Jack Kevorkian to be a moral and legal issue in 1990 in the USA (Brody, 1999; Kevorkian, 1992; Rosenthal, 2020). Euthanasia and especially physician-assisted suicide are also a bioethical issues from the Islamic perspective (Brockop, 2002; Madadin et al., 2020; Padela, 2007; Zia et al., 2024). In many countries, legal regulations for euthanasia and physician-assisted suicide are becoming common (Picón-Jaimes et al., 2022).

Physician-assisted suicide has, therefore, become an important issue in recent years. Do we have the right to end our own lives, request help to do so, and under what conditions? The term *euthanasia* is based on the Greek language and means *good death*, but it has come to mean one person ending another person's life without his or her permission. In contrast, assisted suicide means providing an individual with the means to die by suicide with the individual's consent.

On April 1, 2002, the Netherlands became the first nation to pass a law permitting assisted suicide. The law permitted physicians to assist an individual to die by suicide if certain conditions were met.[4]

- The request is made voluntarily and directly by the person
- The person is psychologically competent at the time of the request
- The wish to end life is sustaining
- There is intolerable suffering with no prospect of improvement
- Only palliative care is possible and rejected by the person
- The helper is a professional
- There have been consultations with colleagues

Physician-assisted suicide is now legal in some countries, in certain situations, including Austria, Belgium, Canada, Luxembourg, the Netherlands, New Zealand, Portugal, Spain, Switzerland, and parts of the United States (California, Colorado, Hawaii, Maine, Montana, New Jersey, New Mexico, Oregon, Vermont, Washington, and Washington, DC). The trend is for more and more countries and states to pass legislation to permit physician-assisted suicide. Switzerland is unique in having a place for people from anywhere in the world to go and obtain assisted suicide if they meet the requirements: *Dignitas* near the town of Zurich.

In the USA, there have been many opponents of physician-assisted suicide, including Herbet Hendin (1996) as well as supporters (e.g., Werth, 1999). There have also been non-professionals involved, including Derek Humphry (1992) who wrote a book (*Final Exit*), a how-to-it guide to suicide, and Jack Kevorkian, who helped people die in his van (Canetto & Hollenshead, 1999).

In Iran, physician-assisted suicide is not specifically criminalized. There is no legal requirement about physician-assisted suicide (for or against), an obvious legal vacuum in this regard in the Iranian legal system (Beigi, 2019).

---

[4] Interestingly, Nico Speijer, a Dutch suicidologist, and his wife died by suicide in 1981 (Diekstra, 1986).

# 9 Other Issues

## 9.1 *Suicide in Prison*

Often individuals die by suicide in response to legal problems. Suicide, for example, is common in prisons and jails (Tartaro, 2019; Tartaro & Lester, 2009), especially on death row while awaiting execution (Lester & Tartaro, 2002; Tartaro & Lester, 2015, 2016). There is a high level of supervision on death row in the USA, but the prisoners on death row have a higher suicide rate than both the male prison population in the USA and the population of males over the age of 14 in the general population. For the years 1978 through 2010, Lester and Tartaro revealed that the suicide rate on death row was 129.7 per 100,000 per year compared to 17.4 for inmates in state prisons and 24.6 for males over the age of 15 in the general population.

In a 17-year national cohort study of the Norwegian prison population, Bukten and Stavseth (2021) reported an increased suicide risk, both in prison and after release. These findings were also confirmed in the study of Miller et al. (2024).

In the penal laws of Iran, attempted suicide and self-harm in prison are seen as a violation of rules and regulations but not as a criminal act. If suicidal behavior occurs in prison, it is considered a disciplinary violation of the prison regulations, and the violator will be evaluated and perhaps punished according to the prison disciplinary council or tried by the judicial authorities.

## 9.2 *Suicide After Being Charged with a Crime*

People occasionally die by suicide after being arrested. Lester and Baker (1989) presented cases of men arrested for child pornography dying by suicide. In an entrapment operation coordinated by law enforcement officials and the post office, the government trapped men into buying child pornography from them, and of 162 arrests, four men died by suicide. The motive for such suicides is most likely shame (Lester, 1997).

# 10 Conclusion

It seems that, at the present time, from the point of view of public health, there is no sound reason to criminalize suicide or attempted suicide. Making attempted suicide a criminal act hinders obtaining professional psychiatric and psychological help for the suicidal person. However, many religions consider the taking of a life is immoral, and this view impacts legal issues concerning completed suicide.

There is evidence that government regulation, intentionally (as in gun control laws) or unintentionally (as in ordering a switch from coal gas for domestic use to natural gas) has a larger impact on suicidal behavior than laws about suicidal behavior. The evidence from countries such as Austria, Canada, and New Zealand indicates that stricter gun control laws do result in a lower firearm suicide rate, and in countries where firearms are a popular method for suicide, there may also be a decline in the overall suicide rate since not all potential suicides will switch to alternative methods.[5]

## References


Anestis, M. D., Khazem, L. R., Law, K. C., Houtsma, C., LeTard, R., Moberg, F., & Martin, R. (2015). The association between state laws regulating handgun ownership and statewide suicide rates. *American Journal of Public Health, 105*(10), 2059–2067. https://doi.org/10.2105/AJPH.2014.302465

Beautrais, A. L. (2001). Effectiveness of barriers at suicide jumping sites. *Australian & New Zealand Journal of Psychiatry, 35*(5), 557–562. https://doi.org/10.1080/0004867010060501

Beautrais, A. L., Fergusson, D. M., & Horwood, L. J. (2006). Firearms legislation and reductions in firearm-related suicide deaths in New Zealand. *Australian & New Zealand Journal of Psychiatry, 40*(3), 253–259. https://doi.org/10.1080/j.1440-1614.2006.01782.x

Beigi, J. (2019). Comparative study of physician-assisted suicide status in the laws of different countries and Iran legal system. *Bioethics Journal, 9*(34), 67–80. https://doi.org/10.22037/bioeth.v9i34.26750

Brockop, J. E. (2002). Islamic ethics of saving life: A comparative perspective. *Medical Law, 21*(2), 225–241. PMID: 12184604.

Brody, H. (1999). Kevorkian and assisted death in the United States. *British Medical Journal, 318*(7189), 953–954. https://doi.org/10.1136/bmj.318.7189.953

Bukten, A., & Stavseth, M. R. (2021). Suicide in prison and after release: A 17-year national cohort study. *European Journal of Epidemiology, 36*(10), 1075–1083. https://doi.org/10.1007/s10654-021-00782-0

Canetto, S. S., & Hollenshead, J. D. (1999). Gender and physician-assisted suicide: An analysis of the Kevorkian cases, 1990–1997. *Omega, 40*(1), 165–208. https://doi.org/10.2190/av9g-cdru-1h83-gq0x

Clarke, R. V., & Lester, D. (1986). Detoxification of motor vehicle exhaust and suicide. *Psychological Reports, 59*(3), 1034. https://doi.org/10.2466/pr0.1986.59.3.1034

Clarke, R. V., & Lester, D. (1989). *Suicide: Closing the exits.* Springer-Verlag. https://psycnet.apa.org/record/1989-98414-000

Diekstra, R. F. (1986). The significance of Nico Speijer's suicide: How and when should suicide be prevented? *Suicide & Life-Threatening Behavior, 16*(1), 13–15. https://doi.org/10.1111/j.1943-278x.1986.tb00716.x

Farberow, N. L., & Shneidman, E. S. (1961). The cry for help. New York: McGraw-Hill.

Gunnell, D., Knipe, D., Chang, S. S., Pearson, M., Konradsen, F., Lee, W. J., & Eddleston, M. (2017). Prevention of suicide with regulations aimed at restricting access to highly hazardous pesticides. *Lancet Global Health, 5*, e1026–e1037. https://doi.org/10.1016/S2214-109X(17)30299-1

Hawton, K., Townsend, E., Deeks, J., Appleby, L., Gunnell, D., Bennewith, O., & Cooper, J. (2001). Effects of legislation restricting pack sizes of paracetamol and salicylate on self poisoning in the United Kingdom: Before and after study. *British Medical Journal, 322*(7296), 1203–1207. https://doi.org/10.1136/bmj.322.7296.1203


[5] A possible reason for this is that suicides using firearms tend more often to be impulsive.

Hendin, H. (1996). Suicide, assisted suicide, and euthanasia. *Crisis, 17*(2), 90–93. https://doi.org/10.1027/0227-5910.17.2.90
Humphry, D. (1992). *Final exit: The practicalities of self-deliverance and assisted suicide for the dying*. Dell. https://archive.org/details/finalexitpractica00hump
Kahn, D. L., & Lester, D. (2013). Efforts to decriminalize suicide in Ghana, India and Singapore. *Suicidology Online, 4*, 110–118. https://api.semanticscholar.org/CorpusID:37307618
Kapusta, N., Etzerdorfer, E., Krall, C., & Sonneck, G. (2007). Firearm legislation reform in the European Union: Impact on firearm availability, firearm suicide and homicide rates in Austria. *British Journal of Psychiatry, 191*, 253–257. https://doi.org/10.1192/bjp.bp.106.032862
Kevorkian, J. (1992). A fail safe model for justifiable medically assisted suicide. *American Journal of Forensic Psychiatry, 13*(1), 7–81. https://www.suicideinfo.ca/resource/siecno-20021271/
Landers, D. (1981). Unsuccessful suicide by carbon monoxide: A secondary benefit of emissions control. *Western Journal of Medicine, 135*(5), 360–363. https://www.ncbi.nlm.nih.gov/pmc/articles/PMC1273253/
Leenaars, A. A., & Lester, D. (1997). The impact of gun control on suicide and homicide across the life span. *Canadian Journal of Behavioural Science, 29*(1), 1–6. https://doi.org/10.1037/0008-400X.29.1.1
Lester, D. (1988). State laws on suicide and suicide rates. *Psychological Reports, 62*(1), 134. https://doi.org/10.2466/pr0.1988.62.1.134
Lester, D. (1992). Decriminalization of suicide in Canada and suicide rates. *Psychological Reports, 71*(3 Pt 1), 738. https://doi.org/10.2466/pr0.1992.71.3.738
Lester, D. (1993). Decriminalization of suicide in New Zealand and suicide rates. *Psychological Reports, 72*(3 Pt 1), 1050. https://doi.org/10.2466/pr0.1993.72.3.1050
Lester, D. (1995). Effects of the detoxification of domestic gas on suicide rates in six nations. *Psychological Reports, 77*(1), 294. https://doi.org/10.2466/pr0.1995.77.1.294
Lester, D. (1997). The role of shame in suicide. *Suicide & Life-Threatening Behavior, 27*(4), 352–361. PMID: 9444730.
Lester, D. (1999). Effect of changing alcohol laws in Iceland on suicide rates. *Psychological Reports, 84*(3 Pt 2), 1158. https://doi.org/10.2466/pr0.1999.84.3c.1158
Lester, D. (2002a). Decriminalization of suicide in seven nations and suicide rates. *Psychological Reports, 91*(3 Pt 1), 898. https://doi.org/10.2466/pr0.2002.91.3.898
Lester, D. (2002b). Guttman scaling national laws on suicide. *Crisis, 23*(2), 89–90. https://doi.org/10.1027/0227-5910.23.2.89
Lester, D. (2009). *Preventing suicide: Closing the exits revisited*. Nova Science Publishers. https://books.google.com/books/about/Preventing_Suicide.html?id=ZWpVPgAACAAJ
Lester, D. (2019). Firearms and suicide: Research in the 20th and 21st centuries. In D. Lester (Ed.), *Firearms and suicide: Is prevention possible?* (pp. 27–64). Nova Science Publishers. https://psycnet.apa.org/record/2019-47423-002
Lester, D., & Baker, G. (1989). Suicide after legal arrest: Implications for suicide prevention. *Medicine, Science & the Law, 29*(1), 78. https://pubmed.ncbi.nlm.nih.gov/2747468/
Lester, D., & Leenaars, A. A. (1994). Gun control and rates of firearms violence in Canada and the United States: A comment. *Canadian Journal of Criminology, 36*(4), 463–464. https://psycnet.apa.org/record/1995-23593-001
Lester, D., & Murrell, M. E. (1980). The influence of gun control laws on suicidal behavior. *American Journal of Psychiatry, 137*(1), 121–122. https://doi.org/10.1176/ajp.137.1.121
Lester, D., & Tartaro, C. (2002). Suicide on death row. *Journal of Forensic Sciences, 47*, 1108–1111. https://archive.org/details/sim_journal-of-forensic-sciences_2002_47_index
Lew, B., Lester, D., Mustapha, F. I., Yip, P., Chen, Y. Y., Panirselvam, R. R., Hassan, R. S., In, S., Chan, L. F., Ibrahim, M., Chan, C. M. H., & Siau, C. S. (2022). Decriminalizing suicide attempt in the 21st century: An examination of suicide rates in countries that penalize suicide, a critical review. *BMC Psychiatry, 22*(1), 424. https://doi.org/10.1186/s12888-022-04060-5

Madadin, M., Al Sahwan, H. S., Altarouti, K. K., Altarouti, S. A., Al Eswaikt, Z. S., & Menezes, R. G. (2020). The Islamic perspective on physician-assisted suicide and euthanasia. *Medical Sciences Law, 60*(4), 278–286. https://doi.org/10.1177/0025802420934241

Makinen, I. H. (1997). Suicide-related crimes in contemporary European criminal laws. *Crisis, 18*(1), 35–47. https://doi.org/10.1027/0227-5910.18.1.35

Miller, T. R., Weinstock, L. M., Ahmedani, B. K., Carlson, N. N., Sperber, K., Lê Cook, B., Taxman, F. S., Arias, A. A., Kubiak, S., Dearing, H. W., Waehrer, G. M., Barrett, H. G., Hulsey, J., & Johnson, J. E. (2024). Share of adult suicides after recent jail release. *JAMA Network Open, 7*(5), e249965. https://doi.org/10.1001/jamanetworkopen.2024.9965

Mirzaie, S. (2020). Examining the suicide sentence and accessory in it in view of Sharia and Iran law. *New Approaches in Islamic Studies, 2*(3), 33–49. http://ensani.ir/fa/article/journal-number/49165

Mundt, R. J. (1990). Gun control and rates of firearms violence in Canada and the United States. *Canadian Journal of Criminology, 32*(1), 137–154. https://psycnet.apa.org/record/1990-19986-001

Padela, A. I. (2007). Islamic medical ethics: A primer. *Bioethics, 21*(3), 169–178. https://doi.org/10.1111/j.1467-8519.2007.00540.x

Pearson, M., Metcalfe, C., Jayamanne, S., et al. (2017) Effectiveness of household lockable pesticide storage to reduce pesticide self-poisoning in rural Asia: A community-based, cluster-randomized controlled trial. *Lancet*. published online Aug 11. https://doi.org/10.1016/S0140-6736(17)31961-X

Pelletier, A. R. (2007). Preventing suicide by jumping: The effect of a bridge safety fence. *Injury Prevention, 13*(1), 57–59. https://doi.org/10.1136/ip.2006.013748

Picón-Jaimes, Y. A., Lozada-Martinez, I. D., Orozco-Chinome, J. E., Montaña-Gómez, L. M., Bolaño-Romero, M. P., Moscote-Salazar, L. R., Janjua, T., & Rahman, S. (2022). Euthanasia and assisted suicide: An in-depth review of relevant historical aspects. *Annals of Medicine & Surgery, 75*, 103380. https://doi.org/10.1016/j.amsu.2022.103380

Rosenthal, M. S. (2020). The Kevorkian chapter: Physician-assisted death in *You Don't Know Jack* (2010). In *Healthcare ethics on film*. Springer. https://doi.org/10.1007/978-3-030-48818-5_3

Tartaro, C. (2019). *Suicide and self-harm in prisons and jails* (2nd ed.). Lexington Books/Rowman & Littlefield. https://psycnet.apa.org/record/2019-35231-000

Tartaro, C., & Lester, D. (2009). *Suicide and self-harm in prisons and jails*. Lexington. https://books.google.com/books/about/Suicide_and_Self_harm_in_Prisons_and_Jai.html?id=7QRBnDfvgCUC

Tartaro, C., & Lester, D. (2015). Suicide on death row. *Psychological Reports, 117*(3), 944–950. https://doi.org/10.2466/12.PR0.117c29z9

Tartaro, C., & Lester, D. (2016). Suicide on death row. *Journal of Forensic Sciences, 61*(6), 1656–1659. https://doi.org/10.1111/1556-4029.13069

Weapons Smuggling and Carrying Act in Iran. (2024). *Penalty law for arms and ammunition smuggling and owners of illegal arms and ammunition*. https://arianalaw.com

Werth, J. L. (1999). Mental health professionals and assisted death: Perceived ethical obligations and proposed guidelines for practice. *Ethics & Behavior, 9*(2), 159–183. https://doi.org/10.1207/s15327019eb0902_6

Yang, B., & Lester, D. (1991). The effect of gun availability on suicide rates. *Atlantic Economic Journal, 19*, 74. https://doi.org/10.1007/BF02299085

Zia, B., Kouser, T., Helal, H., & Awaad, R. A. (2024). A brief overview of the Islamic ethics of suicide and suicide-related contemporary issues from a Sunnī perspective: A primer for clinicians and researchers. *Journal of Religion and Health, 63*(1), 968–984. https://doi.org/10.1007/s10943-024-02007-6

# Chapter 20
# Ecological Perspectives of Suicide Prevention

**Sheikh Shoib, Kanika Handu, and Fahimeh Saeed**

**Abstract** Suicide is a complex public health issue that necessitates a comprehensive approach to prevention. This paper adopts an ecological perspective, emphasizing the interplay of factors across individual, interpersonal, community, and societal levels that contribute to suicidal behavior. By integrating theoretical frameworks such as Bronfenbrenner's Ecological Systems Theory and the Social-Ecological Model, we provide a robust structure for understanding the multifaceted nature of suicidal behaviors. Our analysis highlights the need for policies and interventions that address both immediate and long-term influences on suicidal behavior, with the ultimate goal of reducing suicide rates across diverse populations.

**Keywords** Suicide · Suicide prevention · Ecology · Social-ecological model · Bronfenbrenner's ecological theory · Mental health · Suicide risk factors · Suicide protective factors · Community-based interventions

## 1 Introduction

Suicide is a significant public health issue worldwide, with profound impacts on individuals, families, communities, and societies (World Health Organization, 2025). The consequences of suicide are far-reaching, affecting not only the individual but also their loved ones, social networks, and the broader community. In recent years,

S. Shoib (✉)
Department of Health Services, Srinagar, Kashmir, India
e-mail: Sheikhshoib22@gmail.com

Sharda University, Greater Noida, India

K. Handu
Esic Medical College & PGIMSR, Bangalore, India

F. Saeed
Psychosis Research Center, University of Social Welfare and Rehabilitation Sciences, Tehran, Iran
e-mail: Fa.saeed@uswr.ac.ir



S. M. Y. Arafat and S. K. Kar (eds.), *Ecological and Social Determinants of Suicidal Behavior*, South Asian Perspectives in Mental Health and Psychology,
https://doi.org/10.1007/978-981-96-4028-7_20

there has been a growing recognition of the need for a more comprehensive approach to suicide prevention, one that takes into account the complex interplay of factors that contribute to suicidal behaviors.

The evolution of suicide prevention strategies has shifted from primarily focusing on individual risk factors to adopting a more comprehensive ecological perspective (Cramer & Kapusta, 2017). This shift in perspective acknowledges that suicidal behaviors are influenced by a dynamic interplay of factors across multiple levels of analysis, including individual, interpersonal, community, and societal contexts (Bronfenbrenner, 1979). By recognizing the interconnectedness of these factors, researchers and policymakers can develop more effective prevention strategies that address the complex needs of diverse populations.

By acknowledging the limitations of individual-focused approaches and the importance of systemic interventions, researchers and policymakers can develop more effective prevention strategies that address the root causes of suicidal behaviors (Van Orden et al., 2010). Ultimately, a comprehensive approach to suicide prevention requires a multifaceted strategy that incorporates individual, community, and societal-level interventions. This approach emphasizes the importance of understanding the social and environmental contexts in which individuals live, work, and interact and seeks to promote mental health and well-being through a range of evidence-based interventions.

## 2 Historical Context and Evolution

The evolution of suicide prevention strategies reflects a growing recognition of the limitations of individual-focused approaches and the need for systemic interventions. Early efforts primarily focused on identifying and mitigating individual risk factors such as mental illness, substance abuse, or life crises (Stone & Crosby, 2014). While these efforts yielded some success, they often overlooked broader environmental and social determinants that contribute to suicidal behaviors (Goldsmith et al., 2002). As research advanced, it became evident that factors such as social relationships, community environments, socioeconomic conditions, and cultural attitudes play significant roles in shaping suicide risk (Goldsmith et al., 2002).

The shift toward ecological perspectives in suicide prevention emerged from the understanding that individuals are embedded within multiple interacting systems that influence their behaviors and experiences (Bryan et al., 2020).

### *2.1 Bronfenbrenner's Ecological Systems Theory*

It provided a foundational framework for this approach, emphasizing that individuals are influenced by nested environmental systems, including the microsystem (immediate surroundings), mesosystem (interactions between microsystems), exosystem

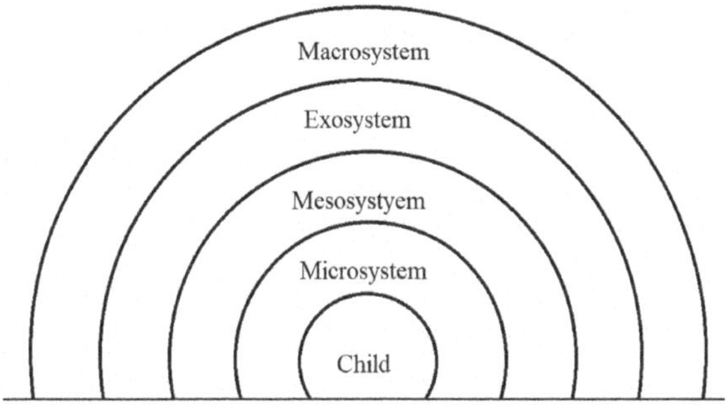


**Fig. 1** Bronfenbrenner's ecological systems

(indirect environments), and macrosystem (cultural norms and values) (Tong & An, 2024). It underscores the dynamic interactions between individuals and their environments, highlighting how changes at one level can impact suicide risk across others. This theory remains pivotal in understanding the multifaceted nature of suicidal behaviors (Harmer et al., 2024) (Fig. 1).

- **Microsystem** involves direct interactions within an individual's immediate environment, such as family dynamics, peer relationships, and school or work settings (Umberson & Montez, 2010). These interactions shape an individual's daily experiences and social relationships, influencing their emotional well-being and sense of belonging (Umberson & Montez, 2010).
- **Mesosystem** examines the interconnections between different microsystems, highlighting how experiences in one setting (e.g., family conflict) can spill over into others (e.g., peer relationships) (Umberson & Montez, 2010). Understanding these interconnections is crucial for identifying protective factors that buffer against suicide risk and risk factors that amplify vulnerability (Sekaran et al., 2018).
- The **exosystem** expands the analysis to include settings in which individuals may not be directly involved but still influence their experiences indirectly, such as parental workplace policies affecting family dynamics or community resources impacting access to support services (Van Orden et al., 2010). These indirect influences can significantly impact an individual's stress levels, coping mechanisms, and access to resources, thereby shaping their risk of suicidal behaviors (Van Orden et al., 2010).
- At the **macrosystem** level, cultural norms, societal values, and broader economic and political contexts shape attitudes toward mental health, help-seeking behaviors, and the availability of resources for suicide prevention (Goldsmith et al., 2002).

**2.2. The Social-Ecological Model builds upon Bronfenbrenner's framework** by integrating individual-level factors with broader environmental influences across multiple levels of analysis as follows:

### 2.1.1 Individual-Level Factors

Includes individual characteristics such as psychological traits (e.g., depression, anxiety, impulsivity) and biological factors (e.g., genetic predispositions, neurobiological processes) (National Center for Chronic Disease Prevention and Health Promotion (US), 2012). These factors contribute to an individual's susceptibility to suicidal ideation and behaviors (Harmer et al., 2024).

- **Psychological Traits**: Certain psychological characteristics, such as hopelessness, emotional distress, and psychiatric disorders (e.g., depression, bipolar disorder), significantly increase an individual's vulnerability to suicidal behaviors. These traits may exacerbate the impact of stressors and life crises, reducing an individual's ability to cope effectively (Harmer et al., 2024).
- **Interpersonal Level:** Encompasses relationships with family, friends, peers, and intimate partners. Positive relationships characterized by support, communication, and trust can serve as protective factors against suicide, while conflict, abuse, or social isolation can increase vulnerability (Van Orden et al., 2010).
- **Biological Influences:** Genetic predispositions, neurobiological factors (e.g., neurotransmitter/hormonal imbalances), and physiological responses to stress play important roles in influencing an individual's susceptibility to suicidal ideation and behaviors (Bryan et al., 2020). Biological vulnerabilities interact with environmental stressors and life experiences to shape an individual's risk profile (National Center for Chronic Disease Prevention and Health Promotion (US), 2012).

### 2.1.2 Interpersonal Dynamics

- **Family Relationships:** Positive family relationships characterized by warmth, support, and effective communication serve as protective factors against suicide (Diamond et al., 2022). Strong family bonds can provide emotional stability, resilience, and a sense of belonging that buffers against stress and adversity (Chen et al., 2017). Conversely, dysfunctional family dynamics, parental conflict, abuse, or neglect can increase an individual's vulnerability to suicidal behaviors by undermining their support network and exacerbating emotional distress (Chen et al., 2017).
- **Peer Influence:** Peer relationships and social networks play a critical role in shaping attitudes, behaviors, and coping mechanisms related to suicide (Shin, 2022). Positive peer relationships characterized by mutual support, empathy, and healthy social norms can promote resilience and protective factors. Conversely, peer pressure, social exclusion, bullying, or involvement in high-risk behaviors may contribute to increased suicide risk, particularly among adolescents and young adults (Lin & Guo, 2024).
- **Social Media Impact:** The pervasive influence of social media platforms introduces new challenges and opportunities in suicide prevention efforts (Memon et al., 2018). Social media can facilitate positive connections, peer support, and

dissemination of mental health resources (Rayland & Andrews, 2023). However, it also exposes individuals to cyberbullying, harmful content (e.g., suicide-related posts, graphic images), and online communities that promote self-harm or suicidal behaviors (Memon et al., 2018). Effective strategies must address these digital environments by promoting responsible online behaviors, enhancing digital literacy skills, and fostering supportive online communities (Nesi, 2020).

### 2.1.3 Community and Societal Influences

The broader contextual factors like community and society-based influences that contribute to suicide risk are essential to understand for developing comprehensive prevention strategies as they play a significant role in developing one's mindset and perceptions:

- **Socioeconomic Factors:** Socioeconomic disparities, such as poverty, unemployment, inadequate housing, and lack of access to healthcare and educational opportunities, increase vulnerability to suicidal behaviors (Alegría et al., 2018). Economic stressors and social inequalities can exacerbate psychological distress, limit coping resources, and reduce access to supportive services and opportunities for social mobility (Alegría et al., 2018).
- **Cultural and Religious Contexts:** Cultural beliefs, values, and norms regarding mental health, suicide, and help-seeking behaviors vary across societies and communities (Goldsmith et al., 2002). Stigma surrounding mental illness, misconceptions about suicide, and religious teachings may influence individuals' attitudes toward seeking help, disclosing emotional distress, and accessing appropriate care (Castillo et al., 2019). Culturally sensitive interventions that respect diverse beliefs, practices, and perspectives are essential for engaging communities and reducing barriers to care (Diamond et al., 2022).
- **Community Resources:** The availability, accessibility, and quality of mental health services, crisis intervention resources, and community support networks significantly impact suicide prevention efforts (Castillo et al., 2019). Strengthening community-based resources, promoting collaborations between healthcare providers, community organizations, and other stakeholders, and enhancing public awareness and education about suicide risk factors and warning signs are critical strategies for reducing suicide rates (U.S. Department of Health & Human Services, 2024).

### 2.1.4 Environmental and Structural Factors

- **Urban vs. Rural Settings:** Geographic location influences suicide risk, with distinct challenges and resources in urban and rural environments (Casant & Helbich, 2022). Rural areas often face barriers such as limited mental health services but offer togetherness and more family support and comfort whereas urban areas may experience higher stress levels, higher risks of social isolation,

and competitive pressures that contribute to mental health challenges (Srivastava, 2009).
- **Access to Lethal Means:** Easy access to lethal means such as firearms, medications, pesticides, and other substances significantly increases the lethality of suicide attempts (Harmer et al., 2024). Restricting access to lethal means through policy measures (e.g., safe storage practices, and firearm legislation) can reduce suicide rates by preventing impulsive acts and promoting safer environments (Yip et al., 2012).

### 2.1.5 Policy and Legislation

- **Suicide Prevention Policies:** Effective suicide prevention policies encompass a range of strategies, including mental health education, early intervention programs, crisis hotline services, and legislative measures to promote firearm safety and restrict access to lethal means (U.S. Department of Health & Human Services, 2024). Policies should be evidence-based, culturally responsive, and integrated across healthcare, education, and community settings to maximize impact (Goldsmith et al., 2002).
- **Healthcare System Roles:** The healthcare system plays a pivotal role in suicide prevention through the integration of mental health services into primary care settings, training healthcare providers in suicide risk assessment and intervention, and ensuring equitable access to quality mental healthcare (U.S. Department of Health & Human Services, 2024). Collaborative efforts between healthcare providers, community organizations, and policymakers are essential for implementing comprehensive suicide prevention strategies (U.S. Department of Health & Human Services, 2024). Health camps, events, and discussions regarding mental health well-being and issues are important measures to spread awareness in masses so that those in need can take appropriate measures and mental health is not being neglected as it corresponds massively to one's growth and physical well-being too (Singh et al., 2022).

## 3 Conclusion

Adopting ecological perspectives in suicide prevention recognizes the complex nature of suicidal behaviors and highlights the importance of addressing interconnected risk and protective factors at individual, interpersonal, community, and societal levels.

At the individual level, psychological traits and biological factors interact with social dynamics. Supportive interpersonal relationships can serve as protective factors, whereas negative family interactions and peer pressures may increase vulnerability.

The community context, including socioeconomic conditions and access to mental health resources, plays a crucial role in how individuals cope with stressors. Additionally, societal factors, such as cultural attitudes and the stigma surrounding mental health, significantly influence individuals' willingness to seek help and the availability of resources.

Effective policies and legislative measures, such as firearm safety regulations and mental health education initiatives, are essential for creating environments that reduce the risk of suicide. By acknowledging the interactions among these various levels, we can create a comprehensive approach to suicide prevention. Collaboration among healthcare providers, community organizations, and policymakers is crucial for developing targeted interventions that address both immediate and systemic influences, ultimately aiming to reduce suicide rates across diverse populations significantly. This ecological perspective not only enhances our understanding of suicidal behaviors but also guides the formulation of more effective and inclusive prevention strategies.

## References


Alegría, M., NeMoyer, A., Falgàs Bagué, I., Wang, Y., & Alvarez, K. (2018). Social determinants of mental health: Where we are and where we need to go. *Current Psychiatry Reports, 20*(11), 95. https://doi.org/10.1007/s11920-018-0969-9

Bronfenbrenner, U. (1979). *The ecology of human development: Experiments by nature and design.* Harvard university press.

Bryan, C. J., Butner, J. E., May, A. M., et al. (2020). Nonlinear change processes and the emergence of suicidal behavior: A conceptual model based on the fluid vulnerability theory of suicide. *New Ideas in Psychology, 57*. https://doi.org/10.1016/j.newideapsych.2019.100758

Casant, J., & Helbich, M. (2022). Inequalities of suicide mortality across urban and rural areas: A literature review. *International Journal of Environmental Research and Public Health, 19*(5), 2669. https://doi.org/10.3390/ijerph19052669

Castillo, E. G., Ijadi-Maghsoodi, R., Shadravan, S., et al. (2019). Community interventions to promote mental health and social equity. *Current Psychiatry Reports, 21*(5), 35. https://doi.org/10.1007/s11920-019-1017-0

Chen, E., Brody, G. H., & Miller, G. E. (2017). Childhood close family relationships and health. *American Psychologist, 72*(6), 555–566. https://doi.org/10.1037/amp0000067

Cramer, R. J., & Kapusta, N. D. (2017). A social-ecological framework of theory, assessment, and prevention of suicide. *Frontiers in Psychology, 8*, 1756. https://doi.org/10.3389/fpsyg.2017.01756

Diamond, G., Kodish, T., Ewing, E. S. K., Hunt, Q. A., & Russon, J. M. (2022). Family processes: Risk, protective and treatment factors for youth at risk for suicide. *Aggressive and Violent Behavior, 64*, 101586. https://doi.org/10.1016/j.avb.2021.101586

Goldsmith, S. K., Pellmar, T. C., Kleinman, A. M., & Bunney, W. E. (Eds.). (2002). *Reducing suicide: A national imperative.* The National Academies Press. https://doi.org/10.17226/10398

Harmer, B., Lee, S., Rizvi, A., et al. (2024). Suicidal ideation. In *StatPearls [Internet].* StatPearls Publishing. https://www.ncbi.nlm.nih.gov/books/NBK565877/

Lin, J., & Guo, W. (2024). The research on risk factors for adolescents' mental health. *Behavioral Sciences (Basel), 14*(4), 263. https://doi.org/10.3390/bs14040263

Memon, A. M., Sharma, S. G., Mohite, S. S., & Jain, S. (2018). The role of online social networking on deliberate self-harm and suicidality in adolescents: A systematized review of literature. *Indian*

*Journal of Psychiatry, 60*(4), 384–392. https://doi.org/10.4103/psychiatry.IndianJPsychiatry_414_17

National Center for Chronic Disease Prevention and Health Promotion (US) Office on Smoking and Health. (2012). *Preventing tobacco use among youth and young adults: A report of the surgeon general*. Centers for Disease Control and Prevention (US). https://www.ncbi.nlm.nih.gov/books/NBK99237/

Nesi, J. (2020). The impact of social media on youth mental health: Challenges and opportunities. *North Carolina Medical Journal, 81*, 116–121. https://doi.org/10.18043/ncm.81.2.116

Rayland, A., & Andrews, J. (2023). From social network to peer support network: Opportunities to explore mechanisms of online peer support for mental health. *JMIR Mental Health, 10*, e41855. https://doi.org/10.2196/41855

Sekaran, V., Kamath, V., Ashok, L., Kamath, A., Hegde, A., & Devaramane, V. (2018). Role of micro- and mesosystems in shaping an adolescent. *Journal of Nepal Paediatric Society, 37*, 178. https://doi.org/10.3126/jnps.v37i2.18307

Shin, H. (2022). Social contagion of academic behavior: Comparing social networks of close friends and admired peers. *PLoS ONE, 17*(3), e0265385. https://doi.org/10.1371/journal.pone.0265385

Singh, V., Kumar, A., & Gupta, S. (2022). Mental health prevention and promotion—A narrative review. *Frontiers in Psychiatry, 13*, 898009. https://doi.org/10.3389/fpsyt.2022.898009

Srivastava, K. (2009). Urbanization and mental health. *Indian Psychiatry Journal, 18*(2), 75–76. https://doi.org/10.4103/0972-6748.64028

Stone, D. M., & Crosby, A. E. (2014). Suicide prevention. *American Journal of Lifestyle Medicine, 8*(6), 404–420. https://doi.org/10.1177/1559827614551130

Suicide. (25 March 2025). Retrieved 10 April 2025, from World Health Organization website: https://www.who.int/news-room/fact-sheets/detail/suicide

Tong, P., & An, I. S. (2024). Review of studies applying Bronfenbrenner's bioecological theory in international and intercultural education research. *Frontiers in Psychology, 14*, 1233925. https://doi.org/10.3389/fpsyg.2023.1233925

U.S. Department of Health and Human Services. (2024). *National strategy for suicide prevention*. U.S. Department of Health and Human Services.

Umberson, D., & Montez, J. K. (2010). Social relationships and health: A flashpoint for health policy. *Journal of Health and Social Behavior, 51*(Suppl), S54–S66. https://doi.org/10.1177/0022146510383501

Van Orden, K. A., Witte, T. K., Cukrowicz, K. C., Braithwaite, S. R., Selby, E. A., & Joiner, T. E., Jr. (2010). The interpersonal theory of suicide. *Psychological Review, 117*(2), 575–600. https://doi.org/10.1037/a0018697

Yip, P. S., Caine, E., Yousuf, S., Chang, S. S., Wu, K. C., & Chen, Y. Y. (2012). Means restriction for suicide prevention. *The Lancet, 379*(9834), 2393–2399. https://doi.org/10.1016/S0140-6736(12)60521-2

The manufacturer's authorised representative in the EU is Springer Nature Customer Service Centre GmbH, Europaplatz 3, 69115 Heidelberg, Germany. If you have any concerns regarding our products, please contact ProductSafety@springernature.com

Printed and bound by CPI Group (UK) Ltd, Croydon, CR0 4YY
01/10/2026
02225929-0008